CASES AND MATERIALS

WHEN MARKETS FAIL:
RACE AND ECONOMICS

by

EMMA COLEMAN JORDAN
Professor of Law
Georgetown University Law Center

ANGELA P. HARRIS
Professor of Law
Boalt Hall–School of Law, University of California, Berkeley

FOUNDATION PRESS

NEW YORK, NEW YORK

2006

© 2006 By FOUNDATION PRESS
        395 Hudson Street
        New York, NY 10014
        Phone Toll Free 1–877–888–1330
        Fax (212) 367–6799
        fdpress.com
Printed in the United States of America
ISBN–13: 978–1–58778–955–7
ISBN–10: 1–58778–955–8

TEXT IS PRINTED ON 10% POST CONSUMER RECYCLED PAPER

For the late E. W. Coleman and M. H. Coleman,
my daughters Kristen and Allison and my sisters Betty, Jean and Earlene

*

INTRODUCTION

We live in a society organized according to two master principles: capitalism and democracy. Although these principles and their associated values, institutions and norms are integral to American life, they often seem to exist in different worlds. Capitalism is often thought of as belonging to the "private" sphere, whereas democracy belongs in the "public" sphere. The business world is full of heroes, like rich and famous C.E.O.s of large corporations and quasi-public (but unelected) figures such as Alan Greenspan, chairman of the Board of Governors of the Federal Reserve. The political world, by contrast, contains very few heroes; important figures in politics and public policy are often regarded by the public with suspicion, even cynicism and hostility. Indeed, we seem to be living in a time when market institutions are more trusted than government institutions to make good policy.

Where should those who are concerned about racial justice put their trust? Some minority leaders in the United States have looked to economic development as the key to equality, while others have looked first to the political system. Consider, for example, the famous disagreement between early twentieth-century African American leaders W.E.B. DuBois and Booker T. Washington: Du Bois argued that racial equality lay in the establishment of legal and political rights for African Americans, while Washington argued that African Americans should temporarily forego political power, insistence on civil rights, and higher education and instead concentrate all their energies on industrial education, with an eye toward economic development. Is capitalism or democracy the royal road to full inclusion in American society? The intellectual heirs of Washington might point out that markets know no color—or rather, the only color they recognize is green. The intellectual heirs of Du Bois might point out that markets fail. Indeed, the persistence of racial discrimination in workplaces and in retail markets casts doubt on the wisdom of the public faith that markets do better than government action at fostering liberty and equality for all.

This book provides the resources for developing a multifaceted approach to racial justice. Race and class have long been inextricably intertwined in American society. From this perspective, Du Bois and Washington were both right: neither political struggles nor economic strategies alone can dissolve the knot of racial inequality. Thus, serious students of inequality should understand the strengths and weaknesses of both market and government regulation. Moreover, students should understand that both market and government institutions are rooted in culture. Belief systems, everyday practices, and social norms undergird the operation of all institutions, public and private; and in the United States, race has historically played an important role in shaping these beliefs, practices, and norms.

The issues discussed in this book highlight the complicated interweaving of public and private institutions with cultural norms. Chapter 2 takes up data concerning economic inequality and class mobility in the United States, and includes the stories of some of those who live on the bottom rung of wealth and income. Chapters 3, 4, and 5 take up specific topics that illuminate the interactions among race, gender, and economic inequality, and the sometimes complementary, sometimes conflicting values of liberty, equality, and community. Chapter 3 concerns the family as an institution with political, economic, and cultural power; Chapter 4 looks directly at questions of culture and identity; and Chapter 5 examines "culture" as an economic issue, from cultural commodities to the economic regulation of cultural difference.

Finally, Chapter 6 addresses questions of remediation and transformation. In the United States, as it has frequently been observed, important social issues quickly become legal issues. As you read and think about all the readings in this book, think about how making a social problem into a legal problem shapes both conceptions of the problem and of possible solutions. Think, as well, about how thinking "outside the box" of conventional legal strategies and arguments might make visible new and more creative paths toward racial justice. For example, how might familiar legal debates like the one over "affirmative action" be transformed when seen from a perspective that incorporates a sophisticated understanding of the relationship between race and class, and a vision that is enriched by both efficiency and justice concerns?

ACKNOWLEDGEMENTS

The idea for creating teaching materials to introduce law students to a systematic examination of the interdisciplinary dimensions of increasing economic inequality and the role of identity in the distribution of wealth first occurred to me more than ten years ago. My decision to create this casebook arose from my mounting frustration with the conceptual limitations of the consumer protection features of commercial law and banking, the two traditional areas in which I had been working over the course of my career. I deeply appreciate the contributions of Nancy Ota who came to Georgetown Law Center in 1992–93 as a graduate Fellow in the Future Law Professor Program to work with me. She invested her unique imagination and commitment to assist me in creating the first set of teaching materials for the first course on Economic Justice.

This casebook owes much to the confidence and support I enjoyed from my publisher, Steven Errick. His enthusiasm and shared vision for the innovations of this effort and his never-failing generosity in responding to and initiating additional publishing opportunities for the Economic Justice topic were important at critical points in the process. Steve's departure in the weeks before this book went to press was a real personal loss. I look forward to working with the new publisher, John Bloomquist in future editions.

I especially want to thank the many Georgetown University Law Center students who enrolled in the early courses in Economic Justice, and who became my most enthusiastic cheering section (offering rap and pop lyrics, African proverbs, Equal Access to Justice/E.A.T. Justice, a socially conscious business venture and strong counterarguments) as this project moved forward to completion. I learned so much from our intense classroom investigations of some of my then forming hypotheses about educational capital, wealth and income inequalities, intergenerational economic effects, linguistic differences, the relationship of the Constitution to economic outcomes, and the limits of conventional market theory. The richness and complexity of this project owe much to my students.

From my Georgetown law students, I chose outstanding research assistants who worked with passion and conviction on the research for this book. They found many truly important additions to the materials. They designed the critical copyright accounting system, chased elusive copyright holders with the zeal of a "repo" man/woman. They kept me laughing when I might have otherwise turned grouchy. They discussed this newly emerging field with me with intelligence and energy. My special thanks go to Angela

Ahern '05, Rashida Baskerville '06, Katherine Buell '04, Cassandra Charles '05, Kenneth Leichter '06, William Morriss '05, Michael Radolinski '06, and Joshua Soszynski '07.

Shaping the boundaries of this project required many hours of conversation with colleagues. Steven Salop was exceptionally generous with his time and the contents of his library on economics. The time we spent talking about economics and shuttling from my office to his across the hall, undoubtedly accelerated my understanding of the intellectual framework of modern economics. I benefited greatly from the expertise and gentle prodding of several colleagues: Alex Aleinikoff, William Braxton, Jerry Kang (during his visit in 2004–5), Carrie Menkel-Meadow, Michael Seidman, Gerry Spann, Rebecca Tushnet, Kathy Zeiler and the colleagues who participated in the Georgetown Law Center Summer Faculty Workshop in 2004. If there are any errors in what follows, it must be because I didn't listen to their sage advice.

This project could not have been finished without the superb institutional arrangements in place at Georgetown University Law Center to support faculty manuscripts. Georgetown enjoys an organizational structure that would be the envy of most casebook writers. I received several summer research grants to allow me to devote time to developing and completing the project. In their capacities as lead manuscript editor and faculty services librarian for this book, Zinta Saulkans and Jennifer Locke and her staff were truly indispensable to achieving a high technical quality for the final manuscript. Diane McDonald, my faculty assistant, Derreck Brown, Sylvia Johnson, Toni Patterson, Ronnie Reese, and Anna Selden in the Office of Faculty Support were always optimistic in the face of frustrations and the unexpected nightmares of formatting, and other technical meltdowns. They were responsive to my many requests during the development of this book. Finally, the Office of Information Systems and Technology introduced me to new equipment and software for managing the project. My special thanks go to Dianne H. Ferro Mesarch, Dimo Michailov, Pablo Molina and Barry Wileman.

In 2001, Angela Harris visited at Georgetown from Boalt Hall at the Univ. of California at Berkeley. As we discussed her work on class and race, it became clear that I could benefit from working with her on this casebook. When she agreed to join the project, I could not know then what a terrific contributor she would be. Her intelligence and humor made the work flow effortlessly to conclusion. We truly had fun doing this work; my only regret is that I didn't think to ask her to join me sooner.

Finally, I want to thank my dear friends Gail, Audrey, Fay and Marta for their support, as well as my two daughters Kristen and Allison for their patience and understanding during the many hours I devoted to completing this project.

EMMA COLEMAN JORDAN

Washington, D.C. August, 2005

I would like to thank my students at Boalt and at Georgetown (Wealth and Class Relations, fall 2000; Wealth and Class Relations, fall 2001; and Law, Markets, and Culture, fall 2004) for their excitement, hard work, and insight as we tried to think through the complicated mutual entanglements of "fairness," "efficiency," "markets," "culture," and "law," and as we struggled toward an institutional theory of human flourishing.

I would like to thank my assistant, Ayn Lowry, for her skill and dedication at tracking down copyright holders across the globe, and for her enthusiasm for this project despite the many last-minute headaches it caused.

I owe a huge debt to my co-author, Emma Coleman Jordan, for talking me into joining and then sticking with the project, and for her wonderful combination of brilliant vision, sisterly solidarity, and can-do spirit.

Last, but not least, I would like to thank my amazing research assistants, Tucker Bolt Culbertson and Naomi Ruth Tsu, for everything: research, pep talks, proofreading, formatting, article suggestions, critical feedback, and, of course, cookies.

ANGELA HARRIS

Berkeley, California
August 2005

*

SUMMARY OF CONTENTS

TABLE OF CONTENTS

TABLE OF CASES

Principal cases are in bold type. Non-principal cases are in roman type. References are to Pages.

CASES AND MATERIALS

WHEN MARKETS FAIL:
RACE AND ECONOMICS

*

CHAPTER 1

RACE, MARKETS AND NEUTRALITY IN TWO DISCIPLINES

Introduction and Overview

Almost fifty years ago, Charles P. Snow, the British novelist and physicist, identified an important communications gap between the literary and scientific cultures. In a now famous lecture, he used the metaphor of "two cultures" to represent the often incompatible world views of science and literature. He worried that the progress of knowledge in the western world would be compromised by the incomprehension then existing between scientists on one hand, and scholars in the humanities on the other. For Snow, science embodied a culture of objectivity, neutrality, and detached factual inquiry. Literary intellectuals, on the other hand were concerned with questions of meaning, identity, and history.

We conclude that an analogous gap exists today between two groups of legal scholars who think seriously about markets. On one hand, traditional law and economics scholars, like economists, are interested in questions of rational choice, efficiency, wealth maximization, and production and transactions costs. On the other hand, legal scholars concerned with questions of identity, including race, gender and sexual orientation have focused their scholarly investigations on issues of subordination, identity, cultural context, and legal indeterminacy. These two groups of scholars might have much to learn from each other. However, these "two cultures" of law, with few exceptions, remain in separate conversations, with separate world views and separate, even antagonistic, operating assumptions about how to evaluate market phenomena.

In this book, we investigate the problems of the market domain with respect for both cultures. We suspect that the economics perspective, with its reliance on scientific measurement and numerical representation of experience, offers much that can be useful. Our vantage point as scholars who have been active in anti-subordination theory, however, also leads us to be attentive to questions of identity, culture, context, history, and dominance.

Central to the tension between the two cultures of law is the question of method. Is legal analysis (or should it be) a science? Or is legal reasoning inherently interpretive, more art than science? Is the law a neutral and objective forum for conflict resolution, or is it a tool of the powerful? Scholars concerned with the problem of subordination—especially subordination based on race and gender identity—have challenged the claims of neutrality of traditional legal theory. This challenge has brought to the surface the conflict between the two cultures of law. In this book we extend the anti-subordination critique to classic market economics and to law and economics. We believe that the question of method—whether there is an objective science of society, or whether knowledge is inherently perspectival—is of such central importance to understanding the structure of economic inequality that it provides a promising field upon which to begin the three-way conversation between the traditionalists in economics, the traditionalists in law, and the anti-subordination-oriented legal theorists.

As legal scholars concerned with the impact of subordination in law and in markets, we want to examine the role that traditional legal analysis plays in reinforcing the rational choice, efficiency, and wealth maximization assumptions of traditional economic views of the operation of markets. It is not surprising to find that claims of neutrality play as central a role in traditional legal theory as they do in traditional economic analysis.

We turn now to the central organizing question of this first chapter: what methods and normative assumptions are most useful in evaluating the complex landscape of law, markets, and culture? What tools are best suited to sort truth from ideology and myth? What would "truth" look like if we found it? We begin with these questions because we believe that unless these intensely .contested, yet often invisible, first premises of analysis are explored, it will be impossible to make sense of the claims and arguments of the traditionalists in economics and in law or the contradictory positions of critical race, feminist and other scholars concerned with the problem of intertwined structures of subordination. Throughout this book we will use a variety of tools to pursue our interest in fostering a conversation between economics and the critical perspectives. We will use methodologies and insights from sociology, psychology, and behavioral economics, as well as the various schools of modern legal thought.

To begin our discussion we have chosen a now-famous narrative account by Professor Patricia Williams. Williams is a part of the critical race theory movement, described below. Our choice to begin with a narrative reflects our view about neutrality and truth. Stories can provide a potent starting point for identifying and examining buried assumptions. As you work through this material keep in mind the structure and sources of the neutrality claims identified above. See if you can detect them on your own.

A.   CRITICAL RACE THEORY: NARRATIVE, NEUTRALITY, AND THE MARKETPLACE

The Death of the Profane

THE ALCHEMY OF RACE AND RIGHTS 44–51 (1991).

■ PATRICIA J. WILLIAMS

Buzzers are big in New York City. Favored particularly by smaller stores and boutiques, merchants throughout the city have installed them as screening devices to reduce the incidence of robbery: if the face at the door looks desirable, the buzzer is pressed and the door is unlocked. If the face is that of an undesirable, the door stays locked. Predictably, the issue of undesirability has revealed itself to be a racial determination. While controversial enough at first, even civil-rights organizations backed down eventually in the face of arguments that the buzzer system is a "necessary evil," that it is a "mere inconvenience" in comparison to the risks of being murdered, that suffering discrimination is not as bad as being assaulted, and that in any event it is not all blacks who are barred, just "17-year-old black males wearing running shoes and hooded sweatshirts."

The installation of these buzzers happened swiftly in New York; stores that had always had their doors wide open suddenly became exclusive or received people by appointment only. I discovered them and their meaning one Saturday in 1986. I was shopping in Soho and saw in a store window a sweater that I wanted to buy for my mother. I pressed my round brown face to the window and my finger to the buzzer, seeking admittance. A narrow-eyed, white teenager wearing running shoes and feasting on bubble gum glared out, evaluating me for signs that would pit me against the limits of his social understanding. After about five seconds, he mouthed "We're closed," and blew pink rubber at me. It was two Saturdays before Christmas, at one o'clock in the afternoon; there were several white people in the store who appeared to be shopping for things for *their* mothers.

I was enraged. At that moment I literally wanted to break all the windows of the store and *take* lots of sweaters for my mother. In the flicker of his judgmental gray eyes, that saleschild had transformed my brightly sentimental, joy-to-the-world, pre-Christmas spree to a shambles. He snuffed my sense of humanitarian catholicity, and there was nothing I could do to snuff his, without making a spectacle of myself.

I am still struck by the structure of power that drove me into such a blizzard of rage. There was almost nothing I could do, short of physically intruding upon him, that would humiliate him the way he humiliated me. No words, no gestures, no prejudices of my own would make a bit of difference to him; his refusal to let me into the store—it was Benetton's, whose colorfully punish ad campaign is premised on wrapping every one of the world's peoples in its cottons and woolens—was an outward manifestation of his never having let someone like me into the realm of his reality. He had no compassion, no remorse, no reference to me; and no desire to acknowledge me even at the estranged level of arm's-length transactor. He saw me only as one who would take his money and therefore could not conceive that I was there to give him money.

In this weird ontological imbalance, I realized that buying something in that store was like bestowing a gift, the gift of my commerce, the lucre of my patronage. In the wake of my outrage, I wanted to take back the gift of appreciation that my peering in the window must have appeared to be. I wanted to take it back in the form of unappreciation, disrespect, defilement. I wanted to work so hard at wishing he could feel what I felt that he would never again mistake my hatred for some sort of plaintive wish to be included. I was quite willing to disenfranchise myself, in the heat of my need to revoke the flattery of my purchasing power. I was willing to boycott Benetton's, random white-owned businesses, and anyone who ever blew bubble gum in my face again.

My rage was admittedly diffuse, even self-destructive, but it was symmetrical. The perhaps loose-ended but utter propriety of that rage is no doubt lost not just to the young man who actually barred me, but to those who would appreciate my being barred only as an abstract precaution, who approve of those who would bar even as they deny that they would bar even as they deny that they would bar *me*.

The violence of my desire to burst into Benetton's is probably quite apparent. I often wonder if the violence, the exclusionary hatred, is equally apparent in the repeated public urgings that blacks understand the buzzer system by putting themselves in the shoes of white storeowners—that, in effect, blacks look into the mirror of frightened white faces for the reality of their undesirability; and that then blacks would "just as surely conclude that they would not let themselves in under similar circumstances." (That some blacks might agree merely shows that some of us have learned too well the lessons of privatized intimacies of self-hatred and rationalized away the fullness of our public, participatory selves.)

On the same day I was barred from Benetton's, I went home and wrote the above impassioned account in my journal. On the day after that, I found I was still brooding, so I turned to a form of catharsis I have always found healing. I typed up as much of the story as I have just told, made a big poster of it, put a nice colorful border around it, and, after Benetton's was truly closed, stuck it to their big sweater-filled window. I exercised my first amendment right to place my business with them right out in the street.

So that was the first telling of this story. The second telling came a few months later, for a symposium on Excluded Voices sponsored by a law review. I wrote an essay summing up my feelings about being excluded from Benetton's and analyzing "how the rhetoric of increased privatization, in response to racial issues, functions as the rationalizing agent of public unaccountability and, ultimately, irresponsibility." Weeks later, I received the first edit. From the first page to the last, my fury had been carefully cut out. My rushing, run-on-rage had been reduced to simple declarative sentences. The active personal had been inverted in favor of the passive impersonal. My words were different; they spoke to me upside down. I was afraid to read too much of it at a time—meanings rose up at me oddly, stolen and strange.

A week and a half later, I received the second edit. All reference to Benetton's had been deleted because, according to the editors and the faculty adviser, it was defamatory; they feared harassment and liability; they said printing it would be irresponsible. I called them and offered to supply a footnote attesting to this as my personal experience at one particular location and of a buzzer system not limited to Benetton's; the editors told me that they were not in the habit of publishing things that were unverifiable. I could not but wonder, in this refusal even to let me file an affidavit, what it would take to make my experience verifiable. The testimony of an independent white bystander? (a requirement in fact imposed in U.S. Supreme Court holdings through the first part of the century).

Two days *after* the piece was sent to press, I received copies of the final page proofs. All reference to my race had been eliminated because it was against "editorial policy" to permit descriptions of physiognomy. "I realize," wrote one editor, "that this was a very personal experience, but any reader will know what you must have looked like when standing at that window." In a telephone conversation to them, I ranted wildly about the significance of such an omission. "It's irrelevant," another editor explained in a voice gummy with soothing and patience; "It's nice and poetic" but it doesn't "advance the discussion of any principle. . . . This is a law review, after all." Frustrated, I accused him of censorship; calmly he assured me it was not. "This is just a matter of style," he said with firmness and finality.

Ultimately I did convince the editors that mention of my race was central to the whole sense of the subsequent text; that my story became one of extreme paranoia without the information that I am black; or that it became one in which the reader had to fill in the gap by assumption, presumption, prejudgment, or prejudice. What was most interesting to me in this experience was how the blind application of principles of neutrality, through the device of omission, acted either to make me look crazy or to make the reader participate in old habits of cultural bias.

That was the second telling of my story. The third telling came last April, when I was invited to participate in a law-school conference on Equality and Difference. I retold my sad tale of exclusion from Soho's most glitzy boutique, focusing in this version on the law-review editing process as a consequence of an ideology of style rooted in a social text of neutrality, I opined:

> Law and legal writing aspire to formalized, color-blind, liberal ideals. Neutrality is the standard for assuring these ideals; yet the adherence to it is often determined by reference to an aesthetic of uniformity, in which difference is simply omitted. For example, when segregation was eradicated from the American lexicon, its omission led many to actually believe that racism therefore no longer existed. Race-neutrality in law has become the presumed antidote for race bias in real life. With the entrenchment of the notion of race-neutrality came attacks on the concept of affirmative action and the rise of reverse discrimination suits. Blacks, for so many generations deprived of jobs based on the color of our skin, are now told that we ought to find it demeaning to be hired, based on the color of our skin. Such is the silliness of simplistic either-or inversions as remedies to complex problems.

> What is truly demeaning in this era of double-speak-no-evil is going on interviews and not getting hired because someone doesn't think we'll be comfortable. It is demeaning not to get promoted because we're

judged "too weak," then putting in a lot of energy the next time and getting fired because we're "too strong." It is demeaning to be told what we find demeaning. It is very demeaning to stand on street corners unemployed and begging. It is downright demeaning to have to explain why we haven't been employed for months and then watch the job go to someone who is "more experienced." It is outrageously demeaning that none of this can be called racism, even if it happens only to, or to large numbers of, black people; as long is it's done with a smile, a handshake and a shrug; as long as the phantom-word "race" is never used.

The image of race as a phantom-word came to me after I moved into my late godmother's home. In an attempt to make it my own, I cleared the bedroom for painting. The following morning the room asserted itself, came rushing and raging at me through the emptiness, exactly as it had been for twenty-five years. One day filled with profuse and overwhelming complexity, the next day filled with persistently recurring memories. The shape of the past came to haunt me, the shape of the emptiness confronted me each time I was about to enter the room. The force of its spirit still drifts like an odor throughout the house.

The power of that room, I have thought since, is very like the power of racism as status quo: it is deep, angry, eradicated from view, but strong enough to make everyone who enters the room walk around the bed that isn't there, avoiding the phantom as they did the substance, for fear of bodily harm. They do not even know they are avoiding; they defer to the unseen shapes of things with subtle responsiveness, guided by an impulsive awareness of nothingness, and the deep knowledge and denial of witchcraft at work.

The phantom room to me is symbolic of the emptiness of formal equal opportunity, particularly as propounded by President Reagan, the Reagan Civil Rights Commission and the Reagan Supreme Court. Blindly formalized constructions of equal opportunity are the creation of a space that is filled in by a meandering stream of unguided hopes, dreams, fantasies, fears, recollections. They are the presence of the past imaginary, imagistic form—the phantom-roomed exile of our longing.

> It is thus that I strongly believe in the efficacy of programs and paradigms like affirmative action. Blacks are the objects of constitutional omission which has been incorporated into a theory of neutrality. It is thus that omission is really a form of expression, as oxymoronic as that sounds: racial omission is a literal part of original intent; it is the fixed, reiterated prophecy of the Founding Fathers. It is thus that affirmative action is an affirmation; the affirmative act of hiring—or hearing—blacks is a recognition of individuality that replaces blacks as a social statistic that is profoundly interconnective to the fate of blacks and whites either as sub-groups or as one group. In this sense, affirmative action is as mystical and beyond-the-self as an initiation ceremony. It is an

act of verification and of vision. It is an act of social as well as professional responsibility.

The following morning I opened the local newspaper, to find that the event of my speech had commanded two columns on the front page of the Metro section. I quote only the opening lines: "Affirmative action promotes prejudice by denying the status of women and blacks, instead of affirming them as its name suggests. So said New York City attorney Patricia Williams to an audience Wednesday."

I clipped out the article and put it in my journal. In the margin there is a note to myself: eventually, it says, I should try to pull all these threads together into yet another law-review article. The problem, of course, will be that in the hierarchy of law-review citation, the article in the newspaper will have more authoritative weight about me, as a so-called "primary resource," than I will have; it will take precedence over my own citation of the unverifiable testimony of my speech.

I have used the Benetton's story a lot, in speaking engagements at various schools. I tell it whenever I am too tired to whip up an original speech from scratch. Here are some of the questions I have been asked in the wake of its telling:

Am I not privileging a racial perspective, by considering only the black point of view? Don't I have an obligation to include the "salesman's side" of the story?

Am I not putting the salesman on trial and finding him guilty of racism without giving him a chance to respond to or cross-examine me?

Am I not using the store window as a "metaphorical fence" against the potential of his explanation in order to represent my side as "authentic"?

How can I be sure I'm right?

What makes my experience the real black one anyway?

Isn't it possible that another black person would disagree with my experience? If so, doesn't that render my story too unempirical and subjective to pay any attention to?

Always a major objection is to my having put the poster on Benetton's window. As one law professor put it: "It's one thing to publish this in a law review, where no one can take it personally, but it's another thing altogether to put your own interpretation right out there, just like that, uncontested, I mean, with nothing to counter it."

————

NOTES AND QUESTIONS

1. Shared claims of neutrality: legal neutrality and economic neutrality. In their declarations of "truth," legal opinions are presented as objective, indifferent, and neutral. Similarly, the market is based on the notion that a willing buyer and a willing seller will participate in an arm's-length transaction according to their preferences. The sum total of these discrete transactions is a market expressing cumulative preferences that are neutral, in that they do not reflect central government control. It was Adam Smith, one of the founding fathers of modern economics, who asserted that the greater good for all could be best achieved through such a market of free exchanges, guided by the invisible hand. But, what happens when only one party is willing to participate in a transaction? How do individual preferences and choices affect the market? What role does legal neutrality play in weakening or reinforcing these preferences?

2. Wechslerian principles of neutrality. Lawyer and legal scholar Herbert Wechsler promoted constitutional interpretation based on neutral principles, not the immediate results of particular cases. He described the "ad hoc evaluation" based on individual outcome as "the deepest problem of our constitutionalism." Herbert Wechsler, *Toward Neutral Principles of Constitutional Law*, 73 HARV. L. REV. 1 (1959).

> A principled decision, in the sense I have in mind, is one that rests on reasons with respect to all the issues in the case, reasons that in their generality and their neutrality transcend any immediate result that is involved. When no sufficient reasons of this kind can be assigned for overturning value choices of the other branches of the Government or of a state, those choices must, of course, survive. Otherwise, as Holmes said in his first opinion for the Court, "a constitution, instead of embodying only relatively fundamental rules of right, as generally understood by all English-speaking communities, would become the partisan of a particular set of ethical or economical opinions...." *Id.* at 19.

Wechsler recognizes the potential for constitutional decisions that do not reflect personal views of justice, and he points to use of the Fourteenth Amendment to remedy racial discrimination as "the hardest test." *Id.* at 26. Though he claimed to be in favor of desegregated schools, he says:

> I find it hard to think the judgment [in *Brown v. Board of Education*] really turned upon the facts. Rather, it seems to me, it must have rested on the view that racial segregation is, in principle, a denial of equality to the minority against whom it is directed; that is, the group that is not dominant politically and, therefore, does not make the choice involved. For many who support the Court's decision this assuredly is the decisive ground. But this position also presents problems. Does it not involve an inquiry into the motive of the legislature, which is generally foreclosed to the courts? Is it alternatively defensible to make the measure of validity of legislation the way it is interpreted by those who are affected by it? In the context of a charge that segregation *with equal facilities* is a denial of equality, is there not a point in *Plessy* in the statement that if "enforced separation stamps the colored race with a badge of inferiority" it is solely because its members choose "to put that construction upon it"? ...
>
> For me, assuming equal facilities, the question posed by state-enforced segregation is not one of discrimination at all. Its human and its

constitutional dimensions lie entirely elsewhere, in the denial by the state of freedom to associate, a denial that impinges in the same way on any groups or races that may be involved.

* * *

But if the freedom of association is denied by segregation, integration forces an association upon those for whom it is unpleasant or repugnant.... Given a situation where the state must practically choose between denying the association to those individuals who wish it or imposing it on those who would avoid it, is there a basis in neutral principles for holding that the Constitution demands that the claims for association should prevail? (I should like to think there is, but I confess that I have not yet written the opinion. To write it is for me the challenge of the school-segregation cases.)

Id, at 33–34.

The requirement of neutrality in law, as described by Wechsler, limits the judiciary's ability to make law based on value judgments. Is it more important for the legal system to make decisions based on neutral principles or outcomes? Are "neutral" principles really neutral, or do they promote value judgments as well? Is the refusal of the courts to inquire into the motive of the legislature a neutral principle or one which upholds the power of the political majority? In what ways has this philosophy influenced the development of the common law? We return to the question of motive in *Washington v. Davis* infra at 44.

Williams challenges the "blind application of principles of neutrality," claiming, "[b]lacks are the objects of a constitutional omission which has been incorporated into a theory of neutrality." WILLIAMS, *supra* at 50. How would Williams respond to Wechsler's question whether there is a neutral principle upon which *Brown v. Board of Education* could have, or should have, been decided?

3. Neutrality of facts in appellate opinions. Courts use the law as a screen through which certain facts emerge as relevant while other facts are sifted out as irrelevant. *See* Richard Delgado, *Storytelling for Oppositionists and Others: A Plea for Narrative*, 87 MICH. L. REV. 2411, 2428 (1989). Sometimes the facts after they pass through this screen are startlingly dissimilar to the experiences of the parties involved.

For example, the Supreme Court's opinion in *United States v. Cruikshank*, 92 U.S. 542 (1875) did not include any significant discussion of the facts, only stating the indictments at issue:

The general charge ... that of "banding," and ... that of "conspiring" together to injure, oppress, threaten, and intimidate Levi Nelson and Alexander Tillman, citizens of the United States, of African descent and persons of color, with the intent thereby to hinder and prevent them in their free exercise and enjoyment of rights and privileges "granted and secured" to them "in common with all other good citizens of the United States by the constitution and law of the United States." United States v. Cruikshank, 92 U.S. 542, 548 (1875).

The Court found that the charges were insufficiently specific under the Civil Rights Enforcement Act of 1870, and the convictions were overturned. *id.* at 559. The Court failed to mention that the charges stemmed from the "bloodiest violence of the Reconstruction." ENCYCLOPEDIA OF AFRICAN AMERICAN CIVIL RIGHTS: FROM EMANCIPATION TO THE PRESENT 541 (Charles D. Lowery & John F. Marszalek, eds., 1992). On Easter Sunday of 1873 in Colfax, Louisiana, 280 African Americans were massacred. *id.* at 541. In *Cruikshank*, the Court overturned the only convictions among scores of federal prosecutions for the Colfax Riot, but the significance of the opinion's blow to the post-Civil War civil rights movement is lost without a factual setting.

Rather than failing to include significant facts, Justice Cardozo seems to have invented his own version of what took place in the famous torts case *Palsgraf v. Long Island Railroad.* After reading Cardozo's impossible account of Mrs. Palsgraf being injured from across the station platform after a small package exploded, her attorney requested a rehearing because "there was an apparent error in the understanding of the facts of the case." Manz, *Palsgraf, Cardozo's Urban Legend?*, 107 DICK. L. REV. 785, at 818 (Spring 2003). Manz asserts that the importance of this case, despite its questionable fact pattern, does not indicate disregard for the truth so much as academic interest in the opinion itself, not the underlying event. Manz, *supra* at 789. As Wechsler advocated, principled reasoning, not the immediate outcome, is important. *See* Wechsler, *supra* text at note 2. Perhaps the outcome of this case is relevant, however. Mrs. Palsgraf was reportedly upset by the lost case for the rest of her life. Manz, *supra* at 840. Additionally, Cardozo's version of the facts has raised questions about his attitudes toward women and the poor. *Id.* at 786. For more on the Palsgraf case factual history, see JOHN T. NOONAN, JR., PERSONS AND MASKS OF THE LAW (1976).

The law review board attempted to screen references to Williams's race as irrelevant and the role of Benetton's as unverifiable. Is Williams correct in asserting that these facts were relevant to her story?

Questioning the neutrality of law, Richard Delgado observed:

Traditional legal writing purports to be neutral and dispassionately analytical, but too often it is not. In part, this is so because legal writers rarely focus on their own mindsets, the received wisdoms that serve as their starting points, themselves no more than stories, that lie behind their quasi-scientific string of deductions. The supposedly objective point of view often mischaracterizes, minimizes, dismisses, or derides without fully understanding opposing viewpoints. Implying that objective, correct answers can be given to legal questions also obscures the moral and political value judgments that lie at the heart of any legal inquiry. Delgado, *supra* at 2440–41.

Delgado is describing the indeterminacy of the law and challenging the notion of neutral application—central themes in the critical legal studies movement. *See* RICHARD W. BAUMAN, CRITICAL LEGAL STUDIES: A GUIDE TO THE LITERATURE 3 (1996). Although "[n]o single manifesto" can summarize the diversity of critical legal thought, "[t]he critique of law, its theories, and its institutions is meant to break down hierarchies of gender, race, class, or so-called merit." *Id.* at 3–4.

4. Challenging neutrality in practice. Law students generally learn the language of law through legal writing courses, which teach the tone, culture, factual analysis, and reasoning of the practice of law. Kathryn M. Stanchi, *Resistance is Futile: How Legal Writing Pedagogy Contributes to the Law's Marginalization of the Outsider*, 103 DICK. L. REV. 1, 11 (1998).

In addition to internalizing the labels of "relevant" and "irrelevant" facts, students learn how to write objectively. The dominant perspective is described as neutral and objective, and the subjective is disregarded as personal, as opposed to professional. *id.* at 40. "[O]bjectivity is a hallmark of legal language, of the professional voice." *id.* at 35.

To counteract the negative effects of objectivity, instructors must incorporate critical legal theory into teaching lawyering skills, but critical writing has generally been focused on legal scholarship instead of the practice of law. Stanchi, *supra* at 56; Brook K. Baker, *Transcending Legacies of Literacy and Transforming the Traditional Repertoire: Critical Discourse Strategies for Practice*, 23 WM. MITCHELL L. REV. 491, 516 (1997).

> Developing a critical discourse is fraught with contradictions arising from lawyers' competing obligations to act and write zealously on behalf of clients on the one hand, and to resist dogma and write transformatively in furtherance of community interests and social justice on the other. Nonetheless, legal writing specialists might consider the efficacy of increased reliance on: (1) using subversive outsider-narratives; (2) confronting and avoiding appeals to bias; and (3) using a more dialogic, less adversarial, more feminist discourse. *Id.* at 517.

Narratives, when subversive instead of hegemonic, use an individual story to reveal a collective wrong. *Id.* at 528–29, 532. The adversarial nature of legal representation allows lawyers to use almost any relevant tactic and prevents only the most blatant appeals to biases. The backlash of color-blind jurisprudence restricts the means to counteract stereotypes, employing biases as well. *Id.* at 543. Using feminist ideals to counteract the male ideology of legal representation as combat, "a nonadversarial advocacy might tone down excessive rhetoric, decrease competitive posturing, and instead engage in a more serious legal, moral, and political dialogue with opponents and legal decision-makers." *Id.* at 555–56.

How might Williams have used her experience in a discrimination suit against Benetton's? Could she find a role for her narrative in the formality of legal documents, thereby avoiding appeals to biases and creating a dialogue about retailers' use of buzzers? *See* Williams at 48, in which she claims omission of her race would make the reader participate in old habits of cultural bias.

5. Narratives in legal discourse. Narratives are a powerful means of constructing moral and social realities, which are indeterminate and therefore subject to interpretation. Richard Delgado, *Storytelling for Opposition-*

ists and Others: A Plea for Narrative, 87 MICH. L. REV. 2411, 2415–16 (1989) (illustrating how the reality of a single event changes with the perspective of five different stories).

The stories of the dominant ingroup are used to construct a "shared reality in which its own superior position is seen as natural," by picking and choosing facts to justify the world as it is. But " 'neutrality' can feel [different] from the perspective of an outsider." *Id.* at 2412, 2421, 2425.

Members of outgroups use counterstories, which directly challenge the stories of the ingroup, as (1) a means of self-preservation and (2) a means of lessening their own subordination. *Id.* at 2436.

> [S]tories about oppression, about victimization, about one's own brutalization—far from deepening the despair of the oppressed, lead to healing, liberation, mental health. They also promote group solidarity. Storytelling emboldens the hearer, who may have had the same thoughts and experiences the storyteller describes, but hesitated to give them voice. Having heard another express them, he or she realizes, I am not alone.

> Yet, stories help oppressed groups in a second way—through their effect on the oppressor. Most oppression ... does not seem like oppression to those perpetrating it. It is rationalized, causing few pangs of conscience. The dominant group justifies its privileged position by means of stories, stock explanations that construct reality in ways favorable to it....

> This story is drastically at odds with the way most people of color would describe their condition.... Counterstories can attack that complacency.

> What is more, they can do so in ways that promise at least the possibility of success. Most civil rights strategies confront the obstacle of blacks' otherness. The dominant group, noticing that a particular effort is waged on behalf of blacks, increases its resistance. Stories at times can overcome that otherness, hold that instinctive resistance in abeyance. Stories are the oldest, most primordial meeting ground in human experience. Their allure will often provide the most effective means of overcoming otherness, of forming a new collectivity based on the shared story.

Id. at 2436–38.

Listeners asked Patricia Williams why she did not feel obligated to include the salesman's side of the story and why her individual experience was worth their attention. How could Williams, had she chosen to answer the questions, have defended putting "[her] own interpretation right out there"?

6. Significance of Williams's self description. While describing her face in a manner that reinforces connections with this country's segregated history, is Williams giving short shrift to descriptive accuracy? What relationship should the accuracy of Williams's self description have with her publication of the Benetton's story in a law review? If the law review editors believe Williams's description was wholly inaccurate, should they refuse to publish her work? Would the answer change if Williams's piece were written in the traditional, "objective" law review style? For an especially heated exchange between two critical legal scholars about exactly the point raised in the notes above, and the credibility of Patricia Williams's Benetton story, see Mark Tushnet, *The Degradation of Constitutional Discourse*, 81 Geo. L.J. 251, 265–78 (1992) and Gary Peller, *The Discourse of Constitutional Degradation*, 81 Geo. L.J. 313 (1992). *See generally* Richard Posner, *The Skin Trade*, The New Republic, Oct. 13, 1997, at 40; Daniel A. Farber and Suzanna Sherry, Beyond All Reason (1997).

One possible criticism that can be made of Williams's decision to describe her face as round and brown is that it paints a much more familiar picture of racism. Discrimination against Patricia Williams implies a difficult problem which can not be solved simply by assimilation or affirmative action. Law review readers who believe in marketplace neutrality will not want to believe in discrimination against Patricia Williams because it may raise issues of their own culpability for not finding ways of combating prejudice beyond assimilation.

Does Williams's article lose some of its effectiveness by perpetuating a comforting picture of racism? *See also* Devon W. Carbado & Mitu Gulati, *The Law and Economics of Critical Race Theory: Crossroads, Directions, and a New Critical Race Theory*, 112 Yale L.J. 1757, 1817 (2003) (book review).

7. Williams and anonymous clerk. In *Death of the Profane*, Williams describes not one, but two transactions. First, there is the actual transaction between her and the clerk: the gift of her commerce in exchange for his permission to enter Benetton's. Second, there is the hypothetical exchange which never took place: Williams's money in exchange for Benetton's sweater. When analyzing the situation in this way, doesn't it seem simply as though Williams didn't meet the clerk's asking price for admittance? Obviously, the clerk undervalued Williams's cultural capital. Since the clerk did not open the door, should Williams have pressed a twenty dollar bill against the window in order to sweeten her offer? Would it indicate that the market was functioning properly, at least in the first exchange, if the clerk who refused Williams entry was fired because of bringing bad publicity to Benetton's?

8. Note on Williams's "marketplace." Williams's poignant personal account details her exclusion from participating in the marketplace, an environment where, theoretically, a willing buyer and a willing seller make a connection based on each of their preferences and enter into agreements to buy and sell products and services. The marketplace is fundamentally associated with freedom, functional objectivity, and deference to personal preference. Deborah Waire Post et al., Contracting Law 1 (1996). In making exchanges for goods and services, willing buyers and sellers usually engage in single transactions or once-only interactions. Craig Calhoun et al.,

STRUCTURES OF POWER AND CONSTRAINT: PAPERS IN HONOR OF PETER M. BLAU 134 (1990). These transactions are not based on personal trust between these buying and selling actors; rather, individuals depend on the independent system of law, official contracts, courts, and enforcement agencies to regulate interaction and exchange in the marketplace. *Id.* In this case, Williams requesting to enter Benetton's was an offer to participate in the marketplace, a manifestation of intent to enter into an exchange of her money for a Benetton's product. POST, *supra* at 196. However, Williams's offer created the power of acceptance in the sales associate—the "narrow-eyed, white teenager"—and in denying her admittance into the store, the young clerk abruptly ended a potential exchange in the retail market. *Id.* Therefore, economists may claim that there was no acceptance on the part of the sales clerk, thereby making no obligation on the part of Benetton's to sell Williams any goods or services. The absence of an acceptance failed to complete the formation of a contract between Benetton's to sell goods and Williams to grant "the gift of her commerce."

Though the marketplace paradigm explicates exchanges between buying and selling actors in a straightforward, ostensibly neutral model, it largely ignores several ideological, cultural, and social implications of everyday human interaction. The simple paradigm assumes that actors voluntarily enter into these transactions and that these buyers and sellers do not consider salient issues, such as the other actor's race, class, gender, or ethnicity. *Id.* at 2. As societal norms, citizens' biases, and the nation's socioeconomic hierarchy play a large role in social life, economic models of exchange in the marketplace fail to consider the varied rule systems that constitute and control social transactions. CALHOUN, *supra* at 142.

Williams challenges the simple economic model by asserting that the market is not an impartial setting, but a partial milieu where market players are significantly influenced by their own prejudices and self-indulgence to exclude certain actors from participating in the process of exchange. Williams claims the white clerk's rejection of her admittance into the store was an overt "manifestation of his never having let someone like me into the realm of his reality"; this clerk was only a willing seller to certain willing buyers, not buyers like Williams. Rather than a simple economic transaction, where two players are interested in generating an efficient exchange with one another, negotiating, and creating bilateral decisions, Williams is not given a chance to enter into the bargain; she is on the receiving end of a unilateral decision. According to Williams, a critical race scholar, the marketplace is not an environment where players are on equal footing and make decisions based on individual preferences, but a place where her "round brown face" banishes her from creating stable economic relationships.

9.   *Death of the Profane* as demonstrating market power. At first glance, Professor Williams's experience seems to imply a market failure. However, market economics does not say that businesses (like Benetton's) always make correct decisions; it says that when businesses make bad decisions, they are punished by lost profits which provide an incentive to make better decisions in the future. According to this model, if a business does not stop making bad decisions, its competitors will eventually drive it out of business. With this in mind, is Williams's story an example of the market in action? Benetton's has certainly suffered for its bad decision. Not only did Professor Williams not patronize Benetton's, she also posted a sign in Benetton's window and immortalized the episode in a law review article. Will the loss of business and bad publicity generated by this incident lead Benetton's to change its ways, demonstrating that there wasn't a market failure after all?

10.   *Death of the Profane* as demonstrating market impotence. If Williams's experience was not a market failure, does that mean that the market provides no means of dealing with any particular act of injustice, and that it can only (theoretically) work to minimize possible future injustice? However, if the market can not deal with actual acts of injustice, does that argue strongly for legislative solutions?

11.   Does a famous black face make any difference? In the summer of 2005, Oprah Winfrey, the billionare entertainer and entrepreneur, went shopping in Paris. Just fifteen minutes after closing, Oprah approached the very exclusive Hermes store, accompanied by a small party of friends. She noticed a group of people still milling about in the store, and she tried to enter. She was firmly turned away by a clerk. Oprah's best friend, Gayle King, who witnessed the incident reports that: " 'People were in the store and they were shopping. **Oprah** was at the door and she was not allowed into the store.' '**Oprah** describes it herself as "one of the most humillating moments of her life." ' "

King said it's unlikely that Winfrey will shop there again. *Store Sorry for Closed Door Policy*, Chi. Trib., June 24, 2005, at p. 23.

Oprah was as enraged as Patricia Williams at this shopping slight. Oprah turned her considerable publicity apparatus to respond to the store's refusal. Although she received an apology, she has promised to devote an entire show to the episode when she begins taping for the new season in the fall of 2005.

Does the Oprah incident reinforce, undercut, or complicate the racial explanation of Patricia Williams story? Like Williams, Oprah concluded that this was an example of racism. What weight should we give the store's explanation that it refused entry to Oprah because it was preparing for a special promotional event? Does it matter that the store did not fire or demote the clerk who denied entry to Oprah and friends?

12.   Buzzer's role in market model. Does the buzzer fit into the conventional model of the market discussed above? Rather than a traditional negotiation between a willing buyer and a willing seller, the buzzer creates a unilateral decision made by an unwilling seller to exclude a willing buyer from the market. What factors might have influenced the clerk's decision to exclude Williams?

13.   Buzzer and racism in marketplace. Williams notes that some deemed the buzzer system to be a "necessary evil" to mitigate the risk of crime in retail establishments. Another possible interpretation of the cultural and social context of the buzzer is that it symbolizes an elevated economic status or a means to establish economic segregation, utilized to prevent theft by excluding people who do not look as if they could afford the merchandise.

If the buzzer system was created to serve this purpose, why did the sales clerk choose to exclude Williams from the store? What is the basis of his belief that a black woman like Williams cannot afford clothes from Benetton's? Did the clerk exclude Williams based on the pervasive cultural representations of African Americans' socioeconomic background in the media or in the courts? Teun A. Van Dijk's study of racism and prejudice at a micro level observed interpersonal communication in everyday life. Van Dijk asserts that the media and the law are major vehicles that create ethnic prejudices in society. TEUN A. VAN DIJK, COMMUNICATING RACISM: ETHNIC PREJUDICE IN THOUGHT AND TALK 361 (1987). These representations of minorities may have a deleterious effect on interpersonal relations in the marketplace:

> Prejudices about aggression and crime of ethic groups largely derive from biased media stories that mention the ethnic backgrounds of suspects, which are again based on police reports or court trials, as well as on media articles about crime statistics or crime "waves" that are also partly derived from information supplied by the authorities. This is one of the most socially destructive ethnic prejudices, and there is much empirical evidence that the law and the media together help construct public attitudes about crime, deviance, or similar negative properties attributed to ethnic minority groups. *Id.* at 364.

Do you share Van Dijk's view? Do court trials aid in creating derogatory beliefs about the socioeconomic status of minorities and thus reinforce the legitimacy of the buzzer system?

An article in the *Washington Post Magazine* created heated debate concerning the buzzer system when it ran a column that supported the use of locks and buzzers as a security measure to discriminatorily screen young black male customers entering retail shops.

> As for me, I'm with the store owners, although I was not at first.... Young black males commit an inordinate amount of urban crime.... [R]ace is only one factor in their admissions policy. Age and sex count, too. And while race is clearly the most compelling factor, ask yourself what their policies would be if young white males were responsible for most urban crime.

> A nation with our history is entitled to be sensitive to race and racism—and we are all wary of behavior that would bring a charge of racism. But the mere recognition of race as a factor—especially if those of the same race recognize the same factor—is not in itself racism. This may apply as much to some opponents of busing or public housing in their own neighborhood as it does to who gets admitted to jewelry stores. Let he who would open the door throw the first stone.

Richard Cohen, *Closing the Door on Crime*, WASH. POST, Sept. 7, 1986 (magazine), at W13; *see also* Jane Gross, *When "By Appointment" Means Keep Out*, N.Y. TIMES, Dec. 17, 1986, at B1.

Was race "only one factor" in the exclusion of Williams, a successful female law professor? How does race as a factor in exclusion affect the model of the market described above? Is using race as a factor in excluding a willing buyer from the market racist? If not, what would meet the commentator's definition of racism?

14.   More screening based on race. Discriminatory screening practices are not an isolated occurrence. In New York, small shops on the Upper Eastside have used, in addition to locks and buzzers, signs that read, "Men by appointment only." *Fear of Blacks, Fear of Crime*, N.Y. Times, Dec. 28, 1986, at § 4, 10. In addition, an African American man in Philadelphia filed a complaint with the Human Rights Commission after he was denied entrance to Mums & Pops Confectionary, which employs a lock and buzzer system. *See* Tamar Charry, *Bitter Sweets Battle*, Philadelphia City Paper, Dec. 7–14, 1995.

The retailers employing such security measures seem to equate blackness with criminality, and the *New York Times* editorial board warned, "discrimination, cumulatively, can be as poisonous as mugging or burglary." *Fear of Blacks, supra.* "Fearful whites need to put themselves in the shoes of innocent blacks. Doing so will not dissipate fear, but it can steadily inspire the understanding and reason that keep fear in its place." *id.* A letter to the editor disagreed "that a society in which prejudice is rampant is as bad as one in which violent crime is rampant." Michael Levin and Margarita Levin, *Howard Beach Turns a Beam on Racial Tension*, N.Y. Times, Jan. 11, 1987, at § 4, 30. The letter concluded that an innocent black person would not let himself into the shop if standing in the owner's shoes. After reading Williams's description of the humiliation and rage she felt, do you think she would agree with the letter's conclusion? For an array of responses to a hypothetical involving decisions to screen customers based on race, see *The Jeweler's Dilemma* in The New Republic, November 10, 1986, at 18.

15.   Law and economics criticisms of critical race narrative methodology. Judge Richard Posner, a leading law and economics scholar, faults the critical race narrative methodology as non scientific, selective, and unreliable when compared to economic methodology. Posner, Overcoming Law, 368–384, "Nuance, Narrative and Empathy in Critical Race Theory." This argument is discussed in the next section of this chapter.

B.   A Law and Economics Challenge to the Neutrality of the Critical Race Narrative Methodology

Nuance, Narrative, and Empathy in Critical Race Theory

Overcoming Law 368–84 (1995).

■ Richard Posner

The Alchemy of Race and Rights describes its author, Patricia Williams, as a young black female law professor of contracts and commercial law whose abiding interest is the plight of the American black. Or plights, for she is particularly concerned with the lack of fit that her condition of being a black professional woman makes with the attitudes and expectations of the predominantly white community in which, as a professor in an academic field that has relatively few women, very few blacks, and therefore almost no black women, she mainly circulates. The lack of fit induces in her at times a sense of disorientation that is almost vertiginous. So it is a book about both "privileged" blacks like herself and her underprivileged coracialists at the bottom of the social totem pole.

The book offers a black feminist perspective on a variety of practices and institutions: law's pretense to objectivity and impersonality, surrogate motherhood, consumerism, constitutional protection of hate speech and condemnation of governmental efforts at affirmative action, the inept and insensitive behavior of well-meaning white liberal academics, and above all white racism in what she considers its hydra-headed manifestations. There is little that is new in the paraphrasable content of her criticisms. The novelty is the form, which can aptly be described as literary, in which Williams has cast her discussion of these legal and social issues. She is not unique in employing literary methods in legal scholarship; earlier and essentially isolated examples of this genre to one side, it is the methodological signature of critical race theory. But she is one of the most skillful practitioners of the genre.

The subtitle of the book—"Diary of a Law Professor"—is a clue to her technique. The book is not literally a diary, although it contains some excerpts from the author's diary. But it is like a diary in presenting the author's analyses of legal and social issues in the form of reactions to her daily experiences, whether as consumer, law professor, television viewer, or daughter. The reader comes to understand that Williams's way of coping with the many stresses of her life is to write down her reactions to stressful or arresting events as soon after they occur as she can. Writing in a diary-like format is thus a form of therapy. But it also gives scope for her powerful gift for narration. * * *

The rhetorical highlight of the book, however, is the description of an episode at a Benetton clothing store. "Buzzers are big in New York City. Favored particularly by smaller stores and boutiques, merchants throughout the city have installed them as screening devices to reduce the incidence of robbery: if the face at the door looks desirable, the buzzer is pressed and the door is unlocked. If the face is that of an undesirable, the door stays locked. Predictably, the issue of undesirability has revealed itself to be a racial determination," as Williams discovers one Saturday afternoon when she

> was shopping in Soho and saw in a store window a sweater that I wanted to buy for my mother. * * *

The power of this sketch lies in its compression, its vivid contrasting of the round brown face with the sales clerk's narrow eyes and pink bubble gum, its use of physical exclusion as a metaphor for social exclusion, its suggestion that the least significant of whites (this gum-chewing bubble-blowing teenage sales clerk) is utterly comfortable with exercising power over an older and more accomplished black, and its elegant summation of the clerk's reaction to her ("evaluating me for signs that would pit me against the limits of his social understanding"). Yet here at the very pinnacle of Williams's art the careful reader will begin to feel a sense of disquiet. Did Williams really press her face against the window—that is, did her face actually touch the glass? Or is she embroidering the facts for dramatic effect—making the insult to her seem even graver than it was because it shattered a childlike eagerness and innocence? Also, how does she know that the sales clerk refused to let her in the store because she's black? The only evidence she cites is that, since Christmas was approaching, it was unlikely that the store had closed, and that there were other shoppers in the store. The second point has no force. Stores normally stop admitting customers before all the customers already in the store have left—otherwise the store might never be able to close. The first point has greater force. Although many stores close early on Saturday, the likelihood that a Benetton store in New York City during the Christmas shopping season would be one of them is slight. Yet Williams does not suggest that she has tried to find out whether the store was open. She does not suggest that she saw any customers admitted after she was turned away. The absence of a sign indicating that the store was closed would be some evidence that it was not, but she doesn't say anything about the presence or absence of a sign. Many stores list their hours on the front door. She makes no mention of this either. In all likelihood the store was open, but I am surprised that she—a lawyer—did not attempt to verify the point.

But of course the attempt might have been futile. And it is even possible, though I find no clues to this in the text, that her anger at the episode reflects in part a pervasive, debilitating uncertainty that confronts blacks in their encounters with whites. Not every disappointment that a black person encounters is a result of discrimination, and yet it may be impossible to determine which is and which is not. We like to know where we stand with other people, and this may be difficult for blacks in their dealings with whites.

Yet she had told us at the outset, in defense of doing legal scholarship in the form of story telling, "that one of the most important results of reconceptualizing from 'objective truth' to rhetorical event will be a more nuanced sense of legal and social responsibility" (p. 11). Unless "nuanced" is a euphemism for fictive, Williams has promised to get the particulars of an event or situation right, rather than submerging them in a generality, such as that whites hate blacks. That promise implies an effort to find out what *really* was going on in that white teenager's mind when he told her the store was closed. Maybe, as I said, it was closed; or maybe it wasn't but the clerk had his hands full with the customers inside. Maybe he was a disloyal employee who wanted to get his employer in trouble; maybe he was lazy, mischievous, rude, irresponsible, or just plain dumb.

The Alchemy of Race and Rights suppresses every perspective other than that of the suffering, oppressed black. * * *

This is a pattern. In discussing the case of Bernhard Goetz, who shot four black youths in a subway car and was acquitted of all but an illegal weapons charge even though he could not have been acting in *reasonable* self-defense, Williams disparages white fear of black crime by characterizing the criminal records of Goetz's victims as mere "allegations" by asking rhetorically how the community would have reacted to Goetz's action if he had been black and his victims white *and the crime had occurred in a department store rather than in the subway*—an added fictive touch that magnifies the malignant irrationality of Goetz's action—and by reciting irrelevant statistics showing that whites commit more crimes than blacks. What is omitted is that the prison population is almost half black, although blacks are only 12 percent of the population, and that urban street (and subway) crime is committed mostly by blacks. Black criminality is a serious social problem. To pretend otherwise is an evasion. AIDS, drug addiction, homophobia, neglect of children, anti-Semitism, and poor political leadership are other problems of the black community that Williams ignores. * * *

Mention of black anti-Semitism brings me back to the question of Beethoven's color. That Beethoven was black is a typical and recurrent claim of the Afrocentrist movement, members of which have also asserted that melanin is positively correlated with intelligence, that the ancient Greeks stole philosophy from black Egyptians and, specifically, that Alexander the Great pillaged the library at Alexandria to steal Egyptian philosophical ideas for his old tutor, Aristotle (never mind that Alexander *founded* Alexandria and that the library was built long after his death), that Napoleon shot off the sphinx's nose so that no one would know that the sphinx had Negroid features, that not only Beethoven but also Haydn, Cleopatra, and Lincoln were black, that Beethoven's blackness is shown by (among other things) his confidence in his abilities, a confidence similar to that of Mohammed Ali, that Dwight Eisenhower's mother was black, that America was first discovered by Africans, that AIDS was invented by whites to exterminate the black race, that the telephone and carbon steel were invented in Africa along with science, medicine, and mathematics, that "the [African] Blacks' conception of God was on a scale too grand to be acceptable to Western minds"—and that Jews controlled the African slave trade and today are plotting with the Mafia the financial destruction of the black race. *Not all Afrocentrists are anti-Semitic; but irresponsible claims appear to be the hallmark of the movement* [emphasis added], and I should have thought that Williams, as a lawyer and an academic, would have wanted to place as much distance as possible between herself and it rather than to embrace uncritically one of its representative wild claims.

Could it be—despite Martha Nussbaum's argument that imaginative literature in general and the novel in particular renders social reality with a degree of balance, nuance, and concreteness that provides a needed antidote to the partial visions furnished by abstract, generalizing social-scientific approaches, such as that of economics—that one-sidedness is an endemic risk of the literary depiction of reality, rather than a particular characteristic of Patricia Williams? * * *

We accept one-sidedness in literature, moreover, because we make allowance for *autres temps*, *autres moeurs* and because factual accuracy and scholarly detachment are not rules of the literature game. But they are rules of the scholarly game, and Williams is writing as a scholar. If my criticisms of her in this chapter should turn out to be one-sided, misleading, and tendentious, she would not be impressed by my rejoining that mine is only one voice in an ongoing conversation and I can leave it to others to rectify any omissions or imbalance in my contribution.

If one-sidedness is the other side of literature's empathetic concreteness, empathetic awareness of strangers' pains and pleasures is the unexpected other side of the economist's Gradgrindian detachment. Consider rent control. The beneficiaries are plain to see: they are the tenants when the rent-control law is adopted. The victims are invisible: they are the future would-be tenants, who will face a restricted supply of rental housing because landowners will have a diminished incentive to build rental housing and owners of existing apartment buildings will prefer to sell rather than to rent the apartments in them. Economics brings these victims before the analyst's eye; literature, and the type of legal scholarship that imitates literature, does not.

Maybe economic scholarship is not *really* empathetic. The economist does not enter imaginatively into the distress of the disappointed quester for rental housing; all he does is tote up some additional costs. But that may be a sounder way of doing policy than by cultivating empathy. A jurisprudence of empathy can foster short-sighted substantive justice because the power to enter imaginatively into another person's outlook, emotions, and experiences diminishes with physical, social, and temporal distance.[30] Compare the maxims *tout comprendre c'est tout pardoner* and no man is a villain in his own eyes (an actor's adage). The second maxim should remind us that when we succeed in looking at the world through another's eyes, we lose the perspective necessary for judgment. We find ourselves in a stew of rationalization, warped perception, and overmastering emotion. (Any lawyer knows the risk of overidentification with his client.) The *tout comprendre* maxim expresses a different point: To understand another person completely is to understand the causality of his behavior, to see that behavior as the end of a chain of causes and thus as determined rather than responsible. It is to understand the person as completely as a scientist understands an animal, which is to say as a phenomenon of nature rather than as a free agent. If we understand a criminal's behavior as well as we understand a rattlesnake's behavior, we are unlikely to accord him much dignity and respect.

---

30. A more basic point is that the internal perspective—the putting oneself in the other person's shoes—that is achieved by the exercise of empathetic imagination lacks normative significance *[Emphasis added]*.

The project of empathetic jurisprudence invites us to choose between achieving a warped internal perspective and an inhumanly clinical detachment: between becoming too hot and too cold. The affective dimension of empathy leads to identification with the person whose fate or welfare is at stake; the intellectual dimension leads to embedding the person in a web of causes that transforms him from a free human being into (in Nietzsche's phrase) an irresponsible piece of fate. I take back nothing I said in discussing the German judges about the importance of remembering that other human beings are—human. That does not require us to be able to crawl into their minds. Indeed, a lively awareness that other people are in an important sense closed to us—that they have their own plans and perspectives, into which we can enter imperfectly if at all—is one of the planks of the liberal platform. It is a presupposition of individuality.

Another problem with Williams's method is a lack of clarity. Here is the ending of the chapter in which Williams stands up for rights against the critical legal studies movement: "Give [rights] to trees. Give them to cows. Give them to history. Give them to rivers and rocks. Give to all of society's objects and untouchables the rights of privacy, integrity, and self-assertion; give them distance and respect" (p. 165). "What does it *mean* to give rights to history, or to entitle cows to privacy, integrity, and self-assertion? Is the reference to cows meant to put us in mind of Hindu doctrine regarding the sacredness of animals? Is Williams an animist, a "Green"? Is she the second coming of Walt Whitman? (likely Carl Sandburg.) How can all this be squared with her being a fashion-conscious shopper. * * *

Narrative has two aspects, Narrative in the sense of the telling of a story is the way we make sense of a sequence of events unfolding in history.31 Black scholars like it because they believe that the current condition of the American black population cannot be understood without reference to the history of Negro slavery. But despite Williams's references to her great-great-grandmother, a slave, her book does not employ historical narration.

Narration is also a literary technique. To present an issue, such as the clash between critical legal studies and critical race theory, in the form of a story, * * * is to reinforce or replace abstract argument with a portrait. Portraits, including the verbal portraits that we call literature—works that depict rather than overtly argue—can change minds. This role of verbal portraiture, as also of photographs, is especially valuable in situations in which we have difficulty *seeing* important aspects of a problem because it involves people whose experiences are remote from ours. In education and occupation Patricia Williams is like other establishment legal figures, but in race and all that that connotes in this country (at least when the race is black) she is not, and maybe one has to learn to see the world through her eyes as well as one's own before one can fully evaluate the arguments pro and con various racial policies. On this view the very one-sidedness of her presentation, however questionable by the conventional standards of scholarship and even by the professed standards of critical race theory (which promised us, remember, nuance), has value in providing insight into the psychology and rhetoric of many blacks. But if whites must acquire a stereoscopic biracial perspective in order to cope effectively with our society's racial problems, blacks must too.

NOTES AND QUESTIONS

1. Standards of proof and burden of persuasion in narrative. What standards of proof and persuasion does Judge Posner rely upon to assess the Williams narrative? *See* Richard H. Gaskins, Burdens of Proof in Modern Discourse (1993) (New Haven, Yale University Press).

2. Throwing rhetorical stones from glass houses? Does Posner's essay exhibit any of the problems that he sees in Williams work? Lack of clarity, exaggeration for rhetorical effect, manipulation of empathy, one-sidedness?

3. Difference between legal and economic standards of proof. Is the Posner essay structured by the standards of economic proof, or legal proof?

4. Finding "truth" in law or economics. What would persuade Judge Posner that a report of racism or microaggression is "true"?

5. Valuing collective experience. What place does group experience with subordination have in the Posnerian schema? *But see* Charles R. Lawrence, III, *The Id, the Ego, and Equal Protection: Reckoning with Unconscious Racism*, 39 Stan. L. Rev. 317 (1987) (arguing for "cultural meaning test" based on a community's collective experience as the targets of racism).

6. Statistics as a scientific form of collective experience. In economics, collective experience is represented in statistical forms of aggregate data, including the mode, mean, average, and regression analysis. *Mode* is the value or item occurring most frequently in a series of observations or statistical data. *Mean* is the sum of all the members of the set divided by the number of items in the set. *Average* is something, as a type, number, quantity, or degree, that represents a midpoint between points on a scale of valuation. In statistics, *regression analysis* is a mathematical method of modeling the relationships among three or more variables. It is used to predict the value of one variable given the values of the others.

C. The Narrative of Post-Modern Racism: The "Microagressions"

Popular Legal Culture: Law as Microaggression
98 Yale L.J. 1559 (1989).

■ Peggy C. Davis

[*The scene is a courthouse in Bronx, New York. A white assistant city attorney "takes the court elevator up to the ninth floor. At the fifth floor, the doors open. A black woman asks: 'Going down?' 'Up,' says [the city attorney]. And then, as the doors close: 'You see? They can't even tell up from down. I'm sorry, but it's true.' "*]

The black woman's words are subject to a variety of interpretations. She may have thought it efficient, appropriate, or congenial to ask the direction of the elevator rather than to search for the indicator. The indicator may have been broken. Or, the woman may have been incapable of competent elevator travel. The city attorney is led, by cognitive habit and by personal and cultural history, to seize upon the pejorative interpretation.

The city attorney lives in a society in which blacks are commonly regarded as incompetent. The traditional stereotype of blacks includes inferior mentality, primitive morality, emotional instability, laziness, boisterousness, closeness to anthropoid ancestors, occupational instability, superstition, care-free attitude, and ignorance. Common culture reinforces the belief in black incompetence in that the black is "less often depicted as a thinking being." If, for example, the city attorney watches television, she has observed that whites, but not blacks, are likely to exert authority or display superior knowledge; that whites, but not blacks, dispense goods and favors; and that blacks are disproportionately likely to be dependent and subservient. Cognitive psychologists tell us that the city attorney shares with all human beings a need to "categorize in order to make sense of experience. Too many events occur daily for us to deal successfully with each one on an individual basis; we must categorize in order to cope." In a world in which sidewalk grates routinely collapsed under the weight of an average person, we would walk around sidewalk grates. We would not stop to inspect them and distinguish secure ones from loose ones: It is more efficient to act on the basis of a stereotyping heuristic. In a world in which blacks are commonly thought to be incompetent (or dangerous, or musical, or highly sexed), it is more efficient for the city attorney to rely on the generalization than to make individuating judgments.

It is likely that the city attorney assimilated negative stereotypes about blacks before she reached the age of judgment. She will, therefore, have accepted them as truth rather than opinion. Having assimilated the stereotypes, the city attorney will have developed a pattern of interpreting and remembering ambiguous events in ways that confirm, rather than unsettle, her stereotyped beliefs. If she sees or hears of two people on a subway, one white, one black, and one holding a knife, she is predisposed to form an impression that the black person held the knife, regardless of the truth of the matter. She will remember examples of black incompetence and may fail to remember examples of black competence.

Psychoanalysts tell us that the stereotype serves the city attorney as a mental repository for traits and impulses that she senses within herself and dislikes or fears. According to this view, people manage normal developmental conflicts involving impulse control by projecting forbidden impulses onto an outgroup. This defense mechanism allows the city attorney to distance herself psychologically from threatening traits and thoughts. In this respect, the pejorative outgroup stereotype serves to reduce her level of stress and anxiety.

Historians tell us of the rootedness of the city attorney's views. During the early seventeenth century, the circumstances of blacks living in what was to become the United States were consistent with principles of open, although not equal, opportunity. African-Americans lived both as indentured servants and as free people. This early potential for egalitarianism was destroyed by the creation of a color-caste system. Colonial legislatures enacted slavery laws that transformed black servitude from a temporary status, under which both blacks and whites labored, to a lifelong status that was hereditary and racially defined. Slavery required a system of beliefs that would rationalize white domination, and laws and customs that would assure control of the slave population.

The beliefs that served to rationalize white domination are documented in an 1858 treatise. In many respects, they echo the beliefs identified one hundred years later as constitutive of the twentieth century black stereotype:

> [T]he negro, ... whether in a state of bondage or in his native wilds, exhibits such a weakness of intellect that ... 'when he has the fortune to live in subjection to a wise director, he is, without doubt, fixed in such a state of life as is most agreeable to his genius and capacity.' ...
>
> ... So debased is their [moral] condition generally, that their humanity has been even doubted.... [T]he negro race is habitually indolent and indisposed to exertion.... * * *
>
> The negro is naturally mendacious, and as a concomitant, thievish....
>
> ... Lust is his strongest passion; and hence, rape is an offence of too frequent occurrence.

The laws and customs that assured control of the slave population reinforced the image of blacks as incompetent and in need of white governance. The master was afforded ownership, the right to command labor, and the virtually absolute right of discipline. Social controls extending beyond the master-slave relationship served to exclude the slave—and in some respects to exclude free blacks—from independent, self-defining activity. * * * Social relationships between whites and blacks were regulated on the basis of caste hierarchy: Breaches of the social order, such as "insolence" of a slave towards a white person, were criminally punishable.

This history is part of the cultural heritage of the city attorney. The system of legal segregation, which maintained caste distinctions after abolition, is part of her life experience. This "new system continued to place all Negroes in inferior positions and all whites in superior positions." The city attorney is among the

> two-thirds of the current population [that] lived during a time when it was legal and customary in some parts of this country to require that

blacks sit in the back of a bus, give up their seats to whites, use different rest rooms and drinking fountains, and eat at different restaurants.

The civil rights movement and post–1954 desegregation efforts are also part of the city attorney's cultural heritage. As an educated woman in the 1980s, she understands racial prejudice to be socially and morally unacceptable. Psychological research that targets her contemporaries reveals an expressed commitment to egalitarian ideals along with lingering negative beliefs and aversive feelings about blacks. "Prejudiced thinking and discrimination still exist, but the contemporary forms are more subtle, more indirect, and less overtly negative than are more traditional forms."

Recent research also suggests that the city attorney can be expected to conceal her anti-black feelings except in private, homoracial settings. Many of her white contemporaries will suppress such feelings from their conscious thoughts. White Americans of the city attorney's generation do not wish to appear prejudiced. "[T]he contemporary form[ ] of prejudice is expressed [at least in testing situations] in ways that protect and perpetuate a nonprejudiced, nondiscriminating self-image." Americans of the city attorney's generation live under the combined influence of egalitarian ideology and "cultural forces and cognitive processes that . . . promote prejudice and racism." Anti-black attitudes persist in a climate of denial.

The denial and the persistence are related. It is difficult to change an attitude that is unacknowledged. Thus, "like a virus that mutates into new forms, old-fashioned prejudice seems to have evolved into a new type that is, at least temporarily, resistant to traditional . . . remedies."

II. THE VIEW FROM THE OTHER SIDE OF THE LENS: MICROAGGRESSION

Return to the fifth floor and to the moment at which the elevator door opened. The black woman sees two white passengers. She inquires and perceives the response to her inquiry. She sees and hears, or thinks she sees and hears, condescension. It is in the tone and body language that surround the word, "Up." Perhaps the tone is flat, the head turns slowly in the direction of the second passenger and the eyes roll upward in apparent exasperation. Perhaps the head remains lowered, and the word is uttered as the eyes are raised to a stare that suggests mock disbelief. The woman does not hear the words spoken behind the closed elevator doors. Yet she feels that she has been branded incompetent, even for elevator travel. This feeling produces anger, frustration, and a need to be hypervigilant against subsequent, similar brandings.

The elevator encounter is a microaggression. "These are subtle, stunning, often automatic, and non-verbal exchanges which are 'put downs' of blacks by offenders." Psychiatrists who have studied black populations view them as "incessant and cumulative" assaults on black self-esteem.

Microaggressions simultaneously sustain defensive-deferential

thinking and erode self confidence in Blacks. . . . [B]y monopolizing . . . perception and action through regularly irregular disruptions, they contribute to relative paralysis of action, planning and self-esteem. They seem to be the principal foundation for the verification of Black inferiority for both whites and Blacks.

The management of these assaults is a preoccupying activity, simultaneously necessary to and disruptive of black adaptation.

> [The black person's] self-esteem suffers ... because he is constantly receiving an unpleasant image of himself from the behavior of others to him. This is the subjective impact of social discrimination.... It seems to be an ever-present and unrelieved irritant. Its influence is not alone due to the fact that it is painful in its intensity, but also because the individual, in order to maintain internal balance and to protect himself from being overwhelmed by it, must initiate restitutive maneuvers ... —all quite automatic and unconscious. In addition to maintaining an internal balance, the individual must continue to maintain a social facade and some kind of adaptation to the offending stimuli so that he can preserve some social effectiveness. All of this requires a constant preoccupation, notwithstanding ... that these adaptational processes ... take place on a low order of awareness.

Vigilance and psychic energy are required not only to marshall adaptational techniques, but also to distinguish microaggressions from differently motivated actions and to determine "which of many daily microaggressions one must undercut."

The microaggressive acts that characterize interracial encounters are carried out in "automatic, preconscious, or unconscious fashion" and "stem from the mental attitude of presumed superiority." They are the product of the factors described in Part I. The elevator incident represents their least insidious form. This is so for three reasons. First, the black woman at the elevator initiated an interaction, thereby providing social cues that would predictably result in an expressed judgment. The microaggression she suffered was avoidable. The black woman can in the future decline to initiate an exchange with a white stranger. To the extent that she minimizes such exchanges, she can protect against further insult. Moreover, the microaggression was arguably content-based. The reaction of the city attorney can be interpreted as a response to the woman's question—to the data gathered in the interaction—rather than a response to the person. Susceptibility to content-based microaggression can be minimized or controlled, not only by avoiding interactions, but also by avoiding ambiguity when interactions occur: The black woman might have said, "The indicator is broken. Is this elevator going up or down?" The more frequent and more insidious microaggressions, however, are unavoidable in that they are neither initiated by blacks nor based in any apparent way on the behavior of blacks. Finally, the elevator incident is benign among microaggressions because the white woman's implicit assertion of superiority did not culminate in an achievement of subordination. A fictitious continuation of the elevator incident illustrates microaggressions that are not only unprovoked in the sense described above but also complete in their achievement of subordination:

[*The city attorney decides to leave the elevator. She is standing at the right side of the car—directly opposite, but several feet away from, the black woman. Although she might easily exit by walking a path angled toward the center of the car, she takes a step directly forward. After a moment's hesitation, the black woman steps aside.*]

This is microaggression in its most potent form. It is the direct descendent of an aspect of color-caste behavior described fifty years ago as "deference":

> The most striking form of ... "caste behavior" is deference, the respectful yielding exhibited by the Negroes in their contacts with whites. According to the dogma and to a large extent actually, the behavior of both Negroes and white people must be such as to indicate that the two are socially distinct and that the Negro is subordinate. Thus ... [i]n places of business the Negro should stand back and wait until the white has been served before receiving any attention, and in entering or leaving he should not precede a white but should stand back and hold the door for him. On the streets and sidewalks the Negro should "give way" to the white person.

The wordless interchange was not initiated by the black woman. It was not based upon any action taken by her. It was a natural manifestation of an imbedded interactive pattern in which "skin color determines whether or not one is expected to operate from an inferior or superior vantage point. Both races have come to expect and accept as unremarkable that the blacks' time, energy, space, and mobility will be at the service of the white." The inferiority of the black is more than an implicit assertion; it is a background assumption that supports the seizure of a prerogative.

* * *

_____

NOTES AND QUESTIONS

1. Neutrality in law: its sources. In the public law debates over constitutional principle, the once well-accepted idea that legal rules are neutral, formal, and even scientific has been a vigorously contested terrain. In the 1980s, critical legal scholars mounted a broad challenge to the neutrality of legal rules. They argued that legal rules are indeterminate, lacking in objective neutrality, controlled instead by context, politics, and discretionary incorporation of the decision maker's perspective. However, when we turn to the debates about the rules that control outcomes in the market, skepticism about neutrality and rationality has emerged among legal scholars more recently.

In what follows we offer a preliminary map, tracing the role of the neutrality claim in legal theory. We start with the formalism of Christopher C. Langdell, a late 19th century dean of Harvard Law School, who introduced the study of appellate cases and the classification of legal subjects into categories that he defined as based upon a scientifically rigorous organization of legal thought, derived from provable "principles" of law. Langdell's formalism thus served to introduce the early framework of the neutrality claim through its assertion that legal reasoning was based upon "scientifically provable premises."

In the practice of law, legal neutrality is featured in several professional norms. First, we have the expectation of professional detachment in which the lawyer serves as a vigorous advocate on behalf of the client, without becoming so identified with the client as to lose perspective on sound professional assessments of what best serves the client's interest. Second, in litigation, neutrality expectations are on display in the rules that govern judicial conduct. Judges are expected to maintain an even temperament. Our chosen garb for judges, black robes, strips them of their ordinary clothing and the signifiers of class status that are a part of ordinary "street" clothing. Thus, the black robe is chosen to signal to participants in the legal process that judges have left behind personal identity in the service of their professional obligation of fair treatment and neutrality for every litigant.

In the dynamics of the courtroom, we can see the contest model of truth-seeking neutrality at work. In the contest model opposing lawyers may introduce palpably false testimony, misleading evidence, and they may use harsh tactics to destroy the credibility of witnesses who speak the objective truth. However, in the contest model, neutrality does not depend upon the truth or unbiased participation of litigants, but depends instead upon the dynamics of contested assertions. Neutrality emerges from the competing vectors of truth introduced by the interested parties. The contest model is also carried over into our expectations for jury deliberation. Juries are expected to rely upon their diverse identities, experience, and preferences to arrive at a verdict in both the criminal and civil cases. The verdict is the product of a contest of competing points of view, ultimately produces a compromise that represents a fair and neutral adjudication of the disputed claims.

In constitutional frameworks, the ideal of neutrality finds its home in the Equal Protection Clause. The equality norm has, at least since Wechsler (see note 2, supra at page 8), merged with legal formalism to insist on the application of "neutral principles." The concept of legal neutrality therefore can be traced to many complex and mutually reinforcing structures in legal theory, legal practice, and doctrine.

2. Neutrality in economics: its sources. In the market domain, belief in the insights of the first modern economist, Adam Smith, is still very firmly entrenched. Smith's central argument, in the 1759 classic the *Theory of Moral Sentiments*, was that private markets operate on the self-interested decisions of each individual participant. He argued that society achieved its maximum productivity when individuals were left alone to figure out from whom they wanted to buy and to whom they wanted to sell. Smith's famous metaphor for the social good that would arise from the cumulative impact of these buyer-seller decisions is the "invisible hand." In the centuries since Smith wrote, the argument that individuals are "led by an invisible hand to promote" what was good for society by choosing what was good for themselves has been enormously influential across all social-science disciplines, such as law, sociology, psychology, and economics.

Traditional economic analysis does not incorporate variables for either culture or identity. The language of economic analysis is built upon the implicit assumption that economic activity is natural and pre-political, and that economic actors possess abstract, identity-free preferences, devoid of the influences of culture or the dynamics of social groups. We adopt an opposing view that economic institutions are suffused with cultural power. We know that identity matters, and that economic subordination is not an abstract preference to those excluded from participation in the material comforts of our wealthy economic system.

As in traditional models of legal practice, traditional economic method-ologies are framed with the claim of neutrality in seeking truth. Truth seeking in the hard sciences, like mathematics, physics, and chemistry depends upon the use of the scientific method, in which researchers do not have a normative stake in the outcome of the investigations. So, empiri-cism, and experimental procedures that can be duplicated by any trained scientist, insure that the "truth" is not subject to manipulation. Economics associates itself with the scientific culture. This association plays a role in advancing the neutrality premises, as well. In this culture, professional detachment is a prerequisite. There is a preference for laboratory experi-ments over *in vivo* (life), in which variables can be controlled, unlike the messy multivariate environments of real human interaction.

Despite the association of economics with the physical sciences and mathematics, we notice that contemporary economics imposes crucial limi-tations upon its fields of inquiry. For example, questions of distribution—who has how much wealth—have been defined as outside the scope of research for the discipline. The problems of economic inequality and the structures of identity-based subordination have no place in the equations featuring wealth maximization, zero transactions costs, rational choice, and perfect competition.

3. Critical race theory objections to neutrality frameworks: sources and central themes. Critical race theory rejects the neutrality and objectivity of law, elevating a personal, subjective, outsider experience to the center of jurisprudence, and demanding non-neutral laws to eradi-cate the ramifications of oppression. In addition to its anti-neutrality position, critical race theory explores other themes, including the following characteristic viewpoints:

   a.   **Race as a social construction.** Critical race theorists deem the notion of race developed as a function of communal needs, econom-ics, and politics. This belief aids in explaining the simplicity and prevalence of race as a social category (the mere existence of race) and the derogatory and positive connotations related to particular racial identities.

Because race is a social construct, it does not exist a priori; rather, it is created by discourses in politics, law, and science. In addition, the constructs that support race formation are mutable and volatile. The meaning of race, the number of racial groupings, and the cultural definition of particular racial personalities have all changed over time.

b. **Narrative.** Critical race scholars write narratives to liberate themselves from the constraining effects of conformity. With narratives, scholars can choose from a range of techniques—autobiographies, parables, and self-portraits—to communicate race and equality issues. Narrative provides a framework about the character of discrimination from the view of those who experience it and also challenges the "truth" (the objective reasoning) of American jurisprudence. Carbado & Gulati, *supra* at 1784–86. Though there is some "storytelling" in the legal world—in the courtroom and in legal documents—stories told through a detached lens fail to capture central experiences.

c. **Color-blind society.** Critical race theorists reject the notion of colorblindness and embrace race consciousness. According to these scholars, colorblindness promotes nonwhites to assimilate and to deny their racial background because association with that group would cause these nonwhites to appear to be different. Critical race theory scholars argue that one simply cannot be "blind" to race because it is impossible not to notice an individual's attributes without having first thought about such traits at least once before. Neil Gotanda elaborates on this notion as he discusses the difference between medical colorblindness and liberal theorists' "nonrecognition" of race:

> A medically color-blind person is someone who cannot see what others can. It is a partial nonperception of what is "really" there. To be racially color-blind, on the other hand, is to ignore what one has already noticed. The medically color-blind individual never perceives color in the first place; the racially color-blind individual perceives race and then ignores it. . . . The characteristics of race that are noticed . . . are situated within an already existing understanding of race. . . . This preexisting race consciousness makes it impossible for an individual to be truly nonconscious of race.

Neil Gotanda, *A Critique of "Our Constitution is Color-Blind,"* 44 STAN. L. REV. 1, 18–19 (1991).

d. **Race as performative identity.** Legal scholars Devon Carbado and Mitu Gulati argue that the social definition of an individual's racial identity is a function of the way that person "performs" his or her race—for example, how an Asian person presents her "Asianness." In everyday encounters, people create or project specific images of race. This implies that the simplicity of an African American's racial identity partly originates from (1) the image of blackness he presents, and (2) how that racial projection is interpreted. Carbado and Gulati argue that they often have to suppress their racial or ethnic attributes in speech, clothing, and hair in order to dispel derogatory stereotypes about their demographic groups. This implies that racial minorities have some power to configure the parameters upon which they are experienced.

The racial "performance" an individual exhibits can span a wide range, and that individual's susceptibility to racism largely depends on where he falls on the racial spectrum:

> On one side of the spectrum are "conventional" black people. They are black prototypes—that is, people who are perceived to be stereotypically black. Their performance of blackness is consistent with society's understanding of who black people really are. On the other side are "unconventional" black people—people who are not stereotypically black. Their performance of blackness is outside of what society perceives to be conventional black behavior. A black person's vulnerability to discrimination is shaped in part by her racial position on this spectrum. The less stereotypically black she is, the more palatable her identity is. The more palatable her identity is, the less vulnerable she is to discrimination. The relationship among black unconventionality, racial palatability, and vulnerability to discrimination creates an incentive for black people to signal—through identity performances—that they are unconventionally black. These signals convey the idea that the sender is black in a phenotypic but not a social sense. Put another way, the signals function as a marketing device. They brand the black person so as to make clear that she is not a black prototype.

Devon W. Carbado & Mitu Gulati, *The Law and Economics of Critical Race Theory*, 112 YALE L.J. 1757, 1769 (2003) (book review).

e. Essentialism. To "essentialize" about race is to assume that a specific racial or gender personality has a singular and particular essence, isolated from other parts of identity. Some critical race scholars choose not to follow this essentialized methodology and are instead committed to intersectionality, a theory that insinuates that people's identities are intersectional—that is raced, gendered, sexually oriented, etc.—and that people's susceptibility to racism is a function of their specific intersectional identities. *id. See* Kimberlé W. Crenshaw, *Mapping the Margins: Intersectionality, Identity Politics, and Violence Against Women of Color*, 43 STAN. L. REV. 1241 (1991); Angela P. Harris, *Race and Essentialism in Feminist Legal Theory*, 42 STAN. L. REV. 581 (1990).

f. Identity privilege. Critical race theorists argue that because racial discrimination is an enduring social predicament, there will be victims and recipients of this discrimination.

g. **Multiracialism.** A primary premise of critical race theory is a multiracial concept. This implies that the effects of racism are larger than any particular racial group. Certain critical race scholars condemn the black/white paradigm, asserting that most legal and political discussions concerning race focus on black and white experiences, failing to consider or marginalizing the experiences of nonblack minorities.

D. Economics and Law: Two Cultures in Tension

Economics and Law: Two Cultures in Tension

54 Tenn. L. Rev. 161 (1986).

■ James Boyd White

* * *

Many people think of economics solely as a scientific, conceptual, and cognitive system, apparently unaware that there are any other dimensions of meaning in economic talk. But all expression is loaded with values, ethical and otherwise; all expression defines a self and another and proposes a relation between them; all expression remakes its language; in these senses all expression proposes the creation of a community and a culture. All expression, in short, is ethical, cultural, and political, and it can be analyzed and judged as such. To claim that economics is a science is perhaps to claim that it cannot be judged in such terms. But "sciences" are cultures too, with their own created worlds and values. One way to describe my aim in this talk, then, is to say that it reverses the usual flow: we are used to economic analyses of this or that aspect of our common life—voting, the family, war, etc. I propose here to begin what I would call a rhetorical or cultural analysis of a certain kind of economics.

* * *

III. Economics as a Language of Theory

Neoclassical microeconomics proceeds upon certain assumptions that can be summarized this way. The universe is populated by a number of discrete human actors, each of whom is competent, rational, and motivated solely by self-interest. External to the human actors is a natural universe that affords what are called "resources," which are acted upon by human actors to create something called "wealth." Partly for reasons of practicality, this kind of economics defines economic activity, and hence wealth, in terms of the process of exchange by which one actor exchanges some item within his dominion for an item within the dominion of another, or, far more commonly, for money which is the medium of exchange. To look at everything from the point of view of exchange is, naturally enough, to regard the universe as a collection of items for potential exchange, and in this sense to itemize it. When an exchange takes place these items enter the economic system and become part of what we mean by productivity. Where no exchange actually takes place—as where wealth is created and consumed by the same person, or where leisure is chosen over work—the economic effect of the actor's decision is not disregarded by professional economics, as it often is in popular economic thought, but it is still measured by the value of an imagined exchange, the one the actor has forgone. The central principle of the system is that everything is at least hypothetically interchangeable and thus of necessity quantifiable in ways that permit meaningful commensuration, at any rate by the actors who are faced with the choices to which economics speaks.

As the natural universe is itemized by these real or imagined exchanges, the social world is atomized, conceived of as a set of actors of equal competence, without race, gender, age, or culture. Each actor is assumed to be motivated by an unlimited desire to acquire or consume. Since each is interested only in its own welfare, each is in structural competition with all the others. This in turn creates a severe scarcity with respect to the resources. Where there is no scarcity, as there once was not with respect to clean air or water, there can be no economics of this kind. The final ingredient is money, a medium in which surplus can be accumulated with convenience and, in principle, without limit. So far as possible, all human interaction is reduced to the single model of exchange. Economics is the study of what life would be like on such assumptions.

Exchange is a method of determining value, which, tautologically, is said to be the price for which items are sold. This is the value that is put upon them by the economic system, and the only kind of value that economics can express. Obviously individuals may put different values on different items—indeed, this is ordinarily necessary for the exchange to occur in the first place—but although these private values drive the economic system, they are not directly expressible in its terms.

In the world of economics individual actors function according to what economists call "rationality." This is a reasoning process that consists of identifying items of potential consumption or dominion in the world, calculating their value in dollar or other common terms, and then estimating various kinds of positive and negative risks. Reason is thus reducible to calculation and risk assessment. * * *

     * * *

IV.   ECONOMICS AS A SYSTEM OF VALUES

We can start with the question of value. In its purest form economics claims to be a value-free social science. But as I suggested earlier I think it in fact enacts a set of values, including political ones, values to which the speaker of the language cannot avoid finding himself at least in part committed.

A.   *In the World*

Think, for example, of the way in which economics defines the economic actor and the processes by which he functions. He is for the most part assumed to be an individual of indeterminate age, sex, race and cultural background, but of adequate competence at manipulating economic relations. He acts as one who is both perfectly aware of his own wishes and wholly rational—in the special sense in which that term is used, to mean "calculating"—in his pursuit of them. He exists as an individual, not as part of a community, except insofar as he establishes contractual or exchange relations with others. He is assumed to be motivated by self-interest, which in turn is defined in terms of competition, acquisition, and dominion, at least in relation to resources and other actors, for in the process of exchange the self is reduced to those desires.

Of course a particular individual may have other values—indeed the economist insists that he must, calling them "tastes" or "preferences"— perhaps including a "taste" for altruism, for peace and quiet, for heavy metal music, for appreciating nature unspoiled, for beautiful or ugly art, and so forth. These values will drive his participation in the exchange process, or his decision to withdraw from it. But in either case they are themselves valued by the method of exchange: either by an actual exchange that takes place or by a hypothetical or imagined exchange that is forgone (or in a more complicated case by a combination of exchanges made and forgone). In both cases these external values are converted by the discourse into the acquisitive or instrumental values—the desire to extend the dominion of the will—that all economic actors are assumed to have, for this is the only kind of value about which economics can directly talk.

With respect to the external values in their original form, the system is purportedly "value neutral." That is, it regards individual values as simply exogenous to the system itself. Economics of course recognizes that these values exist, but it demeans them by calling them "tastes" or "preferences," names that imply that no serious conversation can proceed on such subjects. And economics itself is by definition not about those values, but about the process by which they are reflected in the activity of exchange. This means that economics cannot, in principle, talk about any value other than the acquisitive or instrumental one that it universalizes. (Indeed it does not talk about this value either, but merely assumes and acts upon it.) This is not to be "value free," as its apologists claim, but to make self-interest the central, indeed almost the only, value, for it is the only one that can be talked about in these terms. To come at it the other way, it is to claim that all values can be talked about, at least for some purposes, as if they were selfish, quantifiable, and interchangeable.

* * *

Yet economics is troubling not only for the self-interested values it directly asserts, but also for the very neutrality, the "value freedom," that it claims. It is in principle neutral on all questions of value that are external to the acquisitive and competitive ones enacted in the exchange game, which it lumps together as "tastes" or "preferences" among which no distinctions can be drawn. But this is to be silent on all the great questions of human life: questions of beauty and ugliness in art and music, sincerity and falsity in human relations, wisdom and folly in conduct and judgment, and the greatest of all questions, which is how we ought to lead our lives. Economic analysis assumes as a given the existence of "tastes" or "preferences" which drive the system, but economics as a language can provide no way of talking about these values, whether in oneself or another, no way of thinking about which to prefer and which not. To the extent that economics does reach out for these questions it may be worse than silent, for silence after all can be a mode of controlling a discourse. When economics tries to speak about these matters it does so in the only way it knows how to speak, in purely quantitative terms and on the assumption that all human transactions can be reduced to the model of exchange.

* * *

For the purposes of economic analysis all human wishes and desires are thus reduced to the same level, as though no principled choices could be made among them, as though it didn't matter what choices one made. This in turn means that it is impossible to talk in these terms about our most important choices as individuals and communities, or about the education of mind or heart, for any impulse that we or others may happen to have is as good, valid, and entitled to respect as any other.

* * * We must and do have preferences, as the economist knows; and these necessarily commit those who have them to the inquiry of better and worse, as well as to that of greater and less. To refuse to engage in this inquiry—to privatize it—as economics in its neutral phase necessarily does, is to deny an essential and necessary aspect of human life. To reduce all value to self-interest, as it does the rest of the time, is intellectually and ethically intolerable. How could one educate one's children or oneself to live in a world that was neutral on all the great questions of life, except that it reduced them to acquisition, competition, and calculation?

B.   Among Economists

There is another dimension to economics, as a discourse among economists. Here too, in the discourse, values are of necessity enacted. For example, economics necessarily values the reduction of life to terms such as I describe, for this is what it achieves. It values linear reasoning and competition for dominance. This last is especially so among economists, for it is ostensibly a premise of economic discourse, as a rule of proof appropriate to a science, that we will believe only what we are forced by logic and fact to believe. This means that economic conversations—like certain other academic discussions—are often attempts to compel others to submit to one's views, or to resist such submission. In doing so they necessarily perform a claim that this is the most appropriate and valuable way to converse on these subjects, itself a most dubious position.

* * *

The claim that microeconomics is a value-free science is thus false in at least two ways. First, even as a science it is not value-free, for no science can be. It values the positivist and behaviorist premises from which it functions, the reduction of reason to calculation, the performed conversion of the world into quantifiable units, and so on. Second, economics attributes motives and values to its actors, those of acquisitiveness and self-interest, and invests itself in these attributions, which it assumes to be universal. This assumption is qualified by the recognition that one actor may choose to act for others, but in the end economics always reduces motive to self-interest, the only kind of motive it can conceive of and speak about. The reduction of all human interaction to the model of exchange, actual or imagined, simply erases whole fields of life and thought, from art to morals, for economics recognizes no ground, other than competitive survivability, upon which one can choose one form of life or one work of art over another, or even upon which one can choose to favor the market and its methods of analysis over others.

In saying that "value-free" economics is actually committed to certain values, both in the assumptions it makes about the world and in the conventions by which its own discourse operates, I do not mean to suggest that the field is in this respect peculiar. Quite the contrary. As I say above I think that all systems of discourse commit their users to values and do so in both domains, that is in one's account of the "other world" one talks about and in the here-and-now world one creates by talking. Science does this, and so do law and literary criticism too. Economics is not to be blamed, then, for having values. But no one should be allowed to claim value-neutrality where it does not exist, and economics, like other disciplines, can be praised or blamed for the values it has. All of us, economists and lawyers and lecturers among the rest, should be held responsible for the values we enact in our talking.

All this is not to say that economics is wrong to do what it does, namely, to isolate the practices of exchange for study, especially when its results are applied to spheres of life that are in fact characterized by exchanges that take place on conditions roughly matching the assumptions of the discourse. This is, after all, a good deal of the economic life of the investor or entrepreneur in a capitalist economy. But it is to say that this study would lead to insanity unless it were premised on a recognition that these activities, and the culture they and their study together create, require subordination to other activities and cultures, both at the level of the individual and of the polity.

V. ECONOMICS AS A POLITICAL SYSTEM

An economist might agree with most of this and say that the language and practices in which he engages as an economist must somehow be put together with the languages and practices that make up the rest of his life, both public and private. This would raise the wonderfully interesting and important question, how this might be done, and with what effect on economics itself, a question to which I shall return below.

But another line of justification is possible as well, one that neither denies the political character of this discourse nor seeks to subordinate it to other languages and practices, but affirmatively celebrates the politics and ethics that this kind of economics entails, mainly on the ground that the market is affirmatively desirable both as a model of life and as a political and social institution. The premises of the analytic method, in other words, can be regarded as the proper premises upon which to build our collective life. In talking this way the economist moves off the ground of purportedly pure science. He begins to use his language not as a "filing system" but as a way of expressing overt social and political attitudes, largely in support of the institution of the market. I should stress that not all economists would take this step. But some would. They are of course perfectly entitled to do so, but only to the extent that their politics and ethics, not their economics, persuade us of the rightness of their vision.

A.   *Justifying the Market as a Model of Life*

The institution of the market is celebrated by its proponents because in their view it is democratic—each person brings to the market his own values and can "maximize" them his own way—and because it is creative and open, leaving the widest room for individual choice and action. The market establishes a community based upon a competitive process that allows each person freedom to choose what to do with what is his. These merits mean, for some economists at least, that all social institutions ought to be modified to approximate the market—to conform to the analytic model of life as exchange—or at least to be analyzed and judged on that presumption.

The market is further justified, when such justification is thought necessary, in either of two rather conflicting ways. The first is to say that the market is good because it promotes efficiency, that is to say it maximizes the "welfare" of all participants in the process. It does this by definition, because each person participates in the process only because he thinks he gets more that way than he would any other way, and who are we to tell him differently? In maximizing the welfare of all participants it does the same for society as a whole, which is nothing more or less than the sum of all the participants in the market. The obvious trouble with this is that it takes for granted not only the existing values (or "tastes") of the actors, but also the existing distributions among them of wealth, capacity, and entitlement, which it has no way of criticizing. Yet these may of course be eminently criticizable.

The "welfare" defense of the market would justify all transactions—including the sale of oneself into slavery or prostitution—that are not in an obvious sense "coerced" by another because they are marginal improvements for the actors involved. But an economy might provide a different set of starting points for its actors, so that such degrading activities would no longer be "improvements" for anyone. We would all benefit from living in such a world. But the economist has no way of saying this. On the premises I have described he cannot deny the desirability of redistribution, but he cannot affirm it either. Even to discuss the question requires a shift of discourse, to ways of talking that economics of the sort I have been discussing excludes.

The second ground upon which the market is justified is that not of its gross effects but of its fairness. In one version this justification rests upon the ethical standing of voluntary action and holds that the results of the market process are justified with respect to every actor because the choices by which the market works are voluntary. In another version, it becomes the affirmative celebration of autonomy or liberty: whether or not it is efficient, the market is good because it gives the widest possible range to freedom of choice and action. Here the claim moves beyond justifying market results by the voluntary character of the choices upon which they rest to the point of asserting autonomy as the central social and political value. The obvious trouble with this line of defense, in both of its forms, is that it assumes that all exchanges are for all actors equally voluntary and equally expressive of autonomy, a position that common sense denies.

* * *

The market purports to rest upon an assumption of the equality of all the actors in the system. In fact, it rests upon a different assumption, namely, the equality of every dollar in the system. Since some players have many more dollars, and through this fact are at a competitive advantage, it is a system that actively supports inequality among its actors.

It is not too much to say, I think, that the modern celebration of the market as the central social institution—the most fair, the most respecting of autonomy, and the most efficient—threatens to destroy the single greatest achievement of Western political culture: the discovery that a community can govern itself through a rule of law that attempts to create a fundamental moral and political equality among human beings. The great phrase in the Declaration of Independence—"all men are created equal"— is partly a theological statement about the conditions under which we are created and partly a political statement about the obligation of the government to acknowledge, indeed to create or recreate, that equality. This value is the heart of what is meant both by equality under law and by our democratic institutions more generally, resting as they do on the premise that each person's vote is worth exactly what everyone else's is. The ideology of the market, if it prevailed in its desire to convert all institutions into markets, would destroy this set of political relations and would create another in its stead, based upon the dollar.

* * *

The market ideology claims to be radically democratic and egalitarian because it leaves every person free to do with her own what she will. But this freedom of choice is not equally distributed among all people. The market is democratic not on the principle of one person one vote, but on the far different principle of one dollar, one vote. One could hardly make a greater mistake than to equate, as so much modern public talk carelessly does, the "free market" with democracy.

There are two distinct points here. First, the exchange transactions that the market celebrates are not entitled to the special respect claimed for them as free and voluntary, and hence fair, unless each person has roughly the same amount of money and the same competence and freedom in its use, which is demonstrably not the case. The accumulations of wealth it permits thus cannot be justified by the fairness of the transactions by which the accumulation occurs. Second, if the advocates of the market succeeded in converting other institutions into markets, the result would be to transfer to those who have wealth not only the economic power that inescapably follows it but also the political power that in our democratic tradition the people have claimed for themselves and have exercised through the institutions of self-government. This would validate and institutionalize private economic power held by one person over another, of the rich over the poor. If we were to yield entirely to its claims, we would gradually find our traditional government, which operates by collective deliberation on a premise of fundamental equality of citizens, replaced by a private-sector government of the few over the many, wholly unregulated by collective judgment.

VI.   ECONOMICS AS A SYSTEM OF ECONOMIC ANALYSIS

But it is not only as a system of value and politics that this kind of economics, and the ways of thought it encourages, are troubling. I think that it is distorted and unrealistic as a way of imagining, thinking about, and shaping the processes of production and exchange that we think of as the economy itself.

A.   *The Social and Natural Matrix*

The first distortion I wish to consider has to do with the relationship between the exchange system and the cultural and natural world that it necessarily presupposes. What I mean is this. The economic activity of exchange takes place under natural and cultural conditions that are absolutely essential to it, but about which economics has no way of talking except by itemization, quantification, and conversion into the material of actual or hypothetical exchange. All talk about exchanges, that is, necessarily presupposes that the exchangers live in the natural world of sun, air, and water, subject to the powers of growth and health and disease, a world the organization of which is complex far beyond our understanding. Each of the exchangers is part of that world in another sense as well, for each is himself an organism, and one that incompletely understands both himself and his relation to the natural world upon which he absolutely depends for his existence. The language of economics similarly assumes the existence of a society and culture, a set of human understandings and expectations upon which each exchanger can rely: that promises will normally be kept, that one can get one's money home without being robbed, that it is worth thinking about the future, for oneself or for one's children, and so on. What is more, the actor's motives or values (what the economists call his "preferences") are themselves formed by interactions both with his culture and with nature. This is how we are made as individuals, how we cohere as a community, and how we connect ourselves to the past and to the future.

But on all this economics is silent, for it begins to speak only when an actor has, at least in his mind, identified some item in the world and begun to think of exchanging it for something else. It is his judgment of its worth, in exchanging it or in declining to do so, that is for the economist its value. But what confidence can we have in such judgments of worth, by actors necessarily imperfectly aware both of themselves and of the cultural and natural worlds they inhabit? To put it in epistemological terms, the economist assumes that there is nothing to be known about the natural or cultural world that cannot be known through the process of exchange itself. But in order to judge the value of an item now, or to predict one for the future (which is very much the same thing), one must make estimates about possible changes in the social, cultural, and natural matrix in which all exchange takes place, and about the effect of this and similar exchanges upon that matrix. There is no reason to be especially confident in anyone's capacity to make such estimates.

* * *

This is to talk about it in terms of knowledge, the knowledge that the economist assumes we have. But it can be cast in terms of value as well, for the language of economics assumes that the relation between humanity and nature should be one of dominion, that the expanded assertion of control by individual actors over nature—called "natural resources"—is inherently a good thing. But why should one grant such an assumption? As Wendell Berry repeatedly points out in his works on agricultural economics, modern agriculture can be considered a great technological success only if one uses the measure of present-day output per man-hour, disregarding both the destructive effects of modern farming on soil and water and the costs, natural and economic, of the fossil fuels used for both fertilizer and power. If productivity over decades or per acre is the test, as in a world of five billion perhaps it should be, our agriculture falls well below that of many more "primitive" peoples. If one includes the meaning of the work the farmer does, its rhythms and its harmonies or disharmonies with nature, the picture is complicated further; still further if one asks how important it is in a nuclear age for a particular polity, or for humanity, that the capacity for fruitful and stable survival on a small scale be maintained. Economic language assumes, with what a theologian like James Gustafson might call a foolish pride, that man's wants and wishes are the ultimate measure of value; it then claims that these wishes are constrained only in ways that traders can see and account for. These are assumptions of fact and value that one might generously regard as dubious.

The only kind of meaning economics can reflect is one that can be expressed in the medium of exchange, that is, quantifiable and comparative. This is in turn to give the world itself a meaning of a new kind, reflected in the Japanese phrase for the blue sky that can rarely be seen over Tokyo these days: it is called a "recession sky."

* * *

D. *Erasing Community*

For similar reasons this kind of economics has the greatest difficulty in reflecting the reality of human community and the value of communal institutions. Its necessary tendency seems to be to destroy the idea of public action, indeed the idea of community itself. This is partly because this methodology tends to resolve all communities and organizations into the individual human actors who constitute them, partly because commitment to the market system leads one to think that everything that can be made the subject of the market should be. The idea is that every economic actor should pay for what he wants, and should not have to pay for what he doesn't want. But this tends to destroy our public institutions, all of which extend benefits far beyond those who would pay (if they were reduced to markets) or who do pay (when they are supported by taxes). Such institutions reflect a communal judgment that we need to educate ourselves and each other, that our "tastes" are not all of equal value but need to be formed, and formed well rather than badly. Public universities, libraries, orchestras, museums, parks—all these would fall before the ideology that denies the existence and reality of community and reduces all institutions, all human production, to the language of the market.

Think here of the way economists explain why people who will probably never visit, say, the Everglades or an art museum are happy to have their taxes used to maintain them. The economist says it is because the actor wants to maintain the option of visiting them some day, and calls this an "option demand." But may it not be that the voter simply takes pleasure in what other people have and in what other people can do, in belonging to a community that is good for all its members? Or that he respects their desires and wants a community based on that kind of mutual respect? This possibility is systematically denied by the assumption of economic talk, that individuals and communities are in principle incapable of generosity, or more precisely, that "altruism" can adequately be talked about as a species of selfishness.

The language of self and self-interest not only fails to reflect the reality of community and of shared interests, it draws attention away from those aspects of life and devalues them. To continue to talk on these assumptions, even hypothetically, is to encourage "self-interest" in an ethical sense and to erode the commitments we have to each other that underlie such essential practices of citizenship as the willingness to pay taxes, to work for the local school, or to serve in the army, upon which everything depends. To adopt the economic view would in fact threaten the very existence of community, for on these premises no one would conceivably die or seriously risk his life for his community: at the point of danger one's self-interest in survival would outweigh all other self-interests. And to speak of all "tastes" as if they were equivalent is to invite oneself and others to think that they are, and to confirm the premises of our culture, already drummed into the mind by the consumer economy, that the consumer is king, that whatever you happen to want is a good that you should seek to satisfy, that no distinction can be drawn between the beautiful and ugly, the wise and foolish, and so on. It is to confirm a vulgar view of democracy that makes the preference or will supreme, as if we functioned by instant referendum. It erases the sense that a democracy is a mode of communal self-constitution and self-education that may have higher ends than the satisfaction of wants, namely the creation of a community of a certain sort, at once based upon a set of responsibilities and offering us a set of opportunities for civic and social action.

————

NOTES AND QUESTIONS

1.   Effect of terminology on White's critique. White states that "all systems of discourse commit their users to values . . . [and that] economics is [not] wrong to do what it does." James Boyd White, *Economics and Law: Two Cultures in Tension*, 54 TENN. L. REV. 161, 176 (1986). If all White wishes is for economics to acknowledge that it is no different from other systems of discourse, does his critique of law and economics have any value? Would the problems White identifies with law and economics be solved by acknowledging that law and economics has values without making any substantive changes to the discipline? Would White be satisfied with this solution?

2.   Pernicious nature of law and economics. At the close of his article, White states that "to continue to talk on . . . [law and economics'] assumptions, even hypothetically, is to encourage 'self interest' in an ethical sense and to erode the commitments we have to each other that underlie such essential practices of citizenship as the willingness to pay taxes, to work for the local school, or to serve in the army, upon which everything depends. To adopt the economic view would in fact threaten the very existence of community. . . ." *Id.* at 192. If White is correct about the dire consequences of even hypothesizing in an economic framework, how can he assert that economics is not wrong to "do what it does"? *Id.* at 176.

E.   JUDGING RACE: THE DOCTRINE OF DISCRIMINATORY INTENT

Note About Neutrality in Form, Discriminatory Impact and the Paradox of Statistical Correlation vs. Motivation

The debate about race, neutrality, and markets has not been limited to economic theories of rationality contesting the subjective narratives of critical race scholars. Conflicting perspectives about neutrality also extend to disputes about what evidence can trigger a constitutional violation of the Equal Protection Clause. In this debate, the liberal and conservative positions have been reversed. Civil rights advocates sought to rely upon scientific measures of statistical racial disparity to show that the impact of a facially neutral policy violated the Equal Protection standard. The Court rejected statistical measures of the disparate impact of the employment screening test on black applicants.

For "facially neutral" policies, such as this employment screening test, the Court introduced a motive-focused standard that required evidence of intentional racial discrimination to establish a violation of the Fourteenth Amendment. The demise of disparate impact theory to prove an Equal Protection violation was a major setback for the use of civil rights legal theory seeking to challenge government policies and practices, even though such policies did not contain a race-specific classification.

Consider how this case contributes to our understanding of the uses of the concept of neutrality. Does the fact that scientific tools, such as statistical proof of disproportionate harm to racial minority groups, were rejected in this case turn the conservative (scientific) vs. liberal (empathetic, seeking to enter the subjective experience of another) on its head? As you read the case that follows, recall that it was Judge Posner who said:

> Maybe economic scholarship is not *really* empathetic. The economist does not enter imaginatively into the distress of the disappointed quester for rental housing; all he does is tote up some additional costs. But that may be a sounder way of doing policy than by cultivating empathy. A jurisprudence of empathy can foster short-sighted substantive justice . . . [1]

Posner, OVERCOMING LAW, *supra* at 381.

On the basis of the observations above, had he been a Justice, do you think Judge Posner would have dissented in the following case?

———

Washington v. Davis

426 U.S. 229 (1976).

■ MR. JUSTICE WHITE DELIVERED THE OPINION OF THE COURT.

This case involves the validity of a qualifying test administered to applicants for positions as police officers in the District of Columbia Metropolitan Police Department. The test was sustained by the District Court, but invalidated by the Court of Appeals. We are in agreement with the District Court and hence reverse the judgment of the Court of Appeals.

[The action was filed by black applicants to become police officers in the District of Columbia. The claimants were unsuccessful in passing a test that was designed to measure verbal skills, vocabulary and reading. They introduced evidence in the District Court showing that a greater percentage of blacks failed, than did whites. In addition, the claimants alleged that the

---

1. A more basic point is that the internal perspective—putting oneself in the other person's shoes—that is achieved by the exercise of empathic imagination lacks normative significance.

test had not been validated, by accepted test measurement methodology, to provide reliable test results for predicting future job performance.]

The central purpose of the Equal Protection Clause of the Fourteenth Amendment is the prevention of official conduct discriminating on the basis of race. It is also true that the Due Process Clause of the Fifth Amendment contains an equal protection component prohibiting the United States from invidiously discriminating between individuals or groups. *Bolling* v. *Sharpe,* 347 U.S. 497 (1954). But our cases have not embraced the proposition that a law or other official act, without regard to whether it reflects a racially discriminatory purpose, is unconstitutional *solely* because it has a racially disproportionate impact.

Almost 100 years ago, *Strauder* v. *West Virginia,* 100 U.S. 303 (1880), established that the exclusion of Negroes from grand and petit juries in criminal proceedings violated the Equal Protection Clause, but the fact that a particular jury or a series of juries does not statistically reflect the racial composition of the community does not in itself make out an invidious discrimination forbidden by the Clause. "A purpose to discriminate must be present which may be proven by systematic exclusion of eligible jurymen of the proscribed race or by unequal application of the law to such an extent as to show intentional discrimination." A defendant in a criminal case is entitled "to require that the State not deliberately and systematically deny to members of his race the right to participate as jurors in the administration of justice."

The rule is the same in other contexts [a 1964 case] upheld a New York congressional apportionment statute against claims that district lines had been racially gerrymandered. The challenged districts were made up predominantly of whites or of minority races and their boundaries were irregularly drawn. The challengers did not prevail because they failed to prove that the New York Legislature "was either motivated by racial considerations or in fact drew the districts on racial lines"; the plaintiffs had not shown that the statute "was the product of a state contrivance to segregate on the basis of race or place of origin." * * *

The school desegregation cases have also adhered to the basic equal protection principle that the invidious quality of a law claimed to be racially discriminatory must ultimately be traced to a racially discriminatory purpose. That there are both predominantly black and predominantly white schools in a community is not alone violative of the Equal Protection Clause. The essential element of *de jure* segregation is "a current condition of segregation resulting from intentional state action." *Keyes* v. *School Dist. No. 1,* 413 U.S. 189, 205 (1973). "The differentiating factor between *de jure* segregation and so-called *de facto* segregation ... is *purpose* or *intent* to *segregate*." *Id.,* at 208. See also *id.,* at 199, 211, and 213. The Court has also recently rejected allegations of racial discrimination based solely on the statistically disproportionate racial impact of various provisions of the Social Security Act because "[t]he acceptance of appellants' constitutional theory would render suspect each difference in treatment among the grant classes, however lacking in racial motivation and however otherwise rational the treatment might be."

This is not to say that the necessary discriminatory racial purpose must be express or appear on the face of the statute, or that a law's disproportionate impact is irrelevant in cases involving Constitution-based claims of racial discrimination. A statute, otherwise neutral on its face, must not be applied so as invidiously to discriminate on the basis of race. *Yick Wo v. Hopkins,* 118 U.S. 356 (1886). It is also clear from the cases dealing with racial discrimination in the selection of juries that the systematic exclusion of Negroes is itself such an "unequal application of the law . . . as to show intentional discrimination." A prima facie case of discriminatory purpose may be proved as well by the absence of Negroes on a particular jury combined with the failure of the jury commissioners to be informed of eligible Negro jurors in a community, or with racially nonneutral selection procedures. With a prima facie case made out, "the burden of proof shifts to the State to rebut the presumption of unconstitutional action by showing that permissible racially neutral selection criteria and procedures have produced the monochromatic result."

Necessarily, an invidious discriminatory purpose may often be inferred from the totality of the relevant facts, including the fact, if it is true, that the law bears more heavily on one race than another. It is also not infrequently true that the discriminatory impact—in the jury cases for example, the total or seriously disproportionate exclusion of Negroes from jury venires—may for all practical purposes demonstrate unconstitutionality because in various circumstances the discrimination is very difficult to explain on nonracial grounds. Nevertheless, we have not held that a law, neutral on its face and serving ends otherwise within the power of government to pursue, is invalid under the Equal Protection Clause simply because it may affect a greater proportion of one race than of another. Disproportionate impact is not irrelevant, but it is not the sole touchstone of an invidious racial discrimination forbidden by the Constitution. Standing alone, it does not trigger the rule, that racial classifications are to be subjected to the strictest scrutiny and are justifiable only by the weightiest of considerations. * * *

As an initial matter, we have difficulty understanding how a law establishing a racially neutral qualification for employment is nevertheless racially discriminatory and denies "any person . . . equal protection of the laws" simply because a greater proportion of Negroes fail to qualify than members of other racial or ethnic groups. Had respondents, along with all others who had failed Test 21, whether white or black, brought an action claiming that the test denied each of them equal protection of the laws as compared with those who had passed with high enough scores to qualify them as police recruits, it is most unlikely that their challenge would have been sustained. Test 21, which is administered generally to prospective Government employees, concededly seeks to ascertain whether those who take it have acquired a particular level of verbal skill; and it is untenable that the Constitution prevents the Government from seeking modestly to upgrade the communicative abilities of its employees rather than to be satisfied with some lower level of competence, particularly where the job requires special ability to communicate orally and in writing. Respondents, as Negroes, could no more successfully claim that the test denied them equal protection than could white applicants who also failed. The conclusion would not be different in the face of proof that more Negroes than whites had been disqualified by Test 21. That other Negroes also failed to score well would, alone, not demonstrate that respondents individually were being denied equal protection of the laws by the application of an otherwise valid qualifying test being administered to prospective police recruits.

Nor on the facts of the case before us would the disproportionate impact of Test 21 warrant the conclusion that it is a purposeful device to discriminate against Negroes and hence an infringement of the constitutional rights of respondents as well as other black applicants. As we have said, the test is neutral on its face and rationally may be said to serve a purpose the Government is constitutionally empowered to pursue. Even agreeing with the District Court that the differential racial effect of Test 21 called for further inquiry, we think the District Court correctly held that the affirmative efforts of the Metropolitan Police Department to recruit black officers, the changing racial composition of the recruit classes and of the force in general, and the relationship of the test to the training program negated any inference that the Department discriminated on the basis of race or that "a police officer qualifies on the color of his skin rather than ability."[13] * * *

A rule that a statute designed to serve neutral ends is nevertheless invalid, absent compelling justification, if in practice it benefits or burdens one race more than another would be far reaching and would raise serious questions about, and perhaps invalidate, a whole range of tax, welfare, public service, regulatory, and licensing statutes that may be more burdensome to the poor and to the average black than to the more affluent white. . . .

We also hold that the Court of Appeals should have affirmed the judgment of the District Court granting the motions for summary judgment

---

13. It appears beyond doubt by now that there is no single method for appropriately validating employment tests for their relationship to job performance. Professional standards developed by the American Psychological Association in its Standards for Educational and Psychological Tests and Manuals (1966), accept three basic methods of validation: "empirical" or "criterion" validity (demonstrated by identifying criteria that indicate successful job performance and then correlating test scores and the criteria so identified); "construct" validity (demonstrated by examinations structured to measure the degree to which job applicants have identifiable characteristics that have been determined to be important in successful job performance); and "content" validity (demonstrated by tests whose content closely approximates tasks to be performed on the job by the applicant). These standards have been relied upon by the Equal Employment Opportunity Commission in fashioning its Guidelines on Employee Selection Procedures, 29 CFR pt. 1607 (1975), and have been judicially noted in cases where validation of employment tests has been in issue.

filed by petitioners and the federal parties. Respondents were entitled to relief on neither constitutional nor statutory grounds. * * *

■ MR. JUSTICE STEVENS concurring. . . .

While I agree with the Court's disposition of this case, I add these comments on the constitutional issue discussed. . . .

The requirement of purposeful discrimination is a common thread running through the cases summarized in Part II. These cases include criminal convictions which were set aside because blacks were excluded from the grand jury, a reapportionment case in which political boundaries were obviously influenced to some extent by racial considerations, a school desegregation case, and a case involving the unequal administration of an ordinance purporting to prohibit the operation of laundries in frame buildings. Although it may be proper to use the same language to describe the constitutional claim in each of these contexts, the burden of proving a prima facie case may well involve differing evidentiary considerations. The extent of deference that one pays to the trial court's determination of the factual issue, and indeed, the extent to which one characterizes the intent issue as a question of fact or a question of law, will vary in different contexts.

Frequently the most probative evidence of intent will be objective evidence of what actually happened rather than evidence describing the subjective state of mind of the actor. For normally the actor is presumed to have intended the natural consequences of his deeds. This is particularly true in the case of governmental action which is frequently the product of compromise, of collective decision-making, and of mixed motivation. It is unrealistic, on the one hand, to require the victim of alleged discrimination to uncover the actual subjective intent of the decision-maker or, conversely, to invalidate otherwise legitimate action simply because an improper motive affected the deliberation of a participant in the decisional process. A law conscripting clerics should not be invalidated because an atheist voted for it.

My point in making this observation is to suggest that the line between discriminatory purpose and discriminatory impact is not nearly as bright, and perhaps not quite as critical, as the reader of the Court's opinion might assume. I agree, of course, that a constitutional issue does not arise every time some disproportionate impact is shown. On the other hand, when the disproportion is as dramatic as in *Gomillion* v. *Lightfoot,* 364 U.S. 339, or *Yick Wo* v. *Hopkins,* 118 U.S. 356, it really does not matter whether the standard is phrased in terms of purpose or effect. Therefore, although I accept the statement of the general rule in the Court's opinion, I am not yet prepared to indicate how that standard should be applied in the many cases which have formulated the governing standard in different language. * * *

My agreement . . . rests on a ground narrower than the Court describes. I do not rely at all on the evidence of good-faith efforts to recruit black police officers. In my judgment, neither those efforts nor the subjective good faith of the District administration, would save Test 21 if it were otherwise invalid.

There are two reasons why I am convinced that the challenge to Test 21 is insufficient. First, the test serves the neutral and legitimate purpose of requiring all applicants to meet a uniform minimum standard of literacy. Reading ability is manifestly relevant to the police function, there is no evidence that the required passing grade was set at an arbitrarily high level, and there is sufficient disparity among high schools and high school graduates to justify the use of a separate uniform test. Second, the same test is used throughout the federal service. The applicants for employment in the District Columbia Police Department represent such a small fraction of the total number of persons who have taken the test that their experience is of minimal probative value in assessing the neutrality of the test itself. That evidence, without more, is not sufficient to overcome the presumption that a test which is this widely used by the Federal Government is in fact neutral in its effect as well as its "purpose" as that term is used in constitutional adjudication. * * *

■ MR. JUSTICE BRENNAN and MR. JUSTICE MARSHALL dissent

[I]t should be observed that every federal court, except the District Court in this case, presented with proof identical to that offered to validate Test 21 has reached a conclusion directly opposite to that of the Court today. * * *

Empirical Evidence

PERVASIVE PREJUDICE, UNCONVENTIONAL EVIDENCE OF RACE AND GENDER DISCRIMINATION 3–8 (2001).

■ IAN AYRES

Indeed, there seems to be a widespread, implicit belief (at least among white males) that race and gender discrimination is not a serious problem in retail markets. The civil rights laws of the 1960s focused on only a handful of non-retail markets-chiefly concerning employment, housing, and public accommodation services. Indeed, the most gaping hole in our civil rights law concerns retail gender discrimination. No federal law prohibits gender discrimination in the sale of goods or services. A seller could flatly refuse to deal with a potential buyer of a car or a paperclip because of her gender. And while the civil rights laws of the 1860s prohibited race discrimination in contracting, the civil rights laws a century later only prohibited sex discrimination in a narrow range of "titled" markets. The thousands of other markets that make up our economy are completely unregulated with regard to gender (as well as to religion and national origin) discrimination and only somewhat more regulated with regard to race. And only a handful of cities and states (chief among them California) make up for this failing by prohibiting gender discrimination in contracting generally.

The non-regulation of retail discrimination seems to be premised on a vague coterie of assumptions: (1) retail discrimination does not exist because retailers have no motive to discriminate; (2) retail discrimination does not exist because competition forces retailers not to discriminate; and (3) any retail discrimination that does occur does not have serious consequences because of effective counterstrategies by potential victims. It is also argued that any discrimination in the sale of goods or services is less important than the potential effects of discrimination in the markets for employment and housing. But without denying the primacy of employment, the current regulatory regime leaves approximately 66 percent of the dollars we spend-and 35 percent of the dollars we earn-unregulated (with respect to gender discrimination) or less regulated (with respect to race discrimination).

In this book, I contest the idea that race and gender discrimination in the retail sale of goods is nonexistent or unimportant. My thesis is that race and gender discrimination is neither a thing of the past nor is it limited to the narrow set of "titled" markets regulated by the civil rights legislation of the 1960s (Title VII, Title II, and so on). The book's primary contribution is empirical, but let me begin with a few theoretical reasons why we should take the possibility of retail discrimination seriously.

RETAILERS MAY HAVE A MOTIVE TO DISCRIMINATE

The argument that discrimination in the sale of goods and services does not exist because retailers lack any disparate treatment motive is itself premised on the twin ideas that discriminating against economically marginal groups would not be profitable and that racial animus would not manifest itself in discrete retail transactions.

The latter idea is that while animus might cause race discrimination in the more relational settings employment, apartment rental, and restaurants-which civil rights laws regulate, regulated retail transactions are sufficiently discrete that seller and/or customer prejudice would not induce disparate treatment. There are, however, several problems with this theory. First, as pointed out by Ian MacNeil, contractual arrangements are not as discrete as initially appear. Barbers may have much more tactile and repeated contact with their customers than one-time sellers of a house, but the law much more vigorously regulates the latter transaction. Second, the thought that prejudice is less likely to be acted upon in discrete transactions is premised on a narrow theory of what might be called "associational" animus-that is, that bigots don't like associating with particular groups. But, * * * there are other types of animus that might persist even in discrete markets. For example, if sellers enjoy extracting an extra dollar of profit from people of color more than from whites, we might expect to see disparate racial treatment in pricing or quality of service. Finally, appreciating the pervasive discretion given to employees as agents open up the possibility that even profit-maximizing principals will by necessity countenance some disparate treatment by their subordinates.

Discriminating retailers may also be actuated by profit. Sellers may have a profit-maximizing incentive to price discriminate against minorities and women-even if sellers believe that members of these groups are on average poorer. It has long been known that "statistical discrimination" might cause rational, profit-maximizing sellers to charge more to groups that on average cause sellers to incur higher costs. Thus, as a theoretical matter, the drivers of taxis might discriminate against African American men if the drivers perceive a higher chance of being robbed by such passengers. But, more provocatively, focusing on the example of new car sales, I argue that profit-maximizing sellers may engage in "revenue-based" race and gender disparate treatment. Dealerships may discriminate not because they expect higher costs but because they expect to be able to extract higher revenues. This is a surprising possibility because, as an empirical matter, people of color have a substantially lower ability to pay for new cars. But profit-maximizing sellers care far more about the variability in willingness to pay than in the mean willingness. The presence of a few minority members who are willing to pay a large markup can make it rational for the dealership to offer higher prices to all members of the group-even if group members are on average poorer.

It is correct and useful to ask whether sellers would plausibly be motivated to engage in a particular type of discrimination. But treating this issue seriously opens up a variety of dimensions where discrimination in the retail sale of goods and services could be a plausible seller strategy for either profit or non-profit-based reasons.

COMPETITION MAY NOT DRIVE OUT RETAIL DISCRIMINATION

Nobel-prize winning economist Gary Becker emphasized how competition could provide a much-needed antidote for the disease of discrimination. Non-discriminating sellers could earn higher profits by picking up the sales of those minorities and/or women excluded from equal access to the discriminating sellers. One problem with this theory is that it focuses on the ability of competition to drive out discriminating sellers, but competition may not be as effective at driving out the preferences of discriminating customers. If fixed costs of production limit the number of firms selling and if a substantial number of, say, white customers prefer dealing with a firm that discriminates against (by excluding or offering inferior service to) people of color, then firms may decide that it is more profitable to exclude minorities than to lose the patronage of whites.

As an empirical matter, however, my guess is that most firms would not find overt race or gender discrimination to be a profit-maximizing strategy. While Lester Maddox may have increased his sales by excluding African Americans, in most markets a "whites only" or "males only" policy or overtly charging higher prices to particular demographic groups would lead to a general negative consumer reaction-by both minorities and progressive white consumers.

A more important limitation on competition is consumer information. In order for discrimination to cause the competitive shift of consumers toward nondiscriminatory sellers, consumers must know which sellers are discriminating and which are not. There is thus an important informational prerequisite for competition to have the predicted Beckerian effect. But as described above, there are many aspects of treatment where consumers may not be able to compare how sellers treat similarly situated counter-parts. Retail discrimination is most likely to persist where consumers do not learn the benchmark treatment of fellow consumers. Thus, while there is little opportunity for a single fast food franchise to charge different prices for hamburgers, it is possible for a dealership to charge different prices to potential buyers of cars. Since bargained prices diverge from the list price, it is very difficult for a consumer to know whether she has received a nondiscriminatory price. And it will be more difficult for a nondiscriminatory seller to credibly market itself on the basis that the race or gender of customers do not influence its bargaining strategy.

Markets in which price or other terms of trade are individually bargained for provide much greater opportunities for race or gender dis-crimination than markets with homogeneous product attributes and posted prices. However, even retailers that sell standardized products at posted prices might discriminate on the basis of race or gender with regard to discretionary aspects of service. Anyone watching the *Prime Time* segment could vividly see that record and department stores could substantially increase the "transaction costs" of minority customers. This is not just an issue of whether the retailer provides "service with a smile" but, as in the *Prime Time Live* testing, whether the retailers make minority customers wait substantially longer before being served (or whether the minority customers are conspicuously shadowed to scrutinize whether they are shoplifting).

Retailers may also discriminate in their willingness to accommodate private and somewhat idiosyncratic consumer requests. For example, Jane Connor is currently testing retailers in Binghamton, New York, to see whether there are racial differences in their willingness to accede to a request to use a restroom or a request to return a sweater without a receipt. Economists (and others) tend to ignore or downplay the harms of such discrimination. But nontrivial injury may be visited on people of color in terms of both higher transactions costs and taking more precaution to comply strictly with retailer policies. One audit study showed that African Americans in Washington, D.C., had to wait 27 percent longer to hail a cab If this seems a minor inconvenience, white readers should try to imagine what their life would be like if *every* (or even just many) transactions took 27 percent longer. Even a single incident can impose real psychological costs. Consider, for example, Patricia Williams's story of being denied entrance to an open Benneton store by a gum-chewing, buzzerwielding store clerk.

———

NOTES AND QUESTIONS

1.   Statistical discrimination. Statistical discrimination exists when a seller or provider of services or property owner treats two equally suitable persons differently, solely on the basis of the average characteristics of members of a race, gender, or other subordinated group.

2.   References for statistical discrimination. For more extensive discussion of statistical discrimination, see D.J. Aigner & G.C. Cain, *Statistical Theories of Discrimination in the Labor Market,* 30 Indus. & Lab. Rel. Rev. 175 (1977); K.J. Arrow, *The Theory of Discrimination; in* Discrimination in Labor Markets (Ashenfelter and Rees eds.) (1973); A. Moro & P. Norman, *A General Equilibrium Model of Statistical Discrimination,* 114 J. of Econ. Theory 1 (2004); S. Schwab, *Is Statistical Discrimination Efficient?,* 76 Amer. Econ. Rev. 228 (1986); P. Norman, *Statistical Discrimination and Efficiency,* 70 Rev. of Econ. Studies 615 (2003).

3.   Does statistical discrimination account for the proliferation of stereotypes and the presence of negative cognitive associations for subordinated groups whose average characteristics are the product of a societal history of exclusion from opportunity?

F.   Neutrality Challenges From Other Social Science Methodologies:

1.   Cognitive Psychology—Scientific Evidence of Cognitive Bias?

Racism lost its explicit social endorsement in the aftermath of the civil rights revolution that followed in the more than half-century since the 1954 Supreme Court decision in *Brown v. Board of Education.* Hostile racial attitudes and prejudicial belief systems gradually went underground, flourishing in the subterranean world of personal cognition, family norms, and private conversations in racially homogeneous settings. Until recently, this bias was undetectable by scientifically reliable assessment tools. Moreover, both economic theory and legal theory operated on heuristics that assumed that significant racial bias no longer existed.

As Ian Ayres has shown, with a series of empirical research studies of racial discrimination in retail markets, this assumption is probably false. *See* Ayres, Pervasive Prejudice? Unconventional Evidence of Race and Gender Discrimination, *infra* at 347. However, notwithstanding Ayres pathbreaking empirical research, the difficulty for those seeking to challenge the neutrality heuristics of economics and law has been to find ways to identify individual biases, and more importantly to link those biases to racially harmful behavior.

Note on the Implicit Association Test (I.A.T.)

The development of the Implicit Association Test has provided a method to penetrate the web of latent individual bias. The test, in its most widely used version, is administered to individuals who choose to take it on the internet. Test takers are asked to sort a randomly shown series of faces into two categories: black American or white American. The test instructions encourage speedy responses using two keys on the computer keyboard that require the use of either the left or right hand. In the second stage of the test, a sequence of value-laden words, such as "joy" and "failure" appear on the screen. The test taker is asked to associate these words with a random distribution of the same set of faces representing the two racial groups. In the final step, the words and faces are reversed, and the test taker is asked again to associate the words with the, now racialized faces. The existence of bias is measured by the time difference between the length of time it takes to match the faces to words that are consistent with the racial stereotype, and the length of time required to match the faces with words associated with the other group, so that matching blacks with joy takes longer than matching blacks with "failure." The test is built on the psychological phenomenon of cognitive dissonance, in which there is discrepancy between beliefs, and new facts require more mental effort to process. The test results, from tens of thousands of self-selected test takers who described themselves as liberal, identified 88 percent of white test takers as having an anti-black bias. Perhaps even more interesting than the bias of whites against blacks, were the results of black bias against other blacks, revealing an internalization of the cultural tilt against all blacks. A startling 48 percent of blacks showed an anti-black bias.

The test is not without its critics who charge that even if it accurately measures interior states of mind, it should not be the basis for policymaking, or legal intervention by government, because it only reveals "thoughts". Psychologist, Hal Arkes, argues that the problem with the test is "where we are going to set our threshold of proof for saying something represents prejudice. My view is the implicit prejudice program sets the threshold at a historical low." Quoted in, Shankar Vedantam, "See No Bias", *The Washington Post Magazine*, 12, at 40, January 23, 2005.

Taking the I.A.T. We encourage you to take a moment to take the test for yourself. The website is https://implicit.harvard.edu. A full explanation of the research design can be found at https://implicit.harvard.edu/implicit/demo/faqs.html.

Pro–Black Bias. Courtland Milloy, a black columnist for the *Washington Post*, took the Implict Association Test. He reports that his results told him that: "your data suggest a strong automatic preference for Black relative to White." White notes:

> For some readers, no doubt, this is confirmation that I am a reverse racist ... The last thing I wanted [was] to end up in that group of African Americans who showed a pro-white or anti-black bias [48 percent]. ... A conscious effort is what it has taken for me not to absorb the worst of white society's stereotypes about blacks.

Courtland Milloy, "Out From Under the Thumb of White Bias", *Washington Post*, B1, January 26, 2005.

———

Civil Rights Perestroika: Intergroup Relations After Affirmative Action

86 CAL. L. REV. 1251 (1998).

■ LINDA HAMILTON KRIEGER

Here at the University of California at Berkeley, there was a surreal quality to November 6, 1996, the day after voters, in enacting Proposition 209, elected to end affirmative action in California state hiring, contracting, and education. The few protests that had been organized ended quickly and quietly. At the law school, students seemed uncharacteristically subdued: quietly resigned—or quietly pleased. In the newspapers that morning and on the mornings that followed, articles about Texaco executives referring to their African-American employees as "niggers" and "black jelly beans" were oddly juxtaposed against others in which Proposition 209's triumphant sponsors heralded a glorious new era of truly equal opportunity and the long-awaited dawning of a colorblind society.

Now, many months later and well into the first of Berkeley's "post-affirmative action" years, the atmosphere here is no less strange. On the first day of classes in 1997, the halls and courtyards swarmed with television cameras and reporters, attempting, I noted with a sense of irony, to identify the lone African-American member of Boalt Hall's first "colorblind" class. We were no longer supposed to consider race, but race was everywhere in these halls on that first morning of the new school year. * * *

If history is any guide, the trend started in California will spread to other states and to the national stage in the months ahead. The 105th Congress witnessed the introduction of three separate bills that would have "nationalized" Proposition 209, and, events in Houston notwithstanding, many States are contemplating similar legislation.

But before proceeding further down this road, it might be wise to pause and ask some hard questions. * * * What can we expect to occur with respect to intergroup relations, and with race relations in particular, in a post-affirmative action environment? If affirmative action is eliminated, will remaining policy tools prove adequate to effectuate racial and gender equity and to prevent the resegregation of American society? Will the idea of "colorblindness" suffice as a theoretical model for understanding what it means not to discriminate? Or will we find instead that affirmative action actually served to mask a "multiplicity of sins"—critical failings in our approach to intergroup relations and serious defects in the tools available to make the equal opportunity society a reality instead of a hazy, unattainable dream? * * *

[This article] inquires whether, absent preferential forms of affirmative action, remaining policy tools would prove adequate to control discrimination and prevent the further segregation of American society. It concludes that these remaining tools, which include a colorblindness model of nondiscrimination, an objective concept of merit, and individualized adjudication as a primary policy enforcement tool, are unequal to the task. In short, we still lack adequate tools for coping successfully with the problems of intergroup competition and cooperation in a pluralistic society.

This failure, which I will argue has been masked to a certain extent by preferential forms of affirmative action, derives from a misunderstanding of the nature and sources of intergroup bias, from a failure to recognize its tendency to persist over time, and from over-reliance on limited adjudicatory and regulatory approaches to address what is fundamentally a complex cultural problem. Accordingly, I argue that unless we develop a broadened understanding of intergroup bias and new approaches to reducing it, the problems of discrimination and inequality of opportunity will worsen in a post-affirmative action environment.

[D]iscrimination does not solely derive from stable, dispositional traits internal to actors we call "discriminators." Rather, intergroup bias increases or decreases in response to contextual, environmental factors which shape how social actors perceive, judge, and make decisions about members of their own and other social reference groups. Accordingly, an anti-discrimination policy grounded in an individualized search for discriminatory intent cannot be expected to succeed either in identifying and preventing intergroup bias or in managing social tendencies toward intergroup conflict. If we are to solve the problem of intergroup discrimination, we must attend more closely to the ecology of intergroup relations. Eliminating affirmative action before we have developed an effective alternative theoretical and doctrinal approach to managing intergroup bias is a strategy more risky than many might assume. * * *

II

AFTER AFFIRMATIVE ACTION: RECOGNIZING DISCRIMINATION IN THE LAND OF THE COLORBLIND

What might we expect if every institution in the nation—every college and university, every corporation, every state and local public agency, and every arm and organ of the federal government—suddenly prohibited its employees from considering the race, sex, or national origin of applicants or employees in hiring, contracting, promotion, or admission to educational programs? What would happen if every employment and admissions decision maker was told simply to "be colorblind," to base his or her decisions only on "considerations of merit"? Would they do it? Could they do it? Could we identify those who did not do it, whose decisions were tainted by intergroup bias?

The answers to these questions are, quite simply, "no," "no," and "no." Perhaps constitutions can be colorblind. Perhaps official government or corporate policies can be colorblind. But human beings living in a society in which history, ideology, law, and patterns of social, economic, and political distribution have made race, sex, and ethnicity salient, cannot be colorblind. The "colorblindness" approach to nondiscrimination will prove ineffective because it provides neither a framework for enabling people to recognize the effects of race, gender, or national origin on their perceptions and judgments, nor the tools required to help them counteract those effects. Indeed, a color blindness-centered interpretation of the nondiscrimination principle, coupled with well-meaning people's awareness that they do categorize along racial and ethnic lines, may exacerbate the very intergroup anxiety and ambivalence that lead to what social psychologists refer to as aversive racism.

Furthermore, decision makers cannot base selection decisions only on colorblind considerations of merit for the simple reason that merit has a color. Conceptions of merit are socially and politically constructed and are shaped by the same ingroup preferences that give rise to other subtle forms of intergroup bias. Affirmative action preferences have, in many ways, diverted our attention from the biases inherent in the construction of merit. But if preferences are eliminated, this problem and the inequities it generates will soon rise into sharp relief.

Finally, there is substantial reason to doubt that remaining law enforcement tools, particularly the adjudication of individual disparate treatment cases, will prove effective in identifying and remedying subtle but pervasive forms of intergroup bias. For a variety of reasons, reliance on individual disparate treatment adjudication can be expected to result in the serious underidentification of discrimination by judicial decision makers, victims, and private fact finders.

A.   The Inefficacy of Colorblindness as a Normative Construct

[E]xisting antidiscrimination law constructs intergroup bias as something that occurs when a "discriminatory purpose" motivates a decision. In other words, in order for a decision to be considered "discriminatory" under a statute such as Title VII, the disparate treatment plaintiff must show that the employer chose to take the negative action against him because of his membership in a particular protected class. Thus, to say that discrimination is intentional means that the decision stands in a particular sort of close relation to the target person's group status. Specifically, in the decision maker's mental process, there must be some syllogistic connection between the two.

So, for example, existing antidiscrimination law understands cognitive stereotypes as causing discrimination through the operation of a conscious, syllogistic reasoning process, through which the decision maker uses a person's group status in the following sort of way:

Major Premise: Women with young children are preoccupied with family responsibilities and do not put their jobs first;

Minor Premise: This applicant is a woman with young children;

Conclusion: This applicant cannot be expected to put the job first.

Current antidiscrimination law further conceives gender role expectations, or normative stereotypes, as causing discrimination through the operation of a similar sort of syllogistic reasoning:

Major Premise: Women with young children should be preoccupied with family responsibilities and should not hold jobs that will compete with the responsibilities associated with raising children;

Minor Premise (1) The rigors of this job can be expected to conflict with family responsibilities associated with raising young children;

Minor Premise (2) This applicant is a mother with young children;

Conclusion: This applicant should not hold this job.

According to the existing jurisprudential model of discrimination, personal animosity may also lead to discrimination through the operation of implicit syllogistic reasoning:

Major Premise: Working with black coworkers makes me feel uncomfortable;

Minor Premise: This applicant is black;

Conclusion: Working with him would make me feel uncomfortable.

In each of these contexts, the decision maker's thinking moves directly through the target person's group status. So long as we understand discrimination as operating in this way, we can rely on a color-blindness model of nondiscrimination to function as an effective normative principle. A social decision maker can refrain from discriminating simply by refraining from any syllogistic use of the target person's group status, in other words, by being "colorblind."

But as I have also attempted to demonstrate, not all discrimination is of this sort. Much discrimination has little connection with discriminatory motive or intent. This sort of discrimination occurs when an individual's group status subtly, even unconsciously, affects a decision makers' subjective perception of relevant traits, on which ostensibly non-discriminatory decision are subsequently based. This form of discrimination results from a variety of categorization-related cognitive biases, and can result in disparate treatment based on race, sex, national origin, or other factors, even among the well-intentioned.

I do not wish to rehash the evidence supporting this proposition described at length elsewhere. Rather, using related but more recent research, I wish to demonstrate that only "color-consciousness" can control these cognitive forms of intergroup bias. This research strongly suggests that cognitive biases in social judgment operate automatically, without intention or awareness, and can be controlled only through subsequent, deliberate "mental correction" that takes group status squarely into account.

1.   Automatic Processes in Intergroup Judgment

In his early work on perceptual readiness, Jerome Bruner observed that when a person receives information with the goal of forming an impression, his or her first cognitive task is to fit that information into some existing knowledge structure. As Bruner described, only when behavioral information is encoded in this way does it becomes useful, or even meaningful.

Of course, in many situations incoming information is ambiguous in that it is susceptible to varied interpretations. A student's volunteered but halting response to a question can be interpreted as reflecting dull-wittedness—or courageous engagement with a difficult subject. An employee's hesitancy in the face of an important decision may evince timidity—or prudence. As Bruner suggested, "All perception is generic," meaning that observed actions, like objects, take on meaning only when they are assigned to a particular trait construct—a preexisting knowledge structure residing in the observer's mind.

In their attempts to understand this process more fully, cognitive psychologists originally assumed that assigning an action to a particular trait construct depended primarily on the extent of the "match" between the features of the action and those of the construct. Then in the late 1970s through the early 1980s, encouraged no doubt by Amos Tversky and Daniel Kahneman's seminal work on the availability heuristic, various researchers began investigating the role of trait construct accessibility in social perception. Their work showed that the readiness with which a person will characterize a particular behavior in terms of any given trait construct is a function of that construct's availability in memory at the time the behavior is perceived. Any activity, conscious or unconscious, that "primes" a particular trait construct will tend to increase its accessibility and the corresponding likelihood that ambiguous information will be assimilated or encoded in a manner consistent with that trait.

Social stereotypes bias perception in this general manner. As numerous researchers have demonstrated, one learns at an early age stereotypes of the major social groups in the United States. These stereotypes have a long history of activation, and are likely to be highly accessible, regardless of whether they are believed. They are invoked automatically when people encounter members of a stereotyped outgroup. Once activated, stereotypes serve to "prime" the trait constructs with which they are associated. Incoming behavioral information, especially if capable of various interpretations, is accordingly assimilated into those traits associated with the stereotype.

This tendency to assimilate ambiguous information into stereotypic trait constructs might not be so serious if people were aware that they were doing it. To understand the significance of this process and its implications for the debate over affirmative action, it is useful to understand a phenomenon which attribution theorists refer to as spontaneous trait inference.

People are highly concerned with understanding why things happen in their social environments. Rightly or wrongly, we assume that understanding why something has happened will improve our power to predict or even control what will happen in the future. To the extent that personality traits play an important role in understanding people's actions, one might expect the process of translating observed behaviors into trait-related meanings to occur with great frequency. Given that social perception and judgment processes become increasingly efficient with repeated execution, one might further hypothesize that trait inference processes could become so overlearned as to operate without intention or awareness, much like the processes involved in recognizing a word or a face.

This hypothesis appears to be correct. In a number of studies replicated in a variety of contexts by other researchers, New York University psychologist James S. Uleman and his colleagues demonstrated that European-American subjects spontaneously encode behaviors into stable trait constructs without intention or awareness. Thus, there is a strong tendency, at least among European Americans, to attribute stable dispositional qualities spontaneously, as part of the process of perceiving and encoding information about another person's behavior. To say that trait inference is "spontaneous" however is not quite the same as saying it is "automatic," and the difference is critical to equal opportunity policy.

Through the early-1980s, it was generally believed that a particular mental process was either entirely automatic or entirely deliberate. Over time, however, cognitive processes came to be understood as falling along a continuum. On one side of that continuum lie "controlled processes," which require substantial processing capacity and occur with greater levels of focus and awareness. On the other side lie fully automatic processes, which occur without intention or awareness, are difficult if not impossible to control once triggered, and interfere little with other ongoing mental activity. Eventually, it became apparent that complex mental processes such as causal attribution and other forms of social inference were neither exclusively automatic nor exclusively controlled, but rather combined aspects of both. Specifically, social inference came to be understood as comprising a chain of three sequential subprocesses: "categorization," in which the person perceived is identified and placed within an existing categorical structure; "characterization," in which spontaneous dispositional inferences are drawn from the observed behavior; and "correction," in which those dispositional inferences are adjusted to account for situational factors. While categorization and characterization are automatic, correction is controlled. It requires deliberate, effortful mental processing and will compete for cognitive resources with other information processing demands. * * *

The significance of these processes and their implications for the colorblindness approach to nondiscrimination can hardly be overemphasized. Very little information shapes a social perceiver's impression of a target person. Rather, it is the perceiver's interpretation of the raw information that influences social judgment. If the target's social group membership influences these interpretations, and if one is unaware of the effect of such status on those interpretations, how can we expect a colorblindness approach to nondiscrimination to function successfully as a normative principle? Given the realities of social perception, we can anticipate that similarly situated people will be treated differently based on their group membership, because decision makers, influenced by these subtle forms of intergroup bias, will not perceive them as similarly situated at all.

Nothing in the colorblindness approach to nondiscrimination provides social decision makers with the tools required to recognize or to correct for biases of this sort.

According to spontaneous trait inference theory, only the application of deliberate, controlled, corrective processes can prevent stereotypes and subtle ingroup priming valences from biasing interpersonal judgment. As social cognition researchers Patricia Devine and Susan Fiske observe, it is neither that nonprejudiced individuals "do not notice" such traits as gender or ethnicity nor that the presence of a member of another group does not "prime" the stereotypes associated with those groups. Rather, insofar as cognitive sources of bias are concerned, the difference between people who discriminate and those who do not is that members of the latter group notice the influences of stereotypes on their thinking and counteract those influences by consciously adjusting responses in a nonprejudiced direction. This process, however, is effortful: it requires both strong motivation and a great deal of capacity, attention, and practice. In short, controlling the biases stemming from such processes as spontaneous trait inference is substantially more complicated than it might at first seem.

2.   Controlled Processes and Nondiscrimination: Taming the Beast of Automaticity

The major sources of error in human judgment divide into two broad types. Errors of the first type stem from a failure to know or apply normative rules of inference. Errors of the second type result from a phenomenon which Timothy Wilson and Nancy Brekke refer to as "mental contamination." Mental contamination occurs when a person's judgment or behavior is corrupted by unconscious or uncontrollable mental processes which she would rather not have influence her behavior or decisions. Judgment errors deriving from rule ignorance or incorrect rule application are easier to remedy than those resulting from mental contamination. Normative rules of inference, like the rule of regression to the mean, supply specific procedures for solving the problems to which they pertain and can be consciously learned and deliberately applied.

Correcting judgmental errors resulting from mental contamination is more difficult, in large part because simply teaching people a particular decision rule is unlikely to control biases of which they are unaware. This will be particularly true if the biases in question are difficult to recognize, or easily mistaken for valid, decision-relevant considerations. A supervisor evaluating employees for promotion, or a professor considering which student to hire as a research assistant, may know the rule, "don't discriminate against the black guy." But that kind of rule, in this case the colorblindness rule, cannot be applied in the same way as cost-benefit analysis or the rule of regression to the mean. It can be applied to eliminate facial discrimination—that is, a conscious, explicit policy of excluding a certain group of persons from consideration. It might even be applied to eliminate the conscious, deliberate use of group status as a proxy for decision-relevant traits like initiative or writing ability. But it cannot be applied to prevent or correct biases caused by emotional discomfort, the subconscious effects of stereotypes, causal attribution, or spontaneous trait inference, because it fails to provide a specific set of procedures or techniques which can be applied to the evaluation or decision task at hand. A normative decision rule, such as one prohibiting discrimination on the basis of race, cannot be applied to eliminate a source of bias if the decision maker is unaware that her judgment might be biased or is unable to control the effects of such bias for lack of applicable remedial tools.

As Wilson and Brekke explain, four discrete conditions must be satisfied if people are to control the effects of nonconscious biases. First, one must become aware of the nature of the particular mental process which threatens to bias one's judgment. Second, one must be motivated to correct its unwanted influence once it has been recognized. Third, one must be able to discern the direction and magnitude of the bias, lest it be "overcorrected" and judgment skewed in the opposite direction. And finally, one must have sufficient control over his or her mental processes to correct the effect of the unwanted influences. While it is beyond the scope of this Article to review all of the problems encountered at each of these four stages, those with the most serious implications for the colorblindness model of nondiscrimination warrant attention here.

a.   Unawareness of Mental Process

During the fall of 1996, while the campaign on Proposition 209 swirled around the University, I was teaching a class on employment discrimination law. Every day, I called on a different student to respond to questions about the cases prepared for that day's class. Most of my students were Caucasian; only three of sixty-five were African American. Let us assume for purposes of illustration, that one day I had called on one of these three African-American students, and that he experienced a certain amount of difficulty answering various questions. He was not unprepared, but many of his answers were halting and somewhat confused, leaving me with the initial impression that he was not particularly capable.

I flatly reject the belief that African-American law students are less intelligent than others. If asked at the beginning of the semester to predict how any one of my three African-American students would perform relative to their classmates, I would have vigorously objected to making a prediction in the absence of individuating information. Given that I am familiar with certain normative rules of inference such as the principle of regression to the mean, I would probably, if pushed, have predicted that his or her performance would be about average.

But it is also true that, although I reject them as untrue, I am aware of the stereotypes associated with intelligence, academic achievement, and African-American males. I too was exposed to those stereotypes at a very early age, before I developed my own powers of critical and moral intelligence and made a conscious decision to reject these stereotypes as inaccurate and unfair. But my nonprejudiced beliefs did not displace the stereotypes, which exist alongside and function independently of these beliefs.

The stereotypes are triggered whether I believe in them or not. And, once triggered, those stereotypes prime the trait constructs associated with them, constructs like "not too bright" or "underachieving," rather than "grappling courageously with a difficult subject."

So, what should one conclude if I had taken from this hypothetical encounter the initial impression that the student in question was "not particularly capable?" His performance had not been very good. Why then, should I even question whether the student's race had anything to do with my judgment?

If such a situation were to arise, I would likely question my initial impression only if: (1) I was aware of the possibility that negative stereotypes of African-American males, or some other aspects of the situation had subtly influenced my judgment; and (2) I was motivated to do something about it.

Of course, other subtle cognitive sources of bias besides racial stereotypes could have "contaminated" my judgment as well. If I approached the issue mindfully, I would probably have noticed that over the course of the semester, a number of students I had called on had performed relatively poorly, some just as poorly as the student in question. But try as I might, if I had not made contemporaneous notes, I probably could not now remember just who those students were. I would remember the African-American student, but I would most likely have forgotten the others.

This scenario illustrates a common unconscious source of bias—the polarized evaluation of distinctive members of an otherwise largely homogeneous group. It is well-established that people pay particularly close attention to distinctive stimulus objects, such as a "token" woman or minority group member. And the more attention we pay to something, the more about it we perceive, encode, and store in memory. Indeed, under conditions of high attention, we are more likely to encode an event visually, which makes it more readily available in memory and more influential in the formation of subsequent judgments. Accordingly, the poor performance of a distinctive minority student is more likely to be remembered, and will tend to be charged with a more powerful negative valence, than the poor performance of a majority white student.

If I were unschooled in these sorts of salience or expectancy-related biases, I would likely remain unaware that the student's race had played any role in the formation of my initial impression that he was "not particularly capable." But could I fairly deny that he had been negatively judged, at least in part, because of his race?

The colorblindness approach to nondiscrimination is dangerous because it leads a decision maker to believe that, so long as she is not consciously thinking about race, she is not discriminating. But social cognition theory teaches that, in a culture pervaded by racial stereotypes, or where persons of one race constitute a small minority in an otherwise homogeneous group, one must think about race in order not to discriminate. In short, the colorblindness principle discourages the first step prerequisite to controlling cognitive sources of intergroup bias.

b.   The Role of Motivation

All "dual process" models of social inference posit that in order to correct errors caused by an automatic mental process, people must not only be aware of the process, but must also be motivated to control its biasing effects. Of course, the development of awareness itself requires motivation. Despite early controversy on particular issues, it is now relatively well-accepted that people lack awareness of a large proportion of mental processing, including the processes comprising impression formation.

Developing self-awareness of such processes and correcting for the various biases inherent in them is in any context objectively difficult. Even after they are activated, the controlled processes required for mental correction require a great deal of capacity and attention and will compete for cognitive resources with other mental demands. But in the context of intergroup discrimination, the order is taller still. Increasing awareness of and sustained attention to the biasing effects of racial, ethnic, or gender stereotypes on one's social judgments is apt to engender fear of moral opprobrium and substantial psychological discomfort. Thus, especially in the context of reducing intergroup bias, there is little reason to assume that people will expend the effort or bear the psychological discomfort associated with mental correction unless they have strong motivations for so doing. Thus, the colorblindness approach not only fails to provide incentives for developing an awareness of mental contamination, but the model itself and the rhetoric that often accompanies it actually establish disincentives for so doing. * * *

c.   The Limits of Mental Correction

As Timothy Wilson and Nancy Brekke observe, even if a person becomes aware that some unwanted mental process has tainted her judgment, she may not be able to determine the magnitude of the resulting bias. For example, in my hypothetical interaction with my African-American student, I might have become aware that stereotype or salience-related biases had influenced my assessment of his performance. But assuming that I were eventually required to formulate an evaluation, how far, if at all, should I adjust it? There is really no way for me to assess how much of my impression is fairly attributable to bias and how much to the student's flawed performance.

Even more troubling is the question whether "correction" is feasible at all. Once the initial impression that the student was "not particularly capable" had been formed, would I be able to erase it from my mind, or prevent it from influencing my impressions of him in connection with future interactions?

There is ample reason to fear that I would not. In a series of now classic studies, Stanford psychologist Lee Ross and his colleagues demonstrated that, even after a belief is discredited, the causal explanations generated to support it persist, giving the discredited belief a kind of cognitive life after death. More recently, University of Texas psychologists Daniel Gilbert and Randall Osborne extended these observations to the process of spontaneous trait inference. Their work demonstrates that once a trait inference is made, subsequent efforts to adjust it may prove ineffective. As they observed, misperceptions are "metastatic." Controlled processing may correct the original misperception, but it often fails to eliminate subsidiary changes that the original misperception engendered. These endure and influence subsequent judgments of the person perceived. It is easier to forbear from action based on a biased impression than to eliminate the impression itself.

Assuming I realized that my impression formation process was potentially biased, I might have decided to reject the view that the student was not particularly capable. I might even have decided not to take action based on my initial impression of his in-class performance, for example, deciding not to use it in calculating his grade. But I would probably not be able to erase the impression from my mind. Given its enduring presence, I would likely experience any adjustments in my subsequent behavior toward or expressed beliefs about the student as a form of racial preferencing. "After all," I might tell myself, "if the student weren't African-American, I wouldn't be bending over backwards like this." What the colorblindness perspective would allow me to forget, or never teach me in the first place, is that if the student were not African-American, I probably would not have remembered his performance at all. * * *

[Krieger's discussion of how conceptions of "merit" are "defined and assessed through the same complex, largely unconscious cognitive processes which subtly bias social judgment in other contexts and give rise to more easily recognizable forms of discrimination" is omitted.]

b. Schematic Expectancies and the Problem of Ingroup Favoritism * * *

iii. Ingroup Helping Discrimination and the Leniency Effect

Patterns of modern discrimination turn in large measure on the answer to one simple question: Who gets cut slack, and who does not? What happens when an employee violates a rule? Is she subjected to discipline under established policies, or are her transgressions overlooked, or attributed to factors beyond her control? When an ambiguous aspect of a person's background can be interpreted in various ways, one negative, one neutral, which attribution is made? And when a person simply needs help, does she receive it?

Type II bias in large measure shapes people's tendencies to assist or ignore, to excuse others' transgressions or hold them accountable under objective standards of conduct. The earliest, and perhaps still the most vivid of the studies illustrating this effect, was conducted in the early 1970s, in front of a Kansas supermarket. In this study, one black woman and one white woman, whom researchers matched for age and social class-related appearance, dropped a bag of groceries while leaving a supermarket, right in the path of oncoming shoppers. Researchers investigated whether white shoppers would help a white "bag dropper" more frequently than a black bag dropper.

The results were complex and intriguing. Overall, the experimenters found no significant effect of race on the provision of help per se: approximately the same percentage of incoming white shoppers in either condition stopped to help. Subsequent analysis of the data however, revealed an important, if more subtle, phenomenon. When the bag dropper was white, sixty three percent of those who stopped continued to provide assistance until the job was done. When the bag dropper was black, helpers tended to pick up one or two items and then leave, providing complete assistance only thirty percent of the time.

Additional studies provide further evidence of an ingroup helping bias. In 1977, Samuel Gaertner and John Dovidio conducted an experiment in which white subjects were led to believe that they were participating in an investigation of extrasensory perception (ESP). Researchers assigned subjects to serve as either a "sender" or a "receiver," and paired each with a partner/confederate, who was either white or black. Senders and receivers sat in different rooms. Researchers told some subjects that a second person was sitting with their partner in the other room, and told other subjects that the partner was alone.

During the course of the "ESP" experiment, researchers staged an emergency. Subjects heard the sound of falling chairs and the screams of the partner in the other room, followed by prolonged silence. Researchers investigated whether the partner's race would effect the rates at which subjects would go to the aid of their partner.

When subjects believed that their partner was alone in the other room, the partner's race had no significant effect on responses. However, when subjects believed that there was another person in the room with the partner, race made a dramatic difference. Where the apparently imperiled partner was white, seventy-five percent of subjects offered aid, but where the partner was black, the rate dropped to thirty-seven percent. Perhaps even more significantly, subjects showed greater physiological arousal, measured by change in heart rate, when the partner/confederate was white than when he was black.

Gaertner and Dovidio interpreted these results as indicating that whites do not deliberately avoid providing assistance to blacks. However, when features of the situation are ambiguous, when it is unclear whether help is called for, they tend to resolve uncertainty in favor of helping whites and against helping blacks. * * *

As the tendency to assist is biased, so is the tendency to overlook or excuse transgression. For example, in a 1974 field study of whites' reactions to apparent shoplifting, Max Dertke and his colleagues demonstrated that when the shoplifter/confederate was black, white shoppers spontaneously reported and followed up on an observed shoplifting incident at a much higher rate than when the shoplifter/confederate was white. * * *

One can easily see how over time, these subtle forms of ingroup favoritism would result in markedly different outcomes for ingroup and outgroup members. If decision makers react to members of their own social reference groups with more positive associations, a quicker willingness to help, and a stronger inclination to ignore or excuse shortcomings, it is easy to predict who will be systematically advantaged in hiring and promotion decisions. Disparities will develop even absent hostile animus or negative actions directed towards the outgroup. * * *

[Krieger's discussion of how current anti-discrimination law is poorly equipped to control Type II discrimination is omitted.]

D. Individualized Adjudication, Hypothesis Testing, and Causal Attribution: The Effects of Intergroup Bias

Consider for a moment the judgment task involved in adjudicating an individual employment discrimination suit. Determining in any given case whether discrimination has occurred is fundamentally an exercise in causal attribution. The employer has taken some negative action, most frequently a termination of employment, against the plaintiff. The jury's role is to determine why that negative action was taken. Was it, as the plaintiff alleges, because the decision maker discriminated against her because of her membership in a protected group? Or was it, as the defendant argues, because of some legitimate, nondiscriminatory reason, usually some malfeasance or deficiency on the plaintiff's part? In a hiring case, did the plaintiff fail to get the job because the decision maker took her group status into account in making the challenged decision? Or did the decision maker believe that some other candidate would do a better job? The trial of such a case will essentially entail a battle between two competing causal theories. Seeking to convince the jury that discrimination is to blame, the plaintiff will portray the decision makers as discriminators. Seeking to convince the jury that the plaintiff is to blame, the defendant will do everything possible to make his or her deficiencies salient.

Why should we expect a jury to approach this social decision task free from the various forms of intergroup bias that distort intergroup perception and judgment in other contexts? As we have seen, unconscious stereotypes about members of different social groups create implicit expectancies in the minds of social perceivers. These expectancies in turn distort the perception, interpretation, and recall of information about members of the targeted groups, pulling subsequent social judgments in a stereotype-consistent direction. Stereotypic expectancies and other forms of intergroup bias also affect causal attribution, causing unconscious distortions in the interpretation and perceived predictiveness of past behavior.

Attributing the causes of employment decisions implicates the very processes of social perception and judgment bound up in the challenged employment decisions themselves. Unless the demographic characteristics of fact finders vary in some dramatic way from those of the decision makers, we cannot reasonably expect that the level of intergroup discrimination reflected in employment decisions will vary in any meaningful way from the level reflected in discrimination verdicts. Indeed, the analytical structure and content of disparate treatment adjudications, focusing as it does on the plausibility of defendant's proffered legitimate nondiscriminatory reasons for a challenged employment decision, can be expected to potentiate those forms of intergroup bias caused by stereotypic expectancies. Discrimination adjudications therefore may be even more vulnerable to cognitive forms of intergroup bias than the decision tasks which give rise to them.

An employer's determination, for example, whether a particular employee should be terminated is not much different from a court's determination whether an employer believed in good faith that a particular employee deserved to be terminated. Similarly, an employer judging whether a particular candidate is best qualified for a position is not particularly different from a court judging whether a particular candidate would reasonably have been viewed by a well-intentioned employer as the best qualified person for a position. Expectancy confirmation effects, such as those illustrated in Darley's and Gross's study discussed above, will distort both types of judgments. Thus, there is no reason to believe that the incidence of stereotype-induced judgment error in discrimination adjudications will differ in any significant way from its incidence in employment or educational decision making. Indeed, if as Darley and Gross suggest, exposure to ambiguous but ostensibly diagnostic collections of information potentiates expectancy confirmation bias, we can expect disparate treatment adjudications, with their "information rich texture," to suffer even more from such biases than hiring or educational admissions decisions, where relatively little diagnostic information is available and decision makers may be more on guard against making stereotypic judgments.

In short, from a cognitive process standpoint we cannot expect disparate treatment adjudications to be any less subject to subtle forms of intergroup bias than the decisions which give rise to them. Correspondingly, we cannot expect individualized adjudication of disparate treatment claims to be particularly effective in identifying or redressing cognitive discrimination. For this reason as for others, disparate treatment adjudication, like the colorblindness model of nondiscrimination and reliance on an objective concept of merit, is an extremely weak tool for combating cognitive forms of intergroup bias. We cannot expect these policies to do the work once accomplished by disparate impact theory, numerical standards, and the systematic, self-critical analysis of selection procedures. Unfortunately, when a person is color-blind, there is simply much he will not see.
* * *

———

What is the explanation for the stubborn persistence of pervasive discrimination today? In what follows, R.A. Lenhardt draws on sociological research to argue that the focus should be on the racial harm, including citizenship harms arising from exclusion, instead of either disparate impact, or intent.

2. Sociology and Law: Stigma Theory

Understanding the Mark: Race, Stigma, and Equality in Context

79 N.Y.U. L. Rev. 803 (2005).

■ R.A. Lenhardt

* * *

* * * In fact, we are approaching a state in which many minority youths arguably stand a greater chance of being incarcerated than of obtaining a college degree and entering the economic mainstream. According to a recent study, of the approximately two million people in adult correctional facilities in the United States, an astounding 1.2 million, or 63%, are African-American or Latino, even though these groups together comprise only 25% of the total population.

These statistics paint a devastating picture of increasing racial separation and inequality along several fundamental life axes and demonstrate how far away we actually are from remedying the problem of racial disadvantage. The truth is that, in many ways, we are as racially divided a society today as we were before the Supreme Court's landmark decision in *Brown v. Board of Education* and the enactment of the Civil Rights Act of 1964. Where we live, go to school, and work are all still greatly determined by race. The question we must ask is: Why? What accounts for the stubborn persistence of the color line DuBois identified so many years ago? Why do racial disparities still exist?

For some time, the only legal framework available for understanding questions of racial inequity and disadvantage, reflected in cases such as *Washington v. Davis*, was that of intentional discrimination. Then, more than fifteen years ago, Professor Charles Lawrence revolutionized legal scholarship by arguing that the source of racial harm lay principally in unconsciously racist acts. Drawing on psychoanalytic theory and cognitive psychology, Lawrence's article, *The Id, The Ego, and Equal Protection: Reckoning with Unconscious Racism*, challenged the view that only intentionally discriminatory conduct ran the risk of imposing racial harm. Because of the cognitive processes and meanings associated with race in this country, Lawrence argued, racial motive was most often reflected in unconscious conduct bearing a disparate racial impact. He maintained that the messages communicated by facially neutral governmental actions were the best indicator of racist motive, and he therefore advocated greater judicial attention to the cultural or racial meaning of policy choices and initiatives.

This Article seeks to advance the conversation about the nature and contours of racial harm by asserting that we should be concerned, not with the meanings associated with conduct, but rather with the meanings associated with race itself. My argument is that racial stigma, not intentional discrimination or unconscious racism, is the true source of racial injury in the United States. This theory accounts for the persistence of racial disparities that mark the color line, as well as the incidence of intentionally discriminatory or racialized behavior. It conceives of these problems as a function of racial stigma, not vice versa. In this respect, it is perhaps the most comprehensive theory of racial harm advanced thus far.

[Lenhardt defines racial stigma as consisting of the following 4 characteristics:]

I.   WHAT IS RACIAL STIGMA?

* * * Brands were used as a way of identifying African slaves as human property up until the latter part of the eighteenth century and as a method of punishment well into the nineteenth century. When we talk about racial stigma today, however, we are almost never referring directly to the brands and cuts that were used to demarcate slave or outsider status. We plainly mean something different, something less physical and perhaps more cognitive in nature. The question is: What?

Even as the term racial stigma has become part of common parlance, it has escaped clear definition. An informal survey of individuals on the street likely would generate as many definitions as people interviewed. For some, it refers to demeaning racial insults or stereotypes. For others, it is synonymous with the concept of racial inferiority. Still others see it principally as a by-product of discriminatory treatment that excludes or denies a benefit on the basis of race. The connotation given the term seems to vary by individual and even by context.

Significantly, this holds true even among courts and legal scholars, who ordinarily might be expected to have a more uniform understanding of a concept that has been embraced as a key constitutional principle in the race context. The legal approach to racial stigma, for the most part, has mirrored the strategy that former Justice Potter Stewart infamously adopted in obscenity cases: "I know it when I see it." By contrast, with only a few refinements, social scientists seem to have employed the same basic understanding of stigma for some time. In this Section, I thus look principally outside the legal arena to social science for direction in defining what racial stigma is and how it functions.

1.   DEHUMANIZATION AND THE IMPOSITION OF VIRTUAL IDENTITY

Most lawyers are probably familiar with the social research on racial stigma that Dr. Kenneth Clark completed nearly fifty years ago as an expert in the litigation surrounding *Brown v. Board of Education.* In the social science world, however, the work of another social scientist—Erving Goffman—is most often cited in connection with questions surrounding the problem of racial stigma. Nearly forty years after it was first published, Goffman's book, STIGMA: NOTES ON THE MANAGEMENT OF SPOILED IDENTITY, continues to be regarded as one of the definitive texts in this area.

In Stigma, Goffman concerned himself with a single purpose: defining the problem of stigma. Looking to a variety of psychological, sociological, and historical studies and texts, he explored a range of stigma-inducing conditions and situations, including the so-called "tribal" or group-based stigmas such as "race, nation, and religion." Although Goffman also studied the etiology and function of stigmas relating to physical deformities and character "blemishes" attributed to a variety of conditions, the many insights he garnered through his research are extremely relevant to the race-focused inquiry that I take up here. Even today, virtually all social scientists accept the broad definition of stigma developed through his work, namely that "stigmatized persons possess an attribute that is deeply discrediting and that they are viewed as less than fully human because of it." * * *

2. SHARED NEGATIVE MEANINGS ABOUT THE RACIALLY STIGMATIZED

* * * Racial stigma, at bottom, concerns the relationship between a group of individuals perceived as essentially similar and shared community beliefs about that group and the attributes they possess. While racist attitudes are held at an individual level as well, the group-level responses to racial difference are most important here. Part of the strength of the "societal devaluations" associated with race in this country is that "they cannot be dismissed as the ravings of some idiosyncratic bigot." They are shared and consensual, which means that they cannot easily be ignored. This, perhaps even more than the precise character of the messages conveyed about race, is what makes racial stigma such a powerful social force. The meanings ascribed to an attribute—i.e., that dark skin or an accent provide meaningful evidence of intellectual or moral inferiority—begin to form what constitutes "a socially shared sense of 'reality.'" * * *

3. THE AUTOMATIC NATURE OF RESPONSES TO THE RACIALLY STIGMATIZED

The next stigma factor that contributes to broad-scale racial inequality relates to the automatic or unconscious nature of the responses the no stigmatized—and sometimes even minorities themselves—have to the racially stigmatized. The prevailing constitutional paradigm in the race context is, of course, the discrimination model discussed earlier. Under that model, embodied in cases such as Washington v. Davis, only conduct and policies that reflect discriminatory intent or motive can be actionable. No remedies exist for racialized, unconsciously committed behavior or policies that have merely a discriminatory impact. * * *

4. THE REINFORCING NATURE OF RACIAL STIGMA AND STEREOTYPES

As previously noted, when asked to define racial stigma, people often confuse it with the problem of racial stereotypes, which have historically been defined as inaccurate or overbroad generalizations, but have more recently come to be understood as "cognitive categories" employed in processing information. Most "profoundly stigmatized social identities" have a myriad of well-accepted stereotypes associated with them: "Blacks are dumb"; "Latinos are lazy"; "Asians are smart, but conniving." The terms racial stigma and racial stereotype are, however, two analytically distinct concepts. Whereas racial stigma provides the negative meanings associated with race and accounts for the initial affective reactions individuals often have toward racial minorities, racial stereotypes help to explain the persistence of certain attitudes about and responses toward race and the racially stigmatized. In this way, they also are directly related not just to discrimination but to the broader problem of racial inequality.

Racial stigma and stereotypes, in some sense, play mutually reinforcing roles in the dehumanization and marginalization—social, as well as economic and political—of minority groups. On the one hand, racial stigma contributes to the development of negative racial stereotypes about stigmatized groups. It is thought that the social meanings conveyed by racial stigma actually influence the cognitive processes that lead to stereotype formation. As Glenn Loury notes, "The 'social meaning of race'—that is, the tacit understanding associated with 'blackness' [or dark skin] in the public's imagination, especially the negative connotations—biases the social cognitions and distorts the specifications of observing agents, inducing them to make causal misattributions [or categorizations] detrimental to" racial minorities.

CHAPTER 2

LIFE IN A CLASS SOCIETY

A. DOWN AND OUT

Number of People Living in Poverty Increases in U.S.

N.Y. TIMES, Sept. 25, 2002, at A1.

■ ROBERT PEAR

The proportion of Americans living in poverty rose significantly last year, increasing for the first time in eight years, the Census Bureau reported today. At the same time, the bureau said that the income of middle-class households fell for the first time since the last recession ended, in 1991.

The Census Bureau's annual report on income and poverty provided stark evidence that the weakening economy had begun to affect large segments of the population, regardless of race, region or class. Daniel H. Weinberg, chief of income and poverty statistics at the Census Bureau, said the recession that began in March 2001 had reduced the earnings of millions of Americans.

The report also suggested that the gap between rich and poor continued to grow.

All regions except the Northeast experienced a decline in household income, the bureau reported. For blacks, it was the first significant decline in two decades; non-Hispanic whites saw a slight decline. Even the incomes of Asians and Pacific Islanders, a group that achieved high levels of prosperity in the 1990's, went down significantly last year.

"The decline was widespread," Mr. Weinberg said.

The Census Bureau said the number of poor Americans rose last year to 32.9 million, an increase of 1.3 million, while the proportion living in poverty rose to 11.7 percent, from 11.3 percent in 2000.

Median household income fell to $42,228 in 2001, a decline of $934 or 2.2 percent from the prior year. The number of households with income above the median is the same as the number below it.

A family of four was classified as poor if it had cash income less than $18,104 last year. The official poverty levels, updated each year to reflect changes in the Consumer Price Index, were $14,128 for a family of three, $11,569 for a married couple and $9,039 for an individual.

The bureau's report is likely to provide fodder for the Congressional campaigns. The White House said the increase in poverty resulted, in part, from an economic slowdown that began under President Bill Clinton. But Democrats said the data showed the failure of President Bush's economic policies and his tendency to neglect the economy.

Mr. Bush said today that he remained optimistic. "When you combine the productivity of the American people with low interest rates and low inflation, those are the ingredients for growth," Mr. Bush said.

But Senator Paul S. Sarbanes, Democrat of Maryland, said the administration should "start paying attention to the economic situation." Richard A. Gephardt of Missouri, the House Democratic leader, expressed amazement that Mr. Bush, after being in office for 20 months, was still blaming his predecessor.

Rudolph G. Penner, a former director of the Congressional Budget Office, said: "The increase in poverty is most certainly a result of the recession. The slow recovery, the slow rate of growth, has been very disappointing. Whether that has a political impact this fall depends on whether the election hinges on national conditions or focuses on local issues."

Although the poverty rate, the proportion of the population living in poverty, rose four-tenths of a percentage point last year, it was still lower than in most of the last two decades. The poverty rate exceeded 12 percent every year from 1980 to 1998. As the economy grew from 1993 to 2000, the rate plunged, to 11.3 percent from 15.1 percent, and the poverty rolls were reduced by 7.7 million people, to 31.6 million.

The latest recession showed an unusual pattern, seeming to raise poverty rates among whites more than among minority groups, Mr. Weinberg said.

Increases in poverty last year were concentrated in the suburbs, in the South and among non-Hispanic whites, the Census Bureau said. Indeed, non-Hispanic whites were the only racial group for whom the poverty rate showed a significant increase, to 7.8 percent in 2001, from 7.4 percent in 2000.

Poverty rates for minority groups were once much higher. But last year, the bureau said, they remained "at historic lows" for blacks (22.7 percent), Hispanics (21.4 percent) and Asian Americans (10.2 percent).

With its usual caution, the Census Bureau said the data did not conclusively show a year-to-year increase in income inequality. But the numbers showed a clear trend in that direction over the last 15 years.

The most affluent fifth of the population received half of all household income last year, up from 45 percent in 1985. The poorest fifth received 3.5 percent of total household income, down from 4 percent in 1985. Average income for the top 5 percent of households rose by $1,000 last year, to $260,464, but the average declined or stayed about the same for most other income brackets.

Robert Greenstein, executive director of the Center on Budget and Policy Priorities, a liberal research institute, said, "The census data show that income inequality either set a record in 2001 or tied for the highest level on record."

Median earnings increased 3.5 percent for women last year, but did not change for men, so women gained relative to men.

"The real median earnings of women age 15 and older who worked full time year-round increased for the fifth consecutive year, rising to $29,215— a 3.5 percent increase between 2000 and 2001," Mr. Weinberg said. The comparable figure for men was unchanged at $38,275. So the female-to-male earnings ratio reached a high of 0.76. The previous high was 0.74, first recorded in 1996.

Democrats said the data supported their contention that Congress should increase spending on social welfare programs, resisted by many Republicans. But Wade F. Horn, the administration's welfare director, said the number of poor children was much lower than in 1996, when Congress overhauled the welfare law to impose strict work requirements.

Of the 32.9 million poor people in the United States last year, 11.7 million were under 18, and 3.4 million were 65 or older. Poverty rates for children, 16.3 percent, and the elderly, 10.1 percent, were virtually unchanged from 2000. But the poverty rate for people 18 to 64 rose a half percentage point, to 10.1 percent.

Median household income for blacks fell last year by $1,025, or 3.4 percent, to $29,470. Median income of Hispanics, at $33,565, was virtually unchanged. But household income fell by 1.3 percent for non-Hispanic whites, to $46,305, and by 6.4 percent for Asian Americans, to $53,635.

The Census Bureau report also included these findings:

There were 6.8 million poor families last year, up from 6.4 million in 2000. The poverty rate for families rose to 9.2 percent, from a 26-year low of 8.7 percent in 2000.

The rate in the South rose to 13.5 percent, from 12.8 percent in 2000. The South is home to more than 40 percent of all the nation's poor, and it accounted for more than half of the national increase in the number of poor last year.

The poverty rate for the suburbs rose to 8.2 percent last year, from 7.8 percent in 2000. The number of poor people in suburban areas rose by 700,000, to 12 million. There was virtually no change in the rates in central cities (16.5 percent) and outside metropolitan areas (14.2 percent).

The bureau said the number of "severely poor" rose to 13.4 million last year, from 12.6 million in 2000. People are considered to be severely poor if their family incomes are less than half of the official poverty level.

———

Just Trying to Survive

ROSA LEE: A MOTHER AND HER FAMILY IN URBAN AMERICA 39–47 (1996).

■ LEON DASH

Rosa Lee guided her eleven-year-old grandson through the narrow aisles of a thrift shop in suburban Oxon Hill, Maryland, past the crowded racks of secondhand pants and shirts, stopping finally at the row of children's jackets and winter coats. Quickly, the boy selected a mock-leather flight jacket with a big number on the back and a price tag stapled to the collar.

"If you want it," Ross Lee said, "then you're going to have to help me get it."

"Okay, Grandmama," he said nervously. "But do it in a way that I won't get caught."

Like a skilled teacher instructing a new student, Rosa Lee told her grandson what to do. "Pretend you're trying it on. Don't look up! Don't look around! Don't laugh like it's some kind of joke! Just put it on. Let Grandma see how you look."

The boy slipped off his old, coat and put on the new one. Rosa Lee whispered, "Now put the other one back on, over it." She pushed down the new jacket's collar so that it was hidden.

"What do I do now?" he asked.

"Just walk on out the door," Rosa Lee said. "It's your coat."

Four days later, Rosa Lee is recounting this episode for me, recreating the dialogue by changing her voice to distinguish between herself and her grandson. It is January 1991. By now, I have spent enough time with Rosa Lee that her shoplifting exploits no longer surprise me.

The previous November, Rosa Lee took her eight-year-old granddaughter into the same thrift shop on a Sunday morning to steal a new winter coat for the girl one week after they were both baptized in a Pentecostal church. On the Sunday of the shoplifting lesson, Rosa Lee had decided she did not want to take her granddaughter back to the church because her winter coat was "tacky and dirty."

In the thrift shop, Rosa Lee told her granddaughter to take off her coat and hang it on the coatrack. Next, she told the grinning child to put on the attractive pink winter coat hanging on the rack.

"Are we going to take this coat, Grandma?" asked the skinny little girl.

"Yes," Rosa Lee told her. "We are exchanging coats. Now walk out the door."

A month later, a week before Christmas, Rosa Lee was searching for something in a large shopping bag in her bedroom and dumped the contents onto the bed. Out spilled dozens of bottles of expensive men's cologne and women's perfume, as well as leather gloves with their sixty-dollar price tags still attached. She leaves the tags on when she sells the goods as proof of the merchandise's newness and quality.

"Did you get all this in one trip?" I ask.

"Oh, no," she says. "This is a couple of weeks' worth."

In Rosa Lee's younger years especially, shoplifting was a major source of income, supplementing her welfare payments and the money she made during fifteen years of waitressing at various nightclubs. With eight children to feed and clothe, stealing, she says, helped her survive. Later on, when she began using heroin in the mid-1970s, her shoplifting paid for drugs.

She stole from clothing stores, drugstores, and grocery stores, stuffing items inside the torn liner of her winter coat or slipping them into one of the oversized black purses that she carries wherever she goes. When her children were young—the ages of the grandson and granddaughter—she taught them how to shoplift as well.

"Every time I went somewhere to make some money, I would take my children," she said. "I would teach them or they would watch me. 'Just watch what Mama does. I'm getting food for y'all to eat.' "

In supermarkets, she could count on her children "to distract the security guard while I hit the meat freezer. The guards would always watch groups of children before they'd watch an adult."

Her favorite targets were the department stores. One of her two older brothers, Joe Louis Wright, joked with me one day that Rosa Lee "owned a piece" of Hecht's and had put Lansburgh's out of business. "Man, she would get coats, silk dresses," he recalled. "A cloth coat with a mink collar. She got me a mohair suit. Black. Three-piece. I don't know how the hell she'd get them out of there."

Her stealing has caused divisions and hard feelings in her family, and is one reason why Rosa Lee's relationships with several of her brothers and sisters are strained. They see Rosa Lee's stealing as an extreme and unjustified reaction to their impoverished upbringing. And her sons Alvin and Eric have always refused to participate in any of their mother's illegal activities.

Rosa Lee has served eight short prison terms for various kinds of stealing during the past forty years, dating back to the early 1950s. Her longest stay was eight months for trying to steal a fur coat from a Maryland department store in 1965. She says that she went to prison rehabilitation programs each time but that none had much of an effect on her. "I attended those programs so it would look good on my record when I went before the parole board," she says. "What they were talking about didn't mean anything to me. I didn't have the education they said would get me a job. I couldn't read no matter how many programs I went to."

Nothing seems to deter her from shoplifting, not even the specter of another jail term. On the day she directed her grandson in stealing the flight jacket, she was four days away from sentencing at the city's Superior Court for stealing the bedsheets from Hecht's the previous summer.

"I'm just trying to survive," she says.

Rosa Lee had chosen her clothes carefully for her appearance before Commissioner John Treanor in November. She wanted to look as poor as possible to draw his sympathy.

She wore an ill-fitting winter coat, gray wool overalls and a white wool hat pulled back to show her graying hair. She had removed her upper dental plate to give herself a toothless look when she smiled. "My homey look," she calls it. "No lipstick. No earrings. No nothing!"

Rosa Lee did not expect to go home that day. She saw a heavyset female deputy U.S. marshal move into place behind the defense table when the courtroom clerk called her name. It was a certain sign that Treanor had already decided to "step her back" and send her to jail. She hastily handed me her purse with all her documents.

"Hold on to these papers for me, Mr. Dash," she whispered. "Looks like I'm going to get some jail time. Tell my children where I'm at. You better come see me!"

Her lawyer's statements matched her downtrodden look. Rosa Lee's life was a mess, Elmer D. Ellis told Treanor. She was addicted to heroin, a habit she had developed in 1975. She was HIV positive. She was caring for three grandchildren because their mother was in jail.

Rosa Lee told Treanor that she was trying hard to turn herself around. She was taking methadone every day to control her heroin addition and had turned again to the church. "I got baptized Sunday, me and my three grandchildren," she said, her voice breaking. "And I'm asking you from the bottom of my heart, give me a chance to prove that I'm taking my baptize seriously, 'cause I know I might not have much longer."

Tears ran down her cheeks. "I'm asking you for a chance, please," she begged Treanor. "I know I have a long record."

Rosa Lee was stretching the truth. Yes, she had been baptized, and yes, she was taking methadone. But no, she wasn't caring for her grandchildren alone. Their mother's jail term had ended in July, and she had returned to Rosa Lee's two-bedroom apartment to take care of the children, with help from Rosa Lee.

Treanor looked unimpressed with Rosa Lee's performance. He glowered at her, and Rosa Lee braced for the lecture she knew was coming. Both had played these roles before.

"Every time you pump yourself full of drugs and spend money to do it," he said, "you're stealing from your grandchildren. You're stealing food from their plates, clothes from their backs, and you're certainly jeopardizing their future. You're going to be the youngest dead grandmother in town. And you're going to have three children that will be put up for adoption or going out to some home or some junior village or someplace."

That had been Rosa Lee's opening. "Can I prove to you that my life has changed?"

"Yeah, you can prove it to me, very simply," Treanor answered. "You can stay away from dope. Now I'll make a bargain with you.... You come back here the end of January and tell me what you've been doing, and then we'll think about it. But you're looking at jail time. You're looking at the cemetery."

Rosa Lee had won. Treanor postponed the sentencing. The marshal, who had moved in closer behind Rosa Lee at the start of Treanor's lecture, moved back. Treanor, red-faced with anger, called a ten-minute recess and hurriedly left the bench. Ellis shook Rosa Lee's hand.

Rosa Lee came over to me, her cheeks still tearstained but her face aglow. "Was I good?" she asked.

"Yeah," I said, startled at her boldness.

"Thank you," she said, smiling.

The marshal walked up to Rosa Lee. She too was smiling. She had escorted Rosa Lee and her daughters to the jail several times in the not-so-distant past. "You were going to jail, honey," she said to Rosa Lee. "You stopped him with those three grandchildren. He didn't want to have to deal with making arrangements for those children if he had sent you to jail. Is their mama still over the jail?"

"Yes, she is," Rosa Lee lied, putting on a sad face.

Five days before the hearing Rosa Lee was teaching her grandchild how to shoplift. Through most of November and December, Rosa Lee stole cologne, perfume, gloves, and brightly colored silk scarves to sell to people who used them as Christmas presents. The day before her court appearance, she and a fellow drug-clinic patient, Jackie, were shoplifting in a drugstore one block from the Superior Court building shortly after they had drunk their morning meth.

When she returns for sentencing on January 22, a transformed Rosa Lee enters the courthouse. She looks good. She has a clean report from the methadone clinic. She stopped injecting heroin and cocaine in November, after her last seizure. She seems to have done everything Commissioner Treanor asked.

She always dresses well, but she has outdone herself today: she's wearing a two-piece, white-and-gray cotton knit suit with tan leather boots and a tan pocketbook. A gold-colored watch on a gold-colored chain hangs around her neck, both items she stole from the drugstore.

Before they enter Treanor's courtroom, Elmer Ellis has a word with Rosa Lee. "Please don't cry, Mrs. Cunningham," her lawyer says gently. "If you start crying again, you're only going to make Treanor angry." Rosa Lee laughs and agrees not to cry.

"What would you like to say, Mrs. Cunningham?" Treanor asks Rosa Lee when she stands in front of him.

"Well, Your Honor, I know I haven't been a good person. I know it," she begins.

Treanor cuts her off. His demeanor is softer, his words more sympathetic than in November. "Wait a minute, now. Why do you say that? . . . You're taking care of those three grandchildren, isn't that right?"

"Yes, Sir," Rosa Lee says, keeping up the pretense.

"All right," he says. "Now you've raised one family, and now you have another one."

"Yes, Sir," she says.

"Which is really too much to ask of anybody, so I don't think you should sell yourself short. You're doing the Lord's work. Your daughter's in jail for drugs, right?"

"Yes, sir," Rosa Lee says.

"And you have or have had a bad drug problem yourself."

"Yes, Sir."

Then Treanor launches into another lecture about drugs. He doesn't ask Rosa Lee why she steals. "You steal to support your habit," he says. "It's as plain as the nose on your face."

But it isn't that plain. Rosa Lee began stealing long before she became a drug addict.

Finally, Treanor announces his decision: no jail. Instead, he gives her a suspended sentence and one year of probation with drug counseling. "Now, don't come back here," he says.

Rosa Lee sometimes puts on a public mask, the way she wants the world to see her. She fudges a little here, omits a little there, even when she is trying to be candid about her behavior. By her account, her stealing started when she was a teenager. It was her eldest brother, Ben Wright, who told me that Rosa Lee's stealing started when she was nine years old. Her target: the lunch money that her fourth-grade classmates at Giddings Elementary School kept in their desks.

"JESUS, BEN!" Rosa Lee shouts when I ask her about it.

"What's the matter?" I laugh. "You said I could interview Ben."

It is a late afternoon in January, not long after her court appearance. We are talking in my car, which is parked outside Rosa Lee's apartment. We watch the teenage crack dealers come and go, making the rounds of the low-rent housing complex. Two of Rosa Lee's grandchildren are playing nearby on a patch of dirt where the grass has been worn away. The sun is beginning to sink behind the buildings as she tells me about her first theft.

The year was 1946, and Giddings's imposing red-brick building at Third and G streets, S.E., was a bustling part of the District's then-segregated education system. The school served black children living in Capitol Hill neighborhoods; some, like Rosa Lee, came from poor sharecropping families who had moved to Washington during the Depression, and they did not have the new clothes and spending money that their better-off classmates did.

Rosa Lee's father, Earl Wright, never made much money. He worked for a paving contractor as a cement finisher but he was never given that title; instead, he was always classified as a "helper" and paid a lower wage. Eventually, drinking became the primary activity of his life. Rosa Lee's mother, Rosetta Lawrence Wright, brought in most of the family's money, working as a domestic on Capitol Hill during the day.

"She used to call it 'day work,' " remembers Rosa Lee. "That's what she used to do down in the country" in North Carolina. "Clean white people's houses."

Rosetta also sold dinners from the family's kitchen in the evening and on weekends, always for cash. "She wanted cash because she was getting a welfare check for us," says Rosa Lee. The welfare payments began several years before her father's death because he spent all his time drinking and did not work. After he died, Rosetta had four additional children by another man. "Back in those days, they gave you a check for each child. Seventeen dollars a check. You never want the welfare to know how much money you got. They'll cut the check."

Ben contends that his sister's memory is faulty, that the family did receive monthly deliveries of surplus government food in this period, as did all of the poorest families in Washington, but his mother did not receive a monthly welfare stipend.

Whatever the truth, Rosa Lee and Ben agree that their family—there were eleven children in all—was poor. For much of her childhood, they lived in a ramshackle wooden row house within a mile of the Capitol, since replaced with a public housing project. None of the houses they rented over the years had electricity. The toilet for each dwelling was an outhouse along the edge of the property in the back yard. Water came from a standpipe spigot in the center of the yard.

"I hated them!" says Rosa Lee of the houses, her mouth turning down in a grimace. "No privacy. People knew what you were doing when you went into" the outhouse. "No bathtub. I was always afraid of the kerosene lamps. I was scared they'd turn over and we'd all burn up in those houses."

Other girls came to school with change to buy "brownie-thins"— penny-a-piece cookies that the teachers sold to go with free milk at lunch. Rosa Lee's family was too poor to spare even a few pennies. Rosa Lee was determined to steal her classmates' money so she too could buy cookies. And she did. She knew it was wrong to steal from her classmates' desks, she says. But she couldn't stand being poor, either.

Rosa Lee soon found that she had plenty of opportunities to steal, if she were daring enough. During the summer of 1948, a sinewy Rosa Lee was the only girl among the many "roughneck" boys selling the *Baltimore-Washington Afro–American* newspaper door-to-door on Tuesday and Thursday evenings. She was eleven. The newspaper sales were timed to catch middle-class black people—low-level federal and city civil servants—when they had just come from work.

Rosa Lee was not concerned about tough neighborhood bullies taking her money or trying to force her off the blocks where an *Afro* seller was sure to be successful. "Rosa Lee would fight quick," remembers Ben. "Fight anybody! Beat up most girls and a good many boys. I don't remember ever having to stick up for her."

Selling the *Afro* also gave Rosa Lee a chance to slip into neighborhood row houses and rifle through the pocketbooks that women often left on the dining room table or the living room couch. Washington was a safer place in those days, and Rosa Lee discovered that many families would leave their front screen doors unlatched while they chatted in their back yards, trying to cool off on hot summer evenings after returning home from work.

"I would walk down Fourth Street," says Rosa Lee, in front of the row houses across from Mount Joy Baptist Church, where her family worshipped. "I would go and knock on their screen door. *'Afro!* Anybody want an *Afro?'* I would open the screen door and if no one answered, I'd go in. I could look through the house and see them out back," she remembers. "Some people would leave their pocketbooks on the chair in the front room or on their table. I would go into so many peoples' houses." * * *

Mathematics

Black on Both Sides (Priority Records 1999).

■ Mos Def

   * * *

Yo, it's one universal law but two sides to every story

Three strikes and you be in for life, mandatory

   * * *

Young soldiers tryin' to earn they next stripe

When the average minimum wage is $5.15

You best believe you gotta find a new ground to get cream

The white unemployment rate, is nearly more than triple for black

so frontliners got they gun in your back

Bubblin' crack, jewel theft and robbery to combat poverty

and end up in the global jail economy

Stiffer stipulations attached to each sentence

Budget cutbacks but increased police presence

And even if you get out of prison still livin'

join the other five million under state supervision

This is business, no faces just lines and statistics

from your phone, your zip code, to S-S-I digits

The system break man child and women into figures

Two columns for who is, and who ain't niggaz

Numbers is hardly real and they never have feelings

but you push too hard, even numbers got limits

Why did one straw break the camel's back? Here's the secret:

the million other straws underneath it—it's all mathematics.

* * *

—————

Homelessness and the Issue of Freedom

39 UCLA L. Rev. 295, 299–302 (1991).

■ Jeremy Waldron

Estimates of the number of homeless people in the United States range from 250,000 to three million. A person who is homeless is, obviously enough, a person who has no home. One way of describing the plight of a homeless individual might be to say that there is no place governed by a private property rule where he is allowed to be.

In fact, that is not quite correct. Any private proprietor may invite a homeless person into his house or onto his land, and if he does there *will* be some private place where the homeless person is allowed to be. A technically more accurate description of his plight is that there is no place governed by a private property rule where he is allowed to be whenever *he* chooses, no place governed by a private property rule from which he may not at any time be excluded as a result of someone else's say-so. As far as being on private property is concerned—in people's houses or gardens, on farms or in hotels, in offices or restaurants—the homeless person is utterly and at all times at the mercy of others. And we know enough about how this mercy is generally exercised to figure that the description in the previous paragraph is more or less accurate as a matter of fact, even if it is not strictly accurate as a matter of law.

For the most part the homeless are excluded from *all* of the places governed by private property rules, whereas the rest of us are, in the same sense, excluded from *all but one* (or maybe all but a few) of those places. That is another way of saying that each of us has at least one place to be in a country composed of private places, whereas the homeless person has none.

Some libertarians fantasize about the possibility that *all* the land in a society might be held as private property ("Sell the streets!") This would be catastrophic for the homeless. Since most private proprietors are already disposed to exclude him from their property, the homeless person might discover in such a libertarian paradise that there was literally *nowhere* he was allowed to be. Wherever he went he would be liable to penalties for trespass and he would be liable to eviction, to being thrown out by an owner or dragged away by the police. Moving from one place to another would involve nothing more liberating than moving from one trespass liability to another. Since land is finite in any society, there is only a limited number of places where a person can (physically) be, and such a person would find that he was legally excluded from all of them. (It would not be entirely mischievous to add that since, in order to exist, a person has to be *somewhere*, such a person would not be permitted to exist.)

Our society saves the homeless from this catastrophe only by virtue of the fact that some of its territory is held as collective property and made available for common use. The homeless are allowed to *be*—provided they are on the streets, in the parks, or under the bridges. Some of them are allowed to crowd together into publicly provided "shelters" after dark (though these are dangerous places and there are not nearly enough shelters for all of them). But in the daytime and, for many of them, all through the night, wandering in public places is their only option. When all else is privately owned, the sidewalks are their salvation. They are allowed to *be* in our society only to the extent that our society is communist.

This is one of the reasons why most defenders of private property are uncomfortable with the libertarian proposal, and why that proposal remains sheer fantasy. But there is a modified form of the libertarian catastrophe in prospect with which moderate and even liberal defenders of ownership seem much more comfortable. This is the increasing regulation of the streets, subways, parks, and other public places to restrict the activities that can be performed there. What is emerging—and it is not just a matter of fantasy—is a state of affairs in which a million or more citizens have no place to perform elementary human activities like urinating, washing, sleeping, cooking, eating, and standing around. Legislators voted for by people who own private places in which they can do all these things are increasingly deciding to make public places available only for activities other than these primal human tasks. The streets and subways, they say, are for commuting from home to office. They are not for sleeping; sleeping is something one does at home. The parks are for recreations like walking and informal ball-games, things for which one's own yard is a little too confined. Parks are not for cooking or urinating; again, these are things one does at home. Since the public and the private are complementary, the activities performed in public are to be the complement of those appropriately performed in private. This complementarity works fine for those who have the benefit of both sorts of places. However, it is disastrous for those who must live their whole lives on common land. If I am right about this, it is one of the most callous and tyrannical exercises of power in modern times by a (comparatively) rich and complacent majority against a minority of their less fortunate fellow human beings.

———

NOTES AND QUESTIONS

1. Illicit activity as means for survival. Traditionally, the majority of African American women have been obliged, by necessity, to work outside the home to support their families. Leith Mullings, On Our Own Terms: Race, Class, and Gender in the Lives of African American Women 90 (1997). Due to severe levels of unemployment of black men, the labor force participation rate of black females has become approximately equal to that of black males. *Id.* Though black women comprise a considerable proportion of the labor force, women like Rosa Lee still face several obstacles to achieve economic stability and must therefore resort to either government assistance and/or illicit activity to support their families. In a study performed in Central Harlem in 1990, for example, 54.7 percent of women eligible to work were not in the labor force, with 28.9 percent of individuals residing in Harlem receiving Aid to Families with Dependent Children. *Id.* at 91 (citing *Persons 16 Years and Over by Labor Force Status and Sex, New York City, Boroughs and Community Districts.* (New York: Department of City Planning, no. 317, 1990)). Furthermore, that study found that more than half of all households in Harlem headed by females that include children under age eighteen have incomes below the poverty line. *Id.* (citing *Socioeconomic profiles: A Portrait of New York City's Community Districts from the 1980 and 1990 Census of Population and Housing* (New York: Department of City Planning)). Faced with poor odds of achieving economic stability, and in "just trying to survive," what can women like Rosa Lee do but break the law to support their families?

University of Pennsylvania Professor of Law Regina Austin explains that though illegal activity may be disparaged, it may be the only means for underprivileged African Americans to survive in America:

> [F]or some poor blacks, breaking the law is not only a way of life: it is the only way to survive. Thus, what is characterized as economic deviance in the eyes of a majority of people may be viewed as economic resistance by a significant number of blacks. Regina Austin, *"An Honest Living": Street Vendors, Municipal Regulation, and The Black Public Sphere*, 103 Yale L.J. 2119, 2119 (1994).

Austin reaches this conclusion based on her study of black street vendors in major cities like New York, Washington, D.C., and Philadelphia. These vendors are part of an informal economy where merchants work without a license and in violation of applicable regulations and sales tax laws. Though illegal, street vending by black workers gives people jobs, supplies African Americans with their preferred products, contributes to the maintenance of African American culture, and assists individuals in gaining the necessary capital and knowledge to operate a business in the formal sector. Because of street vending's benefits for afflicted black communities, Austin stresses that such activity should not immediately be written off, and should instead be respected:

> As blacks in America, we must not fall into the trap of automatically equating legitimacy with legality. Just because an enterprise is small,

informal, and illegal does not mean that it is not valuable or that it should be disparaged. *Id.* at 2130.

Based on her comments, how do you think Austin would react to Rosa Lee's illegal behavior? Would she disagree with Rosa Lee's actions because stealing, like street vending, does not achieve legitimate objectives such as promoting African American black entrepreneurial activity?

2.   Sociology of deviance. Are lawbreakers innately inclined to transgress social norms, or are they simply reacting to society's imposed institutions? In other words, are individuals like Rosa Lee instinctively prone to deviate from societal standards, or are they simply products of their insolvent, unstable environments? Howard S. Becker addressed these questions in *Outsiders: Studies in the Sociology of Deviance*, and proposed the premise that deviant peoples violate rules because social groups establish laws whose breach constitutes deviance, and by applying those laws and penalties to an "offender." Becker defines an outsider as an individual who others deem deviant and therefore unworthy of inclusion in society's "normal" social functions.

Would Howard Becker maintain that Rosa Lee is an outsider—one who is judged by law-abiders and stands outside of conventional social groups? Is she more likely to be labeled as an outsider because she is an African American? Becker elaborates on the implications of being an outsider:

> The degree to which an act will be treated as deviant depends also on who commits the act and who feels he has been harmed by it. Rules tend to be applied more to some persons than others. Studies of juvenile delinquency make the point clearly. Boys from middleclass areas do not get as far in the legal process when they are apprehended as do boys from slum areas. The middle-class boy is less likely, when picked up by the police, to be taken to the station; less likely when taken to the station to be booked; and it is extremely unlikely that he will be convicted and sentenced. This variation occurs even though the original infraction of the rule is the same in the two cases. Similarly, the law is differentially applied to Negroes and whites. It is well known that a Negro believed to have attacked a white woman is much more likely to be punished than a white man who commits the same offense; it is only slightly less well known that a Negro who murders another Negro is much less likely to be punished than a white man who commits murder.

Howard S. Becker, Outsiders: Studies in the Sociology of Deviance 12–13 (1973).

Consider Becker's proposition and Rosa Lee's case. Recall that Rosa Lee was acquitted when she returned to court for a shoplifting charge. Though she is African American and a "deviant outsider," she was able to receive approval from the judge and continue to maintain her freedom. However, was Rosa Lee not trying to portray herself as an "insider" by wearing more respectable attire and emotionally appealing to the judge?

3. "Underclass" and "culture of poverty." Since the 1970s, conservative scholars and critics have attempted to highlight the role of "culture" in maintaining poverty, arguing that poverty becomes intergenerational when poor people lack self-discipline, initiative, and "soft skills" required for success in the working world. These arguments played a large part in welfare reform from the 1970s through the turn of the twenty-first century. A similar debate has gone on about the so-called "underclass," identified as a group of people (Marx would have called them an "industrial reserve army") so chronically lacking regular employment that they can be seen as having effectively been marginalized from the economy altogether. In the late 1980s, the media spent a lot of time worrying about the "underclass," which was said to epitomize all the cultural deviance (lack of initiative, dependency, and so on) exhibited by the poor more generally, and which was thought to be a breeding ground for street crime. For scholarly discussions of the "underclass," *see, e.g.*, WILLIAM JULIUS WILSON, THE TRULY DISADVANTAGED: THE INNER CITY, THE UNDERCLASS, AND PUBLIC POLICY (1987); CHRISTOPHER JENCKS, RETHINKING SOCIAL POLICY: RACE, POVERTY, AND THE UNDERCLASS (1992).

Is it "culture" or material conditions that account for the large gaps that remain in family income, wages, and employment between African Americans and whites? For a "cultural" explanation, *see, e.g.*, STEPHEN THERNSTROM & ABIGAIL THERNSTROM, *America in Black and White* (1997); for a "material" explanation, *see, e.g.*, MICHAEL K. BROWN, ET AL., WHITEWASHING RACE: THE MYTH OF A COLOR-BLIND SOCIETY 66–103 (2003). Does a material explanation account for the behavior of people like Rosa Lee?

4. *"Underclass"* and prison industrial complex. Some might argue that to the extent that an underclass exists, it is, ironically, the effect as much as the cause of state policy. The "war on drugs" and the "war on crime" more generally have created an incarceration crisis for many poor communities. African American and Latino men are incarcerated for long periods at dramatic rates, which creates a social ripple effect of poverty: ex-felons find it difficult to get jobs when they get out of prison; the removal of these men from families and neighborhoods places extra economic and social stress on the people left behind. This social disorganization, in turn, leads to more crime in the increasingly impoverished and dangerous neighborhoods of inner cities. *See* Tracey Meares, *Social Organization and Drug Law Enforcement*, 35 AM. CRIM. L. REV. 191 (1998); Dorothy Roberts, *The Social and Moral Cost of Mass Incarceration in African American Communities*, 56 STAN. L. REV. 1271 (2004).

Some scholars argue that this vicious circle is coupled with another vicious circle: the increasing dependency of strapped towns and counties on prisons as economic engines, which leads to the increased political power of prison guards and prison officials unions, which leads in turn to a continuation of punitive criminal justice policies. *See* Stephen C. Thaman, *Is America a Systematic Violator of Human Rights in the Administration of Criminal Justice?* 44 ST. LOUIS L.J. 999 (2000). Another element in the continuing appeal of punitive policies, some scholars argue, is the declining influence of criminal justice experts: criminal justice policy today tends to be seen as a populist issue and not an issue about which experts should have any particular say. In this environment, politicians promising to be "tough on crime" and prosecutors dominate the legislative process. *See* Franklin Zimring, *Populism, Democratic Government, and the Decline of Expert Authority: Some Reflections on "Three Strikes" in California*, 28 PAC. L.J. 243 (1996); William Stuntz, *The Pathological Politics of Criminal Law*, 100 MICH. L. REV. 505 (2001).

5.   Crime, class, and race. The United States mass incarceration policy does not seem to have been either effective at stopping crime nor economically efficient. Why, then, has it persisted? Some scholars argue that punitive criminal justice policy serves ideological functions that are more powerful than their economic or social functions. *See, e.g.*, JEFFREY REIMAN, THE RICH GET RICHER AND THE POOR GET PRISON: IDEOLOGY, CLASS, AND CRIMINAL JUSTICE (7TH ED. 2003); MICHAEL TONRY, MALIGN NEGLECT: RACE, CRIME, AND PUNISHMENT IN AMERICA (1996); DAVID COLE, NO EQUAL JUSTICE: RACE AND CLASS IN THE AMERICAN CRIMINAL JUSTICE SYSTEM (2000).

6.   Homelessness and criminal justice policy. Like "the underclass," "the homeless" are frequently a target of fear and loathing in American culture; like the poor generally, some make an effort to distinguish the innocent or involuntary homeless from those who have "chosen" their situation; and like poverty generally, homelessness and crime are closely connected in the public mind, resulting in, ironically, more criminalization. *See* CHRISTOPHER JENCKS, THE HOMELESS (1995); PETER H. ROSSI, DOWN AND OUT IN AMERICA: THE ORIGINS OF HOMELESSNESS (1991). For a lively discussion of how not only law but architecture and urban planning are affected by the desire to make homeless people invisible in city spaces, see MIKE DAVIS, CITY OF QUARTZ: EXCAVATING THE FUTURE IN LOS ANGELES (1992).

B.   RELATIONS OF (RE)PRODUCTION

The Working Poor: Invisible in America

39–44 50, 64–67 (2004).

■ DAVID K. SHIPLER

Christie did a job that this labor-hungry economy could not do without. Every morning she drove her battered '86 Volkswagen from her apartment in public housing to the YWCA's child-care center in Akron, Ohio, where she spent the day watching over little children so their parents could go to work. Without her and thousands like her across the country, there would have been fewer people able to fill the jobs that fueled America's prosperity. Without her patience and warmth, children could have been harmed as well, for she was more than a baby-sitter. She gave the youngsters an emotionally safe place, taught and mothered them, and sometimes even rescued them from abuse at home.

For those valuable services, she received a check for about $330 every two weeks. She could not afford to put her own two children in the day-care center where she worked.

Christie was a hefty woman who laughed more readily than her predicament should have allowed. She suffered from stress and high blood pressure. She had no bank account because she could not keep enough money long enough. Try as she might to shop carefully, she always fell behind on her bills and was peppered with late fees. Her low income entitled her to food stamps and a rental subsidy, but whenever she got a little pay raise, government agencies reduced the benefits, and she felt punished for working. She was trapped on the treadmill of welfare reform, running her life according to the rules of the Personal Responsibility and Work Opportunity Reconciliation Act of 1996. The title left no doubt about what Congress and the White House saw as poverty's cause and solution.

Initially the new law combined with the good economy to send welfare caseloads plummeting. As states were granted flexibility in administering time limits and work requirements, some created innovative consortiums of government, industry, and charity to guide people into effective job training and employment. But most available jobs had three unhappy traits: They paid low wages, offered no benefits, and led nowhere. "Many who do find jobs," the Urban Institute concluded in a 2002 report, "lose other supports designed to help them, such as food stamps and health insurance, leaving them no better off—and sometimes worse off—than when they were not working."

Christie considered herself such a case. The only thing in her wallet resembling a credit card was a blue-green piece of plastic labeled "Ohio" and decorated with a drawing of a lighthouse projecting a beam into the night. Inside the "O" was a gold square—a computer chip. On the second working day of every month, she slipped the card into a special machine at Walgreen's, Save-A-Lot, or Apple's, and punched in her identification number. A credit of $136 was loaded into her chip. This was the form in which her "food stamps" were now issued—less easy to steal or to sell, and less obvious and degrading in the checkout line.

The card contained her first bit of income in every month and permitted her first expenditure. It could be used for food only, and not for cooked food or pet food. It occupied the top line in the balance sheet she kept for me during a typical October.

"2nd Spent 136.00 food stamps," she wrote. So the benefit was all gone the day she got it. Three days later she had to come up with an additional $25 in cash for groceries, another $54 on October 10, and $15 more on the twelfth. Poor families typically find that food stamps cover only one-half to three-quarters of their grocery costs.

Even the opening balance on the card was chipped away as Christie inched up in salary. It makes sense that the benefit is based on income: the less you need, the less you get. That's the economic side. On the psychological side, however, it produces hellish experiences for the beneficiaries.

Every three months Christie had to take half a day off from work (losing half a day's wages) and carry an envelope full of pay stubs, utility bills, and rent receipts to be pawed over by her ill-tempered caseworker, who applied a state-mandated formula to figure her food stamp allotment and her children's eligibility for health insurance. When Christie completed a training course and earned a raise of 10 cents an hour, her food stamps dropped by $10 a month.

That left her $6 a month ahead, which was not nothing but felt like it. Many former welfare recipients who go to work just say good riddance to the bureaucracies that would provide food stamps, medical coverage, and housing. Some think wrongly that they're no longer eligible once they're off welfare; others would rather forfeit their rights than contend with the hassle and humiliation. Quiet surrender ran against Christie's grain, however. She was smart and insistent, as anyone must be to negotiate her way through the system. She never flinched from appealing to higher authority. When she once forgot to put a utilities bill in her sheaf of papers, her caseworker withheld her food stamps. "I mailed it to her the next day," Christie said. Two weeks passed, and the card remained empty. Christie called the caseworker. "She got really snotty," Christie remembered. " 'Well, didn't I tell you you were supposed to send some documentation?' "

"I was like, 'Have you checked your mail?' " No, as it turned out, the caseworker's mail had piled up unread. "She was like, 'Well, I got people waiting up to two, three months on food stamps.' And she didn't get back with me. I had to go to her supervisor." The benefits were then restored.

It is easy to lose your balance having one foot planted tentatively in the working world and the other still entwined in this thicket of red tape. Managing relations with a boss, finding reliable child care, and coping with a tangle of unpaid bills can be daunting enough for a single mother with little such experience; add surveillance by a bureaucracy that seems more prosecutor than provider, and you have Christie's high blood pressure.

While she invoked the system's rules to get her due, she also cheated— or thought she did. Living with her surreptitiously was her boyfriend, Kevin, the father of her son. She was certain that if the Housing Authority knew, she would be evicted, either because he was a convicted felon (two years for assault) or because his earning power, meager though it was, would have lifted her beyond eligibility. So slight are the margins between government assistance and outright destitution that small lies take on large significance in the search for survival.

Kevin looked like a friendly giant—a solid 280 pounds, a shaved head, and a small earring in his right ear. His income was erratic. In decent weather he made $7.40 an hour working for a landscaper, who rewarded him with a free turkey to end the season at Thanksgiving—and then dumped him onto unemployment for the winter. He wanted to drive a truck or cut meat. He had received a butcher's certificate in a training course during imprisonment, but when he showed the document from the penitentiary, employers didn't rush to put a knife in his hand.

The arithmetic of Christie's life added up to tension, and you had to look hard through her list of expenditures to find fun or luxury. On the fifth she received her weekly child support check of $37.66 from Kevin (she got nothing from her daughter's father, who was serving a long prison sentence for assault). The same day, she put $5 worth of gas in her car, and the next day spent $6 of her own money to take the day-care kids to the zoo. The eighth was payday, and her entire $330 check disappeared in a flash. First, there was what she called a $3 "tax" to cash her check, just one of several such fees for money orders and the like—a penalty for having no checking account. Immediately, $172 went for rent, including a $10 late fee, which she was always charged because she never had enough to pay by the first of the month. Then, because it was October and she had started to plan for Christmas, she paid $31.47 at a store for presents she had put on layaway, another $10 for gasoline, $40 to buy shoes for her two kids, $5 for a pair of corduroy pants at a secondhand shop, another $5 for a shirt, $10 for bell-bottom pants, and $47 biweekly car insurance. The $330 was gone. She had no insurance on her TVs, clothes, furniture, or other household goods.

Utilities and other bills got paid out of her second check toward the end of the month. Her phone usually cost about $43 a month, gas for the apartment $34, electricity $46, and prescriptions between $8 and $15. Her monthly car payment ran $150, medical insurance $72, and cable TV $43. Cable is no longer considered a luxury by low-income families that pinch and sacrifice to have it. So much of modern American culture now comes through television that the poor would be further marginalized without the broad access that cable provides. Besides, it's relatively cheap entertainment. "I just have basic," Christie explained. "I have an antenna, but you can't see anything, you get no reception." And she needed good reception because she and Kevin loved to watch wrestling.

One reason for Christie's tight budget was the abundance of high-priced, well-advertised snacks, junk food, and prepared meals that provide an easy fallback diet for a busy working mother—or for anyone who has never learned to cook from scratch. Besides the staples of hamburgers, and chicken, "I buy sausages," Christie said, "I buy the TV dinners 'cause I might be tired some days and throw it in the oven—like Salisbury steaks and turkey and stuff like that. My kids love pizza. I get the frozen pizzas. . . . I buy my kids a lot of breakfast things 'cause we're up early and we're out the door. You know, those cereal bars and stuff like that, they're expensive! You know? Pop Tarts, cereal bars, Granola." The cheaper breakfasts, like hot cereal, came only on weekends, when she had time. "They eat the hot cereal, but during the week we're on the go. So I give them cereal in the bag. My son likes to eat dry cereal, so I put him some cereal in the lunch bag. Cocoa Puffs. They got Cocoa Dots." She laughed. "Lucky Charms. He's not picky. My daughter's picky." Those candylike cereals soak up dollars. At my local supermarket, Lucky Charms cost dearly: $4.39 for a box of just 14 ounces, while three times as much oatmeal goes for nearly the same price, $4.29. * * *

Her mother, "Gladys," had dropped out of high school, spent years on welfare, and nurtured the fervent dream of seeing her three children in college. The ambition propelled two of them. Christie's brother became an accountant, and her sister, a loan officer. But Christie never took to higher education. She began reluctantly at the University of Akron, lived at home, and finally got fed up with having no money. The second semester of her sophomore year, she went to work instead of to school, a choice that struck her then as less momentous than it turned out to be.

"She didn't take things as serious as they really were," Gladys complained. "Now she sees for herself how serious this is." Just how serious depended on what she wanted to do. She loved working with children but now discovered that without a college degree she would have trouble getting hired at a responsible level in the Head Start preschool program, much less as a teacher in a regular school; she was limited to a YWCA daycare center whose finances were precarious. Since 95 percent of the Y's children came from low-income families, the fees were essentially set by the center's main source of income, Ohio's Department of Human Services, which paid $99 to $114 a week for full-time care. Given the center's heavy expenses, the rates were not enough to pay teachers more than $5.30 to $5.90 an hour.

Christie's previous jobs had also imprisoned her close to the minimum wage as a hostess-cashier at a Holiday Inn, a cashier at Kmart, a waitress in a bar, a cook and waitress and cashier in various restaurants. She had become a veteran of inadequate training programs designed to turn her into a retail salesperson, a bus driver, and a correctional officer, but the courses never enabled her and her classmates to pass the tests and get hired. She had two words to explain why she had never returned to college. "Lazy. Lazy."

It was strange that she thought of herself as lazy, because her work was exhausting, and her low wage required enormous effort to stay afloat. * * *

The new millennium arrived in a crescendo of American riches. The nation wallowed in luxury, burst with microchips, consumed with abandon, swaggered globally. Everything grew larger: homes, vehicles, stock portfolios, life expectancy. Never before in the sweep of human history had so many people been so utterly comfortable.

Caroline Payne was not one of them. A few weeks after New Year's Day, she sat at her kitchen table and reflected on her own history. Two of her three goals had been achieved: She had earned a college diploma, albeit just a two-year associate's degree. And she had gone from a homeless shelter into her own house, although it was mostly owned by a bank. The third objective, "a good-paying job," as she put it, still eluded her. Back in the mid–1970s, she earned $6 an hour in a Vermont factory that made plastic cigarette lighters and cases for Gillette razors. In 2000, she earned $6.80 an hour stocking shelves and working cash registers at a vast Wal-Mart superstore in New Hampshire. * * *

Anyone who walked all the way around the outside of the Wal-Mart superstore on Route 103 would walk a mile, Caroline said. The place was immense. It sold everything from lawn mowers to ground beef, underpricing smaller stores that were struggling to survive in the center of town. Its 300 to 330 employees, who came and went seasonally, wore Wal-Mart's uniform of blue smocks and friendly smiles, trained as they were to be surprisingly helpful to customers.

Mark Brown, the manager, could pay his people more without raising prices, he conceded. He sat at a table in the store's snack bar, watching the part of the grocery section he could see, listening to the public address system's call for help at the registers, his eyes darting around this corner of his fiefdom like a school principal waiting for the next catastrophe. He was thirty-one, but he looked as young as a college kid and spoke with the twang of his native southeast Missouri. He had come from another store in Georgia and was learning to ski here in New Hampshire.

His employees started at $6.25 an hour, earned an extra dollar at night and another 25 cents "for going to the front end," which meant working one of the twenty-four cash registers. And if he started them at $8 an hour, say, instead of $6.25, how would that change the economics of the store? "Hmmmm. I don't think it would change at all." He wouldn't have to raise prices? "No. We've got a corporate pricing structure. And the way we do things, we go out and we check our competition every single week. Every department manager in this store goes out once a week and checks competition, and that's what determines our prices. We have a core price structure that we set regionally, by areas. Definitely the base price here would be probably higher than what it is in Arkansas, where there's a cheap cost of living. So it would be higher here, but it would still be standard to this area. And then after they give us that base, then we go out and check our competition, and if we're gettin' beat, we lower our prices."

So there's enough profit to absorb an increase from $6.25 to $8? "There would be, because if we were having to raise our wages, then evidently everybody else would be too, and if we make sure we're low enough, our competitors' customers are gonna shop with us." Would wage increases have any effect at all? "We'd have to cut corners on other things like, you know, we may not be able to put all the pretty balloons up all over the store. The non-necessities we'd have to cut back on."

Three days later Wal-Mart Stores, Inc., announced a net income of $5.58 billion for 1999, up 26 percent from the previous year.

Caroline was bouncing from one department to another, from one shift to another, but her pay stayed within a narrow range, beginning at $6.25, going to $6.80, sometimes up to $7.50 if she worked at night. So unpredictable were her hours that she couldn't work a second job, which would have helped her cash flow. She kept applying to higher positions and kept hearing that she needed a bit more experience. * * *

In more depressed parts of the country and during recessions, * * * some Wal-Mart managers were accused of forcing employees to work before punching in or after punching out to avoid paying overtime as required by law. "Wal-Mart management doesn't hold itself to the same standard of rectitude it expects from its low-paid employees," wrote Barbara Ehrenreich, who worked at a Wal-Mart in Minnesota while researching her book *Nickel and Dimed*. "When I applied for a job at Wal-Mart in the spring of 2000, I was reprimanded for getting something 'wrong' on this test: I had agreed only 'strongly' to the proposition, 'All rules have to be followed to the letter at all times.' The correct answer was 'totally agree.' Apparently the one rule that need not be slavishly adhered to at Wal-Mart is the federal Fair Labor Standards Act, which requires that employees be paid time and a half if they work more than forty hours in a week." Workers were warned against "time theft," which meant "doing anything other than working during company time, anything at all," she reported. "Theft of *our* time is not, however, an issue."

Caroline never had the overtime problem in her New Hampshire store, but in six Southern states employees filed a class-action suit against the company for ordering them off the clock as their weekly time approached forty hours. Their attorney calculated the benefits to the firm: If each of 250 hourly wage "associates" in a single store worked just one hour of unpaid overtime a week, that would total 250 unpaid hours a week, 1,000 a month, 12,000 a year—and there were over 300 Wal-Mart stores in Texas, producing savings in that state alone of more than $30 million that should have been paid to employees.

Caroline did not suffer from any violations of law, as far as she could tell, but her career went nowhere. Mark Brown, the manager who liked her, got transferred to Pennsylvania, dimming her prospects for advancement. So after a year and a half at Wal-Mart, she signed up with a temp agency, which found her a $7.50–an-hour daytime job Monday through Friday assembling wallpaper sample books. And she had the pleasure of telling Wal-Mart's assistant manager that she was leaving for higher pay.

––––––––

Down and Out in Discount America

The Nation, Dec. 16 2004, http://www.thenation.com/doc.mhtml?i=20050103&s=featherstone.

■ LIZA FEATHERSTONE

On the day after Thanksgiving, the biggest shopping day of the year, Wal-Mart's many progressive critics—not to mention its business competitors—finally enjoyed a bit of schadenfreude when the retailer had to admit to "disappointing" sales. The problem was quickly revealed: Wal-Mart hadn't been discounting aggressively enough. Without low prices, Wal-Mart just isn't Wal-Mart.

That's not a mistake the big-box behemoth is likely to make again. Wal-Mart knows its customers, and it knows how badly they need the discounts. Like Wal-Mart's workers, its customers are overwhelmingly female, and struggling to make ends meet. Betty Dukes, the lead plaintiff in *Dukes v. Wal-Mart*, the landmark sex-discrimination case against the company, points out that Wal-Mart takes out ads in her local paper the same day the community's poorest citizens collect their welfare checks. "They are promoting themselves to low-income people," she says. "That's who they lure. They don't lure the rich.... They understand the economy of America. They know the haves and have-nots. They don't put Wal-Mart in Piedmonts. They don't put Wal-Mart in those high-end parts of the community. They plant themselves right in the middle of Poorville."

Betty Dukes is right. A 2000 study by Andrew Franklin, then an economist at the University of Connecticut, showed that Wal-Mart operated primarily in poor and working-class communities, finding, in the bone-dry language of his discipline, "a significant negative relationship between median household income and Wal-Mart's presence in the market." Although fancy retailers noted with chagrin during the 2001 recession that absolutely everybody shops at Wal-Mart—"Even people with $100,000 incomes now shop at Wal-Mart," a PR flack for one upscale mall fumed— the Bloomingdale's set is not the discounter's primary market, and probably never will be. Only 6 percent of Wal-Mart shoppers have annual family incomes of more than $100,000. A 2003 study found that 23 percent of Wal-Mart Supercenter customers live on incomes of less than $25,000 a year. More than 20 percent of Wal-Mart shoppers have no bank account, long considered a sign of dire poverty. And while almost half of Wal-Mart Supercenter customers are blue-collar workers and their families, 20 percent are unemployed or elderly.

Al Zack, who until his retirement in 2004 was the United Food and Commercial Workers' vice president for strategic programs, observes that appealing to the poor was "Sam Walton's real genius. He figured out how to make money off of poverty. He located his first stores in poor rural areas and discovered a real market. The only problem with the business model is that it really needs to create more poverty to grow." That problem is cleverly solved by creating more bad jobs worldwide. In a chilling reversal of Henry Ford's strategy, which was to pay his workers amply so they could buy Ford cars, Wal-Mart's stingy compensation policies—workers make, on average, just over $8 an hour, and if they want health insurance, they must pay more than a third of the premium—contribute to an economy in which, increasingly, workers can only afford to shop at Wal-Mart.

To make this model work, Wal-Mart must keep labor costs down. It does this by making corporate crime an integral part of its business strategy. Wal-Mart routinely violates laws protecting workers' organizing rights (workers have even been fired for union activity). It is a repeat offender on overtime laws; in more than thirty states, workers have brought wage-and-hour class-action suits against the retailer. In some cases, workers say, managers encouraged them to clock out and keep working; in others, managers locked the doors and would not let employees go home at the end of their shifts. And it's often women who suffer most from Wal-Mart's labor practices. *Dukes v. Wal-Mart*, which is the largest civil rights class-action suit in history, charges the company with systematically discriminating against women in pay and promotions. * * *

SOLIDARITY ACROSS THE CHECKOUT COUNTER

Given the poverty they have in common, it makes sense that Wal-Mart's workers often express a strong feeling of solidarity with the shoppers. Wal-Mart workers tend to be aware that the customers' circumstances are similar to their own, and to identify with them. Some complain about rude customers, but most seem to genuinely enjoy the shoppers.

One longtime department manager in Ohio cheerfully recalls her successful job interview at Wal-Mart. Because of her weight, she told her interviewers, she'd be better able to help the customer. "I told them I wanted to work in the ladies department because I'm a heavy girl." She understands the frustrations of the large shopper, she told them: " 'You know, you go into Lane Bryant and some skinny girl is trying to sell you clothes.' They laughed at that and said, 'You get a second interview!' "

One plaintiff in the *Dukes* lawsuit, Cleo Page, who no longer works at Wal-Mart, says she was a great customer service manager because "I knew how people feel when they shop, so I was really empathetic."

Many Wal-Mart workers say they began working at their local Wal-Mart because they shopped there. "I was practically born in Wal-Mart," says Alyssa Warrick, a former employee now attending Truman State University in Missouri. "My mom is obsessed with shopping.... I thought it would be pretty easy since I knew where most of the stuff was." Most assumed they would love working at Wal-Mart. "I always loved shopping there," enthuses *Dukes* plaintiff Dee Gunter. "That's why I wanted to work for 'em."

Shopping is traditionally a world of intense female communication and bonding, and women have long excelled in retail sales in part because of the identification between clerk and shopper. Page, who still shops at Wal-Mart, is now a lingerie saleswoman at Mervyn's (owned by Target). "I do enjoy retail," she says. "I like feeling needed and I like helping people, especially women."

Betty Dukes says, "I strive to give Wal-Mart customers one hundred percent of my abilities." This sentiment was repeated by numerous other Wal-Mart workers, always with heartfelt sincerity. Betty Hamilton, a 61-year-old clerk in a Las Vegas Sam's Club, won her store's customer service award last year. She is very knowledgeable about jewelry, her favorite department, and proud of it. Hamilton resents her employer—she complains about sexual harassment and discrimination, and feels she has been penalized on the job for her union sympathies—but remains deeply devoted to her customers. She enjoys imparting her knowledge to shoppers so "they can walk out of there and feel like they know something." Like Page, Hamilton feels she is helping people. "It makes me so happy when I sell something that I know is an extraordinarily good buy," she says. "I feel like I've done somebody a really good favor."

The enthusiasm of these women for their jobs, despite the workplace indignities many of them have faced, should not assure anybody that the company's abuses don't matter. In fact, it should underscore the tremendous debt Wal-Mart owes women: This company has built its vast profits not only on women's drudgery but also on their joy, creativity and genuine care for the customer.

Why Boycotts Don't Always Work

Will consumers return that solidarity and punish Wal-Mart for discriminating against women? Do customers care about workers as much as workers care about them? Some women's groups, like the National Organization for Women and Code Pink, have been hoping that they do, and have encouraged the public not to shop at Wal-Mart. While this tactic could be fruitful in some community battles, it's unlikely to catch on nationwide. A customer saves 20–25 percent by buying groceries at Wal-Mart rather than from a competitor, according to retail analysts, and poor women need those savings more than anyone.

That's why many women welcome the new Wal-Marts in their communities. *The Winona* (Minnesota) *Post* extensively covered a controversy over whether to allow a Wal-Mart Supercenter into the small town; the letters to the editor in response offer a window into the female customer's loyalty to Wal-Mart. Though the paper devoted substantial space to the sex discrimination case, the readers who most vehemently defended the retailer were female. From the nearby town of Rollingstone, Cindy Kay wrote that she needed the new Wal-Mart because the local stores didn't carry large-enough sizes. She denounced the local anti-Wal-Mart campaign as a plot by rich and thin elites: "I'm glad those people can fit into and afford such clothes. I can barely afford Shopko and Target!"

A week later, Carolyn Goree, a preschool teacher also hoping for a Winona Wal-Mart, wrote in a letter to the *Post* editor that when she shops at most stores, $200 fills only a bag or two, but at Wal-Mart, "I come out with a cart full top and bottom. How great that feels." Lacking a local Wal-Mart, Goree drives over the Wisconsin border to get her fix. She was incensed by an earlier article's lament that some workers make only $15,000 yearly. "Come on!" Goree objected. "Is $15,000 really that bad of a yearly income? I'm a single mom and when working out of my home, I made $12,000 tops and that was with child support. I too work, pay for a mortgage, lights, food, everything to live. Everything in life is a choice.... I am for the little man/woman—I'm one of them. So I say stand up and get a Wal-Mart."

Sara Jennings, a disabled Winona reader living on a total of $8,000, heartily concurred. After paying her rent, phone, electric and cable bills, Jennings can barely afford to treat herself to McDonald's. Of a recent trip to the LaCrosse, Wisconsin, Wal-Mart, she raved, "Oh boy, what a great treat. Lower prices and a good quality of clothes to choose from. It was like heaven for me." She, too, strongly defended the workers' $15,000 yearly income: "Boy, now that is a lot of money. I could live with that." She closed with a plea to the readers: "I'm sure you all make a lot more than I. And I'm sure I speak for a lot of seniors and very-low-income people. We *need* this Wal-Mart. There's nothing downtown."

FROM CONSUMERS TO WORKERS AND CITIZENS

It is crucial that Wal-Mart's liberal and progressive critics make use of the growing public indignation at the company over sex discrimination, low pay and other workers' rights issues, but it is equally crucial to do this in ways that remind people that their power does not stop at their shopping dollars. It's admirable to drive across town and pay more for toilet paper to avoid shopping at Wal-Mart, but such a gesture is, unfortunately, not enough. As long as people identify themselves as consumers and nothing more, Wal-Mart wins.

The invention of the "consumer" identity has been an important part of a long process of eroding workers' power, and it's one reason working people now have so little power against business. According to the social historian Stuart Ewen, in the early years of mass production, the late nineteenth and early twentieth centuries, modernizing capitalism sought to turn people who thought of themselves primarily as "workers" into "consumers." Business elites wanted people to dream not of satisfying work and egalitarian societies—as many did at that time—but of the beautiful things they could buy with their paychecks.

Business was quite successful in this project, which influenced much early advertising and continued throughout the twentieth century. In addition to replacing the "worker," the "consumer" has also effectively displaced the citizen. That's why, when most Americans hear about the Wal-Mart's worker-rights abuses, their first reaction is to feel guilty about shopping at the store. A tiny minority will respond by shopping elsewhere—and only a handful will take any further action. A worker might call her union and organize a picket. A citizen might write to her congressman or local newspaper, or galvanize her church and knitting circle to visit local management. A consumer makes an isolated, politically slight decision: to shop or not to shop. Most of the time, Wal-Mart has her exactly where it wants her, because the intelligent choice for anyone thinking as a consumer is not to make a political statement but to seek the best bargain and the greatest convenience.

To effectively battle corporate criminals like Wal-Mart, the public must be engaged as citizens, not merely as shoppers. What kind of politics could encourage that? It's not clear that our present political parties are up to the job. Unlike so many horrible things, Wal-Mart cannot be blamed on George W. Bush. The Arkansas-based company prospered under the state's native son Bill Clinton when he was governor and President. Sam Walton and his wife, Helen, were close to the Clintons, and for several years Hillary Clinton, whose law firm represented Wal-Mart, served on the company's board of directors. Bill Clinton's "welfare reform" has provided Wal-Mart with a ready workforce of women who have no choice but to accept its poverty wages and discriminatory policies.

Still, a handful of Democratic politicians stood up to the retailer. California Assemblywoman Sally Lieber, who represents the 22nd Assembly District and is a former mayor of Mountain View, was outraged when she learned about the sex discrimination charges in *Dukes v. Wal-Mart*, and she smelled blood when, tipped off by dissatisfied workers, her office discovered that Wal-Mart was encouraging its workers to apply for public assistance, "in the middle of the worst state budget crisis in history!" California had a $38 billion deficit at the time, and Lieber was enraged that taxpayers would be subsidizing Wal-Mart's low wages, bringing new meaning to the term "corporate welfare."

Lieber was angry, too, that Wal-Mart's welfare dependence made it nearly impossible for responsible employers to compete with the retail giant. It was as if taxpayers were unknowingly funding a massive plunge to the bottom in wages and benefits—quite possibly their own. She held a press conference in July 2003, to expose Wal-Mart's welfare scam. The Wal-Mart documents—instructions explaining how to apply for food stamps, Medi-Cal (the state's healthcare assistance program) and other forms of welfare—were blown up on posterboard and displayed. The morning of the press conference, a Wal-Mart worker who wouldn't give her name for fear of being fired snuck into Lieber's office. "I just wanted to say, right on!" she told the assemblywoman.

Wal-Mart spokespeople have denied that the company encourages employees to collect public assistance, but the documents speak for themselves. They bear the Wal-Mart logo, and one is labeled "Wal-Mart: Instructions for Associates." Both documents instruct employees in procedures for applying to "Social Service Agencies." Most Wal-Mart workers I've interviewed had co-workers who worked full time for the company and received public assistance, and some had been in that situation themselves. Public assistance is very clearly part of the retailer's cost-cutting strategy. (It's ironic that a company so dependent on the public dole supports so many right-wing politicians who'd like to dismantle the welfare state.)

Lieber, a strong supporter of the social safety net who is now assistant speaker pro tempore of the California Assembly, last year passed a bill that would require large and mid-sized corporations that fail to provide decent, affordable health insurance to reimburse local governments for the cost of providing public assistance for those workers. When the bill passed, its opponents decided to kill it by bringing it to a statewide referendum. Wal-Mart, which just began opening Supercenters in California this year, mobilized its resources to revoke the law on election day this November, even while executives denied that any of their employees depended on public assistance.

Citizens should pressure other politicians to speak out against Wal-Mart's abuses and craft policy solutions. But the complicity of both parties in Wal-Mart's power over workers points to the need for a politics that squarely challenges corporate greed and takes the side of ordinary people. That kind of politics seems, at present, strongest at the local level.

Earlier this year, labor and community groups in Chicago prevented Wal-Mart from opening a store on the city's South Side, in part by pushing through an ordinance that would have forced the retailer to pay Chicago workers a living wage. In Hartford, Connecticut, labor and community advocates just won passage of an ordinance protecting their free speech rights on the grounds of the new Wal-Mart Supercenter, which is being built on city property. Similar battles are raging nationwide, but Wal-Mart's opponents don't usually act with as much coordination as Wal-Mart does, and they lack the retail behemoth's deep pockets.

With this in mind, SEIU president Andy Stern has recently been calling attention to the need for better coordination—and funding—of labor and community anti-Wal-Mart efforts. Stern has proposed that the AFL-CIO allocate $25 million of its royalties from purchases on its Union Plus credit card toward fighting Wal-Mart and the "Wal-Martization" of American jobs.   * * *

Such efforts are essential not just because Wal-Mart is a grave threat to unionized workers' jobs (which it is) but because it threatens all American ideals that are at odds with profit—ideals such as justice, equality and fairness. Wal-Mart would not have so much power if we had stronger labor laws, and if we required employers to pay a living wage. The company knows that, and it hires lobbyists in Washington to vigorously fight any effort at such reforms—indeed, Wal-Mart has recently beefed up this political infrastructure substantially, and it's likely that its presence in Washington will only grow more conspicuous.

The situation won't change until a movement comes together and builds the kind of social and political power for workers and citizens that can balance that of Wal-Mart. This is not impossible: In Germany, unions are powerful enough to force Wal-Mart to play by their rules. American citizens will have to ask themselves what kind of world they want to live in. That's what prompted Gretchen Adams, a former Wal-Mart manager, to join the effort to unionize Wal-Mart. She's deeply troubled by the company's effect on the economy as a whole and the example it sets for other employers. "What about our working-class people?" she asks. "I don't want to live in a Third World country." Working people, she says, should be able to afford "a new car, a house. You shouldn't have to leave the car on the lawn because you can't afford that $45 part."

NOTES AND QUESTIONS

1. **Wal-Mart as avatar of new economy.** Simon Head notes the phenomenal success of Wal-Mart:

> Within the corporate world Wal-Mart's preeminence is not simply a matter of size. In its analysis of the growth of U.S. productivity, or output per worker, between 1995 and 2000—the years of the "new economy" and the high-tech bubble on Wall Street—the McKinsey

Global Institute has found that just over half that growth took place in two sectors, retail and wholesale, where, directly or indirectly, Wal-Mart "caused the bulk of the productivity acceleration through ongoing managerial innovation that increased competition intensity and drove the diffusion of best practice." This is management-speak for Wal-Mart's aggressive use of information technology and its skill in meeting the needs of its customers.

In its own category of "general merchandise," Wal-Mart has taken a huge lead in productivity over its competitors, a lead of 44 percent in 1987, 48 percent in 1995, and still 41 percent in 1999, even as competitors began to copy Wal-Mart's strategy. Thanks to the company's superior productivity, Wal-Mart's share of total sales among all the sellers of "general merchandise" rose from 9 percent in 1987 to 27 percent in 1995, and 30 percent in 1999, an astonishing rate of growth which recalls the rise of the Ford Motor Company nearly a century ago. McKinsey lists some of the leading causes of Wal-Mart's success. For example, its huge, ugly box-shaped buildings enable Wal-Mart "to carry a wider range of goods than competitors" and to "enjoy labor economies of scale."

McKinsey mentions Wal-Mart's "efficiency in logistics," which makes it possible for the company to buy in bulk directly from producers of everything from toilet paper to refrigerators, allowing it to dispense with wholesalers. McKinsey also makes much of the company's innovative use of information technology, for example its early use of computers and scanners to track inventory, and its use of satellite communications to link corporate headquarters in Arkansas with the nationwide network of Wal-Mart stores. Setting up and fine-tuning these tracking and distribution systems has been the special achievement of founder Sam Walton's (the "Wal" of Wal-Mart) two successors as CEOs, David Glass and the incumbent Lee Scott.

Simon Head, *Inside the Leviathan,* 51 N.Y. REV. BOOKS 80 (2004), *available at* http://www.nybooks.com/archives. Wal-Mart's success has also, however, crucially relied on its ability to keep wages and benefits low. Like Featherstone, Head argues for stronger and better enforced labor laws, asserting that "Wal-Mart has reached back beyond the New Deal to the harsh, abrasive capitalism of the 1920s." *id.*

2. Wal-Mart and gender discrimination. In the summer of 2004, a federal district court certified a sex discrimination class action against Wal-Mart on behalf of 1.6 million women who had worked at Wal-Mart since December 26, 1998. The plaintiffs in *Dukes v. Wal-Mart,* 222 F.R.D. 137 (N.D. Cal. 2004), the largest private civil rights case in United States history, alleged that Wal-Mart discriminated against its female employees in making promotions, job assignments, pay decisions and training, and retaliated against women who complained about such practices. *See* http://www.walmartclass.com.

3. Markets in poverty. Many services as well as goods are targeted to the poverty market. As David Shipler describes in his book, *The Working*

Poor: Invisible in America (2004), tax preparers, check-cashing outlets, credit card companies, and mortgage and other loan providers often market their services to poor people. Services to the poor, however, tend to cost more money than the same services to the middle-class or the wealthy. The "subprime" market is a lucrative one because the customers have few options, urgent need, and often little information about their rights. Shipler offers an example of how poverty costs money:

> Say you're short of cash, and the bills are piling up, along with some disconnection notices. Payday is two weeks away, and your phone and electricity will be shut off before then. The guy at the local convenience store, who has a booth for cashing checks, throws you a lifeline. If you need $100 now, you write him a check for $120, postdated by two weeks. He'll give you the $100 in cash today, hold your check until your wages are in your bank account, and then put the check through. Or you can give him the $120 in cash when you get it, and he'll return your check. Either way, 20 percent interest for two weeks equals 1.438 percent a day, or 521 percent annually. * * *

> Furthermore, the loans are not technically loans in some states, because there's a check. And if a check bounces, more severe penalties apply than those for unrepaid loans. Borrowing $300, for instance, an Indiana woman paid a $30 fee and wrote a check for $330. When the check bounced, her bank and the payday loan establishment charged $80 in fees. Then the lender took her to court, won triple damages of $990, lawyer's fees of $150, and $60 in court costs. The total charge on the $300 loan: $1,310.

SHIPLER, THE WORKING POOR, *supra* at 18–19.

4. Health care and bankruptcy. A recent study found that about half of personal bankruptcy filers interviewed cited "medical causes" as the reason for their filing bankruptcy. Among those whose illnesses led to bankruptcy, out-of-pocket costs averaged $11,854 since the start of illness; 75.7 percent had insurance at the onset of illness. David U. Himmelstein et al., *Market Watch: Illness and Injury as Contributors to Bankruptcy*, HEALTH AFFAIRS, Feb. 2, 2005, http://content.healthaffairs.org/cgi/content/full/hlthaff.w5.63/DC1. The authors of the study concluded that "Even middle-class insured families often fall prey to financial catastrophe when sick." *Id.*

———

Nanny Diaries and Other Stories: Imagining Immigrant Women's Labor in the Social Reproduction of American Families

52 809, 813, 814–22, 832–47 (2003).

■ MARY ROMERO

> *Wanted: One young woman to take care of four-year-old boy. Must be cheerful, enthusiastic, and selfless—bordering on masochistic. Must*

relish sixteen-hour shifts with a deliberately nap-deprived preschooler. Must love getting thrown up on, literally and figuratively, by everyone in his family. Must enjoy the delicious anticipation of ridiculously erratic pay. Mostly, must love being treated like fungus found growing out of employer's Hermes bag. Those who take it personally need not apply.

Introduction

Two former nannies employed on the Upper East Side of Manhattan offer this want advertisement as an illustration of employers' expectations and working conditions awaiting potential employees. Although it is a fictionalized account of their total six-year experience as nannies while attending college, Emma McLaughlin and Nicola Kraus's *The Nanny Diaries: A Novel* has spurred significant attention from the media. * * *

 * * *

II.   *The Nanny Diaries:* Reality or Fantasy?

Given the media attention and public discourse generated by the novel, it is worth asking the question: How representative is *The Nanny Diaries?* * * *

Given the large number of undocumented immigrants and United States workers employed "off the books," workers with temporary or permanent visas, and the broad category that the Department of Labor and the Census classify as domestic service, precise numbers of domestics and nannies are difficult to obtain. Assessing the United States Bureau of Labor Statistics, Human Rights Watch estimates that 800,000 private household workers were officially recorded in 1998, of which 30% were immigrant women. Regions exporting the largest number of women to labor as domestic servants are Asia, Africa, Latin America, and Eastern Europe. Research conducted on domestics in the United States include immigrants from Latin America, the Caribbean, and the Philippines.

A distinctive characteristic of domestic service in the United States is the race and ethnic differences between employer and employee. The intersection of class, race, and ethnicity has been a prominent component to the study of African-American, Chicana and Japanese-American domestics. Racial distinctions remain a striking feature identifying caregivers from their charges and employers. Reflecting on the playground scene in Central Park depicted in *The Nanny Diaries*, one onlooker contrasted the faces of children and caretakers:

> There are also adults there, but curiously, the faces of the two groups (adults and children) don't match. For every white child in a stroller, there is a black woman leaning down, to guide a juice box into their mouth. If she isn't black, she is Hispanic or Asian. The women are the

children's nannies. In many cases, they are stepping in for white parents, who are working full-time.

Apparent differences between native-born and immigrant women of color employed as maids and nannies are education and previous work experience. African-American, Chicana and Japanese-American women rarely have more than a high school education. A growing number of Latina and Caribbean immigrants are high school and college graduates, and some have held white-collar positions in their homeland. Helma Lutz noted the international trend toward older and better educated third-world immigrant women in her survey of research on the globalization of domestic service. Unlike younger and single European immigrant women at the turn of the twentieth century, these women work to cope with financial crisis, to support families, and to educate their children. Thus, Nan's race, marital status, and citizenship are not characteristic of many women employed as nannies in the United States. With the exception of European women immigrating to the United States with J-1 visas to work as *au pairs* while pursuing their education, most immigrant women are not part-time college students. Nan's career trajectory is obviously destined for a professional or managerial position; whereas, older immigrant working mothers find little if any social mobility. For these women, domestic service is best described as a ghetto occupation rather than a bridging occupation.

Nan informs the reader of the existing continuum of childcare arrangements which she designates as three types of nanny gigs: (1) "a few nights a week for people who work all day and parent most nights;" (2) " 'sanity time' a few afternoons a week to a woman who mothers most days and nights;" and (3) "provide twenty-four/seven 'me time' to a woman who neither works nor mothers." Embedded in this classification are live-in positions (twenty-four hours a day, seven days a week) and day workers that might work solely for one employer full-time or for a number of employers. Employers make arrangements with agencies, franchises, collectives, or directly with the employee. Employees working on their own include some that are bonded and considered self-employed, and others working in the underground economy. However, the actual distinctions are reflected in the working conditions: hours of employment, wages, lack of benefits, and the inclusion of all household work alongside childcare.

Researchers and labor advocates reporting wages for immigrant women over the last decade point to the variability in the market. Grace A. Rosales found wages ranging from $100 to $400 a week in Los Angeles. In her study of immigrant women employed as domestics and nannies in Los Angeles, Pierrette Hondagneu-Sotelo states that many Latina live-in workers do not receive minimum wage, whereas day workers averaged a higher wage of $5.90 an hour. Doreen Mattingly interviewed current and former Latina domestics in San Diego during the same period and found the average hourly rate for day workers was $8.02 and for live-ins was $2.72. Rhacel Salazar Parreñas reports that Filipina women migrating to Los Angeles earned an average of $425 a week for providing elderly care and $350 a week for live-in housekeeping and childcare. In a survey conducted in 2000, the Center for the Childcare Workforce in Washington, D.C., found that half of childcare providers earned less than $4.82 an hour and worked 55 hours a week. Human Rights Watch reviewed 43 egregious cases among domestic workers with special visas in the United States, and found a median hourly rate of $2.14.

Variation in wages and working conditions among employees points to the hierarchical structure in domestic service reinforced by employers' preferences. Obviously the hierarchy was not completely lost by McLaughlin and Kraus. In a reading at a Barnes & Noble bookshop, Kraus acknowledged the privileged subject position she and her colleague experienced: "We were the Hermès bags of nannies.... [A]s white, middle-class and university-educated nannies they [she and McLaughlin] were able to avoid the seamier elements of the industry." Latina and Caribbean immigrants are more vulnerable in the labor market than European immigrants. Skills do appear to be taken into consideration under certain circumstances. For instance, in her study of language between nannies and children in Los Angeles, Patricia Baquedano–López concluded that speaking English and a high school education were assets that domestics used in their negotiations with employers.

McLaughlin and Kraus portray a typical day of nanny tasks as "spent schlepping Grayer to French class, music lessons, karate, swimming, school and play dates." Although consistent with the image of Maria Rainer, the governess that Captain Von Trapp hired to care for his children in the film *The Sound of Music*, most employers with a live-in nanny assign employees a wide range of household tasks. While the distinction between housekeepers and nannies is frequently used to distinguish workers employed primarily to care for children, housekeepers may occasionally be asked to assist in childcare and nannies may be expected to cook, wash dishes, "pick-up," and do other household work directly related to the care of children. A consistent complaint among nannies is the expectation that they do housework and cook, alongside caring for children. Distinctions between domestic workers or private household workers and nannies are blurred in the everyday reality of employees as they engage in a broad range of household and caregiving activities, including cleaning, cooking, laundry, nursing the sick, supervising, playing with children, and grocery shopping.

Obviously, the most lucrative and sought after positions are the ones that make a clear distinction between tasks and recognize employees' skills, expertise, and experience. Immigrant women, particularly those who are undocumented, are more likely to be hired for live-in, as well as day work, positions that do not have clearly defined job descriptions. These nannies are unlikely to have much authority over the children or in planning activities. Instead, they find themselves at the beck and call of children as they serve and wait on them. Given the number of immigrant women nannies that McLaughlin and Kraus saw in the park, it is not surprising that they wrote, "[E]very playground has at least one nanny getting the shit kicked out of her by an angry child." *San Francisco Chronicle* reporter Adair Lara differentiated job descriptions offered to non-immigrant women:

"At the other end of the spectrum, a professional nanny often works weekends, engages the child in imaginative play, knows CPR.... She will want her hours guaranteed, will expect a bonus, and might be persnickety about doing more than the dishes and the baby's laundry."

Nan's life implies that work as a nanny is filled with new learning opportunities and adventures, from learning to cook exotic foods for Grayer to vacationing among the rich and famous. This depiction does not capture the overwhelming sense of isolation reported by immigrant women, particularly among live-in workers. Since Lucy Salmon's sociological study at the turn of the century, extreme isolation continues to be cited among live-in workers as one of the worst aspects of the job. Isolation from relatives, friends, and other domestic workers removes them from gaining resources to find employment elsewhere. Separation from their own children is frequently identified as a major force in developing strong emotional attachment to their charges. Domestics' loneliness is not countered by stimulating tasks. In the transformation of domestic labor from the unpaid work of mothers to low-wage work, physical demands are increased and more creative aspects are eliminated. The transformation from unpaid to paid childcare results in assigning immigrant nannies to the least pleasant tasks. Childcare advocates Suzanne W. Helburn and Barbara R. Bergmann describe the division as follows: "The parents try to reserve the more interesting child-rearing tasks for themselves. They do the storytelling and reading, supervise homework, and organize outings and parties in order to spend 'quality time' with their children."

Like the public discourse generated by the Nannygate scandals over the last decade, *The Nanny Diaries* examined the impact on employers and their children rather than on the employees and their children. Editorials and book reviews focus on employer rights to privacy, poor parenting, and the suffering and deprivation of "the poor little rich boy, Grayer." Since the novel's fictionalized couple who hired the nanny was portrayed as a cheating husband and an unemployed trophy wife, the stage is set against a public debate over the needs of working parents. Labor issues are contexualized as interpersonal gender relationships between women (and their competing expectations and emotions in doing "women's work") and the difficulty of employees identifying as a servant. Reference to immigrant nannies are curtailed to discussions concerning the impact that their limited English skills and cultural differences have on children under their care.

However, when immigrant women speak for themselves, the following list of labor issues are similar to the concerns expressed by workers in the United States: low wages, unpaid hours, lack of decent standards, absence of health insurance and other employee benefits, and constant supervision. In the case of live-in domestics, employer abuses include violations of their human rights. Grievances reported in Bridget Anderson and Philzacklea's international study that are also found in the United States include:

> denial of wages in cases of dismissal following trial or probation periods, refusal by employers to arrange legal resident status (for tax

reasons, etc.); control and sexual harassment; pressure to do additional work (for friends and colleagues); excessive workloads, especially where in addition to caring for children and elderly people they are responsible for all other household chores; and finally the very intimate relationship between the domestic helpers and their employers.

Human Rights Watch cites the following additional employer abuses in the United States: "basic telephone privileges, prohibiting them from leaving employers' homes unaccompanied, and forbidding them to associate or communicate with friends and neighbors." "To prevent domestic workers from leaving exploitative employment situations, employers confiscate the workers' passports and threaten them with deportation if they flee. In the most severe cases of abuse, migrant domestic workers—both live-in and day workers—have reported instances of sexual assault, physical abuse, and rape." Health hazards posed by cleaning chemicals "causing everything from skin irritation and rashes to serious respiratory problems from inhaling toxic fumes" is another grievance reported by human rights and labor advocates.

* * *

IV. Immigrant Nanny Care and the Reproduction of Privilege

Globalization of childcare is based on income inequality between women from poor countries providing low-wage care work for families in wealthier nations. Even with the low wages and variability in the market cited above, hiring a nanny is recognized as the most expensive childcare option. Researchers recognize this reality: "The grim truth is that some women's access to the high-paying, high-status professions is being facilitated through the revival of semi-indentured servitude. Put another way, one woman is exercising class and citizenship privilege to buy her easy way out of sex oppression." The largest number of domestic workers are located in areas of the country with the highest income inequality among women. In regions with minimal income inequality, the occupation is insignificant. Particular forms of domestic labor that affirm and enhance employers' status, shift the burden of sexism to low-wage women workers, and relegate the most physically difficult and dirty aspects of domestic labor. However, little attention has been given to the ways that privilege is reproduced through childcare arrangements and the significance that third-world immigrant women's labor plays in the reproduction of privilege.

Intensive and competitive mothering revolves around individuality, competition, and the future success of their children. Competition and individualism are values embedded in children's activities. Annette Lareau refers to this version of child rearing as "concerted cultivation" geared toward "deliberate and sustained effort to stimulate children's development and to cultivate . . . cognitive and social skills." Concerted cultivation aims to develop children's ability to reason by negotiating with parents and placing value on children's opinions, judgments, and observations. Family leisure time is dominated by organized children activities, such as sports, clubs, and paid lessons (e.g., dance, music, tennis). Most children's time is adult-structured rather than child-initiated play. "Play is not just play anymore. It involves the honing of 'large motor skills,' 'communication skills,' 'hand-eye coordination,' and the establishment of 'developmentally appropriate behavior.'"

Qualities of intensive and competitive mothering are at odds with demanding careers. Everyday practices of intensive mothering [require] immense emotional involvement, constant self-sacrificing, exclusivity, and a completely child-centered environment. These mothering activities are financially draining and time-consuming. Mothers with disposable income use commodities to fulfill areas of intensive and competitive mothering that they find themselves falling short of. In *The Mother Puzzle*, Judith D. Schwartz argues that advertising companies use guilt as significant child leverage:

> Companies who are marketing to our guilt inevitably start marketing the guilt itself in order to keep us shopping. This toy will help your child develop motor skills (implicit message: his motor skills will suffer without it). This line of clothing is made of the softest cotton (implicit message: other, less expensive fabrics may be abrasive).

By the 1990s, "babies and children were firmly entrenched as possessions that necessitated the acquisition of other commodities (and that became more valuable with further investment in goods and services)." Advertisers targeted the new "Skippies" market (*s*chool *k*ids with *i*ncome and *p*urchasing *p*ower). Quoting *People* magazine, Schwartz characterizes parents of these "gourmet children" as "rapaciously grabbing kudos for their kids with the same enterprise applied to creating fortunes on Wall Street." She suggests that, "Teaching values to our children has been replaced by building value into them ... by preparing them to compete and giving them what we think they need to do so."

Hiring a live-in immigrant worker is the most convenient childcare option for juggling the demands of intensive mothering and a career. Purchasing the caretaking and domestic labor of an immigrant [woman] commodificates reproductive labor and reflects, reinforces, and intensifies social inequalities. The most burdensome mothering activities (such as cleaning, laundry, feeding babies and children, and chauffeuring children to their various scheduled activities) are shifted to the worker. Qualities of intensive mothering, such a sentimental value, nurturing, and intense emotional involvement, are not lost when caretaking work is shifted to an employee. Employers select immigrant caretakers on the basis of perceived "warmth," "love for children," and "naturalness in mothering." Different racial and ethnic groups are stereotyped by employers as ideal employees for housework, childcare, or for live-in positions. Stereotyping is based on a number of individual characteristics—race, ethnicity, class, caste, education, religion, and linguistic ability—and results in a degree of "otherness" for all domestic servants. However, such a formalization of difference does not always put workers in the subordinate position, and employers' preferences can vary from place to place. Janet Henshall Momsen notes that, "Professionally-trained British nannies occupy an élite niche in Britain and North America." Interviewing employers in Los Angeles and New York City, Julia Wrigley observed Spanish-speaking nannies were identified by employers for their ability to broaden the cultural experience of their children, particularly in exposing them to a second language in the home. Employers referenced the growing Latino population in their community and the long-term benefits of their children learning Spanish. However, the socialization to race and culture politics may be the most significant consequence of the current commodification of reproductive labor.

The primary mission of reproductive labor in contemporary mothering is to assure their children's place in society. This is partially accomplished through socialization into class, gender, sexual, ethnic and race hierarchies. Employment of immigrant women as caregivers contributes to this socialization. Reinforced by their parents' conceptualization of caretaking as a "labor of love," children learn a sense of entitlement to receiving affection from people of color that is detached from their own actions. Children learn to be "consumers of care" rather than providers of caregiving. Caretaking without parental authority does not teach children reciprocal respect but rather teaches that the treatment of women of color as "merely means, and not as ends in themselves." The division of labor between mother and live-in caretaker domestic stratifies components of reproductive labor and equates burdensome, manual and basic maintenance labor with immigrant women of color. This gendered division of labor serves to teach traditional patriarchal privilege. Privilege is learned as they acquire a sense of entitlement to having a domestic worker always on call to meet their needs.

Stratified reproductive labor of a live-in immigrant domestic assures "learned helplessness and class prejudice in the child," and teaches "[dependence], aggressiveness, and selfishness." Systems of class, racial, ethnic, gender and citizenship domination are taught to children by witnessing "the arbitrary and capricious interaction of parents and servants or if they are permitted to treat domestic servants in a similar manner." As children move from their homes located in class (and frequently racially) segregated neighborhoods to schools (also likely to be segregated), power relationships and the larger community's class and racial etiquette are further reinforced. "As care is made into a commodity, women with greater resources in the global economy can afford the best-quality care for their family." If mothering is directed toward assuring their child's social and economic status in society—a society that is racist, capitalist, and patriarchal—then her goals are strengthened by employing a low wage, full-time or live-in immigrant woman. Conditions under which immigrant women of color are employed in private homes is structured by systems of privilege and, consequently, employers' children are socialized into these norms and values.

V. PROLONGATION OF IMMIGRANT WOMEN SUBORDINATION

Paid reproductive labor in the United States is structured along local, national and international inequalities, positioning third-world immigrant women as the most vulnerable workers. Careworkers are sorted by the degree of vulnerability and privilege. Consequently, paid domestic labor is not only structured around gender but is stratified by race and citizenship status, relegating the most vulnerable worker to the least favorable working conditions and placing the most privileged in the best positions. A major initiative in the American childcare movement is addressing low wages in the childcare industry. However, the plight of live-in caregivers and immigrant women as a specific group is rarely addressed. The solution of hiring a live-in domestic, used by a relatively privileged group, is a component of reproductive labor in the United States, and serves to intensify inequalities between women: first, by reinforcing childcare as a private rather than public responsibility; and second, by reaping the benefits gained by the impact of globalization and restructuring on third-world women. The globalization of domestic service contributes to the reproduction of inequality between nations in transnational capitalism and cases reported of domestic servitude is increasingly characterized as global gender apartheid.

Devaluation of immigrant women in the international division of labor begins in the home as unpaid labor; then is further devalued in the segregated labor forces within third-world countries used by wealthier nations for cheap labor. Women are relegated to low-wage factory work in textiles and electronics industries with no opportunities available for better-paid positions. Migrating and working as domestics becomes the primary strategy for sustaining households for both poor and middle-class women. The demand for low-wage migrant workers expands the pool of cheap labor that unemployment and welfare regulations are unable to maintain. Theorists have traditionally argued that women's unpaid domestic labor in the home served as a reserve labor force. Applying this qualification to immigrant domestic workers, the employment of third-world women becomes a significant source for reproducing a labor reserve, similar to the function of the unemployed and underemployed. Saskia Sassen states this proposition in the following question: "Does domestic service—at least in certain locations—become one of the few alternatives and does it, then, function, as a privatized mechanism for social reproduction and maintenance of a labor reserve?" The transnational export of women from global south to the rich industrialized countries of the north has resulted in promoting domestics as a major "export product." Transnational division of labor is determined "simultaneously by global capitalism and systems of gender inequality in both sending and receiving countries of migration."

A prominent feature of globalized reproductive labor is commodification. Parreñas argues that, "Commodified reproductive labor is not only low-paid work but declines in market value as it gets passed down the international transfer of caretaking." However, Anderson argues that the commodification process in globalization is not limited to the labor but is extended to the worker. In her work on the global politics of domestic labor, she points out that employers "openly stipulate that they want a particular type *person* justifying this demand on the grounds that they will be working in the home." Having hired the preferred racialized domestic caretaker on the basis of personal characteristics rather than former experience or skills, the emotional labor required is not recognized by the employer but the worker's caring "brings with it no mutual obligations, no entry into a community, no 'real' human relations, only money."

Employers' hiring preferences for employees who are a particular race, ethnicity, and nationality contributes to the hierarchical chain of domestic caretakers. Hondagneu-Sotelo notes that African Americans are no longer the preferred employee in Los Angeles homes because [they] are portrayed as "bossy" and with "terrifying images associated with young black men." Similar images are applied to Caribbean women in New York and are cautioned against coming "across in interviews as being in any way aggressive." Latina immigrants in Los Angeles are perceived as "responsible, trustworthy, and reliable" workers as well as "exceptionally warm, patient, and loving mothers." In the case of Filipina women, Dan Gatmaytan argues that their labor is distinctively featured in international division of labor as "docile and submissive," and thus, ideally packaged to be imported "by other countries for jobs their own citizens will not perform and for wages domestic citizens would not accept." Parreñas's findings suggest that employers view Filipinas as providing a "higher-quality" service because they speak English and generally have a higher education than Latina immigrants.

However, without state regulations of labor and immigration policies, employers' preferences are irrelevant in the racialization of reproductive labor in the United States. Joy Mutanu Zarembka, director of the Campaign for Migrant Domestic Workers' Rights, argues that the estimated four thousand special visas issued annually for third-world immigrant women contributes to commodification of these workers into a "maid to order" in the United States. Three visas perpetuating the subordination of immigrant women of color as live-in domestic workers are:

> A–3 visas to work for ambassadors, diplomats, consular officers, public ministers, and their families; G–5 visas to work for officers and employees of international organizations or of foreign missions to international organizations and their families; and B–1 visas to accompany U.S. citizens who reside abroad but are visiting the United States or assigned to the United States temporarily for no more than four years, or foreign nations with nonimmigrant status in the United States.

In contrast to special visas given primarily to third-world immigrant women, the J-1 visa is increasingly used to bring young and middle-class European immigrant women as nannies or *au pairs* with "educational and cultural exchange" their primary purpose. Under this visa, each nanny receives an orientation session and is placed in geographical locations near other nannies. After her placement, she attends an orientation session and "receives information on community resources, educational opportunities and contacts for a local support network." Counselors have monthly sessions with each employer and nanny to "report any problems and resolve disputes." "In contrast, with the G-5, A-1 and B-1 domestic worker programs, there are no official orientations, no information, no contact numbers, no counselors, and no educational programs. In practice, as well, there is often no freedom—many are systematically (though illegally) forbidden from contacting the outside world."

Human Rights Watch further asserts that special visas intensify workers' vulnerability to abuse and facilitate the violation of other human rights. Procedures, guidelines, laws, and regulations governing special domestic worker visas construct circumstances that tolerate and conceal employer abuses, and restrict workers' rights. Among the problems cited by Human Rights Watch are the lack of INS follow-up monitoring or investigations to verify employer compliance with employment contracts, and the Department of Labor's lack of involvement with administrating these visas. Consequently, no governmental agency is responsible for enforcing contracts. Zarembka asserts that the secrecy of the whereabouts of G-5, A-3 and B-1 workers makes "them some of the most vulnerable and easily exploited sectors of the American workforce" and violation of human rights is silenced by their invisibility. In addition to low wages, long hours, and the lack of both privacy and benefits that are common among live-in conditions, immigrant women experience other abuses. They include passport confiscation, limited freedom of movement and ability to communicate with others, employer threats of deportation, assault and battery, rape, servitude, torture, and trafficking. Changing employers under live-in conditions has always been difficult for workers, and for women with employment-based visas, they are faced with weighing "respect for their own human rights and maintaining their legal immigration status." For similar reasons, women are reluctant to report abuse because they fear losing their jobs, deportation, unfamiliarity with the American legal system, social and cultural isolation, and fear that "their retaliation powerful employers will retaliate against their families in their countries of origin."

Exclusion from a number of labor policies contribute to the hardships immigrant women experience as live-in domestics. They are excluded from overtime provisions provided in the Fair Labor Standard Act, from the right to organize, strike, and bargain collectively in the National Labor Relations Act, and from regulations in the Occupational Safety and Health Act. "In practice, too, live-in domestic workers are rarely covered by Title VII protections against sexual harassment in the workplace, as Title VII only applies to employers with fifteen or more workers."

Third-world immigrant domestics experience first hand the inequalities of caregiving as they provide labor for parents in rich industrialized countries while leaving their own children. Sarah Blaffer Hrdy equates mothers leaving their children with relatives in their homelands to European infants left in foundling homes or sent to wet nurses during the eighteenth century: "Solutions differ, but the tradeoffs mothers make, and the underlying emotions and mental calculations, remain the same." Anderson notes that immigrant women's care for their children is limited "in the fruits of hard labour, in remittances, rather than in the cuddles and 'quality time' that provide so much of the satisfaction of care." Transnational mothering cannot provide the "physical closeness, seen as healthy and 'normal' in the Western upbringing of a child, are not given, because most of the women are not allowed to take their children with them." These conditions reduce mothering to the basic function of economic support. In her research on Filipina women in Rome and Los Angeles, Parrenas observed the impact of economic ties rather than affective ties between mother and child departed from each over a long period of time. The use of material good, financial assistance, and school tuition result in commodifying family relationships and motherhood. Inequalities in the distribution and quality of domestic labor and caregiving is a cost borne by the children of live-in workers. The absence of retirement benefits pension assures that workers will not be able to contribute financially to their children's future, but rather will need their assistance.

VI. Conclusion

Before the September 11 attacks, the Federation for American Immigration Reform (FAIR), Patrick Buchanan, Pete Wilson and others vilified immigrants as the cause of all problems in the United States. Homeland security has further fanned the flames of xenophobia and support for vilifying immigrants. Yet, within the intimacy of many American homes, immigrant women (primarily Latina and Caribbean immigrants) continue to provide assisted reproductive labor that fulfills the basic tasks of maintaining families of dual career couples and contribute to middle-upper- and upper-class lifestyles. Popular culture functions to normalize the hiring of immigrant women by depicting domestic service as a bridging occupation that offers social mobility, opportunities to learn English, and other cultural skills that assist in the assimilation process. The characterization of nannies and private household workers in *The Nanny Diaries*, as well as in films and sitcoms, serves to reduce the significance of immigrant women in fulfilling childcare needs in the United States and to erase issues of employee rights from the American imagination. Instead, employers are classified as good or bad: good employers who are benevolent and provide immigrant women with a modernizing experience, or bad employers who are rich couples ignoring their children. Popular culture does not contextualize paid reproductive labor. Economic, political and legal structures surrounding the migration of Latina, Caribbean and Filipina women are ignored along with the circumstances that relegate their labor to low-wage dead-end jobs. Consequently, we can maintain our illusions of Latina domestics as sexually out of control and utterly colorful spitfire, the self-deprecating accented smart-mouthed, or the rosary-praying maid. We can continue to see these images and sing out, "Yes, that's what maids are like."

* * *

Centering immigration on questions of "belonging" (and related concepts, e.g., assimilation, ethnic differences, and ethnic loyalty) blinds us to inquiries into the role of immigration in sustaining systems of privilege and perpetuating myths and ideologies central to national identity. Immigration and labor regulations reproduce race, class, gender and citizenship inequalities and privileges. In the case of immigrant women employed as private household workers or caregivers, the social reproduction of inequalities begins in the employer's home. Managing the contradictions of intimacy and vilification of immigrants through cultural images that falsify employee-employer relationships, allows Americans to reap the benefits of retaining a vulnerable labor force unprotected from exploitation while arguing humanitarian positions. The popular version of nannies depicted in *The Nanny Diaries* assists in normalizing privilege and erases issues of economic injustice. Our complacency in the subordination of immigrant women is once again obtained by our fascination with chatty gossip on sex, drugs, money, and family values of the wealthy on Park Avenue. Moreover, our illusion that there is no greater state of being than Americans is further enhanced by denying the privileges gained by third-world assisted social reproduction.

The Hidden Injuries of Class

79–87 (1972).

■ Richard Sennett & Jonathan Cobb

Josiah Watson Grammar School is an old red-brick building with a simple but well-kept playground. It is a large school, in the midst of an urban neighborhood of mostly three-decker houses. In the community surrounding the school live groups of Irish, Italian, and old-stock New Englanders, but almost all are manual laborers. The median family income in the neighborhood is about $8000—neither poor nor affluent.

The rooms at the Watson School evoke the interiors of the children's homes: old, rather run down, and yet clean, almost austere. In each schoolroom the only decorations consist of an American flag, a bound set of maps, and a plaque with the Pledge of Allegiance. The school desks are new—tubular steel legs holding up flat wooden boxes. In them, children's supplies are neatly arranged, even for the littlest children. The teachers take a certain pride in this, but they apologize to the visitor for the tops scratched with the obscene words, drawings, and initials that children always seem to inflict on such objects.

The classes in Watson School, even as low as the second grade, jolt the outsider who has lost touch with the institutional life of children. Everything that goes on in the second-grade class, from reading preparedness to play with toys, is directed by the teacher. She takes great pains to see that the children act "good and proper." The visitor who is aware of his own presence in these classrooms at first thinks this show of discipline, this constant commanding and watching, is the teacher's response to that presence. After the teacher relaxes and forgets he is there, however, the discipline continues. It varies among the teachers from harsh to loving; but all those in charge of classrooms at the Watson School act like conductors who must bring potentially unruly mobs of musicians under their direction. As the principal remarks, "It is by establishing authority that we make this school work."

In Watson School, teachers restrict the freedom of the children because these figures of authority have a peculiar fear of the children. It is the mass who seem to the teachers to threaten classroom order, by naughty or unruly behavior; only a few are seen as having "good habits" or the right attitude. As one teacher explained, "These children come from simple laborers' homes where the parents don't understand the value of education." Yet in the early grades the observer noticed few examples of disruptive behavior. He sensed among the six-and seven-year olds a real desire to please, to accept the teacher's control and be accepted by her. One pathetic incident, although extreme, stands out. In the middle of a reading-preparedness class, a child wet his pants because he was absorbed in his lesson. "What can you do with children like that?" the teacher later remarked in a tone of disgust.

What happens is that the teachers act on their expectations of the children in such a way as to *make* the expectations become reality. Here is how the process worked in one second-grade class at Watson School—unusual in that it was taught by a young man. In this class there were two children, Fred and Vincent, whose appearance was somewhat different from that of the others: their clothes were no fancier than the other children's, but they were pressed and seemed better kept; in a class of mostly dark Italian children, these were the fairest-skinned. From the outset the teacher singled out these two children, implying that they most closely approached his own standards for classroom performance. He never praised them openly by comparison to the other children, but a message that they were different, were better, was spontaneously conveyed. As the observer watched the children play and work over the course of the school year, he noticed these two boys becoming more serious, more solemn, as the months passed. Obedient and never unruly from the first, by the end of the year they were left alone by the other children.

By then they were also doing the best work in the class. The other children had picked up the teacher's hidden cues that their performance would not be greeted with as much enthusiasm as the work of these two little boys. "It's not true of the other children that they generally have less potential," the teacher remarked. "It's a question of not developing their ability like Fred and Vincent. I know you're right, I tend to encourage them more despite myself, but I—it's obvious to me these little boys are going to make something of themselves."

In the Watson School, by the time the children are ten or eleven the split between the many and the few who are expected to "make something of themselves" is out in the open; the aloofness developing in the second grade has become open hostility by the sixth. Among the boys, this hostility is expressed by images which fuse sex and status. Boys like Fred and Vincent are described by the "ordinary" students as effeminate and weak, as "suck-ups." The kids mean by this both that the Freds and Vincents are getting somewhere in school because they are so docile, and that only a homosexual would be so weak; the image of a "suck-up" crystallizes this self-demeaning, effeminate behavior that to them marks off a student whom the institution can respect.

What has happened, then, is that these children have directed their anger at their schoolmates who are rewarded as individuals rather than at the institution which is withholding recognition of them. Indeed, the majority of boys in the fifth and sixth grades are often not consciously in conflict with the school at all. Something more complex is happening to them.

These "ordinary" boys in class act as though they were serving time, as though schoolwork and classes had become something to wait out, a blank space in their lives they hope to survive and then leave. Their feeling, apparently, is that when they get out, get a job and some money, *then* they will be able to begin living. It is not so much that they are bored in school— many in Watson School like their classes. It is rather that they have lost any expectation that school will help them, that this experience will change them or help them grow as human beings.

One teacher in this school, an enthusiastic young woman who liked to work with "ordinary" students, said her greatest problem was convincing the students that they could trust her. The other teachers and the principal disapprove of her because she runs her class in an informal manner. They feel she lets the students "get away with anything," "that she can't keep discipline." Permissiveness is a vice, order a necessity, in the minds of the other teachers; they believe that most of their charges, due to family class background and past school performances, will resist following the rules which to an educated adult seem so logical and beneficial. It is not that these teachers are intentionally mean, but that they unwittingly set in motion in the classroom a vicious circle that produces exactly the kind of behavior they expect.

There is a counterculture of dignity that springs up among these ordinary working-class boys, a culture that seeks in male solidarity what cannot be found in the suspended time that comprises classroom experience. This solidarity also sets them off from the "suck-ups." Hanging around together, the boys share their incipient sexual exploits, real and imagined; sex becomes a way to compete within the group. What most cements them as a group, however, is the breaking of rules—smoking, drinking, or taking drugs together, cutting classes. Breaking the rules is an act "nobodies" can share with each other. This counterculture does not come to grips with the labels their teachers have imposed on these kids; it is rather an attempt to create among themselves badges of dignity that those in authority can't destroy.

A full circle: outsider observers—parents, teachers, and others—who see only the external aspects of this counterculture, are confirmed in their view that "hanging around" is destructive to a child's self-development. Dignity in these terms exacts a toll by the standards of the outer world.

The division of children, in schools like Watson, into groups with a shared sense of loyalty and individuals alone but "getting somewhere," characterizes many levels of education; it is not something unique to, say, college-bound youth as opposed to vocational school boys. Studies of trade schools show the same phenomenon occurring: boys who are good at car mechanics in school start to feel cut off from others, even though the possession of those skills might make them admired by their less-skilled peers outside of school. It is an institutional process that makes the difference, a question of mere toleration versus active approval from those in power.

The drama played out in the Watson School has as its script the assigning and the wearing of badges of ability like those described earlier, worn by adults. The teachers cast the Freds and Vincents into the role of Andrew Carnegie's virtuous man. Ability will make these children into individuals, and as individuals they will rise in social class. The mass find themselves in a role similar to that which Lipset assigns to adult workers: their class background allegedly limits their self-development, and the counterculture of compensatory respect they create reinforces, in a vicious circle, the judgments of the teachers.

The teacher has the *power* to limit the freedom of development of his or her students through this drama. But why is he or she moved to act in this repressive way? This question is really two questions: it is first a matter of a teacher legitimizing in his own mind the power he holds, and second, a matter of the students taking that power as legitimate.

The teachers are in a terrible existential dilemma. It is true that they are "prejudiced" against most of their students; it is also true that they, like all human beings, want to believe in the dignity of their own work, no matter how difficult the circumstances in which they have to work seem to them. If a teacher believed that every single student would perpetually resist him, he would have no reason to go on teaching—his power in the classroom would be empty. A teacher needs at least a responsive few in order to feel he has a *reason* to possess power. The few will confirm to him that his power to affect other people is real, that he can truly do good. To sort out two classes of ability, then, in fear of the "lower" class of students, is to create a meaningful image of himself as an authority rather than simply a boss.

It is true that an analysis at this level of teachers, or other power figures dealing with working-class people, is by itself inadequate. A teacher may be having an existential crisis, but that doesn't explain why images of social class and classes of ability have come to fuse in his mind, nor does it explain how useful, how convenient, this crisis of self-legitimacy is in keeping the present class structure going. Still, it is important to keep before ourselves the experiential reality facing a person who has power over others. The teachers at Watson did not think of themselves as tools of capitalism, or even as repressive. They felt they had to legitimize their own work's dignity in the face of working-class students; and making a moral hierarchy on the basis of ability—however artificially and unjustifiably—was the natural means they used.

The perceptions the children had of the teachers similarly concerned not their power, but their legitimacy.

The observer is playing marbles with Vinny, a third-grader, described by his teacher as an "unexceptional average student who tolerates school," and Vinny begins absentmindedly to arrange the marbles in sets by color. The observer points out to him that he is doing something like what the teacher had asked him to do in arithmetic hour and he hadn't then been able to do. Vinny replies, "I didn't want to give her no trouble"—an answer the observer notes without, at the time, understanding what Vinny meant. In a class on grammar, Stephanie gives a past participle incorrectly; the teacher asks her to try again, but while she is thinking, one of the bright children interrupts with the right answer. The teacher—the experimental and "permissive" woman already described—tells the bright child to shut up and gives Stephanie another answer to work out. Stephanie looks at her in total surprise, wondering why the teacher should still care about whether *she* can learn to do it, if the right answer has already been provided. Max, an obnoxious fifth-grade bully, has somehow formed an interest in writing doggerel rhymes. During a composition hour he reads one, but when he finishes, the teacher makes no reply, merely smiles and calls on the next pupil. Asked later how he felt, Max looks a little crestfallen and says with characteristic grace, "Lookit, shithead, she ain't got time to waste on me."

————

NOTES AND QUESTIONS

1. "Globalization" at top and bottom of economy. Saskia Sassen argues that "globalization" has produced both transnational marginalized labor classes and transnational privileged classes: while the elite of "global cities" such as New York, Hong Kong, and Paris are increasingly intertwined through networks of education and training, the "underclass" in such cities are also intertwined, through networks of migration and the demand for low-end service work. Saskia Sassen, *Toward a Feminist Analytics of the Global Economy*, 4 IND. J. GLOBAL LEGAL STUD. 7 (1996). Sassen argues that migration (legal and illegal), which is often treated as only a problem for the government sector to be solved through immigration law, should be seen as intimately connected to trade policy and economic policy more generally.

How might the increasing income and wealth inequality brought about by globalization affect women as a group? Sassen is hopeful that the globalizing economy, as it pulls more women into wage work, will empower them within their families and in the public sector. *id.*, at 27. At the same time, she acknowledges that women are "constituted as an invisible and disempowered class of workers in the service of the strategic sectors constituting the global economy." *id.*, at 26.

2.   Modern-day slavery. The very lowest caste of contemporary workers is made up of those whose labor power is forcibly expropriated by others. Kevin Bales argues that slavery is alive and well today, although it takes different legal and social forms than the "old" slavery:

> *My best estimate of the number of slaves in the world today is 27 million.*
>
> This number is much smaller than the estimates put forward by some activists, who give a range as high as 200 million, but it is the number I feel I can trust * * *. The biggest part of that 27 million, perhaps 15 to 20 million, is represented by *bonded labor* in India, Pakistan, Bangladesh, and Nepal. Bonded labor or debt bondage happens when people give themselves into slavery as security against a loan or when they inherit a debt from a relative * * *. Otherwise slavery tends to be concentrated in Southeast Asia, northern and western Africa, and parts of South America (but there are some slaves in almost every country in the world, including the United States, Japan, and many European countries). There are more slaves alive today than all the people stolen from Africa in the time of the transatlantic slave trade. Put another way, today's slave population is greater than the population of Canada, and six times greater than the population of Israel.
>
> These slaves tend to be used in simple, nontechnological, and traditional work. The largest group work in agriculture. But slaves are used in many other kinds of labor: brickmaking, mining or quarrying, prostitution, gem working and jewelry making, cloth and carpet making, and domestic service; they clear forests, make charcoal, and work in shops. Much of this work is aimed at local sale and consumption, but slave-made goods reach into homes around the world. Carpets, fireworks, jewelry, and metal goods made by slave labor, as well as grains, sugar, and other foods harvested by slaves, are imported directly to North America and Europe. In addition, large international corporations, acting through subsidiaries in the developing world, take advantage of slave labor to improve their bottom line and increase the dividends to their shareholders.

KEVIN BALES, DISPOSABLE PEOPLE: NEW SLAVERY IN THE GLOBAL ECONOMY 8–9 (1999).

Bales argues that the new slavery differs from the old slavery in several ways. Among these differences are the following: slaveholders no longer assert legal ownership over their slaves; slaveholders do not contribute to the maintenance costs of their slaves; ethnic differences between slaveholding and slave classes are less important than they were in, for example, American slavery; slaves produce very high profits; the relationship between slaveholder and slave tends to be short-term rather than long-term; and there is a surplus rather than a shortage of potential slaves. *id.*, at 15.

The International Labor Organization defines "forced labor" as "all work or service which is exacted from any person under the menace of any penalty and for which the said person has not offered himself voluntarily." International Labor Organization, Convention Concerning Forced Labor (No. 29). Using this definition, a team of researchers at the University of California at –Berkeley, working with a nonprofit antislavery organization, examined the nature and scope of forced labor in the United States from January 1998 to December 2003. According to their report:

> Over the past five years, forced labor operations have been reported in at least ninety U.S. cities. These operations tend to thrive in states with large populations and sizable immigrant communities, such as California, Florida, New York, and Texas—all of which are transit routes for international travelers.

> Forced labor is prevalent in five sectors of the U.S. economy: prostitution and sex services (46%), domestic service (27%), agriculture (10%), sweatshop/factory (5%), and restaurant and hotel work (4%) * * *. Forced labor persists in these sectors because of low wages, lack of regulation and monitoring of working conditions, and a high demand for cheap labor. These conditions enable unscrupulous employers and criminal networks to gain virtually complete control over workers' lives.

HUMAN RIGHTS CENTER & FREE THE SLAVES: FORCED LABOR IN THE UNITED STATES 1 (2004), *available at* http://www.hrcberkeley.org/download/hiddenslaves _report.pdf. (posted September 2004) (last visited, Mar. 6, 2005). The researchers estimated that approximately 10,000 people are working as forced laborers in the United States at any given time. *id.*, at 10.

In the United States, slavery and human trafficking are subject to the federal Victims of Trafficking and Violence Protection Act of 2000, § 107, 22 U.S.C. §7105 (2004). The act, among other things, establishes mandatory restitution from convicted traffickers, and an amendment allows survivors to sue their captors for civil damages for violations of the statute. *See* Trafficking Victims Protection Reauthorization Act of 2003, 18 U.S.C. § 1595 (2004) (civil damages provision). The act also provides social services and immigration status to victims of a "severe form of trafficking" who cooperate with law enforcement to prosecute the traffickers.

3. Women, prostitution and sex work: abolitionists versus labor activists. Feminists have long argued over whether prostitution and other forms of sex work should be abolished as forms of violence against women, or legalized and regulated as just another kind of labor. Jane Larson argues that the dichotomy is unhelpful and that prostitution, like sweatshop labor, child labor, and various forms of bonded and indentured labor, should be examined more closely to help us think more generally about what kinds of labor are acceptable and why:

> Instead of fruitless debates about the "essential nature" of the commodity relation of prostitution, I urge instead a common project aimed at defining the material, moral, and legal differences between free and unfree labor, describing with empirical depth and range what conditions of work characterize commercial sex in its various forms and

locales, and measuring the sex industry against the free labor standard. What is force and compulsion in the sex labor setting? Is the definition of force such that the exchange of money refutes the claim of compulsion, or can the liberal concern for substantive freedom in labor relations translate into international standards? What working conditions render prostitution a per se unacceptably exploitative practice for children? Is it different for adults? Why or why not? What kinds of discrimination on the basis of sex or race are unacceptable? Does the demographic constitution of the market for sexual labor demonstrate such discrimination? If prostitution is one of women's best economic options, how does this shape other economic opportunities for women? Does female prostitution violate the equality ideal?

Jane E. Larson, *Prostitution, Labor, and Human Rights*, 37 U.C. Davis L. Rev. 673, 698–99 (2004).

4. Public education and construction of failure. Cobb and Sennett were concerned primarily with the education and socialization of the sons of white working class "ethnic" immigrants. Other scholars have found that public education similarly sets up African American and Latino/a working class children, especially boys, to fail. For example, Theresa Glennon observes:

> First, African American boys are much more likely to be identified as disabled or delinquent than other children, including African American girls. Second, they are more likely than other children to be placed in educational, mental health, and juvenile justice programs that exert greater external control and deliver fewer services despite identified needs. Third, these negative experiences lead African American boys to stay away from or exit these institutional settings.

Theresa Glennon, *Knocking Against the Rocks: Evaluating Institutional Practices and the African American Boy*, 5 J. Health Care L. & Pol'y 10, 11 (2002). Glennon argues that these disparities are a result of racism.

Sociologist John Ogbu found another dynamic among African American children similar to that identified by Sennett and Cobb: black students both underperform and pressure one another to underperform by associating school success with "acting white." Signithia Fordham & John U. Ogbu, *Black Students' School Success: Coping with the "Burden of Acting White,"* 18 Urb. Rev. 176 (1986). Ogbu and Fordham's findings have been controversial in African American communities.

———

The Overworked American: The Unexpected Decline of Leisure

17–24 (1991).

■ Juliet B. Schor

Time squeeze has become big news. In summer 1990, the premiere episode of Jane Pauley's television show, "Real Life," highlighted a single father whose computer job was so demanding that he found himself at 2:00 A.M. dragging his child into the office. A Boston-area documentary featured the fourteen-to sixteen-hour workdays of a growing army of moonlighters. CBS's "Forty–Eight Hours" warned of the accelerating pace of life for everyone from high-tech business executives (for whom there are only two types of people—"the quick and the dead") to assembly workers at Japanese-owned automobile factories (where a car comes by every sixty seconds). Employees at fast-food restaurants, who serve in twelve seconds, report that the horns start honking if the food hasn't arrived in fifteen. Nineteen-year-olds work seventy-hour weeks, children are "penciled" into their parents' schedules, and second-graders are given "half an hour a day to unwind" from the pressure to get good grades so they can get into a good college. By the beginning of the 1990s, the time squeeze had become a national focus of attention, appearing in almost all the nation's major media outlets. * * *

The time squeeze surfaced with the young urban professional. These high achievers had jobs that required sixty, eighty, even a hundred hours a week. On Wall Street, they would regularly stay at the office until midnight or go months without a single day off. Work consumed their lives. And if they weren't working, they were networking. They power-lunched, power-exercised, and power-married. As the pace of life accelerated, time became an ever-scarcer commodity, so they used their money to buy more of it. Cooking was replaced by gourmet frozen foods from upscale delis. Eventually the "meal" started disappearing, in favor of "grazing." Those who could afford it bought other people's time, hiring surrogates to shop, write their checks, or even just change a light bulb. They cut back on sleep and postponed having children. ("Can you carry a baby in a briefcase?" queried one Wall Street executive when she was asked about having kids.)

High-powered people who spend long hours at their jobs are nothing new. Medical residents, top corporate management, and the self-employed have always had grueling schedules. But financiers used to keep bankers' hours, and lawyers had a leisured life. Now bankers work like doctors, and lawyers do the same. A former Bankers Trust executive remembers that "somebody would call an occasional meeting at 8 A.M. Then it became the regular 8 o'clock meeting. So there was the occasional 7 A.M. meeting. . . . It just kept spreading." On Wall Street, economic warfare replaced the clubhouse atmosphere—and the pressure forced the hours up. As women and new ethnic groups were admitted into the industry, competition for the plum positions heightened—and the hours went along. Twenty-two-year-olds wear beepers as they squeeze in an hour for lunch or jogging at the health club.

What happened on Wall Street was replicated throughout the country in one high-income occupation after another. Associates in law firms competed over who could log more billable hours. Workaholics set new standards of survival. Even America's sleepiest corporations started waking up; and when they did, the corporate hierarchies found themselves coming in to work a little earlier and leaving for home a little later. As many companies laid off white-collar people during the 1980s, those who remained did more for their monthly paycheck. A study of "downsizings" in auto-related companies in the Midwest found that nearly half of the two thousand managers polled said they were working harder than two years earlier.

At cutting-edge corporations, which emphasize commitment, initiative, and flexibility, the time demands are often the greatest. "People who work for me should have phones in their bathrooms," says the CEO from one aggressive American company. Recent research on managerial habits reveals that work has become positively absorbing. When a deadline approached in one corporation, "people who had been working twelve-hour days and Saturdays started to come in on Sunday, and instead of leaving at midnight, they would stay a few more hours. Some did not go home at all, and others had to look at their watches to remember what day it was." The recent growth in small businesses has also contributed to overwork. When Dolores Kordek started a dental insurance company, her strategy for survival was to work harder than the competition. So the office was open from 7 A.M. to 10 P.M. three hundred and sixty-five days a year. And she was virtually always in it.

This combination of retrenchment, economic competition, and innovative business management has raised hours substantially. One poll of senior executives found that weekly hours rose during the 1980s, and vacation time fell. Other surveys have yielded similar results. By the end of the decade, overwork at the upper echelons of the labor market had become endemic—and its scale was virtually unprecedented in living memory.

If the shortage of time had been confined to Wall Street or America's corporate boardrooms, it might have remained just a media curiosity. The number of people who work eighty hours a week and bring home—if they ever get there—a six-figure income is very small. But while the incomes of these rarefied individuals were out of reach, their schedules turned out to be downright common. As Wall Street waxed industrious, the longer schedules penetrated far down the corporate ladder, through middle management, into the secretarial pool, and even onto the factory floor itself. Millions of ordinary Americans fell victim to the shortage of time.

The most visible group has been women, who are coping with a double load—the traditional duties associated with home and children and their growing responsibility for earning a paycheck. With nearly two-thirds of adult women now employed, and a comparable fraction of mothers on the job, it's no surprise that many American women find themselves operating in overdrive. Many working mothers live a life of perpetual motion, effectively holding down two full-time jobs. They rise in the wee hours of the morning to begin the day with a few hours of laundry, cleaning, and other housework. Then they dress and feed the children and send them off to school. They themselves then travel to their jobs. The three-quarters of employed women with full-time positions then spend the next eight and a half hours in the workplace.

At the end of the official workday, it's back to the "second shift"—the duties of housewife and mother. Grocery shopping, picking up the children, and cooking dinner take up the next few hours. After dinner there's clean-up, possibly some additional housework, and, of course, more child care. Women describe themselves as "ragged," "bone-weary," "sinking in quicksand," and "busy every waking hour." For many, the workday rivals those for which the "satanic mills" of the Industrial Revolution grew justly infamous: twelve-or fourteen-hour stretches of labor. By the end of the decade, Ann Landers pronounced herself "awestruck at the number of women who work at their jobs and go home to another full-time job ... How do you do it?" she asked. Thousands of readers responded, with tales ranging from abandoned careers to near collapse. According to sociologist Arlie Hochschild of the University of California, working mothers are exhausted, even fixated on the topic of sleep. "They talked about how much they could 'get by on': ... six and a half, seven, seven and a half, less, more ... These women talked about sleep the way a hungry person talks about food."

By my calculations, the total working time of employed mothers now averages about 65 hours a week. Of course, many do far more than the average—such as mothers with young children, women in professional positions, or those whose wages are so low that they must hold down two jobs just to scrape by. These women will be working 70 to 80 hours a week. And my figures are extremely conservative: they are the lowest among existing studies. A Boston study found that employed mothers *average* over 80 hours of housework, child care, and employment. Two nationwide studies of white, married couples are comparable: in the first, the average week was 87 hours; in the second, it ranged from 76 to 89, depending on the age of the oldest child.

One might think that as women's working hours rose, husbands would compensate by spending less time on the job. But just the opposite has occurred. Men who work are also putting in longer hours. The 5:00 Dads of the 1950s and 1960s (those who were home for dinner and an evening with the family) are becoming an "endangered species." Thirty percent of men with children under fourteen report working fifty or more hours a week. And many of these 8:00 or 9:00 Dads aren't around on the weekends either. Thirty percent of them work Saturdays and/or Sundays at their regular employment. And many others use the weekends for taking on a second job.

A twenty-eight-year-old Massachusetts factory worker explains the bind many fathers are in: "Either I can spend time with my family or support them—not both." Overtime or a second job is financially compelling: "I can work 8–12 hours overtime a week at time and a half, and that's when the real money just starts to kick in.... If I don't work the OT my wife would have to work much longer hours to make up the differences, and our day care bill would double.... The trouble is, the little time I'm home I'm too tired to have any fun with them or be any real help around the house." Among white-collar employees the problem isn't paid overtime, but the regular hours. To get ahead, or even just to hold on to a position, long days may be virtually mandatory.

Overwork is also rampant among the nation's poorly paid workers. At $5, $6, or even $7 an hour, annual earnings before taxes and deductions range from $10,000 to $14,000. Soaring rents alone have been enough to put many of these low earners in financial jeopardy. For the more than one-third of all workers now earning hourly wages of $7 and below, the pressure to lengthen hours has been inexorable. Valerie Connor, a nursing-home worker in Hartford, explains that "you just can't make it on one job." She and many of her co-workers have been led to work two eight-hour shifts a day. According to an official of the Service Employees International Union in New England, nearly one-third of their nursing-home employees now hold two full-time jobs. Changes in the low end of the labor market have also played a role. Here is less full-time, stable employment. "Twenty hours here, thirty hours there, and twenty hours here. That's what it takes to get a real paycheck," says Domenic Bozzotto, president of Boston's hotel and restaurant workers union, whose members are drowning in a sea of work. Two-job families? Those were the good old days, he says. "We've got four-job families." The recent influx of immigrants has also raised hours. I.N. Yazbeck, an arrival from Lebanon, works ninety hours a week at three jobs. It's necessary, he says, for economic success.

This decline of leisure has been reported by the Harris Poll, which has received widespread attention. Harris finds that since 1973 free time has fallen nearly 40 percent—from a median figure of 26 hours a week to slightly under 17. Other surveys, such as the 1989 Decision Research Corporation Poll, also reveal a loss of leisure. Although these polls have serious methodological drawbacks, their findings are not far off the mark. A majority of working Americans—professionals, corporate management, "working" mothers, fathers, and lower-paid workers—*are* finding themselves with less and less leisure time.

Life.com

THE BERKELEY MONTHLY, October 1999.

■ CLIVE THOMPSON

The elevator door slides open and Jess slides in, looking slightly rumpled. Tara sizes her up.

"Didn't get much sleep last night?"

"You can tell?"

"Well, you're wearing the same clothes as yesterday."

Jess laughs. Her music show, Freq, broadcast live over the internet here at the new-media house Pseudo, went late last night and the staff wound up hanging around till dawn. Now it's 10:30 a.m. and she's back from breakfast to make some calls and set up meetings.

"At some point I'm gonna have to shower," she mutters as she wanders off to her desk.

Tara and I tour the studios, strolling through Pseudo's odd mix of high camp and high tech. The office is a study in chaos and energy, each room reflecting the peculiar pop-cultural animus of the twenty-somethings who work here. There's the room for the women's net shows, done up in late-'70s drag with a rainbow-colored bead-curtain entrance. There's a group of goateed musicians hanging out in one room, holding keyboards and a computer monitor. Who are they? "I have no idea," Tara says.

"Sorry," she apologizes at one point, yawning. "I'm a bit burnt out today."

I'm not surprised. In new media it's difficult to find anyone who can boast a full night's rest. Later in the day I visit a 23-year-old acquaintance at a website design firm across town and find him collapsed on a sofa in the staff room.

Late night? "Yeah." He's been setting up a database for a website that's set to go live in two days. The deadline looms and the client—a major corporation—is getting twitchy. Some deeply caffeinated all-nighters will be called for.

"It's intense but it's going pretty well," he says, his hair out of whack with a minor case of bed-head. "I figure I have another two days like this. But it's cool. It's a really cool project."

He pours himself a thick coffee in the well-stocked kitchen and heads back to his workstation, plopping down beside some two dozen other coders and designers clacking away at their keyboards as a stereo pumps out ambient techno in an endless loop. Most of them figure they'll be here until 4 in the morning.

Working till sunup, destroying your eyesight, playing Quake on the company lan, hanging out in a funky office with your dog: in the modern digital workplace this sort of stuff is de rigueur. Indeed, for young Turks in new media—software, website development or the amorphous zone of "content"—aggressively casual and freewheeling is the signature office style.

On the surface it has to do with making work seem a lot more fun and thus a lot less like work. It is, as it were, the master narrative of the New Work, which we could sketch out like this: young digital employees have thrown off the 9-to-5 straitjacket in which their parents so miserably toiled. No more suits, no more rigid corporate hierarchies, no more dull, repetitive tasks. Today work means getting to wear your Star Wars T-shirt, sport multiple piercings and hang out in an office with homey perks: massage-therapist visits, pets, wacky furniture, toys and lots of beer. The staff dines together and parties together. It works hard, sure, but it plays hard too, and usually at the same time. And the workers aren't chained to one job.

Instead they hop at will from company to company, forcing hapless employers to scramble after them, offering ever more perks and stock options to lure their portable, highly paid talents. These kids hold all the cards.

It's a story that has fascinated the media. Reporters covering the industry regularly marvel at the scenes of controlled chaos and pop-cultural riot. In Mountain View [California], Netscape staff members are willing to quit if they can't bring their dogs to work. *USA Today* once breathlessly noted that the office at Organic Online "has been the scene of a dance party, complete with disc jockeys, for 400 people."

Which is precisely the problem.

The studied hipness of new media is a rather devious cultural illusion. Those ultracool offices cover up a seldom-discussed truth: that the jobs themselves often demand intense work and devotion for relatively low pay and zero security. By making work more like play, employers neatly erase the division between the two, which ensures that their young employees will almost never leave the office.

High-tech employees hang out at work long after the city has gone to bed. They'll kill themselves over deadlines, putting in up to 80 hours a week. Then they'll smile and thank their lucky stars that they're part of the digital revolution, the cultural flashpoint of the '90s. For employers, of course, it's a sweet deal—you can't buy flexibility like that. As more than one worker has told me, a website design company can almost always hold a meeting at 2 o'clock on a Saturday afternoon because, well, everyone's there. Where else would they be?

New-media companies are notorious for employee burnout and nanosecond turnover. It's not surprising: given the insane hours, the payoffs are rather slim. We're hit relentlessly with media hype about digital workers' high pay, desirability and stock options. But none of these myths holds up under statistical scrutiny. The vast majority of new-media workers in New York, for example, make less than junior accountants, enjoy the job security of fast-food workers and have a laughably small chance of getting offered any stock anytime anywhere. As for programmers, most are paid surprisingly little and hurled overboard as soon as they hit their mid-30s.

Enamored of its distorted image, the digital workforce is reluctant to accept the facts. "People do not want to face reality," says Bill Lessard, a veteran of the industry who runs NetSlaves, a website that compiles true tales of new-media burnout. "Someone will tell you, 'Oh, I'm a producer.' But they're just a schmuck who's working 90 hours a week. You give these companies body and soul and you really get nothing back."

These workers are touted as the most renegade, the most entrepreneurial generation in years. Yet they are, in traditional labor terms, amazingly compliant. Chained to their keyboards, working far longer hours than they're paid for and blurring the boundaries between their jobs and their lives, digital employees paradoxically present the kind of servile workforce that would have pleased Henry Ford, Nelson Rockefeller and probably Chairman Mao.

When I visit Fred Kahl he's busy designing a computer game based on the TV cartoon "Space Ghost." I peer over his shoulder at the screen, where Fred is fiddling with a sequence: Space Ghost chasing the arch-villain Lokar, who is impersonating Santa Claus. In a few days this will air on the website of the Cartoon Network, one of the major clients of Funny Garbage, the new-media design firm that Kahl works for.

It's hard to deny that new-media workplaces are, aesthetically anyway, extremely pleasant places to be. Kahl shows me around Funny Garbage—a firm respected for its right-brained, creative web animations—and it's not unlike wandering through a gallery of '70s kitsch. Workstations are cluttered with retro-pop toys and icons. One of the company's founders, 33-year-old Peter Girardi, has three different video-game systems in his office.

This is not to suggest that everyone is horsing around. Over by the animation computers, three designers are hunkering down for a long haul, even though it's already past 5 o'clock on a Friday night. By 9, staff members will likely launch into a Quake tournament on the company lan. ("I had to stop," Kahl says. "I almost destroyed my wrists.") In this context, it's easy to see how work and life inexorably bleed into each other. It's also easy to see how new-media employers can capitalize on the confusion. For people involved in digital culture, a highly wired office—replete with digital toys and fueled by a T1 connection—can be a more inviting place to hang out than a cramped apartment or a bar or club.

In fact, sometimes work offers even better partying than a club.

One of Psuedo's longest-serving staff members, a 29-year-old programmer named Joey Fortuna, remembers arriving on his first day four years ago to find the office in a fantastic mess from a party held the night before. Pseudo CEO Josh Harris staggered in from his on-site apartment wearing nothing but boxer shorts and instantly set Fortuna to work, even though Fortuna had never written a line of code in his life.

To get up to speed on HTML, Fortuna—like most of the staff—put in months of 12-hour days. In 1996 he spent Christmas Day writing code for a video-publishing database. "It was just insane!" he says. "I was working all the time. I lived here. But I didn't mind. It was like a clubhouse."

He gestures around the loft, pointing to its kooky mix of high-and low-tech. "You know, it's ironic," he grins, "but in the last century this used to be a sweatshop."

If there's an archetypal success story in new media it's probably that of Jeff Dachis and Razorfish. In spring 1995, Dachis and his friend Craig Kanarick, both in their late 20s, founded the website design company in their living rooms. Last year they had 350 employees in eight offices and did $30 million in business.

Companies like Razorfish have built the mythos of gold-rush success in new media: start a firm in your garage, wow senior executives at Fortune 500 companies, then take occasional breaks from your PlayStation to watch the dough roll in. "The trappings of power have changed," wrote *Time* magazine in an October 1997 survey of the "cyber-elite."

But here too the hype outstrips the reality. True, there are dozens of fantastic entrepreneurial successes. But when you look at the statistics the New Work starts to look like an old story: low pay, no security and those who no longer suit the company profile pitched instantly overboard.

In 1997 the New York New Media Association did a study of the local scene. It discovered that high-tech jobs paid an average of $37,212. That's middling at best for a city as expensive as New York. It's also far outpaced by the average salaries in other media: advertising, $71,637; periodicals, $69,849; TV broadcasting, $85,938.

The churn rate in new-media jobs is amazingly high. The New York study found that almost half the work in new media is freelance or part time. More than two-thirds of all freelance contracts last fewer than six months, most are three-month stints. Part-time jobs are growing four-times faster than full-time positions.

In place of decent pay and regular work, new media offers the lure of instant wealth—the fabled stock options that turned the creators of Amazon.com or TheGlobe.com into overnight multimillionaires. It's a seductive tale, and those who have won the game have won huge. Berkeley's Adam Sah, who was in on the ground floor at Inktomi, cashed in some stocks when the company went public. The years of 400-hour months paid off. "It wasn't fun," he says, "but it did turn out all right for me."

Sah previously worked at Microsoft, which pretty much invented the stock-options trick, knowing that the lure of the market is one of the few things that will motivate coders to impale themselves upon unshippable products with unmeetable deadlines. "It's amazing what people will do for money," Sah laughs wryly.

The stock payoff, though, is about as chimerical as you can get. There are no stats on new-media stock cash-ins but high-tech hunters counsel their clients that the chance of getting lucrative options are slim.

"To cash in on stock you have to stick around for several years at a company," says Alex Santic, head of Silicon Valley Connections, one of the first headhunting firms to specialize in new media. "But few people really want to. They want to move on after a year. They get lured in by the promise of stock but rarely see it through." Indeed, as the New York new-media study found, the only folks who own substantial equity are management and founders—worker bees have a statistically insignificant slice of the pie.

Perhaps the most persistent myth of recent years, though, is that of the "programmer shortage." According to this tale, the geeks now run the show. There isn't enough programming talent to go around, so companies are fighting tooth and nail over warm bodies. Mainstream media have taken up the story like a mantra. "Business leaders say the shortage has reached near-crisis proportions," wrote the *Washington Post* in an article detailing—with a sort of horrified fascination—the incredible perks offered to lure programmers, from "signing bonuses like professional athletes" to $70-an-hour rates for temp work.

Again, the facts contradict the hype. Last year Norman Matloff, a professor of computer science at UC Davis, released one of the few studies ever done on the programmer job market. He surveyed the hiring practices of software and new-media firms and concluded that there was, in fact, no shortage of programmers. Companies were hiring only two to four percent of the people they interviewed, a rate far below that for other types of engineers.

Older programmers, meanwhile, are ruthlessly squeezed out. Age discrimination, Matloff says, is "amazingly rampant." He found that after age 35 and increasingly as they get older, programmers are ditched in favor of the fresh-scrubbed kids released each year from technical colleges. By their early 40s fewer than one-fifth of all trained programmers are still working in the field. One 47-year-old programmer Matloff talked to was fluent in C++, Perl, Unix and a host of other languages, but when he went looking for a new job he landed only two interviews in 15 months of searching. Another man had been programming since 1976. "I can't get so much as an interview," he told Matloff. "I now earn about $24,000 a year in retail sales and management."

When you look at the facts you begin to realize the incredible power of new-media workplace culture. It sells a lifestyle of liberation and autonomy that is wildly out of sync with reality. Then you begin to realize why those Quake marathons, those cappuccino machines in the staff kitchen and all those dogs at work are important. Absent decent pay and a commitment from your boss, maybe a game of Quake is the best you can get.

———

The Law and Economics of Critical Race Theory

112 YALE L.J. 1757, 1789–93, 1795–96, 1797–99, 1801–14 (2003) (reviewing CROSSROADS, DIRECTIONS, AND A NEW CRITICAL RACE THEORY (Francisco Valdes et al. eds., 2002)).

■ DEVON W. CARBADO & MITU GULATI

A starting point for thinking about workplace discrimination is to raise the question of whether today's workplace is buttressed by institutionalized racial norms. With respect to explicit racial norms, the answer is no: That would violate antidiscrimination law. But do implicit racial norms structure today's workplace culture? [Critical race theory, or CRT] answers this question affirmatively, pointing to workplace practices like English-only rules and grooming regulations (e.g., rules prohibiting employees from braiding their hair) that restrict the expression of particular identities and, in so doing, marginalize them.

There is, however, a subtle form of institutional discrimination to which CRT scholars have not paid attention. This discrimination derives from a commitment on the part of many employers, particularly employers who use teams to manage their workplace culture to achieve trust, fairness, and loyalty (TFL). Why? TFL reduces transaction costs. Empirical evidence suggests that the effectiveness of teams is enhanced when employers engender TFL among their employees. Employees who perceive that they are a part of a "TFL community" work hard, cooperate, police each other, and share valuable information. Based on this evidence, scholars have argued that law should be structured to facilitate the creation of TFL workplaces. In addition to its efficiency gains, TFL values seem normatively appealing.

TFL's normative surface appeal helps to explain why the institutional discrimination story we articulate below has not yet been told. Central to our story is not the fact that employers are invested in TFL but rather how they go about realizing that investment—by aggressively promoting homogeneity. Evidence suggests that, at least in the short term, a manager with a demographically homogeneous work team has a better chance of producing TFL than one with a diverse team. If, as is often suggested, managers focus primarily on short-term results, there is an incentive for managers to seek demographically homogeneous teams.

The relationship between the pursuit of demographic homogeneity and racial discrimination is direct. In short, workplaces organized to achieve homogeneity are likely to discriminate because homogeneity norms, by their very nature, reflect a commitment to sameness (favoring people perceived to be members of the in-group ("insiders")) and a rejection of difference (disfavoring people perceived to be members of the out-group ("outsiders")). Coupled with the fact that, within most professional settings, whites are insiders and nonwhites are outsiders, the relationship between discrimination and homogeneity becomes clear.

The foregoing suggests that race-neutral workplace norms institutionalize insider racial preference. Is this a reason for concern? The answer is not obviously yes. One might argue that, even to the extent that there are incentives for employers to create and maintain homogeneous workplaces, the threat of antidiscrimination sanctions undermines that incentive. Richard Epstein famously worried about exactly this effect of antidiscrimination law. According to Epstein, part of the problem with antidiscrimination law is that it compromises workplace efficiency by preventing employers from establishing homogeneous workplace cultures. One might conclude, then, that given the threat of legal sanctions, the institutionalized racism problem we have identified is theoretical—not real.

Moreover, there are institutional legitimacy concerns that militate against the establishment of homogenous workplaces. White-only work forces can create public relations problems. Perhaps not surprisingly, there is no employer-driven movement afoot to have antidiscrimination laws repealed because they prohibit employers from establishing demographically homogenous workplaces. To the contrary, even a cursory examination of the management and organizational behavior literature reveals (at least rhetorically) an institutional commitment to manage, and not to eliminate, heterogeneity. Thus, all seems well: Law prevents institutions from privileging homogeneity, and institutions perceive the pursuit of homogeneity to be problematic.

Our claim, however, is that all is not well. Neither antidiscrimination law nor the affirmative pursuit of diversity operates as a meaningful barrier to, or substantially undermines the incentives for employers to achieve, workplace homogeneity. Epstein need not worry. To be sure, the law prohibits blatant racial animus in hiring and promotion. But that is a minimal barrier to the managerial pursuit of racial homogeneity. To move from a phenotypic conception of race to a performative conception is to find that, to a significant extent, judges can (and, we surmise, do) apply antidiscrimination law to actually *protect* the pursuit of racial homogeneity. They do so by failing to capture employment discrimination based on *intraracial* distinctions—distinctions employers make among people within a particular racial group.

Driving these distinctions is a question about racial stereotypes and racial salience. Other things being equal, employers prefer nonwhites whose racial identity is not salient and whose identity performance is inconsistent with stereotypes about their racial group. In other words, employers screen for racial palatability. With respect to Asian Americans, for example, employers determine whether, notwithstanding phenotypic difference, a particular Asian American is (based on how she performs her identity) sufficiently like insiders to be successfully assimilated into a homogenized workplace.

To date, there are no Title VII cases that render a racial palatability discrimination claim cognizable. Thus, employers can make these kinds of intraracial distinctions with legal impunity. And to the extent employers engage in this practice, their associated institutional legitimacy remains intact because the practice anticipates and produces at least some workplace racial integration. Finally, because the racial diversity employers achieve by making intraracial distinctions is literally skin deep, it comfortably coexists with their commitment to homogeneity.

The foregoing sets forth a theory of institutional racism—that it is a function of an investment on the part of employers to realize the efficiency gains of homogeneity. Because many institutions operate under what we call a *diversity constraint*—a constraint that requires the firm to hire at least some nonwhites—employers will determine which nonwhites to hire on evidence of racial palatability. The more racially palatable employers perceive a potential employee to be, the less concerned they will be over the possibility that that potential employee will (racially) disrupt workplace homogeneity. * * *

B.   *The Incentive for Employers To Pursue Homogeneity*

　　　* * *

1.   *Theories*

There are at least three theories suggesting that employers are motivated to pursue homogeneity: social identity theory, similarity-attraction theory, and statistical judgments theory.

Social identity theory suggests that people have an affinity for those they perceive to be part of their in-group. In concrete terms, people are more likely to demonstrate TFL (which, again, is shorthand for trust, fairness, and loyalty) to those they perceive to be members of their in-group. Conversely, they are more likely to discriminate against those they perceive to be members of an out-group. Race, being both socially salient and facially visible, is one of the primary categories along which people make initial in-group and out-group categorizations. One explanation is that people assume that those of a similar race are likely to share similar values and to have had similar experiences. As a result, racial outsiders are vulnerable to discrimination from their racial insider colleagues. To avoid this distrust and dislike (which will likely undermine workplace efficiency by increasing transaction costs), employers will want to hire people who are similar to insiders.

The similarity-attraction theory is largely analogous. It posits that people are attracted to those who are similar. The theory is that race is one of the primary categories used to determine similarity and that this similarity, in turn, translates into attraction. * * *

The final theory suggesting that employers are motivated to pursue homogeneity is statistical judgments theory. Most often attributed to economics (though also central to psychology), this theory claims that racial differences often activate *statistical judgments* about likely behavioral tendencies. These statistical judgments are a type of mental shortcut, a resource-saving device. For example, white workers may see a new black colleague as likely to be lazy, untrustworthy, disloyal (especially to her white colleagues), frequently angry (perhaps as a result of oversensitivity about race), and difficult to communicate with (due to her likely having different values, different interests, and different cultural and experiential points of reference). Under this theory, whether an insider-employer will hire a black person turns on the currency of the foregoing statistical judgments. The stronger the statistical judgment, the stronger the employer's perception that a prospective black employee will not fit into the institution.

These theories suggest that there is a disincentive for employers to hire outsiders and a corresponding incentive for employers to hire insiders. Difference engenders distrust, dislike, disconnection, disidentification, and disassociation. Each of these characteristics (and certainly all of them together) undermines a necessary condition for the effective operation of teams—cooperative behavior—and therefore increases the transaction costs of managing the workplace.

2. *Empirical Evidence*

a. *The Basic Story*

In addition to the theoretical literature, there is empirical evidence predicting that racially heterogeneous teams are likely to be less effective than homogenous ones. Studies consistently show what the above theories suggest: Racial heterogeneity undermines trust and cooperation. Team members in heterogeneous teams tend not to communicate as well as team members in homogeneous teams. Turnover rates in heterogeneous teams are higher. And managerial attempts to spur innovation by diversifying their teams have "met with mixed success."

b. *The More Complicated Account*

Recent scholarship on diversity management suggests that the empirical story about workplace homogeneity may be more complicated than we have thus far described. The complication is that heterogeneity can operate as a double-edged sword. To appreciate how this is so, it is helpful to conceptualize heterogeneity/diversity as operating in a two-stage process. At stage one, superficial differences in terms of variables like race cause distrust, difficulties in communication, and a reluctance to cooperate. However, under the right conditions of intergroup contact—equal status, opportunities for self-revelation, egalitarian norms, and tasks that require cooperative interdependence—diverse team members can, at stage two, gain each other's trust, begin to see commonalities, work cooperatively, and realize the benefits of working as a diverse team. Central to this theory is the notion that there are meaningful things an employer can do at stage one—the initial contact stage—to facilitate cooperative behavior at stage two. * * *

C. *Summary*

There is theoretical and empirical evidence suggesting that employers are motivated to pursue homogeneity: Put simply, homogeneous workplaces facilitate trust, loyalty, and cooperative behavior. The story with respect to heterogeneous work teams is different. First, at an institutional level, heterogeneity is difficult and costly to manage. Second, the most cost-effective way for individual supervisors to manage heterogeneity is to "socialize away" outsider difference. Thus, it is more accurate to characterize this strategy as eliminating, rather than managing, heterogeneity. Third, even assuming that heterogeneity can be effectively managed, the benefits of a heterogeneous workplace are speculative, and they are realized primarily over the long term.

Acknowledging the homogeneity incentive is helpful to CRT in at least two ways. First, it provides critical race theorists with a different perspective on colorblindness. The homogeneity incentive exists because of the transaction costs of heterogeneity. Like colorblindness, then, the homogeneity incentive requires the submersion of racial difference. Second, the existence of the homogeneity incentive supports CRT's claim that an employer's preference for racial sameness won't always be motivated by racial animus. One of the most important ideas in CRT is that racism is not just a function of individual bad actors. From here, CRT advances one of two arguments: (1) that discrimination is unconscious and (2) that discrimination is institutional. The homogeneity incentive provides an additional base from which to theorize about the latter. It demonstrates that institutional discrimination can exist in the absence of racial animosity. * * *

IV. HOW EMPLOYERS RESPOND TO THE HOMOGENEITY INCENTIVE

Given antidiscrimination laws and social norms disfavoring racial exclusivity, institutions are unlikely to respond to the homogeneity incentive by hiring only insiders. They will hire outsiders as well. The claim we advance is that employers will use specific mechanisms to screen outsiders for evidence of racial palatability. These mechanisms select "but for outsiders"—outsiders who, but for their racial phenotype, are very similar to the insiders—and they select against "essential outsiders"—outsiders whose personal characteristics are consistent with the image of the prototypical outsider. * * *

A. *The "Race–Neutral" Response to the Homogeneity Incentive*

1. *The Basic Idea: Selection and Socialization*

Broadly speaking, there are two mechanisms employers can use to respond to the homogeneity incentive: "selection" and "socializing" mechanisms. Selection mechanisms operate at the hiring and the promotion stages. Here, an employer screens individuals for particular characteristics that function as proxies for determining whether a given individual (1) is willing to be homogenized into the workplace culture *and* (2) has the capacity to do so. Socializing mechanisms, in turn, are used to initiate and integrate the individual into the workplace. In other words, socializing mechanisms are the rites of passage that structure a new employee's experiential travels through the workplace after selection mechanisms are used to bring her into the firm. Constituting this passage are numerous rituals through which the individual is expected to demonstrate her commitment to homogeneity. More particularly, she must effectively prove that the employer made the right selection decision. Due to space constraints, we do not elaborate further on socialization mechanisms. We focus on selection, identifying four selection mechanisms employers can use to screen potential employees for evidence of performative (and not simply phenotypic) homogeneity.

2. *The Selection Mechanisms*

Four interrelated selection mechanisms that we draw out of the theory and evidence on homogeneity are: similarity, comfort, differentiation, and respectable exoticism.

a. *Similarity*

This mechanism is intuitive. The question is whether the individual exhibits personal characteristics suggesting she is similar to employees already at the firm. The more an individual appears to be similar to existing employees, the more likely an employer is to conclude that the individual has the potential to be assimilated. The potential employee's response to standard interview questions can signal her potential for assimilation to employers. Consider, for example, Johnny, who is being considered for a mid-level associate position at an elite corporate law firm. A senior partner has asked Johnny to "tell us a little bit about yourself." Johnny's response includes the following:

I enjoy tennis and golf, though I confess that both need improvement. I like a good Gore Vidal novel; in fact, I'm in the process of rereading Julian, *which, by the way, I highly recommend. I'm not a huge sports fan, but I try to make time to watch a good basketball game—usually with colleagues and friends. I wasn't always fond of theater, but two years ago my wife took me to see* The Tin Man, *and I've been sold on theater—both high and low—ever since. I enjoy Italian cinema, the old Fellini stuff as well as some of the more contemporary productions. And every so often, I truly enjoy a good B movie—not a B movie masquerading as an A movie, but a B movie that knows it's a B movie. I love going to the museum with my kids. We try to go twice a month. You'd be surprised at the interpretational skills of a six-year old.*

This response provides the employer with signals about Johnny's socialized identity, information that the employer can use to make a determination as to whether Johnny is sufficiently like the firm's existing employees. Johnny plays tennis and golf, the preferred sports of corporate America. The fact that both need improvement suggests that he is available to play both sports with his colleagues and not likely to be unduly competitive when he does so. In this way, both games can function as sites for socialization. Johnny's response also indicates that he is not an avid sports fan, but that he enjoys a good basketball game. Here, Johnny signals respectable (but not hyper-) masculinity and a willingness to participate in group-based spectator sport rituals. Johnny is married with kids, which reveals his heterosexuality and possibly a certain traditionalism. He appears to be cultured (he reads Gore Vidal, watches Italian cinema, attends the theater, and visits museums), but he is not overly elitist or pompous (he enjoys the occasional B movie and attends low-brow (and just barely high-brow) theater). Finally, the fact that Johnny's wife successfully socialized him into the theater, an experience that he was not predisposed to enjoy, suggests that he will likely not resist the firm's socialization efforts.

Not every institution will select for the foregoing qualities: Similarity selection mechanisms will vary from institution to institution. The point here is twofold: (1) Most employers will have a set of characteristics that they perceive to define their workplace, and (2) without much difficulty, employers can screen for these qualities in interviews.

b. *Comfort*

Related to similarity is comfort. Here, employers want to know whether incumbent employees will be comfortable working with the prospective hire. Again, they can select for comfort (or at least select against discomfort) by considering a prospective employee's response to standard interview questions. Stipulate once more that Johnny is interviewing for a job with an elite corporate law firm. The partner asks Johnny: "Tell us what kind of firm you're looking for." Johnny responds:

I am looking for a firm doing high-level, sophisticated corporate work. Quite frankly, most of the firms I am interviewing with seem to fall in that category—certainly your firm does. What becomes important for me, then, is firm culture. I am looking for a firm that values and respects difference. I guess I believe that people shouldn't have to lose themselves at work. They should be permitted to be who they are. I was happy to learn that your firm recently adopted a casual Friday policy.

I am also looking for a firm within which junior associates have a voice—that is, an opportunity to comment on the institutional governance of the firm, for example, the firm's billing, hiring, and pro bono policies. That sort of participation helps to make junior associates invested in the firm.

Employers could interpret Johnny's response in a number of ways. But if they are screening for comfort, a given employer may have concerns about whether Johnny "fits." Johnny's view is that individuals should be permitted to be themselves and that a firm should value difference. However, difference can be uncomfortable or discomforting. To employ what many would consider an extreme example, the firm would likely be uncomfortable with Johnny coming to work as a cross-dresser. If Johnny does cross dress, the firm would expect him to do so (if at all) outside of the workplace.

Recall that Johnny wants a voice in institutional governance and provides an indication of the kinds of issues he hopes to engage. Johnny's representations here might send a positive signal—specifically, that he wants to become a part of the firm. To the extent the employer is selecting for comfort, however, the employer could interpret Johnny's comments to suggest that he will likely make the firm uncomfortable about its hiring, pro bono, and billing practices, among other institutional governance matters.

c. *Differentiation*

Employers are most likely to utilize the differentiation mechanism when they perceive themselves to be making a "risky hire." Here, prospective employees are in a *category* that is presumed to be incapable of homogenization (or that is disinterested in socialization). Imagine that Johnny is seeking an entry-level job with a law firm. He is a third-year law student at State Law School, which is a third-tier law school. He is on law review and has an A-grade point average. His letters of recommendation are effusive; his writing sample is strong.

The firm has never hired a law student from State Law School, in part because the school is insufficiently elite and because most of the students at State Law School are from working-class backgrounds. The firm therefore assumes that these students are likely to have difficulty fitting into an elite corporate law firm. The firm might not be right for them (read: they might not be right for the firm). Given this concern, whether the employer hires Johnny will be a function of whether Johnny can differentiate himself from the category within which he is situated—that is, State law students. Consider the following exchange between Johnny and a senior partner.

Partner: Good of you to stop by. Come in and have a seat. It seems that I've left your resume elsewhere in the office. You wouldn't happen to have an extra copy, would you?

Johnny: Yes, in fact I do.

Partner: Oh yes . . . I am beginning to remember this resume. I see that you went to Harvard undergrad and that you rowed crew. How did we do this year? I graduated Harvard in '75.

Johnny: We lost to Yale, second year in a row, no pun intended. I suppose if we're going to lose to any school, it ought to be Yale. Their heavyweight eight was selected to represent the country at the World Championships in London.

Partner: So you did really well at Harvard—Magna in history, 3.7 GPA, member of the debating team. I suspect that you had a lot of options when you applied to law school.

Johnny: I was fortunate to have a few. In addition to State, NYU, Columbia, and Michigan said yes. Harvard and Stanford placed me on a waiting list. Yale said no.

Partner: I didn't get into Yale, either. What's more, I've lived to tell the tale. You will, too. But, seriously, you had all these options. I'm curious as to how you made your decision.

Johnny: Well, to a considerable extent my decision was a financial one. I couldn't afford to attend any of the other schools. And I didn't want to burden my parents anymore than I had to. Besides, I hoped that if I distinguished myself at State, I would have many of the same opportunities as if I had attended, say, Michigan.

Partner: So, Johnny, tell me about how you're thinking about law firms. Big law firms are not for everyone, and as you know, we're a pretty big law firm.

Johnny: I had the good fortune of clerking for two summers at Bronton, Stevely & Kellog in Chicago.

Partner: Yes, yes, an excellent firm.

Johnny: I had a good time there. People got along well. They had interests similar to mine. I got the sense that the attorneys there felt that they were part of a larger community. Your firm describes itself in precisely that way. Most of my classmates run away from big firms. Why go through that haze, some ask?

Partner: They consider big firms a haze?

Johnny: Some do. Most simply believe that big firms treat individuals as fungible commodities. That's not my assumption but it is the predominant assumption on campus.

Partner: What's your view, then? Let me guess: You love big firms?

Johnny: Of course. Kidding aside, I'd say that, whether it's a big firm or a small firm, the question is really twofold: whether the individual is committed to becoming a part of a team and whether the firm provides him with the opportunity to play ball.

The foregoing reflects enough differentiation on Johnny's part to effectively remove him from, or at least situate him on the periphery of, the outsider group (again, students at State Law School). Presumably, few law students at State attended Harvard. Johnny's Harvard education is significant in at least three respects. First, it signifies Johnny's intellectual capacity. Second, the fact that Johnny graduated from Harvard (and rowed crew) suggests that he has the potential for socialization. Finally, Johnny's Harvard education places Johnny and the partner in a community that has significant cultural capital—the community of Harvard alumni. That the partner recognizes this shared community is evident in his question: "How did we do this year?"

Nor would many students at State have had the opportunity to attend NYU, Michigan, and Columbia or to clerk at an elite corporate law firm. Here, too, Johnny is different. Finally, Johnny is also different in terms of his strong academic performance and the fact that he does not have a bias against big-firm practice. In short, after completing the interview with Johnny, the partner could tell himself that, although, as a formal matter, Johnny belongs to the group of State Law students, in a substantive sense, he is different. It is this kind of information that the differentiation selection mechanism is designed to ascertain.

d. *Respectable Exoticism*

Certain differences do not threaten firm homogeneity. To the extent that a given difference is both exotic (not an awful lot of people are likely to have it) and respectable (the difference is not overdetermined by a negative social meaning), firms can commodify this difference to their advantage. Thus, while hiring too many immigrants might compromise a firm's commitment to homogeneity, hiring an immigrant of royal lineage might not produce that effect. Immigrant difference that is located in the context of royal identity can be marketed—for example, to employees who might feel special because they have a royal coworker.

Another example of respectable exoticism might be an ex-NBA player in a corporate context. Note, however, that while a firm's homogeneity might tolerate one such individual, it may not be able to tolerate several. The incentive for the employer to utilize the exotic difference selection perhaps is not as strong as the employer's incentive to utilize similarity, comfort, or differentiation. In this respect, it might be more accurate to say that a firm will not select against respectable exoticism than it would be to say that the firm will actively select for that characteristic.

B. *Explicitly Racializing the Discussion: Combining CRT Insights*

The preceding discussion does not identify the racial effects of selection mechanisms. These effects can be demonstrated by adopting CRT's methodology of racializing the analysis. To borrow from Jerome Culp, we "raise . . . the race question" and, in the process, make a number of empirical assumptions about race. While we think the assumptions are plausible, the analysis is necessarily tentative and meant only to be illustrative of the type of analysis that might be performed.

1. *How Likely Is It That Johnny Will Be a Racial Minority?*

How likely is it that "Johnny" will be a racial minority? Consider, for example, the Johnny who is a student at State Law School. Recall that this Johnny attended Harvard College and rowed crew. Rowing crew often means that one attended an elite East Coast prep school, and the number of minorities who fit in this category will be small. Further, although Johnny is at State Law School, he had the option of attending first-tier law schools. Not many students of color at a third-tier law school will have had that opportunity. In short, few minorities will have the kind of cultural capital reflected in Johnny's background.

2. *Assuming That the Johnny at State Law School Is Black, Will He Be "Selected"?*

Our hypothetical assumes that an elite corporate firm would select a person like Johnny, notwithstanding the fact that Johnny does not fit the standard profile (that is, a person who has attended a first-tier law school). But if Johnny is black, this issue is far from clear. Few elite corporate firms hire blacks from schools other than those in the first-tier—more specifically, in the top ten. This may be (at least in part) due to two assumptions. The first is an assumption about affirmative action and intellectual competence—namely, that given race-based admission preferences, "smart blacks" should end up at first-tier schools. The second is an assumption about race and class—namely, that a black person at State Law School is likely to be working class and thus may have difficulty fitting into the law firm. While both assumptions can be rebutted, doing so would require an employer to engage in more intensive (read: more costly) screening of Johnny.

3. *As a General Matter, What Kind of Person of Color Is Johnny Likely to Be?*

Except for respectable exoticism, each of the selection mechanisms described above is designed to ascertain the extent to which a prospective employee is different from firm insiders. The outsiders likely to be the least different from the firm's insiders are those on (or who perform their identity as if they are on) the periphery of their outsider group identity. These "most peripheral outsiders" are likely to have grown up in predominantly white neighborhoods and to have attended elite (and predominantly white) high schools, colleges, and law schools. Employers can use these background characteristics as proxies for whether, and to what extent, outsider candidates will fit comfortably into a predominantly white workplace.

But there is a more direct method the employer can use to determine whether an outsider has the capacity to work within a homogenized workplace. There is evidence suggesting that particular types of outsiders are, from an employer's perspective, likely to cause fewer problems in the operation of a team dominated by insiders than are other types of outsiders. Racial outsiders who are "extroverted" and effective at "self-monitoring" are more likely to succeed than those who are not. Good self-monitors assess how others perceive them and adjust their behavior accordingly; extroverts project a strong and identifiable self-identity. Presumably, the reason these types of outsiders cause minimal disruption is that they actively engage in "impression management." That is, they are constantly interacting with others, sending signals about themselves, and reacting to the impressions that others have of them. An employer's selection decision likely will take account of how well outsiders manage impressions about their racial identity (that is, at least in part, how well they disprove racial stereotypes).

4. *How Do People of Color Signal Racial Differentiation?*

The point of differentiation strategies is to convey one of three ideas— that one does not identify as an outsider, that one is a different kind of outsider, or that what others think of outsiders is wrong. To convey the first idea, that one does not identify as an outsider, an employee would engage in disidentification or disassociation strategies—strategies that signal that the employee does not really identify with his outsider group. Imagine that, in the context of an interview with an elite firm, a partner says this to Johnny: "I have to tell you, Johnny, racial diversity at our firm is not good. We do our best. But the numbers are what they are—not pretty." That statement offers Johnny an "opportunity" to articulate his relationship to his outsider identity. To disidentify and disassociate, Johnny can say: "I appreciate your telling me this, but I am more interested in learning about how your firm cultivates and trains junior associates." Johnny's response could also reflect even stronger evidence of outsider disidentification and disassociation. He might have said: "I appreciate your telling me this, but I just don't believe in identity politics. Diversity is fine and good, but people are people." The point is that the earlier response is enough differentiation to suggest to the employer that Johnny is not a "race man."

To convey the second idea of differentiation, that one is a different kind of outsider, the outsider could adopt an individualized stereotype negation strategy. Here, the outsider would attempt to convey to the employer that stereotypes about his outsider identity do not apply to him. Imagine that the employer asks Johnny what he does with his spare time and Johnny responds: "Fishing, golfing, and catching up on foreign cinema." The employer could interpret this response to suggest that Johnny is not an ordinary black man (who, based on stereotypes, would have responded: "Watching basketball, playing basketball, and listening to hip-hop."). To the extent the employer does not perceive Johnny to be a black male prototype, the employer is less likely to attribute negative stereotypes of black men to Johnny.

Johnny can convey the final idea of differentiation—that others' assumptions about outsiders are wrong—through generalized stereotype negation. Under this strategy, Johnny attempts to persuade the employer that stereotypes about the employee's outsider group are inaccurate. This strategy is difficult and risky to perform when one is interviewing for a job. For instance, after articulating what he likes to do in his spare time (fishing, golfing, and catching up on foreign cinema), Johnny could add something like: "Not all black men like basketball. Moreover, most of the stereotypes about blacks are simply inaccurate. Consider, for example, crime...." It is unlikely that, in the context of an interview, Johnny would engage the employer in this way: The statement presupposes that the employer harbors stereotypes about blacks, a presupposition that could engender racial discomfort on the part of the employer ("This black guy thinks I am a racist."). Further, even if Johnny did make such a statement to the employer, it is unlikely that the employer would be persuaded by it. For generalized stereotype negation to work, there needs to be a level of trust, and sustained interaction, between the outsider and the employer.

Performing each of the foregoing differentiation strategies constitutes a form of work—identity work. Among other problems with this work, it can compromise one's sense of identity.

5. *What Are the Racial Community Costs of Differentiation Strategies?*

One of the problems with the first two differentiation strategies (disidentification/disassociation and individual stereotype negation) is that they are individually oriented. To the extent that an employee feels pressured to perform these strategies, he privileges his individual advancement over that of his group. Differentiation strategies are a response to an institutionalized problem—the employer's investment in homogeneity. So long as the homogeneity incentive drives employment decisions, there is little room for racial diversification. Society ends up with minimal (or token) outsider economic advancement into the workplace. The incentives for the outsider group, therefore, should be to engage in a collective struggle to change the system to tolerate (if not welcome) greater expression and representation of outsider identities. The first two differentiation strategies undermine that goal. They encourage outsiders to disidentify with, and disassociate from, the collective interests of the outsider group. In this sense, the problem with homogeneity is not simply that it drives employers to hire only certain kinds of outsiders, but also that the outsiders whom the employer hires are not likely to lift as they climb.

To summarize, the employer's pursuit of a homogenous workforce is likely to produce the following effects (subject to the assumptions made):

- Given the negative presumption that applies to the ability and willingness of outsiders to satisfy the homogeneity requirement (and the positive presumptions that apply to whites), the quantum of cultural capital (or the price of entry) that employers require of outsiders is likely to be higher than that for their white counterparts.

- Within the outsider community, only the elite are likely to possess the quantum of cultural capital necessary to gain entry. Employers seeking to satisfy the diversity constraint will affirmatively pursue this small subset of minorities.

- The strategies that an individual outsider employee is likely to pursue, such as differentiation, may hurt the collective cause of her minority group and compromise her sense of self. The collective cause may be better served by a struggle to reduce and remove barriers, as opposed to a competition among outsiders for a few slots (and which requires outsider homogenization).

* * *

————

NOTES AND QUESTIONS

1. **"Lean" production and new, ruthless economy.** Changes in technology have permitted a steady rise in economic productivity for the United States in recent years. These changes, however, collectively have made labor much more insecure. William Greider discusses the case of labor unions and the manufacturing sector:

> Starting in the 1970s, U.S. companies gravitated toward a different strategy in which global price pressures were offset by extracting more from labor. Corporations discarded their long postwar truce with unions and began moving jobs, first to the low-wage South and then offshore. They closed factories and demanded wage contracts that depressed wages. They mobilized both political and economic power to weaken labor's bargaining position.
>
> American corporate managers might point out that they themselves were driven to these defensive actions by the global economic forces. The "virtuous circle" of the 1950s and 1960s had also been sustained by the existence of industrial oligopolies—a few big companies that dominated major sectors like autos, steel and aircraft and were powerful enough to set prices and wages in a clubby, arbitrary fashion. The rise of foreign producers, especially from Japan, broke up that comfortable arrangement forever.
>
> As firms shifted production to lower-wage workers, organized labor lost members and became steadily less able to discipline managements. The decline in wages was not confined to union members, however, but was more general. Retail sales workers, for instance, experienced a much sharper fall than manufacturing. In 1970, wages constituted 67 percent of all personal income in the United States, a ratio that had held constant for decades. By 1994, wages were less than 58 percent of total incomes. In 1960, wages were about 26 percent of total sales. By 1994, they were about 20 percent.

WILLIAM GREIDER, ONE WORLD, READY OR NOT: THE MANIC LOGIC OF GLOBAL CAPITALISM 77 (1997). Greider argues that these trends are symptomatic of a larger phenomenon: "wage arbitrage." Wage arbitrage "moves the production and jobs from a high-wage labor market to another where the labor is much cheaper. The producers thus reduce their costs and enhance profits by arbitraging these wage differences, usually selling their finished products back into the high-wage markets." *id.* at 57. Since labor is much less mobile than capital, wage arbitrage means the upper hand in bargaining power for capital in particular disputes. Unions, which are usually organized within national boundaries, become vulnerable to the threat of moving jobs to lower-wage countries.

2.   Law firms as internal labor markets. For an extended application of economic theory to explain the hiring and promotion practices of large law firms, see David B. Wilkins & G. Mitu Gulati, *Reconceiving the Tournament of Lawyers: Tracking, Seeding, and Information Control in the Internal Labor Markets of Elite Law Firms*, 84 VA. L. REV. 1581 (1998).

3.   Winner-take-all markets. Some economists argue that a new feature of contemporary labor markets is the existence of the "winner take all" market. In such markets there are many competitors for a very few extremely lucrative slots. The entertainment industry provides many examples: as reality shows like *American Idol* dramatically illustrate, the possibility of fame and fortune in the entertainment world draws many more people than could possibly succeed. As the economists argue, and as *American Idol* also illustrates, winner-take-all markets are socially wasteful because the possibility of extremely high rewards (coupled with the cognitive quirks identified by bounded rationality theory) draws people who would do better for themselves and the rest of society if they put their time and energy elsewhere. Winner-take-all markets also contribute to income inequality, since a very small number of players make a huge amount of money and the rest make very little. Robert Frank and Philip Cook argue that changes in tax policy, tort reform, health care finance, educational finance, and antitrust policy, among other reforms, could promote both efficiency and equity by reducing the spread and impact of winner-take-all markets. *See* ROBERT H. FRANK & PHILIP J. COOK, THE WINNER-TAKE-ALL SOCIETY 211–31 (1995).

4.   Women and emotional labor. Arlie Russell Hochschild, in *The Managed Heart: Commercialization of Human Feeling* (20th anniversary edition 2003), argues that women in the workplace often face demands not placed on men, that they display certain kinds of emotions, usually cheeriness and nurturance. ARLIE RUSSELL HOCHSCHILD, THE MANAGED HEART: COMMERCIALIZATION OF HUMAN FEELING (20th anniv. ed. 2003). Thus, women may be asked to smile, will be expected to be peacemakers in workplace disputes, and are expected to defer to the emotional needs and desires of men. Hochschild argues that the requirement of emotional labor also tends to fall upon occupations that have been heavily feminized, such as secretaries and nurses, without regard to the sex of the people in those occupations. *See also* ARLIE RUSSELL HOCHSCHILD, COMMERCIALIZATION OF INTIMATE LIFE: NOTES FROM HOME AND WORK (2003). Does Carbado and Gulati's analysis suggest a similar burden of emotional labor on racial minorities in the workplace?

5.   Impression management. Carbado and Gulati's analysis is indebted to the work of sociologist Erving Goffman, who coined the phrase "impression management" to describe how individuals attempt to control how they are seen by others, while those others in turn attempt to discern the "real" self behind the front. *See, e.g.,* Erving Goffman, *The Arts of Impression Management, in* THE PRESENTATION OF DELF IN EVERYDAY LIFE 208–37 (1959).

Goffman emphasizes that everyone in social life is constantly engaged in impression management, both in private and in public settings, and uses the metaphor of the dramatic performance throughout his analysis:

> In this report, the individual was divided by implication into two basic parts: he was viewed as a *performer*, a harried fabricator of impressions involved in the all-too-human task of staging a performance; he was viewed as a *character*, a figure, typically a fine one, whose spirit, strength, and other sterling qualities the performance was designed to evoke. The attributes of a performer and the attributes of a character are of a different order, quite basically so, yet both sets have their meaning in terms of the show that must go on. * * *

> A correctly staged and performed scene leads the audience to impute a self to a performed character, but this imputation—this self—is a *product* of a scene that comes off, and is not a *cause* of it. The self, then, as a performed character, is not an organic thing that has a specific location, whose fundamental fate is to be born, to mature, and to die; it is a dramatic effect arising diffusely from a scene that is presented, and the characteristic issue, the crucial concern, is whether it will be credited or discredited.

Id., at 252–53.

C.   Class and Consumption

The Overspent American: Why We Want What We Don't Need

80–91 (1998).

■ Juliet B. Schor

While television has long been suspected as a promoter of consumer desire, there has been little hard evidence to support that view, at least for adult spending. After all, there's not an obvious connection. Many of the products advertised on television are everyday low-cost items such as aspirin, laundry detergent, and deodorant. Those TV ads are hardly a spur to excessive consumerism. Leaving aside other kinds of ads for the moment (for cars, diamonds, perfumes), there's another counter to the argument that television causes consumerism: TV is a *substitute* for spending. One of the few remaining free activities, TV is a popular alternative to costly recreational spending such as movies, concerts, and restaurants. If it causes us to spend, that effect must be powerful enough to overcome its propensity to save us money.

Apparently it is. My research shows that the more TV a person watches, the more he or she spends. The likely explanation for the link between television and spending is that what we see on TV inflates our sense of what's normal. The lifestyles depicted on television are far different from the average American's: with a few exceptions, TV characters are upper-middle-class, or even rich.

Studies by the consumer researchers Thomas O'Guinn and L.J. Schrum confirm this upward distortion. The more people watch television, the more they think American households have tennis courts, private planes, convertibles, car telephones, maids, and swimming pools. Heavy watchers also overestimate the portion of the population who are millionaires, have had cosmetic surgery, and belong to a private gym, as well as those suffering from dandruff, bladder control problems, gingivitis, athlete's foot, and hemorrhoids (the effect of all those ads for everyday products). What one watches also matters. Dramatic shows—both daytime soap operas and prime-time drama series—have a stronger impact on viewer perceptions than other kinds of programs (say news, sports, or weather).

Heavy watchers are not the only ones, however, who tend to overestimate standards of living. Almost everyone does. (And almost everyone watches TV.) In one study, ownership rates for twenty-two of twenty-seven consumer products were generally overstated. Your own financial position also matters. Television inflates standards for lower-, average-, and above-average-income students, but it does the reverse for really wealthy ones. (Among those raised in a financially rarefied atmosphere, TV is almost a reality check.) Social theories of consumption hold that the inflated sense of consumer norms promulgated by the media raises people's aspirations and leads them to buy more. In the words of one Los Angeles resident, commenting on this media tendency, "They try to portray that an upper-class lifestyle is normal and typical and that we should all have it."

Television also affects norms by giving us real information about how other people live and what they have. It allows us to be voyeurs, opening the door to the "private world" inside the homes and lives of others. * * *

Another piece of evidence for the TV-spending link is the apparent correlation between debt and excessive TV viewing. In the Merck Family Fund poll, the fraction responding that they "watch too much TV" rose steadily with indebtedness. More than half (56 percent) of all those who reported themselves "heavily" in debt also said they watched too much TV.

It is partly because of television that the top 20 percent of the income distribution, and even the top 5 percent within it, has become so important in setting and escalating consumption standards for more than just the people immediately below them. Television lets *everyone* see what these folks have and allows viewers to want it in concrete, product-specific ways. Let's not forget that television programming and movies are increasingly filled with product placements—the use of identifiable brands by characters. TV shows and movies are more and more like long-running ads. * * *

Part of what keeps the see-want-borrow-and-buy sequence going is lack of attention. Americans live with high levels of denial about their spending patterns. We spend more than we realize, hold more debt than we admit to, and ignore many of the moral conflicts surrounding our acquisitions. The

importance of denial for dysfunctional consumers has been well documented. We've all heard the stories about people who drive around in cars full of
unpaid credit card bills, who sneak into the guest room at 2:00 A.M. to make
a QVC purchase, or who quietly slip off at lunchtime for a quick trip to the
mall. What is not well understood is that the spending of many normal
consumers is also predicated on denial. (How many times have you heard
someone say, "Oh, I'm not materialistic, I'm just into books and CDs—and
travel"?) * * *

Nowhere is denial so evident as with credit cards. Contrary to economists' usual portrayal of credit card debtors as fully rational consumers
who use the cards to smooth out temporary shortfalls in income, the
finding of the University of Maryland economist Larry Ausubel was that
people greatly underestimate the amount of debt they hold on their cards—
1992's actual $182 billion in debt was thought to be a mere $70 billion.
Furthermore, most people do not expect to use their cards to borrow, but,
of course, they do. Eighty percent end up paying finance charges within any
given year, with just under half (47 percent) always holding unpaid
balances.

Not paying attention to what we spend is also very common. How
many of us really keep track of where the cash from the ATM goes? Most
Americans don't budget. And they don't watch. Many "fritter," as this
downshifter recalled: "All I know is at the end of the month I never had
anything left. And so I have to say I spent it all. I don't know what I
frittered away. I really don't know what I spent the money on." * * *

Finally, denial also helps us navigate the moral conflicts associated
with consumption. Most of our cherished religious and ethical teachings
condemn excessive spending, but we don't really know what that means.
We have a sense that money is dirty and a nagging feeling that there must
be something better to do with our hard-earned dollars than give them to
Bloomingdale's. As our salaries and creature comforts expand, many of us
keep alive our youthful fantasies of doing humanitarian work, continuing
the inner dialogue between God and Mammon. Not looking *too* hard helps
keep that inner conflict tolerable. Squarely facing the fact that you spent
$6,000 on your wardrobe last year and gave less than one-third of that sum
to charity is a lot harder than living with a vague sense that you need to
start spending less on clothes and giving away more money. * * *

In many places, private school is becoming a part of the upper-middle-
(and even middle-) class standard of living—a requisite element in the basic
package. Parents worry that without it their children will fall behind. Fears
about education become magnified because they tap into larger, more deep-
seated anxieties. Class position seems to be at stake. And, of course, as the
middle and upper-middle classes abandon the public schools, the class
divisions widen. Public school becomes tainted with a lower-class image. As
another mother in the Los Angeles study explained, the public schools work
well for her "housekeeper's child," who will have language problems, but
not for her children. "Our concern with the public schools is really the
safety issue. I have blond-haired, blue-eyed children who are not very

physical and not very aggressive, and I worry about interactions on playgrounds.''

At the same time, these parents have to deal with the complications of schooling alongside the super-wealthy. The same woman who is afraid of the public school playgrounds also worries about her children being at the bottom of the economic ladder in their private school. "The wealth of these kids is just mind-boggling. You put them in an environment in which we cannot compete, nor do we *want* them to compete and have those kinds of values. I don't want them to come home and say, 'Why don't we live in a ten-bedroom house?' " * * *

We have no problem acknowledging the "conspicuous consumption" of the early twentieth century that [Thorstein] Veblen wrote about. Middle class Americans shake their heads at what inner-city youths do to obtain expensive sneakers or gold chains. We can even get passionate about the dangers of status symbols in the Third World. Many Americans boycotted Nestle for promoting infant formula, the often deadly status alternative to breast milk. (Nestle and other companies had women in "modern" white uniforms doling out free supplies of formula in hospitals, leading to sickness, malnutrition, and even death among "bottle babies.") Many Americans deplore the entry of soft drinks and fast-food outlets into poor countries because they contribute to comerciogenic malnutrition: the poor spend their few pesos on soft drinks or French fries, forgoing nutritious food and becoming sick in the process. On the lighter side, we can chuckle at Peruvian Indians carrying rocks painted like transistor radios, Chinese who keep the brand tags on their designer sunglasses, Brazilian shanty-town dwellers with television antennae but no TV's, or the Papua New Guineans who substitute Pentel pens for boars' nose pieces. Third World status consumption seems straightforward, unambiguous in motive.

We have more trouble seeing the counterparts of these behaviors in the American middle class, and in ourselves.

No Scrubs

TLC, *on* FANMAIL, LA FACE (1999).

■ KEVIN BRIGGS, KANDI BURRUSS, TAMEKA COTTLE

A scrub is a guy that thinks he's fly
And is also known as a buster
Always talkin' about what he wants
And just sits on his broke ass
So (no)

I don't want your number (no)
I don't want to give you mine and (no)
I don't want to meet you nowhere (no)
I don't want none of your time and (no)

Chorus:
I don't want no scrub
A scrub is a guy that can't get no love from me
Hanging out the passenger side
Of his best friend's ride
Trying to holler at me
I don't want no scrub
A scrub is a guy that can't get no love from me
Hanging out the passenger side
Of his best friend's ride
Trying to holler at me

But a scrub is checkin' me
But his game is kinda weak
And I know that he cannot approach me
Cuz I'm lookin' like class and he's lookin' like trash
Can't get wit' no deadbeat ass
So (no)

I don't want your number (no)
I don't want to give you mine and (no)
I don't want to meet you nowhere (no)
I don't want none of your time (no)

Chorus
If you don't have a car and you're walking
Oh yes son I'm talking to you
If you live at home wit' your momma
Oh yes son I'm talking to you (baby)
If you have a shorty but you don't show love
Oh yes son I'm talking to you
Wanna get with me with no money
Oh no I don't want no (oh)

No scrub
No scrub (no no)
No scrub (no no no no no)
No scrub (no no)
No

* * *

Dress As Success

Beauty Secrets: Women and the Politics of Appearance 79–80, 83–85, 88–93 (1986).

■ Wendy Chapkis

Appearance talks, making statements about gender, sexuality, ethnicity and class. In a sexually, racially and economically divided society all those visual statements add up to an evaluation of power. Economic power, or class position, is easily suggested by a man's use of the standard business suit. An expensive tailored three-piece suit says authority and privilege quietly but unmistakeably. For a woman to get that kind of attention, she must speak up more loudly. Even dressed in designer everything and costly jewelry her appearance makes a less unambiguous statement than a man's $1,000 suit.

Traditionally, a woman dressed in money has been assumed to be making a statement not about herself, but about a man. Her expensive clothing was thought to signal to the world that her husband or other male provider was so wealthy he could afford a clearly useless luxury in the form of this female. In this Veblenesque* interpretation, the woman herself is relegated to the position of a passive object much like a clothes hanger in someone else's closet. While this may well explain a husband's rationale for paying the bills, conspicuous consumption has a special purpose in a wealthy woman's life, too. * * *

Not only has consuming been one of the few pursuits open to women of a certain class, but being dressed in money demonstrates to the viewing public that the woman's one all important investment—marriage—has paid off nicely. Woman to woman we know that the marriage contract is far from an agreement between peers. At least being well-dressed serves as the visual equivalent of a large pay check.

Women in the role of wife establish social position second hand. A wealthy husband provides access to power for the woman married to him. But this ascribed power has to be made visible. If he has it, you flaunt it—not merely to reflect well on him, but to protect yourself. Dressed in money, a woman looks like someone not to be trifled with despite her sex. She is clearly protected by someone with the ability to do the job.

Increasingly, though, women are finding a need to indicate *personal* financial authority through their dress. Many more women now are bread-winners than in the past. This change is due in part to the women's movement. However, perhaps even more important than feminism is rising male unemployment and inflation making a woman's paycheck indispens-able. Higher divorce rates, too, have helped make female financial indepen-dence a necessity.

How a woman should indicate professional power through her appear-ance is still a subject of debate. But all those voices presuming to advise women on how to put together such an image seem to agree on two fundamental things. First, *looking* "successful" is more than half the battle in actually achieving professional success. And second, success is a formula not to be tinkered with—that is, women may now aspire to professional success but should not attempt to redefine it.

Both these precepts have a particular resonance for women. Haven't we always known that how we look is far more important than what we do or how we do it? And as interlopers in the man-made world of business, we

* Thorstein Veblen, author of *The Theory of the Leisure Class,* published in 1899.

tend toward gratitude if someone even takes the time to explain the rules of the game—we may feel in no position to try to change them. Success in these terms is intensely individual and conformity a useful strategy.

* * *

The carefully composed look of success is not without its fashion competition. New Wave culture and punk style are among the most radical forms of visual dissent. At a very minimum, punk is a statement about consumerism. At least initially, the fashion was put together from hand-made or second hand clothing. Jewelry was to be found or created from inexpensive materials like rubber, plastic and cheap metals.

Punk has also been an explicit message on the state of the economy. If there is a possibility of a job interview in the near future, one probably won't choose a fluorescent green hair dye or a Mohawk haircut. But when unemployment becomes a predictable long-term condition, little is put at risk by looking outrageous. Radically transforming one's personal appearance can be an exercise of personal power in a life that feels out of control. While it may not be possible for an individual to change the reality of high unemployment, housing shortages and poverty, it is possible to transform one's body into a visual shout: "No, I do not accept the goodness of your goals and expectations. No, I will not help you feel secure in your choices. Do I look frightening? Do I look angry? Do I look dangerous? Do you still feel safe in thinking that the system works just fine? Think again."

Not surprisingly, it is not the Punk but the young urban professionals—the so-called Yuppies—who have become the darlings of contemporary media. Their aerobic bodies and expensive dress speak confidently of physical and economic health. The image is above all reassuring. The system works just fine if you play by the rules. We accept the goals and the methods and we will be among the winners.

Success as it is known in the contemporary corporate world is dependent on a division between winners and losers, with a built-in guarantee that more will fail than will be rewarded. Women have always been the structural losers in the system. To be a woman was to be slotted for the position of support staff, both professionally and personally. The reality remains that even today most women will not become senior executives. In fact, most women will not even marry senior executives. The majority of working women will remain on a parallel job ladder which ends in the position of executive secretary or senior administrative assistant.

As anyone with experience in the business world knows, these are the women who run the show, without whom many organizations would come to a standstill. Yet they will never have the money or the authority to accompany the responsibility.

As long as success remains an individual characteristic, only one name will go on the by-line, while research assistants will have to be satisfied with a thank you in the acknowledgements. Secretaries will continue to receive lunch invitations or roses once a year instead of colleague-to-colleague respect and recognition of their partnership in the business endeavor. And women who do make it to a position of recognized power will have to quickly switch class and gender allegiance. Too close an identification with the secretarial crowd, too much empathy with those who come up on the short end of the unequal division of rewards will only be detrimental to one's own climb toward success.

It is arguably an improvement if women as a group are no longer automatically relegated to subordinate positions. But only those who find Jeane Kirkpatrick and Margaret Thatcher shining examples of feminism will believe that this sort of individual success is the same thing as women's liberation.

* * *

In the early days of the contemporary women's movement, women created strategies of empowerment that focused on shared experience and collective labor. However, we also longed for the individual perques of authority and prestige. But we were operating in an economic structure that insured that while our efforts might allow some of us to "make it," all of us would not. Western industrial society is based on competition and scarcity; equality not of condition but of opportunity. Taking on male bastions of power like the corporate world and opening them up to women meant collectively breaking down the barriers to women's participation. We worked for and achieved legislation that guaranteed us access. But once we succeeded in opening the door, we stepped through and realized that the stairway to the top was narrow and already crowded.

Still, now that the opportunity was there, failure became evidence of personal inadequacy not a political problem. Nor was class (known in America as one's "background") a political concern—provided one knew how to hide it. An entire literature developed teaching the common woman how to reach uncommon heights by "applying" herself and dressing for the part. * * *

Once inside and part way up the corporate ladder, the need to disguise your origins becomes imperative. In order to become executive materials, you must look as if you come from executive stock—the upper middle class. Enter John T. Molloy and *Dress for Success*:

> We can increase [a woman's] chances of success in the business world; we can increase her chances of being a top executive; we can make her more attractive to various types of men.

Molloy believes at least as firmly as [Helen Gurley Brown, founder of *Cosmopolitan* magazine] that a woman's business success lies in her own hands. Failure, too, is a personal not a structural problem: "If you have to tell your boss not to send you for coffee, you must have already told him non-verbally that you were ready to go." He quotes "Two extremely successful women" to back him up on this; these women expressed the belief that "The reason most young women wouldn't succeed was because they didn't look like they wanted to succeed."

Dressed in the proper outfit and sporting the proper attitude, the political problem of sexism can be sidestepped. The trick is learning to *accept* reality, not trying to change it. "It is a stark reality that men dominate the power structure.... I am not suggesting that women dress to impress men simply because they are men [but rather because men have power] ... It is not sexism; it is realism."

In the chapter entitled "Does Your Background Hurt You," Molloy dismisses class as a political problem as neatly as he does sex. Women who intend to move into "The power ranks of American society" first must "learn the manners and mores of the inner circle. And the inner circle is most emphatically upper middle class." Not to worry; his advice is exceedingly specific:

> My research showed that a woman wearing a black raincoat is definitely not automatically categorized as lower middle class. Raincoats are important for women, but not as important as they are for men.... The country-tweed look is very upper middle class and highly recommended.... The blazer, by its very nature, is upper middle class; every woman should have at least one.... Office sweaters ... say lower middle class and loser. Don't wear lower middle class colors such as purple and gold.

Predictably, the colors that test best are "gray, medium range blue, beige, deep maroon, deep rust." And the colors to avoid are "most pastels, particularly pink and pale yellow, most shades of green, mustard, bright anything, any shade that would be considered exotic." What we end up with as acceptable colors in the business world are those commonly associated with men and with the white upper class. This look is then defined as "serious." Serious becomes a question of conformity not creative difference, of masculinity not femininity and of the bland over the exotic, i.e. the foreign or racially "deviant."

Racial difference is indeed problematic to success and must be minimized. The process begins with learning to lose any ethnic accent and avoiding exotic fashions. But people of color serious about success are also advised to do whatever possible to transform even their bodies. In African women's magazines, advertisements promote the skin lightener Clere:

> Clere for your own special beauty. We are a successful people and have to look successful. We use Clere for a lighter, smoother skin. Now, Clere will work its magic for you, and make you more beautiful and successful.

Of course, it is not only among dress for success advisors that one finds these prejudices. They just help make them respectable. Even among articulate critics of sexism and racism in contemporary society there is evidence that these standards have been internalized. * * *

The shift from full-time homemaking to double duty (working both for wages and in the home) has helped create a need for new symbols of identity. Women are discovering that they are expected to have not one, but several conflicting images: the wholesome mother, the coolly professional businesswoman and the sexy mistress. No wonder women turn to the magic of wardrobe and makeup to provide inspiration for their multiple selves:

"Springfever by Elizabeth Arden ... New make-up. New inspiration." "I can bring home the bacon, fry it up in a pan and never let you forget you're a man ... En Jolie" "Colors that inspire ... Let L'erin do the talking." You almost can hear the poor woman sigh "gladly."

The cosmetics industry has been carefully studying how best to make use of this bewildering set of demands made upon working women. Women's wages have been a mixed blessing for the beauty trade. In 1983, *Advertising Age*, an industry trade journal, noted with some alarm an increase in the number of women working outside the home:

> Today, 49% of America's mothers with children under six years old are employed as opposed to only 18% in 1960 ... Where women in this group once spent middays at the department store, they are now in the office.... Women who formerly had the time to sample and listen and spend money are no longer shoppers. Even when they do visit the store, they do so as buyers.

The subtle distinction between "shopping" and "buying," *Advertising Age* points out, is that the former implies leisure. This distinction seems to be borne out by figures on grocery store cosmetic sales (cheap and fast). In the U.S., they increased by 35 percent from 1980 to 1982.

Without the leisure to linger and shop, a woman may buy what is handy and in the process discover that what she is buying for convenience is not substantially different than the more expensive brand she used to carefully seek out. *Advertising Age* warns: "This is a dangerous conclusion for the industry."

And indeed after decades of constant growth, the beauty trade is now faced with a leveling off of sales and, in some cases, even a slight decline. Not all product lines have felt the squeeze, though. "Customers seem to be turning away from medium price products," the vice-president for marketing of one of America's largest cosmetic companies notes. "They are buying better goods or switching to generic, low-price products." * * *

Often the expensive and cheap products are not only produced by different divisions of the same conglomerate, but they are made of nearly identical ingredients. Even when we know this to be true, we often will buy the more expensive item because the fantasy it offers is more attractive. Psychologist Erika Freeman explains,

> An item that promises a fantasy by definition must be priced fantastically.... If a cream begins to sell at 50 cents it will not sell as well nor will it be considered as miraculous as a cream that sells for $30.
> * * *

Why do women buy costly beauty products that demonstrably have little purpose other than participation in a fantasy? The purchase of a new cosmetic, the decision to change the color or style of one's hair, the start of a new diet are the female equivalent of buying a lottery ticket. Maybe *you* will be the one whose life is transformed. Despite daily experience to the contrary, we continue to hope that maybe this time, maybe this product, will make a difference in our lives. And if it doesn't, it is still a relatively inexpensive way to visit the mysterious orient of Shiseido, the elite circle of Chanel, the smouldering, sensuous world of Dior. Everything that is so difficult to attain in real life is promised for the price of a new perfume or eye shadow.

————

NOTES AND QUESTIONS

1. Thorstein Veblen and social meaning of consumption. Thorstein Veblen [1857–1929] was an American economist whose work focused on the embeddedness of economic activity in a larger social world in which the desire for prestige in the eyes of others is as central as the desire for purely material gain. Two of the concepts he elaborated—"conspicuous consumption" and "pecuniary emulation"—illustrate this focus. Veblen argued that wealthy people desire to signal to others that they are wealthy, and that buying and displaying luxury goods is an important means by which this is done. Thus, "Conspicuous consumption is how the wealthy demonstrate their wealth, and thus their success in war or in business. By purchasing the finest houses, autos, suits, and shoes—all visible and public signs of financial success—they gain the respect and admiration of their peers and subordinates." Janet Knoedler, *Thorstein Veblen and the Predatory Nature of Contemporary Capitalism, in* Introduction to Political Economy 66 (Charles Sackrey & Geoffrey Schneider eds., 3d ed. 2002).

Veblen also argued that people in all economic classes make consumption decisions based not only on their rational desire for goods and services to make their life better, but out of envy of those who are more successful. This desire to be like and to be seen as like those with more money and social success he named "pecuniary emulation":

> [T]he standard of expenditure which commonly guides our efforts is not the average, ordinary expenditure already achieved; it is an ideal of consumption that lies just beyond our reach ... The motive is emulation—the stimulus of an invidious comparison which prompts us to outdo those with whom we are in the habit of classing ourselves ... [e]ach class envies and emulates the class next above it in the social scale, while it rarely compares itself with those below or with those who are considerably in advance.

Thorstein Veblen, The Theory of the Leisure Class 81 (Houghton Mifflin Co. 1973) (1899).

2. Crisis of over-production and creation of desire. Economic historians argue that after 1890, as modern forms of industrial production began to take shape and more and more mass-produced goods began to flood American markets, American business interests began a campaign to change consumption patterns away from patterns of thrift, self-denial, and self-reliance. As William Leach argues:

From the 1890s on, American corporate business, in league with key institutions, began the transformation of American society into a society preoccupied with consumption, with comfort and bodily well-being, with luxury, spending, and acquisition, with more goods this year than last, more next year than this. American consumer capitalism produced a culture almost violently hostile to the past and to tradition, a future-oriented culture of desire that confused the good life with goods. It was a culture that first appeared as an alternative culture—or as one moving largely against the grain of earlier traditions of republicanism and Christian virtue—and then unfolded to become the reigning culture of the United States. It was the culture that many people the world over soon came to see as *the* heart of American life.

WILLIAM LEACH, LAND OF DESIRE: MERCHANTS, POWER, AND THE RISE OF A NEW AMERICAN CULTURE, xiii (1993); *see also* STUART EWEN, CAPTAINS OF CONSCIOUSNESS: ADVERTISING AND THE SOCIAL ROOTS OF THE CONSUMER CULTURE (2001).

Consumer culture is partly a response to what Veblen identified as an incipient crisis within capitalist societies: the threat of overproduction, too many goods chasing too few buyers. As William Greider puts it:

As economist Thorstein Veblen taught several generations ago, the problem of capitalist enterprise is always the problem of supply: managing the production of goods in order to maximize profit and the return on invested capital. * * *

The great virtue of capitalism—the quality that always confounded socialist critics and defeated rival economic systems—is its ability to yield more from less. Its efficient organization of production strives to produce more goods from less input, whether the input is capital, labor or raw resources. Assuming markets are stable, the rising productivity increases the profit per unit, the yields that get distributed as returns to invested capital or as rising wages for labor or in lower product prices for consumers and, in the happiest circumstances, all three.

But this expanding potential to produce more goods also poses the enduring contradiction for capitalist enterprise: how to dispose of the surplus production. You can make more things, but can you sell them? An undisciplined expansion of productive capacity will be self-defeating, even dangerous for a firm, if all it accomplishes are continuing supply surpluses that degrade prices and undermine the rate of return. The problem of surplus capacity drives not only the competition among firms for market shares but also the imperative to discover new markets.

WILLIAM GREIDER, ONE WORLD, READY OR NOT: THE MANIC LOGIC OF GLOBAL CAPITALISM 44–45 (1997).

3. Branding and consumption. As the culture of consumption has matured, advertising strategies have changed as well. In the early 1990s, American corporations began to shift even more profoundly away from advertising what Karl Marx would have called the use-value of their products, to focus instead on using advertising to create an affective link between their products and the consumer's dreams and fantasies. This new technique relied on "branding," and the advertising of the brand rather than the product. As Naomi Klein observes:

> Overnight, "Brands, not products!" became the rallying cry for a marketing renaissance led by a new breed of companies that saw themselves as "meaning brokers" instead of product producers. What was changing was the idea of what—in both advertising and branding—was being sold. The old paradigm had it that all marketing was selling a product. In the new model, however, the product always takes a back seat to the real product, the brand, and the selling of the brand acquired an extra component that can only be described as spiritual. * * *
>
> On Marlboro Friday [a day in 1993 when Marlboro announced plans to dramatically reduce its prices in an attempt to compete with bargain cigarette brands], a line was drawn in the sand between the lowly price slashers and the high-concept brand builders. The brand builders conquered and a new consensus was born: the products that will flourish in the future will be the ones presented not as "commodities" but as concepts: the brand as experience, as lifestyle.

Naomi Klein, No Logo: Taking Aim at the Brand Bullies 21 (1999).

Does the ever-more-ephemeral link between products and the consumer's actual need for them threaten the pursuit of happiness?

Advertising At the Edge of the Apocalypse

Available at http://www.sutjhally.com/onlinepubs/onlinepubs_frame.html (n.d.).

■ Sut Jhally

In this article I wish to make a simple claim: 20th century advertising is the most powerful and sustained system of propaganda in human history and its cumulative cultural effects, unless quickly checked, will be responsible for destroying the world as we know it. As it achieves this it will be responsible for the deaths of hundreds of thousands of non-western peoples and will prevent the peoples of the world from achieving true happiness. Simply stated, our survival as a species is dependent upon minimizing the threat from advertising and the commercial culture that has spawned it. I am stating my claims boldly at the outset so there can be no doubt as to what is at stake in our debates about the media and culture as we enter the new millennium.

Colonizing Culture

Karl Marx, the pre-eminent analyst of 19th century industrial capitalism, wrote in 1867, in the very opening lines of *Capital* that: "The wealth of societies in which the capitalist mode of production prevails appears as an 'immense collection of commodities'". * * * In seeking to initially distinguish his object of analysis from preceding societies, Marx referred to the way the society showed itself on a surface level and highlighted a *quantitative* dimension—the number of objects that humans interacted with in everyday life.

Indeed, no other society in history has been able to match the immense productive output of industrial capitalism. This feature colors the way in which the society presents itself—the way it *appears*. Objects are everywhere in capitalism. In this sense, capitalism is truly a revolutionary society, dramatically altering the very landscape of social life, in a way no other form of social organization had been able to achieve in such a short period of time. (In *The Communist Manifesto* Marx and Engels would coin the famous phrase "all that is solid melts into air" to highlight capitalism's unique dynamism.) It is this that strikes Marx as distinctive as he observes 19th century London. The starting point of his own critique therefore is not what he believes is the dominating agent of the society, *capital*, nor is it what he believes creates the value and wealth, *labor*—instead it is the *commodity*. From this surface appearance Marx then proceeds to peel away the outer skin of the society and to penetrate to the underlying essential structure that lies in the "hidden abode" of production.

It is not enough of course to only produce the "immense collection of commodities"—they must also be sold, so that further investment in production is feasible. Once produced commodities must go through the circuit of distribution, exchange and consumption, so that profit can be returned to the owners of capital and value can be "realized" again in a money form. If the circuit is not completed the system would collapse into stagnation and depression. Capitalism therefore has to ensure the sale of commodities on *pain of death*. In that sense the problem of capitalism is not mass production (which has been solved) but is instead the *problem of consumption*. That is why from the early years of this century it is more accurate to use the label "the consumer culture" to describe the western industrial market societies.

So central is consumption to its survival and growth that at the end of the 19th century industrial capitalism invented a unique new institution— the advertising industry—to ensure that the "immense accumulation of commodities" are converted back into a money form. The function of this new industry would be to recruit the best creative talent of the society and to create a culture in which desire and identity would be fused with commodities—to make the dead world of things come alive with human and social possibilities (what Marx would prophetically call the "fetishism of commodities"). And indeed there has never been a propaganda effort to match the effort of advertising in the 20th century. More thought, effort, creativity, time, and attention to detail has gone into the selling of the immense collection of commodities that any other campaign in human history to change public consciousness. One indication of this is [simple] the amount of money that has been exponentially expended on this effort. Today, in the United States alone, over $175 billion a year is spent to sell us things. This concentration of effort is unprecedented.

It should not be surprising that something this central and with so much being expended on it should become an important presence in social life. Indeed, commercial interests intent on maximizing the consumption of the immense collection of commodities have colonized more and more of the spaces of our culture. For instance, almost the entire media system (television and print) has been developed as a delivery system for marketers—its prime function is to produce audiences for sale to advertisers. Both the advertisements it carries, as well as the editorial matter that acts as a support for it, celebrate the consumer society. The movie system, at one time outside the direct influence of the broader marketing system, is now fully integrated into it through the strategies of licensing, tie-ins and product placements. The prime function of many Hollywood films today is to aid in the selling of the immense collection of commodities. As public funds are drained from the non-commercial cultural sector, art galleries, museums and symphonies bid for corporate sponsorship. Even those institutions thought to be outside of the market are being sucked in. High schools now sell the sides of their buses, the spaces of their hallways and the classroom time of their students to hawkers of candy bars, soft drinks and jeans. In New York City, sponsors are being sought for public playgrounds. In the contemporary world everything is sponsored by someone. The latest plans of Space Marketing Inc. call for rockets to deliver mile-wide Mylar billboards to compete with the sun and the moon for the attention of the earth's population.

With advertising messages on everything from fruit on supermarket shelves, to urinals, and to literally the space beneath our feet (Bamboo lingerie conducted a spray-paint pavement campaign in Manhattan telling consumers that "from here it looks likes you could use some new underwear"), it should not be surprising that many commentators now identify the realm of culture as simply an *adjunct* to the system of production and consumption.

Indeed so overwhelming has the commercial colonization of our culture become that it has created its own problems for marketers who now worry about how to ensure that their *individual* message stands out from the "clutter" and the "noise" of this busy environment. In that sense the main competition for marketers is not simply other brands in their product type, but all the other advertisers who are competing for the attention of an increasingly cynical audience which is doing all it can to avoid ads. In a strange paradox, as advertising takes over more and more space in the culture the job of the individual advertisers becomes much more difficult. Therefore even greater care and resources are poured into the creation of commercial messages—much greater care than the surrounding editorial matter designed to capture the attention of the audience. Indeed if we wanted to compare national television commercials to something equivalent, it [would be] the biggest budget movie blockbusters. Second by second, it costs more to produce the average network ad than a movie like *Jurassic Park*.

The twin results of these developments are that advertising is everywhere and huge amounts of money and creativity are expended upon them.

If Marx were writing today I believe that not only would he be struck by the presence of even more objects, but also by the ever-present "discourse through and about objects" that permeates the spaces of our public and private domains. * * * This commercial discourse is the *ground* on which we live, the space in which we learn to think, the *lens* through which we come to understand the world that surrounds us. In seeking to understand where we are headed as a society, an adequate analysis of this commercial environment is essential.

Seeking this understanding will involve clarifying what we mean by the power and effectiveness of ads, and of being able to pose the right question. For too long debate has been concentrated around the issue of whether ad campaigns create demand for a particular product. If you are Pepsi Cola, or Ford, or Anheuser Busch, then it may be the right question for your interests. But, if you are interested in the social power of advertising—the impact of advertising on society—then that is the wrong question.

The right question would ask about the *cultural* role of advertising, not its marketing role. Culture is the place and space where a society tells stories about itself, where values are articulated and expressed, where notions of good and evil, of morality and immorality, are defined. In our culture it is the stories of advertising that dominate the spaces that mediate this function. If human beings are essentially a storytelling species, then to study advertising is to examine the central storytelling mechanism of our society. The correct question to ask from this perspective, is not whether particular ads sell the products they are hawking, but what are the consistent stories that advertising spins as a whole about what is important in the world, about how to behave, about what is good and bad. Indeed, it is to ask what values does advertising consistently push.

Happiness

Every society has to tell a story about happiness, about how individuals can satisfy themselves and feel both subjectively and objectively good. The cultural system of advertising gives a very specific answer to that question for our society. *The way to happiness and satisfaction is through the consumption of objects through the marketplace.* Commodities will make us happy. * * * In one very [important sense] that is the consistent and explicit message of every single message within the system of market communication.

Neither the fact of advertising's colonization of the horizons of imagination or the pushing of a story about the centrality of goods to human satisfaction should surprise us. The immense collection of goods have to be consumed (and even more goods produced) and the story that is used to ensure this function is to equate goods with happiness. Insiders to the system have recognized this obvious fact for many years. Retail analyst Victor Liebow said, just after the second world war:

Our enormously productive economy ... demands that we make consumption our way of life, that we convert the buying and the selling of goods into rituals, that we seek our spiritual satisfaction, our ego satisfaction in commodities ... We need things consumed, burned up, worn out, replaced, and discarded at an ever increasing rate. * * *

So economic growth is justified not simply on the basis that it will provide employment (after all a host of alternative non-productive activities could also provide that) but because it will give us access to more things that will make us happy. This rationale for the existing system of ever-increasing production is told by advertising in the most compelling form possible. In fact it is this story, that human satisfaction is intimately connected to the provisions of the market, to economic growth, that is the major motivating force for social change as we start the 21st century.

The social upheavals of eastern Europe were pushed by this vision. As Gloria Steinhem described the East German transformation: "First we have a revolution then we go shopping." * * * The attractions of this vision in the Third World are not difficult to discern. When your reality is empty stomachs and empty shelves, no wonder the marketplace appears as the panacea for your problems. When your reality is hunger and despair it should not be surprising that the seductive images of desire and abundance emanating from the advertising system should be so influential in thinking about social and economic policy. Indeed not only happiness but political freedom itself is made possible by access to the immense collection of commodities. These are very powerful stories that equate happiness and freedom with consumption—and advertising is the main propaganda arm of this view.

The question that we need to pose at this stage (that is almost never asked) is, "Is it true?" Does happiness come from material things? Do we get happier as a society as we get richer, as our standard of living increases, as we have more access to the immense collection of objects? Obviously these are complex issues, but the general answer to these questions is "no."

* * *

In a series of surveys conducted in the United States starting in 1945 (labeled "the happiness surveys") researchers sought to examine the link between material wealth and subjective happiness, and concluded that, when examined both cross-culturally as well as historically in one society, there is a very *weak* correlation. Why should this be so?

When we examine this process more closely the conclusions appear to be less surprising than our intuitive perspective might suggest. In another series of surveys (the "quality of life surveys") people were asked about the kinds of things that are important to them—about what would constitute a good quality of life. The findings of this line of research indicate that if the elements of satisfaction were [divided up] into social values (love, family, friends) and material values (economic security and success) the former outranks the latter in terms of importance. What people say they really want out of life is: autonomy and control of life; good self-esteem; warm family relationships; tension-free leisure time; close and intimate friends; as well as romance and love. This is not to say that material values are not important. They form a necessary component of a good quality of life. But above a certain level of poverty and comfort, material things stop giving us the kind of satisfaction that the magical world of advertising insists they can deliver.

These conclusion[s] point to one of the great ironies of the market system. The market is good at providing those things that can be bought and sold and it pushed us—via advertising—in that direction. But the real sources of happiness—social relationships—are outside the capability of the marketplace to provide. The marketplace cannot provide love, it cannot provide real friendships, it cannot provide sociability. It can provide other material things and services—but they are not what makes us happy.

The advertising industry has known this since at least the 1920s and in fact have stopped trying to sell us things based on their material qualities alone. If we examine the advertising of the end of the 19th and first years of the 20th century, we would see that advertising talked a lot about the properties of commodities—what they did, how well they did it, etc. But starting in the 1920s advertising shifts to talking about the relationship of objects to the social life of people. It starts to connect commodities (the things they have to sell) with the powerful images of a deeply desired social life that people say they want.

No wonder then that advertising is so attractive to us, so powerful, so seductive. What it offers us are images of the real sources of human happiness—family life, romance and love, sexuality and pleasure, friendship and sociability, leisure and relaxation, independence and control of life. That is why advertising is so powerful, that is what is real about it. The cruel illusion of advertising however is in the way that it links those qualities to a place that by definition cannot provide it—the market and the immense collection of commodities. The falsity of advertising is not in the appeals it makes (which are very real) but in the answers it provides. We want love and friendship and sexuality—and advertising points the way to it through objects.

To reject or criticize advertising as false and manipulative misses the point. Ad executive Jerry Goodis puts it this way: "Advertising doesn't mirror how people are acting but how they are dreaming." * * * It taps into our real emotions and repackages them back to us connected to the world of things. What advertising really reflects in that sense is the dreamlife of the culture. Even saying this however simplifies a deeper process because advertisers do more than mirror our dreamlife—they help to create it. They translate our desires (for love, for family, for friendship, for adventure, for sex) into our dreams. Advertising is like a fantasy factory, taking our desire for human social contact and reconceiving it, reconceptualizing it, connecting it with the world of commodities and then translating into a form that can be communicated.

The great irony is that as advertising does this it draws us further away from what really has the capacity to satisfy us (meaningful human contact and relationships) to what does not (material things). In that sense advertising reduces our capacity to become happy by pushing us, cajoling us, to carry on in the direction of things. If we really wanted to create a world that reflected our desires then the consumer culture would not be it. It would look very different—a society that stressed and built the institutions that would foster social relationships, rather than endless material accumulation.

Advertising's role in channeling us in these fruitless directions is profound. In one sense, its function is [analogous] to the drug pusher on the street corner. As we try and break our addiction to things it is there, constantly offering us another "hit." By persistently pushing the idea of the good life being connected to products, and by colonizing every nook and cranny of the culture where alternative ideas could be raised, advertising is an important part of the creation of what Tibor Scitovsky * * * calls "the joyless economy." The great political challenge that emerges from this analysis is how to connect our real desires to a truly human world, rather than the dead world of the "immense collection of commodities."

"THERE IS NO SUCH THING AS 'SOCIETY'"

A culture dominated by commercial messages that tells individuals that the way to happiness is through consuming objects bought in the marketplace gives a very particular answer to the question of "what is society?"— what is it that binds us together in some kind of collective way, what concerns or interests do we share? In fact, Margaret Thatcher, the former conservative British Prime Minister, gave the most succinct answer to this question from the viewpoint of the market. In perhaps her most (in)famous quote she announced: "There is no such thing as 'society'. There are just individuals and their families." According to Mrs. Thatcher, there is nothing solid we can call society—no group values, no collective interests— society is just a bunch of individuals acting on their own.

Indeed this is precisely how advertising talks to us. It addresses us not as members of society talking about collective issues, but as *individuals*. It talks about our individual needs and desires. It does not talk about those things we have to negotiate collectively, such as poverty, healthcare, housing and the homeless, the environment, etc.

The market appeals to the worst in us (greed, selfishness) and discourages what is the best about us (compassion, caring, and generosity).

Again this should not surprise us. In those societies where the marketplace dominates then what will be stressed is what the marketplace can deliver—and advertising is the main voice of the marketplace—so discussions of collective issues are pushed to the margins of the culture. They are not there in the center of the main system of communication that exists in the society. It is no accident that politically the market vision associated with neo-conservatives has come to dominate at exactly that time when advertising has been pushing the same values into every available space in the culture. The widespread disillusionment with "government" (and hence with thinking about issues in a collective manner) has found extremely fertile ground in the fields of commercial culture.

Unfortunately, we are now in a situation, both globally and domestically, where solutions to pressing nuclear and environmental problems will have to take a *collective* form. The marketplace cannot deal with the problems that face us at the turn of the millennium. For example it cannot deal with the threat of nuclear extermination that is still with us in the post-Cold War age. It cannot deal with global warming, the erosion of the ozone layer, or the depletion of our non-renewable resources. The effects of the way we do "business" are no longer localized, they are now global, and we will have to have international and collective ways of dealing with them. Individual action will not be enough. As the environmentalist slogan puts it "we all live downstream now."

Domestically, how do we find a way to tackle issues such as the nightmares of our inner cities, the ravages of poverty, the neglect of healthcare for the most vulnerable section of the population? How can we find a way to talk realistically and passionately of such problems within a culture where the central message is "don't worry, be happy." As Barbara Ehrenreich says:

> Television commercials offer solutions to hundreds of problems we didn't even know we had—from 'morning mouth' to shampoo build-up—but nowhere in the consumer culture do we find anyone offering us such mundane necessities as affordable health insurance, childcare, housing, or higher education. The flip side of the consumer spectacle ... is the starved and impoverished public sector. We have Teenage Mutant Ninja Turtles, but no way to feed and educate the one-fifth of American children who are growing up in poverty. We have dozens of varieties of breakfast cereal, and no help for the hungry. * * *

In that sense, advertising systematically relegates discussion of key societal issues to the peripheries of the culture and talks in powerful ways instead of individual desire, fantasy, pleasure and comfort.

Partly this is because of advertising's *monopolization* of cultural life. There is no space left for different types of discussion, no space at the center of the society where alternative values could be expressed. But it is also connected to the failure of those who care about collective issues to create alternative visions that can compete in any way with the commercial vision. The major alternatives offered to date have been a gray and dismal stateism. This occurred not only in the western societies but also in the former so called "socialist" societies of eastern Europe. These repressive societies never found a way to connect to people in any kind of pleasurable way, relegating issues of pleasure and individual expression to the non-essential and distracting aspects of social life. This indeed was the core of the failure of Communism in Eastern Europe. As Ehrenreich reminds us, not only was it unable to deliver the material goods, but it was unable to create a fully human "ideological retort to the powerful seductive messages of the capitalist consumer culture." * * * The problems are no less severe domestically:

> Everything enticing and appealing is located in the (thoroughly private) consumer spectacle. In contrast, the public sector looms as a realm devoid of erotic promise—the home of the IRS, the DMV, and other irritating, intrusive bureaucracies. Thus, though everyone wants national health insurance, and parental leave, few are moved to wage political struggles for them. 'Necessity' is not enough; we may have to find a way to glamorize the possibility of an activist public sector, and to glamorize the possibility of public activism. * * *

The imperative task for those who want to stress a different set of values is to make the struggle for social change fun and sexy. By that I do not mean that we have to use images of sexuality, but that we have to find a way of thinking about the struggle against poverty, against homelessness, for healthcare and child-care, to protect the environment, in terms of *pleasure and fun and happiness*.

To make this glamorization of collective issues possible will require that the present commercial monopoly of the channels of communication be broken in favor of a more democratic access where difficult discussion of important and relevant issues may be possible. While the situation may appear hopeless we should remind ourselves of how important capitalism deems its monopoly of the imagination to be. The campaigns of successive United States government against the Cuban revolution, and the obsession of our national security state with the Sandinista revolution in Nicaragua in the 1980s, demonstrates the importance that capitalism places on smashing the alternative model. Even as the United States government continues to support the most vicious, barbarous, brutal and murderous regimes around the world, it takes explicit aim at those governments that have tried to redistribute wealth to the most needy—who have been prioritized collective values over the values of selfishness and greed. The monopoly of the vision is vital and capitalism knows it.

The End of the World as We Know It

The consumer vision that is pushed by advertising and which is conquering the world is based fundamentally, as I argued before, on a notion of *economic growth*. Growth requires resources (both raw materials and energy) and there is a broad consensus among environmental scholars that the earth cannot sustain past levels of expansion based upon resource-intensive modes of economic activity, especially as more and more nations struggle to join the feeding trough.

The environmental crisis is complex and multilayered, cutting across both production and consumption issues. For instance just in terms of resource depletion, we know that we are rapidly exhausting what the earth can offer and that if the present growth and consumption trends continued unchecked, the limits to growth on the planet will be reached sometime within the next century. Industrial production uses up resources and energy at a rate that had never before even been imagined. Since 1950 the world's population has used up more of the earth's resources than all the generations that came before. * * * In 50 years we have matched the use of thousands of years. The west and especially Americans have used the most of these resources so we have a special responsibility for the approaching crisis. In another hundred years we will have exhausted the planet.

But even more than that even, we will have done irreparable damage to the environment on which we depend for everything. As environmental activist Barry Commoner says:

> The environment makes up a huge, enormously complex living machine that forms a thin dynamic layer on the earth's surface, and every human activity depends on the integrity and proper functioning of this machine.... This machine is our biological capital, the basic apparatus on which our total productivity depends. If we destroy it, our most advanced technology will become useless and any economic and political system that depends on it will flounder. The environmental crisis is a signal of the approaching catastrophe. * * *

The clearest indication of the way in which we produce is having an effect on the eco-sphere of the planet is the depletion of the ozone layer, which has dramatically increased the amount of ultraviolet radiation that is damaging or lethal to many life forms on the planet. In 1985 scientists discovered the existence of a huge hole in the ozone layer over the South Pole that is the size of the United States illustrating how the activities of humans are changing the very make-up of the earth. In his book *The End of Nature* Bill McKibben reminds us that "we have done this ourselves.... by driving our cars, building our factories, cutting down our forests, turning on air conditioners." * * * He writes that the history of the world is full of the most incredible events that changed the way we lived, but they are all dwarfed by what we have accomplished in the last 50 years.

> Man's efforts, even at their mightiest, were tiny compared with the size of the planet—the Roman Empire meant nothing to the Artic or the Amazon. But now, the way of life of one part of the world in one half-century is altering every inch and every hour of the globe.

The situation is so bad that the scientific community is desperately trying to get the attention of the rest of us to wake up to the danger. The Union of Concerned Scientists (representing 1700 of the world's leading scientists, including a majority of Nobel laureates in the sciences) recently issued this appeal:

> Human beings and the natural world are on a collision course. Human activities inflict harsh and irreversible damage on the environment and on critical resources. If not checked, many of our current practices put at serious risk the future that we wish for human society and the plant and animal kingdoms, and may so alter the living world that it will be unable to sustain life in the manner we know. Fundamental changes are urgent if we are to avoid the collision our present course will bring.

It is important to avoid the prediction of immediate catastrophe. We have already done a lot of damage but the real environmental crisis will not hit until some time in the middle of the next century. However to avoid that catastrophe we have to take action *now*. We have to put in place the steps that will save us in 70 years time.

The metaphor that best describes the task before us is of an oil tanker heading for a crash on the shore. Because of its momentum and size, to avoid crashing the oil tanker has to start turning well before it reaches the coast, anticipating [its] own momentum. If it starts turning too late it will smash into the coast. That is where the consumer society is right now. We have to make fundamental changes in the way we organize ourselves, in what we stress in our economy, if [we] want to avoid the catastrophe in 70 years time. We have to take action *now*.

In that sense the present generation has a unique responsibility in human history. It is literally up to us to save the world, to make the changes we need to make. If we do not, we will be in barbarism and savagery towards each other in 70 years time. We have to make short-term sacrifices. We have to give up [our non-essential appliances]. We especially have to rethink our relationship to the car. We have to make *real* changes—not just recycling but fundamental changes in how we live and produce. And we cannot do this individually, we have to do it collectively. We have to find the political will somehow to do this—and we may even be dead when its real effects will be felt. The vital issue is "how do we identify with that generation in the next century?" As the political philosopher Robert Heilbroner says:

> A crucial problem for the world of the future will be a concern for generations to come. Where will such concern arise? ... Contemporary industrial man, his appetite for the present whetted by the values of a high-consumption society and his attitude toward the future influenced by the prevailing canons of self-concern, has but a limited motivation to form such bonds. There are many who would sacrifice much for their children; fewer would do so for their grandchildren. * * *

Forming such bonds will be made even more difficult within our current context that stresses individual (not social) needs and the immediate situation (not the long-term). The advertising system will form *the ground* on which we think about the future of the human race, and there is nothing there that should give us any hope for the development of such a perspective. The time-frame of advertising is very short-term. It does not encourage us to think beyond the immediacy of present sensual experience. Indeed it may well be the case that as the advertising environment gets more and more crowded, with more and more of what advertisers label as "noise" threatening to drown out individual messages, the appeal will be made to levels of experience that cut through clutter, appealing immediately and deeply to very emotional states. Striking emotional imagery that grabs the "gut" instantly leaves no room for thinking about anything. Sexual imagery, especially in the age of AIDS where sex is being connected to death, will need to become even more powerful and immediate, to overcome any possible negative associations—indeed to remove us from the world of connotation and meaning construed *cognitively*. The value of a collective social future is one that does not, and will not, find expression within our commercially dominated culture. Indeed the prevailing values provide no incentive to develop bonds with future generations and there is a real sense of nihilism and despair about the future, and a closing of ranks against the outside.

IMAGINING A DIFFERENT FUTURE

Over a 100 years ago, Marx observed that there were two directions that capitalism could take: towards a democratic "socialism" or towards a brutal "barbarism". Both long-term and recent evidence would seem to indicate that the latter is where we are headed, unless alternative values quickly come to the fore.

Many people thought that the environmental crisis would be the linchpin for the lessening of international tensions as we recognized our interdependence and our collective security and future. But as the Persian Gulf War made clear, the New World Order will be based upon a struggle for scarce resources. Before the propaganda rationale shifted to the "struggle for freedom and democracy," George Bush reminded the American people that the troops were being dispatched to the Gulf to protect the resources that make possible "our way of life." An automobile culture and commodity-based culture such as ours is reliant upon sources of cheap oil. And if the cost of that is 100,000 dead Iraquis, well so be it. In such a scenario the peoples of the Third World will be seen as enemies who are making unreasonable claims on "our" resources. The future and the Third World can wait. Our commercial dominated cultural discourse reminds us powerfully everyday, we need *ours* and we need it *now*. In that sense the Gulf War is a preview of what is to come. As the world runs out of resources, the most powerful military sources will use that might to ensure access.

The destructive aspects of capitalism (its short-term nature, its denial of collective values, its stress on the material life), are starting to be recognized by some people who have made their fortunes through the market. The billionaire turned philanthropist George Soros * * * talks about what he calls "the capitalist threat"—and culturally speaking, advertising is the main voice of that threat. To the extent that it pushes us towards material things for satisfaction and away from the construction of social relationships, it pushes us down the road to increased economic production that is driving the coming environmental catastrophe. To the extent that it talks about our individual and private needs, it pushes discussion about collective issues to the margins. To the extent that it talks about the present only, it makes thinking about the future difficult. To the extent that it does all these things, then advertising becomes one of the major obstacles to our survival as a species.

Getting out of this situation, coming up with new ways to look at the world, will require enormous work, and one response may just be to enjoy the end of the world—one last great fling, the party to end all parties. The alternative response, to change the situation, to work for humane, collective long-term values, will require an effort of the most immense kind.

And there is evidence to be hopeful about the results of such an attempt. It is important to stress that creating and maintaining the present structure of the consumer culture takes enormous work and effort. The reason consumer ways of looking at the world predominate is because there are billions of dollars being spent on it every single day. The consumer culture is not simply erected and then forgotten. It has to be held in place by the activities of the ad industry, and increasingly the activities of the public relations industry. Capitalism has to try really hard to convince us about the value of the commercial vision. In some senses consumer capitalism is a house of cards, held together in a fragile way by immense effort, and it could just as soon melt away as hold together. It will depend if there are viable alternatives that will motivate people to believe in a different future, if there are other ideas as pleasurable, as powerful, as fun, as passionate with which people can identify.

I am reminded here of the work of Antonio Gramsci who coined the famous phrase, "pessimism of the intellect, optimism of the will." "Pessimism of the intellect" means recognizing the reality of our present circumstances, analyzing the vast forces arrayed against us, but insisting on the possibilities and the moral desirability of social change—that is "the optimism of the will," believing in human values that will be the inspiration for us to struggle for our survival

I do not want to be too Pollyannaish about the possibilities of social change. It is not just collective values that need to be struggled for, but collective values that recognize individual rights and individual creativity. There are many *repressive* collective movements already in existence—from our own home-grown Christian fundamentalists to the Islamic zealots of the Taliban in Afghanistan. The task is not easy. It means balancing and integrating different views of the world. As Ehrenreich writes:

> Can we envision a society which values—not "collectivity" with its dreary implications of conformity—but what I can only think to call *conviviality*, which could, potentially, be built right into the social infrastructure with opportunities, at all levels for rewarding, democratic participation? Can we envision a society that does not dismiss individualism, but truly values individual creative expression—including dissidence, debate, nonconformity, artistic experimentation, and in the larger sense, adventure . . . the project remains what it has always been: to replace the consumer culture with a genuinely *human* culture.
> * * *

The stakes are simply too high for us not to deal with the real and pressing problems that face [us as a] species—finding a progressive and humane collective solution to the global crisis and ensuring for our children and future generations a world fit for truly human habitation.

———

Uneasy Ryder! Jury Finds Winona Guilty in Shoplift Case

N.Y. DAILY NEWS, NOV. 6, 2002.

THE ASSOCIATED PRESS

BEVERLY HILLS, Calif.—Actress Winona Ryder was convicted Wednesday of stealing $5,500 worth of high-fashion merchandise from Saks Fifth Avenue last year.

The jury found the star of "Girl, Interrupted" guilty of felony grand theft and vandalism but cleared her of burglary.

She faces anywhere from probation to three years in prison. Sentencing is scheduled for Dec. 6.

Ryder showed no emotion as the verdict was announced. She kept her eyes on the jurors as they were asked whether the verdicts were accurate. They said yes.

She whispered to her attorney, Mark Geragos, took a drink of water and looked briefly toward her supporters in the audience.

The jury reached the verdict after 5 1/2 hours of deliberations over two days. The one count on which she was acquitted required a specific intent to go into the store to steal. District attorney's spokeswoman Sandi Gibbons said jurors often believe burglary is a crime of breaking and entering, but it does not require those circumstances.

"We're gratified with the verdicts," Gibbons added.

Ryder, a two-time Oscar nominee who marked her 31st birthday in the defendant's chair, was arrested Dec. 12 as she left the Beverly Hills store, her arms filled with packages.

Ryder did not testify during the two-week trial.

Prosecutors said Ryder came to Saks with larceny on her mind, bringing shopping bags, a garment bag and scissors to snip security tags off items.

"She came, she stole, she left. End of story," Deputy District Attorney Ann Rundle said. "Nowhere does it say people steal because they have to. People steal out of greed, envy, spite, because it's there or for the thrill."

Jurors were shown videotape of Ryder moving through the store laden with goods, and Saks security workers testified that after she was detained she apologetically told them a director had told her to shoplift to prepare for a movie role.

Her attorney denounced the security guards as liars even before the trial began.

At the start of her shopping trip, she paid more than $3,000 for a jacket and two blouses. The defense said Ryder believed the store would keep her account "open" while she shopped and would charge her later. But there was no evidence of an account.

In closing arguments Monday, Geragos suggested that the store, trying to avoid a lawsuit, conspired with employees to invent a story that would make Ryder appear guilty.

Geragos ridiculed the charge that Ryder vandalized merchandise by cutting holes in clothes when removing the security tags.

"This woman is known for her fashion sense," he said. "Was she going to start a new line of 'Winona wear' with holes in it?"

He carried a hair bow, which she allegedly had stolen, over to her, placed it on her head and said: "Can anyone see Ms. Ryder with this on top of her head? Does that make sense?"

Settlement talks between the defense and prosecution failed, but just before trial the district attorney's office agreed to dismiss a drug charge after a doctor said he had given her two pills found in her possession when she was arrested.

The 12–member jury included several people with Hollywood connections, including producer Peter Guber, who presided over Sony Entertainment Pictures when three successful Ryder films were made there.

Ryder has made some two-dozen films since 1986, including "Beetlejuice," "Heathers," "Mermaids," "Little Women," "The Age of Innocence," "Edward Scissorhands," "Bram Stoker's Dracula," "Reality Bites" and "Mr. Deeds."

She received her Academy Award nominations for "Little Women" (best actress) and for "The Age of Innocence" (supporting actress).

Ryder was raised by parents who were part of the counterculture revolution in the 1960s. Her godfather was LSD guru Timothy Leary.

In 1993, Ryder posted a $200,000 reward in the kidnap-murder case of a 12–year-old girl, Polly Klaas, in Petaluma, Calif., where the actress grew up. When Ryder was charged with shoplifting, Polly's father, Mark, came to legal proceedings to support her.

In recent years, Ryder has been featured frequently in fashion magazines. Her delicate beauty and waiflike persona were on display at the trial along with a wardrobe of appropriate trial clothes—dark sweaters and skirts, soft dresses and, on the climactic day of closing arguments, a cream silk suit with a pleated skirt and short jacket.

———

NOTES AND QUESTIONS

1. **Consumerism and capitalism.** Can capitalism survive without ever-expanding production and ever-expanding consumer demand? William Greider argues that a global crisis is on the way:

> The economic luxury hidden in the capitalist process is space—capitalism's ability to move on and re-create itself, abandoning the old for the new, creating and destroying production, while trailing a broad flume

of ruined natural assets in its wake. Because globalization has narrowed distances, the luxury has diminished visibly. It is now possible for people to glimpse what was always true: the wasteful nature of their own prosperity. So long as the consequences could be kept afar from the beneficiaries, no one had much incentive—neither producers nor consumers—to face the collective implications.

The brilliant possibility of "one world" is the emerging recognition that there is not going to be anyplace to hide. If Thailand becomes rich, where will it ship its toxic wastes? To Vietnam? To Africa? When every nation has industrialized, will they all dump their refuse in the ocean, as the so-called civilized societies now do? If the rain forests are shrinking, will someone invent machines to purify the air and generate rainfall? When the automobile conquers China, will the world be choking on the polluted atmosphere?

The economic dilemma embedded in these questions revolves around price: global producers are caught up in the desperate competition to reduce costs and prices to hold on to market share, yet the earth's imperative asks the economic system to achieve the opposite—to raise the price of goods so that consumers will begin paying the real production costs of their consumption. The marketplace (including most consumers) is naturally hostile to that imperative since it puts enterprises at immediate disadvantage unless all their competitors in the global system are required to accept the same pricing standards. There is at present no mechanism to achieve such harmony of purpose even if everyone agreed on its wisdom.

The social dilemma grows out of the same facts: If the collective interest requires a transformation of the industrial system's values, the poor will likely be injured more profoundly than the rich since they are the new entrants and least able to pay higher prices for consumption. The developing nations, after all, are emulating the rapacious practices they learned from the advanced economies and are understandably skeptical when high-minded reformers urge them not to repeat the same environmental mistakes—"mistakes" that have made Americans and Europeans quite wealthy. The environmental ethic proposes to alter the basic rules of capitalism at the very moment when some impoverished former colonies are at last enjoying the action.

WILLIAM GREIDER, ONE WORLD, READY OR NOT: THE MANIC LOGIC OF GLOBAL CAPITALISM 446–47 (1997).

2. Consumerism and fantasy. Can exhortations like Jhally's and Greider's stand up against the entwining of goods, the good life, fantasies, and dreams?

CHAPTER 3

DEFINING FAMILY

Introduction

The systematic application of economic theory to the complex zone of intimate, cultural, religious, and long term relationships that we call the family has had a checkered history. In macroeconomic theory, the economic implications of human fertility were explored by the eighteenth-century population economist, Thomas Malthus, who argued that the population would outstrip food supply, leading to rising poverty. This proposition was spelled out in his 1798 work, *An Essay on the Principle of Population,* in which he argued:

> Population, when unchecked, increases in a geometrical ratio. Subsistence only increases in an arithmetical ratio. A slight acquaintance with numbers will show the immensity of the first power compared to the second.

He also predicted that fertility would rise and fall in direct correlation with rising and falling incomes. When this early hypothesis was challenged by the dramatic decrease during the late-nineteenth and early-twentieth century in birthrates in industrialized countries with increasing incomes, Malthus's theories fell out of favor and economists of the era concluded that family decisionmaking was unsuited for useful macroeconomic theory.

In the 1960s, economist Gary Becker turned his attention to the microeconomic dynamics of family decision making. Relying on rational choice theory, once thought to be confined to the marketplace, Becker pursued an ambitious research agenda exploring the dynamics of economic activity within spheres of social interaction, in kinship relations, usually thought to be outside of the market domain. These included his seminal idea of measuring "human capital," investments in education, training, and other prerequisites to market competence.

In Becker's 1981 *Treatise on the Family,* work that is directly related to this chapter in which we consider the social norms and legal rules that define the family, he extended rational choice theory to family behavior, previously thought to be dominated by sentiment and irrationality. One famous application of this idea is the "Rotten Kid Theorem" (RKT). The core idea of the RKT is somewhat counterintuitive. The RKT posits that when parents invest altruistically in their children's early development and education, the children, no matter how selfish, will act to maximize the collective income of the entire family. Thus, the Rotten Kid Theorem introduces the concepts of interdependent preferences within a family system, and altruism. Both of these variables have a weak, if not nonexistent role in conventional microeconomic markets shaped by strangers. Needless to say, feminist economists have criticized both Becker's assumptions and conclusions.

In the cases that follow, we take up questions often put on the back burner of analysis in both family law and constitutional doctrine: What are the economic imperatives within living units that foster social cohesion for both individuals and society? Do legal rules incorporate social constructs about the "natural," pre-political norms of how a family should be configured? Does state intervention or refusal to intervene create economic incentives or disincentives for caring bonds that flow outside of conventional arrangements? Do legal rules privilege some family cultural practices over others, thus placing an economic burden on already disfavored groups? How are the tensions we referred to earlier between community, equality and individual rights resolved in these cases? Can Mrs. Moore's decision to provide housing for her grandchild be explained by Becker's rational choice theory?

A. NUCLEAR FAMILY VS. EXTENDED FAMILY

Moore v. City of East Cleveland, Ohio

Supreme Court of the United States, 431 U.S. 494 (1977).

■ MR. JUSTICE POWELL announced the judgment of the Court, and delivered an opinion in which MR. JUSTICE BRENNAN, MR. JUSTICE MARSHALL, and MR. JUSTICE BLACKMUN joined.

[In an earlier, related case, *Village of Belle Terre v. Boraas*, 416 U.S. 1 (1974), the Supreme Court rejected a challenge to the constitutionality of a zoning ordinance of the Village of Belle Terre, New York, restricting land use to one-family dwellings, and prohibiting occupancy of a dwelling by more than two unrelated persons as a "family," while permitting occupancy by any number of persons related by blood, adoption, or marriage. Justice Douglas, expressing the view of seven members of the court, held that the zoning ordinance (a) was not unconstitutional since it did not violate any right of interstate travel; (b) involved no procedural disparity inflicted on some but not on others; (c) involved no fundamental constitutional right, such as the rights of association or privacy; and (d) was reasonable and bore a rational relationship to a permissible state objective, thus not violating equal protection.

Justice Marshall's dissent argued that the challenged ordinance was unconstitutional. Marshall would have found that it unnecessarily burdened tenants' fundamental rights of association and privacy guaranteed by the First and Fourteenth Amendments. Marshall argued that since the village's legitimate interests in controlling land use and population density could be protected by limiting the number of occupants without discriminating on the basis of such occupants' constitutionally protected choices of life style.]

East Cleveland's housing ordinance, like many throughout the country, limits occupancy of a dwelling unit to members of a single family. § 1351.02.[1] But the ordinance contains an unusual and complicated definitional section that recognizes as a "family" only a few categories of related individuals. § 1341.08.[2] Because her family, living together in her home, fits none of those categories, appellant stands convicted of a criminal offense. The question in this case is whether the ordinance violates the Due Process Clause of the Fourteenth Amendment.

I

Appellant, Mrs. Inez Moore, lives in her East Cleveland home together with her son, Dale Moore, Sr., and her two grandsons, Dale, Jr., and John Moore, Jr. The two boys are first cousins rather than brothers; we are told that John came to live with his grandmother and with the elder and younger Dale Moore after his mother's death.

In early 1973, Mrs. Moore received a notice of violation from the city, stating that John was an "illegal occupant" and directing her to comply with the ordinance. When she failed to remove him from her home, the city filed a criminal charge. Mrs. Moore moved to dismiss, claiming that the ordinance was constitutionally invalid on its face. Her motion was overruled, and upon conviction she was sentenced to five days in jail and a $25 fine. The Ohio Court of Appeals affirmed after giving full consideration to her constitutional claims and the Ohio Supreme Court denied review. We noted probable jurisdiction of her appeal, 425 U.S. 949 (1976).

II

The city argues that our decision in *Village of Belle Terre v. Boraas, 416 U.S. 1 (1974),* requires us to sustain the ordinance attacked here. Belle

---

1. All citations by section number refer to the Housing Code of the city of East Cleveland, Ohio.

2. Section 1341.08 (1966) provides:

" 'Family' means a number of individuals related to the nominal head of the household or to the spouse of the nominal head of the household living as a single housekeeping unit in a single dwelling unit, but limited to the following:

"(a) Husband or wife of the nominal head of the household.

"(b) Unmarried children of the nominal head of the household or of the spouse of the nominal head of the household, provided, however, that such unmarried children have no children residing with them.

"(c) Father or mother of the nominal head of the household or of the spouse of the nominal head of the household.

"(d) Notwithstanding the provisions of subsection (b) hereof, a family may include not more than one dependent married or unmarried child of the nominal head of the household or of the spouse of the nominal head of the household and the spouse and dependent children of such dependent child. For the purpose of this subsection, a dependent person is one who has more than fifty percent of his total support furnished for him by the nominal head of the household and the spouse of the nominal head of the household.

"(e) A family may consist of one individual."

Terre, like East Cleveland, imposed limits on the types of groups that could occupy a single dwelling unit. Applying the constitutional standard announced in this Court's leading land-use case, *Euclid v. Ambler Realty Co.*, 272 U.S. 365 (1926),[6] we sustained the Belle Terre ordinance on the ground that it bore a rational relationship to permissible state objectives.

But one overriding factor sets this case apart from *Belle Terre*. The ordinance there affected only *unrelated* individuals. It expressly allowed all who were related by "blood, adoption, or marriage" to live together, and in sustaining the ordinance we were careful to note that it promoted "family needs" and "family values." 416 U.S., at 9. East Cleveland, in contrast, has chosen to regulate the occupancy of its housing by slicing deeply into the family itself. This is no mere incidental result of the ordinance. On its face it selects certain categories of relatives who may live together and declares that others may not. In particular, it makes a crime of a grandmother's choice to live with her grandson in circumstances like those presented here.

When a city undertakes such intrusive regulation of the family, neither *Belle Terre* nor *Euclid* governs; the usual judicial deference to the legislature is inappropriate. "This Court has long recognized that freedom of personal choice in matters of marriage and family life is one of the liberties protected by the Due Process Clause of the Fourteenth Amendment." * * * A host of cases * * * have consistently acknowledged a "private realm of family life which the state cannot enter." * * * Of course, the family is not beyond regulation. * * * But when the government intrudes on choices concerning family living arrangements, this Court must examine carefully the importance of the governmental interests advanced and the extent to which they are served by the challenged regulation. * * *

When thus examined, this ordinance cannot survive. The city seeks to justify it as a means of preventing overcrowding, minimizing traffic and parking congestion, and avoiding an undue financial burden on East Cleveland's school system. Although these are legitimate goals, the ordinance before us serves them marginally, at best.[7] For example, the ordinance permits any family consisting only of husband, wife, and unmarried children to live together, even if the family contains a half dozen licensed drivers, each with his or her own car. At the same time it forbids an adult brother and sister to share a household, even if both faithfully use public

---

6. *Euclid* held that land-use regulations violate the Due Process Clause if they are "clearly arbitrary and unreasonable, having no substantial relation to the public health, safety, morals, or general welfare." 272 U.S., at 395. See *Nectow v. Cambridge*, 277 U.S. 183, 188 (1928). Later cases have emphasized that the general welfare is not to be narrowly understood; it embraces a broad range of governmental purposes. See *Berman v. Parker*, 348 U.S. 26 (1954). But our cases have not departed from the requirement that the government's chosen means must rationally further some legitimate state purpose.

7. It is significant that East Cleveland has another ordinance specifically addressed to the problem of overcrowding. See *United States Dept. of Agriculture v. Moreno*, 413 U.S. 528, 536–537 (1973). Section 1351.03 limits population density directly, tying the maximum permissible occupancy of a dwelling to the habitable floor area. Even if John, Jr., and his father both remain in Mrs. Moore's household, the family stays well within these limits.

transportation. The ordinance would permit a grandmother to live with a single dependent son and children, even if his school-age children number a dozen, yet it forces Mrs. Moore to find another dwelling for her grandson John, simply because of the presence of his uncle and cousin in the same household. We need not labor the point. Section 1341.08 has but a tenuous relation to alleviation of the conditions mentioned by the city.

III

The city would distinguish the cases based on *Meyer* and *Pierce*. It points out that none of them "gives grandmothers any fundamental rights with respect to grandsons," * * * and suggests that any constitutional right to live together as a family extends only to the nuclear family— essentially a couple and their dependent children.

To be sure, these cases did not expressly consider the family relationship presented here. They were immediately concerned with freedom of choice with respect to childbearing, * * * or with the rights of parents to the custody and companionship of their own children, *Stanley v. Illinois, supra,* or with traditional parental authority in matters of child rearing and education. *Yoder, Ginsberg, Pierce, Meyer, supra.* But unless we close our eyes to the basic reasons why certain rights associated with the family have been accorded shelter under the Fourteenth Amendment's Due Process Clause, we cannot avoid applying the force and rationale of these precedents to the family choice involved in this case.

Understanding those reasons requires careful attention to this Court's function under the Due Process Clause. Mr. Justice Harlan described it eloquently:

> "Due process has not been reduced to any formula; its content cannot be determined by reference to any code. The best that can be said is that through the course of this Court's decisions it has represented the balance which our Nation, built upon postulates of respect for the liberty of the individual, has struck between that liberty and the demands of organized society. If the supplying of content to this Constitutional concept has of necessity been a rational process, it certainly has not been one where judges have felt free to roam where unguided speculation might take them. The balance of which I speak is the balance struck by this country, having regard to what history teaches are the traditions from which it developed as well as the traditions from which it broke. That tradition is a living thing. A decision of this Court which radically departs from it could not long survive, while a decision which builds on what has survived is likely to be sound. No formula could serve as a substitute, in this area, for judgment and restraint."

> "... [T]he full scope of the liberty guaranteed by the Due Process Clause cannot be found in or limited by the precise terms of the specific guarantees elsewhere provided in the Constitution. This 'liberty' is not a series of isolated points pricked out in terms

of the taking of property; the freedom of speech, press, and religion; the right to keep and bear arms; the freedom from unreasonable searches and seizures; and so on. It is a rational continuum which, broadly speaking, includes a freedom from all substantial arbitrary impositions and purposeless restraints, ... and which also recognizes, what a reasonable and sensitive judgment must, that certain interests require particularly careful scrutiny of the state needs asserted to justify their abridgment." *Poe v. Ullman,* supra at 542–543 (dissenting opinion).

Substantive due process has at times been a treacherous field for this Court. There *are* risks when the judicial branch gives enhanced protection to certain substantive liberties without the guidance of the more specific provisions of the Bill of Rights. As the history of the *Lochner* era demonstrates, there is reason for concern lest the only limits to such judicial intervention become the predilections of those who happen at the time to be Members of this Court. That history counsels caution and restraint. But it does not counsel abandonment, nor does it require what the city urges here: cutting off any protection of family rights at the first convenient, if arbitrary boundary—the boundary of the nuclear family.

Appropriate limits on substantive due process come not from drawing arbitrary lines but rather from careful "respect for the teachings of history [and] solid recognition of the basic values that underlie our society." * * * Our decisions establish that the Constitution protects the sanctity of the family precisely because the institution of the family is deeply rooted in this Nation's history and tradition.[12] It is through the family that we inculcate and pass down many of our most cherished values, moral and cultural.

---

12. In *Wisconsin v. Yoder,* 406 U.S. 205 (1972), the Court rested its holding in part on the constitutional right of parents to assume the primary role in decisions concerning the rearing of their children. That right is recognized because it reflects a "strong tradition" founded on "the history and culture of Western civilization," and because the parental role "is now established beyond debate as an enduring American tradition." *id.,* at 232. In *Ginsberg v. New York,* 390 U.S. 629 (1968), the Court spoke of the same right as "basic in the structure of our society." *Id.,* at 639. *Griswold v. Connecticut, supra* struck down Connecticut's anticontraception statute. Three concurring Justices, relying on both the Ninth and Fourteenth Amendments, emphasized that "the traditional relation of the family" is "a relation as old and as fundamental as our entire civilization." 381 U.S., at 496 (Goldberg, J., joined by Warren, C.J., and BRENNAN, J., concurring). Speaking of the same statute as that involved in *Griswold,* Mr. Justice Harlan wrote, dissenting in *Poe v. Ullman,* 367 U.S. 497, 551–552 (1961):

"[H]ere we have not an intrusion into the home so much as on the life which characteristically has its place in the home.... The home derives its pre-eminence as the seat of family life. And the integrity of that life is something so fundamental that it has been found to draw to its protection the principles of more than one explicitly granted Constitutional right."

Although he agrees that the Due Process Clause has substantive content, MR. JUSTICE WHITE in dissent expresses the fear that our recourse to history and tradition will "broaden enormously the horizons of the Clause." *Post,* at 549–550. To the contrary, an approach grounded in history imposes limits on the judiciary that are more meaningful than any based on the abstract formula taken from *Palko v. Connecticut,* 302 U.S. 319 (1937), and apparently suggested as an alternative. Cf. *Duncan v. Louisiana, supra* at 149–150, n.14 (rejecting the *Palko* formula as the basis for deciding what procedural protections are required of a State, in favor of a

Ours is by no means a tradition limited to respect for the bonds uniting the members of the nuclear family. The tradition of uncles, aunts, cousins, and especially grandparents sharing a household along with parents and children has roots equally venerable and equally deserving of constitutional recognition.[14] Over the years millions of our citizens have grown up in just such an environment, and most, surely, have profited from it. Even if conditions of modern society have brought about a decline in extended family households, they have not erased the accumulated wisdom of civilization, gained over the centuries and honored throughout our history, that supports a larger conception of the family. Out of choice, necessity, or a sense of family responsibility, it has been common for close relatives to draw together and participate in the duties and the satisfactions of a common home. Decisions concerning child rearing, which *Yoder, Meyer, Pierce* and other cases have recognized as entitled to constitutional protection, long have been shared with grandparents or other relatives who occupy the same household—indeed who may take on major responsibility for the rearing of the children.[15] Especially in times of adversity, such as the death of a spouse or economic need, the broader family has tended to come together for mutual sustenance and to maintain or rebuild a secure home life. This is apparently what happened here.[16]

Whether or not such a household is established because of personal tragedy, the choice of relatives in this degree of kinship to live together may not lightly be denied by the State. *Pierce* struck down an Oregon law requiring all children to attend the State's public schools, holding that the Constitution "excludes any general power of the State to standardize its children by forcing them to accept instruction from public teachers only." 268 U.S., at 535. By the same token the Constitution prevents East Cleveland from standardizing its children—and its adults—by forcing all to live in certain narrowly defined family patterns.

Reversed.

historical approach based on the Anglo–American legal tradition). Indeed, the passage cited in MR. JUSTICE WHITE'S dissent as "most accurately reflect[ing] the thrust of prior decisions" on substantive due process, *post*, at 545, expressly points to history and tradition as the source for "supplying ... content to this Constitutional concept." *Poe* v. *Ullman, supra* at 542 (Harlan, J., dissenting).

14. See generally B. Yorburg, The Changing Family (1973); Bronfenbrenner, The Calamitous Decline of the American Family, Washington Post, Jan. 2, 1977, p. C1. Recent census reports bear out the importance of family patterns other than the prototypical nuclear family. In 1970, 26.5% of all families contained one or more members over 18 years of age, other than the head of household and spouse. U.S. Department of Com-

merce, 1970 Census of Population, vol. 1, pt. 1, Table 208. In 1960 the comparable figure was 26.1%. U.S. Department of Commerce, 1960 Census of Population, vol. 1, pt. 1, Table 187. Earlier data are not available.

15. Cf. *Prince v. Massachusetts*, 321 U.S. 158 (1944), which spoke broadly of family authority as against the State, in a case where the child was being reared by her aunt, not her natural parents.

16. We are told that the mother of John Moore, Jr., died when he was less than one year old. He, like uncounted others who have suffered a similar tragedy, then came to live with the grandmother to provide the infant with a substitute for his mother's care and to establish a more normal home environment. Brief for Appellant 25.

■ MR. JUSTICE BRENNAN, with whom MR. JUSTICE MARSHALL joins, concurring.

I join the plurality's opinion. I agree that the Constitution is not powerless to prevent East Cleveland from prosecuting as a criminal and jailing[1] a 63-year-old grandmother for refusing to expel from her home her now 10-year-old grandson who has lived with her and been brought up by her since his mother's death when he was less than a year old. I do not question that a municipality may constitutionally zone to alleviate noise and traffic congestion and to prevent overcrowded and unsafe living conditions, in short to enact reasonable land-use restrictions in furtherance of the legitimate objectives East Cleveland claims for its ordinance. But the zoning power is not a license for local communities to enact senseless and arbitrary restrictions which cut deeply into private areas of protected family life. East Cleveland may not constitutionally define "family" as essentially confined to parents and the parents' own children.[3] The plurality's opinion conclusively demonstrates that classifying family patterns in this eccentric way is not a rational means of achieving the ends East Cleveland claims for its ordinance, and further that the ordinance unconstitutionally abridges the "freedom of personal choice in matters of . . . family life [that] is one of the liberties protected by the Due Process Clause of the Fourteenth Amendment." *Cleveland Board of Education v. LaFleur*, 414 U.S. 632, 639–640 (1974). I write only to underscore the cultural myopia of the arbitrary boundary drawn by the East Cleveland ordinance in the light of the tradition of the American home that has been a feature of our society since our beginning as a Nation—the "tradition" in the plurality's words, "of uncles, aunts, cousins, and especially grandparents sharing a household along with parents and children. . . ." *Ante,* at 504. The line drawn by this ordinance displays a depressing insensitivity toward the economic and emotional needs of a very large part of our society.

In today's America, the "nuclear family" is the pattern so often found in much of white suburbia. J. Vander Zanden, Sociology: A Systematic Approach 322 (3d ed. 1975). The Constitution cannot be interpreted, however, to tolerate the imposition by government upon the rest of us of white suburbia's preference in patterns of family living. The "extended family" that provided generations of early Americans with social services and economic and emotional support in times of hardship, and was the

1. This is a criminal prosecution which resulted in the grandmother's conviction and sentence to prison and a fine. Section 1345.99 permits imprisonment of up to six months, and a fine of up to $1,000, for violation of any provision of the Housing Code. Each day such violation continues may, by the terms of this section, constitute a separate offense.

3. The East Cleveland ordinance defines "family" to include, in addition to the spouse of the "nominal head of the household," the couple's childless unmarried children, but only one dependent child (married or unmarried) having dependent children, and one parent of the nominal head of the household or of his or her spouse. Thus an "extended family" is authorized in only the most limited sense, and "family" is essentially confined to parents and their own children. Appellant grandmother was charged with violating the ordinance because John, Jr., lived with her at the same time her other grandson, Dale, Jr., was also living in the home; the latter is classified as an "unlicensed roomer" authorized by the ordinance to live in the house.

beachhead for successive waves of immigrants who populated our cities, remains not merely still a pervasive living pattern, but under the goad of brutal economic necessity, a prominent pattern—virtually a means of survival—for large numbers of the poor and deprived minorities of our society. For them compelled pooling of scant resources requires compelled sharing of a household.[5]

The "extended" form is especially familiar among black families.[6] We may suppose that this reflects the truism that black citizens, like generations of white immigrants before them, have been victims of economic and other disadvantages that would worsen if they were compelled to abandon extended, for nuclear, living patterns.[7] Even in husband and wife house-

5. See, *e.g.*, H. Gans, The Urban Villagers 45–73, 245–249 (1962).

"Perhaps the most important—or at least the most visible—difference between the classes is one of family structure. *The working class subculture* is distinguished by the dominant role of the family circle. . . .

"The specific characteristics of the family circle may differ widely—from the collateral peer group form of the West Enders, to the hierarchical type of the Irish, or to the classical three-generation extended family. . . . What matters most—and distinguishes this subculture from others—is that there be a family circle which is wider than the nuclear family, and that all of the opportunities, temptations, and pressures of the larger society be evaluated in terms of how they affect the ongoing way of life that has been built around this circle." *Id.*, at 244–245 (emphasis in original).

6. Yorburg, *supra* n. 4, at 108. "Within the black lower-class it has been quite common for several generations, or parts of the kin, to live together under one roof. Often a maternal grandmother is the acknowledged head of this type of household which has given rise to the term 'matrifocal' to describe lower-class black family patterns." See J. Scanzoni, The Black Family in Modern Society 134 (1971); see also Anderson, The Pains and Pleasures of Old Black Folks, Ebony 123, 128–130 (Mar. 1973). See generally E. Frazier, The Negro Family in the United States (1939); Lewis, The Changing Negro Family, in E. Ginzberg, ed., The Nation's Children 108 (1960).

The extended family often plays an important role in the rearing of young black children whose parents must work. Many such children frequently "spend all of their growing-up years in the care of extended kin. . . . Often children are 'given' to their grandparents, who rear them to adulthood. . . . Many children normally grow up in a three-generation household and they absorb the influences of grandmother and grandfather as well as mother and father." J. Ladner, Tomorrow's Tomorrow: The Black Woman 60 (1972).

7. The extended family has many strengths not shared by the nuclear family.

"The case histories behind mounting rates of delinquency, addiction, crime, neurotic disabilities, mental illness, and senility in societies in which autonomous nuclear families prevail suggest that frequent failure to develop enduring family ties is a serious inadequacy for both individuals and societies." D. Blitsten, The World of the Family 256 (1963).

Extended families provide services and emotional support not always found in the nuclear family:

"The troubles of the nuclear family in industrial societies, generally, and in American society, particularly, stem largely from the inability of this type of family structure to provide certain of the services performed in the past by the extended family. Adequate health, education, and welfare provision, particularly for the two nonproductive generations in modern societies, the young and the old, is increasingly an insurmountable problem for the nuclear family. The unrelieved and sometimes unbearably intense parent-child relationship, where childrearing is not shared at least in part by others, and the loneliness of nuclear family units, increasingly turned in on themselves in contracted and relatively isolated settings, is another major problem." Yorburg, *supra* n. 4, at 194.

holds, 13% of black families compared with 3% of white families include relatives under 18 years old, in addition to the couple's own children.[8] In black households whose head is an elderly woman, as in this case, the contrast is even more striking: 48% of such black households, compared with 10% of counterpart white households, include related minor children not offspring of the head of the household.[9]

I do not wish to be understood as implying that East Cleveland's enforcement of its ordinance is motivated by a racially discriminatory purpose: The record of this case would not support that implication. But the prominence of other than nuclear families among ethnic and racial minority groups, including our black citizens, surely demonstrates that the "extended family" pattern remains a vital tenet of our society. It suffices that in prohibiting this pattern of family living as a means of achieving its objectives, appellee city has chosen a device that deeply intrudes into family associational rights that historically have been central, and today remain central, to a large proportion of our population.

Moreover, to sanction the drawing of the family line at the arbitrary boundary chosen by East Cleveland would surely conflict with prior decisions that protected "extended" family relationships. For the "private realm of family life which the state cannot enter," recognized as protected in *Prince v. Massachusetts*, 321 U.S. 158, 166 (1944), was the relationship of aunt and niece. And in *Pierce v. Society of Sisters*, 268 U.S. 510, 534–535 (1925), the protection held to have been unconstitutionally abridged was "the liberty of parents and *guardians* to direct the upbringing and education of children under their control" (emphasis added). See also *Wisconsin v. Yoder*, 406 U.S. 205, 232–233 (1972). Indeed, *Village of Belle Terre v. Boraas*, 416 U.S. 1 (1974), the case primarily relied upon by the appellee, actually supports the Court's decision. The Belle Terre ordinance barred only unrelated individuals from constituting a family in a single-family zone. The village took special care in its brief to emphasize that its ordinance did not in any manner inhibit the choice of *related* individuals to constitute a family, whether in the "nuclear" or "extended" form. This was because the village perceived that choice as one it was constitutionally powerless to inhibit. Its brief stated: "Whether it be the extended family of a more leisurely age or the nuclear family of today the role of the family in raising and training successive generations of the species makes it more important, we dare say, than any other social or legal institution.... *If any freedom not specifically mentioned in the Bill of Rights enjoys a 'preferred position' in the law it is most certainly the family.*" (Emphasis supplied.) * * * The cited decisions recognized, as the plurality recognizes today, that the choice of the "extended family" pattern is within the "freedom of

---

8. R. Hill, The Strengths of Black Families 5 (1972).

9. *Id.,* at 5–6. It is estimated that at least 26% of black children live in other than husband-wife families, "including foster parents, the presence of other male or female relatives (grandfather or grandmother, older brother or sister, uncle or aunt), male or female nonrelatives, [or with] only *one* adult (usually mother) present...." Scanzoni, *supra* n. 6, at 44.

personal choice in matters of ... family life [that] is one of the liberties protected by the Due Process Clause of the Fourteenth Amendment." 414 U.S., at 639–640.

* * *

■ MR. JUSTICE STEVENS, concurring in the judgment.

In my judgment the critical question presented by this case is whether East Cleveland's housing ordinance is a permissible restriction on appellant's right to use her own property as she sees fit.

Long before the original States adopted the Constitution, the common law protected an owner's right to decide how best to use his own property. This basic right has always been limited by the law of nuisance which proscribes uses that impair the enjoyment of other property in the vicinity. But the question whether an individual owner's use could be further limited by a municipality's comprehensive zoning plan was not finally decided until this century.

The holding in *Euclid v. Ambler Realty Co.*, 272 U.S. 365, that a city could use its police power, not just to abate a specific use of property which proved offensive, but also to create and implement a comprehensive plan for the use of land in the community, vastly diminished the rights of individual property owners. It did not, however, totally extinguish those rights. On the contrary, that case expressly recognized that the broad zoning power must be exercised within constitutional limits.

In his opinion for the Court, Mr. Justice Sutherland fused the two express constitutional restrictions on any state interference with private property—that property shall not be taken without due process nor for a public purpose without just compensation—into a single standard: "[B]efore [a zoning] ordinance can be declared unconstitutional, [it must be shown to be] clearly arbitrary and unreasonable, *having no substantial relation to the public health, safety, morals, or general welfare.*" *Id.*, at 395 (emphasis added). This principle was applied in *Nectow v. Cambridge*, 277 U.S. 183; on the basis of a specific finding made by the state trial court that "the health, safety, convenience and general welfare of the inhabitants of the part of the city affected" would not be promoted by prohibiting the landowner's contemplated use, this Court held that the zoning ordinance as applied was unconstitutional. * * *

Litigation involving single-family zoning ordinances is common. Although there appear to be almost endless differences in the language used in these ordinances, they contain three principal types of restrictions. First, they define the kind of structure that may be erected on vacant land.[4]

---

4. As this Court recognized in *Euclid,* even residential apartments can have a negative impact on an area of single-family homes.

"[O]ften the apartment house is a mere parasite, constructed in order to take advantage of the open spaces and attractive surroundings created by [a single-family dwelling area].... [T]he coming of one apartment house is followed by others, interfering by their height and bulk with the free circulation of air and monopolizing the rays of the

Second, they require that a single-family home be occupied only by a "single housekeeping unit." Third, they often require that the housekeeping unit be made up of persons related by blood, adoption, or marriage, with certain limited exceptions.

Although the legitimacy of the first two types of restrictions is well settled, attempts to limit occupancy to related persons have not been successful. The state courts have recognized a valid community interest in preserving the stable character of residential neighborhoods which justifies a prohibition against transient occupancy. Nevertheless, in well-reasoned opinions, the courts of [several states] have permitted unrelated persons to occupy single-family residences notwithstanding an ordinance prohibiting, either expressly or implicitly, such occupancy.

These cases delineate the extent to which the state courts have allowed zoning ordinances to interfere with the right of a property owner to determine the internal composition of his household. The intrusion on that basic property right has not previously gone beyond the point where the ordinance defines a family to include only persons related by blood, marriage, or adoption. Indeed, as the cases in the margin demonstrate, state courts have not always allowed the intrusion to penetrate that far. The state decisions have upheld zoning ordinances which regulated the identity, as opposed to the number, of persons who may compose a household only to the extent that the ordinances require such households to remain nontransient, single-housekeeping units.

There appears to be no precedent for an ordinance which excludes any of an owner's relatives from the group of persons who may occupy his residence on a permanent basis. Nor does there appear to be any justification for such a restriction on an owner's use of his property. The city has failed totally to explain the need for a rule which would allow a homeowner to have two grandchildren live with her if they are brothers, but not if they are cousins. Since this ordinance has not been shown to have any "substantial relation to the public health, safety, morals, or general welfare" of the city of East Cleveland, and since it cuts so deeply into a fundamental right normally associated with the ownership of residential property—that of an owner to decide who may reside on his or her property—it must fall under the limited standard of review of zoning decisions which this Court preserved in *Euclid* and *Nectow*. Under that standard, East Cleveland's unprecedented ordinance constitutes a taking of property without due process and without just compensation.

sun which otherwise would fall upon the smaller homes, and bringing, as their necessary accompaniments, the distributing noises incident to increased traffic and business, and the occupation, by means of moving and parked automobiles, of larger portions of the streets, thus detracting from their safety and depriving children of the privilege of quiet and open spaces for play, enjoyed by those in more favored localities,—until, finally, the residential character of the neighborhood and its desirability as a place of detached residences are utterly destroyed. Under these circumstances, apartment houses, which in a different environment would be not only entirely unobjectionable but highly desirable, come very near to being nuisances." 272 U.S., at 394–395.

For these reasons, I concur in the Court's judgment.

■ Mr. Chief Justice Burger, with whom Mr. Justice Stewart and Mr. Justice White join, dissenting.

* * *

"... Courts are forced to add more clerks, more administrative personnel, to move cases faster and faster. They are losing ... time for reflection, time for the deliberate maturation of principles." [Department of Justice Committee on Revision of The Federal Judicial System, Report on the Needs of the Federal Courts 3–4 (1977).]

■ Mr. Justice Stewart, with whom Mr. Justice Rehnquist joins, dissenting.

* * *

The *Belle Terre* decision * * * disposes of the appellant's contentions to the extent they focus not on her blood relationships with her sons and grandsons but on more general notions about the "privacy of the home." Her suggestion that every person has a constitutional right permanently to share his residence with whomever he pleases, and that such choices are "beyond the province of legitimate governmental intrusion," amounts to the same argument that was made and found unpersuasive in *Belle Terre*.

To be sure, the ordinance involved in *Belle Terre* did not prevent blood relatives from occupying the same dwelling, and the Court's decision in that case does not, therefore, foreclose the appellant's arguments based specifically on the ties of kinship present in this case. Nonetheless, I would hold, for the reasons that follow, that the existence of those ties does not elevate either the appellant's claim of associational freedom or her claim of privacy to a level invoking constitutional protection.

* * *

The "association" in this case is not for any purpose relating to the promotion of speech, assembly, the press, or religion. And wherever the outer boundaries of constitutional protection of freedom of association may eventually turn out to be, they surely do not extend to those who assert no interest other than the gratification, convenience, and *economy* [emphasis added] of sharing the same residence.

* * *

The appellant also challenges the single-family occupancy ordinance on equal protection grounds. Her claim is that the city has drawn an arbitrary and irrational distinction between groups of people who may live together as a "family" and those who may not. While acknowledging the city's right to preclude more than one family from occupying a single-dwelling unit, the appellant argues that the purposes of the single-family occupancy law would be equally served by an ordinance that did not prevent her from sharing her residence with her two sons and their sons.

This argument misconceives the nature of the constitutional inquiry. In a case such as this one, where the challenged ordinance intrudes upon no substantively protected constitutional right, it is not the Court's business to decide whether its application in a particular case seems inequitable, or even absurd. The question is not whether some other ordinance, drafted more broadly, might have served the city's ends as well or almost as well. The task, rather, is to determine if East Cleveland's ordinance violates the Equal Protection Clause of the United States Constitution. And in performing that task, it must be borne in mind that "[w]e deal with economic and social legislation where legislatures have historically drawn lines which we respect against the charge of violation of the Equal Protection Clause if the law be ' "reasonable, not arbitrary" ' (quoting *Royster Guano Co. v. Virginia*, 253 U.S. 412, 415) and bears 'a rational relationship to a [permissible] state objective.' *Reed v. Reed, 404 U.S. 71, 76.*" *Village of Belle Terre v. Boraas*, 416 U.S., at 8. "[E]very line drawn by a legislature leaves some out that might well have been included. That exercise of discretion, however, is a legislative, not a judicial, function." *Ibid.* (footnote omitted).[8]

Viewed in the light of these principles, I do not think East Cleveland's definition of "family" offends the Constitution. The city has undisputed power to ordain single-family residential occupancy. *Village of Belle Terre v. Boraas, supra; Euclid v. Ambler Realty Co.*, 272 U.S. 365. And that power plainly carries with it the power to say what a "family" is. * * *

* * *

For these reasons, I think the Ohio courts did not err in rejecting the appellant's constitutional claims. Accordingly, I respectfully dissent.

■ Mr. Justice White, dissenting.

The Fourteenth Amendment forbids any State to "deprive any person of life, liberty, or property, without due process of law," or to "deny to any person within its jurisdiction the equal protection of the laws." Both provisions are invoked in this case in an attempt to invalidate a city zoning ordinance.

I

The emphasis of the Due Process Clause is on "process." * * * As Mr. Justice Harlan once observed, it has been "ably and insistently argued in response to what were felt to be abuses by this Court of its reviewing power," that the Due Process Clause should be limited "to a guarantee of procedural fairness." *Poe v. Ullman*, 367 U.S. 497, 540 (1961) (dissenting

---

8. The observation of Mr. Justice Holmes quoted in the *Belle Terre* opinion, 416 U.S., at 8 n. 5, bears repeating here.

"When a legal distinction is determined, as no one doubts that it may be, between night and day, childhood and maturity, or any other extremes, a point has to be fixed or a line has to be drawn, or gradually picked out by successive decisions, to mark where the change takes place. Looked at by itself without regard to the necessity behind it the line or point seems arbitrary. It might as well or nearly as well be a little more to one side or the other. But when it is seen that a line or point there must be, and that there is no mathematical or logical way of fixing it precisely, the decision of the legislature must be accepted unless we can say that it is very wide of any reasonable mark." *Louisville Gas Co. v. Coleman*, 277 U.S. 32, 41 (dissenting opinion).

opinion). These arguments had seemed "persuasive" to Justices Brandeis and Holmes, *Whitney v. California*, 274 U.S. 357, 373 (1927), but they recognized that the Due Process Clause, by virtue of case-to-case "judicial inclusion and exclusion," *Davidson v. New Orleans*, 96 U.S. 97, 104 (1878), had been construed to proscribe matters of substance, as well as inadequate procedures, and to protect from invasion by the States "all fundamental rights comprised within the term liberty." *Whitney v. California*, supra at 373.

* * *

Although the Court regularly proceeds on the assumption that the Due Process Clause has more than a procedural dimension, we must always bear in mind that the substantive content of the Clause is suggested neither by its language nor by preconstitutional history; that content is nothing more than the accumulated product of judicial interpretation of the Fifth and Fourteenth Amendments. This is not to suggest, at this point, that any of these cases should be overruled, or that the process by which they were decided was illegitimate or even unacceptable, but only to underline Mr. Justice Black's constant reminder to his colleagues that the Court has no license to invalidate legislation which it thinks merely arbitrary or unreasonable. And no one was more sensitive than Mr. Justice Harlan to any suggestion that his approach to the Due Process Clause would lead to judges "roaming at large in the constitutional field." *Griswold v. Connecticut, supra* at 502. No one proceeded with more caution than he did when the validity of state or federal legislation was challenged in the name of the Due Process Clause.

* * *

* * * Here the head of the household may house himself or herself and spouse, their parents, and any number of their unmarried children. A fourth generation may be represented by only one set of grandchildren and then only if born to a dependent child. The ordinance challenged by appellant prevents her from living with both sets of grandchildren only in East Cleveland, an area with a radius of three miles and a population of 40,000. Brief for Appellee 16 n. 1. The ordinance thus denies appellant the opportunity to live with all her grandchildren in this particular suburb; she is free to do so in other parts of the Cleveland metropolitan area. If there is power to maintain the character of a single-family neighborhood, as there surely is, some limit must be placed on the reach of the "family." Had it been our task to legislate, we might have approached the problem in a different manner than did the drafters of this ordinance; but I have no trouble in concluding that the normal goals of zoning regulation are present here and that the ordinance serves these goals by limiting, in identifiable circumstances, the number of people who can occupy a single household. The ordinance does not violate the Due Process Clause.

IV

For very similar reasons, the equal protection claim must fail, since it is not to be judged by the strict scrutiny standard employed when a fundamental interest or suspect classification is involved[.] * * * Rather, it is the generally applicable standard of *McGowan v. Maryland*, 366 U.S. 420, 425 (1961):

> "The constitutional safeguard [of the Equal Protection Clause] is offended only if the classification rests on grounds wholly irrelevant to the achievement of the State's objective. State legislatures are presumed to have acted within their constitutional power despite the fact that, in practice, their laws result in some inequality. A statutory discrimination will not be set aside if any state of facts reasonably may be conceived to justify it."

* * * Under this standard, it is not fatal if the purpose of the law is not articulated on its face, and there need be only a rational relation to the ascertained purpose.

On this basis, as already indicated, I have no trouble in discerning a rational justification for an ordinance that permits the head of a household to house one, but not two, dependent sons and their children.

Respectfully, therefore, I dissent and would affirm the judgment.

————

NOTES AND QUESTIONS

1. Teachings of history and sanctity of family. What limits can one expect to impose on the murky concepts of substantive due process as applied to government regulation of family life? Justice Powell, writing for the Court, thought that the "appropriate limits on due process come not from drawing arbitrary lines but rather from careful respect for the 'teachings of history [and] solid recognition of the basic values that under-lie our society.'" *Moore*, supra at ___. *See also* Snyder v. Massachusetts, 291 U.S. 97, 105 (1934); Griswold v. Connecticut, 381 U.S. 479, 501 (1965) (Harlan, J., concurring). Powell goes on to say that the Court's "decisions establish that the Constitution protects the sanctity of the family precisely because the institution of the family is deeply rooted in this Nation's history and tradition." *Moore, supra* at 503.

Is there a cultural consensus about what the "teachings of history" are? Even if we could agree on the definition of the composition of the family, there remain important differences about the norms that should apply within the family system. Disputes about "family values" are a staple of divisive political campaigns today. Families certainly make intensely different decisions as to methods of discipline, breast feeding, intra-family privacy, individual space expectations, the sharing of bathrooms, young children's nakedness in the home, the appropriate age to begin dating, and the willingness of family to discuss biology and emotional components of human sexuality, just to name a few. *See* Gill Jagger & Caroline Wright, CHANGING FAMILY VALUES (eds., 1999).

Has Justice Powell assumed the existence of a stable, widely shared set of values about family in our very diverse society?

Is the model of deference to history likely to produce stagnant or dynamic approaches to constitutional interpretation of state restrictions on family preferences? What should be the role of the legal system in these intra-family debates? What is the role of economic analysis in Justice Powell's approach? What would Fran Olson's arguments about how the law should view the concepts of non-intervention, privacy, and the private/public distinction suggest about Powell's basis of reasoning?

2. Extended family vs. nuclear family. Justices Brennan and Marshall's concurrence focuses on the central role that the extended family has played for immigrant groups throughout American history, as well as African Americans today. The predominance of non-nuclear family structures in America, especially among ethnic and racial minority groups, suggests that the "extended family" pattern remains a vital tenet of our society. *See* Andrew Billingsley, Climbing Jacob's Ladder: The Enduring Legacy of African-American Families (1992); Ronald Angel & Marta Tienda, *Determinants of Extended Household Structure: Cultural Pattern or Economic Need?*, 87 Am. J. Soc. 1360 (1982). Under the reasoning in Brennan's concurrence, should associational forms which have been historically utilized by such populations in this country receive special protection?

If a minority group traditionally practiced polygamy in order to aid in pooling resources and to avoid the social problems associated with destitute widows and single motherhood, would Brennan's reasoning protect that group's definition of family? What about in the opposite case of polyandry? What about membership in a potentially criminal organization? *See* Linda Kelly, *Family Planning, American Style*, 52 Ala. L. Rev. 943 (2001); Alison Harvison Young, *Reconceiving the Family: Challenging the Paradigm of the Exclusive Family*, 6 Am. U. J. Gender & L. 505 (1998).

3. Drawing the line. What sociological theories are and could be employed by the Court to decide where to draw the line defining what is and is not a family? Are courts competent to make use of the often conflicting theories of social science research? Should people not related by blood have similar associational rights as the traditional family? *See* Smith v. Organization of Foster Families, 431 U.S. 816 (1977). What about unmarried parents? *See* Stanley v. Illinois, 405 U.S. 645 (1972). What about people engaging in casual sex? *See* FW/PBS, Inc. v. City of Dallas, 493 U.S. 215 (1990). How would economic theory shape this debate?

4. Strict scrutiny, rational basis, and *Moore v. East Cleveland*. At the time of *Moore v. East Cleveland*, Fourteenth Amendment Due Process analysis required that if a regulation excluded a suspect class of people, then that regulation must satisfy a "strict scrutiny" test. If the regulation did not discriminate against a suspect class, however, it needed only to pass a much more forgiving "rational basis" standard of review. Though the plurality opinion in *Moore* did not state that the ordinance in question should be subjected to strict scrutiny review, it does seem to be advocating more than a rational basis standard. Does *Moore* create another standard of review between strict scrutiny and rational relationship? If so, does the standard extend past the regulation of families? *See* Robert J. Hopperton,

The Presumption of Validity in American Land-Use Law: A Substitute for Analysis, A Source of Significant Confusion, 23 B.C. ENVTL. AFF. L. REV. 301 (1996).

5. Race, economics, and family definitions. Brennan and Marshall decry the "cultural myopia" of the plurality. In today's America, the "nuclear family" is the pattern so often found in much of white suburbia. The Constitution cannot be interpreted, however, to tolerate the imposition by government of white suburbia's preference in patterns of living. *See also* PEGGY COOPER DAVIS, NEGLECTED STORIES: THE CONSTITUTION AND FAMILY VALUES (1997); DOROTHY ROBERTS, KILLING THE BLACK BODIES (1998).

On the relevance of racial variation in patterns of family formation, the dissent of Justices Stewart and Rehnquist takes the opposite position than the plurality and concurring opinions:

> The opinion of MR. JUSTICE POWELL and MR. JUSTICE BRENNAN'S concurring opinion both emphasize the traditional importance of the extended family in American life. But I fail to understand why it follows that the residents of East Cleveland are constitutionally prevented from following what MR. JUSTICE BRENNAN calls the "pattern" of "white suburbia," even though that choice may reflect "cultural myopia." In point of fact, East Cleveland is a predominantly Negro community, with a Negro City Manager and City Commission.

Moore, supra at 537, n.7.

6. Additional reading. For an annotated catalog of cases and articles relating to the definition of "family" in zoning regulations and restrictive covenants, see James L. Rigelhaupt, Jr., *Annotation What Constitutes a "Family" Within Meaning of Zoning Regulation or Restrictive Covenant*, 71 A.L.R.3D 693 (2004). For a description of how housing codes can be used as tools for discrimination, see Ellen J. Pader, *CLUSTER VI: Class, Economics, and Social Rights: Space of Hate: Ethnicity, Architecture and Housing Discrimination*, 54 RUTGERS L. REV. 881 (2002). For an interesting proposal for defining family, see Angie Smolka, Note, *That's the Ticket: A New Way of Defining Family*, 10 CORNELL J. L. & PUB. POL'Y 629 (2001).

B.   UNMARRIED HETEROSEXUAL COUPLES

Marvin v. Marvin

557 P.2d 106 (Cal. 1976).

■ JUSTICE TOBRINER delivered the opinion of the court.

During the past 15 years, there has been a substantial increase in the number of couples living together without marrying. Such nonmarital relationships lead to legal controversy when one partner dies or the couple separates. Courts of Appeal, faced with the task of determining property rights in such cases, have arrived at conflicting positions: two cases * * * have held that the Family Law Act (Civ. Code, § 4000 et seq.) requires division of the property according to community property principles, and one decision * * * has rejected that holding. We take this opportunity to resolve that controversy and to declare the principles which should govern distribution of property acquired in a nonmarital relationship.

We conclude: (1) The provisions of the Family Law Act do not govern the distribution of property acquired during a nonmarital relationship; such a relationship remains subject solely to judicial decision. (2) The courts should enforce express contracts between nonmarital partners except to the extent that the contract is explicitly founded on the consideration of meretricious sexual services. (3) In the absence of an express contract, the courts should inquire into the conduct of the parties to determine whether that conduct demonstrates an implied contract, agreement of partnership or joint venture, or some other tacit understanding between the parties. The courts may also employ the doctrine of quantum meruit, or equitable remedies such as constructive or resulting trusts, when warranted by the facts of the case.

In the instant case plaintiff and defendant lived together for seven years without marrying; all property acquired during this period was taken in defendant's name. When plaintiff sued to enforce a contract under which she was entitled to half the property and to support payments, the trial court granted judgment on the pleadings for defendant, thus leaving him with all property accumulated by the couple during their relationship. Since the trial court denied plaintiff a trial on the merits of her claim, its decision conflicts with the principles stated above, and must be reversed.

1.   *THE FACTUAL SETTING OF THIS APPEAL.*

Since the trial court rendered judgment for defendant on the pleadings, we must accept the allegations of plaintiff's complaint as true, determining whether such allegations state, or can be amended to state, a cause of action. * * *

Plaintiff avers that in October of 1964 she and defendant "entered into an oral agreement" that while "the parties lived together they would combine their efforts and earnings and would share equally any and all property accumulated as a result of their efforts whether individual or combined." Furthermore, they agreed to "hold themselves out to the general public as husband and wife" and that "plaintiff would further render her services as a companion, homemaker, housekeeper and cook to . . . defendant."

Shortly thereafter plaintiff agreed to "give up her lucrative career as an entertainer [and] singer" in order to "devote her full time to defendant . . . as a companion, homemaker, housekeeper and cook;" in return defendant agreed to "provide for all of plaintiff's financial support and needs for the rest of her life."

Plaintiff alleges that she lived with defendant from October of 1964 through May of 1970 and fulfilled her obligations under the agreement.

During this period the parties as a result of their efforts and earnings acquired in defendant's name substantial real and personal property, including motion picture rights worth over $1 million. In May of 1970, however, defendant compelled plaintiff to leave his household. He continued to support plaintiff until November of 1971, but thereafter refused to provide further support.

On the basis of these allegations plaintiff asserts two causes of action. The first, for declaratory relief, asks the court to determine her contract and property rights; the second seeks to impose a constructive trust upon one half of the property acquired during the course of the relationship.

    * * *

2.   *PLAINTIFF'S COMPLAINT STATES A CAUSE OF ACTION FOR BREACH OF AN EXPRESS CONTRACT.*

* * * [W]e established the principle that nonmarital partners may lawfully contract concerning the ownership of property acquired during the relationship. * * * "If a man and woman [who are not married] live together as husband and wife under an agreement to pool their earnings and share equally in their joint accumulations, equity will protect the interests of each in such property."

In the case before us plaintiff, basing her cause of action in contract upon these precedents, maintains that the trial court erred in denying her a trial on the merits of her contention. Although that court did not specify the ground for its conclusion that plaintiff's contractual allegations stated no cause of action, defendant offers some four theories to sustain the ruling; we proceed to examine them.

Defendant first and principally relies on the contention that the alleged contract is so closely related to the supposed "immoral" character of the relationship between plaintiff and himself that the enforcement of the contract would violate public policy. He points to cases asserting that a contract between nonmarital partners is unenforceable if it is "involved in" an illicit relationship. * * * A review of the numerous California decisions concerning contracts between nonmarital partners, however, reveals that the courts have not employed such broad and uncertain standards to strike down contracts. The decisions instead disclose a narrower and more precise standard: a contract between nonmarital partners is unenforceable only *to the extent* that it *explicitly* rests upon the immoral and illicit consideration of meretricious sexual services.

In the first case to address this issue, *Trutalli v. Meraviglia* * * * the parties had lived together without marriage for 11 years and had raised two children. The man sued to quiet title to land he had purchased in his own name during this relationship; the woman defended by asserting an agreement to pool earnings and hold all property jointly. Rejecting the assertion of the illegality of the agreement, the court stated that "The fact that the parties to this action at the time they agreed to invest their earnings in property to be held jointly between them were living together in an unlawful relation, did not disqualify them from entering into a lawful agreement with each other, so long as such immoral relation was not made *a consideration* of their agreement." (Emphasis added.) * * *

In *Bridges v. Bridges, supra,* * * * both parties were in the process of obtaining divorces from their erstwhile respective spouses. The two parties agreed to live together, to share equally in property acquired, and to marry when their divorces became final. The man worked as a salesman and used his savings to purchase properties. The woman kept house, cared for seven children, three from each former marriage and one from the nonmarital relationship, and helped construct improvements on the properties. When they separated, without marrying, the court awarded the woman one-half the value of the property. Rejecting the man's contention that the contract was illegal, the court stated that: "Nowhere is it expressly testified to by anyone that there was anything in the agreement for the pooling of assets and the sharing of accumulations that contemplated meretricious relations as any part of the consideration or as any object of the agreement." * * *

* * * Numerous other cases have upheld enforcement of agreements between nonmarital partners in factual settings essentially indistinguishable from the present case.

* * * Although the past decisions hover over the issue in the somewhat wispy form of the figures of a Chagall painting, we can abstract from those decisions a clear and simple rule. The fact that a man and woman live together without marriage, and engage in a sexual relationship, does not in itself invalidate agreements between them relating to their earnings, property, or expenses. Neither is such an agreement invalid merely because the parties may have contemplated the creation or continuation of a nonmarital relationship when they entered into it. Agreements between nonmarital partners fail only to the extent that they rest upon a consideration of meretricious sexual services. Thus the rule asserted by defendant, that a contract fails if it is "involved in" or made "in contemplation" of a nonmarital relationship, cannot be reconciled with the decisions.

The three cases cited by defendant which have *declined* to enforce contracts between nonmarital partners involved consideration that *was* expressly founded upon an illicit sexual services. In *Hill v. Estate of Westbrook,* * * * the woman promised to keep house for the man, to live with him as man and wife, and to bear his children; the man promised to provide for her in his will, but died without doing so. Reversing a judgment for the woman based on the reasonable value of her services, the Court of Appeal stated that "the action is predicated upon a claim which seeks, among other things, the reasonable value of living with decedent in meretricious relationship and bearing him two children. . . . The law does not award compensation for living with a man as a concubine and bearing him children. . . . As the judgment is at least in part, for the value of the claimed services for which recovery cannot be had, it must be reversed." * * * Upon retrial, the trial court found that it could not sever the contract and place an independent value upon the legitimate services performed by claimant. We therefore affirmed a judgment for the estate. * * *

In the only other cited decision refusing to enforce a contract, * * * the contract "was based on the consideration that the parties live together as husband and wife." * * * Viewing the contract as calling for adultery, the court held it illegal.[6]

The decisions in the *Hill* and *Updeck* cases thus demonstrate that a contract between nonmarital partners, even if expressly made in contemplation of a common living arrangement, is invalid only if sexual acts form an inseparable part of the consideration for the agreement. In sum, a court will not enforce a contract for the pooling of property and earnings if it is explicitly and inseparably based upon services as a paramour. The Court of Appeal opinion in *Hill*, however, indicates that even if sexual services are part of the contractual consideration, any *severable* portion of the contract supported by independent consideration will still be enforced.

The principle that a contract between nonmarital partners will be enforced unless expressly and inseparably based upon an illicit consideration of sexual services not only represents the distillation of the decisional law, but also offers a far more precise and workable standard than that advocated by defendant.

* * * Similarly, in the present case a standard which inquires whether an agreement is "involved" in or "contemplates" a nonmarital relationship is vague and unworkable. Virtually all agreements between nonmarital partners can be said to be "involved" in some sense in the fact of their mutual sexual relationship, or to "contemplate" the existence of that relationship. Thus defendant's proposed standards, if taken literally, might invalidate all agreements between nonmarital partners, a result no one favors. Moreover, those standards offer no basis to distinguish between valid and invalid agreements. By looking not to such uncertain tests, but only to the consideration underlying the agreement, we provide the parties and the courts with a practical guide to determine when an agreement between nonmarital partners should be enforced.

* * * In summary, we base our opinion on the principle that adults who voluntarily live together and engage in sexual relations are nonetheless as competent as any other persons to contract respecting their earnings and property rights. Of course, they cannot lawfully contract to pay for the performance of sexual services, for such a contract is, in essence, an

---

6. Although not cited by defendant, the only California precedent which supports his position is *Heaps v. Toy* * * * In that case the woman promised to leave her job, to refrain from marriage, to be a companion to the man, and to make a permanent home for him; he agreed to support the woman and her child for life. The Court of Appeal held the agreement invalid as a contract in restraint of marriage (Civ. Code, § 1676) and, alternatively, as "contrary to good morals" (Civ. Code, § 1607). The opinion does not state that sexual relations formed any part of the consideration for the contract, nor explain how—unless the contract called for sexual relations—the woman's employment as a companion and housekeeper could be contrary to good morals.

The alternative holding in *Heaps v. Toy, supra,* finding the contract in that case contrary to good morals, is inconsistent with the numerous California decisions upholding contracts between nonmarital partners when such contracts are not founded upon an illicit consideration, and is therefore disapproved.

agreement for prostitution and unlawful for that reason. But they may agree to pool their earnings and to hold all property acquired during the relationship in accord with the law governing community property; conversely they may agree that each partner's earnings and the property acquired from those earnings remains the separate property of the earning partner.[10] So long as the agreement does not rest upon illicit meretricious consideration, the parties may order their economic affairs as they choose, and no policy precludes the courts from enforcing such agreements.

In the present instance, plaintiff alleges that the parties agreed to pool their earnings, that they contracted to share equally in all property acquired, and that defendant agreed to support plaintiff. The terms of the contract as alleged do not rest upon any unlawful consideration. We therefore conclude that the complaint furnishes a suitable basis upon which the trial court can render declaratory relief. * * * The trial court consequently erred in granting defendant's motion for judgment on the pleadings.

3.   * * *

As we have noted, both causes of action in plaintiff's complaint allege an express contract; neither assert any basis for relief independent from the contract. In *In re Marriage of Cary*, * * * however, the Court of Appeal held that, in view of the policy of the Family Law Act, property accumulated by nonmarital partners in an actual family relationship should be divided equally. Upon examining the *Cary* opinion, the parties to the present case realized that plaintiff's alleged relationship with defendant might arguably support a cause of action independent of any express contract between the parties. The parties have therefore briefed and discussed the issue of the property rights of a nonmarital partner in the absence of an express contract. Although our conclusion that plaintiff's complaint states a cause of action based on an express contract alone compels us to reverse the judgment for defendant, resolution of the *Cary* issue will serve both to guide the parties upon retrial and to resolve a conflict presently manifest in published Court of Appeal decisions.

Both plaintiff and defendant stand in broad agreement that the law should be fashioned to carry out the reasonable expectations of the parties. Plaintiff, however, presents the following contentions: that the decisions prior to *Cary* rest upon implicit and erroneous notions of punishing a party for his or her guilt in entering into a nonmarital relationship, that such decisions result in an inequitable distribution of property accumulated during the relationship, and that *Cary* correctly held that the enactment of the Family Law Act in 1970 overturned those prior decisions. Defendant in response maintains that the prior decisions merely applied common law principles of contract and property to persons who have deliberately elected

---

10. A great variety of other arrangements are possible. The parties might keep their earnings and property separate, but agree to compensate one party for services which benefit the other. They may choose to pool only part of their earnings and property, to form a partnership or joint venture, or to hold property acquired as joint tenants or tenants in common, or agree to any other such arrangement. * * *

to remain outside the bounds of the community property system.[11] *Cary*, defendant contends, erred in holding that the Family Law Act vitiated the force of the prior precedents.

* * * This failure of the courts to recognize an action by a nonmarital partner based upon implied contract, or to grant an equitable remedy, contrasts with the judicial treatment of the putative spouse. Prior to the enactment of the Family Law Act, no statute granted rights to a putative spouse.[13] The courts accordingly fashioned a variety of remedies by judicial decision. Some cases permitted the putative spouse to recover half the property on a theory that the conduct of the parties implied an agreement of partnership or joint venture. * * * Others permitted the spouse to recover the reasonable value of rendered services, less the value of support received. * * * Finally, decisions affirmed the power of a court to employ equitable principles to achieve a fair division of property acquired during putative marriage. * * *

Thus in summary, the cases prior to *Cary* exhibited a schizophrenic inconsistency. By enforcing an express contract between nonmarital partners unless it rested upon an unlawful consideration, the courts applied a common law principle as to contracts. Yet the courts disregarded the common law principle that holds that implied contracts can arise from the conduct of the parties.[16] Refusing to enforce such contracts, the courts spoke of leaving the parties "in the position in which they had placed themselves" * * * just as if they were guilty parties *in pari delicto*.

11. We note that a deliberate decision to avoid the strictures of the community property system is not the only reason that couples live together without marriage. Some couples may wish to avoid the permanent commitment that marriage implies, yet be willing to share equally any property acquired during the relationship; others may fear the loss of pension, welfare, or tax benefits resulting from marriage * * * Others may engage in the relationship as a possible prelude to marriage. In lower socio-economic groups the difficulty and expense of dissolving a former marriage often leads couples to choose a nonmarital relationship; many unmarried couples may also incorrectly believe that the doctrine of common law marriage prevails in California, and thus that they are in fact married. Consequently we conclude that the mere fact that a couple have not participated in a valid marriage ceremony cannot serve as a basis for a court's inference that the couple intend to keep their earnings and property separate and independent; the parties' intention can only be ascertained by a more searching inquiry into the nature of their relationship.

13. The Family Law Act, in Civil Code section 4452, classifies property acquired during a putative marriage as " 'quasi-marital property,' " and requires that such property be divided upon dissolution of the marriage in accord with Civil Code section 4800.

16. "Contracts may be express or implied. These terms however do not denote different kinds of contracts, but have reference to the evidence by which the agreement between the parties is shown. If the agreement is shown by the direct words of the parties, spoken or written, the contract is said to be an express one. But if such agreement can only be shown by the acts and conduct of the parties, interpreted in the light of the subject matter and of the surrounding circumstances, then the contract is an implied one." * * * Thus, as Justice Schauer observed in *Desny v. Wilder* * * * in a sense all contracts made in fact, as distinguished from quasi-contractual obligations, are express contracts, differing only in the manner in which the assent of the parties is expressed and proved. * * *

Justice Curtis noted this inconsistency in his dissenting opinion in *Vallera*, pointing out that "if an express agreement will be enforced, there is no legal or just reason why an implied agreement to share the property cannot be enforced." * * * And in *Keene v. Keene* * * * Justice Peters observed that if the man and woman "were not illegally living together . . . it would be a plain business relationship and a contract would be implied."

* * *

Still another inconsistency in the prior cases arises from their treatment of property accumulated through joint effort. To the extent that a partner had contributed *funds* or *property*, the cases held that the partner obtains a proportionate share in the acquisition, despite the lack of legal standing of the relationship. * * * Yet courts have refused to recognize just such an interest based upon the contribution of *services*. As Justice Curtis points out "Unless it can be argued that a woman's services as cook, housekeeper, and homemaker are valueless, it would seem logical that if, when she contributes money to the purchase of property, her interest will be protected, then when she contributes her services in the home, her interest in property accumulated should be protected." * * *

Thus as of 1973, the time of the filing of *In re Marriage of Cary* * * * the cases apparently held that a nonmarital partner who rendered services in the absence of express contract could assert no right to property acquired during the relationship. The facts of *Cary* demonstrated the unfairness of that rule.

Janet and Paul Cary had lived together, unmarried, for more than eight years. They held themselves out to friends and family as husband and wife, reared four children, purchased a home and other property, obtained credit, filed joint income tax returns, and otherwise conducted themselves as though they were married. Paul worked outside the home, and Janet generally cared for the house and children.

In 1971 Paul petitioned for "nullity of the marriage." Following a hearing on that petition, the trial court awarded Janet half the property acquired during the relationship, although all such property was traceable to Paul's earnings. The Court of Appeal affirmed the award.

Reviewing the prior decisions which had denied relief to the homemaking partner, the Court of Appeal reasoned that those decisions rested upon a policy of punishing persons guilty of cohabitation without marriage. The Family Law Act, the court observed, aimed to eliminate fault or guilt as a basis for dividing marital property. But once fault or guilt is excluded, the court reasoned, nothing distinguishes the property rights of a nonmarital "spouse" from those of a putative spouse. Since the latter is entitled to half the " 'quasi marital property' " (Civ. Code, § 4452), the Court of Appeal concluded that, giving effect to the policy of the Family Law Act, a nonmarital cohabitator should also be entitled to half the property accumulated during an "actual family relationship." * * *

* * *

* * * The argument that granting remedies to the nonmarital partners would discourage marriage must fail; as *Cary* pointed out, "with equal or greater force the point might be made that the pre–1970 rule was calculated to cause the income-producing partner to avoid marriage and thus retain the benefit of all of his or her accumulated earnings." * * * Although we recognize the well-established public policy to foster and promote the institution of marriage * * * perpetuation of judicial rules which result in an inequitable distribution of property accumulated during a nonmarital relationship is neither a just nor an effective way of carrying out that policy.

In summary, we believe that the prevalence of nonmarital relationships in modern society and the social acceptance of them, marks this as a time when our courts should by no means apply the doctrine of the unlawfulness of the so-called meretricious relationship to the instant case. As we have explained, the nonenforceability of agreements expressly providing for meretricious conduct rested upon the fact that such conduct, as the word suggests, pertained to and encompassed prostitution. To equate the nonmarital relationship of today to such a subject matter is to do violence to an accepted and wholly different practice.

We are aware that many young couples live together without the solemnization of marriage, in order to make sure that they can successfully later undertake marriage. This trial period, preliminary to marriage, serves as some assurance that the marriage will not subsequently end in dissolution to the harm of both parties. We are aware, as we have stated, of the pervasiveness of nonmarital relationships in other situations.

The mores of the society have indeed changed so radically in regard to cohabitation that we cannot impose a standard based on alleged moral considerations that have apparently been so widely abandoned by so many. Lest we be misunderstood, however, we take this occasion to point out that the structure of society itself largely depends upon the institution of marriage, and nothing we have said in this opinion should be taken to derogate from that institution. The joining of the man and woman in marriage is at once the most socially productive and individually fulfilling relationship that one can enjoy in the course of a lifetime.

We conclude that the judicial barriers that may stand in the way of a policy based upon the fulfillment of the reasonable expectations of the parties to a nonmarital relationship should be removed. As we have explained, the courts now hold that express agreements will be enforced unless they rest on an unlawful meretricious consideration. We add that in the absence of an express agreement, the courts may look to a variety of other remedies in order to protect the parties' lawful expectations.[24]

---

24. We do not seek to resurrect the doctrine of common law marriage, which was abolished in California by statute in 1895. * * * Thus we do not hold that plaintiff and defendant were "married," nor do we extend to plaintiff the rights which the Family Law Act grants valid or putative spouses; we hold only that she has the same rights to enforce contracts and to assert her equitable interest

The courts may inquire into the conduct of the parties to determine whether that conduct demonstrates an implied contract or implied agreement of partnership or joint venture * * * or some other tacit understanding between the parties. The courts may, when appropriate, employ principles of constructive trust * * * or resulting trust * * *. Finally, a nonmarital partner may recover in quantum meruit for the reasonable value of household services rendered less the reasonable value of support received if he can show that he rendered services with the expectation of monetary reward. * * *[25]

Since we have determined that plaintiff's complaint states a cause of action for breach of an express contract, and, as we have explained, can be amended to state a cause of action independent of allegations of express contract,[26] we must conclude that the trial court erred in granting defendant a judgment on the pleadings.

The judgment is reversed and the cause remanded for further proceedings consistent with the views expressed herein.[27]

◼ Mr. Justice Clark, concurring in part and dissenting in part.

The majority opinion properly permit recovery on the basis of either express or implied in fact agreement between the parties. These being the issues presented, their resolution requires reversal of the judgment. Here, the opinion should stop.

This court should not attempt to determine all anticipated rights, duties and remedies within every meretricious relationship—particularly in vague terms. Rather, these complex issues should be determined as each arises in a concrete case.

* * *

The general sweep of the majority opinion raises but fails to answer several questions. First, because the Legislature specifically excluded some parties to a meretricious relationship from the equal division rule of Civil Code section 4452, is this court now free to create an equal division rule? Second, upon termination of the relationship, is it equitable to impose the economic obligations of lawful spouses on meretricious parties when the latter may have rejected matrimony to avoid such obligations? Third, does not application of equitable principles—necessitating examination of the conduct of the parties—violate the spirit of the Family Law Act of 1969, designed to eliminate the bitterness and acrimony resulting from the

in property acquired through her effort as does any other unmarried person.

25. Our opinion does not preclude the evolution of additional equitable remedies to protect the expectations of the parties to a nonmarital relationship in cases in which existing remedies prove inadequate; the suitability of such remedies may be determined in later cases in light of the factual setting in which they arise.

26. We do not pass upon the question whether, in the absence of an express or implied contractual obligation, a party to a nonmarital relationship is entitled to support payments from the other party after the relationship terminates.

27. We wish to commend the parties and amici for the exceptional quality of the briefs and argument in this case.

former fault system in divorce? Fourth, will not application of equitable principles reimpose upon trial courts the unmanageable burden of arbitrating domestic disputes? Fifth, will not a quantum meruit system of compensation for services—discounted by benefits received—place meretricious spouses in a better position than lawful spouses? Sixth, if a quantum meruit system is to be allowed, does fairness not require inclusion of all services and all benefits regardless of how difficult the evaluation?

When the parties to a meretricious relationship show by express or implied in fact agreement they intend to create mutual obligations, the courts should enforce the agreement. However, in the absence of agreement, we should stop and consider the ramifications before creating economic obligations which may violate legislative intent, contravene the intention of the parties, and surely generate undue burdens on our trial courts.

By judicial overreach, the majority perform a nunc pro tunc marriage, dissolve it, and distribute its property on terms never contemplated by the parties, case law or the Legislature.

––––––

NOTES AND QUESTIONS

1. The choice to marry. Rational Choice Theory relies on the assumption that humans have goals and sets of hierarchically ordered preferences or "utilities." In making a choice between one behavior and another, humans will weigh the utility of the behavior against its costs, including the utility of alternate behaviors and the cost of selecting this behavior over another in terms of utility foregone. In an efficient transaction between two parties, the goal is presumably to increase utility for at least one party without sacrificing utility for either party. *See* MICHAEL ALLINGHAM, RATIONAL CHOICE (1999). How do the arguments of Rational Choice Theory apply to *Marvin v. Marvin*? What are the utilities and costs of opting not to marry and instead choosing to contract as the plaintiff in *Marvin* claims? Has utility been maximized in this transaction, given the foregone utility of the alternate behavior of marriage? *See* Margaret F. Brinig, *Unmarried Partners and the Legacy of* Marvin v. Marvin: *The Influence of* Marvin v. Marvin *on Housework during Marriage,* 76 NOTRE DAME L. REV. 1311 (2001). Which sex is most likely to receive the primary benefit of the express and implied contract rules? *See* Debra S. Betteridge, Note, *Inequality in Marital Liabilities: The Need for Equal Protection When Modifying the Necessaries Doctrine,* 17 U. MICH. J.L. REFORM 43 (1983). Are important differences in the transaction costs likely to arise from the enforcement of the express and implied contract theories?

2. History and tradition? Is the court ignoring legal, cultural, and religious arguments in deciding that parties who are eligible to marry but who choose not to should not be given the economic benefits of marriage? Does the court disregard the "history and tradition" of rewarding compliance with the social and legal norms of marriage? *See* Carol Weisbrod,

Gender-Based Analyses of World Religions and the Law: Universals and Particulars: A Comment on Women's Human Rights and Religious Marriage Contracts, 9 S. CAL. REV. L. & WOMEN'S STUD. 77 (1999). What is the role of cultural change and what framework of analysis did this court rely upon to assess the relevance of these changes to its decision in this case? How do the rationales employed by the court in *Marvin* relate to those employed in *Moore v. East Cleveland?*

3. Bargaining. How would you expect the pre-cohabitation bargaining dynamic to be affected by this decision? How do differences in gender correspond to differences in bargaining power? *See* Elizabeth G. Anderson, *Women and Contracts: No New Deal,* 88 MICH L. REV. 1792 (1990). Is there any way for a couple to cohabit without automatically pooling their assets, short of writing an extremely unromantic contract explicitly separating their assets? *See* Jennifer K. Robbennolt & Monica Kirkpatrick Johnson, *Therapeutic Jurisprudence: Legal Planning for Unmarried Committed Partners: Empirical Lessons for a Preventive and Therapeutic Approach,* 41 ARIZ. L. REV. 417 (1999). How does the rule announced in *Marvin* affect the cultural and economic status of the parties? Furthermore, does this rule provide disincentives for parties who have a strong competitive position in the marriage market because of beauty, wealth, or social status to ever marry? *See* Amy L. Wax, *Bargaining in the Shadow of the Market: Is There a Future for Egalitarian Marriage?,* 84 VA. L. REV. 509 (1998).

4. Meretricious consideration and prostitution. The holding of *Marvin* is limited to the extent that it does not mandate the enforcement of contracts which are made expressly in consideration of sexual services. Given that the courts, as a rule, do not examine the adequacy of consideration, does the court's decision in *Marvin* open the door to legalized prostitution? If a prostitute were to say to a client, "Those pants don't look good on you, let's get them off," would that "fashion advice" qualify as separate consideration and thus render a contract between prostitute and client enforceable under *Marvin?* What is the implication of the court referring to the relationship of two unwed cohabitants as "meretricious," defined as "of, relating to, or befitting a prostitute; having the character of a prostitute" or "showily or superficially attractive but having in reality no value or integrity." OXFORD ENGLISH DICTIONARY (drafted. 2001), *available at* www.oed.com.

5. Common law marriage. From 1920 to 1930, Charlotte Fixel-Erlanger and Abraham Lincoln Erlanger lived together. Charlotte abandoned her career as an actress to support Abraham and take care of his house. Charlotte and Abraham never married and, when Abraham died in 1930, Charlotte was left out of his will. However, in 1932, after a three-month trial, Charlotte was given rights in Abraham's estate as his common-law wife. *In re Estate of Erlanger,* 145 Misc. 1, 259 N.Y.S. 610 (N.Y. Surr. Ct. 1932). Does *Marvin* do anything more than sanction adultery? Is *Marvin* the beginning of common-law polygamy?

6. Additional reading. For more information on the law of cohabitation, see generally Ariela R. Dubler, *Wifely Behavior: A Legal History of Acting*

Married, 100 COLUM. L. REV. 957 (2000); Katherine C. Gordon, Note, *The Necessity and Enforcement of Cohabitation Agreements: When Strings Will Attach and How to Prevent Them a State Survey*, 37 BRANDEIS L.J. 245 (1998/1999). For more information on associational rights and marriage, see generally Symposium, *Liberty and Marriage-Baehr and Beyond: Due Process in 1998*, 12 BYU J. PUB. L. 253 (1998); David A. Anderson, Note, *Jail, Jail, The Gang's All Here: Senate Crime Bill Section 521, The Criminal Street Gang Provision*, 36 B.C. L. REV. 527 (1995). For information on how *Marvin* extends to same sex couples, see Sharmila Roy Grossman, Comment, *The Illusory Rights of* Marvin v. Marvin *for the Same-Sex Couple versus the Preferable Canadian Alternative—*M. v. H., 38 CAL. W. L. REV. 547 (2002).

C. SAME-SEX COUPLES

Whorton v. Dillingham

248 Cal.Rptr. 405 (Cal. Ct. App. 1988).

■ JUDGE WORK delivered the opinion of the court.

Donnis G. Whorton appeals a judgment dismissing his action against Benjamin F. Dillingham III after the court sustained a demurrer without leave to amend. Whorton claims property rights based on an oral cohabiters' agreement with which he fully complied but which Dillingham breached after approximately seven years. The trial court found the pleadings showed the contract was unenforceable as expressly and inseparably based on sexual services. We conclude Whorton has alleged consideration for the purported contract substantially independent of sexual services, and reverse the judgment.

I

On appeal from a judgment of dismissal arising from the sustaining of a demurrer, we accept the facts pleaded in the complaint as true. *(Noguera v. N. Monterey County Unified Sch. Dist.* (1980) 106 Cal. App. 3d 64, 66, 164 Cal. Rptr. 808.)

The alleged facts include the following. At the time the parties began dating and entered into a homosexual relationship, Whorton was studying to obtain his Associate in Arts degree, intending to enroll in a four-year college and obtain a Bachelor of Arts degree. When the parties began living together in 1977, they orally agreed that Whorton's exclusive, full-time occupation was to be Dillingham's chauffeur, bodyguard, social and business secretary, partner and counselor in real estate investments, and to appear on his behalf when requested. Whorton was to render labor, skills, and personal services for the benefit of Dillingham's business and investment endeavors. Additionally, Whorton was to be Dillingham's constant companion, confidant, traveling and social companion, and lover, to terminate his schooling upon obtaining his Associate in Arts degree, and to make no investment without first consulting Dillingham.

In consideration of Whorton's promises, Dillingham was to give him a one-half equity interest in all real estate acquired in their joint names, and in all property thereafter acquired by Dillingham. Dillingham agreed to financially support Whorton for life, and to open bank accounts, maintain a positive balance in those accounts, grant Whorton invasionary powers to savings accounts held in Dillingham's name, and permit Whorton to charge on Dillingham's personal accounts. Dillingham was also to engage in a homosexual relationship with Whorton. Importantly, for the purpose of our analysis, the parties specifically agreed that any portion of the agreement found to be legally unenforceable was severable and the balance of the provisions would remain in full force and effect.

Whorton allegedly complied with all terms of the oral agreement until 1984 when Dillingham barred him from his premises. Dillingham now refuses to perform his part of the contract by giving Whorton the promised consideration for the business services rendered.

II

Adults who voluntarily live together and engage in sexual relations are competent to contract respecting their earnings and property rights. Such contracts will be enforced "unless expressly and inseparably based upon an illicit consideration of sexual services...." *(Marvin v. Marvin* (1976) 18 Cal. 3d 660, 672 [134 Cal. Rptr. 815, 557 P.2d 106].) One cannot lawfully contract to pay for the performance of sexual services since such an agreement is in essence a bargain for prostitution. *(Id.* at p. 674, 134 Cal.Rptr. 815, 557 P.2d 106, 134 Cal. Rptr. 815, 557 P.2d 106.)

A standard which inquires whether an agreement involves or contemplates a sexual relationship is vague and unworkable because virtually all agreements between nonmarital (and certainly, marital) cohabiters involve or contemplate a mutual sexual relationship. Further, a compact is not totally invalid merely because the parties may have contemplated creating or continuing a sexual relationship, but is invalid only to the extent it rests upon a consideration of sexual services. *(Id.* at pp. 670–671, 134 Cal. Rptr. 815, 557 P.2d 106.) Thus, "even if sexual services are part of the contractual consideration, any *severable* portion of the contract supported by independent consideration will still be enforced." *(Id.* at p. 672, 134 Cal. Rptr. 815, 557 P.2d 106.) For instance, contracting parties may make a variety of arrangements regarding their property rights—i.e., agree to pool their earnings and to hold all property in accord with the law governing community property, or to treat monetary earnings and property as separate property of the earning partner, or to keep property separate but compensate one party for services which benefit the other, or to pool only a part of their earnings and property, etc. *(Id.* at p. 674, fn. 10, 134 Cal. Rptr. 815, 557 P.2d 106.) "So long as the agreement does not rest upon illicit meretricious consideration, the parties may order their economic affairs as they choose, and no policy precludes the courts from enforcing such agreements." (*id.* at p. 674, 134 Cal. Rptr. 815, 557 P.2d 106.)

Regarding the issue of what constitutes adequate consideration, *Marvin* notes "[a] promise to perform homemaking services is, of course, a lawful and adequate consideration for a contract...." (*Id.* at p. 670, fn. 5, 134 Cal. Rptr. 815, 557 P.2d 106.) *Marvin* expressly rejects the argument that the partner seeking to enforce the contract must have contributed either property or services additional to ordinary homemaking services. (*Ibid.*)

In *Marvin*, the plaintiff alleged the parties orally agreed that while they lived together they would combine their efforts and earnings and would share equally all property accumulated as a result of their efforts, that they would hold themselves out to the general public as husband and wife, that plaintiff would render services as companion, homemaker, housekeeper and cook, that plaintiff would give up her career in order to provide these services full-time, and that in return defendant would provide for all of plaintiff's financial support for the rest of her life. (*Id.* at p. 666.) The court stated:

> "... plaintiff alleges that the parties agreed to pool their earnings, that they contracted to share equally in all property acquired, and that defendant agreed to support plaintiff. The terms of the contract as alleged do not rest upon any unlawful consideration."
> (*Id.* at pp. 674–675, 134 Cal. Rptr. 815, 557 P.2d 106.)

The holding in *Marvin* suggests the court determined that the contract before it did not *expressly* include sexual services as part of the consideration, and thus, it did not need to reach the issue of whether there were severable portions of the contract supported by independent consideration. The only reference to sexual services in *Marvin's* alleged facts was that the parties agreed to hold themselves out to the public as husband and wife, which apparently the court did not interpret as expressly indicating sexual services were part of the consideration. (See *Alderson v. Alderson* (1986) 180 Cal. App. 3d 450, 462–464, 225 Cal. Rptr. 610 [even though couple engaged in sexual relations and plaintiff perceived this as part of her "role," no evidence that implied agreement between the parties explicitly rested upon a consideration of meretricious sexual services].)

III

Unlike the facts of *Marvin*, here the parties' sexual relationship was an express, rather than implied, part of the consideration for their contract. The contract cannot be enforced to the extent it is dependent on sexual services for consideration, and the complaint does not state a cause of action to the extent it asks for damages from the termination of the sexual relationship.

The issue here is whether the sexual component of the consideration is severable from the remaining portions of the contract.[1] We reiterate the

---

1. Dillingham does not assert *Marvin* is inapplicable to same-sex partners, and we see no legal basis to make a distinction.

guiding language of *Marvin v. Marvin, supra* 18 Cal. 3d at page 672, 134 Cal. Rptr. 815, 557 P.2d 106 "[E]ven if sexual services are part of the contractual consideration, any *severable* portion of the contract supported by independent consideration will still be enforced." One test for determining the enforceability of a contract having both lawful and unlawful factors for consideration is stated in the Restatement Second of Contracts, section 183, "If the parties' performances can be apportioned into corresponding pairs of part performances so that the parts of each pair are properly regarded as agreed equivalents and one pair is not offensive to public policy, that portion of the agreement is enforceable by a party who did not engage in serious misconduct." (See also Civ. Code, § 1599: "Where a contract has several distinct objects, of which one at least is lawful, and one at least is unlawful, in whole or in part, the contract is void as to the latter and valid as to the rest.")

Tyranski v. Piggins (1973) 44 Mich. App. 570, 205 N.W.2d 595, 596–597, evaluates the issue of severability as follows:

> "Professor Corbin and the drafters of the Restatement of Contracts both write that while bargains in whole or in part in consideration of an illicit relationship are unenforceable, agreements between parties to such a relationship with respect to money or property will be enforced if the agreement is independent of the illicit relationship.

> "Neither these authorities nor the large body of case law in other jurisdictions ... articulate a guideline for determining when the consideration will be regarded as 'independent' and when it is so coupled with the meretricious acts that the agreement will not be enforced. A pattern does, however, emerge upon reading the cases.

> "Neither party to a meretricious relationship acquires, by reason of cohabitation alone, rights in the property accumulations of the other during the period of the relationship. But where there is an express agreement to accumulate or transfer property following a relationship of some permanence and *an additional consideration in the form of either money or of services, the courts tend to find an independent consideration.*

> "Thus, a plaintiff who can show an actual contribution of money, pursuant to an agreement to pool assets and share accumulations, will usually prevail. Services, such as cooking meals, laundering clothes, 'caring' for the decedent through sickness, have been found to be adequate and independent considerations in cases where there was an express agreement." (Fns. omitted; italics added.)[2]

---

2. In *Tyranski v. Piggins, supra* 205 N.W.2d at pages 596–597, the plaintiff cleaned the house, did the marketing, cooked the food, did the decedent's personal laundry, acted as his hostess, cared for him when he was sick, and contributed money towards the purchase of a house in which the unmarried

Of particular significance is the decision in *Latham v. Latham* (1976) 274 Ore. 421, 547 P.2d 144. In *Latham*, the court overruled a demurrer where complainant pleaded an agreement to live with defendant, to care for, and to furnish him with all the amenities of married life. The court recognized the alleged agreement specifically included the sexual services implicit in cohabitation. (*id.* 547 P.2d at p. 145.) Thus, as here, the sexual aspect of the agreement appeared on the face of the complaint. In overruling a demurrer based on public policy, the court stated it was not validating an agreement in which sexual intercourse was the only or primary consideration, but only one of the factors incident to the burdens and amenities of married life. (*id.* 547 P.2d at p. 147.)

Thus, the crux of our analysis is whether Whorton's complaint negates as a matter of law, a trier of fact finding he made contributions, apart from sexual services, which provided independent consideration for Dillingham's alleged promises pertaining to financial support and property rights. The services which plaintiff alleges he agreed to and did provide included being a chauffeur, bodyguard, secretary, and partner and counselor in real estate investments. If provided, these services are of monetary value, and the type for which one would expect to be compensated unless there is evidence of a contrary intent. Thus, they are properly characterized as consideration independent of the sexual aspect of the relationship. By way of comparison, such services as being a constant companion and confidant are not the type which are usually monetarily compensated nor considered to have a "value" for purposes of contract consideration, and, absent peculiar circumstances, would likely be considered so intertwined with the sexual relationship as to be inseparable. (Cf. *Walters v. Calderon* (1972) 25 Cal. App. 3d 863, 873, 102 Cal. Rptr. 89 [love and affection do not constitute valuable consideration necessary to support validity of contractual promise].)

We hold that Whorton—based on allegations he provided Dillingham with services of a chauffeur, bodyguard, secretary, and business partner— has stated a cause of action arising from a contract supported by consideration independent of sexual services. Further, by itemizing the mutual promises to engage in sexual activity, Whorton has not precluded the trier of fact from finding those promises are the consideration for each other and independent of the bargained for consideration for Whorton's employment.

We believe our holding does not conflict with that in *Jones v. Daly* (1981) 122 Cal. App. 3d 500, 508, 176 Cal. Rptr. 130, where services provided by the complaining homosexual partner were limited to "lover, companion, homemaker, traveling companion, housekeeper and cook. . . ." The court there found the pleadings unequivocally established that plaintiff's rendition of sex and other services naturally flowing from sexual cohabitation was an inseparable part of the consideration for the so-called cohabitor's agreement. The court stated:

plaintiff and the decedent resided. The court held it was proper to enforce the parties' express agreement to convey the house, which was held in the name of the decedent, to the plaintiff.

"According to the allegations of the complaint, the agreement
provided that the parties would share equally the earnings and
property accumulated as a result of their efforts while they lived
together and that Daly would support plaintiff for the rest of his
life. *Neither the property sharing nor the support provision of the
agreement rests upon plaintiff's acting as Daly's traveling companion, housekeeper or cook as distinguished from acting as his lover.*
The latter service forms an inseparable part of the consideration
for the agreement and renders it unenforceable in its entirety."
(*Jones v. Daly, supra* 122 Cal. App. 3d at p. 509, 176 Cal. Rptr. 130
italics added.)

Jones is factually different in that the complaining party did not allege
contracting to provide services apart from those normally incident to the
state of cohabitation itself. Further, Jones's complaint stated the agreement was premised on that they "would hold themselves out to the public
at large as cohabiting mates...." (*Id.* at p. 505, 176 Cal. Rptr. 130.) In
contrast, Whorton's complaint separately itemizes services contracted for
as companion, chauffeur, bodyguard, secretary, partner and business counselor. These, except for companion, are significantly different than those
household duties normally attendant to nonbusiness cohabitation and are
those for which monetary compensation ordinarily would be anticipated.[5]
Accepting Whorton's allegations as true, we cannot say as a matter of law
any illegal portion of the contract is not severable so as to leave the balance
valid and enforceable, especially where it is alleged the parties contemplated such a result when entering into their agreement.

IV

Statute of frauds

Dillingham asserts the oral agreement is invalid under the statute of
frauds, requiring agreements not to be performed within one year or for
the sale of an interest in real property to be written. (Civ. Code, § 1624,
subds. (a) and (c).) In *Marvin v. Marvin, supra* 18 Cal. 3d at page 674,
footnote 10, 134 Cal. Rptr. 815, 557 P.2d 106, the court noted in cases
involving agreements between nonmarital partners, the majority of the
agreements were oral and the courts have expressly rejected defenses
grounded upon the statute of frauds.

Marvin cites *Cline v. Festersen* (1954) 128 Cal. App. 2d 380, 386, 275
P.2d 149. In *Cline*, the court rejected a statute of frauds argument on the
basis of estoppel, reasoning that the nonmarital partner seeking to obtain
her promised share of the property had trusted and worked for many years
in reliance on the promise, and her partner had never repudiated the
agreement. *Cline* relies on the principle that the doctrine of estoppel to

---

5. Most of the numerous cases cited in
Marvin where nonmarital cohabiters' oral
agreements to pool earnings were upheld involved contributions other than normal
homemaking services. However, *Marvin*
states homemaking services alone are lawful
consideration. (*Marvin v. Marvin*, supra 18
Cal. 3d, p. 670, fn. 5; see also *Watkins v.
Watkins* (1983) 143 Cal. App. 3d 651, 655,
192 Cal. Rptr. 54.)

assert the statute of frauds should be applied to prevent fraud and unconscionable injury that would result from refusal to enforce oral contracts in certain circumstances—i.e., after one party has been induced by the other seriously to change position in reliance on the contract, or when unjust enrichment would result if a party who has received the benefits of the other's performance were allowed to rely upon the statute. (*Id.* at p. 387, 275 P.2d 149).

Whorton alleges he stopped his education earlier than planned to assist Dillingham in his business ventures in exchange for promises of support and sharing of accumulated property. These facts are sufficient to estop Dillingham from raising the statute of frauds by way of demurrer to bar enforcement of the contract.

Statute of limitations

Dillingham meritlessly asserts the action is barred by the statute of limitations.

The general rule is that a cause of action for breach of contract accrues at the time of breach. (See 3 Witkin, Cal. Procedure (3d ed. 1985) Actions, § 375, p. 402.) A *Marvin*-type contract is breached when one partner terminates the relationship. (*Estate of Fincher* (1981) 119 Cal. App. 3d 343, 352, 174 Cal. Rptr. 18.) The statute of limitations for an action upon a contract not founded on a writing is two years. (Code Civ. Proc., § 339, subd. 1.) The complaint states the breach occurred "on or about the latter part of 1984." The complaint was filed in June 1986. The complaint on its face does not show the contract cause of action is barred by the statute of limitations.

For the same reasons, the complaint on its face does not show the three-year fraud limitation has expired.[6]

Additionally, a cause of action based on equitable grounds is not barred, for which the statute of limitations is four years. (*Nelson v. Nevel* (1984) 154 Cal. App. 3d 132, 140–141, 201 Cal. Rptr. 93; Code Civ. Proc., § 343; see generally *Marvin v. Marvin*, supra 18 Cal. 3d at p. 684, fn. 25, 134 Cal. Rptr. 815, 557 P.2d 106.)

Terminable at will

Finally, Dillingham contends that under *Labor Code section 2922*, the contract was terminable at will.[7] That section has no applicability to the issues here. This case does not involve an employment contract within the purview of the Labor Code, but rather a cohabiters' agreement regarding

---

6. The caption of the complaint does not refer to fraud, stating: "Complaint for damages for breach of express oral contract; breach of implied in fact contract; to impress a constructive trust; for declaratory relief; and for injunctive relief." However, the body of the complaint states facts in support of, and refers to, a fraud cause of action.

7. Labor Code section 2922 states: "An employment, having no specified term, may be terminated at the will of either party on notice to the other. Employment for a specified term means an employment for a period greater than one month."

how two nonmarital partners have agreed to regulate their economic affairs. Of course, one partner has a right to end the relationship, and the only issue is whether the facts support a monetary and/or property award to one of the partners.

* * *

Domestic Partner Ordinance Quashed: Atlanta to Appeal in Second Defeat

ATLANTA J. & CONST., Jan. 1, 1997 at D2.

■ BILL RANKIN

A Fulton County judge Tuesday struck down Atlanta's domestic partnership ordinance, the second try by the city to extend insurance benefits to live-in partners of city employees.

The city is attempting "to incorporate a 'family relationship' it has created, domestic partners, into the definition of a dependent," Superior Court Judge Isaac Jenrette said. This "is now inconsistent with state law."

The city will appeal the ruling, said Nick Gold, spokesman for Mayor Bill Campbell. Six city employees have signed up for the domestic partnership benefits, he said.

"Georgia law is clear—no matter how the city manipulates the language of its ordinance, domestic partners are neither 'family' nor 'dependents,'" said Atlanta lawyer David Reed, who argued the case for the conservative Southeastern Legal Foundation. "The taxpayers and families of Georgia have had enough of this nonsense."

Foundation lawyers have said the ordinance was an unconstitutional attempt by the city to encourage homosexuality and was a waste of taxpayers' money.

The foundation filed the lawsuit Sept. 10, the same day the U.S. Senate approved a bill denying recognition of same-sex marriages. The lawsuit challenged an ordinance passed by the City Council to authorize insurance benefits to the unmarried, live-in partners of city employees.

The new provision is a revised version of a 1993 city ordinance granting benefits for domestic partners. The Georgia Supreme Court struck down that ordinance in 1995, saying the city "exceeded its power ... by recognizing domestic partners as 'a family relationship.'" The court noted that the state uses several definitions for "dependents" when allowing insurance benefits and "domestic partners do not meet any of these statutory definitions."

On Tuesday, Jenrette said the city's new ordinance is fatally flawed for the same reasons.

Teresa Nelson, executive director of the Georgia chapter of the American Civil Liberties Union, expressed disappointment at the ruling.

"There are a number of individuals who have no dependents who are city employees, and they have shared the burden for the coverage of those employees who have dependents," Nelson said. "For those who are in partnership relationships, whether they are heterosexual or homosexual, their dependents have been denied that coverage. The city's ordinance is not a statement of morality. It is a statement of equality."

But Matthew Glavin, president of the Southeast Legal Foundation, said the City Council should realize this is not something it has the authority to do.

"If the City Council or the mayor want this kind of ordinance, they should march up the street to the state Legislature and convince it to change the law to include domestic partners," he said. "Unless they do that, anything they do will be unconstitutional, and we will stop them at every attempt."

————

NOTES AND QUESTIONS

1. Limits of consideration for homosexual couples. The Court in this case held that "Whorton—based on allegations he provided Dillingham with services of a chauffeur, bodyguard, secretary, and business partner—has stated a cause of action arising from a contract supported by consideration independent of sexual services." Of course, none of those services were provided in *Marvin*, though the services that were provided in *Marvin*—keeping house, functioning as a companion, etc. were also present in *Whorton*. Why, then, would the court choose to focus on these tasks to find consideration, and what are the implications of that decision? *See, e.g.,* Jones v. Daly, 176 Cal.Rptr. 130 (Cal. App. 1981).

2. Impact of *Whorton v. Dillingham*. Is *Whorton* a victory for homosexual rights? After all, the case is specifically premised on the idea of an express contract being enforced even though it was partially based on sexual consideration. Since this holding is completely orientation-neutral, why should *Whorton v. Dillingham* be considered significant? If it is a victory, how far does it extend? *See* Sharmila Roy Grossman, Comment, *The Illusory Rights of* Marvin v. Marvin *for the Same-Sex Couple Versus the Preferable Canadian Alternative*—M. v. H., 38 CAL. W. L. REV. 547, 557 (2002). If homosexual couples are allowed to enter valid marriages in the state in which they reside, does the *Marvin v. Marvin* rationale apply?

3. Additional reading. For additional information on domestic partner ordinances, see generally, Jonathan Andrew Hein, *Caring for the Evolving American Family: Cohabiting Partners and Employer Sponsored Health Care*, 30 N.M. L. REV. 19 (2000); Debbie Zielinski, Note, *Domestic Partnership Benefits: Why not Offer Them to Same-Sex Partners and Unmarried Opposite Sex Partners*, 13 J.L. & HEALTH 281 (1998–99); William V. Vetter, *Restrictions on Equal Treatment of Unmarried Domestic Partners*, 5 B.U. PUB. INT. L.J. 1 (1995).

D. Sex Between Consenting Adults

Lawrence v. Texas

Supreme Court of the United States, 539 U.S. 558 (2003).

■ Justice Kennedy delivered the opinion of the Court.

Liberty protects the person from unwarranted government intrusions into a dwelling or other private places. In our tradition the State is not omnipresent in the home. And there are other spheres of our lives and existence, outside the home, where the State should not be a dominant presence. Freedom extends beyond spatial bounds. Liberty presumes an autonomy of self that includes freedom of thought, belief, expression, and certain intimate conduct. The instant case involves liberty of the person both in its spatial and more transcendent dimensions.

I

The question before the Court is the validity of a Texas statute making it a crime for two persons of the same sex to engage in certain intimate sexual conduct.

In Houston, Texas, officers of the Harris County Police Department were dispatched to a private residence in response to a reported weapons disturbance. They entered an apartment where one of the petitioners, John Geddes Lawrence, resided. The right of the police to enter does not seem to have been questioned. The officers observed Lawrence and another man, Tyron Garner, engaging in a sexual act. The two petitioners were arrested, held in custody over night, and charged and convicted before a Justice of the Peace * * * [of] "deviate sexual intercourse, namely anal sex, with a member of the same sex (man)." App. to Pet. for Cert. 127a, 139a. The applicable state law is Tex. Penal Code Ann. § 21.06(a) (2003). It provides: "A person commits an offense if he engages in deviate sexual intercourse with another individual of the same sex." * * *

* * *

We granted certiorari, 537 U.S. 1044 (2002), to consider three questions:

"1. Whether Petitioners' criminal convictions under the Texas 'Homosexual Conduct' law—which criminalizes sexual intimacy by same-sex couples, but not identical behavior by different-sex couples—violate the Fourteenth Amendment guarantee of equal protection of laws?

"2. Whether Petitioners' criminal convictions for adult consensual sexual intimacy in the home violate their vital interests in liberty and privacy protected by the Due Process Clause of the Fourteenth Amendment?

"3. Whether Bowers v. Hardwick, 478 U.S. 186 (1986), should be overruled?" Pet. for Cert. i.

    * * *

II

We conclude the case should be resolved by determining whether the petitioners were free as adults to engage in the private conduct in the exercise of their liberty under the Due Process Clause of the Fourteenth Amendment to the Constitution. For this inquiry we deem it necessary to reconsider the Court's holding in *Bowers*.

There are broad statements of the substantive reach of liberty under the Due Process Clause in earlier cases, * * * but the most pertinent beginning point is our decision in *Griswold v. Connecticut*, 381 U.S. 479 (1965).

In *Griswold* the Court invalidated a state law prohibiting the use of drugs or devices of contraception and counseling or aiding and abetting the use of contraceptives. The Court described the protected interest as a right to privacy and placed emphasis on the marriage relation and the protected space of the marital bedroom. *Id.*, at 485.

After *Griswold* it was established that the right to make certain decisions regarding sexual conduct extends beyond the marital relationship. In *Eisenstadt v. Baird*, 405 U.S. 438 (1972), the Court invalidated a law prohibiting the distribution of contraceptives to unmarried persons. The case was decided under the Equal Protection Clause, *id.*, at 454; but with respect to unmarried persons, the Court went on to state the fundamental proposition that the law impaired the exercise of their personal rights, *ibid*. It quoted from the statement of the Court of Appeals finding the law to be in conflict with fundamental human rights, and it followed with this statement of its own:

> "It is true that in *Griswold* the right of privacy in question inhered in the marital relationship.... If the right of privacy means anything, it is the right of the *individual*, married or single, to be free from unwarranted governmental intrusion into matters so fundamentally affecting a person as the decision whether to bear or beget a child." *Id.*, at 453.

The opinions in *Griswold* and *Eisenstadt* were part of the background for the decision in *Roe v. Wade*, 410 U.S. 113 (1973). As is well known, the case involved a challenge to the Texas law prohibiting abortions, but the laws of other States were affected as well. Although the Court held the woman's rights were not absolute, her right to elect an abortion did have real and substantial protection as an exercise of her liberty under the Due Process Clause. The Court cited cases that protect spatial freedom and cases that go well beyond it. *Roe* recognized the right of a woman to make certain fundamental decisions affecting her destiny and confirmed once more that the protection of liberty under the Due Process Clause has a substantive dimension of fundamental significance in defining the rights of the person.

In *Carey v. Population Services Int'l*, 431 U.S. 678 (1977), the Court confronted a New York law forbidding sale or distribution of contraceptive devices to persons under 16 years of age. Although there was no single opinion for the Court, the law was invalidated. Both *Eisenstadt* and *Carey*, as well as the holding and rationale in *Roe*, confirmed that the reasoning of *Griswold* could not be confined to the protection of rights of married adults. This was the state of the law with respect to some of the most relevant cases when the Court considered *Bowers* v. *Hardwick*.

The facts in *Bowers* had some similarities to the instant case. A police officer, whose right to enter seems not to have been in question, observed Hardwick, in his own bedroom, engaging in intimate sexual conduct with another adult male. The conduct was in violation of a Georgia statute making it a criminal offense to engage in sodomy. One difference between the two cases is that the Georgia statute prohibited the conduct whether or not the participants were of the same sex, while the Texas statute, as we have seen, applies only to participants of the same sex. Hardwick was not prosecuted, but he brought an action in federal court to declare the state statute invalid. He alleged he was a practicing homosexual and that the criminal prohibition violated rights guaranteed to him by the Constitution. The Court, in an opinion by Justice White, sustained the Georgia law.
* * *

The Court began its substantive discussion in *Bowers* as follows: "The issue presented is whether the Federal Constitution confers a fundamental right upon homosexuals to engage in sodomy and hence invalidates the laws of the many States that still make such conduct illegal and have done so for a very long time." *Id.*, at 190. That statement, we now conclude, discloses the Court's own failure to appreciate the extent of the liberty at stake. To say that the issue in *Bowers* was simply the right to engage in certain sexual conduct demeans the claim the individual put forward, just as it would demean a married couple were it to be said marriage is simply about the right to have sexual intercourse. The laws involved in *Bowers* and here are, to be sure, statutes that purport to do no more than prohibit a particular sexual act. Their penalties and purposes, though, have more far-reaching consequences, touching upon the most private human conduct, sexual behavior, and in the most private of places, the home. The statutes do seek to control a personal relationship that, whether or not entitled to formal recognition in the law, is within the liberty of persons to choose without being punished as criminals.

This, as a general rule, should counsel against attempts by the State, or a court, to define the meaning of the relationship or to set its boundaries absent injury to a person or abuse of an institution the law protects. It suffices for us to acknowledge that adults may choose to enter upon this relationship in the confines of their homes and their own private lives and still retain their dignity as free persons. When sexuality finds overt expression in intimate conduct with another person, the conduct can be but one element in a personal bond that is more enduring. The liberty protected by the Constitution allows homosexual persons the right to make this choice.

Having misapprehended the claim of liberty there presented to it, and thus stating the claim to be whether there is a fundamental right to engage in consensual sodomy, the *Bowers* Court said: "Proscriptions against that conduct have ancient roots." *Id.*, at 192. In academic writings, and in many of the scholarly *amicus* briefs filed to assist the Court in this case, there are fundamental criticisms of the historical premises relied upon by the majority and concurring opinions in *Bowers*. * * * We need not enter this debate in the attempt to reach a definitive historical judgment, but the following considerations counsel against adopting the definitive conclusions upon which *Bowers* placed such reliance.

At the outset it should be noted that there is no longstanding history in this country of laws directed at homosexual conduct as a distinct matter. Beginning in colonial times there were prohibitions of sodomy derived from the English criminal laws passed in the first instance by the Reformation Parliament of 1533. The English prohibition was understood to include relations between men and women as well as relations between men and men. See, *e.g.*, *King v. Wiseman*, 92 Eng. Rep. 774, 775 (K. B. 1718) (interpreting "mankind" in Act of 1533 as including women and girls). Nineteenth-century commentators similarly read American sodomy, buggery, and crime-against-nature statutes as criminalizing certain relations between men and women and between men and men. See, *e.g.*, 2 J. Bishop, Criminal Law § 1028 (1858); 2 J. Chitty, Criminal Law 47–50 (5th Am. ed. 1847); R. Desty, A Compendium of American Criminal Law 143 (1882); J. May, The Law of Crimes § 203 (2d ed. 1893). The absence of legal prohibitions focusing on homosexual conduct may be explained in part by noting that according to some scholars the concept of the homosexual as a distinct category of person did not emerge until the late 19th century. See, *e.g.*, J. Katz, The Invention of Heterosexuality 10 (1995); J. D'Emilio & E. Freedman, Intimate Matters: A History of Sexuality in America 121 (2d ed. 1997) ("The modern terms *homosexuality* and *heterosexuality* do not apply to an era that had not yet articulated these distinctions"). Thus early American sodomy laws were not directed at homosexuals as such but instead sought to prohibit nonprocreative sexual activity more generally. This does not suggest approval of homosexual conduct. It does tend to show that this particular form of conduct was not thought of as a separate category from like conduct between heterosexual persons.

Laws prohibiting sodomy do not seem to have been enforced against consenting adults acting in private. A substantial number of sodomy prosecutions and convictions for which there are surviving records were for predatory acts against those who could not or did not consent, as in the case of a minor or the victim of an assault. As to these, one purpose for the prohibitions was to ensure there would be no lack of coverage if a predator committed a sexual assault that did not constitute rape as defined by the criminal law. Thus the model sodomy indictments presented in a 19th-century treatise, see 2 Chitty, *supra* at 49, addressed the predatory acts of an adult man against a minor girl or minor boy. Instead of targeting relations between consenting adults in private, 19th-century sodomy prosecutions typically involved relations between men and minor girls or minor boys, relations between adults involving force, relations between adults implicating disparity in status, or relations between men and animals.

* * * The longstanding criminal prohibition of homosexual sodomy upon which the *Bowers* decision placed such reliance is as consistent with a general condemnation of nonprocreative sex as it is with an established tradition of prosecuting acts because of their homosexual character.

The policy of punishing consenting adults for private acts was not much discussed in the early legal literature. We can infer that one reason for this was the very private nature of the conduct. Despite the absence of prosecutions, there may have been periods in which there was public criticism of homosexuals as such and an insistence that the criminal laws be enforced to discourage their practices. But far from possessing "ancient roots," *Bowers*, 478 U.S., at 192, American laws targeting same-sex couples did not develop until the last third of the 20th century. * * *

It was not until the 1970's that any State singled out same-sex relations for criminal prosecution, and only nine States have done so. * * * Post-*Bowers* even some of these States did not adhere to the policy of suppressing homosexual conduct. Over the course of the last decades, States with same-sex prohibitions have moved toward abolishing them. * * *

In summary, the historical grounds relied upon in *Bowers* are more complex than the majority opinion and the concurring opinion by Chief Justice Burger indicate. Their historical premises are not without doubt and, at the very least, are overstated.

It must be acknowledged, of course, that the Court in *Bowers* was making the broader point that for centuries there have been powerful voices to condemn homosexual conduct as immoral. The condemnation has been shaped by religious beliefs, conceptions of right and acceptable behavior, and respect for the traditional family. For many persons these are not trivial concerns but profound and deep convictions accepted as ethical and moral principles to which they aspire and which thus determine the course of their lives. These considerations do not answer the question before us, however. The issue is whether the majority may use the power of the State to enforce these views on the whole society through operation of the criminal law. "Our obligation is to define the liberty of all, not to mandate our own moral code." *Planned Parenthood of Southeastern Pa. v. Casey*, 505 U.S. 833, 850 (1992).

Chief Justice Burger joined the opinion for the Court in *Bowers* and further explained his views as follows: "Decisions of individuals relating to homosexual conduct have been subject to state intervention throughout the history of Western civilization. Condemnation of those practices is firmly rooted in Judeao–Christian moral and ethical standards." 478 U.S., at 196. As with Justice White's assumptions about history, scholarship casts some doubt on the sweeping nature of the statement by Chief Justice Burger as it pertains to private homosexual conduct between consenting adults. See, *e.g.,* Eskridge, Hardwick and Historiography, 1999 U. Ill. L. Rev. 631, 656. In all events we think that our laws and traditions in the past half century are of most relevance here. These references show an emerging awareness that liberty gives substantial protection to adult persons in deciding how to conduct their private lives in matters pertaining to sex. "History and tradition are the starting point but not in all cases the ending point of the substantive due process inquiry." *County of Sacramento v. Lewis*, 523 U.S. 833, 857 (1998) (KENNEDY, J., concurring).

* * *

In *Bowers* the Court referred to the fact that before 1961 all 50 States had outlawed sodomy, and that at the time of the Court's decision 24 States and the District of Columbia had sodomy laws. 478 U.S., at 192–193. Justice Powell pointed out that these prohibitions often were being ignored, however. Georgia, for instance, had not sought to enforce its law for decades. Id., at 197–198, n. 2 ("The history of nonenforcement suggests the moribund character today of laws criminalizing this type of private, consensual conduct").

The sweeping references by Chief Justice Burger to the history of Western civilization and to Judeo–Christian moral and ethical standards did not take account of other authorities pointing in an opposite direction. A committee advising the British Parliament recommended in 1957 repeal of laws punishing homosexual conduct. The Wolfenden Report: Report of the Committee on Homosexual Offenses and Prostitution (1963). Parliament enacted the substance of those recommendations 10 years later. Sexual Offences Act 1967, § 1.

Of even more importance, almost five years before *Bowers* was decided the European Court of Human Rights considered a case with parallels to *Bowers* and to today's case. * * * The court held that the laws proscribing [consenting homosexual] conduct were invalid under the European Convention on Human Rights. *Dudgeon* v. *United Kingdom*, 45 Eur. Ct. H. R. (1981) P52. Authoritative in all countries that are members of the Council of Europe (21 nations then, 45 nations now), the decision is at odds with the premise in *Bowers* that the claim put forward was insubstantial in our Western civilization.

In our own constitutional system the deficiencies in *Bowers* became even more apparent in the years following its announcement. The 25 States with laws prohibiting the relevant conduct referenced in the *Bowers* decision are reduced now to 13, of which 4 enforce their laws only against homosexual conduct. In those States where sodomy is still proscribed, whether for same-sex or heterosexual conduct, there is a pattern of nonenforcement with respect to consenting adults acting in private. The State of Texas admitted in 1994 that as of that date it had not prosecuted anyone under those circumstances. *State v. Morales*, 869 S.W.2d 941, 943 .

Two principal cases decided after *Bowers* cast its holding into even more doubt. In *Planned Parenthood of Southeastern Pa. v. Casey*, 505 U.S. 833 (1992), the Court reaffirmed the substantive force of the liberty protected by the Due Process Clause. The *Casey* decision again confirmed that our laws and tradition afford constitutional protection to personal decisions relating to marriage, procreation, contraception, family relationships, child rearing, and education. *Id.*, at 851. In explaining the respect the Constitution demands for the autonomy of the person in making these choices, we stated as follows:

> "These matters, involving the most intimate and personal choices a person may make in a lifetime, choices central to personal dignity and autonomy, are central to the liberty protected by the *Fourteenth Amendment.* At the heart of liberty is the right to define one's own concept of existence, of meaning, of the universe, and of the mystery of human life. Beliefs about these matters could not define the attributes of personhood were they formed under compulsion of the State." *Ibid.*

Persons in a homosexual relationship may seek autonomy for these purposes, just as heterosexual persons do. The decision in *Bowers* would deny them this right.

The second post-*Bowers* case of principal relevance is *Romer v. Evans*, 517 U.S. 620, (1996). There the Court struck down class-based legislation directed at homosexuals as a violation of the Equal Protection Clause. *Romer* invalidated an amendment to Colorado's constitution which named as a solitary class persons who were homosexuals, lesbians, or bisexual either by "orientation, conduct, practices or relationships," *id.*, at 624 (internal quotation marks omitted), and deprived them of protection under state antidiscrimination laws. We concluded that the provision was "born of animosity toward the class of persons affected" and further that it had no rational relation to a legitimate governmental purpose. *Id.*, at 634.

    * * *

Equality of treatment and the due process right to demand respect for conduct protected by the substantive guarantee of liberty are linked in important respects, and a decision on the latter point advances both interests. If protected conduct is made criminal and the law which does so remains unexamined for its substantive validity, its stigma might remain even if it were not enforceable as drawn for equal protection reasons. When homosexual conduct is made criminal by the law of the State, that declaration in and of itself is an invitation to subject homosexual persons to discrimination both in the public and in the private spheres. The central holding of *Bowers* has been brought in question by this case, and it should be addressed. Its continuance as precedent demeans the lives of homosexual persons.

The stigma this criminal statute imposes, moreover, is not trivial. The offense, to be sure, is but a class C misdemeanor, a minor offense in the Texas legal system. Still, it remains a criminal offense with all that imports for the dignity of the persons charged. The petitioners will bear on their record the history of their criminal convictions. * * * We are advised that if Texas convicted an adult for private, consensual homosexual conduct under the statute here in question the convicted person would come within the [sexual-offender] registration laws of a least four States were he or she to be subject to their jurisdiction. * * * This underscores the consequential nature of the punishment and the state-sponsored condemnation attendant to the criminal prohibition. Furthermore, the Texas criminal conviction carries with it the other collateral consequences always following a conviction, such as notations on job application forms, to mention but one example.

* * *

* * * The right the petitioners seek in this case has been accepted as an integral part of human freedom in many other countries. There has been no showing that in this country the governmental interest in circumscribing personal choice is somehow more legitimate or urgent.

The doctrine of *stare decisis* is essential to the respect accorded to the judgments of the Court and to the stability of the law. It is not, however, an inexorable command. *Payne v. Tennessee*, 501 U.S. 808, 828 (1991) ("*Stare decisis* is not an inexorable command; rather, it 'is a principle of policy and not a mechanical formula of adherence to the latest decision'") (quoting *Helvering v. Hallock*, 309 U.S. 106, 119 (1940)). In *Casey* we noted that when a Court is asked to overrule a precedent recognizing a constitutional liberty interest, individual or societal reliance on the existence of that liberty cautions with particular strength against reversing course. 505 U.S., at 855–856; see also *id.*, at 844 ("Liberty finds no refuge in a jurisprudence of doubt"). The holding in *Bowers*, however, has not induced detrimental reliance comparable to some instances where recognized individual rights are involved. Indeed, there has been no individual or societal reliance on *Bowers* of the sort that could counsel against overturning its holding once there are compelling reasons to do so. *Bowers* itself causes uncertainty, for the precedents before and after its issuance contradict its central holding.

The rationale of *Bowers* does not withstand careful analysis. In his dissenting opinion in *Bowers* JUSTICE STEVENS came to these conclusions:

> "Our prior cases make two propositions abundantly clear. First, the fact that the governing majority in a State has traditionally viewed a particular practice as immoral is not a sufficient reason for upholding a law prohibiting the practice; neither history nor tradition could save a law prohibiting miscegenation from constitutional attack. Second, individual decisions by married persons, concerning the intimacies of their physical relationship, even when not intended to produce offspring, are a form of "liberty" protected by the Due Process Clause of the Fourteenth Amendment. Moreover, this protection extends to intimate choices by unmarried as well as married persons." 478 U.S., at 216 (footnotes and citations omitted).

JUSTICE STEVENS' analysis, in our view, should have been controlling in *Bowers* and should control here.

* * *

The present case does not involve minors. It does not involve persons who might be injured or coerced or who are situated in relationships where consent might not easily be refused. It does not involve public conduct or prostitution. It does not involve whether the government must give formal recognition to any relationship that homosexual persons seek to enter. The case does involve two adults who, with full and mutual consent from each other, engaged in sexual practices common to a homosexual lifestyle. The petitioners are entitled to respect for their private lives. The State cannot demean their existence or control their destiny by making their private sexual conduct a crime. Their right to liberty under the Due Process Clause gives them the full right to engage in their conduct without intervention of the government. "It is a promise of the Constitution that there is a realm of personal liberty which the government may not enter." *Casey, supra* at 847. The Texas statute furthers no legitimate state interest which can justify its intrusion into the personal and private life of the individual.

Had those who drew and ratified the Due Process Clauses of the Fifth Amendment or the Fourteenth Amendment known the components of liberty in its manifold possibilities, they might have been more specific. They did not presume to have this insight. They knew times can blind us to certain truths and later generations can see that laws once thought necessary and proper in fact serve only to oppress. As the Constitution endures, persons in every generation can invoke its principles in their own search for greater freedom.

[Reversed.]

It is so ordered.

■ JUSTICE O'CONNOR, concurring in the judgment.

The Court today overrules *Bowers v. Hardwick*, 478 U.S. 186 (1986). I joined *Bowers*, and do not join the Court in overruling it. Nevertheless, I agree with the Court that Texas' statute banning same-sex sodomy is unconstitutional. See Tex. Penal Code Ann. § 21.06 (2003). Rather than relying on the substantive component of the Fourteenth Amendment's Due Process Clause, as the Court does, I base my conclusion on the Fourteenth Amendment's Equal Protection Clause.

The Equal Protection Clause of the Fourteenth Amendment "is essentially a direction that all persons similarly situated should be treated alike." *Cleburne v. Cleburne Living Center, Inc.*, 473 U.S. 432, 439 (1985); see also *Plyler v. Doe*, 457 U.S. 202 (1982). Under our rational basis standard of review, "legislation is presumed to be valid and will be sustained if the classification drawn by the statute is rationally related to a legitimate state interest." *Cleburne v. Cleburne Living Center, supra* at 440; see also *Department of Agriculture v. Moreno*, 413 U.S. 528, 534 (1973); *Romer v. Evans*, 517 U.S. 620, 632–633 (1996); *Nordlinger v. Hahn*, 505 U.S. 1, 11–12 (1992).

* * * We have consistently held * * * that some objectives, such as "a bare ... desire to harm a politically unpopular group," are not legitimate state interests. *Department of Agriculture v. Moreno, supra* at 534. See also *Cleburne v. Cleburne Living Center, supra* at 446–447; *Romer v. Evans, supra* at 632. When a law exhibits such a desire to harm a politically unpopular group, we have applied a more searching form of rational basis review to strike down such laws under the Equal Protection Clause.

* * *

The statute at issue here makes sodomy a crime only if a person "engages in deviate sexual intercourse with another individual of the same sex." Tex. Penal Code Ann. § 21.06(a) (2003). Sodomy between opposite-sex partners, however, is not a crime in Texas. That is, Texas treats the same conduct differently based solely on the participants. Those harmed by this law are people who have a same-sex sexual orientation and thus are more likely to engage in behavior prohibited by § 21.06.

The Texas statute makes homosexuals unequal in the eyes of the law by making particular conduct—and only that conduct—subject to criminal sanction. * * * [W]hile the penalty imposed on petitioners in this case was relatively minor, the consequences of conviction are not. As the Court notes, see *ante*, at 15, petitioners' convictions, if upheld, would disqualify them from or restrict their ability to engage in a variety of professions, including medicine, athletic training, and interior design. * * * Indeed, were petitioners to move to one of four States, their convictions would require them to register as sex offenders to local law enforcement. * * *

And the effect of Texas' sodomy law is not just limited to the threat of prosecution or consequence of conviction. Texas' sodomy law brands all homosexuals as criminals, thereby making it more difficult for homosexuals to be treated in the same manner as everyone else. Indeed, Texas itself has previously acknowledged the collateral effects of the law, stipulating in a prior challenge to this action that the law "legally sanctions discrimination against [homosexuals] in a variety of ways unrelated to the criminal law," including in the areas of "employment, family issues, and housing." *State v. Morales*, 826 S.W.2d 201, 203 (Tex. App. 1992).

Texas attempts to justify its law, and the effects of the law, by arguing that the statute satisfies rational basis review because it furthers the legitimate governmental interest of the promotion of morality. * * *

This case raises a different issue than *Bowers*: whether, under the *Equal Protection Clause*, moral disapproval is a legitimate state interest to justify by itself a statute that bans homosexual sodomy, but not heterosexual sodomy. It is not. Moral disapproval of this group, like a bare desire to harm the group, is an interest that is insufficient to satisfy rational basis review under the Equal Protection Clause. See, *e.g., Department of Agriculture v. Moreno, supra* at 534; *Romer v. Evans*, 517 U.S., at 634–635. Indeed, we have never held that moral disapproval, without any other asserted state interest, is a sufficient rationale under the Equal Protection Clause to justify a law that discriminates among groups of persons.

* * *

Whether a sodomy law that is neutral both in effect and application, see *Yick Wo v. Hopkins*, 118 U.S. 356, 30 L. Ed. 220, 6 S. Ct. 1064 (1886), would violate the substantive component of the Due Process Clause is an issue that need not be decided today. I am confident, however, that so long as the Equal Protection Clause requires a sodomy law to apply equally to the private consensual conduct of homosexuals and heterosexuals alike, such a law would not long stand in our democratic society. * * *

A law branding one class of persons as criminal solely based on the State's moral disapproval of that class and the conduct associated with that class runs contrary to the values of the Constitution and the Equal Protection Clause, under any standard of review. I therefore concur in the Court's judgment that Texas' sodomy law banning "deviate sexual intercourse" between consenting adults of the same sex, but not between consenting adults of different sexes, is unconstitutional.

■ Justice Scalia, with whom the Chief Justice and Justice Thomas join, dissenting.

"Liberty finds no refuge in a jurisprudence of doubt." *Planned Parenthood of Southeastern Pa. v. Casey*, 505 U.S. 833, 844, 120 L. Ed. 2d 674, 112 S. Ct. 2791 (1992). That was the Court's sententious response, barely more than a decade ago, to those seeking to overrule *Roe v. Wade*, 410 U.S. 113, 35 L. Ed. 2d 147, 93 S. Ct. 705 (1973). The Court's response today, to those who have engaged in a 17-year crusade to overrule *Bowers v. Hardwick*, 478 U.S. 186, 92 L. Ed. 2d 140, 106 S. Ct. 2841 (1986), is very different. The need for stability and certainty presents no barrier.

Most of the rest of today's opinion has no relevance to its actual holding—that the Texas statute "furthers no legitimate state interest which can justify" its application to petitioners under rational-basis review. *Ante*, at 18 (overruling *Bowers* to the extent it sustained Georgia's anti-sodomy statute under the rational-basis test). Though there is discussion of "fundamental propositions," *ante*, at 4, and "fundamental decisions," *ibid.* nowhere does the Court's opinion declare that homosexual sodomy is a "fundamental right" under the Due Process Clause; nor does it subject the Texas law to the standard of review that would be appropriate (strict scrutiny) if homosexual sodomy *were* a "fundamental right." Thus, while overruling the *outcome* of *Bowers*, the Court leaves strangely untouched its central legal conclusion: "Respondent would have us announce ... a fundamental right to engage in homosexual sodomy. This we are quite unwilling to do." 478 U.S., at 191. Instead the Court simply describes petitioners' conduct as "an exercise of their liberty"—which it undoubtedly is—and proceeds to apply an unheard-of form of rational-basis review that will have far-reaching implications beyond this case. *Ante*, at 3.

* * *

Today's approach to *stare decisis* invites us to overrule an erroneously decided precedent (including an "intensely divisive" decision) *if:* (1) its foundations have been "eroded" by subsequent decisions, *ante*, at 15; (2) it has been subject to "substantial and continuing" criticism, *ibid.*; and (3) it has not induced "individual or societal reliance" that counsels against overturning, *ante*, at 16. The problem is that *Roe* itself—which today's majority surely has no disposition to overrule—satisfies these conditions to at least the same degree as *Bowers*.

* * *

I do not quarrel with the Court's claim that *Romer v. Evans*, 517 U.S. 620, 134 L. Ed. 2d 855, 116 S. Ct. 1620 (1996), "eroded" the "foundations" of *Bowers'* rational-basis holding. See *Romer, supra at 640–643* (Scalia, J., dissenting). But *Roe* and *Casey* have been equally "eroded" by *Washington v. Glucksberg*, 521 U.S. 702, 721, 138 L. Ed. 2d 772, 117 S. Ct. 2258, 117 S. Ct. 2302 (1997), which held that *only* fundamental rights which are " 'deeply rooted in this Nation's history and tradition' " qualify for anything other than rational basis scrutiny under the doctrine of "substantive due process." *Roe* and *Casey*, of course, subjected the restriction of abortion to heightened scrutiny without even attempting to establish that the freedom to abort *was* rooted in this Nation's tradition.

* * * *Bowers*, the Court says, has been subject to "substantial and continuing [criticism], disapproving of its reasoning in all respects, not just as to its historical assumptions." *Ante*, at 15. * * * Of course, *Roe* too (and by extension *Casey*) had been (and still is) subject to unrelenting criticism, including criticism from the two commentators cited by the Court today. See Fried, *supra* at 75 ("Roe was a prime example of twisted judging"); Posner, *supra* at 337 ("[The Court's] opinion in *Roe* . . . fails to measure up to professional expectations regarding judicial opinions"); Posner, Judicial Opinion Writing, 62 U. Chi. L. Rev. 1421, 1434 (1995) (describing the opinion in *Roe* as an "embarrassing performanc[e]").

* * * It seems to me that the "societal reliance" on the principles confirmed in *Bowers* and discarded today has been overwhelming. Countless judicial decisions and legislative enactments have relied on the ancient proposition that a governing majority's belief that certain sexual behavior is "immoral and unacceptable" constitutes a rational basis for regulation. * * * State laws against bigamy, same-sex marriage, adult incest, prostitution, masturbation, adultery, fornication, bestiality, and obscenity are likewise sustainable only in light of *Bowers'* validation of laws based on moral choices. Every single one of these laws is called into question by today's decision; the Court makes no effort to cabin the scope of its decision to exclude them from its holding. * * * The impossibility of distinguishing homosexuality from other traditional "morals" offenses is precisely why *Bowers* rejected the rational-basis challenge. "The law," it said, "is constantly based on notions of morality, and if all laws representing essentially moral choices are to be invalidated under the Due Process Clause, the courts will be very busy indeed." 478 U.S., at 196.

What a massive disruption of the current social order, therefore, the overruling of *Bowers* entails. * * *

Texas Penal Code Ann. § 21.06(a) (2003) undoubtedly imposes constraints on liberty. So do laws prohibiting prostitution, recreational use of heroin, and, for that matter, working more than 60 hours per week in a bakery. But there is no right to "liberty" under the Due Process Clause, though today's opinion repeatedly makes that claim. * * * The Fourteenth Amendment *expressly allows* States to deprive their citizens of "liberty," *so long as "due process of law" is provided[.]*

Our opinions applying the doctrine known as "substantive due process" hold that the Due Process Clause prohibits States from infringing *fundamental* liberty interests, unless the infringement is narrowly tailored to serve a compelling state interest. *Washington v. Glucksberg*, 521 U.S., at 721. We have held repeatedly, in cases the Court today does not overrule, that *only* fundamental rights qualify for this so-called "heightened scrutiny" protection—that is, rights which are " 'deeply rooted in this Nation's history and tradition,' " *ibid.* See *Reno v. Flores*, 507 U.S. 292, 303 (1993) * * * *United States v. Salerno*, 481 U.S. 739, 751 (1987) * * * See also *Michael H. v. Gerald D.*, 491 U.S. 110, 122 (1989) * * * *Moore v. East Cleveland*, 431 U.S. 494, 503 (1977) (plurality opinion); *Meyer v. Nebraska*, 262 U.S. 390, 399 (1923) * * * All other liberty interests may be abridged or abrogated pursuant to a validly enacted state law if that law is rationally related to a legitimate state interest.

Bowers held * * * that criminal prohibitions of homosexual sodomy are not subject to heightened scrutiny because they do not implicate a "fundamental right" under the Due Process Clause, 478 U.S., at 191–194. * * *

The Court today does not overrule this holding. Not once does it describe homosexual sodomy as a "fundamental right" or a "fundamental liberty interest," nor does it subject the Texas statute to strict scrutiny. Instead, having failed to establish that the right to homosexual sodomy is " 'deeply rooted in this Nation's history and tradition,' " the Court concludes that the application of Texas's statute to petitioners' conduct fails the rational-basis test, and overrules *Bowers'* holding to the contrary, see *id.*, at 196. * * *

* * *

It is (as *Bowers* recognized) entirely irrelevant whether the laws in our long national tradition criminalizing homosexual sodomy were "directed at homosexual conduct as a distinct matter." *Ante*, at 7. Whether homosexual sodomy was prohibited by a law targeted at same-sex sexual relations or by a more general law prohibiting both homosexual and heterosexual sodomy, the only relevant point is that it *was* criminalized—which suffices to establish that homosexual sodomy is not a right "deeply rooted in our Nation's history and tradition." The Court today agrees that homosexual sodomy was criminalized and thus does not dispute the facts on which *Bowers actually* relied.

* * * [T]he Court makes the claim, again unsupported by any citations, that "[l]aws prohibiting sodomy do not seem to have been enforced against consenting adults acting in private." *Ante*, at 8. The key qualifier here is "acting in private"—since the Court admits that sodomy laws *were* enforced against consenting adults (although the Court contends that prosecutions were "infrequent," *ante*, at 9). I do not know what "acting in private" means; surely consensual sodomy, like heterosexual intercourse, is rarely performed on stage. If all the Court means by "acting in private" is "on private premises, with the doors closed and windows covered," it is entirely unsurprising that evidence of enforcement would be hard to come by. (Imagine the circumstances that would enable a search warrant to be obtained for a residence on the ground that there was probable cause to believe that consensual sodomy was then and there occurring.) Surely that lack of evidence would not sustain the proposition that consensual sodomy on private premises with the doors closed and windows covered was regarded as a "fundamental right," even though all other consensual sodomy was criminalized. * * *

* * *

[A]n "emerging awareness" is by definition not "deeply rooted in this Nation's history and traditions," as we have said "fundamental right" status requires. Constitutional entitlements do not spring into existence because some States choose to lessen or eliminate criminal sanctions on certain behavior. Much less do they spring into existence, as the Court seems to believe, because *foreign nations* decriminalize conduct. The *Bowers* majority opinion *never* relied on "values we share with a wider civilization," *ante*, at 16, but rather rejected the claimed right to sodomy on the ground that such a right was not " 'deeply rooted in *this Nation's* history and tradition,' " 478 U.S., at 193–194 (emphasis added). * * *

* * *

The Texas statute undeniably seeks to further the belief of its citizens that certain forms of sexual behavior are "immoral and unacceptable," *Bowers, supra* at 196—the same interest furthered by criminal laws against fornication, bigamy, adultery, adult incest, bestiality, and obscenity. *Bowers* held that this *was* a legitimate state interest. The Court today reaches the opposite conclusion. The Texas statute, it says, "furthers *no legitimate state interest* which can justify its intrusion into the personal and private life of the individual," *ante*, at 18 (emphasis added). * * * This effectively decrees the end of all morals legislation. If, as the Court asserts, the promotion of majoritarian sexual morality is not even a *legitimate* state interest, none of the above-mentioned laws can survive rational-basis review.

* * *

[As for JUSTICE O'Connor's Equal Protection Clause analysis, m]en and women, heterosexuals and homosexuals, are all subject to [the statute's] prohibition of deviate sexual intercourse with someone of the same sex. To be sure, § 21.06 does distinguish between the sexes insofar as concerns the partner with whom the sexual acts are performed: men can violate the law only with other men, and women only with other women. But this cannot itself be a denial of equal protection, since it is precisely the same distinction regarding partner that is drawn in state laws prohibiting marriage with someone of the same sex while permitting marriage with someone of the opposite sex.

* * * A racially discriminatory purpose is always sufficient to subject a law to strict scrutiny, even a facially neutral law that makes no mention of race. See *Washington v. Davis*, 426 U.S. 229, 241–242 (1976). No purpose to discriminate against men or women as a class can be gleaned from the Texas law, so rational-basis review applies. That review is readily satisfied here by the same rational basis that satisfied it in *Bowers*—society's belief that certain forms of sexual behavior are "immoral and unacceptable," 478 U.S., at 196. This is the same justification that supports many other laws regulating sexual behavior that make a distinction based upon the identity of the partner—for example, laws against adultery, fornication, and adult incest, and laws refusing to recognize homosexual marriage.

JUSTICE O'CONNOR argues that the discrimination in this law which must be justified is not its discrimination with regard to the sex of the partner but its discrimination with regard to the sexual proclivity of the principal actor.

"While it is true that the law applies only to conduct, the conduct targeted by this law is conduct that is closely correlated with being homosexual. Under such circumstances, Texas' sodomy law is targeted at more than conduct. It is instead directed toward gay persons as a class." *Ante*, at 5.

Of course the same could be said of any law. A law against public nudity targets "the conduct that is closely correlated with being a nudist," and hence "is targeted at more than conduct"; it is "directed toward nudists as a class." But be that as it may. Even if the Texas law *does* deny equal protection to "homosexuals as a class," that denial *still* does not need to be justified by anything more than a rational basis, which our cases show is satisfied by the enforcement of traditional notions of sexual morality.

* * *

Today's opinion is the product of a Court, which is the product of a law-profession culture, that has largely signed on to the so-called homosexual agenda, by which I mean the agenda promoted by some homosexual activists directed at eliminating the moral opprobrium that has traditionally attached to homosexual conduct. * * *

One of the most revealing statements in today's opinion is the Court's grim warning that the criminalization of homosexual conduct is "an invitation to subject homosexual persons to discrimination both in the public and in the private spheres." *Ante*, at 14. It is clear from this that the Court has taken sides in the culture war, departing from its role of assuring, as neutral observer, that the democratic rules of engagement are observed. Many Americans do not want persons who openly engage in homosexual conduct as partners in their business, as scoutmasters for their children, as teachers in their children's schools, or as boarders in their home. They view this as protecting themselves and their families from a lifestyle that they believe to be immoral and destructive. The Court views it as "discrimination" which it is the function of our judgments to deter. So imbued is the Court with the law profession's anti-anti-homosexual culture, that it is seemingly unaware that the attitudes of that culture are not obviously "mainstream[.]" * * *

* * * [P]ersuading one's fellow citizens is one thing, and imposing one's views in absence of democratic majority will is something else. I would no more *require* a State to criminalize homosexual acts—or, for that matter, display *any* moral disapprobation of them—than I would *forbid* it to do so. What Texas has chosen to do is well within the range of traditional democratic action, and its hand should not be stayed through the invention of a brand-new "constitutional right" by a Court that is impatient of democratic change. It is indeed true that "later generations can see that laws once thought necessary and proper in fact serve only to oppress," *ante*, at 18; and when that happens, later generations can repeal those laws. But it is the premise of our system that those judgments are to be made by the people, and not imposed by a governing caste that knows best.

* * *

■ JUSTICE THOMAS, dissenting.

I join JUSTICE SCALIA'S dissenting opinion. I write separately to note that the law before the Court today "is ... uncommonly silly." *Griswold v. Connecticut*, 381 U.S. 479, 527 (1965) (Stewart, J., dissenting). If I were a member of the Texas Legislature, I would vote to repeal it. Punishing someone for expressing his sexual preference through noncommercial consensual conduct with another adult does not appear to be a worthy way to expend valuable law enforcement resources.

Notwithstanding this, I recognize that as a member of this Court I am not empowered to help petitioners and others similarly situated. My duty, rather, is to "decide cases 'agreeably to the Constitution and laws of the United States.'" *Id.*, at 530. And, just like Justice Stewart, I "can find [neither in the Bill of Rights nor any other part of the Constitution a] general right of privacy," *ibid.*, or as the Court terms it today, the "liberty of the person both in its spatial and more transcendent dimensions," *ante*, at 1.

———

NOTES AND QUESTIONS

1. *Moore* in context of *Lawrence*. The plurality opinion in *Moore* relied on the primary place that the extended family has traditionally occupied in United States history. This reasoning is similar to that used in *Bowers v. Hardwick*, 478 U.S. 186 (1986), where a history and tradition of intolerance for homosexual conduct was used to support an anti-sodomy law. However, now that *Lawrence v. Texas*, 539 U.S. 558 (2003) has overruled *Bowers*, is the history and tradition argument which was invoked by the plurality in *Moore* on shaky ground? *See* David M. Wagner, *Hints, Not Holdings: Use of Precedent in* Lawrence v. Texas, 18 BYU J. PUB. L. 681 (2004); Susan

Austin Blazier, Note, *The Irrational Use of Rational Basis Review in* Lawrence v. Texas, 26 CAMPBELL L. REV. 21 (2004).

2.   Justice O'Connor's concurrence.

a.   Domestic partners and O'Connor's concurrence in *Lawrence*. In her concurring opinion in *Lawrence v. Texas*, 539 U.S. 558 (2003) (O'Connor, J., concurring), Justice O'Connor notes that the conduct targeted by the Texas sodomy law was "closely correlated with being homosexual," and that this contributed to her decision that that law violated the equal protection clause. Under that rationale, it would seem that the state law that forbids recognition of domestic partners as dependants would also violate the equal protection clause, given that, as long as homosexuals are not allowed to marry, they will be forced into domestic partnership arrangements. Does this mean, under O'Connor's equal protection argument, that the state would be required to extend positive benefits (like domestic partner benefits) to homosexuals if those benefits are extended to heterosexuals?

In May 1992, MCA Corporation announced that it would provide health benefits to employees' same-sex partners, but not heterosexual domestic partners. William V. Vetter, *Restrictions on Equal Treatment of Unmarried Domestic Partners*, 5 B.U. PUB. INT. L.J. 1, 3 (1995). Is this asymmetric treatment of same-sex and opposite domestic partnerships discriminatory, or is some level of asymmetry necessary in order to compensate for the asymmetry in marriage laws between same-sex and opposite-sex couples?

b.   Heterosexual domestic partnership. Domestic partnership arrangements are certainly not limited to same-sex couples. Would the "correlated with" approach O'Conner uses to equal protection sweep too broadly and end up refuting legislative intent by requiring domestic partner benefits for all cohabiting couples? However, if you reject a "correlated with" approach to equal protection, what would prevent a legislature from enacting a law which fell much more heavily on some disfavored group but had an ostensibly neutral purpose, like promoting marriage?

3.   Morality as a state interest. Justice Scalia's dissent is longer than the opinion of the court itself, yet in eleven pages of dissent, he devotes only two paragraphs to the majority opinion, and those two paragraphs merely observe that no other society has decreed that morality is a sufficient basis for the enactment of a law. Does this mean that Scalia believes that enforcing public morality should be considered a legitimate state interest? *See* TracyLee Schimelfenig, Note, *Recognition of the Rights of Homosexuals: Implications of* Lawrence v. Texas, 40 CAL. W. L. REV. 149, 158–59 (2003). If that is the case, under Scalia's philosophy, can any law *ever* fail a rational basis review, since, presumably, the public elected the legislature and the legislature writes laws that are consistent with the social norms of the society that elected them? In other words, if morality alone is a legitimate state interest, is there anything left of due process?

4.   Silly laws and legitimate state interests. Justice Thomas' dissent begins by stating that the Texas anti-sodomy law is "uncommonly silly." Given that Justice Thomas does not believe that enforcing this law is a "worthy" use of government resources, how can he support the idea that it survives a due process attack for lacking a rational relation to a legitimate state interest? Is Thomas' version of due process something closer to "a silly relation to an unworthy government interest?" *See* Kris Franklin, *Homophobia and the "Matthew Shepard Effect": In* Lawrence v. Texas, 48 N.Y.L. SCH. L. REV. 657, 667 at n.51 (2004).

5.   The limits of *Lawrence*. The holding of the court in this case is that "[t]he Texas statute furthers no legitimate state interest which can justify its intrusion into the personal and private life of the individual." However, this holding raises an interesting question: is the Texas statute unconstitutional because it furthers no legitimate state interest, or because it intrudes into the private life of the individual? If the former is true, then it would seem that all morals-based legislation is illegitimate and, unless it has some ancillary benefits, will most likely be struck down. If the latter is the case, *Lawrence* is a much more limited victory for gay rights, essentially stating that individuals have the right to be homosexual in their bedrooms, but nowhere else. *See* Wagner, *supra* at 226, n.1.

6.   Response of the church to changing social norms. In response to the decision in *Lawrence v. Texas*, televangelist Pat Robertson issued a national call for Christians to pray for the retirement of Justices O'Connor, Stevens, and Ginsburg. Interview by Paula Zahn with Pat Robertson, *Pat Robertson: Pray For Justices to Retire*, July 17, 2003, *available at* http://www.cnn.com/2003/LAW/07/17/cnna.robertson/. Additionally, the Catholic Church has issued a statement condemning homosexual marriage. Victor L. Simpson, *Vatican Issues Offensive on Gay Marriages*, ASSOCIATED PRESS, July 28, 2003.

7.   Additional reading. For additional information on morality laws, see generally Peter M. Cicchino, *Reason and the Rule of Law: Should Bare Assertions of "Public Morality" Qualify as Legitimate Government Interests for the Purposes of Equal Protection Review?*, 87 GEO. L.J. 139 (1998); Steve Sheppard, *The State Interest in the Good Citizen: Constitutional Balance Between the Citizen and the Perfectionist State*, 45 HASTINGS L.J. 969 (1994). For a look at existing methods of gaining state recognition of same-sex marriages, see Phyllis Randolph Frye & Alyson Dodi Meiselman, *Same–Sex Marriages Have Existed Legally in the United States for a Long Time Now*, 64 ALB. L. REV. 1031 (2001). For an overview of the evolving definition of family with respect to same-sex unions, see Paula Ettelbrick, *Domestic Partnership, Civil Unions, or Marriage: One Size Does Not Fit All*, 64 ALB. L. REV. 905 (2001).

E.   A FAMILY BASED ON SAME–SEX MARRIAGE

Goodridge v. Department of Public Health

798 N.E.2d 941 (Mass. 2003).

■ MARSHALL, C.J.

Marriage is a vital social institution. The exclusive commitment of two individuals to each other nurtures love and mutual support; it brings stability to our society. For those who choose to marry, and for their children, marriage provides an abundance of legal, financial, and social benefits. In return it imposes weighty legal, financial, and social obligations. The question before us is whether, consistent with the Massachusetts Constitution, the Commonwealth may deny the protections, benefits, and obligations conferred by civil marriage to two individuals of the same sex who wish to marry. We conclude that it may not. The Massachusetts Constitution affirms the dignity and equality of all individuals. It forbids the creation of second-class citizens. In reaching our conclusion we have given full deference to the arguments made by the Commonwealth. But it has failed to identify any constitutionally adequate reason for denying civil marriage to same-sex couples.

We are mindful that our decision marks a change in the history of our marriage law. Many people hold deep-seated religious, moral, and ethical convictions that marriage should be limited to the union of one man and one woman, and that homosexual conduct is immoral. Many hold equally strong religious, moral, and ethical convictions that same-sex couples are entitled to be married, and that homosexual persons should be treated no differently than their heterosexual neighbors. Neither view answers the question before us. * * *

[In *Lawrence*,] the Court affirmed that the core concept of common human dignity protected by the Fourteenth Amendment to the United States Constitution precludes government intrusion into the deeply personal realms of consensual adult expressions of intimacy and one's choice of an intimate partner. The Court also reaffirmed the central role that decisions whether to marry or have children bear in shaping one's identity. * * *

Barred access to the protections, benefits, and obligations of civil marriage, a person who enters into an intimate, exclusive union with another of the same sex is arbitrarily deprived of membership in one of our community's most rewarding and cherished institutions. That exclusion is incompatible with the constitutional principles of respect for individual autonomy and equality under law.

I

The plaintiffs are fourteen individuals from five Massachusetts counties. * * *

In March and April, 2001, each of the plaintiff couples attempted to obtain a marriage license from a city or town clerk's office. * * * In each case, the clerk either refused to accept the notice of intention to marry or denied a marriage license to the couple on the ground that Massachusetts does not recognize same-sex marriage. Because obtaining a marriage license is a necessary prerequisite to civil marriage in Massachusetts, denying marriage licenses to the plaintiffs was tantamount to denying them access to civil marriage itself, with its appurtenant social and legal protections, benefits, and obligations.

[The District Court ruled in favor of the defendants, concluding "prohibiting same-sex marriage rationally furthers the Legislature's legitimate interest in safeguarding the 'primary purpose' of marriage, 'procreation.' "]

* * *

III

A

The larger question is whether, as the department claims, government action that bars same-sex couples from civil marriage constitutes a legitimate exercise of the State's authority to regulate conduct, or whether, as the plaintiffs claim, this categorical marriage exclusion violates the Massachusetts Constitution. We have recognized the long-standing statutory understanding, derived from the common law, that "marriage" means the lawful union of a woman and a man. But that history cannot and does not foreclose the constitutional question.

The plaintiffs' claim that the marriage restriction violates the Massachusetts Constitution can be analyzed in two ways. Does it offend the Constitution's guarantees of equality before the law? Or do the liberty and due process provisions of the Massachusetts Constitution secure the plaintiffs' right to marry their chosen partner? In matters implicating marriage, family life, and the upbringing of children, the two constitutional concepts frequently overlap, as they do here. * * *

We begin by considering the nature of civil marriage itself. Simply put, the government creates civil marriage. In Massachusetts, civil marriage is, and since pre-Colonial days has been, precisely what its name implies: a wholly secular institution. * * *

Civil marriage is created and regulated through exercise of the police power. * * * In broad terms, it is the Legislature's power to enact rules to regulate conduct, to the extent that such laws are "necessary to secure the health, safety, good order, comfort, or general welfare of the community." * * *

Without question, civil marriage enhances the "welfare of the community." It is a "social institution of the highest importance." * * * Civil marriage anchors an ordered society by encouraging stable relationships over transient ones. It is central to the way the Commonwealth identifies individuals, provides for the orderly distribution of property, ensures that children and adults are cared for and supported whenever possible from private rather than public funds, and tracks important epidemiological and demographic data.

Marriage also bestows enormous private and social advantages on those who choose to marry. Civil marriage is at once a deeply personal commitment to another human being and a highly public celebration of the ideals of mutuality, companionship, intimacy, fidelity, and family. * * *

Tangible as well as intangible benefits flow from marriage. The marriage license grants valuable property rights to those who meet the entry requirements, and who agree to what might otherwise be a burdensome degree of government regulation of their activities. * * *

The benefits accessible only by way of a marriage license are enormous, touching nearly every aspect of life and death. The department states that "hundreds of statutes" are related to marriage and to marital benefits. With no attempt to be comprehensive, we note that some of the statutory benefits conferred by the Legislature on those who enter into civil marriage include, as to property [including: joint Massachusetts income tax filing, automatic rights to inherit the property of a deceased spouse who does not leave a will, and entitlement to wages owed to a deceased employee].

* * *

Where a married couple has children, their children are also directly or indirectly, but no less auspiciously, the recipients of the special legal and economic protections obtained by civil marriage. Notwithstanding the Commonwealth's strong public policy to abolish legal distinctions between marital and nonmarital children in providing for the support and care of minors, * * * the fact remains that marital children reap a measure of family stability and economic security based on their parents' legally privileged status that is largely inaccessible, or not as readily accessible, to nonmarital children. Some of these benefits are social, such as the enhanced approval that still attends the status of being a marital child. Others are material, such as the greater ease of access to family-based State and Federal benefits that attend the presumptions of one's parentage.

It is undoubtedly for these concrete reasons, as well as for its intimately personal significance, that civil marriage has long been termed a "civil right." * * *

Without the right to marry—or more properly, the right to choose to marry—one is excluded from the full range of human experience and denied full protection of the laws for one's "avowed commitment to an intimate and lasting human relationship." * * * Because civil marriage is central to the lives of individuals and the welfare of the community, our laws assiduously protect the individual's right to marry against undue government incursion. Laws may not "interfere directly and substantially with the right to marry." * * *

B

For decades, indeed centuries, in much of this country (including Massachusetts) no lawful marriage was possible between white and black Americans. That long history availed not when the Supreme Court of California held in 1948 that a legislative prohibition against interracial marriage violated the due process and equality guarantees of the Fourteenth Amendment, *Perez v. Sharp,* * * * or when, nineteen years later, the United States Supreme Court also held that a statutory bar to interracial marriage violated the Fourteenth Amendment, *Loving v. Virginia,* * * * As both *Perez* and *Loving* make clear, the right to marry means little if it does not include the right to marry the person of one's choice, subject to appropriate government restrictions in the interests of public health, safety, and welfare. * * * As it did in *Perez* and *Loving,* history must yield to a more fully developed understanding of the invidious quality of the discrimination. * * *

The individual liberty and equality safeguards of the Massachusetts Constitution protect both "freedom from" unwarranted government intrusion into protected spheres of life and "freedom to" partake in benefits created by the State for the common good. * * * Both freedoms are involved here. Whether and whom to marry, how to express sexual intimacy, and whether and how to establish a family—these are among the most basic of every individual's liberty and due process rights. * * * And central to personal freedom and security is the assurance that the laws will apply equally to persons in similar situations. "Absolute equality before the law is a fundamental principle of our own Constitution." * * * The liberty interest in choosing whether and whom to marry would be hollow if the Commonwealth could, without sufficient justification, foreclose an individual from freely choosing the person with whom to share an exclusive commitment in the unique institution of civil marriage.

* * *

The department posits three legislative rationales for prohibiting same-sex couples from marrying: (1) providing a "favorable setting for procreation"; (2) ensuring the optimal setting for child rearing, which the department defines as "a two-parent family with one parent of each sex"; and (3) preserving scarce State and private financial resources. We consider each in turn.

The judge in the Superior Court endorsed the first rationale, holding that "the state's interest in regulating marriage is based on the traditional concept that marriage's primary purpose is procreation." This is incorrect. Our laws of civil marriage do not privilege procreative heterosexual intercourse between married people above every other form of adult intimacy and every other means of creating a family. * * * People who have never consummated their marriage, and never plan to, may be and stay married. * * * While it is certainly true that many, perhaps most, married couples have children together (assisted or unassisted), it is the exclusive and permanent commitment of the marriage partners to one another, not the begetting of children, that is the sine qua non of civil marriage.

Moreover, the Commonwealth affirmatively facilitates bringing children into a family regardless of whether the intended parent is married or unmarried, whether the child is adopted or born into a family, whether assistive technology was used to conceive the child, and whether the parent or her partner is heterosexual, homosexual, or bisexual. If procreation were a necessary component of civil marriage, our statutes would draw a tighter circle around the permissible bounds of nonmarital child bearing and the creation of families by noncoital means. The attempt to isolate procreation as "the source of a fundamental right to marry," * * * overlooks the integrated way in which courts have examined the complex and overlapping realms of personal autonomy, marriage, family life, and child rearing. Our jurisprudence recognizes that, in these nuanced and fundamentally private areas of life, such a narrow focus is inappropriate.

* * *

The department's first stated rationale, equating marriage with unassisted heterosexual procreation, shades imperceptibly into its second: that confining marriage to opposite-sex couples ensures that children are raised in the "optimal" setting. Protecting the welfare of children is a paramount State policy. Restricting marriage to opposite-sex couples, however, cannot plausibly further this policy. * * * The "best interests of the child" standard does not turn on a parent's sexual orientation or marital status. * * *

The department has offered no evidence that forbidding marriage to people of the same sex will increase the number of couples choosing to enter into opposite-sex marriages in order to have and raise children. There is thus no rational relationship between the marriage statute and the Commonwealth's proffered goal of protecting the "optimal" child rearing unit. Moreover, the department readily concedes that people in same-sex couples may be "excellent" parents. These couples (including four of the plaintiff couples) have children for the reasons others do—to love them, to care for them, to nurture them. But the task of child rearing for same-sex couples is made infinitely harder by their status as outliers to the marriage laws. * * * Given the wide range of public benefits reserved only for married couples, we do not credit the department's contention that the absence of access to civil marriage amounts to little more than an inconvenience to same-sex couples and their children. Excluding same-sex couples from civil marriage will not make children of opposite-sex marriages more secure, but it does prevent children of same-sex couples from enjoying the immeasurable advantages that flow from the assurance of "a stable family structure in which children will be reared, educated, and socialized." * * *

The third rationale advanced by the department is that limiting marriage to opposite-sex couples furthers the Legislature's interest in conserving scarce State and private financial resources. The marriage restriction is rational, it argues, because the General Court logically could assume that same-sex couples are more financially independent than married couples and thus less needy of public marital benefits, such as tax advantages, or private marital benefits, such as employer-financed health plans that include spouses in their coverage.

An absolute statutory ban on same-sex marriage bears no rational relationship to the goal of economy. First, the department's conclusory generalization—that same-sex couples are less financially dependent on each other than opposite-sex couples—ignores that many same-sex couples, such as many of the plaintiffs in this case, have children and other dependents (here, aged parents) in their care. The department does not contend, nor could it, that these dependents are less needy or deserving than the dependents of married couples. Second, Massachusetts marriage laws do not condition receipt of public and private financial benefits to married individuals on a demonstration of financial dependence on each other; the benefits are available to married couples regardless of whether they mingle their finances or actually depend on each other for support.

* * *

It has been argued that, due to the State's strong interest in the institution of marriage as a stabilizing social structure, only the Legislature can control and define its boundaries. * * * The Massachusetts Constitution requires that legislation meet certain criteria and not extend beyond certain limits. It is the function of courts to determine whether these criteria are met and whether these limits are exceeded. In most instances, these limits are defined by whether a rational basis exists to conclude that legislation will bring about a rational result. The Legislature in the first instance, and the courts in the last instance, must ascertain whether such a rational basis exists. To label the court's role as usurping that of the Legislature, * * * is to misunderstand the nature and purpose of judicial review. We owe great deference to the Legislature to decide social and policy issues, but it is the traditional and settled role of courts to decide constitutional issues.

* * *

The history of constitutional law "is the story of the extension of constitutional rights and protections to people once ignored or excluded." * * * As a public institution and a right of fundamental importance, civil marriage is an evolving paradigm. * * * Marriage has survived [many] transformations, and we have no doubt that marriage will continue to be a vibrant and revered institution.

* * *

■ [GREANEY, J. concurred in the opinion]

◗ [SPINA, J. and SOSMAN, J. dissented, with CORDY, JJ. joining both opinions].

■ CORDY, J. (dissenting, with whom Spina and Sosman, JJ., join).

* * *

Civil marriage is the institutional mechanism by which societies have sanctioned and recognized particular family structures, and the institution of marriage has existed as one of the fundamental organizing principles of human society. * * * Marriage has not been merely a contractual arrangement for legally defining the private relationship between two individuals (although that is certainly part of any marriage). Rather, on an institutional level, marriage is the "very basis of the whole fabric of civilized society," * * * and it serves many important political, economic, social, educational, procreational, and personal functions.

Paramount among its many important functions, the institution of marriage has systematically provided for the regulation of heterosexual behavior, brought order to the resulting procreation, and ensured a stable family structure in which children will be reared, educated, and socialized. * * * Admittedly, heterosexual intercourse, procreation, and child care are not necessarily conjoined (particularly in the modern age of widespread effective contraception and supportive social welfare programs), but an orderly society requires some mechanism for coping with the fact that sexual intercourse commonly results in pregnancy and childbirth. The institution of marriage is that mechanism.

The institution of marriage provides the important legal and normative link between heterosexual intercourse and procreation on the one hand and family responsibilities on the other. * * * The alternative, a society without the institution of marriage, in which heterosexual intercourse, procreation, and child care are largely disconnected processes, would be chaotic.

The marital family is also the foremost setting for the education and socialization of children. Children learn about the world and their place in it primarily from those who raise them, and those children eventually grow up to exert some influence, great or small, positive or negative, on society. The institution of marriage encourages parents to remain committed to each other and to their children as they grow, thereby encouraging a stable venue for the education and socialization of children. * * *

It is difficult to imagine a State purpose more important and legitimate than ensuring, promoting, and supporting an optimal social structure within which to bear and raise children. At the very least, the marriage statute continues to serve this important State purpose. * * *

Taking all of this available information into account, the Legislature could rationally conclude that a family environment with married opposite-sex parents remains the optimal social structure in which to bear children, and that the raising of children by same-sex couples, who by definition cannot be the two sole biological parents of a child and cannot provide children with a parental authority figure of each gender, presents an alternative structure for child rearing that has not yet proved itself beyond reasonable scientific dispute to be as optimal as the biologically based marriage norm. * * *

NOTES AND QUESTIONS

1. **Economic framework for same sex marriage.**

   a. **Orderly distribution of property, private support for children's care.**

   "It is central to the way the Commonwealth identifies individuals, provides for the orderly distribution of property, ensures that children and adults are cared for and supported whenever possible from private rather than public funds..."

   b. **Property rights to those who choose to marry.**

   "The marriage license grants valuable property rights to those who meet the entry requirements, and who agree to what might otherwise be a burdensome degree of government regulation of their activities."

2. **Justifications for ban on same sex marriage.**

   a. Providing a "favorable setting for procreation"

    b. Ensuring the optimal setting for child rearing, which the department defines as "a two-parent family with one parent of each sex"

    c. Preserving scarce state and private financial resources

Which of the above listed rationales for banning same-sex marriage are based upon libertarian arguments for limited government and maximum personal autonomy?

3. Neo-classical economics and same sex marriage

Libertarian economist Milton Friedman has argued that there were four duties of government: (1) to protect citizens from military invasion, (2) to protect citizens from violence by fellow citizens, (3) to create and maintain the public works infrastructure and (4) to provide for "irresponsibles." Does a state or federal ban on same-sex marriage fit into any of these categories?

What position would you guess Milton and Rose Friedman take in the same-sex marriage debates? Would their position be consistent with economic libertarianism? If not, what rationale would they give for any inconsistency?

4. Queer theory arguments against same sex marriage?

Can you imagine what the arguments of gay advocates might be against same sex marriage? For a representative selection of such arguments, see WILLIAM H. ESKRIDGE & NAN D. HUNTER, *Families We Choose, in* SEXUALITY, GENDER AND THE LAW 1008–99 (2d ed. 2004), (featuring gay argument and counter arguments for same sex marriage).

Paula Ettelbrick argues that:

> "Marriage runs contrary to two of the primary goals of the lesbian and gay movement: the affirmation of gay identity and culture and the validation of many forms of relationships.... At this point in time, making legal marriage for lesbian and gay couples a priority would set an agenda of gaining rights for a few, but would do nothing to correct power imbalances between those who are married (whether gay or straight) and those who are not. Thus justice would not be gained.... Being queer means pushing the parameters of sex, sexuality, and family, and in the process transforming the very fabric of society.... The thought of emphasizing our sameness to married heterosexuals in order to obtain this 'right' terrifies me. It rips away the very heart and soul of what I believe it is to be a lesbian in this world. It robs me of the opportunity to make a difference. We end up mimicking all that is bad about the institution of marriage in our effort to appear to be the same as straight couples."

    Id. at 1098 (excerpted from Paula Ettelbrick, *Since When is Marriage a Path to Liberation*, OUTLOOK, Autumn 1989, at 8–12).

CHAPTER 4

Culture and Identity

Introduction

The assumptions of conventional economic theory largely ignore questions of race, class, or other variables that affect individual identity. The rational actor of economics is assumed to be, like the reasonable person of law, a male member of the dominant culture. This assumption allows the values and perspectives of the dominant groups to serve as a crude surrogate for a more refined understanding of other perspectives.

The major consequence of omitting identity from economic reasoning is that economic theory has been unable to provide effective tools for diagnosing some of the most critical issues of economic inequality. This omission is present in both theoretical models and empirical research assumptions. The "thin" accounts of how race, gender, and other identity variables play a role in creating economic distribution are now being vigorously challenged by more robust models that for the first time are explicitly concerned with the economic impact of identity.

In 2003, George Akerlof, a Nobel laureate in economics, and Rachel Kranton, a professor of economics, introduced an important model of economic behavior that explicitly addresses critical questions of race, class and other identity factors and their relationship to the distribution of economic resources.

In this chapter, we begin with Akerlof and Kranton's model that offers a persuasive account of identity and culture in the sphere of economic activity. Next, we take up the insights of social norm theory, which draws upon modern sociological theory and turns attention to the dynamics of social group interaction. Finally, we look at race itself, a major identity variable. In this section, we explore the two competing theories about race and economics, and we look at law professor Ian Ayres' pathbreaking empirical study of evidence of pervasive racial discrimination in the market for the second-largest consumer retail purchase: new cars. Ayres has extended his empirical studies of racial discrimination to include transactions as varied as kidney transplants, taxi tipping practices, and bail setting. From these investigations he has argued, with some success in actual litigation, for a more sensitive test of the disparate impact theory of racial discrimination. Ayres' view does not require proof of discriminatory intent, and relies instead upon statistical disparities that show discriminatory impact upon subordinated groups.

A. CULTURE AND IDENTITY

Economics and Identity

115 Q. J. ECON. 715 (2000).

GEORGE A. AKERLOF AND RACHEL E. KRANTON

This paper considers how identity, a person's sense of self, affects economic outcomes. We incorporate the psychology and sociology of identity into an economic model of behavior. In the utility function we propose, identity is associated with different social categories and how people in these categories should behave. We then construct a simple game-theoretic model showing how identity can affect individual interactions. The paper adapts these models to gender discrimination in the workplace, the economics of poverty and social exclusion, and the household division of labor. In each case, the inclusion of identity substantively changes conclusions of previous economic analysis.

I. INTRODUCTION

This paper introduces identity—a person's sense of self—into economic analysis. Identity can account for many phenomena that current economics cannot well explain. It can comfortably resolve, for example, why some women oppose "women's rights," as seen in microcosm when Betty Friedan was ostracized by fellow suburban housewives for writing *The Feminine Mystique*. Other problems such as ethnic and racial conflict, discrimination, intractable labor disputes, and separatist politics all invite an identity-based analysis. Because of its explanatory power, numerous scholars in psychology, sociology, political science, anthropology, and history have adopted identity as a central concept. This paper shows how identity can be brought into economic analysis, allowing a new view of many economic problems.

We incorporate identity into a general model of behavior and then demonstrate how identity influences economic outcomes. Specifically, we consider gender discrimination in the labor market, the household division of labor, and the economics of social exclusion and poverty. In each case, our analysis yields predictions, supported by existing evidence, that are different from those of existing economic models. The Conclusion indicates many other realms where identity almost surely matters.

Our identity model of behavior begins with social difference. Gender, a universally familiar aspect of identity, illustrates. There are two abstract social categories, "man" and "woman." These categories are associated with different ideal physical attributes and prescribed behaviors. Everyone in the population is assigned a gender category, as either a "man" or a "woman." Following the behavioral prescriptions for one's gender affirms one's self-image, or identity, as a "man" or as a "woman." Violating the prescriptions evokes anxiety and discomfort in oneself and in others. Gender identity, then, changes the "payoffs" from different actions.

This modeling of identity is informed by a vast body of research on the salience of social categories for human behavior and interaction. We present in the next section a series of examples of identity-related behavior. These examples, and other evidence, indicate that (1) people have identity-based payoffs derived from their own actions; (2) people have identity-based payoffs derived from others' actions; (3) third parties can generate persistent changes in these payoffs; and (4) some people may choose their identity, but choice may be proscribed for others.

The concept of identity expands economic analysis for at least four corresponding reasons.

First, identity can explain behavior that appears detrimental. People behave in ways that would be considered maladaptive or even self-destructive by those with other identities. The reason for this behavior may be to bolster a sense of self or to salve a diminished self-image.

Second, identity underlies a new type of externality. One person's actions can have meaning for and evoke responses in others. Gender again affords an example. A dress is a symbol of femininity. If a man wears a dress, this may threaten the identity of other men. There is an externality, and further externalities result if these men make some response.

Third, identity reveals a new way that preferences can be changed. Notions of identity evolve within a society and some in the society have incentives to manipulate them. Obvious examples occur in advertising (e.g., Marlboro ads). As we shall explore, there are many other cases, including public policies, where changing social categories and associated prescriptions affects economic outcomes.

Fourth, because identity is fundamental to behavior, choice of identity may be the most important "economic" decision people make. Individuals may—more or less consciously—choose who they want to be. Limits on this choice may also be the most important determinant of an individual's economic well-being. Previous economic analyses of, for example, poverty, labor supply, and schooling have not considered these possibilities. * * *

B. *Psychology and Experiments on Group Identification*

The prominence of identity in psychology suggests that economists should consider identity as an argument in utility functions. Psychologists have long posited a self or "ego" as a primary force of individual behavior. They have further associated an individual's sense of self to the social setting; identity is bound to social categories; and individuals identify with people in some categories and differentiate themselves from those in others.

While experiments in social psychology do not show the existence of a "self" or this identification per se, they do demonstrate that even arbitrary social categorizations affect behavior. Consider the Robbers Cave experiment. In its initial week, two groups of boys at a summer camp in Oklahoma were kept apart. During this period, the boys developed norms of behavior and identities as belonging to *their* group. When they met for a tournament in the second week, the eleven-year-old equivalent of war broke out, with name-calling, stereotyping, and fighting. Later experiments show that competition is not necessary for group identification and even the most minimal group assignment can affect behavior. "Groups" form by nothing more than random assignment of subjects to labels, such as even or odd. Subjects are more likely to give rewards to those with the same label than to those with other labels, even when choices are anonymous and have no impact on own payoffs. Subjects also have higher opinions of members of their own group.

Our modeling of identity exactly parallels these experiments. In the experiments ... there are social categories; there is an assignment of subjects to those social categories; finally, subjects have in mind some form of assignment-related prescriptions, else rewards would not depend on group assignment.

C.   Examples of Identity–Related Behavior

We next present a set of "real-world" examples of four different ways, outlined in the introduction and formalized in our utility function, that identity may influence behavior.

Our *first* set demonstrates that people have identity-related payoffs from their own actions. The impact of an action a_j *on utility* U_j depends in part on its effect on identity I_j.

Self-Mutilation. The first of these examples is perhaps the most dramatic: people mutilate their own or their children's bodies as an expression of identity. Tattooing, body-piercing (ear, nose, navel, etc.), hair conking, self-starvation, steroid abuse, plastic surgery, and male and female circumcision all yield physical markers of belonging to more or less explicit social categories and groups. In terms of our utility function, these practices transform an individual's physical characteristics to match an ideal. The mutilation may occur because people believe it leads to pecuniary rewards and interactions such as marriage. But the tenacity and defense of these practices indicate the extent to which belonging relies on ritual, and people have internalized measures of beauty and virtue.

Gender and Occupations. Female trial lawyer, male nurse, woman Marine—all conjure contradictions. Why? Because trial lawyers are viewed as masculine, nurses as feminine, and a Marine as the ultimate man. People in these occupations but of the opposite sex often have ambiguous feelings about their work. In terms of our utility function, an individual's actions do not correspond to gender prescriptions of behavior. A revealing study in this regard is Pierce's [1995] participant-observer research on the legal profession. Female lawyers thought of themselves as women, yet being a good lawyer meant acting like a man. Lawyers were told in training sessions to act like "Rambo" and to "take no prisoners." In the office, trial attorneys who did not "win big" were described as "having no balls." Intimidation of witnesses was "macho blasts against the other side." A Christmas skit about two partners dramatized the gender conflict:

[O]ne secretary dressed up as Rachel and another dressed up as Michael. The secretary portraying Michael ... ran around the stage barking orders and singing, "I'm Michael Bond, I'm such a busy man. I'm such a busy man." The other secretary followed suit by barking orders and singing. "I'm Rachel Rosen, I'm such a busy man, I mean woman. I'm such a busy man, I mean woman...." Michael responded to the spoof in stride.... Rachel, on the other hand, was very upset [Pierce, 1995, p. 130].

Female lawyers expressed their ambivalence in many discussions. "Candace," another partner, told Pierce: "I had forgotten how much anger I've buried over the years about what happened to the woman who became a lawyer ... To be a lawyer, somewhere along the way, I made a decision that it meant acting like a man. To do that I squeezed the female part of me into a box, put on the lid, and tucked it away" [Pierce 1995, p. 134].

Alumni Giving. Charitable contributions may yield a "warm glow" [Andreoni 1989], but how do people choose one organization over another? Charity to the organization with the highest marginal return would maximize its economic impact. Yet, at least for higher education, contributions may well reflect identity. Graduates give to *their own* alma mater. Alumni giving could enhance the value of a degree by maintaining an institution's reputation. But this explanation suffers from the collective action problem. And it does not account for student loyalty and identification with an institution, as expressed in such lyrics as "For God, for country, and for Yale."

Mountaineering. Why do people climb mountains? Loewenstein [1998] argues that facing the extreme discomfort and danger of mountaineering enhances an individual's sense of self.

Our *second* set of examples demonstrates that people have identity-related payoffs from others' actions. The effect of an action a_j on utility includes an impact on I_j.

Gender and Occupations. A woman working in a "man's" job may make male colleagues feel less like "men." To allay these feelings, they may act to affirm their masculinity and act against female coworkers. In her study of coal handlers in a power plant, Padavic [1991] interpreted the behavior of her male coworkers in this way. On one occasion, they picked her up, tossed her back and forth, and attempted to push her onto the coal conveyer belt (jokingly, of course). In the case of another worker, no one trained her, no one helped her, and when she asked for help, she was refused assistance that would have been routine for male coworkers.

To further assay the reasons for such behavior, we took a random-sample telephone survey relating a vignette about a female carpenter at a construction company who was "baited and teased" by a male coworker. We see in Table I that among the six possible explanations, 84 percent of the respondents said it was "somewhat likely," "likely," or "very likely" that the male worker behaved in this way because he felt less masculine. This explanation was one of the most popular, and more than three-quarters of the respondents thought that a woman in a man's job "frequently" or "almost always" faces such treatment.

Manhood and Insult. For a man, an action may be viewed as an insult which, if left unanswered, impugns his masculinity. As in the example above, an action a_{-j} impacts I_j, which may be countered by an action a_j. Psychologists Nisbett and Cohn [1996] have detected such identity concerns in experiments at the University of Michigan. These experiments, they argue, reveal remnants of the white antebellum Southern "culture of honor" in disparate reactions to insult of males from the U. S. South and North. Their experiments involved variations of the following scenario: an associate of the experimenters bumped subjects in the hallway as they made their way to the experiment. Rather than apologizing, the associate called the subject "asshole." Insulted Southerners were more likely than insulted Northerners and control Southerners to fill in subsequent word-completion tests with aggressive words (for example, g-un rather than f-un), and had raised cortisol levels.

TABLE I

VIGNETTE CONCERNING HARASSMENT AND EVALUATION OF POSSIBLE EXPLANATIONS

Vignette: Paul is a carpenter for a construction company. The company has just hired Christine, its first female carpenter, for 3 dollars *less* per hour than it pays Paul and the other carpenters. On Christine's first day of work, Paul and two of his coworkers bait and tease Christine, making it difficult for her to do her job.

Try to imagine why Paul behaved as he did. Rate each of the following explanations for Paul's behavior as not-at-all likely, not likely, somewhat likely, likely, or very likely.

Explanation	Fraction somewhat likely, likely, or very likely[a,b]	Average Score[c]
Paul put Christine down because he is afraid that by hiring a woman the company can lower his wage.	.36 (.06)	2.5 (.12)
Paul put Christine down because he does not feel that it is fair that Christine is getting a lower wage.	.13 (.04)	1.7 (.12)
Paul put Christine down because he feels less masculine when a woman is doing the same job.	.84 (.04)	3.4 (.12)
Paul put Christine down because he feels he and his friends will not be able to joke around if a woman is present.	.84 (.04)	3.6 (.12)
Paul put Christine down because he is afraid that other men will tease him if a woman is doing the same job.	.76 (.05)	3.3 (.13)
Paul put Christine down because he is afraid that people will think that his	.64 (.06)	2.9 (.12)

Explanation	Fraction likely, likely, or very likely[a,b]	Average Score[c]
requires less skill if a woman is doing the same job.		
Paul put Christine down because he is afraid that if he does not, then his male coworkers will start to tease him.	.80 (.05)	3.4 (.13)
Paul put Christine down because he feels that it is wrong for women to work in a man's job.	.77 (.05)	3.2 (.14)

a. Sample size is 70 households. Households were selected randomly from the Fremont, CA phonebook.

b. Standard errors are in parentheses.

c. Average with not-at-all likely = 1, not likely = 2, somewhat likely = 3, likely = 4, very likely = 5.

Most revealing that the insult affected identity, insulted Southerners were also more likely to fear that the experimenter had a low opinion of their masculinity. They will probably never meet the experimenter or the hallway accomplice again; their encounter in the experiment is otherwise anonymous. Their concern about the experimenter then can only be a concern about how they feel about themselves, about their own sense of identity, as perceived through the "mirror of the opinions and expectations of others" [Gleitman 1996, p. 343]. We see the same psychology in other examples.

Changing Groups or Violating Prescriptions. Because of j's *identification* with others, it may affect j's identity when another person in j's social category violates prescriptions or becomes a different person. A common response is scorn and ostracism, which distances oneself from the maverick and affirms one's own self-image. Such behavior occurs daily in school playgrounds, where children who behave differently are mocked and taunted. Those who seek upward mobility are often teased by their peers, as in *A Hope in the Unseen* [Suskind 1998], which describes Cedric Jennings' progress from one of Washington's most blighted high schools to Brown University. The book opens with Cedric in the high-school chemistry lab, escaping the catcalls of the crowd at an awards assembly. Those who try to change social categories and prescriptions may face similar derision because the change may devalue others' identity, as for the housewives in Betty Friedan's suburb.

Our *third* set of examples demonstrates that to some extent people choose their identity; that is, c_j may be partially a choice. Many women in the United States can choose either to be a career woman or a housewife (see Gerson [1986]). Parents often choose a school—public versus private, secular versus parochial—to influence a child's self-image, identification with others, and behavior. The choice of where to live at college can both reflect and change how students think of themselves. Fraternities, sororities, African-American, or other "theme"-oriented dorms are all associated with social groups, self-images, and prescribed behavior. The list can continue. The choice for an immigrant to become a citizen is not only a change in legal status but a change in identity. The decision is thus often fraught with ambivalence, anxiety, and even guilt.

Identity "choice," however, is very often limited. In a society with racial and ethnic categories, for example, those with nondistinguishing physical features may be able to "pass" as a member of another group. But others will be constrained by their appearance, voice, or accent.

Our *fourth* set of examples demonstrates the creation and manipulation of social categories **C** and prescriptions **P**.

Advertising. Advertising is an obvious attempt to manipulate prescriptions. Marlboro and Virginia Slims advertisements, for example, promote an image of the ideal man or woman complete with the right cigarette.

Professional and Graduate Schools. Graduate and professional programs try to mold students' behavior through a change in identity. As a "one-L" Harvard Law School student said: " 'They are turning me into someone else. They're making me different' " [Turow 1977, p. 73]. In medicine, theology, the military, and the doctorate, a title is added to a graduate's name, suggesting the change in person.

Political Identity. Politics is often a battle over identity. Rather than take preferences as given, political leaders and activists often strive to change a population's preferences through a change in identity or prescriptions. Again, examples abound. Fascist and populist leaders are infamous for their rhetoric fostering racial and ethnic divisions, with tragic consequences. Symbolic acts and transformed identities spur revolutions. The ringing of the Liberty Bell called on the colonists' identities as Americans. Gandhi's Salt March sparked an Indian national identity. The French Revolution changed subjects into *citizens*, and the Russian Revolution turned them into *comrades*.

III.   ECONOMICS AND IDENTITY: A PROTOTYPE MODEL

In this section we construct a prototype model of economic interaction in a world where identity is based on social difference. In addition to the usual tastes, utility from actions will also depend on identity. Identity will depend on two social categories—Green and Red—and the correspondence of own and others' actions to behavioral prescriptions for their category.

A.   *A Prototype Model*

We begin with standard economic motivations for behavior. There are two possible activities, Activity One and Activity Two. There is a population of individuals each of whom has a taste for either Activity One or Two. If a person with a taste for Activity One (Two) undertakes Activity One (Two), she earns utility V. An individual who chooses the activity that does not match her taste earns zero utility. In a standard model of utility maximization, each person would engage in the activity corresponding to her taste.

We next construct identity-based preferences. We suppose that there are two social categories, Green and Red. We assume the simplest division of the population into categories; all persons think of themselves and others as Green. We add simple behavioral prescriptions: a Green should engage in Activity One (in contrast to Reds who engage in Activity Two). Anyone who chooses Activity Two is not a "true" Green—she would lose her Green identity. This loss in identity entails a reduction in utility of I_s, where the subscript s stands for "self." In addition, there are identity externalities. If an i and j are paired, Activity Two on the part of i diminishes j's Green identity. j has a loss in utility I_o, where the subscript o denotes "other." After i has committed Activity Two, j may "respond." The response restores j's identity at a cost c, while entailing a loss to i in amount L.

Figure I represents an interaction between an individual with a taste for Activity One ("Person One") and an individual with a taste for Activity Two ("Person Two"). Person One chooses an activity first.

This model can be expressed by ideas central to the psychodynamic theory of personality, found in almost any psychology text. In personality development, psychologists agree on the importance of *internalization* of rules for behavior. Freud called this process the development of the *superego*. Modern scholars disagree with Freud on the importance of psychosexual factors in an individual's development, but they agree on the importance of *anxiety* that a person experiences when she violates her internalized rules. One's *identity*, or *ego*, or *self*, must be constantly "defended against anxiety in order to limit disruption and maintain a sense of unity" [Thomas 1996, p. 284]. In terms of our model, Person Two's internalization of prescriptions causes her to suffer a loss in utility of I_s if she chooses Activity Two. To avoid this anxiety, she may refrain from that activity.

Identification is a critical part of this internalization process: a person learns a set of values (prescriptions) such that her actions should conform with the behavior of some people and contrast with that of others. If Person One has internalized prescriptions via such identifications, another person's violation of the prescriptions will cause anxiety for Person One. In our model, this anxiety is modeled as a loss in utility of I_o. Person One's response, in our language, restores her identity, and in terms of the psychology textbook relieves her anxiety and maintains her sense of unity. Person One no longer loses I_o, although she does incur c.

* * *

IV.   Identity, Gender and Economics in the Workplace

An identity theory of gender in the workplace expands the economic analysis of occupational segregation. As recently as 1970, two-thirds of the United States' female or male labor force would have had to switch jobs to achieve occupational parity. This measure of occupational segregation remained virtually unchanged since the beginning of the century. Yet, in twenty years, from 1970 to 1990, this figure declined to 53 percent. An identity model points to changes in societal notions of male and female as a major cause.

The model we propose captures the "auras of gender" [Goldin 1990a] that have pervaded the labor market. Occupations are associated with the social categories "man" and "woman," and individual payoffs from different types of work reflect these gender associations. This model can explain patterns of occupational segregation that have eluded previous models. It also directly captures the consequences of the women's movement and affords a new economic interpretation of sex discrimination law.

Identity also provides a microfoundation for earlier models. The "distaste" of men for working with women, as in the crudest adaptations of racial discrimination models [Becker 1971; Arrow 1972], can be understood as due to loss in male identity when women work in a man's job. Similarly women's assumed lower desire for labor force participation (as in Mincer and Polachek [1974], Bulow and Summers [1986], and Lazear and Rosen [1990]) can be understood as the result of their identity as homemakers.

A.   The Model

There are two social categories, "men" and "women," with prescriptions of appropriate activities for each. A firm wishes to hire labor to perform a task. By the initial prescriptions, this task is appropriate only for men; it is a "man's job." Relative to a "woman's job," women lose identity in amount I_s by performing such work. In this situation, male coworkers suffer a loss I_o. They may relieve their anxiety by taking action against women coworkers, reducing everyone's productivity.

To avoid these productivity losses, the firm may change gender-job associations at a cost. The firm is likely to create a "woman's job" alongside the "man's job," rather than render the whole task gender neutral, when a new job description can piggyback on existing notions of male and female. A well-known historical example illustrates. In the nineteenth century, Horace Mann (as Secretary of Education for Massachusetts) transformed elementary school teaching into a woman's job, arguing that women were "more mild and gentle," "of purer morals," with "stronger parental impulses." Secondary school teaching and school administration remained jobs for men.

The model also indicates why gender-job associations may persist. If associations are sector-wide or economy-wide, and not firm-specific, perfectly competitive firms will underinvest in new job categories. Benefits would accrue to other firms. In the absence of market power or technological change, a shift in social attitudes and legal intervention would be necessary for changes in employment patterns.

The model easily extends to the decision to participate in the labor force. If women's identity is enhanced by work inside the home, they will have lower labor force attachment than men. Historically, female labor force participation rates, relative to male rates, have been both lower and more cyclically variable.

B.   Implications for Labor Market Outcomes

This identity model explains employment patterns arising from associations between gender and type of work. These patterns go beyond what can be explained by women's assumed lower labor force attachment as in Mincer and Polachek [1974], where women work in occupations that require little investment in firm-specific human capital.

In our model, women will dominate jobs whose requirements match construed female attributes and inferior social status; men eschew them. Historically, three occupations illustrate: secretaries (97.8 percent female in 1970) have often been called "office wives," and elements of sexuality are inscribed in the working relationship (boss = male, secretary = female) [MacKinnon 1979; Pringle 1988]. Secretaries are expected to serve their bosses, with deference, and to be attentive to their personal needs [Davies 1982; Kanter 1977; Pierce 1996]. Elementary school teachers (83.9 percent female), in contrast to secondary school teachers (49.6 percent female), are supposed to care for young children. Nurses (97.3 percent female) are supposed to be tender and care for patients, as well as be deferential to doctors [Fisher 1995; Williams 1989].

In our model, women do not enter male professions because of gender associations. Historically, many male professions have required similar levels of education and training to female professions and could have been amenable to part-time and intermittent work. Contrast nursing and teaching with accounting and law. All require college degrees and certification, and sometimes have tenure and experience-based pay. Only the very top of these professions have required continuity in employment and full-time work.

Rhetoric surrounding job shifts from male to female further demonstrates the salience of gender-job associations. The recruitment of women into "men's jobs" during World War II, for example, was accompanied by official propaganda and popular literature picturing women taking on factory work without loss of femininity [Milkman 1987; Honey 1984; Pierson 1986]. In addition, the jobs were portrayed as temporary; only the wartime emergency excused the violation of the usual gender prescriptions.

C. Effects of the Women's Movement

The model gives a theoretical structure for how the women's movement may have impacted the labor market. The movement's goals included reshaping societal notions of femininity (and masculinity) and removing gender associations from tasks, both in the home and in the workplace. In the model, such changes would decrease women's gains (men's losses) in identity from homemaking, and decrease the identity loss I_s of women (men) working in traditionally men's (women's) jobs, as well as the accompanying externalities I_o. These shifts would increase women's labor force participation and lead to a convergence of male and female job tenure rates. More women (men) would work in previously male (female) jobs.

All these outcomes are observed coincidental with and following the women's movement. Gender-job associations diminished, reflected in changes in language (e.g., firemen became firefighters). In 1998 the median job tenure of employed women over 25 was 0.4 years lower than that of men; in 1968 that gap had been 3.3 years. Changes in sex composition within occupations accounted for the major share of decline in occupational segregation from 1970–1990 [Blau, Simpson, and Anderson, 1998]. Of the 45 three-digit Census occupations that were 0.0 percent female in 1970, only one (supervisors: brickmasons, stonemasons, and tile setters), was less than 1 percent female twenty years later. Many incursions of females into male-dominated professions were very large. Consider again accounting and law. In 1970 (1990) females were 24.6 (52.7) percent of auditors and accountants, and 4.5 (24.5) percent of lawyers. Not only did the proportion of women in men's jobs increase, but so did the proportion of men in women's jobs (albeit much less dramatically). Of the triumvirate of explanations for such increases—technology, endowments, and tastes—elimination makes tastes the leading suspect, since there was no dramatic change in technology or endowments that would have caused such increased mixing on the job. Legal initiatives discussed next reflect such changes in tastes.

D. Gender–Job Associations and Sex Discrimination Law

Legal interpretations of sex discrimination correspond to earlier economic models as well as our own. Title VII of the Civil Rights Act of 1964 makes it unlawful for an employer to discriminate "against any individual ... with respect to ... compensation, terms, conditions of employment" or "to [adversely] limit, segregate, or classify his employees ... because of ... sex." At its most basic, this law prohibits a discriminatory exercise of "tastes" against women (analogous to Becker [1971] and Arrow [1972]). Courts also interpret Title VII as outlawing statistical discrimination by sex or criteria correlated with sex, even when women on average lack a desirable job qualification. Discriminatory hiring because of women's presumed lower workplace attachment, as in Lazear and Rosen [1990], was precisely the issue addressed in *Phillips v. Martin-Marietta*.

Our model, where sex discrimination occurs because jobs have gender associations, corresponds to a wider interpretation of Title VII. This interpretation is at the forefront of current legal debate and is supported by a number of precedents. In *Diaz v. Pan American World Airways*, the Court outlawed sex bans in hiring. The airline originally pleaded for their prohibition of male flight attendants because women were better at "the nonmechanical aspects of the job." But this association of gender with the job was disallowed on appeal since feminine traits were deemed irrelevant to the "primary function or services offered" (cited in MacKinnon [1979, p. 180]). *Price Waterhouse v. Hopkins* set a precedent for workers already hired. The plaintiff had been denied a partnership after negative evaluations for her masculine deportment. The Supreme Court ruled that "an employer who objects to aggressiveness in women but whose positions require this trait places women in an intolerable and impermissible Catch 22" (cited in Wurzburg and Klonoff [1997, p. 182]). Cases have also involved harassment of women working in men's jobs as, in the terminology of our model, male coworkers protect themselves from loss of identity I_o. *Berkman v. City of New York* reinstated a firefighter who had been dismissed because of substandard work performance. The Court ruled that the interference and harassment by her male coworkers made it impossible for her to perform her job adequately [Schultz 1998, p. 1770]. This expansive interpretation of a "hostile work environment," a category of sexual harassment which is in turn a category of sex discrimination, has been exceptional. Judges have viewed sexual desire as an essential element of sexual harassment. However, Schultz [1998] and Franke [1995] argue that any harassment derived from gender prescriptions has discriminatory implications (as depicted in our model) and are thus violations of Title VII.

V. Identity and the Economics of Exclusion and Poverty

This section will consider identity and behavior in poor and socially excluded communities. In an adaptation of the previous model of Greens and Reds, people belonging to poor, socially excluded groups will choose their identity. Greens identify with the dominant culture, while those with Red identity reject it and the subordinate position assigned to those of their "race," class, or ethnicity. From the point of view of those with Green identities, Reds are often making bad economic decisions; they might even be described as engaging in self-destructive behavior. Taking drugs, joining a gang, and becoming pregnant at a young age are possible signs of a Red identity. This aspect of behavior has not been explored in previous models, but it is implicit in Wilson's account of black ghetto poverty [1987, 1996]. It also is implicit in every study that finds significant dummy variables for "race," after adjustment for other measures of socioeconomic status. The Green/Red model of this section offers an explanation for the significance of such dummy variables. Furthermore, it yields a less monolithic view of poverty than current economic theories that emphasize conformity (e.g., Akerlof [1997] and Brock and Durlauf [1995]).

A. *Motivation for Model*

Our model reflects the many ethnographic accounts of "oppositional" identities in poor neighborhoods. MacLeod's [1987] study of teenagers in a Boston area housing project, for example, contrasts the murderous and alcoholic Hallway Hangers to their obedient and athletic peers, the Brothers. In *Learning to Labour* Willis [1977] describes the antagonism between the unruly "lads" and the dutiful "earholes" in a working-class English secondary school. Similarly, Whyte's [1943] description of Boston's Italian North End circa 1940 contrasts the Corner Boys to the College Boys. Yet earlier, turn-of-the century accounts of the Irish in the United States contrast the "lace curtain" Irish of poor districts to their neighbors (see, e.g., Miller [1985]).

Our model further evokes the psychological effects of social exclusion in the colonial experience analyzed by Bhabha [1983] and Fanon [1967], and in the context of African-Americans in the United States by Anderson [1990], Baldwin [1962], Clark [1965], DuBois [1965], Frazier [1957], Hannerz [1969], Rainwater [1970], Wilson [1987, 1996], and others. In these settings, individuals from particular groups can never fully fit the ideal type, the ideal "Green," of the dominant culture. Some in excluded groups may try to "pass" or integrate with the dominant group, but they do so with ambivalence and limited success. A series of autobiographies tells of the pain and anger of discovering that one is not really "Green." Former *New York Times* editor Mel Watkins [1998] titles the chapter on his freshman year at Colgate as "stranger in a strange land." Gandhi [1966], Fanon [1967], Fulwood [1996], Staples [1994], and Rodriguez [1982] all relate strikingly similar experiences of perceived or real rejection and alienation. This social exclusion may create a conflict: how to work within the dominant culture without betraying oneself. As Jill Nelson [1993, p. 10] explains her exhaustion after a long day of interviewing for a job at *The Washington Post*:

> I've also been doing the standard Negro balancing act when it comes to dealing with white folks, which involves sufficiently blurring the edges of my being so that they don't feel intimidated, while simultaneously holding on to my integrity. There is a thin line between Uncle-Tomming and Mau-Mauing. To fall off that line can mean disaster. On one side lies employment and self-hatred; on the other, the equally dubious honor of unemployment with integrity.

These reactions, it must be emphasized, reflect how dominant groups define themselves by the exclusion of others. The creation and evolution of such social differences are the subject of much historical research. Said [1978] documents the emergence of the Western idea of the "Oriental," a concept that had significant implications for colonialism. In the United States Roediger [1991] and other historians show how workers of European descent in the nineteenth century increasingly were defined as "white." Prior to Emancipation, this identity evoked the contrast between white freedom and African-American enslavement. In the model we construct, the key interaction is between such social differences and the adoption of oppositional identities by those in excluded groups.

Lack of economic opportunity may also contribute to the choice of an oppositional identity. Wilson [1987, 1996] underscores the relation between the decline in remunerative unskilled jobs, the loss of self-respect by men who cannot support their families, and the rise in inner city crime and drug abuse. This process is illustrated in microcosm by "Richard" in *Tally's Corner* [Liebow 1967]. Unable to find decent-paying work, he abandoned his family and joined Tally's group of idlers on the street corner. By adopting a different identity, Richard no longer suffered the guilt of a failed provider.

Red activities have negative pecuniary externalities. Richard's wife and children had to find alternative means of support. The prime goal of the "lads" in Willis' secondary school was to get a "laff," through vandalism, picking fights, and returning drunk to school from the local pub. Running a school with lads is difficult. The situation corresponds to the externalities in Benabou's [1993, 1996] models of high schooling costs in poor neighborhoods. Further externalities accrue from drug dealing, crime, and other "pathological" behavior. In our model, there are also identity-based externalities. A Red is angered by a Green's complicity with the dominant culture, while a Green is angered by a Red's "breaking the rules." Again consider Willis' lads and earholes. As the lads define themselves in contrast to the earholes, the earholes define themselves in contrast to the lads. The earholes are even more proestablishment than the teachers—feeling that the teachers should be stricter. The lads, in turn, bait the earholes. This situation is just one (relatively tame) example of how interaction between the two groups generates antagonism on both sides.

B. Identity Model of Poverty and Social Exclusion

As in the prototype model, there are two activities, One and Two. Activity One can be thought of as "working" and Activity Two as "not working." There is a large community, normalized to size one, of individuals. The economic return to Activity One for individual i is v_i which we assume is uniformly distributed between zero and one, to reflect heterogeneity in the population and to ensure interior solutions. The economic return to Activity Two is normalized to zero.

As for identity, there are two social categories, Green and Red. A Green suffers a loss in identity r, representing the extent to which someone from this community is not accepted by the dominant group in society. Those with the less adaptive Red identity do not suffer this loss. Behavioral prescriptions say that Greens (Reds) should engage in Activity One (Two). Thus, a Green (Red) loses identity from Activity Two (One) in amount I^G_s (I^R_s). Because Reds reject the dominant Green culture, they are also likely to have lower economic returns to Activity One than Greens. A Red individual i will only earn $v_i - a$ from Activity One, as well as suffer the loss I^R_s. There are also identity externalities when Greens and Reds meet. A Green (Red) suffers a loss I^G_o (I^R_o). In addition, Reds who have chosen Activity Two impose a pecuniary externality k on those who have chosen Activity One.

Each person i chooses an identity and activity, given the choices of everyone else in the community. We assume that people cannot modify their identity or activity for each individual encounter. Rather, individuals choose an identity and activity to maximize expected payoffs, given the probabilities of encounters with Greens who choose Activity One, Greens who choose Two, Reds who choose One, and Reds who choose Two.

* * *

D. Further Lessons from the Model

The model and its solution also afford interpretations of policies designed to reduce poverty and the effects of social exclusion.

First, the model indicates why residential Job Corps programs may succeed while other training programs fail [Stanley, Katz, and Krueger 1998]. According to the model, taking trainees out of their neighborhoods would eliminate, at least for a time, the negative effects of interaction with those with Red identities. Moreover, being in a different location may reduce a trainee's direct loss r from being Green and pursuing Activity One. That is, this loss may be both individual-specific and situational, and leaving a poor neighborhood is likely to generate a lower r than otherwise.

In a somewhat controlled experiment, the U.S. government tried to save money with JOBSTART, which preserved many of the features of Job Corps except the expensive housing of trainees. Follow-up studies of JOBSTART show little or no improvement in employment or earnings.

Second, the model affords an interpretation of different education initiatives for minority students. Like Job Corps, the Central Park East Secondary School (CPESS) in East Harlem may succeed because it separates Green students from Red students. Students, for example, must apply to the school, indicating their and their parents' willingness to adopt its rules (see Fliegel [1993] and Meier [1995] for this and other details). Another interpretation of CPESS and other successes (e.g., Comer [1980] in New Haven) parallels the logic of the all-Red equilibrium where some people nonetheless pursue Activity One. The schools take measures to reduce the loss in identity of Red students, I^R_s, in activities such as learning Standard English. Delpit's [1995] award-winning book *Other People's Children* proposes numerous ways to reduce the alienation that minority students may experience in school.

Finally, the model illuminates a set of issues in the affirmative action debate. Much of this debate concerns the success or failure of specific programs (see, e.g., Dickens and Kane [1996]). Yet, more is at stake. The rhetoric and symbolism of affirmative action may affect the level of social exclusion r. On the one hand, Loury [1995] argues that portraying African-Americans as victims, a portrayal necessary to retain affirmative action programs, is costly to blacks. In terms of the model, such rhetoric will increase r and the adoption of Red identities. On the other hand, affirmative action will decrease r, to the extent it is seen as an apology for previous discrimination and an invitation for black admission to the dominant culture. Reversal of affirmative action would negate this effect. To cite a recent example, our analysis suggests that removing affirmative action admissions criteria at the University of California and University of Texas Law Schools could have behavioral implications that far exceed the impact on applicants.

The identity model of exclusion, then, explains why legal equality may not be enough to eliminate racial disparities. If African-Americans choose to be Red because of exclusion and if whites perpetuate such exclusions, even in legal ways, there can be a permanent equilibrium of racial inequality. The negative externalities and their consequences, however, would disappear when the community is fully integrated into the dominant culture, so that $r = \mathbf{a} = 0$, and everyone in the community adopts a Green identity. This, of course, is the American ideal of the melting pot, or the new ideal of a mosaic where difference can be maintained within the dominant culture.

VI.   Identity and the Economics of the Household

An identity model of the household, unlike previous models, predicts an asymmetric division of labor between husbands and wives. Theories based on comparative advantage (e.g., Becker [1965] and Mincer [1962]) predict that whoever works more outside the home will work less inside the home, whether it be the husband or the wife. Yet, the data we present below indicate a gender asymmetry. When a wife works more hours outside the home, she still undertakes a larger share of the housework.

Hochschild's [1990] study *The Second Shift* reveals the details of such asymmetries. One of the couples in her study found an ingenious way to share the housework. "Evan Holt," a furniture salesman, took care of the lower half of the house (i.e., the basement and his tools). His wife "Nancy," a full-time licensed social worker, took care of the upper half. She took care of the child. He took care of the dog.

Quantitative evidence from Hochschild's sample and our data analysis suggest that the Holts conform to a national pattern. Figure III shows the low average of husbands' share of housework and its low elasticity with respect to their share of outside work hours. The figure plots shares of housework reported by married men in the Panel Study of Income Dynamics, as computed from answers to the question(s): "About how much time do you (your wife) spend on housework in an average week? I mean time spent cooking, cleaning, and doing other work around the house?" The intent of the question was to exclude child care. The figure plots men's share of housework as a fourth-order polynomial of their share of outside hours, for households by age of youngest child. When men do all the outside work, they contribute on average about 10 percent of housework. But as their share of outside work falls, their share of housework rises to no more than 37 percent. As shown in the figure the presence of children of different ages makes a small difference to the function. Similar results obtain when the independent variable is shares of income rather than shares of outside work hours.

Predicted values from tobit estimation

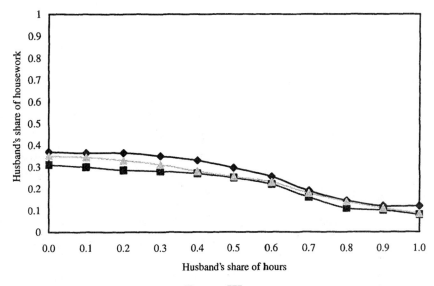

FIGURE III

Husband's Share of Housework versus Their Share of Outside Work Hours

Existing theories do not predict this asymmetry. Consider the following variant based on comparative advantage. Husband and wife both have the same utility function, which is increasing in quantity of a household public good that derives from their joint labor. Utility is decreasing in own labor inputs in outside and home production. We assume equal bargaining power, so that each marriage partner enjoys the same level of utility. With this framework, returns to specialization explain the observed division of labor when a wife has a comparative advantage in home production. Women who put in less than half of the outside work hours put in more than half the housework, as seen in the right-hand side of the graph of Figure III. But this model is inconsistent with the left-hand side of the graph.

Identity considerations can explain the high shares of housework of wives who undertake a large share of outside work hours. Add to the above model two social categories, "men" and "women." Prescriptions dictate that "men" should not do "women's work" in the home and "men" should earn more than their wives. Hochschild's interviews suggest that many men, and some women, hold these prescriptions. In the amended model, the husband loses identity when he does housework and when his wife earns more than half the household income. Equality of utility is restored when the wife undertakes more housework than her husband. Hochschild reports that in the "Tanagawa" household, for example, "Nina" earned more than half the family income, but she worked more than "Peter" at home to assuage his unease with the situation. Eventually, she quit her job.

VII.   CONCLUSION

This paper considers how identity affects economic outcomes. Following major themes in psychology and sociology, identity in our models is based on social difference. A person's sense of self is associated with different social categories and how people in these categories should behave. This simple extension of the utility function could greatly expand our understanding of economic outcomes. In a world of social difference, one of the most important economic decisions that an individual makes may be the type of person to be. Limits on this choice would also be critical determinants of economic behavior, opportunity, and well-being.

Identity affects economic behavior in our models through four avenues. First, identity changes the payoffs from one's own actions. We capture this possibility by a value I_s in our models. In our study of gender in the workplace, for example, a woman working in a "man's" job suffers a loss in utility, affecting the labor supply. Second, identity changes the payoffs of others' actions. We capture this externality by a value I_o in our models. A "Red" in our poverty model, for example, is harmed by a member of his own community who complies with the dominant culture. Third, the choice, or lack thereof, of different identities affects an individual's economic behavior. In our poverty model, while individuals could choose between

Green or Red, they could never be a "true" Green. The greater the extent of this social exclusion, the greater the possibility of equilibria in which individuals eschew remunerative activities. Finally, the social categories and behavioral prescriptions can be changed, affecting identity-based preferences. This possibility expanded the scope of employment policy in our model of gender in the workplace and of education policy in our study of social exclusion.

This paper has only scratched the surface of the economic implications of identity. A first tack in future research would be continued analysis of particular settings. Identity is likely to affect economic outcomes, for example, in areas of political economy, organizational behavior, demography, the economics of language, violence, education, consumption and savings behavior, retirement decisions, and labor relations. As in this paper, models that incorporate well-documented existing social categories and prescriptions could yield new results. A second tack in this agenda is comparative, examining identity across space and time. Researchers, for example, could consider why notions of "class" or "race" vary across countries; why might gender and racial integration vary across industries; what might explain the rise and fall of ethnic tensions. Such comparative studies would be a fruitful way to explore the formation of identity-based preferences.

In peroration, this paper explores how to incorporate identity into economic models of behavior. Many standard psychological and sociological concepts—*self-image, ideal type, in-group and out-group, social category, identification, anxiety, self-destruction, self-realization, situation*—fit naturally in our framework, allowing an expanded analysis of economic outcomes. This framework is then perhaps one way to incorporate many different nonpecuniary motivations for behavior into economic reasoning, with considerable generality and a common theme.

————

Identity in Mashpee

THE PREDICAMENT OF CULTURE: TWENTIETH-CENTURY ETHNOGRAPHY, LITERATURE, AND ART 277–346 (1988).

JAMES CLIFFORD

In August 1976 the Mashpee Wampanoag Tribal Council, Inc., sued in federal court for possession of about 16,000 acres of land constituting three-quarters of Mashpee, "Cape Cod's Indian Town." (The township of Mashpee extends inland from the Cape's southern shore, facing Martha's Vineyard, between Falmouth and Barnstable.) An unprecedented trial ensued whose purpose was not to settle the question of land ownership but rather to determine whether the group calling itself the Mashpee Tribe was in fact an Indian tribe, and the same tribe that in the mid-nineteenth century had lost its lands through a series of contested legislative acts.

The Mashpee suit was one of a group of land-claim actions filed in the late 1960s and 1970s, a relatively favorable period for redress of Native American grievances in the courts. Other claims were being initiated by the Gay Head Wampanoag Tribe on Martha's Vineyard; the Narragansets of Charlestown, Rhode Island; Western Pequots, Schaghticokes, and Mohegans in Connecticut; and Oneidas, St. Regis Mohawks, and Cayugas in New York. The Mashpee action was similar in conception to a much-publicized suit by the Passamaquoddy and Penobscot tribes laying claim to a large portion of the state of Maine. Their suit, after initial successes in Federal District Court, direct intervention from President Jimmy Carter, and five years of hard negotiation, resulted in a favorable out-of-court settlement. The tribes received $81.5 million and the authority to acquire 300,000 acres with Indian Country status.

The legal basis of the Penobscot-Passamaquoddy suit, as conceived by their attorney, Thomas Tureen, was the Non-Intercourse Act of 1790. This paternalist legislation, designed to protect tribal groups from spoliation by unscrupulous whites, declared that alienation of Indian lands could be legally accomplished only with permission of Congress. The act had never been rescinded, although throughout the nineteenth century it was often honored in the breach. When in the 1970s Indian groups appealed to the Non-Intercourse Act, they were attempting, in effect, to reverse more than a century of attacks on Indian lands. The alienations had been particularly severe for eastern groups, whose claim to collective land was often unclear. When court decisions confirmed that the Non–Intercourse Act applied to non-reservation Indians, the way was opened for suits, like those of the Maine tribes, claiming that nearly two centuries of Indian land transfers, even ordinary purchases, were invalid since they had been made without permission of Congress.

Although the Mashpee claim was similar to the Maine Indians', there were crucial differences. The Passamaquoddy and Penobscot were generally recognized Indian tribes with distinct communities and clear aboriginal roots in the area. The Mashpee plaintiffs represented most of the nonwhite inhabitants of what, for over three centuries, had been known as an "Indian town" on Cape Cod; but their institutions of tribal government had long been elusive, especially during the century and a half preceding the suit. Moreover, since about 1800 the Massachusett language had ceased to be commonly spoken in Mashpee. The town was at first largely Presbyterian then Baptist in its public religion. Over the centuries inhabitants had intermarried with other Indian groups, whites, blacks, Hessian deserters from the British Army during the Revolutionary War, Cape Verde islanders. The inhabitants of Mashpee were active in the economy and society of modern Massachusetts. They were businessmen, schoolteachers, fishermen, domestic workers, small contractors. Could these people of Indian ancestry file suit as the Mashpee Tribe that had, they claimed, been despoiled of collectively held lands during the mid-nineteenth century? This was the question a federal judge posed to a Boston jury. Only if they answered yes could the matter proceed to a land-claim trial.

The forty-one days of testimony that unfolded in Federal District Court during the late fall of 1977 bore the name *Mashpee Tribe v. New Seabury et al.,* shorthand for a complex, multipartied dispute. Mashpee Tribe referred to the plaintiffs, the Mashpee Wampanoag Tribal Council, Inc., described by its members as an arm of the Mashpee Tribe. A team of lawyers from the Native American Rights Fund, a nonprofit advocacy group, prepared their suit. Its chief architects were Thomas Tureen and Barry Margolin. In court the plaintiffs' case was argued by the trial lawyer Lawrence Shubow, with assistance from Tureen, Margolin, Ann Gilmore, and Moshe Genauer. New Seabury et al. referred to the New Seabury Corporation (a large development company), the Town of Mashpee (representing over a hundred individual landowners), and various other classes of defendant (insurance companies, businesses, property owners). The case for the defense was argued by James St. Clair (Richard Nixon's Watergate attorney) of the large Boston firm Hale and Dorr, and Allan Van Gestel of Goodwin, Proctor, and Hoar. They were assisted by a team of eight other lawyers.

The presence of the Town of Mashpee among the defendants requires explanation. It was not until 1869 that the community living in Mashpee was accorded formal township status. From 1869 until 1964 the town government was overwhelmingly in the hands of Indians. During this period every selectman but one was an Indian or married to an Indian. Genealogical evidence presented at the trial showed that the families of town officers were closely interrelated. No one contested the fact that before the 1960s Mashpee was governed by Indians. The disagreement was over whether they governed as an "Indian tribe."

This basic demographic and political situation, which had not altered drastically for over three centuries, was revolutionized during the early 1960s. Before then census figures showed a population in Mashpee fluctuating in the neighborhood of 350 Indians and "negroes," "coloreds," or "mulattoes" (the official categories shifted), and 100 or fewer whites. A reliable count of 1859, which served as a benchmark in the trial, listed only one white resident. After 1960 for the first time white were recorded in the majority and by 1970 whites outnumbered Indians and other people of color by 982 to 306. By 1968 two of the town's selectmen were whites, the third Indian. This proportion was in effect at the time of the lawsuit. Mashpee's white selectmen voted that the town should legally represent the non-Indian majority of property holders who were threatened by the land claim.

"Cape Cod's Indian Town" had finally been discovered. For centuries a backwater and a curiosity, in the 1950s and 1960s Mashpee became desirable as a site for retirement, vacation homes, condominiums, and luxury developments. Fast roads now made it accessible as a bedroom and weekend suburb of Boston. The new influx of money and jobs was first welcomed by many of Mashpee's Indian residents, including some of the leaders of the land-claim suit. They took advantage of the new situation. The town government, still run by Indians, enjoyed a surge in tax revenues. But when local government passed out of Indian control, perhaps for good, and as the scale of development increased, many Indians began to feel qualms. What they had taken for granted—that this was their town—no longer held true. Large tracts of undeveloped land formerly open for hunting and fishing were suddenly ringed with "No Trespassing" signs. The New Seabury development, on a choice stretch of coastline, with its two golf courses and expansionist plans, seemed particularly egregious. Tensions between traditional residents and newcomers increased, finally leading to the suit, filed with the support of most, but not all, of the Indians in Mashpee. The land claim, while focusing on a loss of property in the nineteenth century, was actually an attempt to regain control of a town that had slipped from Indian hands very recently.

Earl Mills

Earl Mills has taught high school in the Falmouth Public School system for over twenty-five years. Between 1952 and 1967 he lived in Falmouth, ten miles from Mashpee. Mills has taught physical education, health, and social studies. He advises the student council and directs various other extracurricular activities.

In Mashpee he shares ownership of the town's best restaurant with his ex-wife, Shirley. He is its principal cook.

Since the mid-fifties Mills has held the title of Chief Flying Eagle of the Mashpee Wampanoag Tribe.

On the witness stand he is earnest, engaging, very much the coach or Boy Scout leader. Forty-eight years old, trim, athletic-looking, he wears a striped necktie, blue blazer, loafers.

Mills recalls his youth in Mashpee during the thirties and forties. He was never as good a hunter as his brother, Elwood, so he often skipped the frequent hunting trips. Early on he asked questions and read books. He questioned his grandmother, "the strong arm" behind his uncle (who had held the formal title of chief and was "a drifter"), and also his mother, the treasurer and tax collector of the town, "the strong arm behind me."

In the thirties, Mills recalls, some townspeople wore regalia occasionally, and a few spoke a little Indian dialect. He remembers the festive atmosphere of a close community—selling corn at town meetings, the yearly beach outings, the annual herring run.

As a child he was shown the location of "Indian taverns." These were not drinking places, according to Mills, but just places where paths crossed. You would pick up a stick, spit on it, and throw it on a heap to appease spirits in the area.

Mills says he can still identify two "Indian taverns," but most have long since been cleared away because the sticks, piled high, were a fire hazard.

This is the extent of the Indian rituals Mills reports. Raised a Baptist, he does not now consider himself a Christian; but he believes in a creator, "something greater than me."

Mills says that when he inquired after Indian artifacts, especially the traditional Mashpee plaited baskets, he was told by his father that "those fellows up around Cambridge must've taken them" (a reference probably to the Harvard Anthropology Department). His father showed him how to plait bark baskets, a skill he had acquired as a young man from Eben Queppish, a master basket maker in Mashpee.

Mills recalls that as a boy he made fun of the old-timers, including the medicine man of the period, William James.

In Falmouth High School Mills excelled in athletics. ("You had to be a scrapper to make it.") Sports were a road to confidence in a threatening environment. Outside of school, like his father and other Mashpee Indians, he served as a guide for hunting and fishing parties in the region.

Q.: "How was your youth different from that of any small-town youth?"

A.: "We were different. We knew we were different. We were told we were different."

Only in the late forties did Mills learn Indian dancing—in the army. On a lonely evening during basic training at Fort Dix two comrades, a Montana Chippewa and a New York Iroquois, performed their dances. Mills was chagrined to admit that he knew none himself.

Earl Mills tells about his five children-four by his first wife, who is part Navajo, and one by his second wife, who is Caucasian. The eldest, Roxanne, is married to a Choctaw. Earl Jr. (called "Chiefy") lives in Falmouth and in recent years has become a champion drummer at various Indian gatherings and powwows. Shelly, also a fine drummer, attends Native American festivals all over the Northeast. Robert lives on Commonwealth Avenue in Boston. "He's into quill work, leather work, skins." Nancy, the child of Mills's second marriage, is now six years old. She does Indian dances. Her parents agree that she is a Wampanoag.

Mills explains his duties as tribal chief. He teaches beadwork, leatherwork, and basketry in Mashpee. Overall his job is to be a mediator, to keep his people "on balance."

Under questioning he cannot or will not give any specific examples of his mediations. Mills tells how in the late fifties and early sixties he and three whites formed a committee to restore the Old Indian Meeting House in Mashpee. The meeting house, which had fallen into disrepair, had for many years been the most visible symbol of Indian life in the town.

During the fifties there had been a tribal constitution of some sort (the document is introduced into evidence), but Mills testifies that the tribe did not follow the constitution as written. Tribal meetings were held irregularly, with notice passed by word of mouth. (Where, St. Clair asks on cross-examination, are the minutes for these purported tribal meetings?)

In the early seventies, Mills says, he attended a grant-writing seminar at Dartmouth College, along with Amelia Bingham, a state employee (sister of John Peters, the tribal medicine man, and Russell Peters, chairman of the Tribal Council, Inc.). Mills says he had little originally to do with the land suit. As chief he simply approved the action of the incorporated body on behalf of the tribe. It was discussed in his restaurant kitchen.

Earl Mills testifies that he respects John Peters. The two of them represent the Mashpee traditionalist wing. The modernists, he says, people like Russell Peters, are the legal arm of the tribe and represent its interests in dealings with the government, the courts, and foundations.

St. Clair's questions portray Chief Flying Eagle as an opportunist following rather than leading his people. They reveal that Mills's traditional authority was recently challenged by Russell Peters and others who wanted to sell beer at the annual Mashpee powwow, a festival attended by a considerable number of tourists and other outsiders. Over the chief's objections beer was sold. St. Clair harps on this evidence of lack of leadership. Rebuttals follow, concerning different tribal responsibilities and roles. There are references to President Carter's inability to control the (beer-related) behavior of his brother, Billy.

On the stand Chief Flying Eagle often sounds like a social studies teacher; his speech is larded with pat anecdotes and homilies.

Only once, toward the end of his testimony, does he do something unexpected. Asked whether he often wears Indian regalia, Mills answers no, only at powwows. Then he suddenly tugs at his necktie, pulling two thin strings of beads from under his shirt. One, he says, is turquoise, from the Southwest. The other small strand was a gift from his father.

Many people in the courtroom are surprised by this apparently spontaneous revelation—surprised and, as Mills stuffs the beads back into his shirt and fumbles to readjust his tie, a little embarrassed.

Images

At the end of the trial Federal Judge Walter J. Skinner posed a number of specific questions to the jurors concerning tribal status at certain dates in Mashpee history; but throughout the proceedings broader questions of Indian identity and power permeated the courtroom. Although the land claim was formally not at issue, the lawyers for New Seabury et al. sometimes seemed to be playing on a new nightmare. At the door of your suburban house a stranger in a business suit appears. He says he is a Native American. Your land has been illegally acquired generations ago, and you must relinquish your home. The stranger refers you to his lawyer.

Such fears, the threat of a "giveaway" of private lands, were much exploited by politicians and the press in the Penobscot-Passamaquoddy negotiations. Actually small holdings by private citizens were never in danger; only large tracts of undeveloped land held by timber companies and the state were in question. In Mashpee the plaintiffs reduced their claim to eleven thousand acres, formally excluding all private homes and lots up to an acre in size. Large-scale development, not small ownership, was manifestly the target; but their opponents refused pretrial compromises and the kinds of negotiation that had led to settlement of the Maine dispute.

According to Thomas Tureen the sorts of land claims pursued in Maine, Mashpee, Gay Head, and Charlestown were always drastically circumscribed. At that historical moment the courts were relatively open to Native American claims, a situation unlikely to last. In a decision of 1985 permitting Oneida, Mohawk, and Cayuga Non-Intercourse Act suits the Supreme Court made it abundantly clear, in Tureen's words, "that Indians are dealing with the magnanimity of a rich and powerful nation, one that is not about to divest itself or its non-Indian citizens of large acreage in the name of its own laws." In short, the United States will permit Indians a measure of recompense through the law—indeed, it has done so to an extent far greater than any other nation in a comparable situation—but it ultimately makes the rules and arbitrates the game. (Tureen 1985:147; also Barsh and Henderson 1980:289–293).

Seen in this light, the Mashpee trial was simply a clarification of the rules in an ongoing struggle between parties of greatly unequal power. But beneath the explicit fear of white citizens losing their homes because of an obscure past injustice, a troubling uncertainty was finding its way into the dominant image of Indians in America. The plaintiffs in the Non-Intercourse Act suits had power. In Maine politicians lost office over the issue, and the Mashpee case made national headlines for several months. Scandalously, it now paid to be Indian. Acting aggressively, tribal groups were doing sophisticated, "nontraditional" things. All over the country they were becoming involved in a variety of businesses, some claiming exemption from state regulation. To many whites it was comprehensible for Northwest Coast tribes to demand traditional salmon-fishing privileges; but for tribes to run high-stakes bingo games in violation of state laws was not.

Indians had long filled a pathetic imaginative space for the dominant culture; they were always survivors, noble or wretched. Their cultures had been steadily eroding, at best hanging on in museumlike reservations. Native American societies could not by definition be dynamic, inventive, or expansive. Indians were lovingly remembered in Edward Curtis' sepia photographs as proud, beautiful, and "vanishing." But Curtis, we now know, carried props, costumes, and wigs, frequently dressing up his models. The image he recorded was carefully staged (Lyman 1982). In Boston Federal Court a jury of white citizens would be confronted by a collection of highly ambiguous images. Could a group of four women and eight men (no minorities) be made to believe in the persistent "Indian" existence of the Mashpee plaintiffs without costumes and props? This question surrounded and infused the trial's technical focus on whether a particular form of political-cultural organization called a tribe had existed continuously in Mashpee since the sixteenth century.

The image of Mashpee Indians, like that of several other eastern groups such as the Lumbee and the Ramapough, was complicated **by** issues of race (Blu 1980; Cohen 1974). Significant intermarriage **with** blacks had occurred since the mid-eighteenth century, and the Mashpee were, at times, widely identified as "colored." In court the defense occasionally suggested that they were really blacks rather than Native Americans. Like the

Lumbee (and, less successfully, the Ramapough) the Mashpee plaintiffs had struggled to distinguish themselves from other minorities and ethnic groups, asserting tribal status based on a distinctive political-cultural history. In court they were not helped by the fact that few of them looked strongly "Indian." Some could pass for black, others for white.

* * *

Borderlines

Mashpee Indians suffered the fate of many small Native American groups who remained in the original thirteen states. They were not accorded the reservations and sovereign status (steadily eroded) of tribes west of the Mississippi. Certain of the eastern communities, such as the Seneca and the Seminoles, occupied generally recognized tribal lands. Others—the Lumbee, for example—possessed no collective lands but clustered in discrete regions, maintaining kinship ties, traditions, and sporadic tribal institutions. In all cases the boundaries of the community were permeable. There was intermarriage and routine migration in and out of the tribal center—sometimes seasonal, sometimes longer term. Aboriginal languages were much diminished, often entirely lost. Religious life was diverse—sometimes Christian (with a distinctive twist), sometimes a transformed tradition such as the Iroquois Longhouse Religion. Moral and spiritual values were often Native American amalgams compounded from both local traditions and pan-Indian sources. For example the ritual and regalia at New England powwows now reflect Sioux and other western tribal influences; in the 1920s the feathered "war bonnet" made its appearance among Wampanoag leaders. Eastern Indians generally lived in closer proximity to white (or black) society and in smaller groups than their western reservation counterparts. In the face of intense pressure some eastern communities have managed to acquire official federal recognition as tribes, others not. During the past two decades the rate of applications has risen dramatically.

Within this diversity of local histories and institutional arrangements the long-term residents of Mashpee occupied a gray area, at least in the eyes of the surrounding society and the law. The Indian identity of the Penobscot and Passamaquoddy was never seriously challenged, even though they had not been federally recognized and had lost or adapted many of their traditions. The Mashpee were more problematic. Partisans of their land claim, such as Paul Brodeur (1985), tend to accept without question the right of the tribal council, incorporated in 1974, to sue on behalf of a group that had lost its lands in the mid-nineteenth century. They see the question of tribal status as a legal red herring, or worse, a calculated ploy to deny the tribe its birthright. However procrustian and colonial in origin the legal definition of tribe, there was nonetheless a real issue at stake in the trial. Although tribal status and Indian identity have long been vague and politically constituted, not just anyone with some native blood or claim to adoption or shared tradition can be an Indian; and not just any Native American group can decide to be a tribe and sue for lost collective lands.

Indians in Mashpee owned no tribal lands (other than fifty-five acres acquired just before the trial). They had no surviving language, no clearly distinct religion, no blatant political structure. Their kinship was much diluted. Yet they did have a place and a reputation. For centuries Mashpee had been recognized as an Indian town. Its boundaries had not changed since 1665, when the land was formally deeded to a group called the South Sea Indians by the neighboring leaders Tookonchasun and Weepquish. The Mashpee plaintiffs of 1977 could offer as evidence surviving pieces of Native American tradition and political structures that seemed to have come and gone. They could also point to a sporadic history of Indian revivals continuing into the present.

The Mashpee were a borderline case. In the course of their peculiar litigation certain underlying structures governing the recognition of identity and difference became visible. Looked at one way, they were Indian, seen another way, they were not. Powerful ways of *looking* thus became inescapably problematic. The trial was less a search for the facts of Mashpee Indian culture and history than it was an experiment in translation—part of a long historical conflict and negotiation of "Indian" and "American" identities.

◆

I offer vignettes of persons and events in the courtroom that are obviously composed and condensed. Testimony evoked in a page or two may run to hundreds of pages in the transcript. Some witnesses were on the stand for several days. Moreover, real testimony almost never ends the way my vignettes do; it trails off in the quibbles and corrections of redirect and recross-examination. While I have included for comparison a verbatim excerpt from the transcript, I have generally followed my courtroom notes, checked against the record, and have not hesitated to rearrange, select, and highlight. Where quotation marks appear, the statement is a fairly exact quotation; the rest is paraphrase.

Overall, if the witnesses seem flat and somewhat elusive, the effect is intentional. Using the usual rhetorical techniques, I could have given a more intimate sense of peoples' personalities or of what they were really trying to express; but I have preferred to keep my distance. A courtroom is more like a theater than a confessional.

Mistrustful of transparent accounts, I want mine to manifest some of its frames and angles, its wavelengths.

* * *

History I

The case against the plaintiffs was straightforward: there never had been an Indian tribe in Mashpee. The community was a creation of the colonial encounter, a collection of disparate Indians and other minorities who sought over the years to become full citizens of the Commonwealth of Massachusetts and of the Republic. Decimated by disease, converted to Christianity, desirous of freedom from paternalistic state tutelage, the people of mixed Indian descent in Mashpee were progressively assimilated into American society. Their Indian identity had been lost, over and over, since the mid-seventeenth century.[2]

The plague. When the English Pilgrims arrived at Plymouth in 1620, they found a region devastated by a disease brought by white seamen. The settlers walked into empty Indian villages and planted in already cleared fields. The region was seriously underpopulated. In the years that followed Puritan leaders like Myles Standish pressed steadily to limit Indian territories and to establish clear "properties" for the growing number of newcomers. Misunderstandings inevitably ensued: for example whites claimed to own unoccupied land that had been ceded to them for temporary use.

Richard Bourne of Sandwich, a farmer near what is now Mashpee Pond and a tenant on Indian lands, studied the language of his landlords and soon became an effective mediator between the societies. He was friendly to the area's inhabitants, remnants of earlier groups, who came to be called South Sea Indians by the settlers to the north. He believed that they needed protection; becoming their advocate, he negotiated formal title to a large tract adjoining his farm (which in the meantime he had managed to purchase). His ally in these transactions was Paupmunnuck, a leader of the nearby Cotachesset.

Bourne's "South Sea Indian Plantation" was to become a refuge for Christian converts, for as white power increased, it became increasingly dangerous for Indians to live around Cape Cod unless they came together as a community of "praying Indians." Under Bourne's tutelage the Mashpee plantation was a center for the first Indian church on the Cape, organized in 1666.

Thus Mashpee was originally an artificial community, never a tribe. It was created from Indian survivors in an area between the traditional sachemdoms of Manomet and Nauset—the former centered on the present town of Bourne at the Cape's western edge, the latter near its tip.

Conversion to Christianity. Badly disorganized after the plague and confronted by a growing number of determined settlers, the Cape Cod Indians made accommodations. Live and let live was not the Puritan way, especially once their power had been consolidated. Tensions and conflicts

---

2. The two "histories" that follow represent the best brief interpretive accounts I could construct of the contending versions of Mashpee's past. They draw selectively on the expert testimony presented at the trial—testimony much too long, complex, and contested to summarize adequately. The overall shape of the two accounts reflects the summation provided at the end of the testimony by each side's principle attorney. "History I" owes a good deal to Francis Hutchins' book *Mashpee: The Story of Cape Cod's Indian Town* (1979). This book takes a somewhat more moderate position than the courtroom testimony on which it is based. "History II" owes something to the general approach of James Axtell's book *The European and the Indian* (1981). Axtell was a witness for the plaintiffs.

grew, leading to war in 1675 with the forces of the Wampanoag Supreme Sachem Metacomet ("King Philip"). After Metacomet's defeat Indians who sympathized with him were expelled from their lands. Many, including some who had remained neutral, were sold into slavery.

The price for living on ancestral lands in eastern New England was cooperation with white society. The Mashpee, under Bourne's tutelage became model Christians. By 1674 ninety Mashpee inhabitants were counted as baptized, and twenty-seven were admitted to full communion. The "praying Indians" were entering a new life. They stopped consulting "powwows" (medicine men, in seventeenth-century usage); they respected the Sabbath and other holy days, severed ties with "pagans," altered child-rearing practices, dressed in new ways, washed differently. The changes were gradual but telling. They reflected not only a tactical accommodation but also a new belief, born of defeat, that the powerful white ways must be superior. When Bourne died in 1682, his successor as protestant minister was an Indian, Simon Popmonet, son of Bourne's old ally Paupmunnuck. This was a further sign that the Indians were willingly giving up their old ways for the new faith.

"Plantation" status. Once the South Sea Indian Plantation had been established, its inhabitants' claim to their land rested on a written deed and on English law rather than on any aboriginal sovereignty. Like other "plantations" in New England, the community at Mashpee was a joint-ownership arrangement by a group of "proprietors." Under English law proprietors were licensed to develop a vacant portion of land, reserving part for commons, part for the church, and part for individual holdings. All transfers of land were to be approved collectively. This plantation-proprietory form, as applied to early Cape Cod settlements such as Sandwich and Barnstable, was intended to evolve quickly into a township where freemen held individual private property and were represented in the General Court of the colony. The white plantations around Mashpee did evolve directly into towns. From the late seventeenth century on their common lands were converted into private individual holdings in fee simple. Mashpee followed the same course, but more slowly. As late as 1830 its lands were the joint property of proprietors.

For complex historical reasons Mashpee's progress toward full citizenship lagged almost two centuries behind that of its neighbors. An enduring prejudice against Indians, and their supposed lack of "civility" certainly played a part, for during the early and mid-eighteenth century the Indian plantation was governed in humiliating ways by white "guardians." Nonetheless, development toward autonomy, while delayed, did occur. In 1763, after a direct appeal to King George III, Mashpee won the right to incorporation as a district, a step on the road to township status and a liberation from oppressive meddling by white outsiders. Then, beginning in 1834 and culminating in 1870, a series of acts of the Massachusetts legislature changed the Mashpee plantation into an incorporated town. Its inhabitants had overcome the prejudice and paternalism that had so long hemmed them in. They were now full-fledged citizens of Massachusetts.

Taking the colonists' side. From early on the Indian inhabitants of Mashpee gave signs of active identification with the new white society. During King Philip's War a certain Captain Amos, probably a Nauset from near Sandwich, led a group of Indians against Metacomet. Amos became a prominent inhabitant of Mashpee after the conflict ended. A century later the district of Mashpee sent a contingent to fight in the Revolutionary War against the British, a commitment of troops even greater than that of the surrounding white towns. Reliable accounts estimate that about half the adult male population died in the war. A Mashpee Indian, Joshua Pocknet, served at Valley Forge with George Washington. At these critical moments, therefore, the descendants of the South Sea Indians showed something more than simple acquiescence under colonial rule. Their enthusiastic patriotism strongly suggests that they had identified with white society, relinquishing any sense of a separate tribal political identity.

Intermarriage. Mashpee's population showed two significant periods of expansion. During the 1660s and 1670s there had been an influx of Indians from elsewhere on the Cape. Then after a century of relative equilibrium the population rose again in the 1760s and 1770s. Census figures are inexact and subject to interpretation, but it seems clear that before 1760 the principal newcomers were a steady trickle of New England Indians: Wampanoags from Gay Head and Herring Pond, Narragansets and Mohicans from Connecticut, Long Island Montauks. Immigration was restrained by the tutelage of outside "guardians," some of whom had an interest in keeping Mashpee small so that "unused" Indian lands could be made available for whites. After 1763, however, the newly incorporated district opened its borders to a variety of new settlers. A few whites entered by marriage but maintained a separate legal status. Their progeny, if one parent was Indian, could become proprietors. A least one white man "went native," living in a wigwam—just as the Indian residents of Mashpee were abandoning the last of theirs. Four Hessian mercenaries stayed on after the Revolutionary War and married Mashpee women. It is recorded that they accepted Indian manners.

The 1776 census counted fourteen "negroes" in a total population of 341. Significant intermarriage with freed black slaves occurred in this period, but it is difficult to say how much since common parlance, reflected in the census, sometimes mixed diverse peoples of brownish skin color in categories such as "Indian," "mulatto," or "negro." Intermarriage between blacks and Indians was encouraged by a common social marginality and by a relative shortage of men among the Indians and of women among the blacks. The local racial mix also included Cape Verde islanders and exotic imports resulting from the employment of Mashpee men in the far-flung sailing trades and women in domestic service: a Mexican and an Indian from Bombay are mentioned in the written sources.

By 1789 Mashpee's white minister, the Reverend Gideon Hawley, had become so concerned about Mashpee being overrun by blacks and foreigners that he engineered a return to plantation status, with himself as guardian of the town's threatened authenticity. This return to a restrictive paternalism was a setback for Mashpee's ability to grow and develop into a distinctive, independent nonwhite community. It was not until the 1840s, after a long conflict with Hawley's successor, the Reverend Phineas Fish, that local leaders finally rid themselves of outside tutelage. The struggle for citizenship had been slowed but not stopped. By the time of the final transition from plantation to township status in the four decades after 1830 the American citizens of Mashpee had become a complex mix—"colored" in contemporary parlance—that included several American Indian, black, and foreign ingredients.

Mashpee becomes a town. In 1834, following a popular rebellion against the outside authority of the Presbyterian minister Fish, district status was again accorded by the Massachusetts General Court. The Mashpee were no longer wards of the state and, like other towns, were governed by three elected selectmen. But full citizenship did not follow, largely because the proprietors of Mashpee wished to preserve traditional restraints on the sale of lands to outsiders. Leaders such as Daniel Amos argued that many inhabitants of Mashpee were not yet ready for the responsibilities of citizenship and unrestricted property rights. They might sell their lands irresponsibly or be maneuvered into debt; the community would be invaded and broken up. In practice the entailment on property did not seal off Mashpee from growth. To qualify as a landowner one had to trace ancestry to at least one Indian proprietor; and by the mid-nineteenth century quite a few individuals around the Cape could make this claim. In 1841–42, at the urging of Indian entrepreneurs such as Solomon Attaquin, who had returned to Mashpee with the end of state tutelage, most of the district's common lands were divided among its individual proprietors—men, women, and children. Lands could now be freely bought and sold, but still only among proprietors.

This progress did not go uncontested. Mashpee was divided among those who, like Attaquin—self-made men reflecting the era's dominant laissez-faire capitalist ethos—wanted to move quickly to remove all barriers to individual initiative and others who wanted to move more slowly or who saw in the old plantation entailments a guarantee of community integrity. In 1868 matters finally came to a head. A petition to the General Court from two of Mashpee's three selectmen and twenty-nine residents requested an end to all land-sale restrictions and the granting of full state and federal voting rights. This petition was promptly countered by a "remonstrance" signed by the third selectman and fifty-seven Mashpee residents urging that the district's status not be altered. A public hearing was called to air the differing views.

The hearing, which took place in early 1869, marks a crucial turning point in Mashpee history. Records of its disagreements offer a rare access to a diversity of local voices and opinions. Those who spoke in favor of the proposed changes evoked centuries of degrading state tutelage and second-class status. It was time, they said, for Mashpee inhabitants to be full citizens, to stand on their own. If this meant that some would fail or be displaced from their lands, so be it. They spoke also of the commercial advantages to the region of making portions of its land available for outside capital investment. Representatives of Mashpee's "colored non-proprietors" (a status that gave certain mulattoes and blacks all rights of proprietorship except title to land) also favored the changes in legal status. As valued members of the community they felt the restriction on landholding to be an insult and a reminder of an inferior condition they had in every other respect left behind.

Others opposed the changes. They argued that the influx of outside capital would be a very mixed blessing, and without the present protections many who were not wealthy and wise to the ways of business would soon be displaced. They would find themselves, in the words of one speaker, "ducking and dodging from one city to another, and gain no residence." Some proprietors did not think the right to vote in state and federal elections worth the risk; the present system, providing real control over Mashpee's government, seemed sufficient to local needs. The Reverend Joseph Amos ("Blind Joe" Amos), the community's most influential spiritual voice and leader of a successful Indian Baptist movement three decades earlier, opposed the changes. He said that another generation of preparation was needed before the proposed step could safely be taken. Solomon Attaquin, who owned the Hotel Attaquin, a renowned hunting lodge in Mashpee, spoke for abandoning the district's special status. He evoked a lifelong dream of full citizenship and equality, a dream shared with others in the community. Those who had worked long and hard for this day should not have to die without gaining the status of free men in the commonwealth and the nation.

A vote was taken. Eighteen favored participation in federal and state elections, eighteen were opposed. The removal of land restrictions was sharply rejected, twenty-six to fourteen. Despite this vote by a minority of the total population the recorded discussions clearly showed a consensus in favor of ultimately ending Mashpee's special status, with disagreements only on the timing. The Massachusetts General Court, recognizing this fact and more impressed by Mashpee's "progressive" voices, in 1870 formally abolished the status of "Mashpee proprietor." All lands were henceforth held in fee simple with no restrictions on alienation. All residents, whatever their ancestry, now enjoyed equal status before the law. The transfer of town lands to outsiders began immediately.

This turning point marked the end of Mashpee's distinctive institutional status stemming from its Indian past. Though the community was divided on the change, the most dynamic, forward-looking leaders favored it; whatever their hesitations on timing, community members willingly embraced their future as Massachusetts and United States citizens.

Assimilation. During the years between 1670 and the 1920s Indians throughout the nation were forced to abandon tribal organizations and to become individual citizen-farmers, workers, and businessmen. This was the period of the Dawes Act with its extensive land-allotment projects west of the Mississippi. Not until the twenties was there much evidence anywhere of tribal dynamism. Mashpee residents continued to live as before, working as hunting and fishing guides, servants, and laborers in various trades. The town remained a backwater. To find steady work people often had to move to nearby towns or even farther afield. The historical record contains little evidence of any distinctly Indian life in Mashpee before the Wampanoag revival movements of the twenties. The town apparently did not undergo any major demographic or social changes and remained a rather cohesive community of long-term residents, most of whom were of varying degrees of Indian descent. Significantly, between 1905 and 1960 the category "Indian" disappeared from Mashpee's federal census records. The more than two hundred individuals who had previously been so classified were now listed as either "colored" (distinct from "negro") or "other." Only in 1970 would they again be called Indian. In the eyes of the state the majority of Mashpee's inhabitants were simply Americans of color.

Some of these Americans participated in the founding of the Wampanoag Nation in the late twenties. At that time various more-or-less theatrical revivals of Indian institutions were under way. People in Mashpee showed interest, but the daily life and government of the town were not materially affected. The Wampanoags did not, like many other Indian groups in the thirties, take advantage of the turnaround in policy at John Collier's Bureau of Indian Affairs (BIA) to reorganize themselves as a federally recognized "tribal" unit. The new sense of Indianness around Mashpee was a matter of county fairlike powwows, costumes, and folkloric dances.

The individuals of Indian ancestry from Mashpee who filed suit in 1976 were American citizens similar to Irish-or Italian–Americans with strong ethnic attachments. Individuals such as Earl Mills and John and Russell Peters had simply taken advantage of the latest wave of pan-Indian revivalism and the prospect of financial gain to constitute themselves as a Mashpee Tribe. Mashpee's distinctive history was in fact a story of Indian–Christian remnants who over the centuries had repeatedly given up their customs and sovereignty. Theirs had been a long, hard struggle for equality and respect in a multiethnic America.

Vicky M. Costa

Vicky Costa is seventeen years old; her father is Portuguese, her mother Indian. She considers herself an Indian. She looks like any American teenager.

Q.: How do you know you're an Indian? A.: My mother told me.

She speaks softly. Judge Skinner asks her to speak up so the court can hear. "Think of yourself shouting across a field to those people," indicating the jury, "over there." (The "field" is a courtroom cluttered with lawyers tables, papers, documents, items of evidence.)

Vicky Costa does not shout, and everyone listens closely. She tells about the values she is currently learning in Mashpee: "To walk on Mother Earth in balance, and to respect every living thing."

Q.: How often do you dance? A.: All the time. Q.: When did you dance most recently? A.: Last night.

She describes her Indian dancing. She says she first learned at a powwow "a long time ago." Now she attends powwows regularly.

She names the dances: animal names, "blanket dance," "fancy dance." In the "round dance" they turn and dance to the good and bad spirit, moving in both directions so neither of the spirits will be offended. Is there music? Singing? Just the round-dance song. The purpose of the animal dances? To imitate the animals, mocking them. To thank the Creator for that animal.

(The mood in these questions and answers is conversational, quiet. Is it partly because this time Ann Gilmore of the plaintiffs' trial team is conducting the examination? It is one of the rare moments in the trial when a woman speaks directly with another woman. For whatever reasons the prevailing sense of contest and performance is gone.)

Costa testifies that she has been studying what she calls the "Wampanoag language" for one-and-a-half years. She says that as a girl she had to go to the Baptist church but now believes in Indian values.

On cross-examination she assents to hostile questions with the devastating American teenage shrug: "Yeah . . . yeah . . . yeah . . ."

History II

The case against the Mashpee plaintiffs was based on a reading of Cape Cod history. Documents were gathered, interpreted, and arranged in a coherent sequence. The story emerged of a small mixed community fighting for equality and citizenship while abandoning, by choice or coercion, most of its aboriginal heritage. But a different, also coherent, story was constructed by the plaintiffs, drawing on the same documentary record. In this account the residents of Mashpee had managed to keep alive a core of Indian identity over three centuries against enormous odds. They had done so in supple, sometimes surreptitious ways, always attempting to control, not reject, outside influences.

The plague. Aboriginally the concept of tribe has little meaning. The "political" institutions of Native American groups before contact with Europeans varied widely. Cape Cod Indian groupings seem to have been flexible, with significant movement across territories. Communities formed and reformed. In this context it is unclear whether the elders of local villages or sachems or supreme sachems should be identified as "tribal" leaders. These individuals had supreme power in some situations, limited authority in others. The plague was a disaster, but it did not decimate the Cape to the extent that it did the Plymouth area. In any event the response of the survivors at Mashpee, regrouping to form a cohesive unit, was a traditional political response, albeit to an unusual emergency. Written sources reflect only the views of whites, such as the evangelist Bourne, who saw his "praying Indians" paternalistically as passive remnants. The intentions of leaders such as Paupmunnuck and his kin are not recorded.

Thus it is anachronistic to say that the community gathered at what would later be called Mashpee was not a tribe. It is well known that the political institutions of many bona fide American Indian "tribes" actually emerged during the nineteenth and twentieth centuries in response to white expectations and power. Neat analytic categories such as "political organization," "kinship," "religion," and "economy" do not reflect Indian ways of seeing things. The simple fact remains that Bourne's South Sea Indian Plantation was a discrete community of Cape Cod Indians living on traditional Indian land—an arrangement that, through many modifications, survived until the mid-twentieth century.

Conversion to Christianity. Accounts of conversion as a process of "giving up old ways" or "choosing a new path" usually reflect a wishful evangelism rather than the more complex realities of cultural change, resistance, and translation. Recent ethnohistorical scholarship has tended to show that Native Americans' response to Christianity was syncretic over the long run, almost never a radical either-or choice. Moreover, in situations of drastically unequal power, as on Puritan Cape Cod, one should expect the familiar response of colonized persons: outward agreement and inner resistance.

The disruptions caused by disease, trade, and military conquest were extreme. All Indian societies had to adjust, and they developed varying strategies for doing so. Some passed through revitalization movements in the late eighteenth and early nineteenth centuries, led by messianic figures: the Delaware Prophet or Handsome Lake. These movements incorporated Christian features in a new "traditional" religion. Other groups renewed native culture by using Christianity for their own purposes. The white man's religion could be added on to traditional deities and rites. Beliefs that appeared contradictory to Puritan evangelists coexisted in daily life. Native American religions are generally more tolerant, pragmatic, and inclusive than Christianity, a strongly evangelical, exclusive faith.

This is not to say that groups such as the South Sea Indians did not embrace Christianity in good faith or find there a source of spiritual strength. It is only to caution against the either-or logic of conversion as seen by the outsiders whose accounts dominate the written record. The gain of Christian beliefs did not necessarily mean the loss of Indian spirituality. It is easy to be impressed by surface transformations of clothing and public behavior and to forget that continuous kin ties and life on a familiar piece of land also carry potent "religious" values.

Adopting Christianity in Mashpee was not merely a survival strategy in an intolerant, hostile environment. The faith of the "praying Indians" kept a distinctly indigenous cast. Beginning with Richard Bourne's successor, Simon Popmonet, Indian ministers in Mashpee preached in Massachusett, a practice that continued throughout the eighteenth century. When white missionaries were imposed from outside, they were forced to use some Massachusett or to compromise, like Gideon Hawley, who conducted bilingual services in tandem with a respected Indian pastor, Solomon Briant. Moreover, the historical record before 1850 is filled with conflict between authoritarian missionaries and Indian church members. Hawley, who served from 1757 to 1807, progressively alienated his parishioners, especially after Solomon Briant's death in 1775. His successor, Phineas Fish, lost virtually all local support and in 1840, after a protracted struggle, was physically ejected from the Old Indian Meeting House by irate Indian Christians.

Baptist revivalism had already won over most of the congregation, a change tied to a political assertion of Indian power. As in many nativist revitalization movements, an Indian outsider took a leading role—in this case William Apes, a young Pequot Baptist preacher. Blind Joe Amos had already acquired a larger following for his all-Indian Baptist meetings than the Congregationalist minister, Fish.

The situation was volatile. Apes, a firebrand with a vision of united action by "colored" peoples against white oppressors, stimulated a Masphee "Declaration of Independence" in 1833 on behalf of a sovereign Mashpee Tribe. (This was one of the few times before the twentieth century that the word tribe appears in the historical record.) The effect of the declaration and of the political maneuvers that ensued was to wrest control of the town's religion from the outsider Fish, reclaiming the Meeting House and funds from Harvard University supporting Indian Christianity for the majority faith, which was now Baptist. Mashpee returned to district status, free of outside governors.

Over the centuries Indians in Mashpee fought to keep control first of their Presbyterian and then their Baptist institutions. Religion was a political as well as a spiritual issue. Well into the 1950s the New England Baptist Convention habitually referred to Mashpee as "our Indian church." The exact nature of Mashpee Christian belief and practice over the centuries is obscure. The historical record does not inform us, for example, of exactly what took place in Blind Joe Amos' insurgent Baptist services during the 1830s; but even the partial written record makes it clear that Christianity in Mashpee, symbolized by the Old Indian Meeting House, was a site of local power and of resistance to outsiders. At recurring intervals it was a focus of openly Indian, or "tribal," power.

"Plantation" Status. Leaders of the South Sea Indians probably recognized, with Bourne, that title to land under white law was needed if it was not to be despoiled by an aggressive colonization; but seventeenth-century English proprietory forms did not unduly restrict their ability to function as an Indian community. Collective ownership of land, with individual use rights, could be maintained. The legal status that to some appeared an impediment to progress in fact protected the traditional life ways of Indian proprietors.

Although eastern Indians were not accorded reservation lands, Mashpee's plantation status created a de facto reservation. Unlike all its neighbors Mashpee did not quickly become a town but had the status forced on it in 1869. The plantation was widely considered to be Indian land held collectively in a distinctive manner. The reasons for keeping Mashpee "backward," a pupil of the state, were often racist and paternalist; but from the viewpoint of a small group struggling to maintain its collective identify, the proprietorship arrangement was an effective way of having legal status while also maintaining a difference. While there was internal disagreement at times, the majority of Mashpee proprietors consistently favored keeping the plantation land system. This was changed only by legislative fiat in 1969, against their expressed wishes. Until then an "archaic" status had been effectively used to preserve Indian lands in a collective form through rapidly changing times. The land claim suit aimed to restore a situation illegally altered by the Massachusetts legislature.

Taking the colonists' side. The fact that some South Sea Indians fought against Metacomet in King Philip's War does not prove that they were abandoning their Indian sovereignty or independence. More did not fight, and the motivations of those who did are a matter of speculation. There was nothing new about Indians making war on other Indians. Moreover they may have had little choice. Puritan authorities were on the warpath, and even "loyal" Indians were punished during and after the war by loss of lands and slavery.

As for the war against England, again we should be wary of imputing motives. The Mashpee Indians who served in the Revolutionary Army may not have done so primarily as "American" patriots. They were, among other things, rebelling against the authority of their missionary Hawley, an ardent Tory. Moreover, as Indian status has evolved in the United States, it has been legally recognized that the privileges of citizenship (including the decision to unite in war against a common enemy) do not contradict other arrangements establishing special group identity and status. One can be fully a citizen and fully an Indian.

To expect Cape Cod Indians to hold themselves apart from the historical currents and conflicts of the dominant society would be to ask them to commit suicide. Survival in changing circumstances meant participation, wherever possible on their own terms. Staying separate or uninvolved would be to yield to the dangerous fantasies of protectors, like Hawley, who worked to keep the Mashpee pure—and under his tutelage. The inhabitants of Mashpee again and again resisted this restrictive "authenticity." The record confirms that they wanted integrity but never isolation.

Intermarriage. There was a good deal of racial mixing In Mashpee, but the exact extent is hard to determine, given the shifting categories of different censuses and doubts about how race was actually measured. Mashpee was a refuge for misfits, refugees, and marginal groups. At certain times a natural alliance against dominant white society formed between the town's Indian "survivors" and newly freed blacks. The crucial issue is whether the core Indian community absorbed the outsiders or were themselves absorbed in the American melting pot.

Historical evidence supports the former conclusion. Since whites and people of color who settled in Mashpee during the eighteenth and most of the nineteenth centuries could not become proprietors, this limited the influx; non-Indians remained a significant but small minority. Children with one Indian parent could become full community members. Intermarriage frequently occurred, and thus the purity of Indian blood was much diluted; but the legal and social structure consistently favored Indian identification. With land entailment and the maintenance of close kin ties among property holders a core was maintained. In any event blood is a debatable measure of identity, and to arrive at quotas for determining "tribal" status is always a problematic exercise. There are federally recognized tribes as mixed as the Mashpee, and organized Indian groups vary widely in the amount of traceable ancestry they actually require for membership.

Ethnohistorical studies show that in New England mixing of different communities was common well before the Pilgrims' arrival. Adoption was frequent, and it was customary to capture and incorporate opponents in war. Indians were in this respect color blind. In colonial times a large number of white captives stayed with their captors, adopting Indian ways, some even becoming chiefs. Mashpee's later openness to outsiders—as long as the newcomers intermarried and conformed to Indian ways—was a continuation of an aboriginal tradition, not a loss of distinct identity.

In 1859, after more than a century of intermarriage and sporadic population growth (the dilution of Indian stock lamented by the missionary Hawley), a detailed report by the commissioner for Indian affairs, John Earle, offered a census of the "Mashpee Tribe" that included 371 "natives" and 32 "foreigners." The latter were people living on the land without proprietary rights and not lineal descendants of Indians. They were described as "Africans" and "colored." Only one "white" was listed. The names of "natives" listed on the 1859 census served in the trial as a benchmark of continuous "tribal" kinship ties.

Mashpee becomes a town. There is strong documentary evidence that most of the proprietors between 1834 and 1869 wanted to hold on to Mashpee's special land restrictions. Commissioner Earle asserts this in his report. "Progressives" such as Attaquin were more vocal, and their testimony thus receives more weight in the record than the less articulate majority who in 1869 voted decisively against township status. Spokesmen (note how few female voices are "heard" by history, although the role of women at the center of community life was undoubtedly crucial) such as Blind Joe Amos and his brother Daniel urged postponing the transition. They argued that most people in Mashpee were too "immature," not "ready" to dispose of their land individually. Give us just one more generation, Daniel Amos asked in the 1830s. His brother asked the same thing in the late 1860s. What do these arguments signify?

For those who see Mashpee's "development" and assimilation as inevitable, such statements require no interpretation: they simply show that even the traditionalists in Mashpee were ready eventually to give up their special status. But this is to assume the historical outcome. The Indian proprietors of Mashpee valued community integrity and possessed effective public and informal leadership. They had shown much strength and initiative in dealing with their various "protectors." The early historical record reveals a steady stream of petitions—1748, 1753, 1760—on behalf of the "poor Indians of Mashpee called the South Sea Indians" protesting abuses by the agents appointed to watch over them. More recently they had successfully asserted their autonomy against the missionaries Hawley and Fish. They were hardly "immature." Yet throughout the mid-nineteenth century Mashpee proprietors temporized, hesitated in the face of an "inevitable" progress. Their ability to protect their community from the coercions and enticements of white society was evidently precious to them.

The modified plantation status they had secured in 1834 gave them a way of keeping collective control over land and immigration while not isolating the community from interaction with the surrounding society. Even the "allotment" of lands sanctioned at that time reproduced an aboriginal land arrangement. Parcels were traditionally given to families for exclusive use while ultimate collective ownership was maintained. (In 1834, moreover, three thousand acres were formally kept as common land.) Continuing entailments on land sales outside the community guaranteed a flexible nineteenth-century tribalism. In this context public arguments about Mashpee's "immaturity" should be seen as ways of addressing an outside audience, the Massachusetts General Court, which still thought of the plantation as a ward of the state and which had already decided and again would arbitrarily decide its fate. It would be impolitic in addressing this body to say that Mashpee rejected full township status in the name of a distinctive vision of Indian community and citizenship. An argument for delay couched in paternalist rhetoric was more likely to succeed.

This interpretation of the debates in 1869 is at least as plausible as a literal reading of the recorded public utterances. Mashpee, like Indian communities throughout their recent history, was split between modernists and traditionalists. The traditionalists prevailed in the vote, but the modernists swayed the authorities. In changing Mashpee's land entailment the legislature violated both simple democracy and, the Federal Non–Intercourse Act of 1790. But even the forced change—although it ultimately brought much land into non-Indian hands—was not fatal. The Mashpee Indians used their new imposed status as they had their former one. For almost a century local government was kept firmly in the hands of a closely interrelated group of town officers. Mashpee remained "Cape Cod's Indian Town."

Assimilation. The Mashpee Indians did not "assimilate." The term's linear, either-or connotations cannot account for revivalism and for changes in the cultural and political climate between 1869 and 1960. There have been better and worse times in the United States to be publicly Indian. The late nineteenth and early twentieth centuries were among the worst. Government policy strongly favored tribal termination and the dispersal of collective lands. It was not until the late 1920s that the failure of allotment schemes was recognized and a "New Indian Policy" instituted at the BIA that favored tribal reorganization. If there is little evidence in the historical record of "tribal" life in Mashpee between 1869 and 1920, it is no surprise. Many groups all over the nation that would emerge later as tribes kept a low profile during these years. Mashpee seemed to be simply a sleepy town run by Indians, known for its good hunting and fishing. There was no political need or any wider context for them to display their Indianness in spectacular ways. Everyone knew who they were. A few attended the Carlisle Indian School in Pennsylvania during this period. Traditional myths and stories were told around kitchen tables; the piles of sticks at Mashpee's "Indian taverns" or "sacrifice heaps" grew into enormous mounds; life close to the land went on.

The history of Indian tribes in the United States has been punctuated by revival movements. The 1920s saw the organization of the Wampanoag Nation, with various explicit tribal institutions including a supreme sachem and a renewed interest in more public Indian displays: dances, regalia, powwows, and the like. As in all revitalization movements "outside" influences from other Indian groups played a major role. Eben Queppish, who had once ridden with Buffalo Bill's Wild West Show, taught traditional basket making and on demand donned his Sioux war bonnet. Individuals from Mashpee participated in nationally known groups such as the Thunderbird Indian Dancers. The effects of these revivals were largely cultural. There was little need for political reorganization in Mashpee, for the town was still governed by an unchallenged Indian majority. Political reorganization of a more explicit "tribal" structure would occur during a later revivalist period, the ferment spurred by the loss of town control after 1968.

Like other tribal groups the Mashpee have been opportunists, taking advantage of propitious historical contexts and undergoing external influences. They have survived as Indians because they have *not* conformed to white stereotypes. They have lived since aboriginal times in a traditional locale. They have maintained their own hybrid faith. Over the centuries they have controlled the rate of intermarriage and have fought for the political autonomy of their community. Explicitly tribal political structures have sometimes been visible to the outside world, as in 1833, the 1920s, and the 1970s, but for the most part these structures have been informal. Often the "tribe" in Mashpee was simply people deciding things by consensus in kitchens or at larger ad hoc gatherings where no records were kept. The chief in Mashpee, when there was one, shared authority with a variety of respected leaders, women and men. Politics was not hierarchical and did not need much in the way of institutional forms. The "tribe" in Mashpee was simply shared Indian kinship, place, history and a long struggle for integrity without isolation. Sometimes the Baptist parish served as an arm of the tribe; so did the town government. When the Mashpee Wampanoag Tribal Council, Inc. filed suit in 1976, it did so as a new legal arm of the tribe.

* * *

◆

The jurors were sequestered, accompanied by a large pile of documents. After twenty-one hours of deliberation they emerged with a verdict:

Did the proprietors of Mashpee, together with their spouses and children, constitute an Indian tribe on any of the following dates:

July 22, 1790? No.   June 23, 1869? No.
March 31, 1834? Yes.   May 28, 1870? No.
March 3, 1842? Yes.

Did the plaintiff groups, as identified by the plaintiff's witnesses, constitute an Indian tribe as of August 26, 1976? No.

If the people living in Mashpee constituted an Indian tribe or nation on any of the dates prior to August 26, 1976, did they continuously exist as a tribe or nation from such date or dates up to and including August 26, 1976? No.

◆

The verdict was a clear setback for the Indians' suit. But as a statement about their tribal history it was far from clear. Judge Skinner, after hearing arguments, finally decided that despite its ambiguity—the apparent emergence of a tribe in 1834—the jury's reply was a denial of the required tribal continuity. His dismissal of the suit has since been upheld on appeal.

The verdict remains, however, a curious and problematic outcome. We can only speculate on what happened in the jury room—the obscure chemistry of unanimity. What was done with the pile of historical documents during the twenty-one hours of discussion? Did the jurors search for a false precision? Asked to consider specific dates, did they conscientiously search the record for evidence of tribal institutions, for mention of the word *tribe*? If so, their literalism was nonetheless different from that encouraged by the particularist history of the defense, for the jury found that Mashpee Indians were inconsistently a tribe. Violating the judge's instructions, they found that a tribe first did not, then did, then did not again exist in Mashpee. Historical particularism does not by itself yield coherent developments or stories. Entities appear and disappear in the record.

The jurors' response contained an element of subversion. In effect it suggested that the trial's questions had been wrongly posed. Asked to apply consistent criteria of tribal existence over three centuries of intense change and disruption, the jury did so and came up with an inconsistent verdict.

Afterthoughts

The court behaved like a philosopher who wanted to know positively whether a cat was on the mat in Mashpee. I found myself seeing a Cheshire cat now a head, now a tail, eyes, ears, nothing at all, in various combinations. The Mashpee "tribe" had a way of going and coming; but something was persistently, if not continuously, there.

The testimony I heard convinced me that organized Indian life had been going on in Mashpee for the past 350 years. Moreover a significant revival and reinvention of tribal identity was clearly in process. I concluded that since the ability to act collectively as Indians is currently bound up with tribal status, the Indians living in Mashpee and those who return regularly should be recognized as a "tribe."

Whether land improperly alienated after 1869 should be transferred to them, how much, and by what means was a separate issue. I was, and am, less clear on this matter. A wholesale transfer of property would in any case be politically unthinkable. Some negotiation and repurchase arrangement—such as that in Maine involving local, state, and federal governments—could eventually establish a tribal land base in some portion of Mashpee. But that, for the moment, is speculation. In the short run the outcome of the trial was a setback for Wampanoag tribal dynamism.

In Boston Federal Court, Cape Cod Indians could not be seen for what they were and are. Modern Indian lives—lived within and against the dominant culture and state—are not captured by categories like tribe or identity. The plaintiffs could not prevail in court because their discourse and that of their attorneys and experts was inevitably compromised. It was constrained not simply by the law, with its peculiar rules, but by powerful assumptions and categories underlying the common sense that supported the law.

Among the underlying assumptions and categories compromising the Indians' case three stand out: (1) the idea of cultural wholeness and structure, (2) the hierarchical distinction between oral and literate forms of knowledge, and (3) the narrative continuity of history and identity.

The idea of cultural wholeness and structure. Although the trial was formally about "tribal" status, its scope was significantly wider. The *Montoya* definition of tribe, featuring race, territory, community and government, did not specifically mention "cultural" identity. The culture concept in its broad anthropological definition was still new in 1901; but the relatively loose *Montoya* definition reflected this emerging notion of a multifaceted, whole way of life, determined neither by biology nor politics. By 1978 the modern notion of culture was part of the trial's common sense.

In the courtroom an enormous amount of testimony from both sides debated the authenticity of Indian culture in Mashpee. Often this seemed to have become the crucial point of contention. Had the Mashpee lost their distinct way of life? Had they assimilated? In his summation for the plaintiffs Lawrence Shubow took time to define the term culture anthropologically, distinguishing it from the "ballet and top hat" conception. Closely paraphrasing E. B. Tylor's classic formula of 1871, he presented culture as a group's total body of behavior. He said that it included how people eat as well as how they think. Using the anthropological definition, he argued that ecology, the special feeling for hunting and fishing in Mashpee, the herring eaten every year, spitting on a stick at an "Indian tavern," these and many other unremarkable daily elements were integral parts of a whole, ongoing way of life.

It is easy to see why the plaintiffs focused on Indian culture in Mashpee. Culture, since it includes so much, was less easily disproven than tribal status. But even so broadly defined, the culture concept posed problems for the plaintiffs. It was too closely tied to assumptions of organic form and development. In the eighteenth century culture meant simply "a tending to natural growth." By the end of the nineteenth century the word could be applied not only to gardens and well-developed individuals but to whole societies. Whether it was the elitist singular version of a Matthew Arnold or the plural, lower-case concept of an emerging ethnography, the term retained its bias toward wholeness, continuity, and growth. Indian culture in Mashpee might be made up of unexpected everyday elements, but it had in the last analysis to cohere, its elements fitting together like the parts of a body. The culture concept accommodates internal diversity and an "organic" division of roles but not sharp contradictions, mutations, or emergences. It has difficulty with a medicine man who at one time feels a deep respect for Mother Earth and at another plans a radical real estate subdivision. It sees tribal "traditionalists" and "moderns" as representing aspects of a linear development, one looking back, the other forward. It cannot see them as, contending or alternating futures.

Groups negotiating their identity in contexts of domination and exchange persist, patch themselves together in ways different from a living organism. A community, unlike a body, can lose a central "organ" and not die. All the critical elements of identity are in specific conditions replaceable: language, land, blood, leadership, religion. Recognized, viable tribes exist in which any one or even most of these elements are missing, replaced, or largely transformed.

The idea of culture carries with it an expectation of roots, of a stable, territorialized existence. Weatherhead (1980:10–11) shows how the *Montoya* definition of tribe was designed to distinguish settled, peaceful Indian groups from mobile, marauding "bands." This political and military distinction of 1901 between tribe and band was debated again, in technical, anthropological terms, during the Mashpee trial. How rooted or settled should one expect "tribal" Native Americans to be—aboriginally, in specific contact periods, and now in highly mobile twentieth century America? Common notions of culture persistently bias the answer toward rooting rather than travel.

Moreover the culture idea, tied as it is to assumptions about natural growth and life, does not tolerate radical breaks in historical continuity. Cultures, we often hear, "die." But how many cultures pronounced dead or dying by anthropologists and other authorities have, like Curtis' "vanishing race" or Africa's diverse Christians, found new ways to be different? Metaphors of continuity and "survival" do not account for complex historical processes of appropriation, compromise, subversion, masking, invention, and revival. These processes inform the activity of a people not living alone but "reckoning itself among the nations." The Indians at Mashpee made and remade themselves through specific alliances, negotiations, and struggles. It is just as problematic to say that their way of life "survived" as to say that it "died" and was "reborn."

The related institutions of culture and tribe are historical inventions, tendentious and changing. They do not designate stable realities that exist aboriginally "prior to" the colonial clash of societies and powerful representations. The history of Mashpee is not one of unbroken tribal institutions or cultural traditions. It is a long, relational struggle to maintain and recreate identities that began when an English-speaking Indian traveler, Squanto, greeted the Pilgrims at Plymouth. The struggle was still going on three-and-a-half centuries later in Boston Federal Court, and it continues as the "Mashpee Tribe" prepares a new petition, this time for recognition from the Department of the Interior.

The hierarchical distinction between oral and literate. The Mashpee trial was a contest between oral and literate forms of knowledge. In the end the written archive had more value than the evidence of oral tradition, the memories of witnesses, and the intersubjective practice of fieldwork. In the courtroom how could one give value to an undocumented "tribal" life largely invisible (or unheard) in the surviving record?

As the trial progressed the disjuncture of oral and literate modes sharpened. The proceedings had been theatrical, full of contending voices and personalities, but they ended with a historian's methodical recitation of particulars. In the early portions of the trial the jurors had been asked to piece together and imagine a tribal life that showed recurring vitality but no unimpeachable essence or institutional core. Indianness in Mashpee often seemed improvised, ad hoc. The jury heard many wishful, incomplete memories of childhood events and debatable versions of recent happenings. In what may be called the "oral-ethnographic" parts of the trial many—too many—voices contended, in its "documentary" ending too few. A historian's seamless monologue was followed by attorneys' highly composed summations, two fully documented stories. There was no way to give voice to the silences in these histories, to choose the unrecorded.

The court imposed a literalist epistemology. Both sides searched the historical records for the presence or absence of the word and institution *tribe*. In this epistemology Indian identity could not be a real yet essentially contested phenomenon. It had to exist or not exist as an objective documentary fact persisting through time. Yet oral societies—or more accurately oral domains within a dominant literacy—leave only sporadic and misleading traces. Most of what is central to their existence is never written. Thus until recently nearly everything most characteristically Indian in Mashpee would have gone unrecorded. The surviving facts are largely the records of missionaries, government agents, outsiders. In the rare instances when Indians wrote—petitions, deeds, letters of complaint—it was to address white authorities and legal structures. Their voices were adapted to an imposed context. The same is true even in the rare cases in which a range of local *voices* was recorded, for example the public debates of 1869 on township status.

History feeds on what finds its way into a limited textual record. A historian needs constant skepticism and a willingness to read imaginatively, "against" the sources, to divine what is not represented in the accumulated selection of the archive. Ultimately, however, even the most imaginative history is tied to standards of textual proof. Anthropology, although it is also deeply formed and empowered by writing, remains closer to orality. Fieldwork—interested people talking with and being interpreted by an interested observer—cannot claim to be "documentary" in the way history can. For even though the origin of evidence in an archive may be just as circumstantial and subjective as that in a field journal, it enjoys a different value: archival data has been found, not produced, by a scholar using it "after the fact."

The distinction between historical and ethnographic practices depends on that between literate and oral modes of knowledge. History is thought to rest on past—documentary, archival—selections of texts. Ethnography is based on present—oral, experiential, observational—evidence. Although many historians and ethnographers are currently working to attenuate, even erase this opposition, it runs deeper than a mere disciplinary division of labor, for it resonates with the established (some would say metaphysical) dichotomy of oral and literate worlds as well as with the pervasive habit in the West of sharply distinguishing synchronic from diachronic, structure from change. As Marshall Sahlins (1985) has argued, these assumptions keep us from seeing how collective structures, tribal or cultural, reproduce themselves historically by risking themselves in novel conditions. Their wholeness is as much a matter of reinvention and encounter as it is of continuity and survival.

The narrative continuity of history and identity. Judge Skinner instructed the jury to decide whether the Indians of Mashpee had continuously constituted a tribe prior to filing suit in 1976. For the land claim to go forward the same tribal group had to have existed, without radical interruption, from at least the eighteenth century. The court's common sense was that the plaintiffs' identity must be demonstrated as an unbroken narrative, whether of survival or change. Both attorneys in their summations duly complied.

St. Clair's story of a long struggle for participation in plural American society and Shubow's "epic of survival and continuity" had in common a linear teleology. Both ruled out the possibility of a group existing discontinuously, keeping open multiple paths, being both Indian and American.

An either-or logic applied. St. Clair argued that there had never been a tribe in Mashpee, only individual Indian Americans who had repeatedly opted for white society. His story of progress toward citizenship assumed a steady movement away from native tradition. Identity as an American meant giving up a strong claim to tribal political integrity in favor of ethnic status within a national whole. Life as an American meant death as an Indian. Conversely Shubow's Mashpee had "survived" as a living tribe and culture from aboriginal times; but the historical record often contradicted his claim, and he sometimes strained to assert continuity. The plaintiffs could not admit that Indians in Mashpee had lost, even voluntarily abandoned, crucial aspects of their tradition while at the same time pointing to evidence over the centuries of reinvented "Indianness." They could not show tribal institutions as relational and political, coming and going in response to changing federal and state policies and the surrounding ideological climate. An identity could not die and come back to life. To recreate a culture that had been lost was, by definition of the court, inauthentic.

But is any part of a tradition lost if it can be remembered, even generations later, caught up in a present dynamism and made to symbolize a possible future?

The Mashpee were trapped by the stories that could be told about them. In this trial "the facts" did not speak for themselves. Tribal life had to be emplotted, told as a coherent narrative. In fact only a few basic stories are told, over and over, about Native Americans and other "tribal" peoples. These societies are always either dying or surviving, assimilating or resisting. Caught between a local past and a global future, they either hold on to their separateness or "enter the modern world." The latter entry—tragic or triumphant—is always a step toward a global future defined by technological progress, national and international cultural relations. Are there other possible stories?

Until recently the "history" accorded to tribal peoples has always been a Western history. They may refuse it, embrace it, be devastated by it, changed by it. But the familiar paths of tribal death, survival, assimilation, or resistance do not catch the specific ambivalences of life in places like Mashpee over four centuries of defeat, renewal, political negotiation, and cultural innovation. Moreover most societies that suddenly "enter the modern world" have already been in touch with it for centuries.

The Mashpee trial seemed to reveal people who were sometimes separate and "Indian," sometimes assimilated and "American." Their history was a series of cultural and political transactions, not all-or-nothing conversions or resistances. Indians in Mashpee lived and acted between cultures in a series of ad hoc engagements. No one in Boston Federal Court, expert or layperson, stood at the end point of this historical series, even though the stories of continuity and change they told implied that they did. These stories and the trial itself were episodes, turns in the ongoing engagement. Seen from a standpoint not of finality (survival or assimilation) but of emergence, Indian life in Mashpee would not flow in a single current.

Interpreting the direction or meaning of the historical "record" always depends on present possibilities. When the future is open, so is the meaning of the past. Did Indian religion or tribal institutions disappear in the late nineteenth century? Or did they go underground? In a present context of serious revival they went underground; otherwise they disappeared. No continuous narrative or clear outcome accounts for Mashpee's deeply contested identity and direction. Nor can a single development weave together the branching paths of its past, the dead ends and hesitations that, with a newly conceived future, suddenly become prefigurations.

◆

(Hesitations. In 1869 Blind Joe Amos and the majority of Mashpee proprietors agreed that they were not yet ready to become citizens of

Massachusetts, separate entrepreneurs with individual control over their lands. They held back, declining a "progressive" step imposed by the legislature. Was it from backwardness? Confusion? Fear? Or something else: an alternate vision? A different voice?

What Susan Howe (1985) has written about a woman—Emily Dickinson, working during the same decade from another place of New England "isolation"—echoes strangely the Indian predicament: the problem of finding a different way through capitalist America.

> HESITATE from the Latin, meaning to stick. Stammer. To hold back in doubt, have difficulty speaking. "*He* may pause but *he* must not hesitate"—Ruskin. Hesitation circled back and surrounded everyone in that confident age of aggressive industrial expansion and brutal Empire building. Hesitation and Separation. The Civil War had split America in two. *He* might pause, *She* hesitated. Sexual, racial, and geographical separation are at the heart of Definition. Tragic and eternal dichotomy—if we concern ourselves with the deepest Reality, is this world of the imagination the same for men and women? What voice when we hesitate and are silent is moving to meet us? (p. 22)

In 1869 Joe Amos and the others did not go on record as resisting full citizenship. Separation and dichotomy were not their agenda: they were already more than half-caught up in a new America. It is important to distinguish hesitation from resistance, for hesitation need not oppose or acquiesce in the dominant course. It can be an alert waiting, thinking, anticipating of historical possibilities. Along with the history of resistances we need a history of hesitations.)

Stories of cultural contact and change have been structured by a pervasive dichotomy: absorption by the other *or* resistance to the other. A fear of lost identity, a Puritan taboo on mixing beliefs and bodies, hangs over the process. Yet what if identity is conceived not as a boundary to be maintained but as a nexus of relations and transactions actively engaging a subject? The story or stories of interaction must then be more complex, less linear and teleological. What changes when the subject of "history" is no longer Western? How do stories of contact, resistance, and assimilation appear from the standpoint of groups in which exchange rather than identity is the fundamental value to be sustained? Events are always mediated by local cultural structures. By focusing on the peripheral places, the neglected "islands of history" In Sahlins' words, "we ... multiply our conceptions of history by the diversity of structures. Suddenly there are all kinds of new things to consider" (1985:72).

In the diversity of local histories—like that of Mashpee—we find distinctive processes and directions. The channeled, inevitable flow of events begins to loop, waver, and fork. In 1830, for example, was the proprietary status of the Mashpee Indians an eroded "survival" from archaic English law, a social form destined to disappear? Or by the nineteenth century had it become a specific invention, a novel way to live on Indian land in modern America, a possible future? Neither story is false; both can be amply documented from the historical record. To say that the strange "tribal" integrity of the Mashpee Plantation was destined to disappear is to accept the history of the victors. But the suit filed a century later was an attempt to reopen this foregone conclusion. Mashpee's semiautonomous plantation, a specific mix of individual citizenship and collective entailment, now appeared not as a historical dead end but as a precursor of reinvented tribalism. No return to a pure Wampanoag tradition was at issue, but rather a reinterpretation of Mashpee's contested history in order to act—with other Indian groups—powerfully, in an impure present-becoming-future.

Whatever the trial's outcome "tribal" life had once again become powerful in Mashpee. Only a literal, backward-looking sense of authenticity (one no group would willingly apply to itself, only to others) could deny this emergent reality. The Wampanoag Supreme Sachem, Elsworth Oakley, commented after the verdict: "How can a white majority decide on whether we are a tribe? We know who we are."

The future of Native American life on Cape Cod after the setback in court is uncertain.

◆

The years immediately following the verdict were marked by disarray in Mashpee. An anticipated petition to the Department of the Interior for tribal status was slow to emerge. During this period the Bureau of Indian Affairs standardized its procedure for recognition claims, following criteria similar to those required by the court in *Mashpee v. New Seabury et al.* (Weatherhead 1980:17). The Indians in Mashpee watched with misgivings the progress of a petition by their fellow Wampanoags at Gay Head. In 1986 the petition was turned down in a preliminary finding. Government experts cited an insufficient degree of community specificity over the years and a loss of tribal political authority after Gay Head became a township in 1870. Gay Head's history was similar to Mashpee's.

Appealing the preliminary finding, the Native American Rights Fund presented additional evidence, compiled by Jack Campisi, of continuing social networks among Gay Head Indians and of a line of tribal authority after 1870. On February 8, 1987, for the first time ever the Bureau of Indian Affairs reversed a negative preliminary finding. The Gay Head Wampanoags were given full tribal recognition.

Quotations from a Native American Rights Fund press release:

Henry Sockbeson, the Penobscot attorney representing the tribe: "This decision means that the Gay Head will be able to settle their land claim within a few months. Under the terms of the settlement the Tribe will receive approximately 250 acres of land that can be developed. We anticipate that they will use it for housing and economic development."

Gladys Widdiss, chairperson of the Wampanoag Tribal Council of Gay Head, Inc.: "I am delighted. This now means that the Tribe can function in a formally recognized manner. Our status as a tribe can no longer be in doubt. Recognition means that our survival as a tribe for generations to come is assured."

Jack Campisi and Native American Rights Fund attorneys are working on Mashpee's petition.

TWO SNAPSHOTS

Mrs. Pells is an Indian born in Mashpee. She is seventy-one years old, now living eighteen miles away near the Bourne Bridge, and is an active member of the Tribal Council, Inc. She is dignified, slow-speaking.

She shows an enlarged photograph of her grandmother, Rebecca Hammond, Blind Joe Amos' daughter.

She has been a member of the Mashpee Wampanoag tribe "since birth."

She testifies that she lived in New York between 1928 and 1972 where she was active in a number of Native American organizations. During the 1940s she was secretary of the "American Indian Thunderbird Dancers." Most of the dancers did not originate in Massachusetts, and only one of the dancers was from Cape Cod.

◆

"Chiefy" Mills is Earl Mills's teenage son. He says he knows he is an Indian because his father told him. He likes to hunt and hang around with his cousins in Mashpee. A champion drummer, he participates often in Native American gatherings around New England. Recently he was among the young people arrested at a camping retreat held to promote Indian consciousness on the fifty-five acres of tribal land in Mashpee.

* * *

Whiteness as Property

106 Harv. L. Rev. 1707 (June 1993).

Cheryl I. Harris

Issues regarding race and racial identity as well as questions pertaining to property rights and ownership have been prominent in much public discourse in the United States. In this article, Professor Harris contributes to this discussion by positing that racial identity and property are deeply interrelated concepts. Professor Harris examines how whiteness, initially constructed as a form of racial identity, evolved into a form of property, historically and presently acknowledged and protected in American law. Professor Harris traces the origins of whiteness as property in the parallel systems of domination of Black and Native American peoples out of which were created racially contingent forms of property and property rights. Following the period of slavery and conquest, whiteness became the basis of racialized privilege—a type of status in which white racial identity provided the basis for allocating societal benefits both private and public in character.

These arrangements were ratified and legitimated in law as a type of status property. Even as legal segregation was overturned, whiteness as property continued to serve as a barrier to effective change as the system of racial classification operated to protect entrenched power.

Next, Professor Harris examines how the concept of whiteness as property persists in current perceptions of racial identity, in the law's misperception of group identity and in the Court's reasoning and decisions in the arena of affirmative action. Professor Harris concludes by arguing that distortions in affirmative action doctrine can only be addressed by confronting and exposing the property interest in whiteness and by acknowledging the distributive justification and function of affirmative action as central to that task.

she walked into forbidden worlds

impaled on the weapon of her own pale skin

she was a sentinel

at impromptu planning sessions

of her own destruction ...

Cheryl I. Harris, *poem for alma*[1]

[P]etitioner was a citizen of the United States and a resident of the state of Louisiana of mixed descent, in the proportion of seven eighths Caucasian and one eighth African blood; that the mixture of colored blood was not discernible in him, and that he was entitled to every recognition, right, privilege and immunity secured to the citizens of the United States of the white race by its Constitution and laws ... and thereupon entered a passenger train and took possession of a vacant seat in a coach where passengers of the white race were accommodated.

Plessy v. Ferguson[2]

I. INTRODUCTION

In the 1930s, some years after my mother's family became part of the great river of Black migration that flowed north, my Mississippi-born grandmother was confronted with the harsh matter of economic survival for herself and her two daughters. Having separated from my grandfather, who himself was trapped on the fringes of economic marginality, she took one long hard look at her choices and presented herself for employment at a major retail store in Chicago's central business district. This decision would have been unremarkable for a white woman in similar circumstances, but for my grandmother, it was an act of both great daring and self-denial, for in so doing she was presenting herself as a white woman. In the parlance of racist America, she was "passing."

1. Cheryl I. Harris, *poem for alma* (1990) (unpublished poem, on file at the Harvard Law School Library).

2. 163 U.S. 537, 538 (1896).

Her fair skin, straight hair, and aquiline features had not spared her from the life of sharecropping into which she had been born in any-where/nowhere, Mississippi—the outskirts of Yazoo City. But in the burgeoning landscape of urban America, anonymity was possible for a Black person with "white" features. She was transgressing boundaries, crossing borders, spinning on margins, traveling between dualities of Manichean space, rigidly bifurcated into light/dark, good/bad, white/Black. No longer immediately identifiable as "Lula's daughter," she could thus enter the white world, albeit on a false passport, not merely passing, but *tres*passing.

Every day my grandmother rose from her bed in her house in a Black enclave on the south side of Chicago, sent her children off to a Black school, boarded a bus full of Black passengers, and rode to work. No one at her job ever asked if she was Black; the question was unthinkable. By virtue of the employment practices of the "fine establishment" in which she worked, she could not have been. Catering to the upper-middle class, understated tastes required that Blacks not be allowed.

She quietly went about her clerical tasks, not once revealing her true identity. She listened to the women with whom she worked discuss their worries—their children's illnesses, their husbands' disappointments, their boyfriends' infidelities—all of the mundane yet critical things that made up their lives. She came to know them but they did not know her, for my grandmother occupied a completely different place. That place—where white supremacy and economic domination meet—was unknown turf to her white co-workers. They remained oblivious to the worlds within worlds that existed just beyond the edge of their awareness and yet were present in their very midst.

Each evening, my grandmother, tired and worn, retraced her steps home, laid aside her mask, and reentered herself. Day in and day out, she made herself invisible, then visible again, for a price too inconsequential to do more than barely sustain her family and at a cost too precious to conceive. She left the job some years later, finding the strain too much to bear.

From time to time, as I later sat with her, she would recollect that period, and the cloud of some painful memory would pass across her face. Her voice would remain subdued, as if to contain the still remembered tension. On rare occasions she would wince, recalling some particularly racist comment made in her presence because of her presumed, shared group affiliation. Whatever retort might have been called for had been suppressed long before it reached her lips, for the price of her family's well-being was her silence. Accepting the risk of self-annihilation was the only way to survive.

Although she never would have stated it this way, the clear and ringing denunciations of racism she delivered from her chair when advanced arthritis had rendered her unable to work were informed by those experiences. The fact that self-denial had been a logical choice and had made her complicit in her own oppression at times fed the fire in her eyes when she confronted some daily outrage inflicted on Black people. Later, these painful memories forged her total identification with the civil rights movement. Learning about the world at her knee as I did, these experiences also came to inform my outlook and my understanding of the world.

My grandmother's story is far from unique. Indeed, there are many who crossed the color line never to return. Passing is well-known among Black people in the United States and is a feature of race subordination in all societies structured on white supremacy. Notwithstanding the purported benefits of Black heritage in an era of affirmative action, passing is not an obsolete phenomenon that has slipped into history.

The persistence of passing is related to the historical and continuing pattern of white racial domination and economic exploitation that has given passing a certain economic logic. It was a given to my grandmother that being white automatically ensured higher economic returns in the short term, as well as greater economic, political, and social security in the long run. Becoming white meant gaining access to a whole set of public and private privileges that materially and permanently guaranteed basic subsistence needs and, therefore, survival. Becoming white increased the possibility of controlling critical aspects of one's life rather than being the object of others' domination.

My grandmother's story illustrates the valorization of whiteness as treasured property in a society structured on racial caste. In ways so embedded that it is rarely apparent, the set of assumptions, privileges, and benefits that accompany the status of being white have become a valuable asset that whites sought to protect and that those who passed sought to attain—by fraud if necessary. Whites have come to expect and rely on these benefits, and over time these expectations have been affirmed, legitimated, and protected by the law. Even though the law is neither uniform nor explicit in all instances, in protecting settled expectations based on white privilege, American law has recognized a property interest in whiteness that, although unacknowledged, now forms the background against which legal disputes are framed, argued, and adjudicated.

My Article investigates the relationships between concepts of race and property and reflects on how rights in property are contingent on, intertwined with, and conflated with race. Through this entangled relationship between race and property, historical forms of domination have evolved to reproduce subordination in the present. * * * I examine the emergence of whiteness as property and trace the evolution of whiteness from color to race to status to property as a progression historically rooted in white supremacy and economic hegemony over Black and Native American peoples. The origins of whiteness as property lie in the parallel systems of domination of Black and Native American peoples out of which were created racially contingent forms of property and property rights. I further argue that whiteness shares the critical characteristics of property even as the meaning of property has changed over time. In particular, whiteness and property share a common premise—a conceptual nucleus—of a right to exclude. This conceptual nucleus has proven to be a powerful center around which whiteness as property has taken shape. Following the period of slavery and conquest, white identity became the basis of racialized privilege that was ratified and legitimated in law as a type of status property. After legalized segregation was overturned, whiteness as property evolved into a more modern form through the law's ratification of the settled expectations of relative white privilege as a legitimate and natural baseline.

[I examine] the two forms of whiteness as property—status property and modern property—that are the submerged text of two paradigmatic cases on the race question in American law, *Plessy v. Ferguson* and *Brown v. Board of Education*. As legal history, they illustrate an important transition from old to new forms of whiteness as property. Although these cases take opposite interpretive stances regarding the constitutional legitimacy of legalized racial segregation, the property interest in whiteness was transformed, but not discarded, in the Court's new equal protection jurisprudence.

[I then consider] the persistence of whiteness as property. I first examine how subordination is reinstituted through modern conceptions of race and identity embraced in law. Whiteness as property has taken on more subtle forms, but retains its core characteristic—the legal legitimation of expectations of power and control that enshrine the status quo as a neutral baseline, while masking the maintenance of white privilege and domination. I further identify the property interest in whiteness as the unspoken center of current polarities around the issue of affirmative action. As a legacy of slavery and de jure and de facto race segregation, the concept of a protectable property interest in whiteness permeates affirmative action doctrine in a manner illustrated by the reasoning of three important affirmative action cases—*Regents of the University of California v. Bakke, City of Richmond v. J. A. Croson & Co.,* and *Wygant v. Jackson Board of Education.*

* * *, I offer preliminary thoughts on a way out of the conundrum created by protecting whiteness as a property interest. I suggest that affirmative action, properly conceived and reconstructed, would de-legitimate the property interest in whiteness. I do not offer here a complete reformulation of affirmative action, but suggest that focusing on the distortions created by the property interest in whiteness would provoke different questions and open alternative perspectives on the affirmative action debate. The inability to see affirmative action as more than a search for the "blameworthy" among "innocent" individuals is tied to the inability to see the property interest in whiteness. Thus reconstructed, affirmative action would challenge the characterization of the unfettered right to exclude as a legitimate aspect of identity and property.

II. THE CONSTRUCTION OF RACE AND THE EMERGENCE OF WHITENESS AS PROPERTY

The racialization of identity and the racial subordination of Blacks and Native Americans provided the ideological basis for slavery and conquest. Although the systems of oppression of Blacks and Native Americans differed in form—the former involving the seizure and appropriation of labor, the latter entailing the seizure and appropriation of land—undergirding both was a racialized conception of property implemented by force and ratified by law.

The origins of property rights in the United States are rooted in racial domination. Even in the early years of the country, it was not the concept of race alone that operated to oppress Blacks and Indians; rather, it was the *interaction* between conceptions of race and property that played a critical role in establishing and maintaining racial and economic subordination.

The hyper-exploitation of Black labor was accomplished by treating Black people themselves as objects of property. Race and property were thus conflated by establishing a form of property contingent on race—only Blacks were subjugated as slaves and treated as property. Similarly, the conquest, removal, and extermination of Native American life and culture were ratified by conferring and acknowledging the property rights of whites in Native American land. Only white possession and occupation of land was validated and therefore privileged as a basis for property rights. These distinct forms of exploitation each contributed in varying ways to the construction of whiteness as property.

A. Forms of Racialized Property: Relationships Between Slavery, Race, and Property

1. *The Convergence of Racial and Legal Status.*—Although the early colonists were cognizant of race, racial lines were neither consistently nor sharply delineated among or within all social groups. Captured Africans sold in the Americas were distinguished from the population of indentured or bond servants—"unfree" white labor—but it was not an irrebuttable presumption that all Africans were "slaves" or that slavery was the only appropriate status for them. The distinction between African and white indentured labor grew, however, as decreasing terms of service were introduced for white bond servants. Simultaneously, the demand for labor intensified, resulting in a greater reliance on African labor and a rapid increase in the number of Africans imported into the colonies.

The construction of white identity and the ideology of racial hierarchy also were intimately tied to the evolution and expansion of the system of chattel slavery. The further entrenchment of plantation slavery was in part an answer to a social crisis produced by the eroding capacity of the landed class to control the white labor population. The dominant paradigm of social relations, however, was that, although not all Africans were slaves, virtually all slaves were not white. It was their racial otherness that came to justify the subordinated status of Blacks. The result was a classification system that "key[ed] official rules of descent to national origin" so that "[m]embership in the new social category of 'Negro' became itself sufficient justification for enslaveability." Although the cause of the increasing gap between the status of African and white labor is contested by historians, it is clear that "[t]he economic and political interests defending Black slavery were far more powerful than those defending indentured servitude."

By the 1660s, the especially degraded status of Blacks as chattel slaves was recognized by law. Between 1680 and 1682, the first slave codes appeared, codifying the extreme deprivations of liberty already existing in social practice. Many laws parceled out differential treatment based on racial categories: Blacks were not permitted to travel without permits, to own property, to assemble publicly, or to own weapons; nor were they to be educated. Racial identity was further merged with stratified social and legal status: "Black" racial identity marked who was subject to enslavement; "white" racial identity marked who was "free" or, at minimum, not a slave. The ideological and rhetorical move from "slave" and "free" to "Black" and "white" as polar constructs marked an important step in the social construction of race.

2. *Implications for Property.*—The social relations that produced racial identity as a justification for slavery also had implications for the conceptualization of property. This result was predictable, as the institution of slavery, lying at the very core of economic relations, was bound up with the idea of property. Through slavery, race and economic domination were fused.

Slavery produced a peculiar, mixed category of property and humanity—a hybrid possessing inherent instabilities that were reflected in its treatment and ratification by the law. The dual and contradictory character of slaves as property and persons was exemplified in the Representation Clause of the Constitution. Representation in the House of Representatives was apportioned on the basis of population computed by counting all persons and "three-fifths of all other persons"—slaves. Gouveneur Morris's remarks before the Constitutional Convention posed the essential question: "Upon what principle is it that slaves shall be computed in the representation? Are they men? Then make them Citizens & let them vote? Are they property? Why then is no other property included?"

The cruel tension between property and humanity was also reflected in the law's legitimation of the use of Blackwomen's bodies as a means of increasing property. In 1662, the Virginia colonial assembly provided that "[c]hildren got by an Englishman upon a Negro woman shall be bond or free according to the condition of the mother...." In reversing the usual common law presumption that the status of the child was determined by the father, the rule facilitated the reproduction of one's own labor force. Because the children of Blackwomen assumed the status of their mother, slaves were bred through Blackwomen's bodies. The economic significance of this form of exploitation of female slaves should not be underestimated. Despite Thomas Jefferson's belief that slavery should be abolished, like other slaveholders, he viewed slaves as economic assets, noting that their value could be realized more efficiently from breeding than from labor. A letter he wrote in 1805 stated: "I consider the labor of a breeding woman as no object, and that a child raised every 2 years is of more profit than the crop of the best laboring man."

Even though there was some unease in slave law, reflective of the mixed status of slaves as humans and property, the critical nature of social relations under slavery was the commodification of human beings. Productive relations in early American society included varying forms of sale of labor capacity, many of which were highly oppressive; but slavery was distinguished from other forms of labor servitude by its permanency and the total commodification attendant to the status of the slave. Slavery as a legal institution treated slaves as property that could be transferred, assigned, inherited, or posted as collateral. For example, in *Johnson v. Butler,* the plaintiff sued the defendant for failing to pay a debt of $496 on a specified date. Because the covenant had called for payment of the debt in "money or negroes," the plaintiff contended that the defendant's tender of one negro only, although valued by the parties at an amount equivalent to the debt, could not discharge the debt. The court agreed with the plaintiff. This use of Africans as a stand-in for actual currency highlights the degree to which slavery "propertized" human life.

Because the "presumption of freedom [arose] from color [white]" and the "black color of the race [raised] the presumption of slavery," whiteness became a shield from slavery, a highly volatile and unstable form of property. In the form adopted in the United States, slavery made human beings market-alienable and in so doing, subjected human life and personhood—that which is most valuable—to the ultimate devaluation. Because whites could not be enslaved or held as slaves, the racial line between white and Black was extremely critical; it became a line of protection and demarcation from the potential threat of commodification, and it determined the allocation of the benefits and burdens of this form of property. White identity and whiteness were sources of privilege and protection; their absence meant being the object of property.

Slavery as a system of property facilitated the merger of white identity and property. Because the system of slavery was contingent on and conflated with racial identity, it became crucial to be "white," to be identified as white, to have the property of being white. Whiteness was the characteristic, the attribute, the property of free human beings.

B.   Forms of Racialized Property: Relationships Between Native American Land Seizure, Race, and Property

Slavery linked the privilege of whites to the subordination of Blacks through a legal regime that attempted the conversion of Blacks into objects of property. Similarly, the settlement and seizure of Native American land supported white privilege through a system of property rights in land in which the "race" of the Native Americans rendered their first possession rights invisible and justified conquest. This racist formulation embedded the fact of white privilege into the very definition of property, marking another stage in the evolution of the property interest in whiteness. Possession—the act necessary to lay the basis for rights in property—was defined to include only the cultural practices of whites. This definition laid the foundation for the idea that whiteness—that which whites alone possess—is valuable and is property.

Although the Indians were the first occupants and possessors of the land of the New World, their racial and cultural otherness allowed this fact to be reinterpreted and ultimately erased as a basis for asserting rights in land. Because the land had been left in its natural state, untilled and unmarked by human hands, it was "waste" and, therefore, the appropriate object of settlement and appropriation. Thus, the possession maintained by the Indians was not "true" possession and could safely be ignored. This interpretation of the rule of first possession effectively rendered the rights of first possessors contingent on the race of the possessor. Only particular forms of possession—those that were characteristic of white settlement— would be recognized and legitimated. Indian forms of possession were perceived to be too ambiguous and unclear.

The conquest and occupation of Indian land was wrapped in the rule of law. The law provided not only a defense of conquest and colonization, but also a naturalized regime of rights and disabilities, power and disadvantage that flowed from it, so that no further justifications or rationalizations were required. A key decision defending the right of conquest was *Johnson and Graham's Lessee v. M'Intosh,* in which both parties to the action claimed the same land through title descendant from different Indian tribes. The issue specifically presented was not merely whether Indians had the power to convey title, but to whom the conveyance could be made—to individuals or to the government that "discovered" land. In holding that Indians could only convey to the latter, the Court reasoned that Indian title was subordinate to the absolute title of the sovereign that was achieved by conquest because "[c]onquest gives a title which the Courts of the conqueror cannot deny. . . ." If property is understood as a delegation of sovereign power—the product of the power of the state—then a fair reading of history reveals the racial oppression of Indians inherent in the American regime of property.

In *Johnson* and similar cases, courts established whiteness as a prerequisite to the exercise of enforceable property rights. Not all first possession or labor gave rise to property rights; rather, the rules of first possession and labor as a basis for property rights were qualified by race. This fact infused whiteness with significance and value because it was solely through being white that property could be acquired and secured under law. Only whites possessed whiteness, a highly valued and exclusive form of property.

C. *Critical Characteristics of Property and Whiteness*

The legal legacy of slavery and of the seizure of land from Native American peoples is not merely a regime of property law that is (mis)informed by racist and ethnocentric themes. Rather, the law has established and protected an actual property interest in whiteness itself, which shares the critical characteristics of property and accords with the many and varied theoretical descriptions of property.

Although by popular usage property describes "things" owned by persons, or the rights of persons with respect to a thing, the concept of property prevalent among most theorists, even prior to the twentieth century, is that property may "consist[] of rights in 'things' that are intangible, or whose existence is a matter of legal definition." Property is thus said to be a right, not a thing, characterized as metaphysical, not physical. The theoretical bases and conceptual descriptions of property rights are varied, ranging from first possessor rules, to creation of value, to Lockean labor theory, to personality theory, to utilitarian theory. However disparate, these formulations of property clearly illustrate the extent to which property rights and interests embrace much more than land and personality. Thus, the fact that whiteness is not a "physical" entity does not remove it from the realm of property.

Whiteness is not simply and solely a legally recognized property interest. It is simultaneously an aspect of self-identity and of personhood, and its relation to the law of property is complex. Whiteness has functioned as self-identity in the domain of the intrinsic, personal, and psychological; as reputation in the interstices between internal and external identity; and, as property in the extrinsic, public, and legal realms. According whiteness actual legal status converted an aspect of identity into an external object of property, moving whiteness from privileged identity to a vested interest. The law's construction of whiteness defined and affirmed critical aspects of identity (who is white); of privilege (what benefits accrue to that status); and, of property (what *legal* entitlements arise from that status). Whiteness at various times signifies and is deployed as identity, status, and property, sometimes singularly, sometimes in tandem.

1. Whiteness as a Traditional Form of Property.—Whiteness fits the broad historical concept of property described by classical theorists. In James Madison's view, for example, property "embraces every thing to which a man may attach a value and have a right," referring to all of a person's legal rights. Property as conceived in the founding era

> included not only external objects and people's relationships to them, but also all of those human rights, liberties, powers, and immunities that are important for human well-being, including: freedom of expression, freedom of conscience, freedom from bodily harm, and free and equal opportunities to use personal faculties.

Whiteness defined the legal status of a person as slave or free. White identity conferred tangible and economically valuable benefits and was jealously guarded as a valued possession, allowed only to those who met a strict standard of proof. Whiteness—the right to white identity as embraced by the law—is property if by property one means all of a person's legal rights.

Other traditional theories of property emphasize that the "natural" character of property is derivative of custom, contrary to the notion that property is the product of a delegation of sovereign power. This "bottom up" theory holds that the law of property merely codifies existing customs and social relations. Under that view, government-created rights such as social welfare payments cannot constitute legitimate property interests because they are positivistic in nature. Other theorists have challenged this conception, and argued that even the most basic of "customary" property rights—the rule of first possession, for example—is dependent on its acceptance or rejection in particular instances by the government. Citing custom as a source of property law begs the central question: whose custom?

Rather than remaining within the bipolar confines of custom or command, it is crucial to recognize the dynamic and multifaceted relationship among custom, command, and law, as well as the extent to which positionality determines how each may be experienced and understood. Indian custom was obliterated by force and replaced with the regimes of common law that embodied the customs of the conquerors. The assumption of American law as it related to Native Americans was that conquest *did* give rise to sovereignty. Indians experienced the property laws of the colonizers and the emergent American nation as acts of violence perpetuated by the exercise of power and ratified through the rule of law. At the same time, these laws were perceived as custom and "common sense" by the colonizers. The Founders, for instance, so thoroughly embraced Lockean labor theory as the basis for a right of acquisition because it affirmed the right of the New World settlers to settle on and acquire the frontier. It confirmed and ratified their experience.

The law's interpretation of those encounters between whites and Native Americans not only inflicted vastly different results on them, but also established a pattern—a *custom*—of valorizing whiteness. As the forms of racialized property were perfected, the value and protection extended to whiteness increased. Regardless of which theory of property one adopts, the concept of whiteness—established by centuries of custom (illegitimate custom, but custom nonetheless) and codified by law—may be understood as a property interest.

2. Modern Views of Property as Defining Social Relations.—Although property in the classical sense refers to everything that is valued and to which a person has a right, the modern concept of property focuses on its function and the social relations reflected therein. In this sense, modern property doctrine emphasizes the more contingent nature of property and has been the basis for the argument that property rights should be expanded.

Modern theories of property reject the assumption that property is "objectively definable or identifiable, apart from social context." Charles Reich's ground-breaking work, *The New Property,* was an early effort to focus on the function of property and note the changing social relations reflected and constructed by new forms of property derived from the government. Property in this broader sense encompassed jobs, entitlements, occupational licenses, contracts, subsidies, and indeed a whole host of intangibles that are the product of labor, time, and creativity, such as intellectual property, business goodwill, and enhanced earning potential from graduate degrees. Notwithstanding the dilution of new property since *Goldberg v. Kelly* and its progeny as well as continued attacks on the concept, the legacy of new property infuses the concept of property with questions of power, selection, and allocation. Reich's argument that property is not a natural right but a construction by society resonates in current theories of property that describe the allocation of property rights as a series of choices. This construction directs attention toward issues of relative power and social relations inherent in any definition of property.

3. Property and Expectations.—"Property is nothing but the basis of expectation," according to Bentham, "consist[ing] in an established expectation, in the persuasion of being able to draw such and such advantage from the thing possessed." The relationship between expectations and property remains highly significant, as the law "has recognized and protected even the expectation of rights as actual legal property." This theory does not suggest that all value or all expectations give rise to property, but those expectations in tangible or intangible things that are valued and protected by the law are property.

In fact, the difficulty lies not in identifying expectations as a part of property, but in distinguishing which expectations are reasonable and therefore merit the protection of the law as property. Although the existence of certain property rights may seem self-evident and the protection of certain expectations may seem essential for social stability, property is a legal construct by which selected private interests are protected and upheld. In creating property "rights," the law draws boundaries and enforces or reorders existing regimes of power. The inequalities that are produced and reproduced are not givens or inevitabilities, but rather are conscious selections regarding the structuring of social relations. In this sense, it is contended that property rights and interests are not "natural," but are "creation[s] of law."

In a society structured on racial subordination, white privilege became an expectation and, to apply Margaret Radin's concept, whiteness became the quintessential property for personhood. The law constructed "whiteness" as an objective fact, although in reality it is an ideological proposition imposed through subordination. This move is the central feature of "reification": "Its basis is that a relation between people takes on the character of a thing and thus acquires a 'phantom objectivity,' an autonomy that seems so strictly rational and all-embracing as to conceal every trace of its fundamental nature: the relation between people." Whiteness was an "object" over which continued control was—and is—expected. The protection of these expectations is central because, as Radin notes: "If an object you now control is bound up in your future plans or in your anticipation of your future self, and it is partly these plans for your own continuity that make you a person, then your personhood depends on the realization of these expectations."

Because the law recognized and protected expectations grounded in white privilege (albeit not explicitly in all instances), these expectations became tantamount to property that could not permissibly be intruded upon without consent. As the law explicitly ratified those expectations in continued privilege or extended ongoing protection to those illegitimate expectations by failing to expose or to radically disturb them, the dominant and subordinate positions within the racial hierarchy were reified in law.

When the law recognizes, either implicitly or explicitly, the settled expectations of whites built on the privileges and benefits produced by white supremacy, it acknowledges and reinforces a property interest in whiteness that reproduces Black subordination.

4. *The Property Functions of Whiteness.*—In addition to the theoretical descriptions of property, whiteness also meets the functional criteria of property. Specifically, the law has accorded "holders" of whiteness the same privileges and benefits accorded holders of other types of property. The liberal view of property is that it includes the exclusive rights of possession, use, and disposition. Its attributes are the right to transfer or alienability, the right to use and enjoyment, and the right to exclude others. Even when examined against this limited view, whiteness conforms to the general contours of property. It may be a "bad" form of property, but it is property nonetheless.

(a) Rights of Disposition.—Property rights are traditionally described as fully alienable. Because fundamental personal rights are commonly understood to be inalienable, it is problematic to view them as property interests. However, as Margaret Radin notes, "inalienability" is not a transparent term; it has multiple meanings that refer to interests that are non-salable, non-transferable, or non-market-alienable. The common core of inalienability is the negation of the possibility of separation of an entitlement, right, or attribute from its holder.

Classical theories of property identified alienability as a requisite aspect of property; thus, that which is inalienable cannot be property. As the major exponent of this view, Mill argued that public offices, monopoly privileges, and human beings—all of which were or should have been inalienable—should not be considered property at all. Under this account, if inalienability inheres in the concept of property, then whiteness, incapable of being transferred or alienated either inside or outside the market, would fail to meet a criterion of property.

As Radin notes, however, even under the classical view, alienability of certain property was limited. Mill also advocated certain restraints on alienation in connection with property rights in land and probably other natural resources. In fact, the law has recognized various kinds of inalienable property. For example, entitlements of the regulatory and welfare states, such as transfer payments and government licenses, are inalienable; yet they have been conceptualized and treated as property by law. Although this "new property" has been criticized as being improper—that is, not appropriately cast as property—the principal objection has been based on its alleged lack of productive capacity, not its inalienability.

The law has also acknowledged forms of inalienable property derived from nongovernmental sources. In the context of divorce, courts have held that professional degrees or licenses held by one party and financed by the labor of the other is marital property whose value is subject to allocation by the court. A medical or law degree is not alienable either in the market or by voluntary transfer. Nevertheless, it is included as property when dissolving a legal relationship.

Indeed, Radin argues that, as a deterrent to the dehumanization of universal commodification, market-inalienability may be justified to protect property important to the person and to safeguard human flourishing. She suggests that non-commodification or market-inalienability of personal property or those things essential to human flourishing is necessary to guard against the objectification of human beings. To avoid that danger, "we must cease thinking that market alienability is inherent in the concept of property." Following this logic, then, the inalienability of whiteness should not preclude the consideration of whiteness as property. Paradoxically, its inalienability may be more indicative of its perceived enhanced value, rather than its disqualification as property.

(b) Right to Use and Enjoyment.—Possession of property includes the rights of use and enjoyment. If these rights are essential aspects of property, it is because "the problem of property in political philosophy dissolves into . . . questions of the will and the way in which we use the things of this world." As whiteness is simultaneously an aspect of identity and a property interest, it is something that can both be experienced and deployed as a resource. Whiteness can move from being a passive characteristic as an aspect of identity to an active entity that—like other types of property—is used to fulfill the will and to exercise power. The state's official recognition of a racial identity that subordinated Blacks and of privileged rights in property based on race elevated whiteness from a passive attribute to an object of law and a resource deployable at the social, political, and institutional level to maintain control. Thus, a white person "used and enjoyed" whiteness whenever she took advantage of the privileges accorded white people simply by virtue of their whiteness—when she exercised any number of rights reserved for the holders of whiteness. Whiteness as the embodiment of white privilege transcended mere belief or preference; it became usable property, the subject of the law's regard and protection. In this respect whiteness, as an active property, has been used and enjoyed.

(c) Reputation and Status Property.—In constructing whiteness as property, the ideological move was to conceptualize white racial identity as an external thing in a constitutive sense—an "object [] or resource [] necessary to be a person." This move was accomplished in large measure by recognizing the reputational interest in being regarded as white as a thing of significant value, which like other reputational interests, was intrinsically bound up with identity and personhood. The reputation of being white was treated as a species of property, or something in which a property interest could be asserted. In this context, whiteness was a form of status property.

The conception of reputation as property found its origins in early concepts of property that encompassed things (such as land and personalty), income (such as revenues from leases, mortgages, and patent monopolies), and one's life, liberty, and labor. Thus, Locke's famous pronouncement, "every man has a 'property' in his own 'person,'" undergirded the assertion that one's physical self was one's property. From this premise, one's labor, "the work of his hands," combined with those things found in the common to form property over which one could exercise ownership, control, and dominion. The idea of self-ownership, then, was particularly fertile ground for the idea that reputation, as an aspect of identity earned through effort, was similarly property. Moreover, the loss of reputation was capable of being valued in the market.

The direct manifestation of the law's legitimation of whiteness as reputation is revealed in the well-established doctrine that to call a white person "Black" is to defame her. Although many of the cases were decided in an era when the social and legal stratification of whites and Blacks was more absolute, as late as 1957 the principle was reaffirmed, notwithstanding significant changes in the legal and political status of Blacks. As one court noted, "there is still to be considered the social distinction existing between the races," and the allegation was likely to cause injury. A Black person, however, could not sue for defamation if she was called "white." Because the law expressed and reinforced the social hierarchy as it existed, it was presumed that no harm could flow from such a reversal.

Private identity based on racial hierarchy was legitimated as public identity in law, even after the end of slavery and the formal end of legal race segregation. Whiteness as interpersonal hierarchy was recognized externally as race reputation. Thus, whiteness as public reputation and personal property was affirmed.

(d) The Absolute Right to Exclude.—Many theorists have traditionally conceptualized property to include the exclusive rights of use, disposition, and possession, with possession embracing the absolute right to exclude. The right to exclude was the central principle, too, of whiteness as identity, for mainly whiteness has been characterized, not by an inherent unifying characteristic, but by the exclusion of others deemed to be "not white." The possessors of whiteness were granted the legal right to exclude others from the privileges inhering in whiteness; whiteness became an exclusive club whose membership was closely and grudgingly guarded. The courts played an active role in enforcing this right to exclude—determining who was or was not white enough to enjoy the privileges accompanying whiteness. In that sense, the courts protected whiteness as any other form of property.

Moreover, as it emerged, the concept of whiteness was premised on white supremacy rather than mere difference. "White" was defined and constructed in ways that increased its value by reinforcing its exclusivity. Indeed, just as whiteness as property embraced the right to exclude, whiteness as a theoretical construct evolved for the very purpose of racial exclusion. Thus, the concept of whiteness is built on both exclusion and racial subjugation. This fact was particularly evident during the period of the most rigid racial exclusion, as whiteness signified racial privilege and took the form of status property.

At the individual level, recognizing oneself as "white" necessarily assumes premises based on white supremacy: It assumes that Black ancestry in any degree, extending to generations far removed, automatically disqualifies claims to white identity, thereby privileging "white" as unadulterated, exclusive, and rare. Inherent in the concept of "being white" was the right to own or hold whiteness to the exclusion and subordination of Blacks. Because "[i]dentity is ... continuously being constituted through social interactions," the assigned political, economic, and social inferiority of Blacks necessarily shaped white identity. In the commonly held popular view, the presence of Black "blood"—including the infamous "one-drop"—consigned a person to being "Black" and evoked the "metaphor ... of purity and contamination" in which Black blood is a contaminant and white racial identity is pure. Recognizing or identifying oneself as white is thus a claim of racial purity, an assertion that one is free of any taint of Black blood. The law has played a critical role in legitimating this claim.

D. White Legal Identity: The Law's Acceptance and Legitimation of Whiteness as Property

The law assumed the crucial task of racial classification, and accepted and embraced the then-current theories of race as biological fact. This core precept of race as a physically defined reality allowed the law to fulfill an essential function—to "parcel out social standing according to race" and to facilitate systematic discrimination by articulating "seemingly precise definitions of racial group membership." This allocation of race and rights continued a century after the abolition of slavery.

The law relied on bounded, objective, and scientific definitions of race—what Neil Gotanda has called "historical race"—to construct whiteness as not merely race, but race plus privilege. By making race determinant and the product of rationality and science, dominant and subordinate positions within the racial hierarchy were disguised as the product of natural law and biology rather than as naked preferences. Whiteness as racialized privilege was then legitimated by science and was embraced in legal doctrine as "objective fact."

Case law that attempted to define race frequently struggled over the precise fractional amount of Black "blood"—traceable Black ancestry—that would defeat a claim to whiteness. Although the courts applied varying fractional formulas in different jurisdictions to define "Black" or, in the terms of the day, "Negro" or "colored," the law uniformly accepted the rule of hypodescent—racial identity was governed by blood, and white was preferred.

This legal assumption of race as blood-borne was predicated on the pseudo-sciences of eugenics and craniology that saw their major development during the eighteenth and nineteenth centuries. The legal definition of race was the "objective" test propounded by racist theorists of the day who described race to be immutable, scientific, biologically determined—an unsullied fact of the blood rather than a volatile and violently imposed regime of racial hierarchy.

In adjudicating who was "white," courts sometimes noted that, by physical characteristics, the individual whose racial identity was at issue appeared to be white and, in fact, had been regarded as white in the community. Yet if an individual's blood was tainted, she could not claim to be "white" as the law understood, regardless of the fact that phenotypically she may have been completely indistinguishable from a white person, may have lived as a white person, and have descended from a family that lived as whites. Although socially accepted as white, she could not *legally* be white. Blood as "objective fact" dominated over appearance and social acceptance, which were socially fluid and subjective measures.

But, in fact, "blood" was no more objective than that which the law dismissed as subjective and unreliable. The acceptance of the fiction that the racial ancestry could be determined with the degree of precision called for by the relevant standards or definitions rested on false assumptions that racial categories of prior ancestors had been accurately reported, that those reporting in the past shared the definitions currently in use, and that racial purity actually existed in the United States. Ignoring these considerations, the law established rules that extended equal treatment to those of the "same blood," albeit of different complexions, because it was acknowledged that, "[t]here are white men as dark as mulattoes, and there are pure-blooded albino Africans as white as the whitest Saxons."

The standards were designed to accomplish what mere observation could not: "That even Blacks who did not look Black were kept in their place." Although the line of demarcation between Black and white varied from rules that classified as Black a person containing "any drop of Black blood," to more liberal rules that defined persons with a preponderance of white blood to be white, the courts universally accepted the notion that white status was something of value that could be accorded only to those persons whose proofs established their whiteness as defined by the law. Because legal recognition of a person as white carried material benefits, "false" or inadequately supported claims were denied like any other unsubstantiated claim to a property interest. Only those who could lay "legitimate" claims to whiteness could be legally recognized as "white," because allowing physical attributes, social acceptance, or self-identification to determine whiteness would diminish its value and destroy the underlying presumption of exclusivity. In effect, the courts erected legal "No Trespassing" signs.

In the realm of *social* relations, racial recognition in the United States is thus an act of race subordination. In the realm of *legal* relations, judicial definition of racial identity based on white supremacy reproduced that race subordination at the institutional level. In transforming white to whiteness, the law masked the ideological content of racial definition and the exercise of power required to maintain it: "It convert[ed] [an] abstract concept into [an] entity."

1. Whiteness as Racialized Privilege.—The material benefits of racial exclusion and subjugation functioned, in the labor context, to stifle class tensions among whites. White workers perceived that they had more in common with the bourgeoisie than with fellow workers who were Black. Thus, W. E. B. Du Bois's classic historical study of race and class, *Black Reconstruction,* noted that, for the evolving white working class, race identification became crucial to the ways that it thought of itself and conceived its interests. There were, he suggested, obvious material benefits, at least in the short term, to the decision of white workers to define themselves by their whiteness: their wages far exceeded those of Blacks and were high even in comparison with world standards. Moreover, even when the white working class did not collect increased pay as part of white privilege, there were real advantages not paid in direct income: whiteness still yielded what Du Bois termed a "public and psychological wage" vital to white workers. Thus, Du Bois noted:

> They [whites] were given public deference . . . because they were white. They were admitted freely with all classes of white people, to public functions, to public parks. . . . The police were drawn from their ranks, and the courts, dependent on their votes, treated them with . . . leniency. . . . Their vote selected public officials, and while this had small effect upon the economic situation, it had great effect on their personal treatment. . . . White schoolhouses were the best in the community, and conspicuously placed, and they cost anywhere from twice to ten times as much per capita as the colored schools.

The central feature of the convergence of "white" and "worker" lay in the fact that racial status and privilege could ameliorate and assist in "evad[ing] rather than confront[ing] [class] exploitation." Although not accorded the privileges of the ruling class, in both the North and South, white workers could accept their lower class position in the hierarchy "by fashioning identities as 'not slaves' and as 'not Blacks.'" Whiteness produced—and was reproduced by—the social advantage that accompanied it.

Whiteness was also central to national identity and to the republican project. The amalgamation of various European strains into an American identity was facilitated by an oppositional definition of Black as "other." As Hacker suggests, fundamentally, the question was not so much "who is white," *but* "who may be considered white," as the historical pattern was that various immigrant groups of different ethnic origins were accepted into a white identity shaped around Anglo–American norms. Current members then "ponder[ed] whether they want[ed] or need[ed] new members as well as the proper pace of new admissions into this exclusive club." Through minstrel shows in which white actors masquerading in blackface played out racist stereotypes, the popular culture put the Black at " 'solo spot centerstage, providing a relational model in contrast to which masses of Americans could establish a positive and superior sense of identity[,]' . . . [an identity] . . . established by an infinitely manipulable negation comparing whites with a construct of a socially defenseless group."

It is important to note the effect of this hypervaluation of whiteness. Owning white identity as property affirmed the self-identity and liberty of whites and, conversely, denied the self-identity and liberty of Blacks. The attempts to lay claim to whiteness through "passing" painfully illustrate the effects of the law's recognition of whiteness. The embrace of a lie, undertaken by my grandmother and the thousands like her, could occur only when oppression makes self-denial and the obliteration of identity rational and, in significant measure, beneficial. The economic coercion of white supremacy on self-definition nullifies any suggestion that passing is a logical exercise of liberty or self-identity. The decision to pass as white was not a choice, if by that word one means voluntariness or lack of compulsion. The fact of race subordination was coercive and circumscribed the liberty to self-define. Self-determination of identity was not a right for all people, but a privilege accorded on the basis of race. The effect of protecting whiteness at law was to devalue those who were not white by coercing them to deny their identity in order to survive.

   2. Whiteness, Rights, and National Identity.—The concept of whiteness was carefully protected because so much was contingent upon it. Whiteness conferred on its owners aspects of citizenship that were all the more valued because they were denied to others. Indeed, the very fact of citizenship itself was linked to white racial identity. The Naturalization Act of 1790 restricted citizenship to persons who resided in the United States for two years, who could establish their good character in court, and who were "white." Moreover, the trajectory of expanding democratic rights for whites was accompanied by the contraction of the rights of Blacks in an ever deepening cycle of oppression. The franchise, for example, was broadened to extend voting rights to unpropertied white men at the same time that Black voters were specifically disenfranchised, arguably shifting the property required for voting from land to whiteness. This racialized version of republicanism—this Herrenvolk republicanism—constrained any vision of democracy from addressing the class hierarchies adverse to many who considered themselves white.

   The inherent contradiction between the bondage of Blacks and republican rhetoric that championed the freedom of all men was resolved by positing that Blacks were different. The laws did not mandate that Blacks be accorded equality under the law because nature—not man, not power, not violence—had determined their degraded status. Rights were for those who had the capacity to exercise them, a capacity denoted by racial identity. This conception of rights was contingent on race—on whether one could claim whiteness—a form of property. This articulation of rights that were contingent on property ownership was a familiar paradigm, as similar requirements had been imposed on the franchise in the early part of the republic.

   For the first two hundred years of the country's existence, the system of racialized privilege in both the public and private spheres carried through this linkage of rights and inequality, and rights and property. Whiteness as property was the critical core of a system that affirmed the hierarchical relations between white and Black.

   * * *

IV. THE PERSISTENCE OF WHITENESS AS PROPERTY

   In the modern period, neither the problems attendant to assigning racial identities nor those accompanying the recognition of whiteness have disappeared. Nor has whiteness as property. Whiteness as property continues to perpetuate racial subordination through the courts' definitions of group identity and through the courts' discourse and doctrine on affirmative action. The exclusion of subordinated "others" was and remains a central part of the property interest in whiteness and, indeed, is part of the protection that the court extends to whites' settled expectations of continued privilege.

The essential character of whiteness as property remains manifest in two critical areas of the law and, as in the past, operates to oppress Native Americans and Blacks in similar ways, although in different arenas. This Part first examines the persistence of whiteness as valued social identity; then exposes whiteness as property in the law's treatment of the question of group identity, as the case of the Mashpee Indians illustrates; and finally, exposes the presence of whiteness as property in affirmative action doctrine.

A.   The Persistence of Whiteness as Valued Social Identity

Even as the capacity of whiteness to deliver is arguably diminished by the elimination of rigid racial stratifications, whiteness continues to be perceived as materially significant. Because real power and wealth never have been accessible to more than a narrowly defined ruling elite, for many whites the benefits of whiteness as property, in the absence of legislated privilege, may have been reduced to a claim of relative privilege only in comparison to people of color. Nevertheless, whiteness retains its value as a "consolation prize": it does not mean that all whites will win, but simply that they will not lose, if losing is defined as being on the bottom of the social and economic hierarchy—the position to which Blacks have been consigned.

Andrew Hacker, in his 1992 book *Two Nations,* recounts the results of a recent exercise that probed the value of whiteness according to the perceptions of whites. The study asked a group of white students how much money they would seek if they were changed from white to Black. "Most seemed to feel that it would not be out of place to ask for $50 million, or $1 million for each coming black year." Whether this figure represents an accurate amortization of the societal cost of being Black in the United States, it is clear that whiteness is still perceived to be valuable. The wages of whiteness are available to all whites regardless of class position, even to those whites who are without power, money, or influence. Whiteness, the characteristic that distinguishes them from Blacks, serves as compensation even to those who lack material wealth. It is the relative political advantages extended to whites, rather than actual economic gains, that are crucial to white workers. Thus, as Kimberlé Crenshaw points out, whites have an actual stake in racism. Because Blacks are held to be inferior, although no longer on the basis of science as antecedent determinant, but by virtue of their position at the bottom, it allows whites—all whites—to "include themselves in the dominant circle. [Although most whites] hold no real power, [all can claim] their privileged racial identity."

White workers often identify primarily as white rather than as workers because it is through their whiteness that they are afforded access to a host of public, private, and psychological benefits. It is through the concept of whiteness that class consciousness among white workers is subordinated and attention is diverted from class oppression.

Although dominant societal norms have embraced the idea of fairness and nondiscrimination, removal of privilege and antisubordination principles are actively rejected or at best ambiguously received because expectations of white privilege are bound up with what is considered essential for self-realization. Among whites, the idea persists that their whiteness is meaningful. Whiteness is an aspect of racial identity surely, but it is much more; it remains a concept based on relations of power, a social construct predicated on white dominance and Black subordination.

B.   Subordination Through Denial of Group Identity

Whiteness as property is also constituted through the reification of expectations in the continued right of white-dominated institutions to control the legal meaning of group identity. This reification manifests itself in the law's dialectical misuse of the concept of group identity as it pertains to racially subordinated peoples. The law has recognized and codified racial group identity as an instrumentality of exclusion and exploitation; however, it has refused to recognize group identity when asserted by racially oppressed groups as a basis for affirming or claiming rights. The law's approach to group identity reproduces subordination, in the past through "race-ing" a group—that is, by assigning a racial identity that equated with inferior status, and in the present by erasing racial group identity.

In part, the law's denial of the existence of racial groups is predicated not only on the rejection of the ongoing presence of the past, but is also grounded on a basic tenet of liberalism—that constitutional protections inhere in individuals, not groups. As informed by the Lockean notion of the social contract, the autonomous, free-will of the individual is central. Indeed, it is the individual who, in concert with other individuals, elects to enter into political society and to form a state of limited powers. This philosophical view of society is closely aligned with the antidiscrimination principle—the idea being that equality mandates only the equal treatment of individuals under the law. Within this framework, the idea of the social group has no place.

Although the law's determination of any "fact," including that of group identity, is not infinitely flexible, its studied ignorance of the issue of racial group identity insures wrong results by assuming a pseudo-objective posture that does not permit it to hear the complex dialogue concerning the identity question, particularly as it pertains to historically dominated groups.

Instead, the law holds to the basic premise that definition from above can be fair to those below, that beneficiaries of racially conferred privilege have the right to establish norms for those who have historically been oppressed pursuant to those norms, and that race is not historically contingent. Although the substance of race definitions has changed, what persists is the expectation of white-controlled institutions in the continued right to determine meaning—the reified privilege of power—that reconstitutes the property interest in whiteness in contemporary form.

In undertaking any definition of race as group identity, there are implicit and explicit normative underpinnings that must be taken into account. The "riddle of identity" is not answered by a "search for essences" or essential discoverable truth, nor by a search for mere "descriptions and re-descriptions." Instead, when handling the complex issue of group identity, we should look to "purposes and effects, consequences and functions." The questions pertaining to definitions of race then are not principally biological or genetic, but social and political: what must be addressed is who is defining, how is the definition constructed, and why is the definition being propounded. Because definition is so often a central part of domination, critical thinking about these issues must precede and adjoin any definition. The law has not attended to these questions. Instead, identity of "the other" is still objectified, the complex, negotiated quality of identity is ignored, and the impact of inequitable power on identity is masked. These problems are illustrated in the land claim suit brought by the Mashpee, a Massachusetts Indian tribe.

In *Mashpee Tribe v. Town of Mashpee,* the Mashpee sued to recover land that several Indians had conveyed to non-Indians in violation of a statute that barred alienation of tribal land to non-Indians without the approval of the federal government. In order to recover possession of the land, the Mashpee were required to prove that they were a tribe at the time of the conveyance. Although the trial judge admitted to some preliminary confusion about the appropriate definition of "tribe," he ultimately accepted the standard articulated in prior case law that defined tribe as "a body of Indians of the same or similar race, united in a community under one leadership or government, and inhabiting a particular though sometimes ill-defined territory." The Mashpee were held not to be a tribe at the time the suit was filed, so that their claim to land rights based on group identity were rejected.

The Mashpee's experience was filtered, sifted, and ultimately rendered incoherent through this externally constituted definition of tribe that incorporated outside criteria regarding race, leadership, territory, and community. The fact that the Mashpee had intermingled with Europeans, runaway slaves, and other Indian tribes signified to the jury and to the court that they had lost their tribal identity.

But for the Mashpee, blood was not the measure of identity: their identity as a group was manifested for centuries by their continued relationship to the land of the Mashpee; their consciousness and embrace of difference, even when it was against their interest; and, their awareness and preservation of cultural traditions. Nevertheless, under the court's standard, the tribe was "incapable of *legal* self-definition." Fundamentally, then, the external imposition of definition maintained the social equilibrium that was severely challenged by the Mashpee land claims.

The Mashpee case presents new variations on old themes of race and property. Previous reified definitions of race compelled abandonment of racial identity in exchange for economic and social privilege. Under the operative racial hierarchy, passing is the ultimate assimilationist move— the submergence of a subordinate cultural identity in favor of dominant identity, assumed to achieve better societal fit within prevailing norms. The modern definition of "tribe" achieved similar results by misinterpreting the Mashpee's adaptation to be assimilation. The Mashpee absorbed and managed, rather than rejected and suppressed, outsiders; yet the court erased their identity, assuming that, by virtue of intermingling with other races, the Mashpee's identity as a people had been subsumed. The Mashpee were not "passing," but were legally determined to have "passed"—no longer to have distinct identity. This erasure was predicated on the assumption that what is done from necessity under conditions of established hierarchies of domination and subordination is a voluntary surrender for gain.

Beyond the immediate outcome of the case lies the deeper problem posed by the hierarchy of the rules themselves and the continued retention by white-controlled institutions of exclusive control over definitions as they pertain to the identity and history of dominated peoples. Although the law will always represent the exercise of state power in enforcing its choices, the violence done to the Mashpee and other oppressed groups results from the law's refusal to acknowledge the negotiated quality of identity. Whiteness as property assumes the form of the exclusive right to determine rules; it asserts that, against a framework of racial dominance and unequal power, fairness can result from a property rule, or indeed any other rule, that imposes an entirely externally constituted definition of group identity. Reality belies this presumption. In *Plessy,* the Court affirmed the right of the state to define who was white, obliterating aspects of social acceptance and self-identification as sources of validation and identity. The Mashpee were similarly divested of their identity through the state's exclusive retention of control over meaning in ways that reinforced group oppression. When group identity is a predicate for exclusion or disadvantage, the law has acknowledged it; when it is a predicate for resistance or a claim of right to be free from subordination, the law determines it to be illusory. This determinist approach to group identity reproduces racial subordination and reaffirms whiteness as property.

C. *Subjugation Through Affirmative Action Doctrine*

The assumption that whiteness is a property interest entitled to protection is an idea born of systematic white supremacy and nurtured over the years, not only by the law of slavery and "Jim Crow," but also by the more recent decisions and rationales of the Supreme Court concerning affirmative action. In examining both the nature of the affirmative action debate and the legal analysis applied in three Supreme Court cases involving affirmative action—*Regents of University of California v. Bakke, City of Richmond v. J. A. Croson Co.,* and *Wygant v. Jackson Board of Education,* it is evident that the protection of the property interest in whiteness still lies at the core of judicial and popular reasoning.

* * *

VI.   CONCLUSION

Whiteness as property has carried and produced a heavy legacy. It is a ghost that has haunted the political and legal domains in which claims for justice have been inadequately addressed for far too long. Only rarely declaring its presence, it has warped efforts to remediate racial exploitation. It has blinded society to the systems of domination that work against so many by retaining an unvarying focus on vestiges of systemic racialized privilege that subordinates those perceived as a particularized few—the "others." It has thwarted not only conceptions of racial justice but also conceptions of property that embrace more equitable possibilities. In protecting the property interest in whiteness, property is assumed to be no more than the right to prohibit infringement on settled expectations, ignoring countervailing equitable claims that are predicated on a right to inclusion. It is long past time to put the property interest in whiteness to rest. Affirmative action can assist in that task. Affirmative action, if properly conceived and implemented, is not only consistent with norms of equality, but is essential to shedding the legacy of oppression.

NOTES AND QUESTIONS

1.   **Identity, economics, and multiculturalism.** If, as this article seems to imply, non-market-oriented identities will invariably arise in response to economic discrimination, does that mean that economic developments that tend to reduce the incidence of such non-market identities are desirable as a means of reducing discrimination? Would the aggressively paternalistic practices that led to the partial assimilation of the Mashpee tribe discussed on pages 266–267 be viewed as desirable practices because they reduce the incidence of the "Red" identity? What about even more intrusive measures such as taking children away from "Red" parents so that they can be raised in a "Green" environment?

2.   **Akerlof, Kranton and McAdams.** The identity payoff model presented in this paper, and the group-status production model presented by McAdams, *infra* at 315, both attempt to explain the persistence of economic inequality when classical economic theory states that the free market should eliminate discrimination. However, while the goals of the two papers might be similar, their approaches are quite different. First, McAdams' approach is group based; all individuals are looked upon as basically the same, with differences created by quasi-market forces. By contrast, the model presented by Akerlof and Kranton focuses on individuals and assumes that, even in the absence of markets, some individuals would have a predisposition to be "Red" while others would be "Green." Additionally, McAdams sees discrimination as the result of self-interested behavior on

the part of the majority, while Akerlof and Kranton see identity differentiation as arising partially as a survival strategy by the minority. Given these differences between the two explanations for discrimination, is there any way that the Akerlof–Kranton and McAdams positions can be reconciled?

3.   Different identities or different settings? Are the "Red" and "Green" cultures of the Akerlof-Kranton model necessarily representative of different identities, or could they be thought of more accurately as different manifestations of the same identity when faced with different circumstances? When Malcolm X began hustling, his mentor gave him the following advice: "[g]et here early ... everything in place ... you never need to waste motion." ALEX HALEY & MALCOLM X, THE AUTOBIOGRAPHY OF MALCOLM X 46 (1965). When Malcolm X became a more successful drug dealer he demonstrated considerable capitalist acumen. He reinvested his profits into his business, developed rational strategies for dealing with law enforcement and entered new markets when government regulation became too tight. *Id.* at 99–102. Given the effort and business skills required to succeed as a hustler, as well as Malcolm X's success when he was able to find non-criminal employment with the Nation of Islam, does it seem more likely that Malcolm's "Red" identity was different from a mainstream "Green" identity, or that it was simply a "Green" identity expressing itself in "Red" surroundings?

4.   Definition of tribe. This case was presented as a contest between history and anthropology, with history winning in the end. However, aren't broad historical and anthropological definitions of the word tribe ultimately beside the point? Shouldn't the definition of tribe be that used by the drafters of the Non-Intercourse Act?

5.   Performative identity. The Indians of Mashpee lost their case because they didn't behave in a way that comported with the jury's view of how an Indian tribe should act, thus their performative identity was not that of a tribe. Isn't this a rather odd way to structure a lawsuit? Modern anti-discrimination laws generally take the opposite approach: the more a minority has assimilated into mainstream culture, the greater chance that minority has of winning an anti-discrimination claim. Devon W. Carbado & Mitu Gulati, *The Law and Economics of Critical Race Theory: Crossroads, Directions, and a New Critical Race Theory*, 112 YALE L.J. 1757, 1822 (2003) (book review). Why is it that in this case, assimilation was (from the standpoint of the outcome of the suit) a bad thing? Does a legal regime which encourages rejection of mainstream culture provide perverse incentives from an anti-discrimination viewpoint?

6.   The point of all this. How did the disposition of this case effect the "tribe?" According to the plaintiffs, the tribe was based on culture, shared traditions, kinship, and other intangible bonds. Would those bonds have been strengthened if the "tribe" had won its suit? Would they have been diluted by the effects of a large settlement? Since the "tribe" was not simply an amalgam of individuals, could it possibly have been aided in any way by a positive verdict? Is it more likely that the "tribe" would have been destroyed by the ascendancy of Tribal Council, Inc., which was organized specifically to provide a structure for interaction with the non-tribal world? Would victory for the corporation have helped the "tribe" of Mashpee?

7. Taint of whiteness. According to Professor Harris, "[a]t the individual level, recognizing oneself as 'white' necessarily assumes premises based on white supremacy ... privileging 'white' as unadulterated, exclusive, and rare." *Supra* p. 300. Is it constructive to tar all people who recognize themselves as white with the implication of white supremacy? It would seem likely that recognition of the social power of whiteness is necessary in order to try to eliminate discrimination against blacks. How, under Professor Harris' conception of whiteness as property, is it possible for a white person to work against racism, when by acknowledging the social privileges accorded to whiteness, white people assume the premises of white supremacy?

8. Neutrality of affirmative action. Professor Harris asserts that, "[b]ecause affirmative action can only be implemented through conscious intervention and requires constant monitoring and reevaluation, it does not function behind a mask of neutrality in the realm beyond scrutiny." Of course, chattel slavery was also implemented through conscious intervention and required constant monitoring and reevaluation (not to mention terroristic violence). The same is true of Jim Crow segregation. Does this mean that segregation and slavery did not function to distort white expectations because they did not "function behind a mask of neutrality?" Further, how could any meaningful affirmative action program not change black expectations? Will expectations not change if affirmative action is effective and reliable? Is Professor Harris arguing that blacks can never be beneficiaries of racism in the future because they have been its victims in the past?

9. Additional reading. For a non-technical perspective on economics and identity, see Gerald D. Jaynes, *Identity and Economic Performance*, 568 ANNALS AM. ACAD. POL. & SOC. SCI. 128 (2000). For an interesting description of an interaction between cultures, see *Ann Southerland, Complexities of U.S. Law and Gypsy Identity*, 45 AM. J. COMP. L. 393 (1997). For additional information on anthropological issues in the courts, see generally Larry Cata Backer, *Chroniclers in the Field of Cultural Production: Courts, Law and the Interpretive Process*, 20 B.C. THIRD WORLD L.J. 291 (2000); Glen Stohr, Comment, *The Repercussions of Orality in Federal Indian Law*, 31 ARIZ. ST. L.J. 679 (1999). For additional information on Indian tribes in the courts, see generally Jennifer L. Tomsen, Note, *"Traditional" Resource Uses and Activities: Articulating Values and Examining Conflicts in Alaska*, 19 ALASKA L. REV. 167 (2002); Neu Jessup Newton, *Sovereignty and the Native American Nation: Memory and Misrepresentation: Representing Crazy Horse*, 27 CONN. L. REV. 1003 (1995). For additional information on the Mashpee case, see Gerald Torres & Kathryn Milun, *Frontier of Legal Thought III: Translating Yonnondio by Precedent and Evidence: The Mashpee Indian Case*, 1990 DUKE L.J. 625 (1990). For an approach to white privilege outside of the property framework, see Sylvia A. Law, *White*

Privilege and Affirmative Action, 32 AKRON L. REV. 603 (1999). For an article that, notwithstanding Harris, espouses the idea of Blackness as property, see Jim Chen, *Affirmative Action: Diversity of Opinions: Embryonic Thoughts on Racial Identity as New Property*, 68 U. COLO. L. REV. 1123 (1997). For a Marxist approach to identity as property, see e. christi cunningham, *Identity Markets*, 45 HOW. L.J. 491 (2002). For an analysis of whiteness as property explored through a fictionalized dialogue with a space alien, see Derrick Bell, *Xerces and the Affirmative Action Mystique*, 57 GEO. WASH. L. REV. 1595 (1989).

B. RACIAL DISCRIMINATION: TWO COMPETING THEORIES AND EMPIRICAL EVIDENCE OF DISPARATE RACIAL IMPACT

A major dispute between scholars who are interested in the problem of persistent racial discrimination is whether the market can be expected to provide a self-correction for racial discrimination that locks members of racial minorities out of participation in basic transactions and therefore wealth accumulation. We return to economics Nobel laureate, Gary Becker for his economic model which treats racial discrimination like any other private preference that can be expressed as a "taste" with monetary value in the marketplace. Legal scholar Richard McAdams draws on sociological theories of group status production to offer an alternative view of the mechanisms fueling persistent racial discrimination. Legal scholar and economist Ian Ayres enters this debate with a powerful new tool: empirical studies of actual marketplace racial dynamics in important transactions.

1. A RATIONAL CHOICE THEORY OF RACIAL DISCRIMINATION IN THE MARKETPLACE

The Forces Determining Discrimination in the Market Place

THE ECONOMICS OF DISCRIMINATION 13–18 (2d ed. 1971).

GARY BECKER

In the socio-psychological literature on this subject one individual is said to discriminate against (or in favor of) another if his behavior toward the latter is not motivated by an "objective" consideration of fact. It is difficult to use this definition in distinguishing a violation of objective facts from an expression of tastes or values. For example, discrimination and prejudice are not usually said to occur when someone prefers looking at a glamorous Hollywood actress rather than at some other woman; yet they are said to occur when he prefers living next to whites rather than Negroes. At best calling just one of these actions "discrimination" requires making subtle and rather secondary distinctions. Fortunately, it is not necessary to get involved in these more philosophical issues. It is possible to give an unambiguous definition of discrimination in the market place and yet get at the essence of what is usually called discrimination.

1. THE ANALYTICAL FRAMEWORK

Money, commonly used as a measuring rod, will also serve as a measure of discrimination. If an individual has a "taste for discrimination," he must act *as if* he were willing to pay something either directly or in the form of a reduced income, to be associated with some persons instead of others. When actual discrimination occurs, he must, in fact, either pay or forfeit income for this privilege. This simple way of looking at the matter gets at the essence of prejudice and discrimination.

Social scientists tend to organize their discussion of discrimination in the market place according to their disciplines. To the sociologist, different levels of discrimination against a particular group are associated with different levels of social and physical "distance" from that group or with different levels of socioeconomic status; the psychologist classifies individuals by their personality types, believing that this is the most useful organizational principle. The breakdown used here is most familiar to the economist and differs from both of these: all persons who contribute to production in the same way, e.g., by the rent of capital or the sale of labor services, are put into one group, with each group forming a separate "factor of production." The breakdown by economic productivity turns out to be a particularly fruitful one, since it emphasizes phenomena that have long been neglected in literature on discrimination.

By using the concept of a *discrimination coefficient* (this will be abbreviated to "DC"), it is possible to give a definition of a "taste for discrimination" that is parallel for different factors of production, employers, and consumers. The *money* costs of a transaction do not always completely measure *net* costs, and a DC acts as a bridge between money and net costs. Suppose an *employer* were faced with the money wage rate π of a particular factor; he is assumed to act as $\pi(1 + d_i)$ were the net wage rate, with di as his DC against this factor. An *employee*, offered the money wage rate π_i for working with this factor, acts as if $\pi(1-d_j)$ were the *net* wage rate, with dj as his DC against this factor. A *consumer*, faced with a unit money of p for the commodity "produced" by this factor, acts as if the net price were $p(1 + d_k)$ with dk as his DC against this factor. In all three instances a DC gives the percentage by which either money costs or money returns are changed in going from money to net magnitudes: the employer uses it to estimate his net wage costs, the employee his net wage rate, and the consumer the net price of a commodity.

A DC represents a non-pecuniary element in certain kinds of transactions, and it is positive or negative, depending upon whether the non-pecuniary element is considered "good" or "bad." Discrimination is commonly associated with *dis*utility caused by contact with some individuals and this interpretation is followed here. Since this implies that d_i, d_j, and d_k are all greater than zero, to the employer this coefficient represents a non-monetary cost of production, to the employer a non-monetary cost of employment, and to the consumer a non-monetary cost of consumption. "Nepotism" rather than "discrimination" would occur if they were less than zero, and they would then represent non-monetary returns of production, employment, and consumption to the employer, employee, and consumer, respectively.

The quantities πd_i, $\pi j d_j$, and $p d_k$ are the exact money equivalents of these non-monetary costs; for given wage rates and prices, these money equivalents are larger, the larger di, dj, and dk are. Since a DC can take on any value between zero and plus infinity, tastes for discrimination can also vary continuously within this range. This quantitative representation of a taste for discrimination provides the means for empirically estimating the quantitative importance of discrimination.

2.   TASTES FOR DISCRIMINATION

The magnitude of a taste for discrimination differs from person to person, and many investigators have directed their energies toward discovering the variables that are most responsible for these differences. I also attempt to isolate and estimate the quantitative importance of some of these variables; the following discussion briefly describes several variables that receive attention in subsequent chapters.

The discrimination by an individual against a particular group (to be called N) depends on the social and physical distance between them and on their relative socioeconomic status. If he works with N in production, it may also depend on their substitutability in production. The relative number of N in the society at large also may be very important: it has been argued that an increase in the numerical importance of a minority group increases the prejudice against them, since the majority begins to fear their growing power; on the other hand, some argue that greater numbers bring greater knowledge and that leads to a decline in prejudice. Closely related to this variable are the frequency and regularity of "contact" with N in different establishments and firms.

According to our earlier definition, if someone has a "taste for discrimination," he must act *as if* he were willing to forfeit income in order to avoid certain transactions; it is necessary to be aware of the emphasis on the words "as if." An employer may refuse to hire Negroes solely because he erroneously underestimates their economic efficiency. His behavior is discriminatory not because he is prejudiced against them but because his is ignorant of their true efficiency. Ignorance may be quickly eliminated by the spread of knowledge, while a prejudice (i.e. preference) is relatively independent of knowledge. This distinction is essential for understanding the motivation of many organizations, since they either explicitly or implicitly assume that discrimination can be eliminated by a wholesale spread of knowledge.

Since a taste for discrimination incorporates both prejudice and ignorance, the amount of knowledge available must be included as a determinant of tastes. Another proximate determinant is geographical and chronological location: discrimination may vary from country to country, from region to region within a country, from rural to urban areas within a region, and from one time period to another. Finally, tastes may differ simply because of differences in personality.

3.   MARKET DISCRIMINATION

Suppose there are two groups, designated by W and N, with members of W being perfect substitutes in production for members of N. In the absence of discrimination and nepotism and if the labor market were perfectly competitive, the equilibrium wage rate of W would equal that of N. Discrimination could cause these wage rates to differ; the market discrimination coefficient between W and N (this will be abbreviated "MDC") is defined as the proportional difference between these wage rates. If π_w and π_n represent the equilibrium wage rates of W and N, respectively, then

$$\text{MDC} = \pi_w - \pi_n \ \pi_w -$$

If W and N are imperfect substitutes, they may receive different wage rates even in the absence of discrimination. A more general definition of the MDC sets it equal to the difference between the ratio of W's and N's wage rate with and without discrimination. In the special case of perfect substitutes, this reduces to the simpler definition given previously, because

$$\pi_{\overset{*}{w}} \text{ would equal } \pi_{\overset{*}{n}}$$

It should be obvious that the magnitude of the MDC depends on the magnitude of individual DC's. Unfortunately, it is often implicitly assumed that it depends only on them; the arguments proceed as if a knowledge of the determinants of tastes was sufficient for a complete understanding of market discrimination. This procedure is erroneous; many variables in addition to tastes take prominent roles in determining market discrimination, and, indeed, tastes sometimes play a minor part. The abundant light thrown on the other variables by the tools of economic analysis has probably been the major insight gained from using them.

The MDC does depend in an important way on each individual's DC; however, merely to use some measure of the average DC does not suffice. The complete distribution of DC's among individuals must be made explicit because the size of the MDC is partly related to individual *differences* in tastes. It also depends on the relative importance of competition and monopoly in the labor and product markets, since this partly determines the weight assigned by the market to different DC's. The economic and quantitative importance of N was mentioned as one determinant of tastes for discrimination; this variable is also an independent determinant of market discrimination. This independent effect operates through the number of N relative to W and the cost of N per unit of output relative to the total cost per unit of output. Both may be important, although for somewhat different reasons, in determining the weight assigned by the market to different DC's. Reorganizing production through the substitution of one factor for another is a means of avoiding discrimination; the amount of substitution available is determined by the production function.

The MDC is a direct function of these variables and an indirect function of other variables through their effect on tastes. Our knowledge of the economic aspects of discrimination will be considered satisfactory only when these relationships are known exactly. In subsequent chapters I present the results of my own attempts to close some gaps in this knowledge.

* * *

2.   A SOCIOLOGICAL THEORY OF RACIAL DISCRIMINATION IN THE MARKETPLACE

Cooperation and Conflict: The Economics of Group Status Production and Race Discrimination

108 HARV. L. REV. 1003 (1995).

RICHARD H. MCADAMS

In Shakespeare's history of King Henry V, when the time comes for the young King to ready his troops to battle a much larger French force at Agincourt, he delivers a stirring speech that many regard as a masterpiece of inspirational rhetoric. Rejecting his advisor's lament for more men, he responds: "No, my fair cousin:/ If we are marked to die, we are enow/ To do our country loss: and if to live,/ The fewer men, the greater share of honour." The King proclaims his personal desire for honor, offers safe passage back to England for those who do not wish to fight, and then describes how those who stay will be celebrated on future anniversaries of this day of battle, known as the Feast of St. Crispian:

> And Crispin Crispian shall ne'er go by,
>
> From this day to the ending of the world,
>
> But we in it shall be remembered;
>
> We few, we happy few, we band of brothers:
>
> For he to-day that sheds his blood with me
>
> Shall be my brother. . . .
>
> And gentlemen in England, now a-bed,
>
> Shall think themselves accursed they were not here;
>
> And hold their manhoods cheap, whiles any speaks
>
> That fought with us upon Saint Crispin's day.

For those of us who strive to be hard-headed theorists of human behavior, and who use economics and game theory to reveal the consequences of legal rules, our initial response to this speech is likely to be: "What a disaster." The King and his soldiers are about to risk their lives.

Yet he denies wanting more men though additional troops would obviously better their odds of surviving and winning. Such a non sequitur can only raise doubts about the clarity of Henry's thinking, which in turn can only increase the chances that his officers will question his commands. And, one might ask, what are the meaning and value of "honor" and "brotherhood"? If Henry wishes to motivate his men, a better strategy would be to spell out the potential material benefits (perhaps promising them more pay) or to remind them of the serious penalties for breaking their promise to fight. Offering to pay their way home, after the enhanced risk of loss has caused Henry's troops to regret their decision to join him in France, is sheer insanity. Finally, those "gentlemen in England now a-bed" will likely count themselves lucky for the opportunity to free-ride on a victory. After all, most of the benefits of victory—the general peace and prosperity of England—cannot be withheld from those who do not fight.

Economics, especially "law and economics," prides itself on the universal application of its method. Yet a theory of human motivation that did not grasp the meaning and power of this speech would be seriously flawed. Military leaders are among the more pragmatic and hard-headed people around and would likely scoff at this economic analysis of Henry's speech. Military rhetoric frequently appeals to honor and brotherhood. If such words prod men and women to risk their lives, one can only imagine how much greater is the power of such words relative to smaller material sacrifices. Consider, for example, the possible economic consequences of the following words:

> Standing in the presence of this multitude, sobered with the responsibility of the message I deliver to the young men of the South, I declare that the truth above all others to be worn unsullied and sacred in your hearts, to be surrendered to no force, sold for no price, compromised in no necessity, but cherished and defended as the covenant of your prosperity, and the pledge of peace to your children, is that the white race must dominate forever in the South, because it is the white race, and superior to that race by which its supremacy is threatened.

A principal purpose of this Article is to illuminate the economic power of this white supremacist oration by Henry Grady and of Henry V's justly celebrated speech, as well as to examine the precise parallel between the two.

Each speech appeals to *group* interests, *group* loyalty, and *group* identity. The ubiquity of social groups says something of their importance: groups include not just firms, trade associations, and families, but groups based on demographic traits such as race, gender, or age, and those based on membership, such as fraternities or sororities, amateur sports teams, gangs, the Rotary or Elks Clubs, or private lunch clubs. Undoubtedly, some or all of these groups, like the firm, serve the individual's interest by minimizing the transaction costs she incurs while acting to satisfy her preference for whatever interest or function the group facilitates. But that explanation offers no insight into the meaning or power of the speeches of Henry V and Henry Grady.

This Article offers an economic theory to explain why individuals make material sacrifices for group welfare. My thesis is that a material view of human motivation underestimates both the level of cooperation that groups elicit from their members and the level of conflict that groups elicit from each other. A single group dynamic connects these added increments of cooperation and conflict: groups achieve solidarity and elicit loyalty beyond what economic analysis conventionally predicts, but solidarity and loyalty within groups lead predictably, if not inevitably, to competition and conflict between groups. The connection is the desire for esteem or status. Groups use intra-group status rewards as a non-material means of gaining material sacrifice from members, but the attendant desire for inter-group status causes inter-group conflict. This theory explains the power of King Henry's speech, which appeals to the individual's identification with the group ("we band of brothers") and effectively describes the status reward by contrasting other members of the group (those gentlemen left in England) who will not share in it. At the same time, the war itself was the product of England's desire for esteem and status—more specifically, Henry's desire for honor—which can only be achieved by conquering France.

This two-fold importance of status is essential to a genuine understanding of race discrimination, which has eluded economics. Discrimination is a means by which social groups produce status for their members, but pivotal to understanding this form of inter-group *conflict* is the role that status plays in generating the intra-group *cooperation* necessary to make discrimination effective. Absent the desire for intra-group status, selfish individuals would not make the material sacrifices that discrimination requires. In this context, Henry Grady's racist speech is an economically explicable (if unusually candid) means of enlisting white troops in the ongoing status warfare, urging them to "compromise[ ] in no [material] necessity" the process of discriminating against, and thereby subordinating, the blacks whose inferior position produces a status gain for whites. The rhetoric helps establish a norm of white behavior, the abrogation of which will lower the in-group status of non-conforming whites.

Race discrimination is the best and most important illustration of what I view as a more general phenomenon of intra-group cooperation and inter-group conflict. Before discussing race, however, I must articulate the general theory—to establish empirically that, because of concern for status, cooperation arises within groups and conflict occurs between groups. Part I sets forth puzzling instances of intra-group cooperation in experimental "dilemma" situations and elsewhere, which are not explained by existing economic theory but are well explained by concern for the esteem of other group members. Part I then proposes a model that describes how "esteem payments" afford groups a novel means of solving their collective action problems and, finally, how this same mechanism leads inevitably to inter-group status conflict. Part II considers the particular problem of race discrimination—the deficiencies in existing economic theory, the superior ability of a status-production model to explain many race-related phenomena, and the implications of such a model. In particular, if race discrimination is a means of producing group status—if groups are engaged in a form of status "warfare"—then discrimination presents the same case for government prohibition that exists for more traditional government restraints on force and fraud.

I.   EXPLAINING "EXCESS" COOPERATION AND CONFLICT:
AN ECONOMIC THEORY OF SOCIAL GROUPS

Current economic theory fails to predict the prevalence of cooperation and conflict in human affairs. Considerable evidence supports David Hume's observation that "[w]hen men are once inlisted on opposite sides, they contract an affection to the persons with whom they are united, and an animosity against their antagonists: And these passions they often transmit to their posterity." Economics has been slow to address the function of social groups and the means by which they engender levels of loyalty and hostility in apparent defiance of conventional notions of material selfishness. But the psychic motivations that explain these "passions"— and the resulting intra-group cooperation and inter-group conflict—are reconcilable with rational self-interest.

This Part presents the modern evidence that supports Hume's claim. Initially, section A examines the empirical evidence that people cooperate beyond conventionally predicted levels. This "excess" cooperation is explained neither by sophisticated rational choice mechanisms such as reciprocity, nor by unselfish motives such as altruism. Instead, the experimental data indicate that cooperation is related to group membership. Section B advances a theory to account for this data: individuals who seek to maximize the esteem they receive from others have selfish reasons to contribute to group status. Two concepts of "group" are advanced: one defined externally by common characteristics observable by third-parties, and one defined internally by relationships among the members. In each case, there are selfish but non-pecuniary reasons for cooperating with one's group members. Finally, section C suggests reasons that the very mechanisms that increase cooperation within groups also increase conflict between groups, and considers evidence that such status-based "excess" conflict exists.

A.   The Empirical Evidence of "Excess" Cooperation

To understand conflict among social groups, we must first understand how groups elicit cooperation from their members. Game theorists study the strategic interactions of individuals, and their most compelling contribution is their description of the difficulties groups face in procuring the cooperation of members. In contrast to Adam Smith's "invisible hand," which guides society to desirable outcomes though individuals are selfishly motivated, game theory describes "collective action problems"—situations in which individually rational decisions lead to sub-optimal collective outcomes. The classic example is the prisoner's dilemma, but the basic problem exists in more complex situations with more than two parties: each individual faces a choice essentially between cooperation and defection, where the dominant strategy for each individual is defection, but where mutual defection is worse for everyone than mutual cooperation. The interest in studying such "games" is generated by the belief that they represent a fundamental feature of social life. Whether it is the undersupply of "public goods," the overconsumption of common resources, or related difficulties, the problem of collective action is commonly offered as a rationale for government regulation. Conversely, many private economic practices can best be understood as mechanisms for solving collective action problems.

The focus of this section and the next is a particular mechanism for solving collective action problems commonly ignored by legal economists: groups achieve cooperation by allocating intra-group status. To persuade the skeptical that the desire for esteem exists and is necessary to explain important examples of cooperation, I could begin with a number of real-world examples of group cooperation. It is difficult, however, to distinguish subtle motivations in complex, uncontrolled events. Some might plausibly assert that, for any number of reasons, the individual's pecuniary self-interest in such examples happens to conform to the group interest. Others, including some critics of economic analysis, would argue that cooperation indicates the existence, not of a selfish interest in status, but of genuine altruism. Given these difficulties, I turn first to laboratory experiments, which can control for alternative motivations for cooperation.

1.   Dilemma Experiments: Evidence of Non–Material Motivations for Cooperation.—Since the 1950s, social scientists have conducted experiments with the prisoner's dilemma game, its multi-party variants, public goods problems, and common resource problems. In each test, experimenters structure monetary payoffs to make defection or free-riding the dominant strategy. Despite the logical force of the monetarily dominant strategy, researchers have not found uniform defection. Many individuals defect, but a significant proportion—one-quarter to two-thirds—chooses to cooperate. After more than two thousand social dilemma experiments, one of the "generally accepted" conclusions is that, when pecuniary incentives appear to compel defection, "many subjects do *not* defect." For those who employ game theory to predict the consequences of legal rules, this residuum of cooperation demands explanation.

One immediate and material explanation is *reciprocity*. When future interactions are likely, reciprocity is possible, and defection may no longer be the dominant strategy. One reciprocal strategy is "tit-for-tat," in which one begins by cooperating and then responds in future rounds by doing whatever the other player did in the previous round. Considerable evidence demonstrates the success of tit-for-tat in preventing mutual defection in iterated prisoner's dilemmas.

Reciprocity does not, however, explain the cooperation observed in the dilemma experiments discussed above. Reciprocity requires future interaction in which players can reciprocate past decisions. Theorists still predict mutual defection for "one-shot" prisoner's dilemmas. Yet a large number of the empirical tests of collective action problems were intentionally designed as "one-shot" games to exclude the opportunity for reciprocity, and these tests have repeatedly found significant amounts of cooperation. In the very circumstance in which there is no material reason to cooperate, there is the undeniable fact of cooperation. Thus, however powerful reciprocity may be in some contexts, a significant residual level of cooperation remains unexplained.

One might note, finally, that the material stakes in these experiments typically involve only a few dollars or less. Though higher stakes might cause people to free-ride, the question is what explains subjects' consistent failure to free-ride when low material stakes suggest they should. After all, entire industries arise to capture stakes of a similar size; what seems low in isolation is vast when aggregated over a large population. Whether we can say the same of the motivations causing this residual cooperation requires us first to discover what those motivations are.

2. Dilemma Experiments: Evidence of Non–Altruistic Motivations for Cooperation.—Critics and reformers of economic modeling have pointed to the dilemma experiments described above as proof of altruism or a commitment to principles of fairness. Yet a full review of the psychological research on collective dilemmas refutes this thesis. Some sense of "group identity," rather than altruism or fairness, explains the variations in cooperation researchers have observed. Of particular note are studies revealing that individuals cooperate more frequently in dilemma games than do groups of individuals and studies revealing that discussion increases the level of cooperation in dilemma games.

First, many prisoner's dilemma studies have contrasted games between individual subjects with games between groups of subjects. Holding the payoffs constant, these studies consistently find significantly more cooperation when individuals play individuals than when teams play teams. One study, for example, found that three-person groups defected an average of 8.73 times in twenty rounds, compared to an average of 1.8 defections out of twenty when individuals played each other. This individual-group "discontinuity" is consistent with research finding that the formation of a purely experimental "group" can elicit a bias in favor of in-group members, against out-group members, or both. Psychologists discovered this when they set out to create a base line in which individuals would have no reason to favor their own group. To their surprise, whenever subjects were divided into groups, people consistently evaluated members of their own group more favorably than members of other groups. Summarizing this effect, one pair of researchers stated that "mere awareness of the presence of an out-group is sufficient to provoke intergroup competitive or discriminatory responses on the part of the in-group."

Additional confirmation of the importance of groups is provided by dilemma experiments in which researchers elicited differences in cooperation by symbolically invoking "real-world" group memberships. In one study, psychologists observed significantly more cooperation from subjects sharing a common resource when they told the subjects that they were being evaluated as a single group against groups not then a part of the experiment (for example, college students versus non-students) than when they told the subjects that they were being evaluated as members of one of two subgroups in the experiment (for example, psychology majors versus economics majors).

These studies appear to confirm David Hume's insight that individuals "have such a propensity to divide into personal factions, that the smallest appearance of real difference will produce them." The experimenter's arbitrary division of subjects into groups is sufficient to "factionalize" them, causing more competitive behavior between groups than between individuals and favoritism for members of one's own "group." Neither a general concern for the welfare of others nor a concern for fairness explains why subjects were so much less cooperative with other subjects whom the experimenter placed in a different group.

The second body of studies that challenge the altruism-fairness explanation are those involving discussion. Repeated study shows that permitting communication between the subjects in a prisoner's dilemma situation dramatically increases the level of cooperation; indeed, discussion as much as doubles cooperation rates. Yet "in none of these experiments does group discussion change the fact of defection's dominance"; given the structure of the experiments, there is no reason for any threat or promise to be credible.

To explain this puzzle, researchers varied the conditions of discussion in multi-party prisoner's dilemmas. In one study, the experimenters randomly divided subjects into two groups and placed each group in a separate room. The experimenters permitted ten minutes of discussion in half the groups and no discussion in the others. In addition, half the groups were told that their decisions would affect the payoff for their own group, while the other half were told that their decisions would determine the payoff for the other group and, conversely, that the decisions of the other group would determine the payoff for their group. The results were striking. When subjects believed their decisions would affect the payoffs of members of their own group, discussion increased cooperation from thirty-four percent to sixty-nine percent. But when subjects believed that their decisions affected payoffs for the *other* group, discussion slightly reduced cooperation. The researchers concluded that "discussion does *not* enhance contribution when beneficiaries are strangers." Of course, *all* of these subjects were "strangers" to each other in the sense that they had never met before the experiment and were randomly assigned to the different groups. Yet with ten minutes of discussion about their upcoming decisions, they were, in an important economic sense, no longer strangers. Limited discussion was sufficient to dramatically increase cooperation if and only if the discussants were the beneficiaries of the cooperation.

These findings further demonstrate that altruism and fairness do not fully explain excess cooperation in the prisoner's dilemma. If discussion invoked a general concern for others or for fairness, it should not matter that the beneficiaries are arbitrarily placed in another room. Instead, discussion seems to permit formation of a group identity that creates a special reason for discussants to cooperate. In the transcripts of the subjects' pre-decision discussion, people frequently referred to what "we"—the members of the group—should do. Moreover, where one group knew that its decisions would affect only the other group, there were "frequent statements that the best results would occur if we all keep and they all give to us." The motive seems to fall far short of altruism or fairness. The kind of speech that so effectively increases cooperation tends to be an appeal not to principle, but to solidarity. Thus, successful inspirational rhetoric—like Henry Grady's racist speech—is often centered around repeated invocations of an "us against them" image.

3. *Cooperation Outside the Laboratory: Further Evidence That Groups Matter.*—Although laboratory experiments more easily control for alternative explanations, it is also appropriate to consider two real-world collective action problems: social protest and war. Although law and economics scholars have criticized Title VII, none has attempted to explain why individual blacks participated in the civil rights protests that led to its enactment. Social protests—such as marches, boycotts, and "sit-ins"—are costly to the individual. Although a group may benefit from collective protest, the gains will likely be enjoyed by all members of the group, regardless of whether they participated in the protest. Thus, social movements are rife with collective action problems, which usually prevents such movements from forming or succeeding. Posing this problem, Dennis Chong inquires how the civil rights movement of the 1950s and 1960s succeeded in mobilizing considerable collective action. Given the violence of white resisters, Chong rejects the possibility that material rewards explain the participation, recounting instead the importance of social incentives within small, pre-existing groups such as black churches.

Consider also the high-stakes collective action problems in war. If all soldiers attempt to free-ride on the combat efforts of others, the result is a rout. S.L.A. Marshall argues forcefully that, for the bulk of soldiers, the only thing that stops them from fleeing in the face of fire is the *opinion* of those with whom the soldiers have formed social ties. Marshall's evaluation is based on the fighting effectiveness of "battle stragglers," soldiers separated from their fighting unit who temporarily join an unfamiliar company. He found that individual stragglers had almost no "combat value" in a new unit, while small squads of stragglers "tended to fight as vigorously as any element:"

> Within the group increments the men were still fighting alongside old friends, and though they were now joined to a new parent body, they were under the same compulsion to keep face and share in the common defense. The individual stragglers were simply responding to the first law of nature which began to apply irresistibly the moment they were separated from the company of men whom they knew and who knew them.

Even in the face of death—high stakes indeed—individuals cooperate not merely to secure material rewards, but also to preserve the opinion that group members hold of them. This, of course, is the very dynamic King Henry manipulates in his St. Crispian speech.

B. *Economic Explanations of "Excess" Cooperation: The Production of Inter-Group and Intra-Group Status*

If neither material self-interest nor altruism explains the residuum of cooperation, what can? And why does the level of cooperation vary so significantly with the manner in which individuals are categorized by group? This section proposes an answer: group-based status production. In the experiments discussed above, individuals behave selfishly, not altruistically, but their selfish end is the production of the non-material good of esteem. If individuals seek such non-material ends, members of social groups have another means of solving collective action problems—by allocating esteem to induce members to make contributions to group welfare. Once we add esteem consequences to the material payoffs of individual decisions in such settings, we can explain both the fact and the nature of residual cooperation.

This section argues that human beings seek esteem from others; in aggregate terms, they seek social status. Individuals derive status from groups in two ways: first, individuals gain esteem from strangers based on visible group memberships; and second, within a socially connected group, individuals are especially concerned with the esteem of fellow members. In each case, though for different reasons, status production creates a non-material incentive for group cooperation.

1. The Individual Preference for Esteem and Status.—If one assumes that individuals behave rationally, the only explanation for the subjects' behavior in the experiments discussed in Part I.A is that the subjects receive benefits from cooperation, or avoid costs from defection, that are not part of the formal, pecuniary payoff structure of the game. One simple way of explaining the cooperation is that the benefit they receive is the esteem of their fellow game-players.

In an earlier article, I described the pervasiveness and power of what I called "negative relative preferences—preferences for approaching or surpassing the consumption level of others." In particular, I offered evidence that people care greatly about achieving a relative social rank or social status. What one gains by attaining 'status,' however, is merely a state of mind—the opinion of others in society—that one is particularly worthy in some way. To understand "excess" cooperation, we should start with precisely this point: that one of the "basic pleasures" people seek in life is the esteem of others.

That people care what others think of them is a parsimonious explanation of many phenomena. The desire for esteem explains, for example, why people are obsessed with the impression their goods make on others. The desire for esteem also underlies the common emotion of embarrassment: individuals feel a momentary but acute pain from loss of esteem at having others observe their missteps or indiscretions. And this desire for esteem helps explain the well-established finding that individuals conform dramati-

cally in the face of a group judgment. Even when there is no material cost
to disagreement, individuals appear to fear that dissent will adversely affect
how others view them.

Given this behavior, it is not implausible to say that some individuals
would cooperate in what is nominally a prisoner's dilemma solely to
preserve the minimal esteem strangers (in that community) normally feel
for one another. Individuals add the "esteem rewards" and "esteem penalties" to the material payoffs and choose accordingly. Esteem concerns may
change the total payoffs enough to make cooperation rational.

2. *Members of "Shared-Trait" Groups Cooperate to Produce Inter-
Group Status.*—To explain the dilemma experiments adequately, an esteem
theory must also explain why the level of cooperation varies with "group
identity" measures. The concept of "shared-trait groups" explains the
existence and variation in the level of cooperation observed in the experiments. By "shared-trait" group, I mean a collection of individuals who have
in common some readily observable feature. In American society, people
can roughly agree on how to group individuals—for example, by age, by
language, or by physical characteristics we refer to as "race." In each case,
on the basis of casual observation, one can determine reasonably well
whether individuals fall within the category.

Observable traits are important because, when individuals encounter a
stranger, they have no other basis for making an esteem judgment. If
individuals feel particularly high or low esteem for others with the same
trait, they tend to extend that judgment to the stranger. I am not
describing irrational prejudice, but a simple application of the economics of
information. Given the scarcity of information, it is rational to use cheaper
information—proxies—to infer the existence of more expensive, individualized information. The economics literature describes the use of proxies for
making decisions of material consequence (such as employment), but proxies can also be used for the allocation of status. Shared-trait group
membership is a proxy people use for granting or withholding esteem to
individuals they do not know personally.

The use of observable traits as proxies gives individuals a reason to
care about the esteem-generating behavior of those with whom they share
an observable trait. If an individual shares a trait with others, she expects
strangers to extend her the esteem they have for the group that shares the
trait. If these third-party observers know only an individual's putative
group membership, the individual expects them to judge her entirely on the
basis of that membership. She therefore has a selfish concern that the
group be highly esteemed in comparison to other groups. Even though the
"members" of a group may not know or feel any affinity for each other,
third-party categorization gives these members a reason to care about the
group's status.

This proxy effect provides a parsimonious explanation of the variation
in cooperation observed in the experiments reviewed above: in the labora-
ry, the experimenter is the third party who categorizes individuals. Any set
of subjects the experimenter designates as constituting a group has a

"shared trait" for purposes of the experiment. The subjects know that the researcher is observing and evaluating them as members of the group she created. In collective action experiments, the only means of distinguishing successful from unsuccessful groups is the extent to which the group cooperates and achieves the best collective result. Subjects in such experiments may earn additional benefits for cooperating or face additional costs for defecting—thus, esteem consequences may make cooperation a rational strategy.

Further, in the prisoner's dilemma studies, individuals playing the game against individuals cooperated at higher levels than teams playing the same game against teams. With team-play, individuals expect that the esteem they receive depends on the success of the arbitrarily created groups to which they belong. The proxy effect works to raise the payoff of defecting when the other team cooperates (the one way of "beating" the other team) and to lower the payoff of cooperating when the other team defects (thereby "losing"). With individual play, however, either there is no cognizable "group," or the group contains both of the subjects in the game. Thus any proxy effect works toward cooperation. If subjects understand that the experimenter will have other pairs play the game, they may imagine themselves being evaluated as a pair against other pairs, which raises the payoff of mutual cooperation (the best "pair" outcome) and lowers the payoff of mutual defection (the worst "pair" outcome).

To the experiments previously reviewed, we may now add studies on relative deprivation as a cause of social protest. Relative deprivation refers to the fact that individuals react strongly to deprivation when others have what they lack. "Psychologists hypothesize that a central component of people's angry feelings over deprivation is a comparison between themselves and others who have the desired thing." Numerous studies have demonstrated the importance of comparison with others to feelings of relative deprivation and to behavior motivated by such feelings. Most important, many of these studies find that attitudes about inter-group comparisons predict participation in social protest, whereas attitudes about interpersonal comparisons do not. People are more likely to protest when they feel that the group to which they belong is relatively deprived than when they simply feel that they as individuals are relatively deprived.

In sum, laboratory experiments show that, even when the group is an entirely arbitrary construct, individuals seek to acquire esteem from "nongroup" members by raising the status of what, in the eyes of those nongroup members, is the individuals' group. Outside the laboratory, concern with how one's shared-trait group is regarded also motivates significant action.

3. Members of "Socially Connected" Groups Cooperate to Produce Intra–Group Status.—A second, more conventional understanding of the group posits that the members are, in some manner, socially connected. These socially connected groups are comprised of people who know each other, the paradigm cases being families, networks of friends, or social clubs. Such groups have two noteworthy features, each of which contributes to the group's ability to overcome collective action problems: individuals tend to care especially about the esteem of their fellow group members, and individuals tend to grant esteem to members who contribute to group welfare.

The first feature of socially connected groups is that individuals tend to value the esteem of fellow group members more than they value the esteem of non-members. If we care what others think of us, we care more intensely the more well-informed an opinion is; those with whom we have frequent interaction—group members—know us best. Moreover, the dilemma experiments in which the simple act of discussion generated greater cooperation among discussants indicate that even minimal social connection can significantly increase the concern for the esteem of another. In addition, the very reason many social groups exist is that the members share some skill, trait, or interest; members tend to value the esteem of in-group members more than outsiders because members share a sense of what skills or traits are worth possessing. Finally, there is a self-reinforcing aspect to the concern for intra-group status: we tend to value most the opinion of those we esteem highly, and we prefer to belong to social groups including such people.

Given the especially high concern for esteem from socially connected group members, we can better understand high-stakes cooperation in the collective action problems presented by social protest and war. Military and social protest groups elicit cooperation by rewarding members with esteem or prestige based on how much they contribute to the group's welfare. Yet even if people *seek* intra-group esteem, the question remains why individual group members *provide* intra-group esteem to those who contribute to group welfare. The second noteworthy feature of socially connected groups is that members readily provide esteem to those who benefit the group; even without a central authority, members tend not to free-ride completely on the "esteem payments" of other members.

People provide esteem to members who benefit the group because, up to a point, thinking well of others is not a cost. To the contrary, esteeming others is a valuable "consumption good." A person deprived of this good—who finds no one in the world worth esteeming—is far less happy than one who has located a small collection of worthy souls. Nor is an individual who esteems twenty others necessarily poorer than someone who esteems only ten others to the same degree. To the extent that esteem is not costly, there is no reason to free-ride by withholding esteem from others. Instead, group members tend to allocate esteem in a way that brings them some return by rewarding those who contribute materially to group welfare and, at a secondary level, by rewarding those who allocate esteem in a manner that benefits the group. Imagine, as an analogy, that people have a kind of currency that is useless except for making group members feel better. It would be irrational to keep the currency or to distribute it randomly; one might as well provide it as a reward for those who contribute to group welfare and withhold it to punish those who do not.

Departing briefly from an economic description of human behavior, I can state the point in more realistic psychological terms. "Thinking well of others" is often reflexive rather than deliberate. People who might free-ride on material payments tend not to free-ride on esteem "payments" because they reflexively admire and respect those who benefit the group. Imagine, for example, a chessmaster, a person who not only intensely studies the game, but also socializes predominantly with others who do the same. Taking egoism seriously means that this person will consider chess-playing ability to be an important measure by which others can be judged. Individuals elevate the importance of those traits or skills that they possess. This process helps the individual secure self-esteem. But a consequence of thinking that a particular trait is desirable is to esteem *others* who possess the trait and to esteem them in relation to how much of the trait they possess. It is neither plausible nor coherent for the chessmaster to withhold esteem from other people who excel in chess. Barring an overshadowing negative trait, an individual will more or less *automatically* esteem others who have the traits the individual most values in herself, or the traits the individual would most like to acquire for herself.

Frequently, people reflexively esteem traits or behaviors that increase the welfare of the group. A player's success at chess tournaments raises the prestige of the chess club to which she belongs and earns her esteem within the club. A soldier whose skill or effort saves the lives of his fellow squad members earns their esteem. Moreover, if one who is known to value a particular trait withholds esteem from those who possess it, she risks appearing envious and losing the esteem of others. Especially within a group of people who desire a particular trait, refusing to esteem the trait (or at least to appear to esteem it) calls into question the dissenter's commitment to or understanding of shared values. Of course, some members may nonetheless be envious and refuse to provide esteem. But since esteem is at least partially reflexive, there is less than complete free-riding in allocating esteem, and the group can achieve a significant level of coordination.

Sociological evidence supports the theory that socially connected groups allocate esteem to overcome collective action problems. Socially connected groups, as I have defined them, consist of relatively small numbers of people who know each other. Sociologists have long been interested in how, within larger groups in society, "norms" arise as an important decentralized mechanism of social control. Esteem allocation, it turns out, provides the necessary micro-level explanation for social norms; the functioning of social norms, in turn, demonstrates the full power of intra-group cooperation.

Although economically inclined theorists have mostly ignored norms, one important exception is Robert Ellickson. *In Order Without Law*, Ellickson summarizes and supplements the empirical literature on the success of norms in regulating individual behavior. Ellickson's empirical contribution is his study of norms that govern the resolution of various disputes over livestock between neighbors in Shasta County, California. Like other social norms that arise within "close-knit groups," the Shasta County norms are a means of enhancing group welfare. The norms are a non-legal means by which the group facilitates desirable collective action. To some degree, what Ellickson and others identify as efficient norms are enforced by reciprocity between neighbors who expect to interact indefinitely, and the norms are therefore explicable in material terms. But the unique contribution norms make to cooperation—the additional power of norms beyond reciprocity—is third-party enforcement. What Ellickson has in mind are sanctions administered not by the immediate "victim" of a norm violation, but by "friends, relatives, gossips, vigilantes, and other nonhierarchical third-party enforcers." Third parties sanction—by gossip, scorn, ostracism, or physical retaliation—those who violate the norms or informal rules of the group.

My point, however, is that this informal third-party enforcement cannot exist without the desire for esteem. There is no material incentive to obey norms unless there is a material cost attached to violating them. There is no material cost associated with violation unless someone imposes a material penalty. And there is no material incentive for others to bear the cost of inflicting such a penalty; after all, norm-enforcement is, for the group, a public good, and like all public goods, faces the problem of free-riding. Ellickson says that there is a secondary enforcement norm that compels people to punish those who violate norms and that those who fail to do so will also be sanctioned. But then the question arises why anyone would bear the cost of sanctioning those who failed to sanction a substantive norm violator. As Jon Elster argues, "People do not frown upon others when they fail to sanction people who fail to sanction people who fail to sanction people who fail to sanction a norm violation." As one moves away from the original norm violation, "the cost of receiving disapproval falls rapidly to zero." Yet if the cost of refusing to enforce a norm at any level falls to zero, there is no reason for anyone to enforce the norm, and hence no reason for anyone to follow the norm.

A concern for esteem as an end in itself, however, is sufficient to defend norm enforcement against the infinite regress Elster describes. Elster's argument assumes that mechanisms like gossip, scorn, and ostracism work only to signal who is to be subject to material sanctions and are only as effective as those material sanctions. But if disapproval *itself* exerts a real force, then the gossip, scorn, and ostracism are themselves sufficient to enforce norms; they punish the violator by lowering the esteem she receives from the community. In addition to this direct support, the desire for esteem may produce a secondary enforcement norm that requires material sanctions for violators of the primary norm. To avoid esteem punishment, individuals may have to bear some cost incurred by imposing material sanctions on norm violators. Thus, the considerable body of evidence that shows that social norms govern behavior further supports the significance of esteem motives, especially within socially connected groups.

In sum, individuals care particularly for esteem within socially connected groups. Even without a central authority, individuals tend to provide esteem to those who contribute to the welfare of such groups, and this process of esteem allocation facilitates wider social norms that bring about further cooperation. Of course, group members will still free-ride when their desire for material well-being outweighs their desire for intra-group status, but esteem allocation will ameliorate, if not eliminate, collective action problems.

C.   The Consequences of Intra–Group Cooperation: Inter–Group Conflict

Intra-group cooperation increases inter-group conflict. Status is both an additional *means* of ensuring intra-group cooperation and a new *end* of intra-group cooperation, and it contributes in both ways to conflict between groups. Given that social groups often conflict over material resources, the desire for intra-group status means that group members will cooperate more effectively in such disputes, which ensures that groups will be more effective "combatants" whenever material conflict arises. More important, the very mechanism that facilitates greater intra-group cooperation will ensure a new form of conflict: competition for *inter-group* status. This latter result is the unfortunate and inevitable connection between cooperation and conflict.

Groups sometimes engage in zero-sum competition with other groups. A classic example is lobbying. When interest groups pursue what economists call "rent-seeking" legislation, such as farm subsidies and tax "loopholes," they seek merely to transfer resources from one group to another. Cartels similarly seek to extract the profits of non-competitive pricing from consumers. For lobbying groups and cartels, individual contributions to the group's rent-seeking endeavor tend to be undersupplied; selfish members free-ride on the efforts of other members. But the cooperation secured by intra-group status production means that individuals contribute more heavily than they otherwise would toward their group's effort to win a conflict.

Indeed, intra-group esteem production, and social norms based on such esteem, may provide the only explanations for the success of very large groups in lobbying despite powerful incentives for individuals to free-ride. Judge Richard Posner has conceded some uncertainty, for example, in explaining how farmers cooperate in legislative activities. I propose that the answer is the same for farmers as it is for the ranchers Ellickson studied in Shasta County. Although the occupational status of farmers or ranchers is not as observable as, for example, their race, it is one of the first things strangers detect about them. And within a geographic area, farmers and ranchers tend to be socially connected. Thus, farmers and ranchers have an interest in the status generally accorded their occupation and a means of inducing contributions to that status. Intra-group esteem allocation elicits material contributions to group material welfare, such as monetary contributions to lobbying efforts. For individual farmers and ranchers, the amount contributed may be small, but multiplication by a large number produces considerable political clout.

There is a second reason intra-group esteem allocation increases group conflict. Individuals compete for esteem. One arena of competition is *group* status competition, in which individuals seek to produce status for themselves by raising the status of their groups. Under certain conditions, status is zero-sum, so that satisfaction of the status preferences of one group's members necessarily means non-satisfaction of the status preferences of another group's members.

In another article, I detailed the conditions under which relative preferences "inherently" conflict—that is, the circumstances under which the relative position is genuinely zero-sum. Although I focused there primarily on individual status-seeking, those conditions exist for social groups when members of different groups seek incompatible positions for their groups along some common, observable, and reasonably objective dimension. When these conditions do not hold, group status production is socially benign. But the conditions do hold, for example, when groups compare themselves along the "common dimension" of generalized social status and seek a position of superiority on that scale. Under such circumstances, social status is entirely relative. Investment in such zero-sum competition is therefore socially wasteful; the extent of the investment measures the size of the inefficiency. In particular, note the social waste of an obvious group optimizing strategy: *one way to raise the status of one's group is to invest in lowering the status of other groups.* Thus, the desire for esteem may lead to "subordination" as groups attempt to sabotage each other's general social position.

The status theory of cooperation and conflict may now be summarized. First, individuals seek, as an end, the esteem of others; in aggregate terms, they seek social status. Second, because socially connected group members are a key source of esteem, individuals will make material sacrifices on behalf of the group to gain intra-group status. Conversely, the group will reward such status to those who contribute to its welfare. Third, because another source of status is the larger society beyond one's social groups, one measure of group welfare is its status within society. Consequently, groups will use intra-group status "payments" to encourage members to contribute materially to inter-group status. Finally, because general social status is relative, one group can raise its inter-group status by lowering the status of other groups.

* * *

The novelty of these otherwise non-instrumental beliefs is that the normal economic correctives to false belief formation do not apply. For expressive purposes, a "good" belief is not necessarily an accurate belief, but rather one that is pleasurable to express. Of course, even if a category of beliefs serves only expressive ends, there are some constraints on belief formation. Our cognitive mechanisms may make it difficult for us to believe certain things that are manifestly contradicted by experience. Moreover, we may not experience the full pleasure of expressing our beliefs if others find them palpably false in an uninteresting way.

Most important for our purposes, however, is the constraint of self-esteem. Some beliefs are more pleasant than others. For expressive purposes, people are more likely to adopt beliefs that enhance, rather than degrade, their self-esteem. If the issue is the talent of a celebrity, for example, a person is more likely to think highly of the celebrity if, through some connection—having attended the same school, for example—the celebrity's talent will enhance the individual's self-esteem. If esteem can influence expressive belief formation in this manner, esteem can also affect conventionally instrumental beliefs—beliefs concerning how best to satisfy one's preferences. As long as the gain in esteem from the bias toward esteem-producing beliefs is larger than any instrumental loss from the bias, then such a bias serves the individual's overall interests. There is considerable evidence to support this claim: research shows, for example, that people tend systematically to overevaluate their own performance and characteristics. Such a bias may even be essential to mental well-being. Self-evaluation is clearly an instrumental belief—one needs to know what one's talents and abilities are—yet the need for self-esteem is sufficient to create some deviation from strictly impartial beliefs about oneself.

If esteem production favorably biases one's self-evaluations, esteem production may also cause a positive bias toward the social groups to which one belongs. One may gain pleasure from believing positive things about one's groups. Moreover, groups will reward status to those who hold beliefs that are conducive to group welfare. A favorable bias regarding group members may strengthen intra-group cooperation by increasing the apparent material advantage available from transacting with members rather than non-members.

But groups may encourage and reward beliefs more complex than simple bias. For example, although he does not explain how belief distortion occurs, Richard Posner has invoked such distortion to explain how certain cartels solve collective action problems. According to Posner, the distinguishing feature of certain successful cartels—which he terms "guilds"—is their having an "ideology." A guild is a social as well as an economic institution in which members have adopted a common "personal morality" of loyalty, conformity, and craftsmanship, and which has achieved a certain "mystique" involving the idealization of quality over quantity. The "mutually reinforcing combination" of this morality and mystique comprises "the *ideology* of guild production," which serves the "the self-interest of producers in the cartelization of production."

Posner appears to mean that guild members convince themselves that the public interest is served by the restrictions on market entry and production necessary to cartelize an industry. This analysis implies that a principled concern for the public good has some force in motivating behavior, so that cartel members would be even more likely to free-ride if they realized that cartel pricing is contrary to the public interest. Ideology, however, turns the moral force against free-riding. An ideological commitment to quality allows the guild member to believe that conduct that would undermine the cartel—lowering quality and expanding output—would harm the public. Self-interested self-deception thus serves the cartel's long run interests by curbing the individual's impulse to free-ride on the restraint of others.

Return now to racial beliefs. In Posner's terms, negative stereotypes are part of a racial "guild's" efforts to monopolize production of esteem. Even for beliefs that serve an instrumental purpose (such as evaluating potential employees), the desire for esteem will cause an individual to adopt distorted beliefs about racial groups as long as the esteem benefit exceeds the instrumental cost. Consequently, the status-production model can explain differences in voting behavior between blacks and whites. A person may gain esteem by believing positive things about political candidates from her own group and, at least in a relative sense, negative things about politicians of other races. If people do not vote for instrumental reasons, there is no instrumental check on the accuracy of these beliefs. A small bias may suffice to explain a significant difference in voting behavior because, for different racial groups, the bias works in opposite directions.

If one assumes that this analysis correctly explains the existence and direction of racial bias, the question remains how to explain the *evolution* of white attitudes regarding race. Recall that status production commonly involves the denial that one's motive is status production. When one seeks to gain status by lowering the status of others, it is all the more important to deny that one is degrading others in order to look better by comparison. Consequently, "guild ideology" never acknowledges its self-serving nature. Members of Posner's representative guild do not openly declare, even among themselves, that they desire to restrain competition in order to charge higher prices and earn monopoly profits. Similarly, whites never explain their discriminatory behavior as serving the function of status production. Even in the Jim Crow South, whites attempted to justify segregation not by reference to naked self-interest but by claims that blacks were inherently inferior, that blacks preferred segregation, or that segregation somehow reflected the natural order of things. Toward this end, the Jim Crow doctrine of "separate but equal" was ideal. Separation was a means of expressing contempt; the pretense of equality served to deny the status motivation.

When proponents of a status-driven ideology can no longer confidently deny the status motivation of their beliefs, the ideology fails and proponents must search for another ideology. This insight may explain the evolution of white attitudes toward segregation. Although the exact causal strands are difficult to disentangle, events leading up to and including the modern civil rights movement undermined the ability of whites to believe that their existing racial beliefs were anything other than a self-serving ideology. World War II provided one ideological shock, as revulsion to Nazi claims of racial superiority was difficult to square with rationalization of southern racial practices. Rising levels of black education and job skills put a material strain on racial ideology by raising the attractiveness of black labor and thus the cost of absolute racial exclusion. I suspect the most immediate cause of ideological breakdown occurred during the civil rights movement, when photographs captured segregation extremists using violent means, often against women and children, to suppress peaceful protests. Violence against peaceful demonstrators was, even for some southern supporters of Jim Crow, irrefutable evidence that whites were not (at least morally) superior, that blacks were indisputably unhappy with segregation, and that segregation was not a naturally ordained moral order. One of the constraints I have suggested for non-instrumental beliefs is "palpable falsity"; the events of the 1950s and 1960s made salient to whites the falsity of the belief that intentional racial segregation is something other than selfishly hurtful.

Whatever the causal mechanism, many whites have come genuinely to believe that segregation is wrong. This shift does not mean, however, that a psychological veil of prejudice has simply been lifted from their eyes. The expressive beliefs whites adopt about race can no longer be of the crude form needed to justify segregation, but the quest for the production of status continues. Having abandoned the older ideology, whites still tend to oppose policies and candidates that would increase the social status of blacks. Whites can give up old, extreme stereotypes and still embrace negative views of blacks. Unless one consciously scrutinizes the statistical validity of one's generalizations about other groups—an unlikely scenario— even false stereotypes will rarely be *palpably* false. Thus, one may acknowledge the good faith and intellectual integrity of conservative arguments on political issues concerning race—like busing, affirmative action, and welfare—and still worry that the same status-maximizing bias that first rationalized slavery and then segregation infects much of the public thinking on these matters. It is more pleasant to believe that one lives in a society in which everyone (or at least everyone else) is being treated as well as she deserves, that past transgressions have been righted, and that fairness and justice require no further sacrifice. The evolution of white attitudes, therefore, reflects an ideological adjustment to status production under changed circumstances. The final descriptive virtue of the status-production theory is that it offers some insight into this otherwise puzzling evolution of white attitudes.

C. Implications of the Status Production Model of Discrimination

The associational model of discrimination has two key implications: market competition will erode discrimination and, partly for that reason, prohibiting race discrimination is inefficient. The status-production model leads to different conclusions on both points.

1. The Persistence of Race Discrimination.—Becker drew an analogy between race discrimination and transportation costs, both of which increase the cost of certain trades. It is uncontroversial that, other things being equal, those who can minimize transportation costs achieve a competitive advantage over those who cannot. If the analogy with discrimination is sound, we should also expect that whites with less intense tastes for discrimination will enjoy a competitive advantage over those with more intense tastes and will tend to dominate a competitive market.

Under the status-production model, discrimination is not the result of costs that discriminators incur from contact with members of other groups, but is a means of producing status. The discriminator does bear a cost in discriminating—forgoing otherwise beneficial trade with the objects of the discrimination—but that cost is an *investment* in the production of status. As long as such investments are cost-effective for the discriminator, the status-production model predicts that race discrimination will persist in the face of market competition. Consequently, the transportation analogy is inapt. Discrimination may exist in a competitive equilibrium for at least three reasons: the power of discriminatory social norms; the existence of reciprocity between whites; and, under certain circumstances, the effect of esteem-producing racial biases. I will examine each of these in turn.

(a) *The Stability of Discriminatory Norms.*—This section presents a theory of discriminatory social norms. I begin with George Akerlof's economic theory of a racial caste system. I then raise and respond to two key objections to Akerlof's theory—that it does not explain why anyone enforces the caste-based norms, and that it does not capture the complexities of modern American society. I conclude that, despite market competition, status production can support a stable system of discriminatory norms.

Akerlof has provided an explanation for the resiliency of the discriminatory customs of a caste society. It is the essence of a caste-system, Akerlof says, that "any transaction that breaks the caste taboos changes the subsequent behavior of uninvolved parties" who may act to punish the caste-breaker. Third party reactions change the calculus for those who have not internalized the norm:

> Those who fail to follow, or even to enforce the caste customs do not gain the profits of the successful arbitrageur but instead suffer the stigma of the outcaste. If the punishment of becoming an outcaste is predicted to be sufficiently severe, the system of caste is held in equilibrium irrespective of individual tastes, by economic incentives; the predictions of the caste system become a self-fulfilling prophecy.

Thus, Akerlof applies to race discrimination the same view of social norm enforcement that Ellickson has applied to property law—because people boycott norm breakers, it often pays to follow norms.

This insight would be trivial, however, if it only applied when *everyone* in society was willing to boycott those who break the caste rules. Surely a few individuals will always be willing to deal with social outcasts (such as other social outcasts or near outcasts). One could argue that, as long as the number of people willing to violate the discriminatory norms exceeds the number of people targeted by the norm, violators need suffer no harm. Further, one might predict that if a few people violate the norm intially, their violation will weaken the norm and induce other violations to follow, eventually leading to the norm's complete unraveling.

Akerlof responds to these arguments with a simple point that depends merely on the existence of transaction costs. Suppose there are search costs for firms seeking buyers or sellers; because of imperfect information about the existence and reputation of buyers and sellers, firms cannot instantly replace existing trading partners but must incur costs inversely proportional to the number of potential trading partners in the relevant geographic market. Under these circumstances, assuming that there are any parties who will boycott "innovators" (those who violate discriminatory norms), the innovators necessarily incur higher search costs in finding trading partners. Thus, each boycotter raises the likely search costs the innovator will incur before locating a trading partner. Further, when the innovator locates a non-boycotter, its higher search costs will place it "in a weaker bargaining position, since the cost of failing to make a trade is greater to [it] than to noninnovators." If the costs of innovation are higher than the benefits, the discriminatory norm will be stable in a competitive market.

There are, however, weaknesses in Akerlof's explanation. First, Akerlof simply posits that some discriminators will boycott those who fail to follow the discriminatory norm. He offers no explanation of why these boycotters are willing to bear such costs. The status-production model does offer such an explanation. The model shows how individuals gain from adhering to and enforcing certain norms, why the kind of norms individuals benefit from enforcing include norms of discrimination, and why the groups for which this process is frequently employed are racial groups. As I argued above, individuals within racial groups benefit from raising the status of their shared traits. One means of contributing to one's racial status is by subordinating members of other races. With sufficient overlap between racial and socially connected groups, whites have a status benefit to exploit and the cooperative means to exploit it.

Consider, however, a second possible weakness in Akerlof's model. A simple caste society is an appropriate starting point, but American society is more complex. Unquestionably, a norm exists against racial discrimination (or at least against certain forms of racial discrimination), and some whites, as well as blacks, boycott those who overtly discriminate. Given this reality, one might reject the Akerlof caste model.

Yet, even with blacks and some whites "counter-boycotting" discriminators, the equilibrium may entail significant discrimination. Discriminators will bear a cost when targeted for a counter-boycott (or other sanction), but unless that cost exceeds the cost that discriminators create for non-discriminators, it will pay to continue discriminating. The relative costs depend largely on the relative size and economic power of the two groups. Because whites constitute a large majority and possess disproportionate wealth, the costs from white boycotts is likely to exceed the costs from black counter-boycotts. At some point, the participation by a sufficient number of whites in the counter-boycott would tip the balance the other way, but this outcome seems unlikely. First, one cannot infer from the fact that opponents of discrimination are more vocal today—when discrimination in various forms is illegal—that white opponents of discrimination exceed supporters. Second, those who rely on the power of white counter-boycotts rely on the force of moral principle (or altruism) to overcome the selfish force of status production. Under existing theory, selfishness is thought to undermine discrimination. But given the status productivity of discrimination, the power of selfishness suggests the more pessimistic outcome.

One might object that discriminatory norms do not exist if any whites are willing to act against them. That some whites will boycott discriminators merely reflects, however, the fact that American whites do not constitute a single group. "Whites" include various ethnic, religious, political, regional, and class subgroups. How much a particular subgroup invests in subordination as a means of producing status will depend on what its various status options are. Low-status whites have fewer options and tend to discriminate more than high-status whites. Further, white condemnation of the blatant racial discrimination common in an earlier era is consistent with a more subtle discriminatory norm. Subordination works only as long as one can deny that one is acting for the purpose of producing status. Whites are less able to deny this function of racial derogation now than in the past; consequently, overt discrimination is no longer as productive of status as it once was. Just as a "nouveau riche" may undermine her own status by engaging in ostentatious and wasteful consumption, a "redneck" or bigot undermines her own status by expressing contempt solely on the basis of race. But, there is still status in wealth if one displays it more deftly, with the appearance of not calculating to make a display. Likewise, there is status to be gained from race discrimination of a more subtle form, especially when one can plausibly deplore its more flagrant manifestations.

One might nevertheless assert that there are significant numbers of whites who oppose even subtle forms of discrimination. One interpretation of this behavior is that high-status whites who condemn low-status whites for their discrimination may gain more by distinguishing themselves from other whites than by investing in the subordination of blacks or other minorities. In fact, certain classes of whites may enjoy free-riding on the status that other whites secure and then further increase their status by subordinating those whites for being discriminatory. A second, more sanguine interpretation begins with Ellickson's claim that norms tend to be efficient, at least from the perspective of the group in which they arise. Ellickson does not discuss norms that span a group as large as an entire society, but a weaker concern for the esteem of strangers might give rise to norms between strangers. If a weak counter-norm arises against discrimination, perhaps it is because discrimination is inefficient from the perspective of the entire society. But because the norm arises at a different and more diffuse level, it can exist alongside more powerful discriminatory norms that arise within or between socially connected groups.

Becker's model does not contemplate the existence of discriminatory social norms. Thus, I cannot be certain how he would respond to the claim I make here. But Robert Cooter, who embraces Becker's prediction that competition will drive out discrimination, does consider social norms. Cooter argues that the proper economic model for discrimination is that of a cartel and that during the Jim Crow era, southern whites advanced their material ends by using law to gain monopoly power in various markets. Like all cartels, whites faced the inherent problem of instability—that is, the incentive for each member to cheat. Cooter agrees that discriminatory social norms countered the incentives to free-ride, but asserts that the effectiveness of the norms probably depended on their being supported by

Jim Crow legislation. Thus, Cooter expresses the conventional economic skepticism that the norms that supported the white "cartel" could survive absent such legal restrictions. The material incentives in an unfettered market, in his view, provide a strong lure for individuals to defect from the group enterprise.

The theory of intra-group cooperation and inter-group conflict offers a reason for thinking otherwise. Cooter's skepticism about the independent strength of social norms would be well-founded if the only ends that individuals seek are material. Indeed, I argued previously that social norms add nothing to our understanding of cooperation beyond what can be explained by reciprocity unless people value the esteem of others as an end in itself. Therefore Cooter's argument might be right if the only purpose of the white cartel were to advance the material ends of whites and the only means of inducing cooperation were material rewards. The whole thrust of the status-production model, however, is that the cartel-like behavior of whites serves to maximize the non-material end of status production (the cartel seeks to monopolize social status) and that the cartel employs the non-material means of intra-group status rewards and punishments. If this fundamental point is right, then social norms can support discrimination notwithstanding market competition.

Nevertheless, Cooter's basic insight is quite helpful. Whites do act like a cartel. But whites are more accurately described as the subset of cartels that Posner calls "guilds," that is, cartels with "social cohesiveness." Based on a morality emphasizing loyalty and conformity, these guilds have an "ideology"—a set of beliefs that serves to inhibit free-riding—specifically that blacks tend to be inferior, that whites should not interact with blacks in certain ways, and that whites must "stick together." Posner contends that farmers and lawyers—very large industrial groups—manage to cooperate in legislative lobbying efforts despite incentives to free-ride. Racial groups may similarly succeed. For reasons explained above, the more observable the trait that links a group of people, the more status members have to gain by cooperating and the greater the reason to expect such groups to become socially connected as a means of achieving cooperation. Given that race is more observable than these industrial affinities, there is reason to believe racial groups can better succeed in overcoming their collective action problems despite their large size.

Consider, then, a new economic analogy for race discrimination: not transportation costs, but an analogy to the acquisition of a public reputation. An entrepreneur donates a large sum of money to a local museum, or a corporate president agrees to sponsor a marathon. No doubt, the economically inclined theorist would assert that such behavior occurs not because it serves an individual's "taste" for fame, but because it produces greater profits for entrepreneurs and firms by bolstering their reputation or name recognition. I suspect the main force behind this view, however, is nothing as contingent as empirical data on the profitability of such donations, but an inference that economic actors would not give money away unless it was productive to do so. I merely argue for a similar inference with respect to race discrimination. Discrimination exists because it is productive for its practitioners.

(b) Reciprocity as a Basis for Market Discrimination.—There is a second reason to believe that race discrimination will persist in the face of market competition. Becker's theory does not argue that market competition erodes social discrimination. Yet because social interaction facilitates more commercial reciprocity, social discrimination may cause persistent "market" discrimination.

According to Axelrod's analysis of iterated prisoner's dilemmas, it often pays to seek cooperation through a reciprocal strategy such as tit-for-tat when there is sufficient likelihood of future interaction with another. Axelrod emphasizes that the more likely future interactions are, the more likely it is that those who employ reciprocal strategies will prosper. Thus, to increase the prospects of cooperation with a particular individual, Axelrod advises (consciously) increasing the durability and frequency of interactions with that individual. One time-honored means of implementing Axelrod's strategy is to pursue social interaction with the group of individuals with whom one wishes to cooperate. When prospective business partners eat, talk, or play together, they are not merely acquiring information about each other. Social interaction also supports reciprocity; by joining a social group, one increases the likelihood of future interaction with members of the group. Most important, social interactions may themselves be relatively inexpensive but might increase the chance of cooperation's emerging in a business or market setting, where the benefits of cooperation are greater. Joining a country club, a "businessman's" club, or a particular neighborhood may "lock" one into a particular social group, raising one's ability to cooperate with members in non-social settings.

We can now understand more fully the power of discriminatory norms. Even in the absence of a social norm that restrains market trading with other racial groups, social norms could significantly impede such trades. A norm limited to preventing social contacts with members of another race is sufficient to harm such members economically. Since social contacts affect the probability of reciprocity, the absence of such contacts places the isolated individual or the disfavored group at a comparative disadvantage in economic trades. Consequently, norm-based discrimination in one setting, such as social clubs or housing, may cause discrimination in other settings, such as business or employment. Social clubs that exclude women and minorities thus cause them more harm than simply denying them information about, and the chance to become known to, market players. They deny them the opportunity to make reciprocity work.

(c) The Power of Esteem-Producing Racial Biases.—A final factor that contributes to the persistence of discrimination is racially biased beliefs or stereotypes. As noted above, discriminatory norms invoke rationalization mechanisms; discriminators prefer to have reasons for discriminating other than a bare interest in status production. Indeed, because status production is inconsistent with an overt strategy of subordination, it is important that discriminators have an explanation—an "ideology"—apart from status

production. Such an explanation can most easily take the form of negative stereotypes—that the failure of blacks to succeed is their own fault, due to their own shortcomings in ability, integrity, or dependability. This ideology buttresses discriminatory norms. Whatever the social cost of violating the norm, biased evaluations of blacks make it appear that the material benefits of norm violation are less than they are. Self-deception prevents cheating that would undermine the cartel.

Indeed, even if there were no discriminatory social norms, ideologically based racial stereotypes might sustain a stable level of discrimination. One might argue, to the contrary, that absent norms, market competition would discipline whites whose evaluations of blacks were biased. If some white employers fail to perceive black workers accurately, for example, they will lose a competitive advantage to more discerning whites. Yet there is one condition under which stereotypes alone will sustain discrimination—when the material costs of one's miscalculation is zero. In the employment setting, for example, the employer may believe in some cases that the applicants are essentially "tied," that is, they appear to have equal marginal productivities. A white employer would suffer no harm from the decision to hire a white applicant who was tied with a black applicant. Of course, given the white employer's ideology, the employer may not actually perceive the two candidates as being equal, but rather will think that the white candidate is better. The point, however, is that there will be no market correction for such a perception; having white job applicants win all "ties" is a market equilibrium. The question remains how frequently such ties occur in the real world—an interesting empirical question that I, like opponents of Title VII, leave to be answered by others. I simply note that, if such ties were frequent, stereotyping could itself add to the persistence of race discrimination.

In sum, the status-production model provides three reasons to suppose that race discrimination will survive market competition: the power of discriminatory social norms; the existence of reciprocity between whites; and, under certain circumstances, the effect of esteem-producing racial biases.

2. The Efficiency of Anti-Discrimination Laws.—Many legal economists have contended that federal anti-discrimination laws are efficient only to the extent that they nullify state laws mandating discrimination. These theorists view such laws as inefficient when they prohibit private discrimination because their only function is to frustrate discriminatory preferences. But the new descriptive theory I propose requires a rethinking of this normative claim. The status-production model views anti-discrimination laws as potentially correcting a market failure in which individuals invest in essentially confiscatory behavior. That discrimination is a market failure would not itself prove that government action is desirable. We must consider whether the regulation can correct the failure and whether the benefits of such intervention exceed the costs.

(a) Discrimination as Market Failure: The Theft Analogy.—Welfare economics provides a justification for laws that prohibit theft (and other

forms of force and fraud) that is not dependent on discounting the gains to the thief (or other criminals). Even assuming that the transfer accomplished by theft itself causes no wealth loss, because the thief gains what the owner loses, a system that permits theft "results in a very substantial diversion of resources to fields where they essentially offset each other, and produce no positive product." In other words, absent laws against theft, individuals must expend resources merely to protect their property from seizure. They will also forgo certain wealth-creating activities to protect what they already have and because it may be too costly to protect some forms of wealth from theft. In response, the thief invests in gaining tools and knowledge to circumvent anti-theft practices and technology. These dynamic reactions to the risk of theft result in deadweight losses to society. Less is produced, and part of what is produced (burglar alarms and burglars' tools) provides no greater satisfaction of an individual's preferences, but merely helps the individual to retain or confiscate goods that will satisfy preferences. The net effect is to decrease wealth. The same argument applies for laws against violence. It is, of course, Thomas Hobbes's justification for the state: that the only alternative, the "warre ... of every man, against every man," is worse.

It follows from the status-production model that a society without discrimination laws permits an unfettered status war of "every group against every group." What is striking about Richard Epstein's *Forbidden Grounds*, which argues for the repeal of laws that prohibit employment discrimination, is not so much his controversial claim that the only role of government is to prevent force or fraud, but that he never considers how laws against race discrimination may fall precisely within this libertarian principle. Status "warfare" may not be as violent as literal combat, but the term is more than just a metaphor. Hobbes identifies competition for honor as one of the three causes of war; he warns that violent conflict results from attempted subordination. Similarly, Hume warned of the tendency of factions to produce "the fiercest animosities." Competition for group status has generated much of America's history of interracial violence, as when whites lynched blacks to preserve their social position or when blacks retaliated against repeated acts of derogation and dishonor.

Of course, laws prohibit such violence. But even with such laws, unregulated status competition mirrors the inefficiency of a regime without laws prohibiting theft. First, racial status preferences inherently conflict. Race discrimination exists because members of (at least) one race seek for their group a status position that is incompatible with the position sought by members of one or more other groups. Even when only one group seeks superiority, if the other group seeks equality, the struggle for social status is zero sum. Consequently, the appropriation of status by subordinating behavior is, like theft, a mere wealth transfer; the gain to the discriminator is at least matched by the loss to the victim. Second, this form of transfer—using discrimination as a mechanism of subordination—generates extremely high costs. By definition, the discriminator makes a material sacrifice (giving up an otherwise favorable trade or engaging in costly behavior) as a means of lowering the status of the victim. The size of the material sacrifice measures the investment that the discriminator makes in status appropriation. This investment determines the initial cost of the process of racial group status production.

But that is not the whole story. As I noted at the outset of this Part, economic analysis of discrimination strikes many non-economists as barren because it fails to acknowledge the full benefit to its practitioners or the full harm to its victims. The status-production model takes as its central premise that whites gain status by discriminating against blacks. To determine the full extent of the investment in, and therefore the costs of, status competition, we must consider the full range of status defense mechanisms employed by victims of discrimination. Such defense mechanisms include the sometimes desperate reactions of those who live as targets of discrimination. These reactions represent further investment in status production and increase the wastefulness of the unregulated process, much like added investment in theft-protection devices constitute waste in a society without theft laws. Of course, the psychological mechanisms at work are vastly more complex. I will attempt merely a brief summary of the reactions within the framework of the status-production model.

First, enraged victims may respond in kind by attempting to disparage and subordinate the original discriminator. Such behavior may take the form of discrimination, which means the victim also makes a wasteful material sacrifice for the sake of status. The victim may, however, lack the opportunity or wealth to respond in kind and may seek a cheaper means of disparagement such as an insult. Violence is the extreme form of such an insult; it inflicts the loss of dignity inherent in an intentional deprivation of bodily integrity. Even if an African American counters with some means other than violence, the original subordinator may resort to violence to ensure the effectiveness of the original insult and to counter any responsive insult. Hobbes identified this escalation over dishonor as a primary source of war.

A second response is to seek to regain status by subordinating someone *other* than the original discriminator. If whites present too difficult a target, other minority groups may be within reach. Thus, the long and unpleasant history of status competition between minority groups exemplifies a predictable response to subordination. The original victim may also focus on vulnerable members of her own group, such as women or those of a different economic class. Evidence suggests, for example, that African Americans discriminate against one another on the basis of the relative lightness or darkness of their skin. Finally, because the original victim may lack any non-violent means of responding to discrimination, some of what appears to be "senseless violence" among discrimination victims may actually be a rational attempt to produce status by subordinating others.

The victim's responses are not limited to subordinating others. The victim may also withdraw from competition—by which status is generally determined—by adopting beliefs that such competitions are without merit. When a subordinated subgroup fails according to the prevailing cultural values, its members may decide to reject those values completely. For example, minorities facing discrimination may decide, rather than be judged by standards of academic or economic success, that education or employment is an overrated "white" value. Like the processes of rationalization, the belief that academics is unimportant may preserve self-esteem; however, such a belief may prove destructive in the long run because it depresses efficient investment in human capital.

Finally, a victim of subordination may wholeheartedly adopt the beliefs of the subordinators, including those that members of her group are deserving of their low status. Such a response might seem unlikely; however, for some it may be easier to accept a lower status with the belief that such a role is natural and proper than to live out such a role every day believing it is arbitrarily imposed. The result, however, is a form of self-loathing.

In sum, many of the effects of discrimination, well-explored in other disciplines, should be of central concern to an economic assessment of the system of race discrimination. In many cases, these effects represent investments that the victims make in defending their status. Combined with the investments made by the original discriminators, these resources represent the deadweight loss of race discrimination. Consequently, considerable evidence demonstrates that race discrimination is a grossly inefficient market failure.

(b) An Efficiency Argument for Anti-Discrimination Laws.—As with laws against theft, the benefit of prohibiting a form of discrimination is to prevent the wasteful investment of resources in such discrimination. When laws prohibit theft, the primary alternative by which the former thief can make material gains is to engage in lawful, productive activity. The argument for laws that prohibit subordination as a means of acquiring status is exactly parallel: by raising the costs of subordination, such laws induce people to switch to socially productive, or at least socially benign, means of acquiring status (either at an individual or a group level). Subordination is not the only means of group status production, and inter-group status production is not the only means of gaining esteem.

A possible distinction from theft, however, is the availability of equally wasteful substitutes to blatant discrimination. A group with a disproportionately large share of political power, economic wealth, and symbols of status will have at its disposal a number of alternative means of subordinating a minority group. Prohibiting one form of subordinating behavior may simply cause a shift to an equally wasteful form of acquiring status. Such a concern, however, may be overstated. After all, common law larceny initially required a trespass in the taking and thus exempted what we now think of as embezzlement and fraud. Even though thieves were free to switch to non-trespassory means of confiscation, the initial prohibition was nonetheless efficient. The opportunities remaining were more limited and costly; a complete substitution would not occur. The same argument can be made for prohibiting private discrimination in certain key areas, such as employment and housing. These forms of discrimination probably represent the most productive means of subordination and therefore induce the greatest "investment" by whites. As I previously pointed out, employment discrimination offers for whites a double insult to blacks: not only the insult inherent in shunning someone, but also the consequence of lowering black income in a society that accords status to wealth. Similarly, excluding blacks from neighborhoods is not only a very public symbol of subordination, but also denies them the material benefits of reciprocity that may arise among neighbors. Effectively prohibiting employment and housing discrimination would deprive whites of their most productive private means of subordination and would thereby lower the resources invested in this wasteful confiscatory activity.

Second, anti-discrimination laws may lower the investment in status confiscation by increasing the incidence of "cross-membership." *Ceteris paribus*, an individual prefers subordinating a group to which she does not belong to subordinating a group to which she does belong. An individual always bears a cost from subordination of her own group and that cost gives her an incentive to avoid such behavior. In fact, an individual who is a member of group A and group B might find it in her interest to invest in efforts to prevent members of group A from seeking to subordinate group B. Therefore, the more "cross-membership" between two groups, the fewer the resources that will be invested by the two groups in subordinating each other.

Laws forbidding race discrimination may increase the occurrence of cross-membership and thereby undermine the effectiveness of racial subordination as a status strategy. Race has been and remains highly correlated with other demographic factors. If a white individual lives in an all-white neighborhood, attends an all-white school, works in an all-white firm, worships at an all-white church, belongs to an all-white amateur sports league, and patronizes all-white hobby clubs, she will never face the problem of cross-membership. If, however, anti-discrimination laws were to integrate neighborhoods, schools, firms, and private clubs, more whites would find themselves in a position in which racial minorities belong to some of *their* groups. Consequently, racial subordination would lower the status of these integrated groups. One response will be for whites to flee the groups that become integrated, but if the costs are too high, as when the law integrates a number of social groups at the same time, the effect might be to lower the effectiveness of racial subordination as a status strategy for many whites.

Finally, anti-discrimination laws may serve to correct the market failure of discrimination by undermining the credibility of rationalizations for discrimination. Several commentators have noted that the law shapes preferences, and that Title VII and other civil rights laws may have reduced the preference for discrimination. The status-production model explains this evolution not as a change in the taste for discrimination, but as a change in the productive capacity of certain forms of subordination. Individuals who seek status require some rationalization for their behavior. Admitting that one seeks to subordinate others for the sake of status conflicts with obtaining such status. Law affects the credibility of any alternative explanation. Take Posner's example of a guild that survives on an ideology of quality to justify restrictions on competition. Consider the long-term effect Posner's critique might have on such ideology were it sufficiently publicized. Exposing the naked self-interest behind platitudes of public concern erodes their effectiveness.

Law is more crude than an intellectual critique, yet it is inherently more public, and can carry more weight. When Jim Crow laws mandated certain forms of segregation, whites confidently spoke of segregation as the natural order of things; when the laws forbade segregation, discriminatory whites had a greater difficulty believing their own ideology. Rationalizations can be fragile things; sometimes they require that dissent be held to a minimum. In the South and elsewhere, Title VII constituted a very powerful "dissent," an indication that a large number, perhaps a majority, of Americans no longer believed the explanations of discrimination. If people care about esteem, the law can change behavior merely by signaling on what grounds the majority will henceforth give and withhold esteem.

In sum, law may correct the market failure of discrimination in three ways: by raising the costs and lowering the productive returns of certain forms of subordination; by increasing the racial diversity of socially connected groups, which raises selfish resistance to the subordination strategy; and by symbolizing a consensus that the rationalizations for the subordination strategy are, in fact, mere rationalizations. Whether such laws are efficient depends on the magnitude of these benefits relative to the administrative and opportunity costs of the system that adjudicates discrimination claims. But under the status-production model, the efficiency question is, like it is for the prohibition of theft, an empirical one; one can no longer simply assert that laws prohibiting satisfaction of discriminatory preferences are presumptively inefficient.

One might inquire about the implications of the status-production model of discrimination for affirmative action. In what may seem like an evasion, I believe the model provides no clear answer for affirmative action, but does reveal the consequential tensions the policy represents. The "cross-membership" effect of anti-discrimination laws provides a theoretical foundation for the claim that affirmative action serves to combat discrimination more effectively than a mere non-discrimination policy. Indeed, the benefit of cross-membership might justify a very aggressive affirmative action program. The utility of integrating social groups by race is not limited by any principle of past wrongful discrimination. The status-production model indicates that we can reduce investment in future status subordination by decreasing racial stratification in society.

Conversely, affirmative action creates a "common fate" for those of the same race and thus raises the salience of race. As critics of affirmative action have claimed, this fact may cause whites to identify themselves more fully with their race. The status-production model adds this insight: raising the salience of race may increase the return from racial subordination and enhance the power of whites to elicit intra-group cooperation for the remaining avenues of racial subordination. Affirmative action likely has already had this effect, which offsets the positive effects of cross-member-ship. However difficult it is to ascertain the present net effect, the more important and difficult question is what the future effects will be. Affirmative action has, so far, done little to integrate effectively American society. Therefore, we have no reason to expect the positive consequences of that policy to have emerged. In the end, the status-production model reveals what I think we knew already: affirmative action is an investment in which we bear certain costs today for the hope of a greater return tomorrow. The model illuminates, but does not resolve, the empirical question of whether the future benefits will outweigh the present costs.

III.   CONCLUSION

Groups inherently tend to elicit a level of cooperation from their members and to incur a level of conflict with other groups. The coopera-tion, in fact, facilitates the conflict. Intra-group esteem allocation permits groups to overcome certain collective action problems that would otherwise make conflict impossible. At the same time, the desire for esteem provides a new objective of group conflict—competition over social status.

What I have termed the theory of intra-group cooperation and inter-group conflict is merely the logical extension of three other steps in political and economic theory. First, Hobbes, among others, justified the state as necessary to avoid perpetual conflict in the state of nature; thus the state's role is to facilitate peaceful cooperation. Second, economists have persuasively contended that certain forms of peaceful cooperation, such as price-fixing, are detrimental to society. Consequently, the govern-ment should act in such cases to prevent cooperation. Third, Ellickson, among others, has written that groups use social norms to solve collective action problems without the centralized coercive power of the state, namely to bring about a cooperative "order without law." The next step, I propose, is to recognize that significant instances of this decentralized cooperation will inevitably be socially destructive and, therefore, that government should obstruct these forms of cooperation. Groups inherently tend to use their powers of decentralized cooperation to produce status through the socially wasteful process of subordination. As with cartels, cooperation in such cases is a social threat that justifies state action.

Aside from these general political implications, the theory of intra-group cooperation and inter-group conflict illuminates the complex problem of race discrimination. Status production explains both the historic and contemporary contours of race discrimination far better than the prevailing associational model of discrimination. Understanding race discrimination as a means of producing status helps us explain its tenacity in the face of market competition and reveals, within an economic model, the full costs of the practice of discrimination. The effort to gain status by taking status away from others, and the responsive measures this effort elicits, are socially wasteful in the same way that confiscation of material property is wasteful. The inefficiency in the system of status competition is measured by the investments each group makes in gaining or protecting its status.

Prohibiting the more productive forms of investments can reduce the wastefulness of such actions even if it does not eliminate it.

In criticizing the associational preference model of discrimination, I focused intensively on a single form of discrimination—racial discrimination—and within that category, exclusively on discrimination against African Americans. The points I made in this context, however, apply to other forms of racial and ethnic discrimination. When substantial overlap exists between groups that share publicly observable traits and groups that are socially connected, the theory predicts substantial investment in status production, including the subordination of other groups. With more than two racial and ethnic groups, greater opportunity exists for movement in social position, and there is, therefore, reason to expect greater investment in maintaining or improving status.

* * * * *

Groups matter. Groups form for simple informational reasons, as economics describes in considerable detail: to minimize the transaction costs people incur in the course of satisfying their preferences. Yet the formation of groups has another consequence. People have a loyalty to groups that goes beyond what serves their narrow pecuniary self-interest. I have sought to explain that solidarity in self-interested terms; doing so requires an expanded understanding of self-interest that includes a powerful desire for esteem and status. Given the ubiquity of groups, this broader social science perspective on their function should prove useful in understanding legal issues beyond racial discrimination. For now, I have argued for a sober appreciation that solidarity for some often means enmity for others.

NOTES AND QUESTIONS

1. Comparing Rational Choice Theory with Group Status Production Theory. Is it possible to compare the Becker and McAdams Models? What are the starting assumptions of each piece? Does McAdams accept any part of the rational choice heuristic?

2. Groups vs. individuals. One possible difference between the Becker and McAdams models is how they treat groups. McAdams is primarily concerned with the operation of intergroup processes for enforcing subordination. In contrast, Becker treats the individual as the central unit of measuring preferences for discrimination. Becker does, however, note that "it has been argued that an increase in the numerical importance of a minority group increases the prejudice against them, since the majority begins to fear their growing power; on the other hand, some argue that greater numbers bring greater knowledge and that leads to a decline in prejudice." To what use does Becker's theory of discrimination put this observation about group size?

3.   Racial discrimination, the moral argument. If racial discrimination is simply a preference with exactly the same entitlement to expression in the marketplace as a taste for strawberry ice cream, how does rational choice distinguish between morally repugnant choices (child pornography) and morally neutral choices? Does rational choice theory require a normative view of racial discrimination to work?

Becker observes that: "[f]or example, discrimination and prejudice are not usually said to occur when someone prefers looking at a glamorous Hollywood actress rather than at some other woman; yet they are said to occur when he prefers living next to whites rather than Negroes. At best, calling just one of these actions 'discrimination' requires making subtle and rather secondary distinctions. Fortunately, it is not necessary to get involved in these more philosophical issues."

4.   Adam Smith and Group Status Production Theory. Recall that Adam Smith argued, self interest, modified by benevolence born of conscience, or the influence of the moral spectator are the primary motivations for human economic behavior. Now, compare Smith to McAdams' thesis "that a material view of human motivation underestimates both the level of cooperation that groups elicit from their members and the level of conflict that groups elicit from each other. A single group dynamic connects these added increments of cooperation and conflict: groups achieve solidarity and elicit loyalty beyond what economic analysis conventionally predicts, but solidarity and loyalty within groups lead predictably, if not inevitably, to competition and conflict between groups. The connection is the desire for esteem or status. Groups use intra-group status rewards as a non-material means of gaining material sacrifice from members, but the attendant desire for inter-group status causes inter-group conflict."

---

3.   AN EMPIRICAL STUDY OF RACIAL DISCRIMINATION

Fair Driving: Gender and Race Discrimination in Retail Car Negotiations

104 HARV. L. REV. 817 (1991).

IAN AYRES

The struggle to eradicate discrimination on the basis of race and gender has a long history in American law. Based on the widely held belief that such discrimination will occur only in markets in which racial or gender animus distorts competition, regulatory efforts have been limited to areas in which interpersonal relations are significant and ongoing, such as housing and employment. In this Article, Professor Ayres offers empirical evidence that seriously challenges faith in the ability of competitive market forces to eliminate racial and gender discrimination in other markets. His Chicago based research demonstrates that retail car dealerships systematically offered substantially better prices on identical cars to white men than they did to blacks and women. Professor Ayres details the nature and startling degree of the discrimination his testers encountered and evaluates various theoretical explanations for their disparate treatment. Based on his conclusions, Professor Ayres explores routes by which "fair driving" plaintiffs might bring suits against dealerships and mechanisms through which regulators might effectively rid the retail car market of such discrimination.

[The] civil rights laws of the 1960s prohibit race and gender discrimination in the handful of markets—employment, housing, and public accommodations—in which discrimination was perceived to be particularly acute. In recent years, lawsuits have increasingly presented claims of more subtle and subjective forms of discrimination within these protected markets. Both legislators and commentators, however, have largely ignored the possibility of discrimination in the much broader range of markets left uncovered by civil rights laws. Housing and employment may be the two most important markets in which people participate, but women and racial minorities may also be susceptible to discrimination when spending billions of dollars on other goods and services. Of these unprotected markets, the market for new cars is particularly ripe for scrutiny because, for most Americans, new car purchases represent their largest consumer investment after buying a home. In 1986, for example, more than $100 billion was spent on new cars in the United States.

This Article examines whether the process of negotiating for a new car disadvantages women and minorities. More than 180 independent negotiations at ninety dealerships were conducted in the Chicago area to examine how dealerships bargain. Testers of different races and genders entered new car dealerships separately and bargained to buy a new car, using a uniform negotiation strategy. The study tests whether automobile retailers react differently to this uniform strategy when potential buyers differ only by gender or race.

The tests reveal that white males receive significantly better prices than blacks and women. As detailed below, white women had to pay forty percent higher markups than white men; black men had to pay more than twice the markup, and black women had to pay more than three times the markup of white male testers. Moreover, the study reveals that testers of different race and gender are subjected to several forms of nonprice discrimination. Specifically, testers were systematically steered to salespeople of their own race and gender (who then gave them worse deals) and were asked different questions and told about different qualities of the car.

At the outset it is difficult to choose how, linguistically, to characterize the results that black and female testers were treated differently from white male testers using the same bargaining strategy. The term "discrimination," although surely a literal characterization, unfortunately connotes to many the notion of animus (even though in antitrust, for example, "price discrimination" is not taken to imply any hatred by sellers). "Disparate treatment," in contrast, connotes to others a strictly technical legal meaning developed in civil rights case law. For the moment, the terms "discrimination" and "disparate treatment" are both used to refer to the result that sellers' conduct was race-and gender-dependent; sellers took race and gender into account and treated differently testers who were otherwise similarly situated. These terms are not meant to imply that salespeople harbored any animus based on race or gender.

In recent years, the Supreme Court has struggled in the employment context to enunciate workable evidentiary standards to govern claims of subtle and possibly unconscious forms of discrimination. Although the 1960s civil rights laws do not reach retail car sales, the finding that car retailers bargain differently with different races might give rise to disparate treatment suits under 42 U.S.C. §§ 1981 and 1982, which originated in the 1866 Civil Rights Act. The test results, by focusing on an unexplored manifestation of disparate treatment, push us to define more clearly what constitutes discrimination generally.

Furthermore, the results highlight a gaping hole in our civil rights laws regarding gender discrimination. Although sections 1981 and 1982 prohibit racial discrimination in contracting and the sale of real and personal property, no federal laws bar intentional discrimination on the basis of gender in the sale of most goods or services. The civil rights laws of the 1960s fail to fill this gap, leaving unregulated a legion of markets in which women contract. Put simply, car dealers can legally charge more or refuse to sell to someone *because* she is a woman. Intentional gender (or race) discrimination of this kind might alternatively be attacked as an "unfair or deceptive" trade practice under state and federal consumer protection laws. In the end, however, courts might perceive that the quintessentially individualized and idiosyncratic nature of negotiation places such disparate treatment entirely outside the purview of either the civil rights or consumer protection laws.

The goal of Congress in passing the Civil Rights Act of 1866 was to guarantee that "a dollar in the hands of a Negro will purchase the same thing as a dollar in the hands of a white man." The standard argument against enacting civil rights laws has been grounded in the conviction that the impersonal forces of market competition will limit race and gender discrimination to the traditionally protected markets, in which there is significant interpersonal contact. Yet the results of this study give lie to such an unquestioning faith in competition: in stark contrast to congressional objectives, this Article indicates that blacks and women simply cannot buy the same car for the same price as can white men using identical bargaining strategies. The price dispersion engendered by the bargaining process implicates basic notions of equity and indicates that the scope of the civil rights laws has been underinclusive. The process of bargaining, already inefficient in many ways, becomes all the more problematic when it works to the detriment of traditionally disadvantaged members of our society.

Part I of this Article describes how the tests of race and gender discrimination were conducted. Part II reports the results of the tests. An analysis of disparate treatment in price, sales tactics, and steering is combined with a regression analysis focusing on the determinants of final offers. Part III explores theoretical explanations of the results. Animus-based theories of disparate treatment are compared with theories of statistical discrimination and tested against the results of the study. Particular attention is paid to the role of competition at both the wholesale and retail level in limiting and channeling the form of race and gender discrimination. Finally, Part IV explores the legal implications of the study. This Part considers whether and how "fair driving" plaintiffs could legally challenge this disparate treatment under consumer protection laws and sections 1981 and 1982. The Article concludes by considering the need for legal reform.

I. METHODOLOGY OF THE TEST

To test whether there is disparate treatment by car retailers on the basis of race or gender, pairs of consumers/testers (for example, a white male and a black female) used the same bargaining strategy in negotiating at new car dealerships. A white male tester was included in each pair of testers. The white male results provide a bench-mark against which to measure the disparate treatment of the non-"whitemale" tester. Three consumer pairs (black female and white male, black male and white male, and white female and white male) conducted approximately 180 tests at ninety Chicago dealerships.

Each tester followed a bargaining script designed to frame the bargaining in purely distributional terms: the only issue to be negotiated was the price. The script instructed the testers to focus quickly on buying a particular car, and testers offered to provide their own financing. The testers elicited an initial price from the dealers and then, after waiting five minutes, the testers responded with an initial counteroffer that equalled an estimate of the dealer's marginal cost. After the tester's initial counteroffer, the salesperson could do one of three things: (1) attempt to accept the tester's offer, (2) refuse to bargain further, or (3) make a lower offer. If the salesperson attempted to accept the tester's offer or refused to bargain further, the test was over (and the tester left the dealership). If the salesperson responded by making a lower offer, the script instructed the tester to wait five minutes and to split the difference. After the tester split the difference, the salesperson again had the same three choices, and the rounds of bargaining continued until the salesperson accepted a tester offer or refused to bargain further. Testers jotted down each offer and counteroffer, as well as options on the car and the sticker price. Upon leaving the dealership, the testers completed a survey recording information about the test.

This design produced results that permit two tests for discrimination. The first, "short test" of discrimination simply compares the dealer's response to the testers' initial question, "How much would I have to pay to buy this car?" The "long test" of discrimination, on the other hand, compares instead the final offers given to testers after the multiple rounds of concessionary bargaining. By focusing on the initial offer, the short test is well controlled because salespeople had little information from which to draw inferences. By focusing on the final offer, the long test isolates more closely the price a real consumer would pay, but it increases the risk that individual differences among the testers influenced the results.

In order to minimize the possibility of non-uniform bargaining, particular attention was paid to issues of experimental control. A major goal of the study was to choose uniform testers and to train them to behave in a standardized manner. Testers were chosen to satisfy the following criteria for uniformity:

1. *Age*: All testers were twenty-four to twenty-eight years old.

2. *Education*: All testers had three or four years of college education.

3. *Dress*: All testers were dressed similarly during the negotiations. Testers wore casual "yuppie" sportswear: the men wore polo or buttondown shirts, slacks, and loafers; the women wore straight skirts, blouses, minimal make-up, and flats.

4. *Economic Class*: Testers volunteered that they could finance the car themselves.

5. *Occupation*: If asked by a salesperson, each tester said that he or she was a young urban professional (for example, a systems analyst for First Chicago Bank).

6. *Address*: If asked by the salesperson, each tester gave a fake name and an address for an upper-class, Chicago neighborhood (Streeterville).

7. *Attractiveness*: Applicants were subjectively ranked for average attractiveness.

The testers were trained for two days before visiting the dealerships. The training included not only memorizing the tester script, but also participating in mock negotiations designed to help testers gain confidence and learn how to negotiate and answer questions uniformly. The training emphasized uniformity in cadence and inflection of tester response. In addition to spoken uniformity, the study sought to achieve tester uniformity in non-verbal behavior.

   * * *

Readers should focus, therefore, not merely on statistical significance but also on the *amount* of the reported discrimination. Although perfect control of such complex bargaining is impossible, the amounts of discrimination reported in the next Part cannot be plausibly explained by idiosyncratic divergence from uniform bargaining.

II.   Results of the Test

The results from the tester surveys provide a rich database for investigating how salespeople bargain and whether they treat testers of a different race or gender differently. This Part presents the results of these tests in three sections. The first section reports disparate treatment regarding the prices that dealerships were willing to offer the testers. This section includes an analysis of both initial and final offers as well as refusals to bargain and differences in the bargaining paths (the sequence of offers made in succeeding rounds). In the second section, nonprice dimensions of the bargaining process are analyzed. The tests reveal that salespeople asked testers different types of questions and used different tactics in attempting to sell the cars. Finally, the third section uses multivariate regression analysis to analyze the determinants of the final offers. The regressions reveal a fairly sophisticated seller strategy. In particular, the size of final offers is sensitive not only to the race and gender of both the tester and the salesperson, but also to the information revealed by the tester in the course of bargaining.

A.   Price Discrimination

1.   Final Offers.—The final offer of each test was the lowest price offered by a dealer after the multiple rounds of bargaining. By comparing these final offers with independent estimates of dealer cost, it was possible to calculate the dealer profit associated with each final offer (final offer minus dealer cost). For a sample of 165 tester visits, the average dealer profits for the different classes of tester are presented in Table 1.

TABLE 1: AVERAGE DEALER PROFIT FOR FINAL OFFERS	
White Male	$ 362
White Female	504
Black Male	783
Black Female	1237

Black female testers were asked to pay over three times the markup of white male testers, and black male testers were asked to pay over twice the white male markup. Moreover, race and gender discrimination were synergistic or "superadditive": the discrimination against the black female tester was greater than the combined discrimination against both the white female and the black male tester.

The reliability of these results is buttressed by an analysis of the relative unimportance of individual effects. The average dealer profits on the non-"white male" testers were statistically different from the average profits on the white males at a five percent significance level. The average profits for the three individual white males were, however, not significantly different from each other. This last result lends support to the proposition that the idiosyncratic characteristics of at least the white male testers did not affect the results.

* * *

Dealer discrimination in early rounds will cause disparate concessions by testers that may preclude equal treatment in final rounds. The possibility that early offers matter, however, is not an embarrassment of design.

Bargainers engage in time consuming initial rounds of bargaining because they individually believe that these rounds will affect the final price. The tests provide strong evidence that if consumers use the same "split the difference" strategy, they will receive different final offers that are determined by their race and gender. * * *

2. *Initial Offers.*—This study also constructed a test of disparate treatment on the basis of the initial offers sellers made to the testers. * * *

The average dealer profit on offers made to white female testers was not significantly different from the average profit on offers made to white male testers. Sellers, however, offered both black males and black females significantly higher prices: sellers asked black males to pay almost twice the markups they charged white males, and they asked black females to pay two and one-half times that markup.

TABLE 2: AVERAGE DEALER PROFIT FOR FINAL OFFERS	
White Male	$ 818
White Female	829
Black Male	1534
Black Female	2169

3. *Willingness to Bargain.*—Another potentially important form of disparate treatment concerns the sellers' willingness to bargain. Consumers are hurt if the sellers either refuse to bargain or force the consumers to spend more time bargaining to achieve the same price. An analysis of the number of bargaining rounds reveals that the average number of rounds for different types of testers did not differ significantly, as shown in Table 3. The amount of time black male and white female testers spent bargaining (both total and per round) was not statistically longer than the amount spent by white male testers. Although black female testers clearly had to pay the most for cars, it was not because dealers refused to spend time bargaining with them. * * *

TABLE 3: DIFFERENCES IN ROUNDS			
	Average Number of Rounds	Average Length of Test (Minutes)	Average Length per Round (Minutes)
White Male	2.43	35.8	14.8
White Female	2.21	32.9	14.9
Black Male	2.32	49.1	21.2
Black Female	3.08	34.6	11.2

* * *

B.   *Nonprice Discrimination*

The study also examined other ways in which sellers may have treated the testers differently. Although these other types of disparate treatment do not directly concern the sales price, they could facilitate price discrimination. Moreover, these comparisons suggest something about the racial and sexual perceptions that determine the behavior of salespeople.

1. *Customer Steering.*—As designed, the script allowed dealerships to steer testers to different types of salespeople or different types of cars. The script instructed testers to go to the center of the showroom and wait for a salesperson to approach them. The salespeople chose the tester, so that the testers could be steered to salespeople of a particular race or gender. In the sample of 119 encounters, sellers paired with testers as reported in Table 4.

The salesperson's race and gender was not randomly distributed across testers. Instead, sellers steered testers to persons of their own race and gender: white male sellers were more likely to serve white male testers; white female sellers were more likely to serve white female testers; and black male sellers were more likely to serve black testers.

TABLE 4: STEERING TO PARTICULAR TYPES OF SALESPEOPLE			
	Seller Type Percentages		
	White Male	White Female	Black Male
All testers	83.2%	7.5%	9.3%
White Male	89.5	3.5	7.0
White Female	71.4	19.1	9.5
Black Male	83.4	5.5	11.1
Black Female	82.6	4.3	13.1

In addition, the study was designed to uncover a second type of dealer steering. Upon entering the dealership, the testers told the salesperson that they were interested in buying a certain car model with certain options and then allowed the salesperson to show them specific cars. However, no statistically significant disparate treatment was found. The test results reveal that dealers did not systematically steer different types of testers to cars of different cost.

2. *Disparate Questioning.*—The testers recorded how often they were asked specific types of questions. Statistical tests were then conducted to evaluate whether sellers asked non-"white male" testers particular questions significantly more or less often than white male testers. These tests indicate the following:

Sellers asked black female testers *more* often about their occupation, about financing, and whether they were married. Sellers asked black female testers *less* often whether they had been to other dealerships and whether they had offers from other dealers.

Sellers asked black male testers *less* often if they would like to test drive the car, whether they had been to other dealerships, and whether they had offers from other dealers.

Sellers asked white female testers *more* often whether they had been to other dealerships. Sellers asked white female testers *less* often what price they would be willing to pay.

These differences may indicate ways that dealers try to sort consumers in order to price discriminate effectively. For example, the fact that salespeople asked black testers less often about whether they had been to other dealerships (or had other offers) may indicate that salespeople do not think that interdealer competition is as much of a threat with black customers as with white customers. Because the price that sellers are willing to offer any customer may be sensitive to that customer's responses, the disparity among who is questioned may facilitate a seller's attempt to price discriminate.

   3. *Disparate Sales Tactics.*—The testers also recorded the different tactics that the salespeople used in trying to sell the car. Test statistics were calculated to evaluate whether particular sales tactics were used significantly more or less often with white male testers than with non-"white male" testers. These tests indicate the following:

   Salespeople tried to sell black female testers *more* often on gas mileage, the color of the car, dependability, and comfort, and asked them more often to sign purchase orders.

   Salespeople tried to sell white female testers more often on gas mileage, the color of the car, and dependability.

   With black male testers, salespeople *more* often offered the sticker price as the initial offer and forced the tester to elicit an initial offer from the seller. Salespeople asked black male testers to sign a purchase order less often.

   These tests suggest that salespeople believe women are more concerned with gas mileage, color, and dependability than are men. The tests also indicate that salespeople try to "sucker" black males into buying at the sticker price by offering the sticker price or refusing to make an initial offer until asked.

   4. *Cost Revelation.*—The script also elicited information about the dealers' willingness to reveal their marginal cost to consumers. In half of the bargaining sessions, the testers were told to ask the seller (at the end of the test) what the dealer had paid the car manufacturer. Thirty-five per cent of the sellers represented a specific dollar cost in response to the testers' inquiries. These disclosures, however, were not evenly distributed across the tester groups. Disaggregated by tester type, the disclosure rates indicate that salespeople were less willing to disclose cost data to black testers, especially black female testers, as presented in Table 5.

TABLE 5: DISCLOSURE OF COST DATA	
Tester Type	Percentage of Salespeople Disclosing Cost Figure
All Testers	35%
White Male	47
White Female	42
Black Male	25
Black Female	0

Instead of disclosing their cost information to black testers, the salespeople were more likely to dissemble and claim that they did not know the car's cost. To the extent that such cost disclosure is valuable, the failure to disclose costs to black testers undermines their ability to bargain as effectively as white testers and thus facilitates price discrimination based on race.

Based on this sample, however, it is unclear whether such disclosure would actually put white testers at a competitive advantage. When the seller did reveal his cost, the represented cost was substantially higher than independent estimates of seller cost for the same models, as seen in Table 6. Thus, although salespeople are more likely to disclose cost figures to white testers, they systematically overstate their costs. The greatest mis-representations were made to white female testers.

* * *

Although the individual interaction variables are not statistically sig-nificant, the regressions indicate that the linear constraints in Model Two are binding. * * *

TABLE 6: SELLER MISREPRESENTATION OF COST DATA	
	Average Misrepresentation
White Male Tester	$ 849
White Female Tester	1046
Black Male Tester	752
Black Female Tester	—

White male testers received best deals from white female sellers.

White female testers received best deals from black male sellers.

Black male testers received best deals from white female sellers.

Black female testers received best deals from white male sellers.

The social psychology literature would not suggest this result to be expected. Several studies, for example, have shown that parties tend to bargain more cooperatively with an opponent of their own race and gender than with a person of a different race or gender. The interaction effects revealed in Model Three (although not statistically significant) suggest, however, that salespeople may try to take strategic advantage of consum-ers' perceptions. This result is especially plausible when combined with the earlier finding that testers were systematically steered to salespeople of the same race and gender. The data thus paints a clear picture: sellers steered testers to salespeople of their own race and gender, who then proceeded to give them the worst deals.

III.   TOWARD A THEORETICAL EXPLANATION

The preceding Part detailed race and gender discrimination that was not only statistically significant but also surprisingly pronounced. This Part explores possible explanations for why dealers would discriminate in this manner. Only with an accurate understanding of the reasons for dealer behavior can regulators hope to determine what, if any, governmental intervention can effectively protect black and female customers. With this goal in mind, this Part examines two broad theories of discrimination: animus-based theories and theories of statistical discrimination.

A. Animus–Based Theories of Discrimination

Animus theories of discrimination posit that a certain group is treated differently because that group is disliked or hated. A variety of market participants can interject animus into a market. A dealership, for example, might charge blacks more because the dealership dislikes blacks, because the dealership's employees dislike blacks, or because the dealership's other customers dislike blacks. As originally formulated by Gary Becker, these sources of bigotry could force sellers to charge blacks higher prices as an animus-compensating tax.

The source of bigotry might partially determine the specific form that animus-based discrimination takes. For example, in the fair housing context, consumer animus has led to steering and refusals to bargain. In the "fair driving" context, employee animus against blacks or women might cause salespeople to bargain frivolously. Because testers visited the dealerships during the least busy times of the day, bigoted dealers—with nothing better to do with their time—might have gained satisfaction in frustrating or wasting the time of women or blacks. Finally, the testers also might have experienced "role-based" bigotry: dealers might have discriminated against buyers who acted in ways that diverged from the dealer's expectation. Female testers could have faced prejudice for speaking with "a male voice"; black testers could have faced prejudice for not "staying in their place." In sum, the animus of various market participants can manifest itself as disparate treatment not only in the prices offered but also in other aspects of seller behavior.

* * *

C. A Tentative Explanation

1. Statistical Discrimination as an Explanation for Dealer Behavior.—The preceding discussion presented three broad theories of discrimination: animus-based, cost-based, and revenue-based. The fair driving tests, like their fair housing analogues, were designed primarily to identify the existence of disparate treatment—not to determine its cause. As a result, ancillary evidence must be used to determine which of the three competing theories best explains seller behavior. Although more study is warranted, it appears that the revenue-based theory best explains the discrimination that the testers encountered.

The cost-based theories of statistical discrimination are perhaps the weakest. The testers' script was explicitly structured to eliminate cost-based differences among the testers. The testers volunteered that they did not need financing—a potentially major source of disparate dealer cost. Notwithstanding these uniform representations, it is possible that the dealers inferred residual differences among the tester types. As an empirical matter, however, differences in net dealership cost simply do not explain why black female testers paid over three times the markup of white male testers. Moreover, on a cost-based theory, the observed seller inferences about profits from ancillary sales might predict a different pattern of disparate treatment.

Animus theories find more support in the data. The testers, for example, recorded several instances of overtly sexist and racist language by sellers. Nonetheless, animus theories do not appear to explain the magnitude of the discrimination. For example, under a theory of salesperson animus, the seller required a higher price from black females as compensation for having to deal with a black customer whom the seller disliked. The data would then imply that the dealer-required compensation must have been an implausible $900 per hour.

Consumer-based animus also fails to explain adequately disparate treatment by sellers. First, each class of testers received its best treatment from salespeople of a different race and gender and, in many cases, the worst treatment from salespeople of the same race and gender. For example, although all salespeople discriminated against black male testers, black salesmen gave them their worst deals. This result runs counter to the standard notion that a person's bigotry is usually directed at another race. Second, the amount of price discrimination black testers encountered at all dealerships did not vary with the racial makeup of the dealership's customer base. One-third of Chicago dealerships are located in neighborhoods with a greater than ninety percent black population, yet the offers these dealerships made to black testers did not differ from offers black testers received elsewhere. If disparate treatment were caused by white consumers' dislike of blacks, there should be less discrimination by sellers in neighborhoods where most consumers are black. Because the data do not confirm this prediction, the animus theory seems an unlikely explanation for the disparate treatment. Finally, consumer animus is inconsistent with observed salesperson behavior: salespeople did not attempt to reduce the length of bargaining sessions with the non-"white male" testers. If disparate treatment of black consumers were caused by sellers' concern for white consumers' desire not to associate with blacks, dealerships should have discouraged black consumers from bargaining for lengthy periods.

Although any conclusions based on this evidence must remain tentative, the case for revenue-based statistical discrimination is strongest. Despite the large amount of randomness (or unexplained variance) in bargaining outcomes, the dealerships seem to display a great deal of sophistication in bargaining. The systematic steering of customers to salespeople who charge them higher markups may be evidence of revenue-based statistical discrimination. Salespeople of the consumer's race and gender may, for example, be better able to infer that consumer's willingness to pay—and thus more finely tune the price discrimination.

* * *

Yet the conundrum persists as to why race and gender would be proxies for consumers' firm-specific reservation price that disfavor women and blacks. Even accepting that firm-specific willingness to pay is more a function of search costs than of ability to pay, why would blacks and women be disfavored? George Stigler has predicted that consumers with high opportunity costs will search less for a particular good than those consumers with lower opportunity costs. Because white males earn more on average than other tester types, under Stigler's theory a dealer should rationally infer that white males search less than members of other race and gender classes. If race and gender serve as proxies for dealer-specific willingness to pay, these proxies would seem to lead sellers to charge higher prices to white males, and not the lower prices revealed by this study.

Nevertheless, group differences in search costs, information, and aversion to bargaining may explain why profit-maximizing dealers charge white males less. The caricatured assertion that white males have higher opportunity costs (because they forgo higher wages when searching) ignores other effects that on balance may make it more difficult for blacks and women to search for a car. For example, white males may have a greater ability to take time off from work or family responsibilities to search for a car. Moreover, blacks are less likely to have a trade-in car with which to search when purchasing a new car. If, on net, blacks and women experience higher search costs than do white males, revenue-based statistical discrimination might lead dealers to make lower offers to white males. Knowing that blacks and women tend to incur higher search costs, a dealer could "safely" charge members of those groups higher prices, because the dealer would effectively have less competition for members of those groups from other dealers. White men may also have superior access to information about the car market. A large proportion of white men know that automobiles can be purchased for less than the sticker price, and white men may more easily be able to discover the customary size of negotiated discounts from the sticker price.

* * *

2. The Reinforcing Role of Dealer Competition.—Many commentators have argued that competition among sellers will tend to eliminate certain forms of race and gender discrimination against buyers. The following discussion examines how market competition among dealerships may in fact reinforce the opportunities for statistical discrimination.

As a first intuition, competition should quickly eliminate revenue-based statistical discrimination, slowly eliminate animus-based discrimination, and never eliminate cost-based statistical discrimination. Competition should quickly eliminate revenue-based discrimination because rival dealers would immediately move to undercut any supra-competitive prices offered to high-valuing car buyers. Competition should slowly eliminate animus discrimination because bigoted sellers would be at a competitive disadvantage and so would eventually be driven out of the market. By contrast, competition should not eliminate cost-based statistical discrimination because no dealer would have a market-based incentive to offer prices that fall below the best estimates of that dealer's actual costs.

The preceding analysis, however, tentatively suggested just the opposite causal ordering. Cost-based statistical discrimination is the least plausible explanation, and revenue-based statistical discrimination is the most plausible. The simple competitive story thus poses a major challenge to the assertion that revenue-based statistical discrimination caused the disparate treatment. In a large city such as Chicago, with hundreds of car dealerships, how could rival dealerships successfully charge individual consumers significantly more than dealership marginal costs?

* * *

The dealers' reliance on high-markup buyers lends additional credibility to the notion that dealership disparate treatment of consumers might be a form of revenue-based statistical discrimination. The dealers' search for high-markup buyers may be tailored to focus on specific racial or gender groups. In their quest to locate high-markup buyers, dealers are not guided by the amount that the *average* black woman is willing to pay. Rather, they focus on the proportion of black women who are willing to pay close to the sticker price. Even a small difference in the percentage of high-markup buyers represented by consumers of any one race or gender class may lead to large differences in the way dealers treat that entire class. Thus, the previous explanations of racial- or gender-based differences in search costs, information, or aversion to bargaining need not be true for the average members of a consumer group in order for those differences to generate significant amounts of revenue-based disparate treatment. The Consumer Federation of America recently completed a survey which revealed that thirty-seven percent of consumers do not understand that the sticker price is negotiable. These responses varied greatly across both race and gender. Sixty-one percent of black consumers surveyed did not realize that the sticker price is negotiable, whereas only thirty-one percent of white consumers made this error. This fact by itself could easily explain dramatic disparate treatment by sellers. Profit maximizing dealers may rationally quote higher prices to blacks even if the average black consumer in fact has a lower willingness to pay.

In sum, although simple economic theory suggests that dealer competition should quickly eliminate price dispersion, dealers in the market for new cars nevertheless sell the same car for different prices. Highly concentrated profits give dealers incentives to search for high-markup buyers through the process of bargaining. In particular, the dealers' search for high-markup buyers may reinforce incentives to discriminate on the basis of race or gender. The concentration of profits is a central pathology of retail car sales and one to which we will return below.

IV. LEGAL IMPLICATIONS

The results of the bargaining tests show that car dealerships treat black and female testers differently than they do white men who use the same bargaining strategy. Whether these findings constitute actionable racial or gender discrimination in a traditional legal sense, however, is a separate matter. The differential treatment of consumers might be seen as a natural consequence of any bargaining process. Market economies sanction such treatment by allowing sellers to pursue high-markup sales through a variety of bargaining methods. The pre-contractual interplay between a potential buyer and seller may seem, in some sense, outside the purview of the law.

This Part argues, however, that the findings presented in this Article constitute compelling evidence of unlawful racial and gender discrimination under both the civil rights and consumer protection laws. In particular, the following section explores whether the car sellers' dealings with black testers constitute unlawful disparate treatment violative of sections 1981 and 1982. Such a claim does not necessarily imply that sellers dislike black or female customers—only that sellers take their customers' race and gender into account when deciding how to bargain. Section B then proposes legal reforms to strengthen sections 1981 and 1982 and to extend their coverage to currently unprotected groups.

A. Liability Under Sections 1981 and 1982

Sections 1981 and 1982 mandate that all people shall have the same rights "to make and enforce contracts" and to "purchase ... personal property," respectively, "as is enjoyed by white citizens." Although a racial discrimination suit has never been brought against a retail car dealership under section 1981 or section 1982, there seems little doubt that one or both these laws covers discrimination relating to retail car price bargaining between private parties. In *Jones v. Alfred H. Mayer Co.*, the Supreme Court emphatically stated that section 1982 (and by implication section 1981) applies to acts of private discrimination. Since *Jones*, courts have applied these sections' prohibitions of private discrimination to contexts similar to retail car price bargaining.

Even if car dealership bargaining falls within the scope of sections 1981 and 1982, a fair driving plaintiff would have a number of hurdles to overcome in winning a claim under these statutes. The substantive legal standard under sections 1981 and 1982 is straightforward: plaintiffs claiming disparate treatment must prove that the defendant intentionally discriminated against them and caused them an identifiable injury. Although the Supreme Court has stated that intentional discrimination "can *in some situations* be inferred from the mere fact of differences in treatment," no civil rights case has ever concluded that a showing of disparate treatment was insufficient to establish intentional discrimination. Thus, it appears that courts will find intentional discrimination whenever the defendant's conduct was conditioned on the plaintiff's race. To establish liability in this context, the typical fair driving plaintiff would need to show that the specific car dealer with whom he or she had bargained considered the plaintiff's race in deciding how to bargain.

On the other hand, because of the difficulties in obtaining direct proof that a defendant's conduct was race-dependent, the law has developed a method for allocating the burdens of proof under sections 1981 and 1982 that in effect allows intent to be inferred from indirect evidence. In particular, courts hearing section 1981 or 1982 claims have imported from the title VII context the shifting burdens of proof scheme articulated in *McDonnell Douglas v. Green.*

Applying the *McDonnell Douglas* reasoning to fair driving suits, the plaintiff bears the initial burden of establishing disparate treatment: that sellers took race into account when deciding how to bargain. If the plaintiff can establish a prima facie violation of section 1981 or section 1982, a burden of production shifts to the defendant "to articulate some legitimate, nondiscriminatory reason" for its differential behavior. Finally, if the defendant can offer such a reason, the burden shifts back to the plaintiff to show that the defendant's response is a mere "pretext."

A black tester from the present study who wanted to make out a successful prima facie case against a particular dealership would have to persuade the court of two things. First, she would have to persuade the court that the study was sufficiently controlled—that is, that she and the white tester visiting the defendant's car dealership appeared similar in every objective respect except for the color of their skin. If courts' attitudes in housing cases under sections 1981 and 1982 are any indication, the fair driving tests conducted in this study were more than sufficiently controlled. Although the typical fair housing test is similarly controlled with respect to timing of the tests, it is less controlled with respect to verbal and nonverbal conduct than was the testing in this study.

Second, fair driving plaintiffs would have to persuade the court that the instances of differential treatment are sufficiently numerous so that the results can not be explained by chance. Again, analogy to the fair housing context suggests that the results of one pair of well controlled testers should suffice. Under this standard, the present study could theoretically give rise to dozens of actionable instances of discrimination against individual dealers.

Although comparisons with the fair housing context are generally apposite, courts may be much more reluctant to find the existence of prima facie cases in the fair driving context because society has differing presumptions about the pervasiveness of the two kinds of discrimination. The long and ongoing history of housing discrimination in the United States is so well known and well documented that courts may require relatively less proof. Discrimination in car negotiations may have a similarly long and deep-seated history, but the size and nature of such discrimination may be masked by the processes of bargaining. As a result, a court hearing a fair driving claim may require that the tests be that much more controlled, that the disparity of treatment be that much greater, or that there be that many more instances of disparate treatment by the same dealer.

Once a court finds that a fair driving plaintiff has made out a prima facie case of disparate treatment, the burden shifts to the defendant-dealer to articulate a legitimate, nondiscriminatory explanation for why it treated white buyers and black buyers differently. If the defendant does not directly rebut the plaintiff's evidence of disparate treatment, it might put forward two distinct arguments that the disparate treatment was not "intentional" discrimination. First, the dealer may argue that the disparate treatment was unintentional because the dealer's motive was to make money, not to harm black people. Under this theory, the dealer might openly admit that its behavior flowed from consciously drawn, economically rational inferences based on the race of prospective buyers—revenue-based inferences, for example, about the proportion of blacks willing to pay a higher markup. It is, however, precisely these sorts of inferences—inferences based on the color of a person's skin—that sections 1981 and 1982 do not countenance. As Judge Posner recently held, "[d]iscrimination may be instrumental to a goal not itself discriminatory, just as murder may be instrumental to a goal not itself murderous (such as money); it is not any less—it is, indeed, more clearly—discriminatory on that account."

Alternatively, defendants might claim that their disparate treatment was unintentional in the sense that they were not conscious of it. The D.C. Circuit rejected this argument in *Hopkins v. Price Waterhouse*:

> [Plaintiff demonstrated] that she was treated less favorably than male candidates because of her sex. This is sufficient to establish discriminatory motive; the fact that some or all of the partners at Price Waterhouse may have been unaware of that motivation, even within themselves, neither alters the fact of its existence nor excuses it.

Once a plaintiff has proven that a defendant has treated blacks differently from identically situated whites, it is fair and reasonable to conclude as a matter of law that the dealer at some level of consciousness must have been aware of the testers' race. Such a legal inference conforms with our common moral intuition that a dealer who must consciously decide what initial price to offer every customer who walks through the door must be aware of the skin color of those to whom it consistently offers a higher initial price. Thus, so long as the fair driving plaintiff can persuade the factfinder that sellers treated similarly situated blacks differently from whites, the disparate treatment discussed in this Article violates sections 1981 and 1982.

B.   Legal Reform

1.   Modernizing Civil Rights Laws.—Lawmakers could respond to bargaining discrimination by expanding the current coverage of the civil rights and consumer protection laws. Most important, Congress could amend sections 1981 and 1982 to extend to women (and other protected classes) the right to be free from discrimination in contracting to buy and sell services as well as goods. Modernized versions of sections 1981 and 1982 could also allow plaintiffs to bring disparate impact suits, currently actionable under title VII, which require no showing of intent. Disparate impact litigation would allow suits to challenge the bargaining practices of sellers that are facially neutral (in the sense that they do not consciously take a buyer's race or gender into account) but have significant discriminatory effects. In sum, creating an additional roman numeraled civil rights "title" to cover the sale of goods and services would provide a remedy for the kinds of discrimination examined in this Article.

Although this Article has argued that the sellers' search for high-markup consumers causes sellers to discriminate against blacks and women, the proposal to extend civil rights protection to the sale of all goods and services is based on the notion that racial and gender-based disparate treatment may well exist in a broader variety of markets. The problem of disparate treatment in new car sales has been perpetuated by the fact that the bargaining process conceals from black and female consumers the prices received by their white male counterparts. Without such information, blacks and women cannot directly learn of disparate treatment. Black and female consumers may also be deprived of this crucial bench-mark in retail markets in which bargaining does not occur. Although uniform stated-pricing eliminates the potential for gender or race discrimination in pricing for most goods, such discrimination may still exist along such different dimensions as product or service quality. Again, although blacks and women can gather information about how other retailers treat them, they face difficulty in learning how retailers treat white men.

The 1960s civil rights laws outlawed discrimination in those markets—most notably housing and employment—in which conspicuous accessible bench-marks disclosed disparate treatment. But the absence of a manifest bench-mark does not imply the absence of discrimination; there is no reason to think that animus or statistical causes of discrimination manifest themselves only in markets in which interracial comparisons of treatment can be readily made. Indeed, as various overt forms of discrimination have become illegal, more subtle and covert manifestations have often replaced them. This Article seeks fundamentally to expand the domain of the civil rights inquiry.

2. Reinvigorating Consumer Protection Laws.—State and federal governments might also attempt to enforce more rigorously consumer protection laws to reduce the type of discrimination revealed in this Article. Indeed, recent Supreme Court decisions hostile to civil rights suits suggest the wisdom of pursuing a remedy under consumer protection laws. In *Patterson v. McLean Credit Union*, for example, the Court, although refusing to apply section 1981 to what it considered "postformation conduct," suggested instead that the victims of discrimination turn to traditional contractual remedies. To the extent that consumer protection laws codify common law remedies such as fraud and duress, they may provide a viable alternative to civil rights remedies. Thus, although consumer protection laws have not yet been used to attack racial disparate treatment as a "deceptive" misrepresentation, this history does not preclude more extensive governmental intervention in the future.

The Federal Trade Commission (FTC) Act and the numerous baby FTC acts passed by the individual states outlaw the use of "unfair or deceptive" trading practices. Utilizing such acts to reach discrimination in bargaining for a new car purchase will require a reconceptualization of what we consider unfair or deceptive. Attacking sellers' disparate treatment in bargaining as being "deceptive" strikes at closely held beliefs about what is appropriate in the normal course of negotiations. The complexity of these beliefs is demonstrated by contrasting the effect of seller misrepresentation in the context of car sales with seller misrepresentation in housing sales. Fair housing cases often gain their moral authority from the egregious nature of seller misrepresentations such as "the apartment is no longer available." In the retail car bargaining context, however, some forms of misrepresentation are broadly accepted. Few would believe, for example, that a seller would be held liable for misrepresenting "I can't reduce the price any further"—even if the seller did reduce the price for another consumer. Seller misrepresentation is present in both the housing market and in the new car market. The distinction in our response turns, if at all, on which types of misrepresentation we deem acceptable.

Nevertheless, consumer protection laws do provide a framework for attacking disparate treatment in bargaining. Courts have construed consumer protection statutes to prohibit implied as well as express misrepresentation. Courts could attack disparate treatment in negotiations for new cars by finding an implied representation that the dealer would not treat black consumers differently from white consumers. In other words, courts may preserve the "essence" of bargaining—by conceding that all consumers should expect inconsistent and unpredictable treatment at the hands of car dealers—but refuse to sanction "discrimination" by rejecting regimes in which the unpredictable behavior is in fact predicated on race or gender.

Such a finding would be completely consistent with freedom of contract. Sellers could avoid making this implicit representation by expressly reserving the right to bargain differently with customers of different races. A judicial or legislative finding of an implicit representation of no racial disparate treatment would simply be "filling a gap" in the parties' contract. Finding an implied representation of no racial disparate treatment is at least as reasonable as finding an implied representation that sellers reserve the right to treat different races differently: few explicit contracts would ever opt for the latter provision. Once lawmakers established a default rule of no disparate treatment, plaintiffs bringing implied misrepresentation cases would then face the same burden as traditional section 1981 plaintiffs: the burden of demonstrating disparate treatment.

The Supreme Court's decision in *Patterson v. McLean Credit Union* strongly supports this analysis. In restricting civil rights protection under section 1981 to discrimination in the formation of a contract, the *Patterson* Court suggested that victims of discrimination should turn to traditional contractual remedies: racial harassment "amounting to a breach of contract under state law is precisely what the language of § 1981 does not cover. That is because, in such a case . . . the plaintiff is free to enforce the terms of the contract in state court." Although the contract at issue was silent as to whether post-formation discrimination was permissible, the court implied that nondiscrimination provisions could be read into state contract remedies. Following the *Patterson* rationale, finding an implicit representation not to treat consumers differently in bargaining because of their race or gender would offer a free market alternative to civil rights interventionism.

3. Structural Reforms.—The expansion of traditional civil rights and consumer protection laws is unlikely to completely eliminate disparate treatment in bargaining based on race or gender. Victims of disparate bargaining treatment will most likely be restricted to suing individual dealerships—instead of manufacturers or groups of dealerships. Even if plaintiffs bring class actions and courts consistently grant testers standing to sue, the piecemeal approach of such suits, combined with the protracted nature of litigation, is unlikely to be sufficient to deter race- and gender-dependent behavior.

In light of these conditions, policymakers might consider structural reforms to improve the workings of the market. Structural changes should grow out of specific causal theories of disparate treatment in order quickly and effectively to erase such treatment. For example, if animus is inducing price discrimination, a law that outlawed price discrimination might induce some sellers to refuse to bargain. However, if the disparate treatment is caused by inferences about different consumer demand, then outlawing price discrimination should not generate such refusals. Simply put, to formulate effective intervention, policymakers must understand why sellers discriminate.

The earlier analysis of competition suggested that high-markup customers (and the ensuing concentration of profits) are a central cause of dealer price discrimination. As a result, if policymakers can find a way to reduce significantly the profits on these sucker sales, the manner in which dealerships conduct the retail sale of *all* cars would become dramatically more competitive. Without the pathological effects of highly concentrated profits, dealers would no longer have an incentive to force consumers to expend real and psychic resources in bargaining.

Policymakers could use three different strategies to eliminate high-markup sales. Most directly, courts could strengthen current notions of substantive unconscionability to prohibit high-markup sales. This strategy, however, is unlikely to occur: courts in the past have shown extreme reluctance to distinguish conscionable from unconscionable markups. Although courts voided contracts for unconscionable markups in two well-known cases, *Frostifresh Corp. v. Reynoso* and *American Home Improvement v. MacIver*, few courts since the early 1960s have reached similar holdings. The likelihood of courts taking the dramatic step of expanding this rarely used doctrine becomes even smaller in light of the special nature of bargaining for retail cars and society's solicitude toward such bargaining.

As a second regulatory strategy, policymakers might restrict the amount of price dispersion permissible in the car market. Regulators might, for example, allow dealerships to engage in bargaining, but void sales with markups that are more than twenty percent above the average markup. Unlike direct unconscionability regulation, firms would retain the freedom to set the average markup for any one model as high as the market would bear but would be prohibited from selling similar cars at significantly different prices. At its most extreme, this form of regulation would prohibit bargaining and mandate that dealerships sell at advertised prices. Restraining price dispersion is an attractive form of regulation because it might benefit all would-be car buyers. If the number of high-markup sales is reduced, sellers may find that bargaining (and the transaction costs that it imposes on all consumers) is no longer profitable. Once high-markup consumers are protected, sellers may no longer subject their low-markup consumers to costly and unpleasant bargaining.

Finally and least intrusively, regulators might reduce the number of sales with disparately high markups by mandating various types of disclosure from dealerships to consumers. Dealerships, for example, might be required to reveal the average price for which each make of car is sold. Knowing that the dealership is attempting to charge $3000 more than the average price would allow high-markup consumers to protect themselves. Alternatively, regulation might force dealerships to reveal the size of the markup on each individual transaction. Clay Miller and I have argued elsewhere that markup disclosure could improve both the equity and efficiency of retail car sales: "markup revelation would truncate the bargaining process at each dealership. The possibility of hoodwinking uninformed buyers into purchasing at a high markup would diminish as the excessive profits would be directly revealed."

In sum, mandating disclosure and restraining price dispersion are plausible strategies to reduce the importance that dealerships place on high-markup sales. A central prediction of this Article is that at some point reducing the concentration of dealership profits would rationalize dealership competition by giving individual dealerships an incentive to opt for high-volume, stated-price selling strategies. The relatively unintrusive nature of disclosure and price-dispersion regulation makes them politically and administratively more viable.

Before choosing a strategy to eliminate price dispersion, policy-makers should determine whether a single price equilibrium is "sustainable": that is, whether competitive dealerships that charge a single price could break even and thus survive price dispersion. In markets with high fixed costs, if sellers were required (directly or indirectly through disclosure) to charge a single price, competition might drive that price to a level below sellers' average cost. Such markets have "hollow cores" (because the "core" set of viable single-price equilibriums is empty or "hollow").

If the retail car market has a hollow core, government intervention to eliminate price dispersion would tend to drive dealerships from the market. In such markets, high-markup sales help dealers cover their fixed costs. In the airline industry, for example, the high-markup sales to business travelers may be necessary to meet industry fixed costs. Indeed, business travelers may benefit from the presence of lower-price tourist fares because "cheap" seats defray part of these fixed costs. If regulation eliminated price dispersion and mandated a single fare per route, business travelers might have to pay higher prices than under the current regime. Tourist travelers would stop buying, and the airline would then pass its fixed costs along to the smaller group of business travelers.

Regulator concerns should be allayed, however, because the retail car market does not resemble hollow core markets. Retail car dealerships do not experience significant high fixed costs (especially when compared to many other single price markets such as the market for electronic appliances and stereo equipment). Moreover, it is implausible that white males would (like tourist travelers) stop purchasing in a single price equilibrium. Mandating a single fare for airlines might lead to an inflated price that only businesspeople could afford, but mandating a single price for automobiles would not leave blacks and females alone to shoulder even higher proportions of the retailers' fixed costs.

Although this discussion of potential regulatory strategies is impressionistic, at the very least it suggests that regulators have a variety of choices beyond traditional civil rights and consumer protection remedies to attack the inequalities uncovered in this Article. Naturally, implementing one of these structural interventions would impose enforcement costs that must be weighed against the benefits of regulation. Dealers may attempt to circumvent such regulations in several ways. Nevertheless, in evaluating the efficacy of structural changes, policymakers should pay particular attention to the concentration of profits and the prevalence of high-markup sales.

V. CONCLUSION

The negotiation of contracts occupies a mysterious and somewhat mythical position in the law and in our society. In *The Wealth of Nations*, Adam Smith opined that people have a natural propensity to "truck and barter" over the sale of goods. Law-and-economic scholars at times extend this insight, suggesting that people will tend to negotiate whenever resources are misallocated: if I want to sit on a crowded subway, I will negotiate with the other passengers for a seat.

Common experience indicates, however, that many people in the United States are averse to bargaining. The frustration that many consumers experience in bargaining for a car is largely attributable to the ludicrously inefficient manner in which cars are marketed. Although Smith and others attach almost mythic qualities to the process of bargaining, this Article has thrown the equity and efficiency of car negotiations into question. The process of retail car negotiations becomes even more problematic when traditionally disadvantaged members of our society effectively pay a bargaining tax whenever they purchase a new car.

Earlier this year, I asked a car dealer during an interview whether the bulk of his profits were concentrated in a few sales. He told me that his dealership made a substantial number of both "sucker" and "non-sucker" sales. He added: "My cousin, however, owns a dealer-ship in a black neighborhood. He doesn't sell nearly as many [cars], but he hits an awful lot of home runs. You know, sometimes it seems like the people that can least afford it have to pay the most." Although it is dangerous to extrapolate from the results of a single study, the amounts of discrimination uncovered, if representative of a larger phenomenon, are truly astounding. A $500 overcharge per car means that blacks annually pay $150 million more for new cars than they would if they were white males. There are substantial reasons to uncover *and eliminate* such discrimination.

———

For further reading, *see also* Peter Siegelman, *Gender and Race Discrimination in Retail Car Negotiations, in* PERVASIVE PREJUDICE?: UNCONVENTIONAL EVIDENCE OF RACE AND GENDER DISCRIMINATION 19 (Ian Ayres ed., 2001).

CHAPTER 5

THE MARKET VALUE OF CULTURE

Introduction

Between culture and commerce lies an ocean of mostly unexplored misunderstandings. In a thousand ways, the captains of commerce and the giants of creative invention live in the perpetual paradox of mutual hostility and mutual dependence. When race and ethnic pluralism are tossed into this already volatile mix, the questions multiply even as the answers diminish in inverse proportion.

This chapter takes up some of the most troublesome issues at the intersection of culture, race, gender and identity in the marketplace. In what follows we consider four central queries: *First*, can economic behavior be fully understood, without an attentive account of the cultural context in which economic transactions occur? The paucity of attention of neoclassical strands of economic analysis to the cultural variables that we discuss in what follows has produced a largely impotent set of models for predicting many crucial items of economic behavior. These thin models, devoid of cultural context, have dominated the legal discourse about economics. We identify a more complex set of ideas that incorporates culture and its tension with commerce. *Second*, what is the impact of racial dominance on the ownership and control of cultural property? We ask whether the rules of intellectual property support or undermine the growth of economic autonomy for members of culturally subordinated groups. Is the economic structure that frames the labor of musicians, artists, singers, songwriters, actors, and other creators just? *Third*, how does subordination express its effect in the valuation of the human capital components of language, hairstyle, sexual difference, and modes of expressive autonomy in the workplace? *Fourth,* if we reconceptualize the relationship of culture and markets, can we elevate the level of human flourishing for a broader group of citizens?

A. ACCENTS

In this passage, novelist Amy Tan vividly captures the problem of an immigrant mother's effort to communicate her hope for cultural transformation, even while clinging to the project of symbolic and creative preservation of cultural memory. The mother dreams of speaking without an accent.

370

The old woman remembered a swan she had bought many years ago in Shanghai for a foolish sum. This bird, boasted the market vendor, was once a duck that stretched its neck in hopes of becoming a goose, and now look! It is too beautiful to eat.

Then the woman and the swan sailed across an ocean many thousands of *li* wide, stretching their necks toward America. On her journey she cooed to the swan: 'In America, I will have a daughter just like me. But over there nobody will say her worth is measured by the loudness of her husband's belch. Over there nobody will look down on her, because I will make her speak perfect American English. And over there she will always be too full to swallow any sorrow! She will know my meaning, because I will give her this swan—a creature that became more than what was hoped for.'

But when she arrived in the new country the immigration officials pulled her swan away from her, leaving the woman fluttering her arms and with only one swan feather for a memory. And then she had to fill out so many forms she forgot why she had come and what she had left behind.

Now the woman was old. And she had a daughter who grew up speaking only English and swallowing more Coca–Cola than sorrow. For a long time now the woman had wanted to give her daughter the single swan feather and tell her, 'This feather may look worthless, but it comes from afar and carries with it all my good intentions.' And she waited, year after year, for the day she could tell her daughter this in perfect American English.

AMY TAN, *Feathers From a Thousand* Li *Away, in* THE JOY LUCK CLUB (1989).

Voices of America: Accent, Antidiscrimination Law, and a Jurisprudence for the Last Reconstruction

100 YALE L.J. 1329 (1991).

■ MARI J. MATSUDA

I. INTRODUCTION

* * * This Article opens with stories of some of the accents that gave rise to the existing judicial decisions. The influence of the "turn to narrative"—the suggestion that human beings understand and form their worlds through stories—is evident here. These narratives create a doctrinal puzzle. * * * The puzzle is this: Courts recognize that discrimination against accent can function as the equivalent of prohibited national origin discrimination. The fact that communication is an important element of job performance, however, tends to trump this prohibition against discrimination, such that it is impossible to explain when or why plaintiffs will ever win in accent cases. In fact, they almost never do. Much of this section will sound like a positivist's plea for logic.

[This article] attempts to understand the cultural context of accent discrimination by considering the role of speech in society, and the ways in which prejudice and status assumptions are tied inextricably to speech evaluation. Given this sociolinguistic reality, I argue * * * for a doctrinal reconstruction that will apply Title VII to accent cases in a rational way. I criticize the current, conclusory reasoning of most accent decisions, while acknowledging the difficulties courts face. This is positivism plus sociology of law—a kind of thinking I associate with the Yale Law School. It demands that we apply our faculties of reason to the social reality of lived experience.

Having set forth what I believe is a rational and just application of Title VII principles to accent cases, [I will then] consider the ethical implications of accepting or rejecting a doctrinal scheme intended to promote linguistic pluralism. [This article] explores liberal justifications for linguistic tolerance, and * * * considers accent from within the perspective of emerging progressive theories of law, including Critical Legal Studies, Critical Race Theory, and feminist jurisprudence. Utilizing these critical theories, I inquire into the deeper meaning of accent discrimination as situated in structures of subordination. This part is influenced by the critical theorists who have confronted the issue of audience: for whom do we write, and why? I attempt to make explicit my intended and multiple audiences, and my political goals.

> * * *

II.   The Stories

I come from a place that is farther away from any place than any place. The islands of Hawaii, geographically isolated and peopled from all corners of the world, are a linguist's dream. The linguistic and ethnic heritage of the islands is more diverse than that of any other state in the United States. In the voices of the islands one hears traces of Hawaiian, Portuguese, New England English, Japanese, Chinese, Filipino, and Spanish. It is thus no accident that two significant Title VII cases falling in the middle of the doctrinal puzzle of accent discrimination come from Hawaii.

Perhaps in explaining the puzzle, it is best to begin where all cases begin, with a person and the story they bring to court.

A.   *Manuel Fragante's Story*
> * * *

In 1981 Manuel Fragante took a civil service examination along with over 700 other applicants. He is an intelligent and educated man, and he was not surprised when he received the highest score of all applicants who took the test. Fragante was ranked first on the list of eligibles, but, after a brief interview, he was turned down for the job of clerk in the Division of Motor Vehicles. When he asked why, he learned that he was rejected because of his Filipino accent. Manuel Fragante, combat veteran of two wars and true believer in the rhetoric of equality, promptly contacted a

Filipino American state legislator, who in turn recommended that Fragante visit the run-down office of a neighborhood public interest law firm.

* * *

Because the DMV creates constant demand for new employees, the personnel department sent a specialist to study the job and devise a screening test to help identify a large pool of prospective clerks. This is a well-established procedure used by large employers. The specialist observed clerks on the job. The key skills she identified included alphabetizing, reproducing numbers and letters with accuracy, making change, exhibiting courtesy, and other routine clerical skills. A test was devised to measure these skills.

* * *

This was the premise Manuel Fragante relied on when he took the civil service examination and out-tested his 700 competitors. He was proud of his score and felt assured of the job. While others thought the job was beneath him given his age and experience, he was looking forward to the simplicity of its tasks, to the official feel of working for the government in an air-conditioned building, and to the chance to earn some spending money instead of wasting his time in boring idleness. He found warnings that the job was stressful mildly amusing. Having lived through invasion, war, and economic uncertainty, Manuel Fragante figured he could handle an irate taxpayer complaining about a long wait in line. He thus walked in for his interview with a calm and assured dignity. He knew the job was his.

* * *

Manuel Fragante was passed over for the job. The administrator in charge of hiring recommendations stated, "because of his accent, I would not recommend him for this position." The interviewers heard what any listener would hear in a brief conversation with Mr. Fragante: he speaks with a heavy Filipino accent, one that he is unlikely to lose at his age.

* * *

The linguist sat through the trial and noted the proceedings with interest. Attorneys for both sides suffered lapses in grammar and sentence structure, as did the judge. Mr. Fragante's English, a review of the transcript confirmed, was more nearly perfect in standard grammar and syntax than any other speaker in the courtroom. Mr. Fragante testified for two days, under the stress of both direct and cross-examination. The judge and the examiners spoke to Fragante in English and understood his answers. A court reporter understood and took down his words verbatim. In the functional context of the trial, everyone understood Manuel Fragante's speech. Yet the defendant's interviewers continued to claim Fragante could not be understood well enough to serve as a DMV clerk.

In an irony particularly noticeable to the linguist, lawyers for both sides, as well as the defendant's witnesses, spoke with the accent characteristic of non-whites raised in Hawaii—the Hawaiian Creole accent that would become the subject of another significant Title VII accent case discussed below. * * * The linguist, trained as he was to recognize accents as intriguing differences rather than handicaps, was troubled by the legal result in the *Fragante* case.

* * * The judge was on assignment from Arizona. He listened to four days of testimony and concluded that Manuel Fragante was denied the job *not* because of national origin, but because of legitimate difficulties with his accent. The opinion was somewhat of a puzzle. The judge found, as fact, that Manuel Fragante "has extensive verbal communication skill in English" but paradoxically that he has a "difficult manner of pronunciation" and a "military bearing," and that some listeners would "stop listening" when they hear a Filipino accent. The court made much of the high-stress communication required for the job, and found that speech was a bona fide occupational qualification. Finally, the court applied the *McDonnell Douglas* test, and found no proof of discriminatory intent or subterfuge.

Manuel Fragante was upset by the opinion. Soon after losing out on the DMV job, he was hired by the State of Hawaii as a statistician. Much of his work involved telephone interviews. Fragante felt his employment with the State proved his claim that the city misjudged his accent. He told his attorneys he wanted to press forward with his case.

Fragante lost on appeal before the Ninth Circuit although he did gain the symbolic victory of the court's sympathetic recognition that accent discrimination could violate Title VII. The U.S. Supreme Court denied certiorari.

* * *

B.   *The Weather Forecasters*

* * *

In 1985, the National Weather Service advertised for a vacancy in the Honolulu forecast office. Coursework in meteorology, climatology, physics, and mathematics was identified in the vacancy announcement as relevant to the position, as was meteorology experience. James Kahakua, a native Hawaiian, proudly possessed years of experience in meteorology, and a Bachelor of Science degree with coursework in all of the areas identified in the announcement. He applied for a promotion to the open position, but was turned down in favor of a "haole"—or white—newcomer to Hawaii. A speech consultant had rated Kahakua's Creole-tinged speech unacceptable for weather broadcasts. The white applicant had no college degree, and minimal experience in meteorology. He was selected because of his "excellent" broadcasting voice. Kahakua, along with other applicants who felt that the promotion of a neophyte constituted discrimination, sued the Weather Service and lost.

* * *

The district judge, a visitor from Fresno, found that race was not a factor in the promotion. The white candidate was selected because he had "better diction, better enunciation, better pronunciation, better cadence, better intonation, better voice clarity, and better understandability." The judge credited the testimony of speech experts that "standard English is that used by radio and TV announcers" and that "standard English pronunciation should be used by radio broadcasters." The court added, "there is no race or physiological reason why Kahakua could not have used standard English pronunciations." The judge discounted the testimony of the linguist who stated that Hawaiian Creole pronunciation is not incorrect, rather it is one of the many varieties of pronunciation of standard English. The linguist, the judge stated, was not an expert in speech.

C. *More Stories, More Voices*

In 1988, A. L. Hahn, a young Korean American, ran for city council in Santa Clara, California. The editorial page of the San Jose Mercury News, an award-winning California newspaper, recommended against voting for Hahn, in spite of the paper's general agreement with Hahn on the issues. This seemed odd in an editorial that welcomed change and opened with criticism of the "old guard" of "powerful insiders," arguing against candidates with established real estate and institutional ties. Why would a pro-change editor reject a bright newcomer? The editorial stated:

> *We like Hahn, 34, who was born in South Korea and whose positions on controlling growth are much like our own. Unfortunately, we think his heavy accent and somewhat limited contacts would make it difficult for him to be a councilman.*

* * *

III. THE DOCTRINAL PUZZLE OF ACCENT AND ANTIDISCRIMINATION LAW

This is the doctrinal puzzle presented by these stories:

1. Title VII absolutely disallows discrimination on the basis of race and national origin.

2. A fortiori, Title VII absolutely disallows discrimination on the basis of traits, like accent, when they are stand-ins for race and national origin.

3. Title VII absolutely allows employers to discriminate on the basis of job ability.

4. Communication, and therefore accent, employers will insist, are elements of job ability.

The puzzle in accent cases is that accent is often derivative of race and national origin. Only Filipino people speak with Filipino accents. Yet, within the range of employer prerogatives, it is reasonable to require communication skills of employees. The claim that accent impedes job ability is often made with both sincerity and economic rationality. How, then, should Title VII squeeze between the walls of accent as protected trait and speech as job requirement?

This puzzle is evident in every reported case considering accent and Title VII. The courts recognize that discrimination against a trait that is a stand-in for a protected category is prohibited. An employer who says, "I'm not discriminating against people of color, I just don't want to hire people with dark skin," is in violation of Title VII. The EEOC has found that discrimination against an accent associated with foreign birth is the equivalent of discrimination against foreign birth, relying in part on evidence that it is nearly impossible for an adult to eliminate their natural accent. Even the skilled mimics of new accents frequently overcorrect. That is, they blanketly apply stereotypical traits of the acquired accent, even in circumstances in which native speakers would drop the trait. To acquire natural, unself-conscious, and native-sounding speech with a new accent is a feat accomplished easily only by young children, who are still in the process of language acquisition. Given this near-immutability, discrimination against accent is the functional equivalent of discrimination against foreign origin.

* * *

A second complicating factor is the role of speech in the job. In some jobs—say a 911 operator—speech is a critical and central job function. In other jobs, such as a bricklayer or a graphic artist, speech is helpful but not central to the work. In some cases the employer may want a certain accent because of its prestige value—say a French accent in a French restaurant. The range of reasons for wanting speech clarity will vary with the range of jobs.

* * *

Given the pervasive, unconscious bias against low-status accents, it is reasonable to inquire of employers exactly what they mean when they declare an accent nonfunctional for the job. If they mean consciously or unconsciously "I don't like foreign sounds and neither will my customers," they are arguing that discrimination is a justification for discrimination. This kind of tautology is obviously insufficient to surmount Title VII's prohibition against discrimination.

* * *

IV. WHAT IS SPEECH?

* * *

B. *What is Accent?*

Accent, as used in this Article, refers to pronunciation rather than choice of words. A linguist might break down the lay concept of accent into smaller components of phonology, including intonation, stress, and rhythm. While this Article focuses on accent, much of the analysis is also relevant to dialect, or word choice. There are many dialects of English, some more prestigious than others, providing many opportunities for discrimination.

As feminist theorists have pointed out, everyone has a gender, but the hidden norm in law is male. As critical race theorists have pointed out, everyone has a race, but the hidden norm in law is white. In any dyadic relationship, the two ends are equidistant from each other. If the parties are equal in power, we see them as equally different from each other. When the parties are in a relationship of domination and subordination we tend to say that the dominant is normal, and the subordinate is different from normal.

And so it is with accent. Everyone has an accent, but when an employer refuses to hire a person "with an accent," they are referring to a hidden norm of non-accent—a linguistic impossibility, but a socially constructed reality. People in power are perceived as speaking normal, unaccented English. Any speech that is different from that constructed norm is called an accent.

The unstated norm—the so-called standard American accent—is an odd choice for a norm, because only a minority of citizens speak it. Most speakers of North American English have an accent that reflects their regional affiliations, their ethnicity, or their age. An odd recent phenomenon, the geographically dispersed, upper-middle-class, youth-based accent known as "valley" or "sunbelt-speak" is heard increasingly among law students across the country. Because I grew up in a world in which accents tended to attach to races, it seems odd to me as a teacher to hear my students of different races speaking in this new, youth-based accent. (They might characterize a racist decision, for example, as "ruhley" unfair or "see-oh" ridiculous.)

If almost no one speaks with standard pronunciation—or, as they call it in Great Britain, "received pronunciation"—the claim that standardization is important for comprehension loses some force. Variability is the master rule of spoken North American English, and if variability impedes comprehension, then we are already living in the tower of Babel.

We are not. We understand each other, particularly when we are motivated to do so. One of the interesting lessons of sociolinguistics is that comprehension is as much a function of attitude as it is of variability. Human beings can and do adjust to marked variation in pitch, intonation, and pronunciation in ways that scores of computer engineers working in the fields of fuzzy logic and artificial intelligence have been unable to duplicate. The seemingly simple ability of a tiny child to recognize its own name whether spoken at Mom's pitch or at Dad's, is in actuality a complex feat of comprehension. The magnificent switchboard that converts sound to understanding in the human mind can account for gaps, pauses, variations, and distortions of many kinds.

Thus a twentieth-century North American can listen to the long-dead accents in a Shakespeare play and—after perhaps a moment of disorientation—soon follow the dialogue with ease. A traveler to a new region of English-speakers, after a sometimes hilarious miscue, will understand more and more of the local speech, especially if motivated by the need to get a bite to eat or a moment of human company. We have all, at various times, performed the miracle of comprehension across a vast sea of phonological difference.

The ability to comprehend across variations is accompanied by a clumsy inability to alter speech across variations. Most of us feel noticeably uncomfortable and phony when we try to imitate other accents, and few succeed at the task of acquiring a permanent, unself-conscious, new accent.

When the Beatles were an unknown Liverpool band trying to make it in the new world of rock and roll, they inserted "R's" in their pronunciation in order to sound more American. As the British invasion captured the fancy of young whites in America, it became more acceptable to sound British. By the time the Beatles hit superstar status, they had reverted to the "R" dropping that characterized their working class, British backgrounds. The Sergeant Pepper album—which established the Beatles as musicians destined to go down in popular history as more than just another pretty band—is notably authentic in its "R"-lessness.

Meanwhile, back in the midwest, U.S.A.—land of "R" pronunciation so abundant it appears even in words like "wash"—a young white musician named Bob Dylan regularly dropped "R's" in his singing. He did this not because he wanted to sound British, but because he wanted to sound like his idols—the African Americans who regularly dropped "R's" in their creation of the indigenous American art form known as the blues. The boys from Liverpool had made a characteristic imitator's error of overcorrection. In adding R's prodigiously to their early recordings they ended up sounding more like Pat Boone than like their African American inspiration, Little Richard. Bob Dylan, more sophisticated in his understanding of "R" usage in the United States, knew that in the world of contemporary American music, status moved south in more ways than one. Sounding Black, sounding down in the power hierarchy, sounding blue, was the definition of cool among the truly down, downtown, non-"R" pronouncers.

The view of most sociolinguists, grounded as they are in the field of anthropology, is that accent is a societal and cultural creation. It situates people socially and helps them sort through social contexts. Most of us do this unconsciously—we speak differently at work, at play, to children, to authority figures.

Sitting on my porch in Honolulu one day, I was talking long distance to my friend Barb in California. Because I lived in L.A. as a child, it's easy for me to shift into a voice that matches hers when we talk. Shifting closer in accent to someone we like is a common signal of intimacy. As we spoke, the newspaper girl, a thirteen-year-old Tongan-Samoan immigrant, walked by and I called out a friendly greeting and asked her a question.

"Oh, how cute, you're talking local," Barb said over the phone. I laughed, because I hadn't realized I had made a shift, but Barb recognized the melodic, inquiring intonation of "local" Hawaii talk that was so absent when I was speaking to an L.A. friend. Because she has lived in Hawaii and liked it, the accent had a good connotation for her.

Accents sometimes charm us with difference. Barb and I both laugh over the accent of the man who cuts our hair. His is a marked Italian accent, sometimes incomprehensible to both of us. In the West L.A. shop where he works, his accent adds the cachet of difference that recalls an old

Beverly Hills joke about the patient who refused a local anesthetic, insisting instead on the imported.

At other times accents can repel us. In that same West L.A. salon, I overheard a beautiful stylist complaining to a client in Brooklynese, "I can't stand the way I talk, it sounds so low class." Media stereotyping can make some accents sound ignorant or threatening. These evaluations are imposed, not natural. As much as we may believe that certain accents "just sound better" or "sound so harsh," our judgments are mediated judgments. The evidence suggests there is no such thing as an inherently pleasant accent. What sounds "low-class, vulgar, rough" in one culture can sound "interesting, pretty" to someone from another culture unfamiliar with the status position of the accent.

I cling to certain notions of accent attitudes as pure and not culturally generated. I am fond of saying that the Hawaiian language sounds beautiful, as though this were absolutely true rather than true to my ears, in relation to the English I am used to, and in connection with my knowledge of the generous, loving aspects of Hawaiian culture that infuse the language. Similarly, I am fond of saying that a particular person has a beautiful voice or a sexy voice as though that were absolutely true, rather than true as a convocation of Hollywood, Madison Avenue, Motown, and my own desires.

We want to believe, when we say of an accent that it is good, or bad, or easy, or difficult, that we are speaking of facts rather than social constructions. Facts, especially when the alternative conclusion is that our evaluations are produced by bigotry or our own feelings of fear and inadequacy.

While the sociolinguists tell us that accent is a social phenomenon, some experts in the field called "speech" or "communications" hold quite a different view. Books on accents are typically found in two separate places in the libraries: under Sociolinguistics and under Speech Pathology. In the Speech Pathology section, accent is considered a disease in need of a cure. There, chapters on accent are side-by-side with chapters on stuttering and aphasia. Rather than seeing accent as a social phenomenon marking speakers as equidistant from each other, the speech pathology view sees an "accent" as an unfortunate deviation from a standard. This deviation is at once labeled disease and declared curable with a series of exercises and manipulations. This view persists in spite of the evidence that eliminating one's native accent is nearly impossible for most adults.

The presumption behind the speech pathology view is that variability is harmful, both for the speaker and the community. Private accent-elimination classes now exist in some cities to help immigrants sound "less foreign." Speech consultants help employers pick "good" voices. In the *Kahakua* case, the employer's speech consultant discussed the joys of eradicating an ethnic accent in almost sexual tones. Writing of one Japanese American candidate, she stated:

> [H]e needs specific help in the area of developing good speech habits through deleting "pidgin" from his daily vocabulary in order to

insure that Standard English can become his automatic model. This will take disciplined work by means of professional help, but he should make every effort to receive such help. It is my belief that he would experience a most gratifying surge of renewed self-confidence and pride in his accomplishment.

* * *

The language of "control" and "handicap" is typical of the speech pathology view. In referring to the accent as "pidgin" the speech consultant shows unfamiliarity with linguistic terminology. Pidgin is a broken English that is spoken by non-native speakers. Neither speaker evaluated in the passages above was speaking pidgin when evaluated. Both were lifelong, native speakers of English. They were reading a weather report written in standard English. The horrible handicap, subject to control through disciplined study, was simply the local accent native to most non-whites who grow up in Hawaii.

The linguist's evaluation of speakers in the *Kahakua* case differed notably from the speech consultant's. The linguist found that both speakers used an acrolectal variety of Hawaiian Standard English. That is, their speech was quite close to standard mainland pronunciation with certain phonological features characteristic of Hawaiian Creole speakers, such as occasional substitution of the "d" sound for the "th" sound.

The linguist concluded that both speakers

speak what a large portion of Hawaiian-born, educated, professional people (e.g. the governor and most state legislators) speak: Hawaii Standard English ... both use an acrolectal and highly intelligible English. The HCE [Hawaiian Creole English] features that are observable are phonetic ones that do mark their identity as non-Caucasians, however, they are not accurately viewed as linguistic deficiencies of any kind. Just as one would not fault the southern accent of former President Jimmy Carter or Jim Lehrer (of the McNeil/Lehrer News Hour)....

The linguist thus viewed the accents as acceptable and intelligible, while the speech consultant viewed them as handicaps in need of correction. The linguist's view is supported by research that shows that language variability is inevitable and that moderate accent differences rarely impede communication when listeners are motivated and nonprejudiced. The speech consultant's view is supported by a widely held belief that speech standardization is necessary, good, and attainable, and that accent interferes with intelligibility.

* * *

V.   TOWARD A DOCTRINAL RECONSTRUCTION

* * *

This doctrinal framework is not intended as a complete guide to the intricacies of Title VII as applied to accent cases. Title VII is one of the most litigated of all federal statutes, and the many significant nuances of Title VII litigation are beyond the scope of this piece. Rather, the intent here is to suggest the critical areas of inquiry that must be part of the analysis of any Title VII accent case, and to suggest why and how a conscientious court would conduct such inquiry.

I suggest that courts should consider four separate questions in accent cases:

1. What level of communication is required for the job?

2. Was the candidate's speech fairly evaluated?

3. Is the candidate intelligible to the pool of relevant, nonprejudiced listeners, such that job performance is not unreasonably impeded?

4. What accommodations are reasonable given the job and any limitations in intelligibility?

* * *

A. *Step One: The Level of Communication Required for the Job*

There are many jobs that people do in silence. In some work places, the level of industrial noise is so high that conversation is impossible. Jobs that rely on visual, manual, and intellectual skills have traditionally comprised the employment of the deaf. The deaf, however, are proving that even jobs that require regular communication can be done by individuals with little or no speech. Our assumption that speech is integral to a job may reflect "hearie" bias.

There are some jobs, however, in which speech is central. Broadcasters and telephone operators, for example, regularly use speech in their jobs.

* * *

The paradigmatic job requiring maximum oral clarity is the 911 operator. Several elements mark the importance of speech in that position:

1. The consequences of miscommunication are grave.

2. Giving and receiving oral communication are a substantial part of the job.

3. The speech interactions are under high stress, where time is of the essence, increasing probability of miscommunication.

4. The interactions are typically one-time calls, such that the caller has little time to adjust in listening and comprehension patterns.

If one or more of these elements is absent, the degree of importance of speech decreases. For example, if time is not of the essence, but clarity of communication is important to avoid grave consequences, forms of communication other than speech—such as writing—may be more appropriate. If interactions are repeated, such that listeners can adjust, again a difference in speech style becomes less of a barrier. Consider, for example, the way in which the regulars at a pier-side fish auction can understand an auctioneer's rapid-fire babble, while newcomers find it incomprehensible.

As one moves farther away from the 911 paradigm, there are a range of jobs in which facility in oral communication is useful but not critical if other job skills are present. Computer programmers, word processors, janitors, dancers, assembly line workers, parking lot attendants, architects, and laboratory technicians, for example, all fall somewhere between the polar opposites of "speech is critical" and "speech is inconsequential."

* * *

In a range of jobs in which speech seems critical—doctor, bank teller, police officer, teacher, lawyer—consideration of the actual job tasks and needs of patients/customers/clients is useful. Is "bedside manner" the equivalent of oral facility? Not necessarily. Some very articulate doctors have weak skills in empathy. Care, concern, and understanding are communicated by nonspeech—posture, eye contact, touch, and taking the time to listen—as well as speech.

* * *

The principle that there are gradations of communication skills required in different jobs was recognized by the Ninth Circuit Court of Appeals in *Nanty v. Barrows*. In that case, the employer refused to hire Mr. Nanty, a Native American, for a job as a furniture mover, claiming, among other things, that Nanty was "inarticulate." That claim alone, without any evidence of why articulate speech was essential for the job, was unpersuasive to the court. The applicant was an experienced furniture mover. The court was suspicious of the claim that Mr. Nanty was inarticulate, especially given the fact that the employer had not even conducted an interview. An employer who is serious about the necessity for oral communication will have some job screening mechanism that rationally measures oral skills. The next section discusses applicant screening and fair evaluation.

B. *Step Two: Fair Evaluation*

An employer who claims speech is a critical job function, but who does not fairly evaluate speech of candidates, is behaving irrationally, or discriminatorily, or both. As Justice Rehnquist suggested in the *Furnco* case, we reasonably presume that economic entities act rationally. When they do not—when they prefer less-qualified applicants, for example—it is probable that prejudice is entering into the process. Evaluation of accent is particularly susceptible to bias and distortion, and thus it is appropriate for courts to examine the evaluation process.

* * *

When we hear a different voice we are likely to devalue it, particularly when it triggers the collective xenophobic unconscious that is the ironic legacy of a nation populated largely by people from other continents. Because misevaluation of speech, and particularly of speech associated with historical targets of discrimination, is common, claims that accent impedes job performance are not credible unless they stem from fair evaluation. An informal answer-a-few-questions interview is less reliable than an evaluation of on-the-job performance, whether simulated or actual. Rather than assuming an accent would be unintelligible over the phone, for example, a candidate might be asked to complete an actual or simulated phone call to see whether breakdowns in communication occur.

Similarly, evaluations that rely on subjective impressions of untrained interviewers are less credible. Interviewers and others making employment decisions can be trained to avoid accent bias. The State of California, for example, has produced a training manual that explains in simple language the danger of bias and prejudice in evaluation of accents.

> * * *

C.   *Step Three: Comprehension by the Relevant, Nonprejudiced Listener at the Level Required for the Job*

If the employer fairly evaluates the speaker, and if speech is an important job function, then it is reasonable to reject a speaker whose accent impedes intelligibility by the relevant, nonprejudiced listener.

> * * *

In public contact jobs, the listener pool is identifiable by region and demography. A bank teller, for example, generally serves clientele from within one city. Having a regional accent, when most of one's clients are from the same region, can enhance rather than impede communication. The point here is that intelligibility is not absolute. It is relational. To whom we speak determines whether our accent helps or hurts communication.

> * * *

The testimony of experts familiar with speech interactions in the relevant listener pool is thus entitled to considerable weight in meeting the plaintiff's burden of persuasion. In the *Kahakua* case, the speech pathologist who declared the Creole-accented speech substandard was not from Hawaii, nor did she purport to speak from knowledge of the relevant listener pool. Instead, she used a generic "broadcasting" standard to conclude that a white candidate's accent was superior.

The plaintiff's expert was a linguist whose field of expertise was speech interactions within the relevant listener pool. She testified that the local-accented speech of the plaintiffs was easily intelligible to *all* residents of Hawaii, including white newcomers, and that for the majority of residents who themselves have some level of a local accent, communication was enhanced by speech in that accent.

The court in *Kahakua* apparently applied the speech pathologist's generic standard, rather than the linguist's contextualized standard. The problem with the court's approach is that it imposes a standard on the community without any rationale for choosing the standard. It is not a majoritarian standard, since most Americans speak with an ethnic or regional accent. It is not an intelligibility standard, because there is no evidence that there is a generic accent that is always more intelligible than any other accent in a given listener pool.

The hidden rationale thus becomes a nationalist/monocultural one. That is, holding people in a nation as radically diverse in accents as ours to one standard of pronunciation is a declaration that this is a nation of one voice. In the same way that some insist ours is a Christian nation with Christianity the norm against which all other religions are seen as different, the fiction of a generic American accent implies that this is a white, upper-class nation, and all non-white, ethnic, regional, and lower-class accents are subnormal. Rather than imagining a fictional generic listener, the unbiased court would look to the actual listeners.

* * *

D. *Rejecting the Gift: The Problem of the Prejudiced Listener*

What should we do when members of the relevant listener pool are prejudiced and can't or won't tolerate an accent? In applying Step 3 above, the principles of Title VII require removing prejudiced listeners from analysis of the relevant listener pool.

It is well established under Title VII that bigoted preferences of customers, however real and economically effective, may not govern employment decisions. Even when employers can prove that they will lose customers who prefer not to do business with women, for example, Title VII requires employers to hire qualified women. By holding all employers to this nondiscriminatory standard, Title VII intervenes in the market and disallows an economic advantage to those employers who are otherwise eager to accede to the racist or sexist demands of customers. Title VII was designed to alter business practices in order to eliminate racism and sexism as a factor in hiring, promotion, and setting conditions of work.

* * *

The claim that customers will refuse to do business with employees with ethnic accents raises two problems. First is the problem that customer preference claims are often made without empirical foundation, reflecting false assumptions about the inability of customers to comprehend certain accents. Given the linguistic evidence that comprehension adjustments are relatively easy for motivated listeners, claims of customer preference, at a minimum, should be supported by some evidence of actual refusal to deal.

At the second level is the problem of actual prejudice. Certain accents, to certain listeners, sound "untrustworthy," for example, regardless of the sincerity of the speaker. An employer concerned with establishing customer confidence might be tempted to exclude from the workplace ethnic accents that key customers find untrustworthy. This is not allowed under Title VII. A particular accent sounds untrustworthy, or lazy, or ignorant to a listener when the listener has attached a cultural meaning, typically a racist cultural meaning, to the accent. In matched guise tests, linguists have shown that these cultural meanings rather than any combination of pronunciation or inflection, create the negative impression. Under the matched guise method, listeners hear tapes of the same words spoken by an actor using different accents. The listeners are not told that one person is acting out the different accents. They are then asked to evaluate what they assume are different speakers for qualities such as intelligence, confidence, trustworthiness, and warmth. The use of the same text and same speaker eliminates the role of personality traits or voice quality of the speaker in evaluation. The subjects are also tested separately to determine what racial stereotypes and prejudices they harbor. In repeated studies of this type, there is a high correlation between negative stereotyping of certain races and negative evaluation of accents associated with those races. The listener who thinks X people are lazy will evaluate a speaker with an X accent as lazy. Listeners can even internalize stereotypes about themselves. Members of subordinated groups in one study evaluated speakers of their own accent as "less intelligent" and "more warm" indicating in-group loyalties, as well as internalization of dominant group stereotypes about intellect.

* * *

E. *Step Four: Can the Employee Be Understood with Reasonable Accommodation of Linguistic Difference?*

To determine whether prejudice rather than unintelligibility motivates linguistic discrimination, it is useful to ask whether the employer can make reasonable changes in the workplace that would increase communication within the relevant listener pool. The concept of reasonable accommodation is well developed in the law governing employment of the differently-abled. It asks not that employers go broke in order to accommodate physical differences. Rather, it asks that employers make those alterations which are either costless or impose costs that, while they may cut into short-term returns, will have the long-term benefit of bringing qualified handicapped individuals into the labor force. Wheelchair ramps, braille in elevators, and grab-bars in restroom stalls are all accommodations we have grown accustomed to in recent years. We have made a collective decision that the costs, while not inconsequential, are reasonable in light of the benefits gained.

* * *

There are several specific inquiries that help separate legitimate communication difficulty from biased evaluation. First, as discussed above, expert witnesses can help in identifying the relevant, nonprejudiced listeners, and in determining whether the accent discrepancies are so divergent as to impede communication. Second, accommodations, including assistance to both speakers and listeners in bridging communication gaps, help show that any residual non-understanding reflects a genuine, irremediable intelligibility problem. Finally, the court can inquire into the level of prejudice against the accent. If the accent is one historically subjected to discrimination, for example, this cautions particular scrutiny and special efforts at accommodation in order to avoid the probability of biased evaluations. Again, experts are useful in determining whether there is a demonstrable history of prejudice against a particular accent, and in identifying kinds of phonological differences that actually do impede comprehension.

* * *

G. *Application*

How would the doctrinal reconstruction suggested above apply to the facts of the existing cases? This section will suggest briefly the ways in which the framework of inquiry presented in this Article would have altered the outcome in cases like *Fragante* and *Kahakua*.

1. Fragante *Reconsidered*

* * * The evaluation of *Fragante* was shoddy. Given the care and effort put into the civil service examination process, the cursory interview by untrained office workers seems an irrational allocation of resources. The interviewers who found Fragante's accent "difficult" did not identify any incidences of misunderstanding during the interview. The lack of standard interview questions, the irrationality of the rating sheet, and the absence in the interview process of training or instruction in either speech assessment or the obligation of nondiscrimination, reveal a weak system of evaluation. This weakness is unjustified given the size and the resources of the employer, and the regular turnover in the job. Significantly, the evaluation process did not include a functional component. That is, Fragante's speech was never tested in a real or simulated job setting. There was no evidence other than presumption that Fragante could not communicate with customers at the DMV.

* * *

The trial judge, as well as the employer's interviewers, found Fragante's accent "difficult." There is no distinction in the trial court opinion between "difficult" meaning "foreign, unusual, a strain on my ears because it is not how most people I know talk," and intelligibility at the level necessary to perform job tasks. The failure to make this critical distinction would, at a minimum, require a remand for clarification. The only legitimate inquiry, given the Title VII rule of nondiscrimination, is whether the speaker can communicate at the level required for the job.

The Ninth Circuit opinion in *Fragante* fails to make this distinction. The court found that there was no proof of discriminatory pretext and that the individuals selected in lieu of Fragante "had superior qualifications." The only "superior qualification" on record is speaking without a Filipino accent. The opinion seems to allow the employer to select a favored accent in lieu of a "foreign" accent. If the intent of the court is to prohibit accent discrimination, clarification is required on this point. The court should state unequivocally that once a person's speech is found functional, the employer may not reject it because a competitor's speech is "less foreign."

* * *

Finally, if the courts had considered the possibility of reasonable accommodation, they might well have altered their ultimate conclusions in *Fragante*. If, as the employer claims, customers are frequently frustrated and confused when they visit the DMV, perhaps there are other alterations to procedures, written information, and staffing, that could ease this burden. If a Filipino accent will "turn off" some listeners, those listeners could, perhaps, be directed to another line, or they could ask for a slower repetition of instructions.

* * *

VII. ACCENT AND ANTISUBORDINATION: A RADICAL CRITIQUE

This Article is written out of contradiction, and this part enters the theoretical world that sees contradiction at the core of meaning in life and law. The contradiction in this Article, the irony of it, is that a self-conscious radical, schooled in the postmodern world, argues from cases, rules, and principles for a result that she sees as liberating. That same system of cases, rules, and principles has enslaved and excluded, taken lives and stilled dissent. That same system of cases, rules, and principles has entrenched ideas of objectivity, neutrality, necessity, and right that have made enslavement, exclusion, murder, and oligarchy seem natural and inevitable. These are the teachings of the feminists, critical legal scholars, and critical race scholars who are the voices of dissent in the world of legal theory. These critical voices constitute the community of scholar-activists whom I consider my colleagues in a most-serious quest for a just world. This part is my tribute to them.

It looks at accent discrimination from within that critical world, to try to understand what is really going on in accent cases, and to suggest an explicitly political justification for the doctrinal position set forth above. If the doctrinal section was "do the logical thing," and the preceding section was "do the liberal thing," I add now, not in jest and not because I reject either logic or liberalism, a section to plead, "do the right thing." This Article is an attempt to do legal scholarship using the tools of critical legal analysis. The method of the following sections follows a pattern emerging within such scholarship:

— First, it attempts to unmask false claims of objectivity, merit, neutrality, and necessity in the rhetoric of accent cases;

— Second, it examines the context of power in which accent cases arise, and draws from an emerging phenomenonology of subordination to understand how accent discrimination fits into broader social, historical, and psychological structures of subordination;

— Third, it is explicit, partisan, and non-neutral in its commitment to the ends of dismantling structures of subordination and promoting radical pluralism;

— Fourth, it understands doctrinal puzzles concerning accent and Title VII as cites of contestation with both ideological and material consequences; and

— Finally, it employs a strategy of legal analysis designed to promote both reformist and radical agendas by exploiting existing tensions in civil rights law. More specifically, by delineating a fair and logical application of Title VII doctrine to accent cases, I hope to affect three constituencies:

a. Readers—including judges, lawyers, possible litigants, and legal theorists of goodwill—who are committed to the values I draw upon in this Article but who are unclear about how or whether those values should apply in accent cases;

b. Activists and theorists seeking to form and critique strategies for radical social change; and

c. Gatekeepers of the established order, whom I hope to reveal as self-interested and politically motivated should they choose to reject a logical argument for accent egalitarianism.

A. *Accent and the Critique of Objectivity*

Which accent is seen as normal, intelligent, most-likely-to-succeed, is a function of power distribution. Thus the key inquiry in understanding accent cases is "what are the power distributions." Attempting to apply Title VII without asking that question is what allows courts to suggest that employers can pick the best accent out of many, without seeing that "best" points up the racial hierarchy. Unmasking the hidden center reveals accent evaluation for what it is: an exercise in power.

Seeing accent evaluation as an exercise of power helps refute the typical justifications for excluding or repressing certain accents, which include:

1. *The inherent superiority of the standard accent.* The claim here is that the standard accent is more pure, more eloquent, more expressive, more valuable.

2. *The universality of the standard accent.* Most people speak it and everyone understands it, therefore it is reasonably designated the national standard.

3. *Standardization is efficient.* Even if the standard is somewhat arbitrary, having a standard increases communication among diverse speakers. It reduces misunderstanding and saves time.

4. *The standard is unifying.* Having a standard helps forge a national identity and avoids the balkanizing disarray that comes with language variation.

The concept of positioned perspective, developed by feminists and critical race theorists, and the critique of neutrality associated with Foucault and the critical legal theorists, rejects the idea of a universal measure of accent quality. Add to this critique the empirical work of sociolinguists, and the argument that standard pronunciation is inherently superior and universal disappears. While most people in power speak the standard, the critical technique of challenging false norms as creations of power helps show how the seemingly absolute universality of standard pronunciation is actually an imposed universality.

This leaves the final two arguments of efficiency and unity. The argument that uniformity is efficient presumes that uniformity is attainable and that variability impedes communication. Both claims are historically and empirically false. Uniformity never has been and by all indications never will be the reality of spoken English. Language is a living, moving thing. Linguistic geographers show this graphically in an obscure but fascinating form of cartography that charts the journeys of words and pronunciation over space and time. The names we call things by are born, expand outward gathering more speakers of those names, and die, as other names take over. The word "orts" for scraps of garbage traveled from England to Massachusetts in the time of the colonies, where it thrived and then faded until only one informant in Bar Harbor and one in New Bedford could tell field researchers what it meant. Similarly, "standard pronunciation" varies both regionally in our time and historically over time. The teachers of "correct enunciation" of fifty years ago would hang their heads in sorrow over what passes for correct on Cable News Network today.

* * *

B. *What Fear Is This? Accent and the Culture of Domination*

* * *

When certain accents are deemed inappropriate for the workplace, for political life, for use in schools and boardrooms, a policing of public and private boundaries occurs. Who may speak, when, and where, is a typical mechanism for distributing power. Who is competent to testify in court, who may speak at political meetings, who is an expert authority—answers to these questions stand at the border between the public realm of power and the private realm of the personal.

As it has become increasingly unacceptable to deny public speech on the basis of race or gender, accent becomes a significant means of maintaining boundaries. The recent push for English-only laws, and the attack on bilingual education, may represent new outlets for racial anxiety now that many traditional outlets are denied. The angry insistence that "they" should speak English serves as a proxy for a whole range of fears displaced by the social opprobrium directed at explicit racism.

* * *

Accents thus construct social boundaries, and social boundaries reinforce accents. The circumstances that perpetuate accents—including residential segregation, tracking systems in schools, and social distancing—are socially created. In distributing social standing according to accent, we distribute according to accents we have, in part, created.

* * *

C. *Producing Counter-Ideology: Antisubordination Strategies in Law*

* * *

Progressive legal theorists seek to include antisubordination ideology in the law through such strategies as affirmative action, reparations, and restriction of hate speech. All of these legal positions recognize that ours is a non-neutral world in which legal attention to past and present injustice requires rules that work against the flood of structural subordination.

Anyone who has swum against the tide knows that it requires effort. Staying still means moving backward.

The accent cases illustrate some of what we know about subordination. We know that subordination has material and ideological dimensions. In the case of accent, the material dimensions include the real denial of life chances: jobs, housing, and educational opportunity may depend on talking the right way. Whether one can speak persuasively before the law—before a police officer or a judge or a legislature or a jury—may determine life or death, freedom or jail, protection or neglect. The ideological dimension of accent discrimination is the creation and maintenance of a belief system that sees some as worthy and others as unworthy based on accent, such that disparities in wealth and power are naturalized.

* * *

Immutability arguments feed into this hierarchical ideology. In arguing for accent tolerance, the rationale of accent as immutable is thus a dangerous one. A more progressive argument is that even if accent is changeable, no citizen should have to alter core parts of identity in order to participate in society. A true antisubordination agenda would apply reasonable accommodation to all differences, whether chosen or immutable, that are historically subject to exploitation or oppression by dominant groups.

In arguing that Title VII should prohibit accent discrimination, the more powerful justification is a notion of radical pluralism, not a notion of charitable concern for the immutably afflicted. Indeed, I am coming to see the antisubordination principle and the radical pluralism principle as necessarily linked.

D. *Accent and Radical Pluralism*

* * *

If language is the nest of culture, and cultural diversity is an absolute good, than linguistic tolerance is a legitimate end of the law. Saying this raises questions of how radical pluralism will work in practice as our imaginations call up much that is ugly when we speak of pluralism, including bitter cultural clashes and domination disguised as cultural expression, to name two.

* * *

In summary, the antisubordination rationale for accent tolerance suggests a radically pluralistic re-visioning of national identity. The only center, the only glue, that makes us a nation is our many-centered cultural heritage. Just as our use of language is rich, varied, interactive, and changeable, so is our national culture. We are the only country in which an Okinawan vendor serves Kosher pastrami and stir-fried vegetables wrapped in a tortilla to young white punk rockers at 3:00 a.m. in the morning. We are the only country in which a white child sleeps blissfully under a quilt lovingly stitched by his aunt, emblazoned with a life-sized portrait of an African American basketball star. We are the only country in which a group of parents planning a little league fundraiser around a transvestite beauty contest would call the ACLU to defend their right to use a public park for the event, and convince a mayor named Hannibal Tavares to change his mind about a permit. From the oversized plaster chickens and donuts that mark our highways to the exquisite wisps of nouvelle Franco-Latin-Japanese cuisine set before our expense-account diners, we are a nation fantastic and wide-ranging in our vernacular and our juxtapositions. From the Grand Ole Opry to neo-metal, from zydeco to the Met, we are a range of tastes and sounds wider than ever before known to the nations of this planet. That is the defining centrality of the American culture I grew up in and love: a broad and delightfully incongruous coming together of difference. In acknowledging plural culture as a strength, and in recognizing and dismantling the false hierarchies that place one culture over another, it may come to pass that we live together in celebration and peace.

E. *To Save Our Own Souls: Law for the Last Reconstruction*

Throughout this Article, I have written to persuade readers of good will to adopt legal rules and ethical positions that promote linguistic pluralism. I have used existing legal doctrine, traditional liberal theory, and new critical theories in this effort. This eclecticism might seem as odd as the kosher burrito and as dangerous as the Ku Klux Klan to those who see impassioned pleas for favored constituencies and eclectic borrowing from many traditions as unprincipled and undisciplined. I believe the antisubordination principle is a principle, and that it can inform our law in a way that is as principled and as disciplined as the ideas of property, equality, and due process that are our constitutional legacy. I have tried to show that accent discrimination is rooted in a culture of dominance fundamentally at odds with the creed of this nation—at odds both with the Enlightenment ideals of liberalism that attended our national birth and the ideal of antisubordination that has constituted the core of our defining struggles against slavery, against fascism, against Jim Crow.

* * *

In suggesting a reconstructed interpretation of Title VII that responds to both liberal and radical critiques, I intended to suggest a model of what law can be and what lawyers can do to work toward justice. The great legal historians of our time have said of Americans that they are users of law. They use it, they believe in it, they constructed a nation around it. Law is part of our culture and it is, therefore, a place to begin in making the changes we need to make.

* * *

VIII. EPILOGUE: VOICES OF AMERICA

* * *

In recounting the tale of the world's many languages coming to America, I have not forgotten that the journey was often hard. We lost most of our native American languages, as we lost their speakers, in a dark part of our history. Also in darkness, the round sounds of West African languages came to America in the bellies of slave ships. Out of pain and poverty, waves of immigrants came from all corners of the earth. Refugees from war came, survivors of persecution came, all came with their tongues and palates shaping newly-learned English words in ways that echoed their years in other places. That is the American accent, the multiplicity of sound bearing the history of our nation, bearing the struggle of its many-voiced people.

NOTES AND QUESTIONS

1.   Differences in accents. In her discussion of the accent and the anti-subordination principle, Matsuda argues that the unequal evaluation of differences in accents is directly linked to the frame work of racism and ethnic power relationships. Do you have an accent? What is your accent? Is your accent associated with power and authority in our settings? Consider the complaint of a mafia member's child who was in the witness protection program from New Jersey, to Salt Lake City, then Seattle, and asked to "blend in."

2.   Preference of some accents to others. Matsuda discusses minorities who were discriminated against for having accents. But she also distinguishes between minority accents and those associated with Europeans. She writes that a plaintiff is most likely to be successful with:

> a slight trace of a European accent, but for the most part . . . has adopted the speech patterns associated vaguely with North American television newscasters. She is qualified in every other respect for a job that requires some basic communication ability. Speech, is not however, a major job function.

Matsuda, supra at 1351. This suggests that not all accents are created equal. As the case law demonstrates, a large number of the plaintiffs are members of minority groups. Is it safe to say that a Norwegian or Swedish person would be treated differently upon applying for a communication position than a Hispanic or Filipino? According to Sandra Del Valle, language and accent are not separate from national origin. Because of this, an accent easily marks minorities as the "other." *See* SANDRA DEL VALLE, LANGUAGE RIGHTS AND THE LAW IN THE UNITED STATES: FINDING OUR VOICES 144 (2003).

3.   Immutability of accents. Del Valle argues that accents are immutable traits. Foreigners, whether they are Hispanic, European, or Asian, will retain traces of their native origins and language. The immutable nature of accents suggests that it is not a choice when people speak with accents. So, why do courts regard accents differently than they do an Afro? In particular, courts have ruled that employees cannot prohibit Afros because they are an immutable trait of blacks. However, numerous courts have ruled that accents can validly eliminate job applicants from consideration. What concept lies within in the court's distinction? Del Valle asserts that regardless of how vital public speaking is to the position, whenever it is just a small component of the job, courts have allowed employers to eliminate candidates with accents without much debate or question.

4. Can Title VII and the Equal Employment Opportunity Commission interpretation be read as contradictory? As Del Valle argues, Title VII does not ban accent discrimination, but the EEOC bans discrimination based on "cultural or linguistic characteristics." Does that not ban accent discrimination? After all, accents stem from one's cultural background and constitute a linguistic characteristic.

5. The four-pronged test articulated by the Supreme Court in *McDonnell Douglas Corp. v. Green* is not always a clear cut indicator that discrimination can be successfully proven. The Court laid out these requirements to have a *prima facie* case of discrimination:

1. That the plaintiff belongs to a protected class;

2. That he or she applied and was qualified for the position sought or held;

3. That despite such qualifications, he or she was rejected or fired; and

4. that after his or her rejection, the position sought or terminated from either remained open and the employer continued to seek similarly qualified applicants or was filled by equally or less qualified individuals not of the protected group.

See 411 U.S. 792, 802 (1973). The fact that fulfilling the four-pronged test can be insufficient is exemplified by *Fragante*. The employer felt he spoke with a heavy, difficult to comprehend Filipino accent that would be difficult to understand. However, it was noted in court that the plaintiff was only asked to repeat his answer on two occasions. Matsuda, *supra* at 1338, n.28.

B. English-Only Rules

Garcia v. Spun Steak Co.

998 F.2d 1480 (9th Cir. 1993).

■ O'Scannlain, Circuit Judge, delivered the opinion of the court.

* * *

I

Spun Steak Company ("Spun Steak") is a California corporation that produces poultry and meat products in South San Francisco for wholesale distribution. Spun Steak employs thirty-three workers, twenty-four of whom are Spanish-speaking. Virtually all of the Spanish-speaking employees are Hispanic. While two employees speak no English, the others have varying degrees of proficiency in English. Spun Steak has never required job applicants to speak or to understand English as a condition of employment.

Approximately two-thirds of Spun Steak's employees are production line workers or otherwise involved in the production process. Appellees Garcia and Buitrago are production line workers; they stand before a conveyor belt, remove poultry or other meat products from the belt and place the product into cases or trays for resale. Their work is done individually. Both Garcia and Buitrago are fully bilingual, speaking both English and Spanish.

Appellee Local 115, United Food and Commercial Workers International Union, AFL–CIO ("Local 115"), is the collective bargaining agent representing the employees at Spun Steak.

Prior to September 1990, these Spun Steak employees spoke Spanish freely to their co-workers during work hours. After receiving complaints that some workers were using their bilingual capabilities to harass and to insult other workers in a language they could not understand, Spun Steak began to investigate the possibility of requiring its employees to speak only English in the workplace. Specifically, Spun Steak received complaints that Garcia and Buitrago made derogatory, racist comments in Spanish about two co-workers, one of whom is African-American and the other Chinese-American.

The company's president, Kenneth Bertelson, concluded that an English-only rule would promote racial harmony in the workplace. In addition, he concluded that the English-only rule would enhance worker safety because some employees who did not understand Spanish claimed that the use of Spanish distracted them while they were operating machinery, and would enhance product quality because the U.S.D.A. inspector in the plant spoke only English and thus could not understand if a product-related concern was raised in Spanish. Accordingly, the following rule was adopted:

> [I]t is hereafter the policy of this Company that only English will be spoken in connection with work. During lunch, breaks, and employees' own time, they are obviously free to speak Spanish if they wish. However, we urge all of you not to use your fluency in Spanish in a fashion which may lead other employees to suffer humiliation.
>
> * * *

In November 1990, Garcia and Buitrago received warning letters for speaking Spanish during working hours. For approximately two months thereafter, they were not permitted to work next to each other. Local 115 protested the English-only policy and requested that it be rescinded but to no avail.

* * *

Garcia, Buitrago, and Local 115, on behalf of all Spanish-speaking employees of Spun Steak, (collectively, "the Spanish-speaking employees") filed suit, alleging that the English-only policy violated Title VII. On September 6, 1991, the parties filed cross-motions for summary judgment.

The district court denied Spun Steak's motion and granted the Spanish-speaking employees' motion for summary judgment, concluding that the English-only policy disparately impacted Hispanic workers without sufficient business justification, and thus violated Title VII. Spun Steak filed this timely appeal and the EEOC filed a brief amicus curiae and participated in oral argument.

II

As a preliminary matter, we must consider whether Local 115 has standing to sue on behalf of the Spanish-speaking employees at Spun Steak. If Local 115 does not have standing, we will consider the application of the policy only to Garcia and Buitrago, both of whom speak English fluently.

* * * [T]he claim asserted and the relief requested do not require the participation of individual members. Local 115 claims that the policy has a per se discriminatory impact on all Spanish-speaking employees. Further, the union is seeking only injunctive relief on behalf of its members, not damages.

In short, Local 115 has standing.

III

Sections 703(a)(1) and (2) of Title VII provide:

(a) It shall be an unlawful employment practice for an employer—

(1) to fail or refuse to hire or to discharge any individual, or otherwise to discriminate against any individual with respect to his compensation, terms, conditions, or privileges of employment, because of such individual's race, color, religion, sex or national origin; or

(2) to limit, segregate, or classify his employees or applicants for employment in any way which would deprive or tend to deprive any individual of employment opportunities or otherwise adversely affect his status as an employee, because of such individual's race, color, religion, sex, or national origin.

42 U.S.C. § 2000e–2(a). It is well-settled that Title VII is concerned not only with intentional discrimination, but also with employment practices and policies that lead to disparities in the treatment of classes of workers. *See, e.g., Griggs v. Duke Power Co.*, 401 U.S. 424, 430–31, (1970). Thus, a plaintiff alleging discrimination under Title VII may proceed under two theories of liability: disparate treatment or disparate impact. *Watson v. Fort Worth Bank & Trust*, 487 U.S. 977, 986–87 (1987). While the disparate treatment theory requires proof of discriminatory intent, intent is irrelevant to a disparate impact theory. *Id. at 988.* "[I]mpact analysis is designed to implement Congressional concern with 'the consequences of employment practices, not simply the motivation.' " *Rose v. Wells Fargo & Co.*, 902 F.2d 1417, 1424 (9th Cir. 1990) (citations omitted).

A

The Spanish-speaking employees do not contend that Spun Steak intentionally discriminated against them in enacting the English-only policy. Rather, they contend that the policy had a discriminatory impact on them because it imposes a burdensome term or condition of employment exclusively upon Hispanic workers and denies them a privilege of employment that non-Spanish-speaking workers enjoy.

* * *

This case, by contrast, does not fall within the language of section 703(a)(2). While policies that serve as barriers to hiring or promotion clearly deprive applicants of employment opportunities, we cannot conclude that a burdensome term or condition of employment or the denial of a privilege would "limit, segregate, or classify" employees in a way that would "deprive any individual of employment opportunities" or "otherwise adversely affect his status as an employee" in violation of section 703(a)(2). *See Nashville Gas Co. v. Satty*, 434 U.S. 136, 144 (1977) (deprivation of benefits does not fall under § 703(a)(2)). Such claims, therefore, must be brought directly under section 703(a)(1). We have never expressly considered, however, whether disparate impact theory applies to claims under section 703(a)(1), and the Supreme Court has explicitly reserved the issue. *Id.*

* * *

B

To make out a prima facie case of discriminatory impact, a plaintiff must identify a specific, seemingly neutral practice or policy that has a significantly adverse impact on persons of a protected class. *Teal*, 457 U.S. at 446. If the prima facie case is established, the burden shifts to the employer to "demonstrate that the challenged practice is job related for the position in question and consistent with business necessity." 42 U.S.C.A. § 2000e–2(k)(1)(A) (Supp. 1992). In this case, the district court granted summary judgment in favor of the Spanish-speaking employees, concluding that, as a matter of law, the employees had made out the prima facie case and the justifications offered by the employer were inadequate.

1

We first consider whether the Spanish-speaking employees have made out the prima facie case. "[T]he requirements of a prima facie disparate impact case . . . are in some respects more exacting than those of a disparate treatment case." *Spaulding v. University of Washington*, 740 F.2d 686, 705 (9th Cir. 1984) (citation omitted). In the disparate treatment context, a plaintiff can make out a prima facie case merely by presenting evidence sufficient to give rise to an inference of discrimination. *McDonnell Douglas Corp. v. Green*, 411 U.S. 792, 802–06 (1973). In a disparate impact case, by contrast, plaintiffs must do more than merely raise an inference of discrimination before the burden shifts; they "must actually prove the discriminatory impact at issue." *Rose*, 902 F.2d at 1421. In the typical disparate impact case, in which the plaintiff argues that a selection criterion excludes protected applicants from jobs or promotions, the plaintiff proves discriminatory impact by showing statistical disparities between the number of protected class members in the qualified applicant group and those in the relevant segment of the workforce. *Wards Cove Packing Co. v. Atonio*, 490 U.S. 642, 650 (1988). While such statistics are often difficult to compile, whether the protected group has been disadvantaged turns on quantifiable data. When the alleged disparate impact is on the conditions, terms, or privileges of employment, however, determining whether the protected group has been adversely affected may depend on subjective factors not easily quantified. The fact that the alleged effects are subjective, however, does not relieve the plaintiff of the burden of proving disparate impact. The plaintiff may not merely assert that the policy has harmed members of the group to which he or she belongs. Instead, the plaintiff must prove the existence of adverse effects of the policy, must prove that the impact of the policy is on terms, conditions, or privileges of employment of the protected class, must prove that the adverse effects are significant, and must prove that the employee population in general is not affected by the policy to the same degree.

* * *

The crux of the dispute between Spun Steak and the Spanish-speaking employees, however, is not over whether Hispanic workers will disproportionately bear any adverse effects of the policy; rather, the dispute centers on whether the policy causes any adverse effects at all, and if it does, whether the effects are significant. The Spanish-speaking employees argue that the policy adversely affects them in the following ways: (1) it denies them the ability to express their cultural heritage on the job; (2) it denies them a privilege of employment that is enjoyed by monolingual speakers of English; and (3) it creates an atmosphere of inferiority, isolation, and intimidation. We discuss each of these contentions in turn.

* * *

a

The employees argue that denying them the ability to speak Spanish on the job denies them the right to cultural expression. It cannot be gainsaid that an individual's primary language can be an important link to his ethnic culture and identity. Title VII, however, does not protect the ability of workers to express their cultural heritage at the workplace. Title VII is concerned only with disparities in the treatment of workers; it does not confer substantive privileges. *See, e.g., Garcia v. Gloor*, 618 F.2d 264, 269 (5th Cir. 1980), cert. denied, 449 U.S. 1113 (1981). It is axiomatic that an employee must often sacrifice individual self-expression during working hours. Just as a private employer is not required to allow other types of self-expression, there is nothing in Title VII which requires an employer to allow employees to express their cultural identity.

b

Next, the Spanish-speaking employees argue that the English-only policy has a disparate impact on them because it deprives them of a privilege given by the employer to native-English speakers: the ability to converse on the job in the language with which they feel most comfortable. It is undisputed that Spun Steak allows its employees to converse on the job. The ability to converse—especially to make small talk—is a privilege of employment, and may in fact be a significant privilege of employment in an assembly-line job. It is inaccurate, however, to describe the privilege as broadly as the Spanish-speaking employees urge us to do.

* * *

c

Finally, the Spanish-speaking employees argue that the policy creates an atmosphere of inferiority, isolation, and intimidation. Under this theory, the employees do not assert that the policy directly affects a term, condition, or privilege of employment. Instead, the argument must be that the policy causes the work environment to become infused with ethnic tensions. The tense environment, the argument goes, itself amounts to a condition of employment.

i

The Supreme Court in *Meritor Savings Bank v. Vinson*, 477 U.S. at 66, held that an abusive work environment may, in some circumstances, amount to a condition of employment giving rise to a violation of Title VII. The Court quoted with approval the decision in *Rogers v. EEOC*, 454 F.2d 234, 238 (5th Cir. 1971), cert. denied, 406 U.S. 957 (1972):

> [T]he phrase 'terms, conditions or privileges of employment' in [Title VII] is an expansive concept which sweeps within its protective ambit the practice of creating a working environment heavily charged with ethnic or racial discrimination.... One can readily envision working environments so heavily polluted with discrimination as to destroy completely the emotional and psychological stability of minority group workers.

Although *Vinson* is a sexual harassment case in which the individual incidents involved behavior that was arguably intentionally discriminatory, its rationale applies equally to cases in which seemingly neutral policies of a company infuse the atmosphere of the workplace with discrimination. The *Vinson* Court emphasized, however, that discriminatory practices must be pervasive before an employee has a Title VII claim under a hostile environment theory.

* * *

The Spanish-speaking employees in this case have presented no evidence other than conclusory statements that the policy has contributed to an atmosphere of "isolation, inferiority or intimidation." The bilingual employees are able to comply with the rule, and there is no evidence to show that the atmosphere at Spun Steak in general is infused with hostility toward Hispanic workers. Indeed, there is substantial evidence in the record demonstrating that the policy was enacted to prevent the employees from intentionally using their fluency in Spanish to isolate and to intimidate members of other ethnic groups. In light of the specific factual context of this case, we conclude that the bilingual employees have not raised a genuine issue of material fact that the effect is so pronounced as to amount to a hostile environment. * * *

ii

* * *

We do not reject the English-only rule Guideline lightly. We recognize that "as an administrative interpretation of the Act by the enforcing agency, these Guidelines . . . constitute a body of experience and informed judgment to which courts and litigants may properly resort for guidance." *Meritor Sav. Bank*, 477 U.S. 57 at 65 (internal quotations and citations omitted). But we are not bound by the Guidelines. *See Espinoza v. Farah Mfg. Co., Inc.*, 414 U.S. 86, 94 (1973). We will not defer to "an administrative construction of a statute where there are 'compelling indications that it is wrong.'" *Id.*

* * *

2

Because the bilingual employees have failed to make out a prima facie case, we need not consider the business justifications offered for the policy as applied to them. On remand, if Local 115 is able to make out a prima facie case with regard to employees with limited proficiency in English, the district court could then consider any business justification offered by Spun Steak.

IV

In sum, we conclude that the bilingual employees have not made out a prima facie case and that Spun Steak has not violated Title VII in adopting an English-only rule as to them. Thus, we reverse the grant of summary judgment in favor of Garcia, Buitrago, and Local 115 to the extent it represents the bilingual employees, and remand with instructions to grant summary judgment in favor of Spun Steak on their claims. * * *

REVERSED and REMANDED.

■ BOOCHEVER, CIRCUIT JUDGE, dissenting in part:

I agree with most of the majority's carefully crafted opinion. I dissent, however, from the majority's rejection of the EEOC guidelines. The guidelines provide that an employee establishes a prima facie case in a disparate impact claim by proving the existence of an English-only policy, thereby shifting the burden to the employer to show a business necessity for the rule. *See* 29 C.F.R. § 1606.7(b) (1991) ("An employer may have a rule requiring that employees speak only in English at certain times where the employer can show that the rule is justified by business necessity."). I would defer to the Commission's expertise in construing the Act, by virtue of which it concluded that English-only rules may "create an atmosphere of inferiority, isolation and intimidation based on national origin which could result in a discriminatory working environment." *Id.* § 1606.7(a).

* * *

It is true that EEOC regulations are entitled to somewhat less weight than those promulgated by an agency with Congressionally delegated rulemaking authority. *General Elec. Co. v. Gilbert*, 429 U.S. 125, 141 (1976). Nevertheless, the EEOC guideline is entitled to "great deference" in the absence of "compelling indications that it is wrong." *Espinoza v. Farah Mfg. Co.*, 414 U.S. 86, 94–95 (1973). While one may reasonably differ with the EEOC's position as a matter of policy, I can find no such "compelling indications" in this case. The lack of directly supporting language in § 703(a)(1) or the legislative history of Title VII, relied on by the majority, does not in my opinion make the guideline "inconsistent with an obvious congressional intent not to reach the employment practice in question." *id.* at 94.

I conclude that if appropriate deference is given to the administrative interpretation of the Act, we should follow the guideline and uphold the district court's decision that a prima facie case was established. I believe, however, that triable issues were presented whether *Spun Steak* established a business justification for the rule, and I would remand for trial of that issue.

———

Yniguez v. Arizonans For Official English

69 F.3d 920 (9th Cir. 1995), *vacated by* 520 U.S. 43 (1997).

■ REINHARDT, Circuit Judge:

I.

* * *

State employees who fail to obey the Arizona Constitution are subject to employment sanctions. For this reason, immediately upon passage of Article XXVIII, Yniguez ceased speaking Spanish on the job. She feared that because of Article XXVIII her use of Spanish made her vulnerable to discipline.

In November 1988, Yniguez filed an action against the State of Arizona, Governor Rose Mofford, Arizona Attorney General Robert Corbin, and Director of the Arizona Department of Administration Catherine Eden, in federal district court. She sought an injunction against state enforcement of Article XXVIII and a declaration that the provision violated the

First and Fourteenth Amendments of the Constitution, as well as federal civil rights laws.

* * *

II.

* * *

We agree with the district court's construction of Article XXVIII. The article's plain language broadly prohibits all government officials and employees from speaking languages other than English in performing their official duties, save to the extent that the use of non-English languages is permitted pursuant to the provision's narrow exceptions section. * * *

III.

* * *

Arizonans for Official English argues vehemently that First Amendment scrutiny should be relaxed in this case because the decision to speak a non-English language does not implicate pure speech rights. Rather, the group suggests, "choice of language . . . is a mode of conduct"—a *"nonverbal* expressive activity." * * * Accordingly, it compares this case to those involving only "expressive conduct" or "symbolic speech." E.g., *Texas v. Johnson,* 491 U.S. 397 (1989) (burning American flag for expressive reasons); *Tinker v. Des Moines Independent Community School Dist.,* 393 U.S. 503 (1969) (wearing arm band for expressive reasons); *United States v. O'Brien*, 391 U.S. 367 (1968) (burning draft card for expressive reasons). In such cases, the government generally has a wider latitude in regulating the conduct involved, but only when the regulation is not directed at the communicative nature of that conduct. *Johnson*, 491 U.S. at 406.

We find the analysis employed in the above cases to be inapplicable here, as we are entirely unpersuaded by the comparison between speaking languages other than English and burning flags. Of course, speech in any language consists of the "expressive conduct" of vibrating one's vocal chords, moving one's mouth and thereby making sounds, or of putting pen to paper, or hand to keyboard. Yet the fact that such "conduct" is shaped by a language—that is, a sophisticated and complex system of understood meanings—is what makes it speech. Language is by definition speech, and the regulation of any language is the regulation of speech.

* * *

In sum, we most emphatically reject the suggestion that the decision to speak in a language other than English does not implicate pure speech concerns, but is instead akin to expressive conduct. Speech in any language is still speech, and the decision to speak in another language is a decision involving speech alone.

* * *

Arizonans for Official English next contends, incorrectly, that Yniguez seeks an affirmative right to have government operations conducted in foreign tongues. Because the organization misconceives Yniguez's argument, it relies on a series of cases in which non-English-speaking plaintiffs have unsuccessfully tried to require the government to provide them with services in their own language. *See Guadalupe Org. Inc.*, 587 F.2d at 1024 (no right to bilingual education); *Carmona v. Sheffield*, 475 F.2d 738 (9th Cir. 1973) (no right to unemployment notices in Spanish); *Toure v. United States*, 24 F.3d 444 (2d Cir. 1994) (no right to notice of administrative seizure in French); *Soberal-Perez v. Heckler*, 717 F.2d 36 (2d Cir. 1983) (no right to Social Security notices and services in Spanish), *cert. denied*, 466 U.S. 929 (1984); *Frontera v. Sindell*, 522 F.2d 1215 (6th Cir. 1975) (no right to civil service exam in Spanish). These cases, however, hold only that (at least under the circumstances there involved) non-English speakers have no affirmative right to compel state government to provide information in a language that they can comprehend. The cases are inapplicable here.

In the case before us, there is no claim of an affirmative right to compel the state to provide multilingual information, but instead only a claim of a negative right: that the state cannot, consistent with the First Amendment, gag the employees currently providing members of the public with information and thereby effectively preclude large numbers of persons from receiving information that they have previously received. *Cf. Board of Educ. Island Trees Union Free School Dist. No. 26 v. Pico*, 457 U.S. 853, 866–67 (1982). Such a claim falls squarely within the confines of traditional free speech doctrine, and is in no way dependent on a finding of an affirmative duty on the part of the state.

* * *

If this case involved a statewide ban on all uses of languages other than English within the geographical jurisdiction of the state of Arizona, the constitutional outcome would be clear. A state cannot simply prohibit all persons within its borders from speaking in the tongue of their choice. Such a restriction on private speech obviously could not stand. *Meyer v. Nebraska*, 262 U.S. 390, 401 (1923). However, Article XXVIII's restraint on speech is of more limited scope. Its ban is restricted to speech by persons performing services for the government. Thus, we must look beyond first principles of First Amendment doctrine and consider the question of what limitations may constitutionally be placed on the speech of government servants.

* * *

Thus, the Court has made it clear that it is the government's interest in performing its functions efficiently and effectively that underlies its right to exercise greater control over the speech of public employees. * * *

In deciding whether to afford constitutional protection to prohibited employee speech, we must consider both the general interest of the public servant in speaking freely, as described in *Perry* and *Rutan*, and the importance to the public of the speech involved. *See Connick*, 461 U.S. at 149 (considering the public's interest in the speech in determining whether to protect it); *Pickering*, 391 U.S. at 571–72 (same). The employee speech banned by Article XXVIII is unquestionably of public import. It pertains to the provision of governmental services and information. Unless that speech is delivered in a form that the intended recipients can comprehend, they are likely to be deprived of much needed data as well as of substantial public and private benefits. The speech at issue is speech that members of the public desire to hear. Indeed, it is most often the recipient, rather than the public employee, who initiates the dialogue in a language other than English. * * *

For example, monolingual Spanish-speaking residents of Arizona cannot, consistent with the article, communicate effectively with employees of a state or local housing office about a landlord's wrongful retention of a rental deposit, nor can they learn from clerks of the state court about how and where to file small claims court complaints. They cannot obtain information regarding a variety of state and local social services, or adequately inform the service-givers that the governmental employees involved are not performing their duties properly or that the government itself is not operating effectively or honestly. Those with a limited command of English will face commensurate difficulties in obtaining or providing such information. * * * Moreover, as we suggested earlier, the restrictions that Article XXVIII imposes severely limit the ability of state legislators to communicate with their constituents concerning official matters. For example, the provision would preclude a legislative committee from convening on a reservation and questioning a tribal leader in his native language concerning the problems of his community. A state senator of Navajo extraction would be precluded from inquiring directly of his Navajo-speaking constituents regarding problems they sought to bring to his attention. So would his staff. The legislative fact-finding function would, in short, be directly affected.

Arizonans for Official English claims, as it and others did when the initiative was on the ballot, that Article XXVIII promotes significant state interests. The organization enumerates these interests as; protecting democracy by encouraging "unity and political stability"; encouraging a common language; and protecting public confidence. We note at the outset that the sweeping nature of Article XXVIII's restriction on public employee speech weighs significantly in our evaluation of the state's alleged interests. In *National Treasury Employees Union,* the Court explained that when the government seeks to defend a "wholesale deterrent to a broad category of expression by a massive number of potential speakers," 513 U.S. at __, 115 S.Ct. at 1013, its burden is heavier than when it attempts to defend an isolated disciplinary action. *id.* Thus, we must examine the state's asserted justifications with particular care.

There is no basis in the record to support the proponents' assertion that any of the broad societal interests on which they rely are served by the provisions of Article XXVIII. * * *

Accordingly, the appellants have not demonstrated that the benefits to be obtained outweigh the burdens imposed on First Amendment rights, particularly given the all-encompassing scope of the restriction they seek to defend. *See National Treasury Employees Union,* 513 U.S. at ___, 115 S.Ct. at 1014 (explaining that the government's "burden is greater" in such cases).

We also reject the justifications for even more basic reasons. Our conclusions are influenced primarily by two Supreme Court cases from the 1920s in which nearly identical justifications were asserted in support of laws restricting language rights. *See Meyer v. Nebraska,* 362 U.S. 390 (1923); *Farrington v. Tokushige,* 273 U.S. 284 (1927). *Meyer* involved a Nebraska statute that prohibited the teaching of non-English languages to children under the eighth grade level; *Tokushige,* similarly, involved a Hawaii statute that singled out "foreign language schools," such as those in which Japanese was taught, for stringent government control.

Like the Court in *Meyer* and *Tokushige, we* recognize the importance of (1) promoting democracy and national unity and (2) encouraging a common language as a means of encouraging such unity. *See Guadalupe Organization, Inc., supra.* The two primary justifications relied on by the article's proponents are indeed closely linked. We cannot agree, however, that Article XXVIII is in any way a fair, effective, or appropriate means of promoting those interests, or that even under a more deferential analysis its severely flawed effort to advance those goals outweighs its substantial adverse effect on first amendment rights. As we have learned time and again in our history, the state cannot achieve unity by prescribing orthodoxy. * * * (forced "Americanization" violates American tradition of liberty and toleration). Notwithstanding this lesson, the provision at issue here "promotes" English only by means of proscribing other languages and is, thus, wholly coercive. Moreover, the goals of protecting democracy and encouraging unity and stability are at most indirectly related to the repressive means selected to achieve them. Next, the measure inhibits rather than advances the state's interest in the efficient and effective performance of its duties. Finally, the direct effect of the provision is not only to restrict the rights of all state and local government servants in Arizona, but also to severely impair the free speech interests of a portion of the populace they serve.

* * *

V.

* * *

We affirm the district court's judgment that Article XXVIII of the Arizona Constitution is facially overbroad and violates the First Amendment, and that the article is unconstitutional in its entirety. We reverse and remand the district court judgment insofar as it denies Yniguez an award of nominal damages.

AFFIRMED IN PART, REVERSED IN PART AND REMANDED.

* * *

■ FERNANDEZ, CIRCUIT JUDGE, with whom CHIEF JUDGE WALLACE and JUDGES HALL and KLEINFELD join, dissenting:

* * * Maria–Kelley F. Yniguez does not like Article XXVIII as a matter of policy. I can understand and sympathize with that. It is when she goes beyond the realm of policy and seeks to show that the Article violates the First Amendment to the United States Constitution that she goes astray. It is there that we part company.

She, in effect, proceeds from the fundamentally flawed assumption that while performing government business an official or employee has much the same freedom as a private citizen. That leads her into a thicket of incorrect assumptions and assertions about the nature of her speech rights, the nature of language, and the rights and duties of the State when it chooses to speak for itself. As a result, she has left the proper analytical pathway and become hopelessly lost in a forest of her own hopes.

* * * Certainly, if the State can require teaching in a particular language, it can itself choose to use a particular language to express the content of what it has to say.

In fine, the people of the State of Arizona did not violate the First Amendment when they adopted Article XXVIII. For good or ill, it was a question "for the people to decide." *Id.*

Therefore, I respectfully dissent.

NOTES AND QUESTIONS

1.   English-only rules as route to socioeconomic mobility? Arizona Representative Dave Carson (R–Prescott) was the key supporter of the bill in 1987. *See* RAYMOND TATALOVICH, NATIVISM REBORN: THE OFFICIAL ENGLISH LANGUAGE MOVEMENT AND THE AMERICAN STATES 131 (1995). Tatalovich, Carson and his supporters argued English-only rules would serve as a positive impetus to draw Hispanics out of the "language and economic ghettoes" of Arizona. *id.* at 132. The bill's supporters regarded English-only rules as a barrier against social and economic segregation in the state. But, it did not seem to take into account the tools needed when immigrants did not understand English. The notion that English is needed to combat segregation and marginalization is reasonable but it ignores the fact that people need the tools, i.e., English fluency, to participate in the marketplace.

2.   Bilingual education initiatives and counterinitiatives—the first rung on the ladder. In the primary and secondary public school arena, advocates of bilingual education have made the argument that children from homes in which English is a second language will secure the full benefit of educational opportunity only if they are given a graduated educational experience, in which they are taught in both their primary language and English in the same curriculum. The opponents of bilingual education, like the English-only advocates for government communication, insist that English is the official language, and that other languages should be banished to the margins of authoritative discourse.

For an explanation of the dynamics of these two political positions, see Charu A. Chandrasekhar, Comment, *The Bay State Buries Bilingualism:*

Advocacy Lessons from Bilingual Education's Recent Defeat in Massachusetts, 24 CHICANO-LATINO L. REV. 4 (2003). Chandrasekhar argues that:

> by a vote of 68 to 32 percent, Massachusetts voters endorsed Question 2, a ballot initiative sponsored by anti-bilingual education activist Ron Unz that eviscerates bilingual education and erodes parents' and teachers' rights. . . . The successful passage in Massachusetts of Question 2 marked another legislative triumph for Unz, who previously crafted Propositions 227 and 203 (successful bills similar to Question 2 banning bilingual education as an instructional method in California and Arizona, respectively).

2.   Effectiveness of the EEOC when English-only rules are applied in the workplace. *Garcia* illustrates the success employers can have by enforcing English-only rules. This was especially the case in *Garcia* because the court placed emphasis on the fact that bilingual employees would not be negatively impacted by an English-only rule. In particular, the court argued bilingual employees have the freedom and choice to switch to English while in the workplace. It was noted that only one of Spun Steak's employees did not speak English. The *Garcia* ruling suggests that the EEOC's guidelines cannot be assumed to be automatically applied in English-only environments.

3.   Additional reading. *See* Drucilla Cornell & William W. Bratton, *Deadweight Costs & Intrinsic Wrongs of Nativism: Economics, Freedom and Legal Suppression of Spanish*, 84 CORNELL L. REV. 595, 629–34 (1999).

C.   CULTURAL PROPERTY

Protecting Folklore of Indigenous Peoples: Is Intellectual Property the Answer?

30 CONN. L. REV. 1 (1997).

■ CHRISTINE HAIGHT FARLEY

INTRODUCTION

What can the Navajos do to prevent non-Navajos from using Navajo rug patterns to produce rugs overseas using cheap materials and labor, thereby undercutting the Navajos themselves in a market for their famous rugs? What can the Australian Aboriginal peoples do when their sacred and secret imagery is reproduced on carpets they did not make, and sold to non-Aboriginals, who will inevitably walk on them? Do these communities have any legal rights to these pieces of their culture? Does the law provide any means for them to take back their culture or to prevent further poaching?

Due to the increasingly widespread commercial appropriation of indigenous images, patterns, designs, and symbols, indigenous rights groups have turned to intellectual property schemes for protection. But indigenous art and folklore present many problems for intellectual property protection, and existing western legal mechanisms may be illsuited to protect certain types of indigenous art.

* * *

[T]he Article begins by recounting a recent incident of commercial use of indigenous art in order to both illustrate the harm caused by this phenomenon and to suggest the challenges in achieving meaningful protection. Part II of this Article describes the particular situation of the indigenous populations and the growing trend toward commercialization and commodification of their art forms. It also explains the particular nature of indigenous art and why this use is so troubling to them. Part III provides an in-depth analysis of the obstacles to copyright protection of folklore, including the duration of the rights, the originality requirement, the fixation requirement, the individual nature of the rights, the fair use exception, the economic focus of the remedies, and considers possible ways of overcoming these obstacles. Part IV evaluates international proposals to develop *sui generis* rights to protect folklore. Part V appraises the possibility of coupling copyright with other laws to achieve protection of folklore. It analyzes moral rights, public domain statutes, and unfair competition laws. Finally, Part VI assesses these strategies with regard to the particular motivations of the indigenous peoples and concludes that the existing intellectual property regime is well-suited to protect those groups who want to participate in and control the marketing of their arts and crafts. But for those who want to preclude any use of their imagery, the existing intellectual property regime is deficient. Application of intellectual property laws, whose underlying logic is to facilitate dissemination, is fundamentally inappropriate to prevent sacred indigenous images from circulation and re-use.

I. A Case of Pirating Cultural Heritage

The Australian carpet incident alluded to earlier presents an excellent illustration of the harm caused by the commercial poaching of indigenous art. In 1991, Mr. Bethune, an Australian entrepreneur, went into the business of importing hand-knotted, wool carpets into Australia. After a failed attempt to sell carpets with traditional Oriental designs, he decided to have Australian Aboriginal designs reproduced on the carpets, which he thought would generate more interest. After selecting ten designs from reproductions of Aboriginal artists' paintings, Bethune instructed a factory in Vietnam to produce carpets copying these designs, only making them "less busy." In all, he had 266 carpets manufactured. These carpets were sold for up to $4,252 each. Each carpet was affixed with a swing tag that read:

> These unique wall hangings and rugs have been designed by Aboriginal artists from areas throughout Australia. These artists are paid royalties on every carpet sold.... As carpet weaving is not a tradition of the Aboriginal people, the rugs are produced in Vietnam where we can combine the artistic skills of the Aboriginal people with

the weaving traditions of the Vietnamese.... [W]e have achieved a blending of the talents of these peoples to produce original artistic creations. Each carpet is a unique piece of art.

But Bethune had no agreement with the Aboriginal artists whose paintings he copied. He neither had their authorization to reproduce the designs, nor did he pay them any royalties.

* * *

The artists whose paintings were copied sued Bethune, his company, and its two directors in federal court for copyright infringement. They claimed they had a valid copyright in the paintings and that Bethune had violated their exclusive rights under the Australian Copyright Act. The court agreed, and *Milpurrurru v. Indofurn Pty. Ltd.* became the first case in which a court declared that Aboriginal artists must be compensated for the unauthorized use of their art. This case was seen as a big victory for Aboriginal peoples and as marking the end to the continued pilfering of their heritage. But has it solved the problem? Although the indigenous artists were able to assert copyright successfully, its requirements may still pose problems for other indigenous works. In addition, other copyright problems that are not present in this case have yet to be overcome.

II.   THE USES AND ABUSES OF INDIGENOUS ART

The *Milpurrurru* case is not an isolated example. Instead, it is indicative of a trend. Over the last decade there has been a proliferation of reproductions of indigenous peoples' artworks. Increasingly, indigenous designs are being appropriated and used commercially throughout the world. Technological advances have only fanned this fire. Indigenous motifs are used to sell everything from Japanese automobiles like the Mazda Navajo to Barbie dolls to back-to-school clothes. Indigenous art has been reproduced and sold as art reproductions and as craft items, but more commonly it has been reproduced and sold as cheaper commodities, such as T-shirts, tea towels, and other souvenirs. Indigenous art has also been reproduced and used in advertising and marketing. Thus we are seeing indigenous designs more often and in new contexts.

* * *

Significantly, nearly all of these reproductions are unauthorized. Most are reproduced without so much as a request for permission. The consequence is that the indigenous peoples who created the art are not being compensated for its use. Another consequence is that indigenous communities are not exercising control over how their art is being used. This lack of control means that they cannot refuse to have their work put to particular uses and that they cannot ensure that their work is reproduced in a way that maintains its integrity or the reputation of the creator. To better understand the consequences of this unauthorized use, we need to better understand the traditional place of art in indigenous communities.

A. *The Nature of Indigenous Art*

Art is central to the practice of religion in most indigenous communities. Most spiritual rituals involve visual displays, dance, and/or music and song. In the words of one well-known Aboriginal artist, "In song and dance, in rock engraving and bark painting we re-enact the stories of the Dreamtime, and myth and symbol come together to bind us inseparably from our past, and to reinforce the internal structures of our society."

* * *

Often, due to the spiritual connections to art, a song, dance, or image may be reserved for special ceremonies. Often "certain works of folklore ... cannot be shown, nor can the themes in them be disclosed, except to those few who have been admitted to knowledge of ritual secrets and mysteries by undergoing initiation or other special ceremonies" due to the sacred nature of the work. Only members of the community who have achieved a certain level of initiation may be permitted to observe these rituals. Thus, the "law of art" will also dictate who may see these images and dances and who may hear these songs.

* * *

B. *The Poaching of Indigenous Culture*

The theft of cultural symbols and art must be placed in historical perspective to grasp its implications fully. Many would agree that the survival of indigenous folklore is threatened. For the indigenous communities, the theft of their folklore represents the final blow to their civilization from "invaders." It is simply an extension of the plunder mentality. It signifies "that culture is open to pillage in the same way that Aboriginal lands and resources have been for over 200 years. Survival for indigenous peoples the world over is not merely a question of physical existence, but depends upon maintaining spiritual links with the land and their communities." Protection of their culture has become recognized as a fundamental human right.

* * *

III. Copyright Protection for Folklore

Over the last few decades there has been an outcry in the United States, Canada, and Australia for governments to do something to protect indigenous communities from the poaching of their artworks. Naturally, indigenous peoples and advocacy groups are concerned about this problem and have sought legal avenues of redress. In an effort to prevent the appropriation and manipulation of their cultural images and texts, indigenous peoples, fighting for their cultural survival, are increasingly turning to intellectual property laws to protect their cultural heritage from external poaching. Significantly, indigenous groups are willing to participate in the western intellectual property rights scheme from which they feel they have been excluded and therefore disadvantaged. They have invoked intellectual property laws to use as a shield to prevent further intrusions into their already pillaged culture.

* * *

What to the consumer market may look like the same problem actually involves two different sets of concerns. First, some indigenous peoples want to be able to benefit from the economic rights provided by intellectual property laws. They want to be compensated for their contribution to the artwork through licensing, and they want to exclude non-indigenous competitors from the market by preventing unauthentic products from being marketed as made by indigenous people. Assuming that the circulation of indigenous art is inevitable, some indigenous artists want to be sure to participate in this celebration of indigenous culture. By gaining control over the circulation of their imagery, they want to ensure that the public gets an accurate account of indigenous culture and that the investment in that culture goes back to their communities. These concerns are illustrated in the first example described at the beginning of this Article involving the use of the Navajo rug patterns. Perhaps a subset of this group is the individual artists who want to be able to draw on and develop the imagery of their ancestors in a way that may lead to commercial success. Throughout this Article, I will refer to this first group as the "realist group."

But the second set of concerns is more profound. Some indigenous peoples also want to use intellectual property laws to prevent what may be characterized as a cultural or psychological harm caused by the unauthorized use of their art. They see intellectual property laws as offering a means to control the circulation of their art. * * *

It is said that indigenous communities are vulnerable to this kind of theft because their artworks do not enjoy comprehensive protection under existing intellectual property regimes. Unfortunately, this claim has been made without supporting analysis. Most commentators begin with the normative question of whether indigenous art should be protected with intellectual property laws. Few even get to the descriptive question of whether or not indigenous art is protected by simply assuming that it is not. By beginning from the standpoint that indigenous art should be protected by intellectual property laws, and by accepting that it is not currently protected based on generalized notions of the originality of indigenous works as a unified group, commentators have failed to understand how indigenous peoples will best be able to meet their needs. Thus this Article will now proceed to that descriptive level and analyze whether some indigenous art is excluded from protection under existing intellectual property laws, whether the protection intellectual property laws offer is adequate and appropriate, or whether intellectual property laws must be reformulated to accommodate the unique challenges that folklore poses.

Of all the existing legal mechanisms, copyright law initially appears to be the best suited to protect indigenous folklore. Copyright law is a logical choice because copyright law is designed to protect artistic works from unauthorized reproduction. Likewise, indigenous groups are seeking to control the reproduction of their paintings, songs, and dances. Why shouldn't copyright law protect indigenous art? Indigenous artists feel that they should be protected to the same extent as non-indigenous artists. In one article, a well-known Aboriginal artist argued that Aboriginal artists should be accorded "the same recognition [as non-Aboriginal artists], that our works be respected and that we be acknowledged as the rightful owners of our own works of art." Thus the question arises as to whether copyright law is capable of accommodating this art form and satisfactorily meeting the needs of the community.

The copyright doctrine, however, presents a myriad of barriers to the full protection of indigenous art and folklore. These barriers include the duration of the protection, the originality requirement, the fixation requirement, the individual nature of the rights, the fair use exception, and the economic focus of the remedies. Each of these barriers will be analyzed in turn to understand whether they are preclusive or whether they can be overcome.

A. *The Duration of the Rights*

The first problem of affording copyright protection to folklore is the term of protection. In all Berne Convention member states, the term of the protection is the life of the author plus fifty years. In addition to the problem of identifying a particular author by whose life the term may be measured, the more significant problem is that the term is insufficient. Many indigenous rights advocates argue that perpetual protection should be granted to folklore because "the protection of the expression of folklore is not for the benefit of individual creators but a community whose existence is not limited in time." Even assuming that works would be protected, say, for one hundred years as an unpublished anonymous work, that period is still insignificant in the life of artistic traditions that date back thousands of years. One hundred years from now, indigenous peoples will not want to release their sacred texts to the outside to be exploited. Thus, this term of protection is insufficient for the "traditional group." It is also inadequate for the "realist group." This limited term of protection means that most folkloric works may already be in the public domain and may therefore be used without authorization. Therefore, the "realist group" will not be able to prevent outsiders from copying their works or their basic underlying symbols.

    * * *

B. *The Originality Requirement*

The second barrier to the protection of folklore is that copyright law requires that a work be original to be eligible for protection. As the U.S. Supreme Court pronounced in its most recent decision concerning the subject matter of copyright: "The sine qua non of copyright is originality." And, indeed, American (and Continental) copyright law is premised on the concept of authorship and the concomitant notion of originality. The Copyright Act provides protection only to "original works of authorship."

    * * *

Still, this requirement may present problems for folklore. Folkloric work is most often ancient, many of the art forms having been developed generations ago. Australian Aboriginal art, for instance, "draw[s] upon custom and tradition" and "represent[s] a ... continuation of ... time-honoured myths and legends." Although folklore can be entirely new, it is most often directly derived from preexisting works. Folklore is the product of a slow process of creative development. It is not stagnant, but evolves slowly.

* * *

Therefore, to protect folklore adequately, copyright would need to be extended "beyond the borders of originality." Furthermore, because the underlying work is unprotected, an outsider could adapt a public domain work and copyright her new translation, thereby obtaining a monopoly over the use of those designs. This would obviously be very problematic for indigenous groups.

* * *

C. *The Fixation Requirement*

Often it may be an outsider who first fixes an indigenous work in a tangible medium—a documentary film maker who videotapes a ritual, or a researcher who notes the steps of a dance, or a musician who writes down the words or notes of a song for the first time. These persons, however, are not the authors, and therefore not the initial copyright owners just as a stenographer is not the "author" for copyright purposes of what he or she transcribes. Under the copyright doctrine, the author is the party who actually "creates" the work. The "fixer" is the author in only the original expression that originates with her. That is, the film-maker is the author of the film, not of the underlying dances or music that she captures on film. Furthermore, the U.S. Copyright Act, for example, requires that the work be fixed "by or under the authority of the author." So, unauthorized fixation will not result in copyright, nor will it preclude indigenous artists from thereafter fixing and copyrighting the work.

* * *

D. *Group Rights*

The fourth problem for the application of copyright to folklore is more fundamental. Copyright law is premised on individual rights, and recognizes group rights only in limited situations. At its core, copyright is intended to reward individual authors for their creation of intellectual property. Indigenous art, in contrast, is not thought to be owned by the particular artist who created it. Instead, it is seen as the property of the group or clan. That is, it is something passed down through the generations for the enrichment of all.

* * *

This custom poses a problem for copyright law since copyright law vests the rights in the one who executes the work. It is this owner alone who has the exclusive right to reproduce the work. But this formulation is contrary to indigenous custom where the art is seen as something owned by the community.

* * *

Three mechanisms in copyright law could be utilized to attempt to overcome this problem: (1) joint authorship; (2) the transfer of rights; and (3) the work made-for-hire provision. These mechanisms may, however, in the end, be unsatisfactory. The most logical possibility is the provision for joint authorship. This provision is the only nod to collective ownership in the acts. It allows the multiple authors of a work to be co-owners of the copyright in the work. Unfortunately, this provision is very narrow. In order to be deemed a joint author, two requirements must be satisfied. First, the joint authors must in fact collaborate in the work's preparation, and second, they must intend, at the time the work is prepared, that their contributions be merged into "inseparable or interdependent parts of a unitary whole." Thus, under the first requirement, joint authorship vests the rights only in the persons who actually make the work (or their designees). That is, only those clan members who are involved in the creation of the work can be joint authors. The rest of the clan or community could not be considered co-owners unless they actually contributed to the creation of the work. Furthermore, to be a joint author each person's contribution must be copyrightable. Thus, a clan elder who dictates the composition to an artist who executes it will not be a joint author with the artist.

* * *

E. *Fair Use*

Under most copyright regimes, the monopoly on speech that the law permits is balanced by a provision that allows the unauthorized use of a copyrighted work where that use is fair—the so-called "fair use" exception. Whether or not an unauthorized use is deemed fair is determined on a case-by-case basis by considering various factors such as the purpose of the use, the nature of the copyrighted work, the amount of the copyrighted work used, and the effect of the use on the value of the copyrighted work. Thus, where a copyrighted work is used for comment or criticism or for an educational purpose, the author of the work may not be able to preclude its use.

* * *

In all instances, the nature of the copyrighted work also makes a harder case for fair use because creative works are thought to deserve more protection than informational works. Even though most indigenous art is used to communicate information to the community, as in the case of art that depicts creation stories, the work itself will still be judged to be creative. Original songs, dances, and paintings, unlike most databases, have a creative element that is impossible to separate from their underlying facts. That is, it is impossible to take only the information about the creation without also taking the design or expression. Moreover, courts are more prone to protect works that are not yet published. Thus, where unpublished sacred texts are used, it will mitigate against a finding of fair use.

* * *

F.   *Damages*

Lastly, some copyright laws may not provide adequate remedies for the unauthorized use of indigenous art. Surely, injunctive relief and the impounding and destruction of infringing works would be helpful. However, the threat of injunctions and destruction of infringing goods may not be enough to deter individuals and companies from using indigenous art without authorization. Damages may be the only way to ensure that outsiders will respect the copyright in indigenous art. For instance, a small company that manufactures infringing T-shirts at a profit may deliberately do so, knowing that the worst that can happen is that it may be ordered to cease at some point. If it were threatened with surrendering its profits, it might not embark on that plan.

Recovering significant damages, however, may not be possible for infringement of indigenous art. Under some copyright laws, only actual damages are awarded for economic harm caused by infringement. The "realist group" will not be negatively affected by this regime since it will be able to show economic harm. But the "traditional group" will fare worse. Where indigenous art would never be put to a economical use by the copyright owners, it may not be possible to prove that the infringement caused any economic loss. That is, where a work is a sacred text, reproduction of which would never be allowed for commercial gain, an infringing use of their work would not deprive the copyright owners of any financial gain. Thus, the true harm done to the copyright owners—the denigration and release of sacred texts—would go unpunished, although it would be halted. This lack of punishment may not adequately deter future infringements.

* * *

IV.   INTERNATIONAL PROPOSALS

* * *

B.   *Model Law on Copyright*

The Tunis Model Law on Copyright (1976) was written to provide a model for developing countries to enact comprehensive copyright legislation. This model act explicitly refers to folklore at several places "because in developing countries national folklore constitutes an appreciable part of the cultural heritage and is susceptible of economic exploitation, the fruits of which should not be denied to those countries." In Section 6(2) the act provides that "[w]orks of national folklore are protected by all means in accordance with subsection (1), without limitation in time." Thus it seems that the protection of folklore is perpetual under this act. There is, however, no mention of retroactivity of protection. Therefore, although newer works will be protected forever, much folklore will already be in the public domain.

    * * *

C. *Model Provisions*

    * * *

The Model Provisions enable the collective ownership and control of folklore, grant perpetual protection, and do not require fixation. The major tenet of the Model Provisions is that utilizations of folklore are subject to authorization by the competent authority "when they are made ... with gainful intent and outside their traditional or customary context." According to the Working Group on the Intellectual Property Aspects of Folklore Protection, three criteria should be used to determine whether a use is unauthorized: (1) whether the intent is gainful; (2) whether the use was made by members or non-members of the community where the expression is derived from; and (3) whether the use is outside of the traditional context of the usual use.

    * * *

D. *The Mataatua Declaration*

In June 1993, over 150 representatives from indigenous populations of fifteen countries convened in New Zealand for the first International Conference on Cultural and Intellectual Property Rights of Indigenous Peoples. There they passed The Mataatua Declaration on Cultural and Intellectual Property Rights of Indigenous Peoples. The Declaration states that existing intellectual property regimes are inadequate to the needs of indigenous peoples and calls for, among other things, new intellectual property mechanisms that provide for collective ownership, retroactive coverage of historical works, protection against debasement of culturally significant items, and multigenerational coverage span. Moreover, the Declaration urges indigenous peoples to define for themselves their own intellectual property and develop a code of ethics that outsiders must observe when interacting with that property. This document thus identifies the key challenges in reconciling the copyright regime with the needs of the indigenous community. However, because it is more a call to action than a proposal, it offers little guidance as to how to achieve a reconciliation. Unfortunately, no action has been taken in response to this declaration thus far.

V. STRETCHING THE BOUNDARIES OF COPYRIGHT LAW

Another possibility in the protection of folklore may be to look beyond copyright law. Without reformulating the copyright law, it may be that the law, when coupled with other rights, provides sufficient protection to folklore. The following mechanisms may provide a means to stretch and strengthen copyright law's protection of folklore.

A. *Moral Rights*

Moral Rights, although distinct from economic rights, are usually grouped in with copyright. Moral Rights basically consist of the rights of divulgation, paternity, and integrity. These rights, which are usually inalienable, allow artists to protect their artwork from being denigrated. Indigenous artists may be protected under this doctrine from having their work first published without their authorization, published without attribution, reproduced in poor quality, reproduced only partially causing the message to be distorted, or put to a use which would be inappropriate to the nature of the original work.

* * * The term of protection may also be a problem for folklore, as protection may be extinguished upon the death of the author, or after a set time. The indigenous community, however, would want to ensure the integrity of the work beyond this limited time since it is the community's interest in the work and not the reputation of the artist with which they are concerned. The community's interest in the work is perpetual. On the other hand, moral rights, if applied too zealously, may frustrate the interests of the "realist group" by protecting sacred imagery from any commercial exploitation.

B. *Public Domain Statutes and Domaine Public Payant*

Public Domain statutes basically provide moral rights in perpetuity. Public Domain legislation is intended to "prevent or sanction use of public domain works in such a way as to prejudice their authenticity or identity." Public domain works can be used as the basis of derivative works so long as the use does not violate the work's essence, cultural value, or reputation. Thus, this scheme appears to provide the appropriate safeguard to the indigenous community's cultural interests, especially those who want to protect sacred imagery. Protection is extended, however, only to works whose copyright protection has expired and to works that would have qualified for copyright protection had the legislation existed at the time they were created. For these reasons, folklore will have the same difficulties that it does with copyright law. Namely, the originality and fixation requirements may prevent it from enjoying protection. Furthermore, authority to control public domain works rests with a designated state agency. Public Domain legislation therefore does not present the problem of individual ownership for indigenous peoples, but it may be problematic to have the state exercise this degree of control over indigenous folklore, especially where the state is not representative of the indigenous community.

* * *

C. *The Law of Unfair Competition*

Combining copyright protection with an additional source of intellectual property protection may be a means of providing adequate protection to folklore. Trademark law may provide additional protection against some kinds of unauthorized copying.

In the United States, Canada, and Australia, indigenous arts and crafts have faced competition in their market from cheaper imitations made by non-indigenous persons, often from overseas. The problem is that as soon as any of their art forms gains popularity with the general public, the market is flooded with imitations. Each of these governments has taken special measures to ensure the authenticity of indigenous products.

In the United States, for example, the Indian Arts and Crafts Act of 1935 was enacted to protect Native American Arts and Crafts. The Act attempts to assure authenticity of Native American works by issuing certification marks * * *. The Act provides civil and criminal penalties for counterfeiting the Board's marks and for misrepresenting the works as "Indian made." The Act, however, appears to be "only a paper tiger" since there has never been a single prosecution in the history of the Act. In fact, after more than sixty years on the books, the Interior Department has not even promulgated any regulations for its enforcement.

　* * *

Another possible means of supplementing copyright law's protection is through general unfair competition laws. Unfair competition laws are designed to protect consumers and competitors from the misrepresentation of products on the market. Indigenous groups may use these laws to prevent outsiders from marketing goods as "Indian made" or as being produced on indigenous lands. Trademark law has the advantage of granting rights collectively and of providing perpetual protection. To gain protection under these laws, however, folklore must qualify as a commercial good or service. Some aspects of folklore, however, such as rituals or dance, may not generally qualify as commercial activities. Thus this law would benefit the first group of concerns more than it would the second.

　* * *

VI.   ARRIVING AT THE NORMATIVE QUESTION

Finally, with the benefit of an analysis of the extent to which indigenous art and folklore are currently protected by intellectual property regimes, we can now ask the normative question: Should indigenous art and folklore be protected by intellectual property regimes? The answer to this question should not be assumed. Along with it one might ask: What are the implications of the application of existing intellectual property laws to folklore? Stated otherwise, what are the consequences of fitting folklore into the existing scheme?

One consequence is that these artistic traditions will be forced to conform to a set of assumptions that are at odds with their traditions. The underlying rationale of intellectual property law privileges individual ownership, economic exploitation, and the dissemination of new expressions of ideas. Intellectual property rights are driven by the economics of free enterprise and profit. The objective is the creation of a limited monopoly right as an incentive for individuals to disseminate their original expressions. However, indigenous art, especially in its sacred forms, is not something that can be owned by any individual, is not something that should be commercially exploited, is not something that can be freely disseminated, and is not something that can be reinterpreted or adapted. These works, which are often sacred in nature, are unlike the types of works anticipated by the copyright law and may require different types of protections. Thus, in some cases, indigenous groups may seek to use intellectual property laws, which imply dissemination, to withhold the circulation of their art. Although they may use the intellectual property regime to get partial protection, they are using it for a purpose that is alien to it.

* * *

CONCLUSION

* * *

The first revelation that the analysis unveils is that those indigenous peoples who want to gain control of their imagery in order to participate in its circulation are, in fact, adequately protected by the existing legal regime. Certainly their protection could be strengthened, but anything more may inhibit free expression and upset the delicate balance that the copyright law has achieved. To the extent we want to grant special protection to these works, this goal may be better achieved through unfair competition law.

———

NOTES AND QUESTIONS

1. **Copyright law as a Western concept.** Copyrights are widely used in Western countries to protect artists' creations and works but this does not easily translate to indigenous cultures. *See* Dieter Dambiec, *Protecting indigenous peoples' folklore through copyright law, available at* http://www.proutworld.org/features/copyrightindigen.itra (1999). According to Dambiec, copyright law does not easily apply in indigenous cultures because of the differences in the concept of ownership. Western cultures tend to think of ownership in individual terms while many indigenous cultures think in terms of community ownership. An intriguing argument at this point can be found in MICHAEL I. BROWN, WHO OWNS NATIVE CULTURE, Harvard University Press (2003).

2. **Questions of identity and ownership.** Another important issue in indigenous folklore is identification of the artists and ownership. Unlike Western cultures, it is not as easy to identify work that may have been created hundreds of years ago in indigenous communities. Some works contain the contribution of a successive groups of artists, whose work accumulates overtime in a serial dynamic process of revision and change. Dambiec says that New Zealand's Maori society has assumed ownership of tribal creations through various levels, meaning different people in the tribe control specific aspects of the creations. This is a possible avenue in

giving ownership to indigenous tribes in a manner that allows community ownership and participation.

3.   Moral rights or copyrights? As Dambiec argues, copyrights are often insufficient when dealing with indigenous culture and folklore. Because of this, a viable solution could be to merge the moral and legal to best meet the needs of indigenous cultures. According to Dambiec, moral rights comprise three types of rights: the power to control the publication or dissemination of a work; the right to have the artist's or tribe's name associated with the work; and the right to prevent misuse, mutilation or distortion of a work. *See* Dambiec, *supra* at 418, n.1. Because of the various issues involved in ownership and folklore culture, the most viable means of compensating indigenous peoples is to merge Western and indigenous concepts to best protect their interests. Obviously, the Western concept of ownership and copyright is often insufficient to address indigenous people's concerns, just as their ideas of ownership and identity are often dismissed in the Western legal system.

D.   BUSINESS-LIKE IMAGE

Rogers v. American Airlines, Inc.

Southern District of New York, 527 F.Supp. 229 (S.D.N.Y. 1981).

■ JUDGE SOFAER delivered the opinion of the court:

Plaintiff is a black woman who seeks $10,000 damages, injunctive, and declaratory relief against enforcement of a grooming policy of the defendant American Airlines that prohibits employees in certain employment categories from wearing an all-braided hairstyle. Plaintiff has been an American Airlines employee for approximately eleven years, and has been an airport operations agent for over one year. Her duties involve extensive passenger contact, including greeting passengers, issuing boarding passes, and checking luggage. She alleges that the policy violates her rights under the Thirteenth Amendment of the United States Constitution, under Title VII of the Civil Rights Act, 42 U.S.C. § 2000e et seq. (1976), and under 42 U.S.C. § 1981 (1976), in that it discriminates against her as a woman, and more specifically as a black woman. She claims that denial of the right to wear her hair in the "corn row" style intrudes upon her rights and discriminates against her. * * *

[The court dismissed the plaintiff's Thirteenth Amendment claim]. The [motion to dismiss] is also meritorious with respect to the statutory claims insofar as they challenge the policy on its face.   * * * The policy is addressed to both men and women, black and white. Plaintiff's assertion that the policy has practical effect only with respect to women is not supported by any factual allegations. Many men have hair longer than many women. Some men have hair long enough to wear in braids if they choose to do so. Even if the grooming policy imposed different standards for men and women, however, it would not violate Title VII.   * * * The complaint does not state a claim for sex discrimination.

The considerations with respect to plaintiff's race discrimination claim would clearly be the same, see *Smith v. Delta Air Lines*, 486 F.2d 512 (5th Cir. 1973), except for plaintiff's assertion that the "corn row" style has a special significance for black women. She contends that it "has been, historically, a fashion and style adopted by Black American women, reflective of cultural, historical essence of the Black women in American society."   * * * "The style was 'popularized' so to speak, within the larger society, when Cicely Tyson adopted the same for an appearance on nationally viewed Academy Awards presentation several years ago.   * * * It was and is analogous to the public statement by the late Malcolm X regarding the Afro hair style.   * * * At the bottom line, the completely braided hair style, sometimes referred to as corn rows, has been and continues to be part of the cultural and historical essence of Black American women."   * * * "There can be little doubt that, if American adopted a policy which foreclosed Black women/all women from wearing hair styled as an 'Afro/bush,' that policy would have very pointedly racial dynamics and consequences reflecting a vestige of slavery unwilling to die (that is, a master mandate that one wear hair divorced from ones historical and cultural perspective and otherwise consistent with the 'white master' dominated society and preference thereof)."   * * *

Plaintiff is entitled to a presumption that her arguments, largely repeated in her affidavit, are true. But the grooming policy applies equally to members of all races, and plaintiff does not allege that an all-braided hair style is worn exclusively or even predominantly by black people. Moreover, it is proper to note that defendants have alleged without contravention that plaintiff first appeared at work in the all-braided hairstyle on or about September 25, 1980, soon after the style had been popularized by a white actress in the film "10." Plaintiff may be correct that an employer's policy prohibiting the "Afro/bush" style might offend Title VII and section 1981. But if so, this chiefly would be because banning a natural hairstyle would implicate the policies underlying the prohibition of discrimination on the basis of immutable characteristics.   * * * An all-braided hair style is an "easily changed characteristic," and, even if socioculturally associated with a particular race or nationality, is not an impermissible basis for distinctions in the application of employment practices by an employer.   * * * The Fifth Circuit recently upheld, without requiring any showing of business purpose, an employer's policy prohibiting the speaking of any language but English in the workplace, despite the importance of Spanish to the ethnic identity of Mexican–Americans.   * * *

Although the Act may shield "employees' psychological as well as economic fringes" from employer abuse * * * plaintiff's allegations do not amount to charging American with "a practice of creating a working environment heavily charged with ethnic or racial discrimination," or one "so heavily polluted with discrimination as to destroy completely the emotional and psychological stability of minority group workers."   * * * If an even-handed English-only policy that has the effect of prohibiting a Mexican–American from speaking Spanish during working hours is valid without a showing of business purpose, the policy at issue here, even if ill-advised, does not offend the law.

Moreover, the airline did not require plaintiff to restyle her hair. It suggested that she could wear her hair as she liked while off duty, and permitted her to pull her hair into a bun and wrap a hairpiece around the bun during working hours. * * *

Plaintiff has failed to allege sufficient facts to require defendants to demonstrate that the policy has a bona fide business purpose. * * * In this regard, however, plaintiff does not dispute defendant's assertion that the policy was adopted in order to help American project a conservative and business-like image, a consideration recognized as a bona fide business purpose. E.g., *Fagan v. National Cash Register Co.*, 481 F.2d 1115, 1124–25 (D.C. Cir. 1973). * * *

Plaintiff also asserts in her complaint that the regulation has been applied in an uneven and discriminatory manner. She claims that white women in particular have been permitted to wear pony tails and shag cuts. She goes on to claim, in fact, that some black women are permitted to wear the same hairstyle that she has been prohibited from wearing. These claims seriously undercut her assertion that the policy discriminates against women, and her claim that it discriminates against black women in particular. Conceivably, however, the complaint could be construed as alleging that the policy has been applied in a discriminatory manner against plaintiff because she is black by some representative of the defendant. On its face, this allegation is sufficient, although it might be subject to dismissal on a summary judgment motion if it is not supplemented with some factual claims.

This remaining claim-of racially discriminatory application-by its nature is not appropriate for class action treatment. In light of plaintiff's assertions that both white and black women in the purported class have been permitted to wear the all-braided style, she seems to be saying, ultimately, that there are no similarly situated people, and she does not identify any. Therefore, the motion for class certification is denied. * * * Indeed, even as broadly alleged, plaintiff's claims would not warrant certification of a class. Plaintiff seeks specific retroactive monetary relief only for herself and not for any class members. With respect to the class, plaintiff seeks a change in company policy, and a victory in plaintiff's case, with an injunctive and declaratory order, would afford relief to all similarly situated people. * * *

A Hair Piece: Perspective on the Intersection of Race and Gender

1991 DUKE L.J. 365.

Paulette M. Caldwell

I. OF SMALL BEGINNINGS

A. *Rediscovering My Hair*

    When will I cherish my hair again, the way my grandmother cherished it, when fascinated by its beauty, with hands carrying centu-

ries-old secrets of adornment and craftswomanship, she plaited it, twisted it, cornrowed it, finger-curled it, olive-oiled it, on the growing moon cut and shaped it, and wove it like fine strands of gold inlaid with semiprecious stones, coral and ivory, telling with my hair a lost-found story of the people she carried inside her?

* * *

B.   *On Being the Subject of a Law School Hypothetical*

The case of *Rogers v. American Airlines* upheld the right of employers to prohibit categorically the wearing of braided hairstyles in the workplace. The plaintiff, a black woman, argued that American Airline's policy discriminated against her specifically as a black woman. In effect, she based her claim on the interactive effects of racial and gender discrimination. The court chose, however, to base its decision principally on distinctions between biological and cultural conceptions of race. More importantly, it treated the plaintiff's claims of race and gender discrimination in the alternative and independent of each other, thus denying any interactive relationship between the two.

* * *

I discovered *Rogers* while reading a newspaper article describing the actual or threatened firing of several black women in metropolitan Washington, D.C. solely for wearing braided hairstyles. The article referred to *Rogers* but actually focused on the case of Cheryl Tatum, who was fired from her job as a restaurant cashier in a Hyatt Hotel under a company policy that prohibited "extreme and unusual hairstyles."

The newspaper description of the Hyatt's grooming policy conjured up an image of a ludicrous and outlandishly-coiffed Cheryl Tatum, one clearly bent on exceeding the bounds of workplace taste and discipline. But the picture that accompanied the article revealed a young, attractive black woman whose hair fell neatly to her shoulders in an all-American, common, everyday pageboy style, distinguished only by the presence of tiny braids in lieu of single strands of hair.

* * *

C.   *Why Would Anyone Want to Wear Their Hair That Way?*

* * *

Hair seems to be such a little thing. Yet it is the little things, the small everyday realities of life, that reveal the deepest meanings and values of a culture, give legal theory its grounding, and test its legitimacy.

II.   To Choose Myself: Interlocking Figurations in the Construction of Race and Gender

A.   *A Black Woman's Hair, A Black Woman's Place*

SUNDAY. School is out, my exams are graded, and I have unbraided my hair a few days before my appointment at the beauty parlor to have it braided again. After a year in braids, my hair is healthy again: long and thick and cottony soft. I decide not to french roll it or twist it or pull it into a ponytail or bun or cover it with a scarf. Instead, I comb it out and leave it natural, in a full and big "Angela Davis" afro style. I feel full and big and regal. I walk the three blocks from my apartment to the subway. I see a white male colleague walking in the opposite direction and I wave to him from across the street. He stops, squints his eyes against the glare of the sun and stares, trying to figure out who has greeted him. He recognizes me and starts to cross over to my side of the street. I keep walking, fearing the possibility of his curiosity and needing to be relieved of the strain of explanation.

MONDAY. My hair is still unbraided, but I blow it out with a hair dryer and pull it back into a ponytail tied at the nape of my neck before I go to the law school. I enter the building and run into four white female colleagues on their way out to a white female lunch. Before I can say hello, one of them blurts out, "It IS weird!" Another drowns out the first: "You look so young, like a teenager!" The third invites me to join them for lunch while the fourth stands silently, observing my hair. I mumble some excuse about lunch and, interject, almost apologetically, that I plan to get my hair braided again the next day. When I arrive at my office suite and run into the white male I had greeted on Sunday, I realize immediately that he has told the bunch on the way to lunch about our encounter the day before. He mutters something about how different I look today, then asks me whether the day before I had been on my way to a ceremony. He and the others are generally nice colleagues, so I half-smile, but say nothing in response. I feel a lot less full and big and regal.

TUESDAY. I walk to the garage under my apartment building, again wearing a big, full "Angela Davis" afro. Another white male colleague passes me by, not recognizing me. I greet him and he smiles broadly saying that he has never seen me look more beautiful. I smile back, continue the chit chat for a moment more and try not to think about whether he is being disingenuous. I slowly get into my car, buckle up, relax, and turn on the radio. It will take me about forty-five minutes to drive uptown to the beauty parlor, park my car, and get something to eat before beginning the long hours of sitting and braiding. I feel good, knowing that the braider will be ecstatic when she sees the results of her healing handiwork. I keep my movements small, easy, and slow, relishing in a rare, short morning of being free.

B.   *When Race and Gender Intersect*

My initial outrage notwithstanding, *Rogers* is an unremarkable decision. Courts generally protect employer-mandated hair and dress codes, and
they often accord the greatest deference to codes that classify individuals
on the basis of socially-conditioned rather than biological differences. And
although *Rogers* rests on one line of authority without acknowledging the
existence of another, grooming codes are governed by decisional law that
clearly lacks conceptual coherence. All in all, such cases are generally
considered only marginally significant in the battle to secure equal employment rights.

But *Rogers* is regrettably unremarkable in an important respect. It
rests on suppositions that are deeply imbedded in American culture—
assumptions so entrenched and so necessary to the maintenance of inter-
locking, interdependent structures of domination that their mythological
bases and political functions have become invisible, especially to those to
whom their existence is most detrimental. *Rogers* proceeds from the
premise that, although racism and sexism share much in common, they are
nonetheless fundamentally unrelated phenomena—a proposition proved
false by history and contemporary reality. Racism and sexism are interlock-
ing, mutually-reinforcing components of a system of dominance rooted in
patriarchy. No significant and lasting progress in combating either can be
made until this interdependent aspect of their relation is acknowledged,
and until the perspectives gained from considering their interaction are
reflected in legal theory and public policy.

* * *

C.   *The Limitations of the Assumptions of Race–Sex Correspondence and Independence*

* * *

Correlative to the assumption of race-sex correspondence, there exists
an equally powerful assumption of race-sex independence or distinctive-
ness. Also rooted in American history, particularly in the politics of emancipation and suffrage, this assumption has contemporary manifestations in
the existence of distinct political movements against racism and sexism, the
development of social policy along exclusively gender or race lines, and the
legal conceptualization of distinct approaches to issues of race and gender.

* * *

Problems arise in the development of legal theory and social policy
when the possibility of other relationships between race and gender, such
as intersection, are not considered. Black women's issues "slip through the
cracks" of legal protection, and the gender components of racism and the
race components of sexism remain hidden.

* * *

In one category, courts have considered whether black women may
represent themselves or other race or gender discriminatees. Some cases

deny black women the right to claim discrimination as a subgroup distinct from black men and white women. Others deny black women the right to represent a class that includes white women in a suit based on sex discrimination, on the ground that race distinguishes them. Still other cases prohibit black women from representing a class in a race discrimination suit that includes black men, on the ground of gender differences. These cases demonstrate the failure of courts to account for race-sex intersection, and are premised on the assumption that discrimination is based on either race or gender, but never both.

A second category of cases concerns the interaction of race and gender in determining the limits of an employer's ability to condition work on reproductive and marital choices associated with black women. Several courts have upheld the firing of black women for becoming pregnant while unmarried if their work involves association with children—especially black teenage girls. These decisions rest on entrenched fears of and distorted images about black female sexuality, stigmatize single black mothers (and by extension their children) and reinforce "culture of poverty" notions that blame poverty on poor people themselves. They also reinforce the notion that the problems of black families are attributable to the deviant and dominant roles of black women and the idea that racial progress depends on black female subordination.

A third category concerns black women's physical images. These cases involve a variety of mechanisms to exclude black women from jobs that involve contact with the public—a tendency particularly evident in traditionally female jobs in which employers place a premium on female attractiveness—including a subtle, and often not so subtle, emphasis on female sexuality. The latter two categories sometimes involve, in addition to the intersection of race and gender, questions that concern the interaction of race, gender, and culture.

* * *

D.   *The Rogers Opinion*

The *Rogers* decision is a classic example of a case concerning the physical image of black women. Renee Rogers, whose work for American Airlines involved extensive passenger contact, claimed that American's prohibition of braided hairstyles in certain job classifications discriminated against her as a woman in general, and as a black woman in particular. The court did not attempt to limit the plaintiff's case by forcing her to proceed on either race or gender grounds, nor did it create a false hierarchy between the two bases by treating one as grounded in statutory law and the other as a "plus" factor that would explain the application of law to a subgroup not technically recognized as a protected group by law. The court also appeared to recognize that the plaintiff's claim was not based on the cumulative effects of race and gender.

* * *

The court gave three principal reasons for dismissing the plaintiff's claim. First, in considering the sex discrimination aspects of the claim, the court disagreed with the plaintiff's argument that, in effect, the application of the company's grooming policy to exclude the category of braided hairstyles from the workplace reached only women. Rather, the court stressed that American's policy was even-handed and applied to men and women alike. Second, the court emphasized that American's grooming policy did not regulate or classify employees on the basis of an immutable gender characteristic. Finally, American's policy did not bear on the exercise of a fundamental right. The plaintiff's racial discrimination claim was analyzed separately but dismissed on the same grounds: neutral application of American's anti-braid policy to all races and absence of any impact of the policy on an immutable racial characteristic or of any effect on the exercise of a fundamental right.

* * *

In support of its view that the plaintiff had failed to establish a factual basis for her claim that American's policy had a disparate impact on black women, thus destroying any basis for the purported neutral application of the policy, the court pointed to American's assertion that the plaintiff had adopted the prohibited hairstyle only shortly after it had been "popularized" by Bo Derek, a white actress, in the film "10." Notwithstanding the factual inaccuracy of American's claim, and notwithstanding the implication that there is no relationship between braided hair and the culture of black women, the court assumed that black and white women are equally motivated (i.e., by the movies) to adopt braided hairstyles.

* * *

The court's reference to Bo Derek presents us with two conflicting images, both of which subordinate black women and black culture. On the one hand, braids are separated from black culture, and, by implication are said to arise from whites. Not only do blacks contribute nothing to the nation's or the world's culture, they copy the fads of whites. On the other hand, whites make fads of black culture, which, by virtue of their popularization, become—like all "pop"—disposable, vulgar, and without lasting value. Braided hairstyles are thus trivialized and protests over them made ludicrous.

* * *

III.   TRUTHS AND SOJOURNS: STEREOTYPING AT THE INTERSECTION OF RACE AND GENDER

A.   *Of Changes and More*

1985.   In a few days I will teach in a four-day workshop for fifty black women. The participants have been chosen primarily because of their status in the corporate world of business and finance. My feelings of performance anxiety seem greatly overshadowed by feelings of happy excitement and expectancy at the prospect of navigating my peers through the murky waters of possibilities and pitfalls for black women in leadership positions. I arrive at the beauty parlor for the grooming of my hair, which, after a year in braids, has grown to my shoulders. Time is short and the hairdresser is late. When she arrives, on impulse, I decide to forgo braids and ask her to apply a chemical straightener to my virgin hair. I return to work a day later and the "significant other" of a male colleague addresses me in that chastising, condescending tone of voice reserved for slaves and women in domestic service: "Every time I see you, you've done something else to your hair!"

Days later I arrive at the workshop site and greet the participants, my hair arranged in a style reminiscent of my former for-profit corporate self. Over the next four days, I am frequently complimented for my competence, unusual insights, and mastery of subject matter, but mostly—especially from those who over the years have watched me alternate between closely-cropped Afros and short, straight bobs—for the beauty of my long, straight hair.

B.   *Hair and the Timeless Search for Legitimacy*

* * *

Unlike skin color and other physical manifestations of race, hair has both mutable and immutable characteristics. Change in the mutable and in the appearance of the immutable characteristics of hair can be accomplished with relative ease, albeit, for many blacks, not without long-term consequences. Hair can be cut off, straightened out, curled up, or covered over either in the exercise of individual preference or to comply with the tastes or preferences of others. The uniqueness of hair among physical characteristics correlating with race lies not only in the ability of its true nature to be disguised, but also in its susceptibility to external control.

* * *

Today, Afro hairstyles—or at least some of them—are widely accepted in all forms of employment, although the extent of their legal protection is far from certain. They are considered by many to reflect personal style—aesthetic choice—and are not generally associated with the politics of the period of their origin. However, the rationalizations that accompanied opposition to Afro hairstyles in the 1960s—extreme, too unusual, not businesslike, inconsistent with a conservative image, unprofessional, inappropriate with business attire, too "black" (i.e., too militant), unclean—are used today to justify the categorical exclusion of braided hairstyles in many parts of the workforce, particularly in jobs that are either traditionally conservative or highly structured, involve close immediate supervision, or require significant contact with the public.

C.   *In Whose Image? The Application of Antidiscrimination Principles to Employer Grooming and Image Preferences*

By focusing on neutrality, immutability, and the exercise of fundamental rights, the *Rogers* court obscured an underlying principle in the application of antidiscrimination law to a variety of employer image preferences, including—but not limited to—those expressed through grooming codes. A careful analysis of cases in this area reveals that courts pay close attention to the eradication of stereotypes, attention in no way evidenced in *Rogers*. These cases also make clear that stereotyping is impermissible whether or not the standards set forth in *Rogers* are satisfied.

* * *

* * * *Image Discrimination in the Airline Industry.* The fact that the *Rogers* case was brought against a major airline is itself of considerable significance. The airline industry's history of discrimination against women is nothing short of malevolent. Perhaps no industry has fought as hard to control its image and to seek competitive advantage by exploiting stereotypical cultural attitudes concerning the physical appearance, proper place in society, and supposed personal characteristics of blacks and women.

* * *

D.   *Public Degradation of Black Women*

Many employers express shock that black women who refuse to unbraid their hair take such a strong stance, one that could cost them their jobs, in defense of a hairstyle. More shocking is the recurrence among unrelated employers of virtually identical solutions to the issue of braids, solutions that embody overt racist caricatures of the past expressed in the subtle, symbolic code of contemporary racism. Invariably, black women are told either to unbraid their hair or to disguise their braids by pulling them into a bun or cover them up with a wig or hairpiece. This latter solution—the forcible covering up of a black woman's hair—connotes a demeaning servitude that persists even in the face of changes in one of America's most cherished and enduring symbols. For the first time in the more than one hundred years of the Aunt Jemima trademark's existence, its current owner has deemed it profitable to reveal Aunt Jemima's hair. But for the color of her skin, the new Aunt Jemima could pass for Betty Crocker. There is nothing wrong or offensive about the similarity of these trademarks, but the marketing judgment of Aunt Jemina's owner does reflect the assumption that the public equates progress for black women with the imitation of white women. Because being black is an occasion for oppression, avoiding blackness and its attached cultural associations becomes the essential mechanism of liberation.

* * *

Judgments about aesthetics do not exist apart from judgments about the social, political, and economic order of a society. They are an essential part of that order. Aesthetic values determine who and what is valued, beautiful, and entitled to control. Thus established, the structure of society at other levels also is justified. What appears to be merely an aesthetic judgment in *Rogers* is part of the subordination of black women and is inextricably connected to the more obvious economic judgments reflected in other cases that affect black women.

IV.   THE NATURE OF KINSHIP

The issues in *Rogers* defy resolution by resort to arguments about mere aesthetic judgments, doctrinal confusion, or minimal effect on employment rights. The application of *Willingham* in *Rogers* reflects patriarchal assumptions about women generally and competing stereotypical images about womanhood determined by race. These competing images limit black women's choices in ways far more fundamental than is readily apparent in controversies about hair. And although *Willingham* and *Rogers* appear to reserve to white women the privilege of their personal and cultural choices, these cases are based on stereotypes that constitute a ready mechanism for denying employment opportunity to white women who refuse to express themselves in ways that satisfy their employers' notions of "white femaleness." These decisions effectively lock men—black and white—and black women out of choices associated with "true" womanhood; read in reverse, they lock white women into such choices.

* * *

V.   HEALING THE SHAME

Eliminating the behavioral consequences of certain stereotypes is a core function of antidiscrimination law. This function can never be adequately performed as long as courts and legal theorists create narrow, inflexible definitions of harm and categories of protection that fail to reflect the actual experience of discrimination. Considering the interactive relationship between racism and sexism from the experiential standpoint and knowledge base of black women can lead to the development of legal theories grounded in reality, and to the consideration by all women of the extent to which racism limits their choices *as women* and by black and other men of color of the extent to which sexism defines their experiences as men of subordinated races.

* * *

NOTES AND QUESTIONS

1.   Impact of *Rogers*. The ruling in the case upheld employers' right to ban prohibit their employees from wearing braided hairstyles. The case relied on *Carswell v. Peachford Hospital*, which upheld the right of a psychiatric hospital to dismiss an employee for wearing beads in their braided hairstyle. The court held that the decision was based on a rule that banned the wearing of jewelry by employees. According to the hospital, the rule was mandated for the patients' safety rather than as a form of racial discrimination. Both cases rely on the premise that braided hairstyles are not the exclusive province of black women. For example, American Airlines claimed the plaintiff only began wearing the braided hairstyle after it was "popularized" by Bo Derek in the movie 10. This argument succeeded because it operated on the premise that braided hairstyles are not immutable physical traits such as an Afro. *See* Caldwell, *supra*.

2.   Employee discrimination or customer preference? Caldwell learned of the *Rogers* decision while reading an article concerning Cheryl

Tatum, a black woman dismissed from Hyatt Hotel in Washington, D.C. for wearing an inappropriate hairstyle. According to Caldwell, the accompanying picture showed a black woman with a pageboy hairstyle that had small braids also. Tatum claims a Hyatt manager said, "I can't understand why you would want to wear your hair like that anyway. What would our guests think if we allowed you all to wear your hair like that?" *See* Caldwell, *supra* at 421, n.7. The managers' statements exhibit the frequency in which employers invoke customer preference as the reason for banning certain hairstyles. But as Caldwell states, customer preference is usually nothing more than the employer stating its appearance preferences.

3.   Black women's place in appearance-focused industries. In the article, Caldwell argues that black women often experience a precarious position in appearance-focused, feminine industries such as airline stewardesses. For example, do the appearance regulations speak to gender or race? Caldwell's article seems to suggest that gender and race are significant factors in the regulations and that black women particularly face both issues. As mentioned in the article, scores of black women have been dismissed from jobs for having inappropriate hairstyles such as braids. In addition, these appearance rules are seen as particularly restricting upon women and decided by men. In this sense black women's appearance has to be pleasing to the white and male eye.

4.   Distinction between immutable and mutable traits. American Airlines and the court felt the plaintiff's hairstyle was a voluntary choice. It was not like an Afro which is an immutable biological trait of blacks. In this sense, the court distinguished between physical and cultural traits and choices. Furthermore, the argument concerning Bo Derek was used by the court and American Airlines to suggest that the prohibition against braided hairstyles was not racial in nature because it was also a style popular with white women. Because of this, it was difficult for the plaintiff to successfully argue that black women were exclusively targeted by the prohibition.

5.   Narrow definition of discrimination. Caldwell's article suggests that Rogers was unsuccessful because the court used such a narrow scope of the harm caused by discrimination. She suggests that a more flexible interpretation would take into account the reality of racism and the manner in which it constricts the choices and options of black women and other minorities. Upon suing under the Thirteenth Amendment prohibition on slavery, Rogers' arguments were not supported because the court ruled she was not forced to stay on the job.

E.   THE MARKET VALUE OF POPULAR IMAGES

Madonna: Plantation Mistress or Soul Sister?

BLACK LOOKS: RACE AND REPRESENTATION 157–64 (1992).

BELL HOOKS

White women "stars" like Madonna, Sandra Bernhard, and many others publicly name their interest in, and appropriation of, black culture as yet another sign of their radical chic. Intimacy with that "nasty" blackness good white girls stay away from is what they seek. To white and other non-black consumers, this gives them a special flavor, an added spice. After all it is a very recent historical phenomenon for any white girl to be able to get some mileage out of flaunting her fascination and envy of blackness. The thing about envy is that it is always ready to destroy, erase, take-over, and consume the desired object. That's exactly what Madonna attempts to do when she appropriates and commodifies aspects of black culture. Needless to say this kind of fascination is a threat. It endangers. Perhaps that is why so many of the grown black women I spoke with about Madonna had no interest in her as a cultural icon and said things like, "The bitch can't even sing." It was only among young black females that I could find die-hard Madonna fans. Though I often admire and, yes at times, even envy Madonna because she has created a cultural space where she can invent and reinvent herself and receive public affirmation and material reward, I do not consider myself a Madonna fan.

* * *

Fascinated yet envious of black style, Madonna appropriates black culture in ways that mock and undermine, making her presentation one that upstages. This is most evident in the video "Like a Prayer." Though I read numerous articles that discussed public outrage at this video, none focused on the issue of race. No article called attention to the fact that Madonna flaunts her sexual agency by suggesting that she is breaking the ties that bind her as a white girl to white patriarchy, and establishing ties with black men. She, however, and not black men, does the choosing. The message is directed at white men. It suggests that they only labeled black men rapists for fear that white girls would choose black partners over them. Cultural critics commenting on the video did not seem at all interested in exploring the reasons Madonna chooses a black cultural backdrop for this video, i.e., black church and religious experience. Clearly, it was this backdrop that added to the video's controversy.

* * *

Eager to see the documentary *Truth or Dare* because it promised to focus on Madonna's transgressive sexual persona, which I find interesting, I was angered by her visual representation of her domination over not white men (certainly not over Warren Beatty or Alek Keshishian), but people of color and white working-class women. I was too angered by this to appreciate other aspects of the film I might have enjoyed. In *Truth or Dare* Madonna clearly revealed that she can only think of exerting power along very traditional, white supremacist, capitalistic, patriarchal lines. That she made people who were dependent on her for their immediate livelihood submit to her will was neither charming nor seductive to me or the other black folks that I spoke with who saw the film. We thought it tragically ironic that Madonna would choose as her dance partner a black male with dyed blonde hair. Perhaps had he appeared less like a white-identified black male consumed by "blonde ambition" he might have upstaged her. Instead he was positioned as a mirror, into which Madonna and her audience could look and see only a reflection of herself and the worship of "whiteness" she embodies-that white supremacist culture wants everyone to embody. Madonna used her power to ensure that he and the other non-white women and men who worked for her, as well as some of the white subordinates would all serve as the backdrop to her white-girl-makes-good drama. Joking about the film with other black folks, we commented that Madonna must have searched long and hard to find a black female that was not a good dancer, one who would not deflect attention away from her. And it is telling that when the film directly reflects something other than a positive image of Madonna, the camera highlights the rage this black female dancer was suppressing. It surfaces when the "subordinates" have time off and are "relaxing".

* * *

I can only say this doesn't sound like liberation to me. Perhaps when Madonna explores those memories of her white working-class childhood in a troubled family in a way that enables her to understand intimately the politics of exploitation, domination, and submission, she will have a deeper connection with oppositional black culture. If and when this radical critical self-interrogation takes place, she will have the power to create new and different cultural productions, work that will be truly transgressive—acts of resistance that transform rather than simply seduce.

————

NOTES AND QUESTIONS

1. Minority gay males in the image of white women. The hooks essay suggests that minority gay males often impersonate and aspire to white womanhood. She also suggests that Madonna capitalizes on this by using a black male dancer who sports blond hair. According to hooks, Madonna is able to look into a mirror and see a similar reflection staring back. *See* bell hooks, *Madonna: Plantation Mistress or Soul Sister?*, in BLACK LOOKS: RACE AND REPRESENTATION, 157–64 (1992). As a doubly oppressed minority, many impoverished minority gay males impersonate famous white women including Madonna. In particular, if one looks at the "drag ball" phenomenon depicted in *Paris Is Burning*, it seems that many poor minority gay males aspire to the "power that is clustered around whiteness, wealth and heterosexuality." *See* Darren Lenard Hutchinson, *Out Yet Unseen: A Racial Critique of Gay and Lesbian Legal Theory and Political Discourse*, CONN. L. REV. 561 (1997). Similarly, hooks contends that Madonna uses her whiteness as power and property that enable her dominance over her minority subordinates. In particular, hooks criticizes the manner in which Madonna often humiliates and condescends to her minority dancers and backup singer. It somewhat echoes Hutchinson's argument that subjugated minorities will often suffer various harms to gain entry into the white world. *See* hooks, *supra*.

2.   Class as a division between women. In *Feminist Theory: From Margin to Center*, hooks suggests that class is a divider in addition to race between white and black women. bell hooks, FEMINIST THEORY FROM MARGIN TO CENTER (1984). According to hooks, to deny that there is a class division is equivalent to denial of a class struggle in the United States. To hooks, it is insufficient for an affluent woman to take a poor woman to lunch and cite this as an example of female unity. In the same sense, it is insufficient for Madonna to hire the services of minorities and still subjugate them to abuse. In hooks' opinion, the documentary film *Truth or Dare: In Bed with Madonna* only reinforces the notion of white dominance over minorities. In particular, she argues that the movie and its images connote white patriarchal power. hooks, *supra* at 159.

3.   The different perceptions of black and white female sexuality. Perhaps an excellent example of this is the recent Super Bowl controversy over Janet Jackson and Justin Timberlake's performance. Here is a sample of some of the headlines in leading national and international newspapers: *FCC is Investigating Super Bowl Show*, THE WASH. POST, Feb. 3, 2004, at A1; *Singer's Boob Sparks Outrage in US*, THE GUARDIAN, Feb. 3, 2004; *Halftime incident sparks FCC inquiry*, ATLANTA J–CONST., Feb. 3, 2004; *Janet's Sorry for Super strip*, N.Y. DAILY NEWS, Feb. 3, 2004. Interestingly enough, Timberlake's participation was notably absent in much of the outrage and debate. A majority of media outlets treated Jackson as if she were the lone participant in the performance. A number of reasons could explain this. Some view her as solely responsible for the planning of the performance and him as an unknowing accomplice. On the other hand, some argue that Jackson has been severely criticized due to her race. In particular, some have wondered if this would have happened if she were white or Timberlake black. Another issue has been whether Timberlake would have been criticized if he were a black man ripping the bodice of a white female performer.

4.   Race, sex and advertising hyperbole: crossing the line. Although hooks's essay was written in 1992, sexuality, race, and power continue to be very controversial topics. The Super Bowl controversy illustrates the notion that the public still rejects certain presentations of female sexuality. In the essay, hooks asserts that Madonna has built a career on bold sexuality while still being able to retreat to her whiteness. For hooks, this means Madonna has been able to project sexuality without having the same derogatory labels and exploitation affixed to her suffered by generations of black women.

What accounts for the different reactions to black and white sexuality? The reactions to Madonna and Janet Jackson were disparate. The latter was pilloried and drew major criticism in terms of her morals and values. Of course, there are several possible reasons for this. First, it occurred during the "family hour" of the Super Bowl. Many adults contend that the half-time show was inappropriate for children. Second, it occurred during one of the biggest events of the year. It is the highest rated show and that could account for the large outpouring of reaction and opinion. Third, she is a black woman who was exposed on national television. The last possibility is one that has been mainly voiced by minority groups. The majority of the mainstream press has not discussed the event as a racial issue. Regardless, the aftermath of the Super Bowl suggests that the public has different standards and notions regarding black and white sexuality.

By contrast to the nearly uniform negative outcry over the Janet Jackson nipple baring "wardrobe malfunction," public reaction was mixed in response to an ad that aired during ABC's Monday Night Football. The ad featured white actress Nicollette Sheridan dropping her towel to flash her naked body to black Philadelphia Eagles receiver Terrell Owens. One columnist thought that the initial public criticism was an "overaction." *Moral Standards; Under Assault, But Holding Their Own*, ORLANDO SENTINEL, Dec. 7, 2004, at A15. Other critics called the "towel-dropping teaser everything from racist to pornographic."

F.   MARKET VALUE OF SEXUAL DIFFERENCES

The Sexual Continuum: Transsexual Prisoners

Note, 24 NEW ENG. J. ON CRIM. & CIV. CONFINEMENT 599 (1998).

■ ANITA C. BARNES

I.   INTRODUCTION

In a society so bent on the absolute, within a legal system so dependent on identifiable categories, the transsexual prisoner presents a serious problem. Transsexualism protests the confines of gender and sex, questioning the very essence of what is man and what is woman, what is masculine and what is feminine. Transgendered individuals challenge the relationship of sex to gender, specifically, sex does not control gender.

The transsexual inmate faces an even greater struggle due to the narrow definition of sex employed by prison authorities. Courts and prisons strain to place pre-and postoperative transsexuals into recognizable categories and fail to appreciate the uniqueness that transsexualism creates. In effect, transgendered prisoners encounter two forms of imprisonment: (1) they are trapped in a body not their own, and (2) they are oppressed within a legal system just beginning to understand their plight.

     * * *

II.   LEGAL RECOGNITION OF GENDER AND SEX

A.   *The Definition of Sex and Gender*

Sex refers to one's anatomy, biology, and physiology. This includes one's genitalia, chromosomal structure, and internal sexual organs. Gender refers to an individual's self-image, how others perceive the individual, and the underlying stereotypes surrounding sex. Gender represents the social construction of sex, "gender is to sex as feminine is to female and masculine is to male." Sex defines the system, and gender the function: "sex is the act and gender is the classification."

* * *

Yet gender is largely more determinative of a person's sex than anatomy or biology. In underestimating the importance of gender in defining sex, "the legal community refuses to accept ... that one's gender is as much an indication of sex as is biology." Gender encompasses one's private experience of sexual roles and his or her public expression of them. Gender influences how sex is perceived, and, ultimately, how society determines identity. Gender identity—the sense of maleness or female-ness—" 'pervades one's entire concept of one's place in life, of one's place in society.' " This pervasiveness culminates in actual facts of biology becoming secondary. As Dr. Richard Green, Director of the Gender Identity Research and Treatment Clinic at the University of California School of Medicine in Los Angeles noted, "[g]ender is the usually unshakable conviction of being male or female." The social construction of gender challenges the notion that sex is somehow irrevocably assigned at birth, and that sex in its biological sense exclusively dictates the formation of gender. The medical profession acknowledges that gender identity is generally established early in life. Medical practitioners also recognize that genetic make-up does not wholly determine gender or sexual identity; rather, socialization plays a crucial role as well. In order to better understand the dilemma of the transsexual prisoner, the legal community must embrace the notion that anatomy does not conclusively define gender, and gender identity does not necessarily stem from biological sex. As Leslie Pearlman concluded:

> It is the semantic distinction between sex and gender and the subsequent jurisprudential construction of gender which the legal community has failed to understand, but that cannot be ignored. The separate concepts of gender and sex must be respected and accorded their true, individual meanings. If they are not, the uniqueness of the transsexual situation cannot be understood.

B.   *Legal Recognition of Gender: Gender Discrimination*

Though the United States Supreme Court hesitates to differentiate gender from sex or to acknowledge gender as separate from sex, Supreme Court cases implicitly focus on gender stereotyping as grounds for sex discrimination. In *Orr v. Orr*, for example, the Court struck down an Alabama statute that required husbands, but not wives, to pay alimony. Recognizing traditional gender roles of men as breadwinners, and women as homemakers as the impetus behind the statute, the Court reasoned that, in order to survive constitutional scrutiny, the statute must rest on some basis other than antiquated gender stereotypes. The Court in *Orr* concentrated on whether sex is a viable criteria for judging financial need. In analyzing this viability, the Court focused on sex not in terms of biology, but rather in terms, of how society dictates gender *on the basis of sex.*

III.   LEGAL DYNAMICS OF TRANSSEXUALISM

A.   *The Definition of Transsexualism*

* * *

Much of the debate surrounding how the law should recognize transsexuality revolves around the search for the root causes of transsexualism, particularly, whether the origin is psychological or physical. Regardless, transsexualism occurs early in life. Though transsexualism is traditionally viewed as a mental disorder, the medical profession recognizes neurological causes for transsexualism. Studies point to brain size and the role of sexual differentiation during fetal development as the sources of transsexuality. Specifically, research concludes that gender identity is the result of "an interaction between the developing brain and sex hormones." Studies suggest that " 'transsexuals are right. Their sex was judged in the wrong way at the moment of birth because people look only to the sex organs and not to the brain' " to determine sex. Given the medical research regarding brain structure and the sexual differentiation of the brain which occurs after birth, assigning a child's sex on the basis of external genitalia amounts to "an act of faith."

* * *

In *Pinneke v. Preisser*, the United States Court of Appeals for the Eighth Circuit concluded that sex reassignment surgery is medically necessary, therefore, Medicaid cannot deny coverage. Likewise, in *G.B. v. Lackner*, the California Court of Appeals rejected the California Department of Health's argument that sex reassignment amounted to cosmetic surgery, which is excluded from Medi–Cal coverage. Instead, the court concluded that transsexual surgery constitutes a reasonable and medically necessary approach to treating transsexuality.

B.   *Transsexualism and Sex Discrimination*

* * *

In analyzing sex discrimination claims brought by transgendered individuals, courts employ circular reasoning. Courts disallow claims of discrimination on the basis of transsexuality, yet would recognize similar actions if based on a transsexual's anatomic or perceived sex. To succeed, transgendered individuals must prove discrimination due to their sex, whether male or female, not their transsexuality. *Dobre* attests to how difficult a burden this places on transsexuals. In *Dobre* the court went so far as to assume that the plaintiff was female and still found that Dobre failed to state an adequate claim that she was discriminated against as a female. The court concluded, "[if] the plaintiff was discriminated against at all, it was because she was perceived as a male who wanted to become a female."

* * *

By clinging to narrow definitions of sex and gender, courts fail to understand the continuum of sexual identity that transgendered individuals create. Instead, courts continue to struggle to assign pre-and postoperative transsexuals an identifiable "sex" according to the traditional definitions of gender and sex. Some courts adopt the rule that completion of surgery determines sex, recognizing postoperative transsexuals with their new sex while classifying preoperative transsexuals according to their anatomy. For the transitioning transsexual, however, this assignment of gender based on biology and genitalia is essentially a form of "institutionalized oppression."

    * * *

C.   Transsexualism and Disability Discrimination

Title VII of the Americans with Disabilities Act (ADA), which bars discrimination against people with disabilities, expressly excludes transsexuals from such protection. Meanwhile, state and federal courts have struggled to define transsexualism and determine whether it is a handicap. In *Leyland v. Orr*, the Ninth Circuit recognized transsexuality as a disability when it upheld the honorable discharge of a postoperative transsexual from the Air Force Reserves. The Air Force concluded that undergoing transsexual surgery significantly impairs an individual's ability to perform his or her duties, and that such surgery rendered Leyland "psychologically unsuitable and physically unfit" for military service.

    * * *

In *Doe v. Blue Cross & Blue Shield of Rhode Island*, a Rhode Island district court recognized the "highly sensitive" nature of transsexuality and the stigma associated with the condition when it allowed a transsexual litigant to pursue his claim under a fictitious name. The judge noted the need for anonymity "[p]articularly in this era of seemingly increased societal intolerance toward 'unconventional' sexual behavior." The judge concluded, "I will not strip [the] plaintiff of the cloak of privacy, which, shields him from the stigmatization he. might otherwise endure."

    * * *

Transsexuality should fall within this protection. Transsexual individuals are socially marginalized due to intolerance, prejudice, and stereotypes surrounding gender and sexual identity. Transgendered individuals are likely to face any or all of the following pervasive social problems: dismissal from employment upon discovery of their transsexuality, termination of parental rights, being labeled as handicapped by the military due to sex reassignment, and being discriminated against by school boards which perpetuate intolerance. Unfortunately, these consequences all occur with the approval of the legal system. This tolerated marginalization challenges Title VII's exclusion of transsexuality as a disability. Transsexualism, therefore, should fall within the definition of a perceived disability.

IV.   The Transsexual Prisoner

    * * *

The Eighth Amendment directly addresses the treatment of prisoners and the conditions surrounding incarceration. Specifically, it prohibits the infliction of cruel and unusual punishment, thereby imposing on prison authorities a duty to provide humane conditions of confinement and to ensure that inmates receive adequate food, clothing, shelter, and medical care. The Eighth Amendment also requires that prison officials "'take reasonable measures to guarantee the safety of the inmates.'" As noted:

> "[W]hen the State by the affirmative exercise of its power [through incarceration] so restrains an individual's liberty that it renders him unable to care for himself, and at the same time fails to provide for his basic human needs ... it transgresses the substantive limits on state action set by the Eighth Amendment."

The Supreme Court defines cruel and unusual punishment as the wanton and unnecessary infliction of pain, which includes harm that serves no legitimate penological interest and treatment that is grossly disproportionate to the sentence imposed. The standard underlying the Eighth Amendment is not static; rather, its meaning derives from the evolving principles of dignity, decency, and humanity.

* * *

A. *Placement of Transsexual Prisoners*

In *Farmer v. Brennan*, the Court articulated the standard for use with the Eighth Amendment as one of "deliberate indifference." Under this standard, the petitioner must prove that the deprivation was serious and also show that prison officials acted with a culpable state of mind. In defining culpability, the Court rejected an objective test-that prison officials knew or should have known of the risk—and instead set out that to be culpable, an official must be aware of, yet disregard, an excessive risk to a prisoner's health or safety. This subjective standard requires that an officer "be aware of facts from which the inference could be drawn that a substantial risk of serious harm exists, and he [or she] must also draw the inference." A showing of reckless disregard of a substantial risk satisfies this "culpable state of mind" requirement.

* * *

The Court further stated that an official would not escape liability by refusing to verify, or failing to confirm, a strong suspicion that a substantial risk existed. Likewise, the Court recognized that membership within an identifiable group from which members are frequently singled out for attack, establishes a sufficiently serious risk that warrants Eighth Amendment protection.

* * *

Placing preoperative transsexuals with prisoners of the same anatomical sex exacerbates the risk of harm to transsexual prisoners and challenges the constitutionality of this practice. Adherence to the strict construction that genitalia determines sex places transitioning transsexuals in a "Catch–22." The inevitable dangers of being placed in the general population forces prison officials to segregate transsexual prisoners into protective custody. As the court in Crosby concluded, due to the inherent risk involved in placing preoperative transsexuals according to their biological sex and the limitations associated with segregation, the best solution is to house transsexual prisoners according to their gender identity.

B. *Medical Care of Transsexual Prisoners*

In *Phillips v. Michigan Department of Corrections*, a district court in Michigan granted a transsexual's preliminary injunction for the continued use of female hormones. In so doing, the court recognized that transsexualism represents a serious medical disorder and that failure to provide treatment constitutes cruel and unusual punishment. The court specifically ordered prison officials to continue estrogen therapy and to afford the plaintiff with "the same standard of care she was receiving prior to incarceration." The *Phillips* court further observed that the failure to provide female hormones to the plaintiff reversed the transitional process, thus adversely affecting the plaintiff by worsening her physical and emotional state. As the court noted,

> [i]t is one thing to fail to provide an inmate with care that would improve his or her medical state, such as refusing to provide sex reassignment surgery or to operate on a long-endured cyst. Taking measures which actually reverse the effects of years of healing medical treatment ... is measurably worse, making the cruel and unusual determination much easier.

Ironically, prisons continue to support treatment approaches that the medical profession and most courts recognize as futile. Outside the prison walls, courts denounce policies that summarily dismiss hormone treatment and sex reassignment as unnecessary and inappropriate treatment for transsexualism. Instead, courts conclude that such treatment is medically necessary and required to "cure" transsexualism. Prison officials' insistence on providing counseling alone, a treatment recognized as unsuccessful, constitutes the unnecessary and wanton infliction of pain, in violation of the Eighth Amendment.

* * *

C. *Use of Protective Custody*

Administrative segregation, also known as protective custody or administrative detention, is a form of confinement utilized to separate an inmate from the general population. It is designed to segregate inmates for short periods of time. Where protective custody is not voluntary, heightened standards will attach. Prison officials may place an inmate in administrative detention when that inmate poses a serious threat to the security of the institution, the lives of staff, other inmates, or to him or herself. In addition, prisoners may voluntarily choose segregation for their own protection. Wherever possible, the conditions of administrative detention should mirror those of the general population. Administrative segregation, for nonpunitive reasons, "is the sort of confinement that inmates should reasonably anticipate receiving at some point in their incarceration." Accordingly, the Fourteenth Amendment does not independently protect inmates from such segregation. Conditions of confinement, however, fall under the scrutiny of the Eighth Amendment. The " 'evolving standards of decency' " and human dignity govern such protective custody.

* * *

States may create liberty interests governing the use of protective custody. In *Hewitt v. Helms*, for example, the United States Supreme Court held that a Pennsylvania statute created a liberty interest for a prisoner to remain in the general prison population. Focusing on the mandatory language contained in the statute, the Court recognized that the Pennsylvania legislature went "beyond simple procedural guidelines" toward creating a liberty interest in not being held in administrative segregation without first complying with due process requirements. The Court also, recognized how administrative detention puts restraints on an inmate's freedom. As dictated by the statute, the Court emphasized that "administrative segregation may not be used as a pretext for indefinite confinement of an inmate." Prison officials, however, must conduct periodic reviews to prevent such abuse. The lower court in *Hewitt* analogized protective custody with solitary confinement absent a showing of misconduct, and concluded that "inmates' interests in avoiding confinement in Administrative Custody are no less real" than those of the prisoner seeking to avoid solitary confinement.

* * *

The United States Supreme Court has recognized that conditions beyond one's control are not punishable. For example, punishing someone for uncontrollable conduct resulting from a disease or illness violates the Eighth Amendment. In *Robinson v. California*, the Court struck down a California statute making drug addiction a criminal offense. The Court determined that addiction represents a status or condition and not a punishable offense. As such, to punish addiction imposes " 'a continuing offense . . . [that] is chronic rather than acute; that it continues after it is complete and subjects the offender to arrest at any time.' " Addiction may also occur innocently or involuntarily, further implicating the Eighth Amendment. In concluding that the punishment of addiction violated the Eighth Amendment, the Court analogized that a statute criminalizing mental illness would undoubtedly entail cruel and unusual punishment as well. As the Court explained:

> A state law which imprisons a person thus afflicted [with addiction] as a criminal, inflicts a cruel and unusual punishment in violation of the Fourteenth Amendment. To be sure, imprisonment for ninety days is not, in the abstract, a punishment which is either cruel or unusual. But the question cannot be considered in the abstract. Even one day in prison would be a cruel and unusual punishment for the "crime" of having a common cold.

* * *

Transsexualism falls within the definition of a status. Specifically, it is beyond the person's control, it is acquired innocently and involuntarily, possibly at birth, and those afflicted are powerless to overcome the condition. Transsexualism is the constant, inflexible, and immutable conviction of imprisonment in the wrong body. Placing transsexual prisoners in protective custody, given their status, compounds the unconstitutionality of such a practice.

* * *

V.   CONCLUSION

Present policies regarding the placement, treatment, and conditions of confinement of transsexual prisoners raise serious constitutional issues. Prisons house transsexual prisoners according to their sex as assigned at birth without recognizing the significance of gender in determining identity. This practice ignores the fact that gender plays a far more crucial role than sex in an individual's self-definition, and in how others perceive that individual. Transsexual prisoners constitute an identifiable group due to their gender identity. Intolerance by other inmates sets transsexual inmates apart and encourages attacks' upon them. Prison authorities' insistence on placing preoperative transsexuals according to their biology represents a conscious disregard, or deliberate indifference, toward the obvious risks inherent in such a policy.

Refusal to Hire, or Dismissal From Employment, on Account of Plaintiff's Sexual Lifestyle or Sexual Preference As Violation of Federal Constitution or Federal Civil Rights Statutes

Annotation, 42 A.L.R. FED. 189, 191, 204–05 (1979 & Supp. 2004).

■ RUSSELL J. DAVIS

[a] Scope

This annotation collects and analyzes the federal and state cases, and relevant decisions of the Equal Employment Opportunity Commission which decide whether it is a violation of the United States Constitution or of any federal civil rights statute to dismiss an employee or to refuse to hire an applicant for employment because of his "sexual lifestyle" or "sexual preference." The latter terms are given a rather broad definition for purposes of this annotation and include such matters as homosexuality, transsexuality, "adulterous" relationships, and cohabitation without benefit of marriage; however, the annotation does not include decisions involving isolated instances of unorthodox or disapproved sexual behavior.

* * *

5. Transsexuality

* * *

In *Grossman v. Bernards Township Board of Education*, [538 F.2d 319 (D.C.N.J. 1975)], the court dismissed the civil rights action of an elementary school music teacher who was dismissed from the school system after undergoing a "sex reassignment operation," holding that jurisdiction over the action could not be based on 42 U.S.C.A. § 1981. The court pointed out that the purpose of § 1981 was clearly to afford protection from discrimination based on race, and that no allegation of racial discrimination appeared anywhere in the plaintiff teacher's pleading.

Plaintiff, who was prospective transsexual and employee in beauty salon operated on premises of department store and who was terminated from employment for not dressing and acting as man while at work, failed to state cause of action under 42 U.S.C.A. § 1985(3), where, under statute, plaintiff must allege that defendants' refusal to allow her to continue work while dressing and acting as woman denied her equal protection, or equal privileges and equal immunities, and where there was no allegation that any other employees who were biologically men, were protected, privileged, or immune so as to have right to work while dressed and acting as women (or vice versa); therefore, plaintiff had failed to allege any manner in which she was treated other than as all other (biological) men were. Further, transsexuals are not suspect class for purposes of equal protection analysis and clearly there was rational basis for employer's requiring its employees who dealt with public to dress and act as persons of their biological sex since allowing employees to do otherwise would disturb customers and cause them to take their business elsewhere. *Kirkpatrick v. Seligman & Latz, Inc.*, [475 F.Supp. 145 (M.D. Fla. 1979)].

[b] Title VII of Civil Rights Act of 1964

Finding a failure to state a cause of action under Title VII of the Civil Rights Act of 1964, 42 U.S.C.A. § 2000e–2(a)(1), the court in *Grossman v. Bernards Township Board of Education*, [538 F.2d 319 (D.C.N.J. 1975)], dismissed an action brought by a transsexual who had been discharged from her position as a music teacher for elementary schools after undergoing a "sex reassignment operation." As affirmed by the state's commissioner of education, the dismissal resulted from school officials' conclusion that the plaintiff teacher was incapable of teaching children because of the potential that her presence in the classroom would cause them psychological harm. Assuming for the purpose of the instant case that the plaintiff teacher was "a member of the female gender," the court found it apparent that she was discharged by the school board not because of her status as a female, but rather because of her change in sex. Noting the scarcity of legislative history relating to the inclusion of sex as a prohibited source of employment discrimination in Title VII, the court expressed its reluctance to ascribe import to this term other than its plain meaning.

Defendant former employer was entitled to dismissal of sex-discrimination complaint by transsexual, since discrimination against sex-change process is not discrimination based on stereotypic notions of males and females and not within congressional intent in prohibiting "sex" discrimination under Title VII. *Dobre v. National R.R. Passenger Corp.*, [850 F.Supp. 284 (E.D. Pa. 1993)].

———

NOTES AND QUESTIONS

1. Transsexual prisoners' rights and housing. One of the most divisive and controversial issues concerning imprisoned transsexuals is their housing. It is a highly delicate issue in terms of the prisoners' concerns for safety and other inmates' concern for privacy. A determinate of where to place the prisoners is whether the prisoner has had genital replacement surgery. Under *Farmer v. Brennan*, 511 U.S. 825, 829 (1994), prisoners who have not had the surgery will be placed according to their birth sex while those who have will be placed in the reassigned gender space. However positive that sounds, there are also negative aspects. In particular, those reassigned are often excluded from educational and occupational opportunities and associational rights. *See* Darren Rosenblum, *"Trapped" in Sing Sing: Transgendered Prisoners Caught in the Gender Binarism,* 6 Mich. J. Gender & L. 499, 530 (2000).

2. Hormone therapy use in prison. Like housing, the issue of hormone use for transsexual prisoners has not been clear-cut. While courts have ruled that transsexual prisoners have a right to continue hormone therapy, prison officials have not been strictly required to provide the treatments. Because of this, scores of prisoners have not received hormone therapy while imprisoned. *See* Rosenblum, *supra* at 545, note 62.

3. Placement rights over privacy issues. Whose rights should receive priority in housing situations? Many female prisoners have felt threatened by male to female prisoners sharing the same quarters with them. On the other hand male to female prisoners are threatened in male quarters. For many, the issue of providing separate quarters for transsexuals rings of special treatment that is unfair. None of these issues are simplified by the overcrowding and violence that are prevalent in the United States prison system. If transsexual prisoners are placed in separate facilities, does that mean people should be segregated by race, handicaps, and sexual orientation also?

4. Impact of unconscious attitudes on sexual orientation discrimination. Some argue that it has been difficult to prove sexual orientation discrimination because courts take a narrow view that overlook the impact of unconscious attitudes toward gays. *See* Elvia R. Arriola, *Gendered Inequality Lesbians, Gays, and Feminist Legal Theory,* 9 Berkeley Women's L.J. 103 (1994). Arriola contends that courts should examine how attitudes toward sexual identity and stereotypes lead to discrimination.

G.   THE MARKET FOR COUNTERCULTURE

"The price we pay when pursuing any art or calling, is an intimate knowledge of its ugly side"

—James Baldwin

Black But Not Beautiful: Negative Black Stereotypes Abound in Rap Lyrics, on Music Videos, in Movies and on Cable—and Blacks Are Among Those Doing the Stereotyping

NEWSDAY, Oct. 24, 1993, at 6.

■ ESTHER IVEREM

Spike Lee Tells a college audience that Hollywood only wants to make black films about urban violence and drugs.

Bill Cosby calls "Russell Simmons' Def Comedy Jam" a "minstrel show."

The Rev. Calvin Butts thunders from his Harlem pulpit about black musical artists who refer to all women as "bitches" and "whores."

Is this Blaxploitation II?

* * *

"What's happening now I call the black-on-black film crime, the black-on-black television crime, because a lot of people creating this stuff happen to be African-American," Townsend says. "Nobody wants to blow the whistle because they say, 'Hey, that's a brother trying to make some money. He's getting paid.' "

Women in the entertainment industry are concerned about how young female fans will build self-esteem and self confidence in the face of misogynist lyrics characterizing women as sex-for-sale gold diggers—lyrics embraced by many young male artists who find that their newfound money and fame attract groupies who would otherwise shun them. In a recent interview, rapper Dr. Dre described his Los Angeles-area home as a place where he hangs out with friends "and about twenty to thirty women."

Another element that distinguishes the new blaxploitation from that of 20 years ago is the degree to which much of the art by blacks is also consumed by whites. Artists such as Ice-T, Ice Cube and L.L. Cool J. generate more sales in America's suburban malls than in city shopping districts. "Def Comedy Jam" has an audience that is 60 percent white.

* * *

MUSIC

* * *

To pinpoint the beginning of the current cultural wave is difficult, but by 1989, there was already criticism of artists in the male-dominated world of rap such as Slick Rick, Too Short, and the group N.W.A. for their sexist lyrics.

Slick Rick, for example, included on his 1989 album, "The Great Adventures of Slick Rick," the cut, "Treat Her Like a Prostitute." The group N.W.A. was one of the first groups to refer to all women as "bitches" and "hos" in its seminal "Straight Outta Compton." Even after N.W.A. disbanded, solo acts spawned by the group, including Dr. Dre, continued the tradition. And as the first popular gangster rappers, N.W.A. also launched a barrage of violent images across the country: "When I'm called off / I gotta sawed off / Squeeze the trigger / And bodies are hauled off," the group also rapped in "Straight Outta Compton."

* * *

But most of the violence in black video (and film) depicts black-on-black crime. And rather than being afraid, young white America embraced gangster rap. During the late '80s, as hip-hop's popularity grew, many white pop and dance-music stations played controversial rap groups banned on black radio stations—and lured young black listeners. Though white pop stations traditionally target youth, black radio stations such as New York's WBLS have historically served a wide variety of musical tastes. Even as some black stations have loosened their restrictions to woo back listeners, it's not uncommon for Onyx, Ice-T and 2Pac to receive their first airplay on white pop stations.

* * *

VIDEO AND PERFORMANCE

Nothing has had a greater impact on the overall music industry in the past decade than music videos. Though record companies were slower to provide video budgets for black artists and MTV was slow to give videos by blacks airplay, videos are now an integral part of the marketing strategy for most artists. Today "MTV Jams," which highlights black music, is one of the most popular programs on the cable channel. Like radio, MTV competes successfully against black-owned BET for young black listeners, even though BET plays a wider variety of black artists.

* * *

Butts, pastor of Harlem's Abyssinian Baptist Church, a leader in the black community's response to offensive messages, says that coming across three videos—one by Luther Campbell, Apache's "Gangsta Bitch" and "Ain't Too Proud to Beg" by TLC—in part spurred him to get involved.

"I was appalled at what I saw and heard," says Butts, sitting at his desk at the church's office. "It was so vulgar. I had seen some things in music before that didn't quite jibe with my sensibilities, but I knew that these things were doing important commentary. However, what I saw that particular night had no socially redemptive value at all.''

* * *

FILM

Taken as a whole, the new wave of black filmmakers is producing diverse films such as Mario Van Peebles' "Posse," Spike Lee's "Malcolm X" and Charles Lane's "Sidewalk Stories." But there is no doubt that Hollywood sees green in what some directors call "hood" films, centering on criminal elements of the black community—starting with "New Jack City," and "Boyz in the Hood" in 1991 and followed by films such as "Juice," "South-Central," "Trespass," "A Rage in Harlem" and, this year, "Menace II Society." Some have starred rap artists.

"It becomes a self-fulfilling prophecy," says Helena Echegoyen, director of development for New Line Cinema, which released "Menace II Society." "We have to look at the movies being made, at what is making money, and you make movies like those."

* * *

And once their films are in the market, black filmmakers contend with a virtually all-white corps of arts writers and critics, many of whom, directors say, feel more comfortable with ghetto stereotypes and violence than with other depictions of black life.

For example, when Kenneth Turan panned "Boomerang" last year in the Los Angeles Times, he cited his feeling that the movie's star, Eddie Murphy, had been better in his previous hustler roles, and his sense that an all-black cast playing successful professionals was "silly and arbitrary." The review provoked a rare written outcry from Murphy, Hudlin and members of the public.

"If this were a movie about gun-totin' drug dealers, it would be praised for its gritty authenticity while the complaints would be about encouraging violent behavior in the wake of national riots," Hudlin wrote in a letter to the Times.

* * *

COMEDY

At 36 years of age, Russell Simmons is certainly old enough to have been shaped by the race debates of the 1960s and 1970s. But, in his role as head of Rush Communications, which includes the record label and "Def Comedy Jam," he finds himself championing artists and trends of what writer Nelson George calls the post-soul culture of black America. And Simmons is not concerned that many of his artists as well as "Def Comedy Jam" serve a largely white audience. Reflecting a general comedy explosion in this country, several black comedy shows have cropped up in the past two years, including The Uptown Comedy Club, The Apollo Comedy Hour and Comic View. But none of these draws the audience or controversy of HBO's "Def Comedy Jam." A recent show, for example, peppered with what is the standard profanity, included several comedians graphically illustrating oral sex.

Responding to criticism leveled by Bill Cosby, Simmons says of his program, "I don't feel it's a minstrel show. If he's offended by their language or whatever they do, hey, those are real people. And they are mostly moral and very straightforward people."

Stan Lathan, director and executive producer of "Comedy Jam," says the show fairly represents the kinds of material being presented in black comedy clubs across the country. "The problem is that people zero in on the raunchy material," Lathan says.

* * *

Sandy Wernick, another executive producer of the show and president of Brillstein–Grey Entertainment, which manages several "Saturday Night Live" artists, including Dana Carvey and Adam Sandler, says the show appeals to whites in part because blacks have become secure enough to laugh at themselves.

Wernick, who is white, says he was intrigued by Simmons' idea because of its crossover appeal, and thought Simmons, who sold rap music to white America, was the right man to make the concept successful.

* * *

WHAT'S NEXT

If those concerned about black messages and images in pop culture are searching for relief, they might find it in the fact that the entertainment machine has to get new parts when the current ones wear down. What is coming could be a backlash against current artists who have reduced the panorama of black life to a single grim snapshot.

Artists who followed Public Enemy in the last wave of "conscious rap," such as X–Clan, A Tribe Called Qwest, Chubb Rock, Heavy D, Queen Latifah, De La Soul, and Poor Righteous Teachers, are being joined by newer artists rejecting images of death and nihilism, such as Arrested Development, Nefertitti, Das EFX and Get Set V.O.P.

"People are tired of hearing about people shooting somebody with their nine," said the rapper Heavy D. "Now it's getting monotonous. In the beginning, it was creative because it was somebody telling the rest of the world about a certain place they are from. Now you have a million and one people making those records who aren't even from the ghettos."

* * *

———

Status Censorship Report

Entertainment Weekly, June 29, 1990.

In an unprecedented legal decision, a federal judge in Florida ruled on June 6 that As Nasty as They Wanna Be, the controversial, sexually explicit rap album by the Miami-based 2 Live Crew, violated community obscenity laws. Within days, three members of the band and a local record-store owner had been arrested for their involvement in the performance and sale of the record, which has been bought by nearly 2 million people nation-wide—and has jumped 29 places on the Billboard chart since the ruling.

With that announcement, the music censorship movement appeared to lose steam-everywhere but in Florida. There, the 2 Live Crew has been at the center of an antiporn campaign by Gov. Bob Martinez (who called Nasty "audio pornography") and Miami attorney Jack Thompson since the release of the album last year. In March, a record-store clerk in Sarasota, Fla., was arrested for selling Nasty to an 11–year-old girl; charges were dropped, but the message to the record business was clear. In response to that incident and other attempts by local police to quell album sales, Luther Campbell (leader of the 2 Live Crew and owner of Luke's Records, which released Nasty) brought a civil suit against Broward County Sheriff Nick Navarro for prohibiting sales of the album by threatening arrest. But on June 6, in a 62–page decision (which began "This is a case between two ancient enemies: Anything Goes and Enough Already"), U.S. District Court Judge Jose Gonzalez ruled that the album's lyrics were legally obscene under the 1973 Miller v. California Supreme Court decision.

In a related development, police attended a Madonna concert in Toron-to on May 29 after complaints of "lewdness" during her Blond Ambition tour, including simulations of masturbation and other sexual acts. No legal action followed. For the moment Madonna is safe, as are most rap albums in local record stores. But developments in the censorship battle have proven that the law can be as nasty as it wants to be, too.

———

A NOTE ON CONFLICTING VALUES WITHIN AFRICAN AMERICAN COMMUNITIES

A discernable tension has developed between some traditional civil rights leaders and the performers in the Gangsta Rap genre of hip-hop. The conflict of values is in part generational. Older civil rights leaders see the sex and violence-laden lyrics of rappers as an affront to more conservative, traditional values of many church-based civil rights activists.

The conflicts between these opposing views within the black communi-ty have often included intellectual property litigation and tort claims for interference with contract, trademark infringement, violation of rights of publicity, defamation, with countercharges of conspiracy, extortion, and fraud.

How would critical race theorists analyze the Rosa Parks and C. Delores Tucker's legal disputes described below? How would law and economics scholars analyze these disputes? Are these primarily economic disputes with political implications, or primarily political disputes with economic implications?

———

Parks v. LaFace Records

329 F.3d 437 (6th Cir. 2003).

■ Judge Holschuh delivered the opinion of the court:

This is a dispute over the name of a song. Rosa Parks is a civil rights icon who first gained prominence during the Montgomery, Alabama bus boycott in 1955. She brings suit against LaFace Records, a record producer, and OutKast, a "rap" (or "hip-hop") music duo, as well as several other named affiliates, for using her name as the title of their song, *Rosa Parks*. Parks contends that Defendants' use of her name constitutes false advertising under § 43(a) of the Lanham Act, 15 U.S.C. § 1125(a), and intrudes on her common law right of publicity under Michigan state law. Defendants argue that they are entitled to summary judgment because Parks has failed to show any violation of the Lanham Act or her right of publicity. Defendants further argue that, even if she has shown such a violation, their First Amendment freedom of artistic expression should be a defense as a matter of law to each of these claims. Parks also contends that Defendants' conduct renders them liable under Michigan law for defamation and tortious interference with a business relationship; Defendants have also denied liability with respect to these claims.

* * *

For the reasons hereafter set forth, [the court concludes that the district court erred in granting Defendants' motion for summary judgment on the Lanham Act and right of publicity claim, but that that the district court properly granted summary judgment in favor of Defendants on Rosa Parks' state law claims of defamation and tortious interference with a business relationship].

I. BACKGROUND

A. Facts

Rosa Parks is an historical figure who first gained prominence as a symbol of the civil rights movement in the United States during the 1950's and 1960's. In 1955, while riding in the front of a segregated bus in Montgomery, Alabama, she refused to yield her seat to a white passenger and move to the back of the bus as blacks were required to do by the then-existing laws requiring segregation of the races. A 381-day bus boycott in Montgomery flowed from that one event, which eventually became a catalyst for organized boycotts, sit-ins, and demonstrations all across the South. Her single act of defiance has garnered her numerous public accolades and awards, and she has used that celebrity status to promote various civil and human rights causes as well as television programs and books inspired by her life story. She has also approved a collection of gospel recordings by various artists entitled *Verity Records Presents: A Tribute to Mrs. Rosa Parks* (the *"Tribute"* album), released in 1995.

Defendants are OutKast, comprised of recording artists André "Dré" Benjamin and Antwan "Big Boi" Patton; their record producers, LaFace— * * * and LaFace's record distributors, Arista Records and BMG Entertainment—* * *. In September 1998, Defendants released the album *Aquemini*. The album's first single release was a song titled *Rosa Parks,* described as a "hit single" by a sticker on the album. The same sticker that contained the name *Rosa Parks* also contained a Parental Advisory warning of "explicit content." Because, as later discussed, the critical issue in this case is a determination of the artistic relevance of the title, *Rosa Parks,* to the content of the song, the lyrics obviously must be considered in their entirety. They are as follows:

(Hook)

Ah ha, hush that fuss
Everybody move to the back of the bus
Do you wanna bump and slump with us
We the type of people make the club get crunk

Verse 1: (Big Boi)

Many a day has passed, the night has gone by
But still I find the time to put that bump off in your eye
Total chaos, for these playas, thought we was absent
We takin another route to represent the Dungeon Family
Like Great Day, me and my nigga decide to take the back way
We stabbing every city then we headed to that bat cave
A–T–L, Georgia, what we do for ya
Bull doggin hoes like them Georgetown Hoyas
Boy you sounding silly, thank my Brougham aint sittin pretty
Doing doughnuts round you suckas like then circles around titties
Damn we the committee gone burn it down
But us gone bust you in the mouth with the chorus now

(Hook)

Verse 2: (André)

I met a gypsy and she hipped me to some life game
To stimulate then activate the left and right brain
Said baby boy you only funky as your last cut
You focus on the past your ass'll be a has what
Thats one to live by or either that one to die to
I try to just throw it at you determine your own adventure
Andre, got to her station here's my destination
She got off the bus, the conversation lingered in my head for hours
Took a shower kinda sour cause my favorite group ain't comin with it
But I'm witcha you cause you probably goin through it anyway
But anyhow when in doubt went on out and bought it
Cause I thought it would be jammin but examine all the flawsky-wawsky

Awfully, it's sad and it's costly, but that's all she wrote
And I hope I never have to float in that boat Up shit creek it's weak is
the last quote
That I want to hear when I'm goin down when all's said and done
And we got a new joe in town
When the record player get to skippin and slowin down
All yawl can say is them niggas earned that crown but until then . . .
* * *

II. DISCUSSION
* * *

B. The Lanham Act

Section 43(a) of the Lanham Act creates a civil cause of action against
any person who identifies his or her product in such a way as to likely
cause confusion among consumers or to cause consumers to make a
mistake or to deceive consumers as to association of the producer of the
product with another person or regarding the origin of the product or the
sponsorship or approval of the product by another person. * * *

[The court discusses the Lanham Act's primary application to "disputes between producers of commercial products and their competitors,"
but states that it] also permits celebrities to vindicate property rights in
their identities against allegedly misleading commercial use by others.
* * *

In order to prevail on a false advertising claim under § 43(a), a
celebrity must show that use of his or her name is likely to cause confusion
among consumers as to the "affiliation, connection, or association" between the celebrity and the defendant's goods or services or as to the
celebrity's participation in the "origin, sponsorship, or approval" of the
defendant's goods or services. * * *

Parks contends that Defendants have violated the Lanham Act because
the *Rosa Parks* title misleads consumers into believing that the song is
about her or that she is affiliated with the Defendants, or has sponsored or
approved the *Rosa Parks* song and the *Aquemini* album. * * *

Defendants respond that Parks' Lanham Act claim must fail for two
reasons. First, they claim that Parks does not possess a trademark right in
her name and Defendants have not made a trademark use of her name, as
allegedly required for a cause of action under the Lanham Act. Second, they
contend that even if use of the title posed some risk of consumer confusion,
the risk is outweighed by Defendants' First Amendment right to free
expression.

1. *Trademark Right In and Trademark Use of Parks' Name*
* * *

We find Parks' prior commercial activities and international recognition as a symbol of the civil rights movement endow her with a trademark
interest in her name the same as if she were a famous actor or musician.

* * * We turn then to Defendants' second argument, that even if Parks could establish some likelihood of confusion, the First Amendment protects Defendants' choice of title.

2. *The First Amendment Defense—Three Approaches*

* * *

[The court discusses the defendants' First Amendment defenses at length, and determines that the *Rogers v. Grimaldi*, 875 F.2d 994 (1989) test should apply.]

* * * The *Rogers* court, finding that overextension of Lanham Act restrictions in the area of titles might intrude on First Amendment values * * * adopted a two-pronged test:

> In the context of allegedly misleading titles using a celebrity's name, that balance [between avoiding consumer confusion and protecting free expression] will normally not support application of the Act unless [1] the title has no artistic relevance to the underlying work whatsoever, or, if it has some artistic relevance, unless [2] the title explicitly misleads as to the source or the content of the work.

* * *

3. Application of the Rogers Test

a. Artistic Relevance Prong

The first prong of Rogers requires a determination of whether there is any artistic relationship between the title and the underlying work. Parks contends that a cursory review of the *Rosa Parks* title and the lyrics demonstrates that there is no artistic connection between them. Parks also submits two articles in which members of OutKast are purported to have admitted that the song was not about her. As further evidence, she offers a "translation" of the lyrics of the song *Rosa Parks,* derived from various electronic "dictionaries" of the "rap" vernacular to demonstrate that the song truly has nothing to do with Parks herself. * * *

Defendants respond that their use of Parks' name is "metaphorical" or "symbolic." They argue that the historical association between Rosa Parks and the phrase "move to the back of the bus" is beyond dispute and that Parks' argument that the song is not "about" her in a biographical sense is simply irrelevant.

* * *

Contrary to the opinion of the district court, we believe that the artistic relationship between the title and the content of the song is certainly not obvious and, indeed, is "open to reasonable debate" for the following reasons.

It is true that the phrase "move to the back of the bus" is repeatedly used in the "hook" or chorus of the song. When the phrase is considered *in the context of the lyrics,* however, the phrase has absolutely nothing to do with Rosa Parks. * * * The composers did *not* intend it to be about Rosa Parks, and the lyrics are *not* about Rosa Parks. The lyrics' sole message is that OutKast's competitors are of lesser quality and, therefore, must "move to the back of the bus," or in other words, "take a back seat." We believe that reasonable persons could conclude that there is no relationship of any kind between Rosa Parks' name and the content of the song—a song that is nothing more and nothing less than a paean announcing the triumph of superior people in the entertainment business over inferior people in that business.... Choosing Rosa Parks' name as the title to the song unquestionably enhanced the song's potential sale to the consuming public.

* * *

While Defendants' lyrics contain profanity and a great deal of "explicit" language (together with a parental warning), they contain absolutely nothing that could conceivably, by any stretch of the imagination, be considered, explicitly or implicitly, a reference to courage, to sacrifice, to the civil rights movement or to any other quality with which Rosa Parks is identified. If the requirement of "relevance" is to have any meaning at all, it would not be unreasonable to conclude that the title *Rosa Parks* is *not* relevant to the content of the song in question. The use of this woman's name unquestionably was a good marketing tool—*Rosa Parks* was likely to sell far more recordings than *Back of the Bus*—but its use could be found by a reasonable finder of fact to be a flagrant deception on the public regarding the actual content of this song and the creation of an impression that Rosa Parks, who had approved the use of her name in connection with the *Tribute* album, had also approved or sponsored the use of her name on Defendants' composition.

It is certainly not dispositive that, in response to an interview following the filing of this lawsuit, one of the OutKast members said that using Rosa Parks' name was "symbolic." Where an artist proclaims that a celebrity's name is used merely as a "symbol" for the lyrics of a song, and such use is highly questionable when the lyrics are examined, a legitimate question is presented as to whether the artist's claim is sincere or merely a guise to escape liability. Our task, it seems to us, is not to accept without question whatever purpose Defendants may now claim they had in using Rosa Parks' name. It is, instead, to make a determination as to whether, applying the law of *Rogers,* there is a genuine issue of material fact regarding the question of whether the title is artistically relevant to the content of the song. * * *

There is a genuine issue of material fact whether the use of Rosa Parks' name as a title to the song and on the cover of the album is artistically related to the content of the song or whether the use of the name Rosa Parks is nothing more than a misleading advertisement for the sale of the song.

b.   Misleading Prong

In *Rogers,* the court held that if the title of the work is artistically relevant to its content, there is no violation of the Lanham Act *unless* the "title explicitly misleads as to the source or the content of the work." * * *

We considered all the facts presented to us and concluded that, with reference to the first prong of the *Rogers* analysis, the issue of artistic relevance of the title *Rosa Parks* to the lyrics of the song is highly questionable and cannot be resolved as a matter of law. However, if, on remand, a trier of fact, after a full evidentiary hearing, concludes that the title *is* used in some symbolic or metaphorical sense, application of the *Rogers* analysis, under the particular facts of this case, would appear to be complete. In the present case, the title *Rosa Parks* "make[s] no explicit statement that the work is about that person in any direct sense." In other words, Defendants did not name the song, for example, *The True Life Story of Rosa Parks* or *Rosa Parks' Favorite Rap.*

* * *

C.   Right of Publicity

1.   *Applicable Law*

The right of publicity protects the identity of a celebrity from exploitive commercial use. *See Carson v. Here's Johnny Portable Toilets, Inc.,* 698 F.2d 831, 835 (6th Cir.1983). "The theory of the right is that a celebrity's identity can be valuable in the promotion of products, and the celebrity has an interest that may be protected from the unauthorized commercial exploitation of that identity." *Id.* As such, the common law right of publicity forms a species of property right. * * *

Parks' right of publicity argument tracks that of her Lanham Act claim. She alleges that Defendants have profited from her fame by using her name solely for a commercial purpose. * * *

2.   *Analysis*

A right of publicity claim is similar to a false advertising claim in that it grants a celebrity the right to protect an economic interest in his or her name. However, a right of publicity claim does differ from a false advertising claim in one crucial respect; a right of publicity claim does not require any evidence that a consumer is likely to be confused. All that a plaintiff must prove in a right of publicity action is that she has a pecuniary interest in her identity, and that her identity has been commercially exploited by a defendant.

The parties have stipulated that Parks is famous and that she has used her name to promote other goods and services. She has therefore established an economic interest in her name. Furthermore, Defendants admit that they have used Parks' name as the name of their song, and have used that name to sell the song and their album. * * *

For the same reasons we have stated earlier and need not repeat, we believe that Parks' right of publicity claim presents a genuine issue of material fact regarding the question of whether the title to the song is or is not "wholly unrelated" to the content of the song. A reasonable finder of fact, in our opinion, upon consideration of all the evidence, could find the title to be a "disguised commercial advertisement" or adopted "solely to attract attention" to the work.

D. Other Michigan State Law Claims

* * *

1. Defamation

Parks argues that the song defames her character or places her in a false light. To succeed on a defamation claim, a public figure must prove actual malice. *See New York Times Co. v. Sullivan*, 376 U.S. 254, 279–80 (1964). In turn, actual malice requires a showing, by clear and convincing evidence, that a defendant made a false statement with knowledge of the falsity or with reckless disregard for the truth. * * * The song is plainly not about Parks in any biographical sense of the term, and certainly does not make any factual statements about her. As there is no factual statement about her, Parks cannot show even the first element of a defamation claim. Therefore, we find this argument meritless.

Parks' defamation-by-implication argument is likewise meritless. As with a traditional defamation claim, a plaintiff in a defamation-by-implication claim must establish a material falsity. Parks has not done so. * * *

[The court found the plaintiff's claim of intentional interference with a business relationship meritless because there was no "wrongful act" must have hastened a contract breach or another breakdown of a business relationship].

For the reasons stated, as to Rosa Parks' Lanham Act claim and her common law right of publicity claim, the judgment of the District Court is REVERSED and this case is REMANDED for future proceedings not inconsistent with this Opinion. With respect to Rosa Parks' claims of defamation and tortious interference with a business relationship, the judgment of the District Court is AFFIRMED.

———

Delores Tucker, Gangsta Busta: She's Playing Defense in Her Offensive Against Rap

Wash. Post, Nov. 29, 1995, at C1.

■ Judith Weinraub

* * *

C. Delores Tucker, 68, entered the fight for civil rights more than 50 years ago and never left. She is a glamorous, well-to-do master of fund-raising—for black causes, black mayors, Democrats, anyone whose needs matched her own need to make a difference. She says she's motivated by "a passionate love affair for God and my people," but she's ready to give it up. "I wish other people could do what I'm doing so I could step back and retire," she says.

Instead she finds herself in deeper than ever. Through the National Political Congress of Black Women, an organization she co-founded more than a decade ago, Tucker has waged her latest and perhaps loudest battle—the one against gangsta rap, the one that has made her the target of two lawsuits.

The plaintiffs are Interscope Records and Death Row Records, music companies whose controversial artists she has campaigned against. They charge Tucker with conspiracy and extortion. Though she has high-profile allies in her campaign—notably former secretary of education William Bennett and Connecticut Sen. Joseph Lieberman—only Tucker is being sued.

The suits contend that last summer Tucker tried to persuade rap impresario Suge Knight, head of Death Row Records, to take his business away from Interscope, a distributor. They charge that Tucker offered to distribute Knight's records through a new company that Tucker would control and from which she would profit. They also allege conspiracy, threats, extortion and bribery.

"The allegations are fictional," says Tucker. "The whole charge was simply to restrain me. They were afraid I was going to damage their business."

* * *

She's been crusading for more than two years, picketing stores that sell the music, blocking their entrances and risking arrest. Distributing anti-gangsta-rap petitions and getting statements of support from dozens of African American organizations. Demanding congressional hearings. Buying stock in Nobody Beats the Wiz, Musicland, Sony and Time Warner in order to protest at shareholder meetings.

* * *

Each side in the legal battle, of course, presents a different version. David Kenner, an attorney for Knight and Death Row Records, says he heard Tucker offer $80 million to Knight to leave Interscope and join her in a black-owned distribution company that Time Warner would back.

But Tucker describes a more benign version: She agreed to a meeting with Knight, along with Warwick and Moore. She encouraged Knight to get his gangsta rap clients to use their talents to deliver positive messages. When she asked him what it would take to produce such music, he said he needed distribution. So Tucker asked Warwick and Moore to identify women in the business who might be interested.

"I was trying to assist [the record industry women] in getting what they came to me to get in the first place," she says.

* * *

THE MAKING OF A LEADER

* * *

Her husband of 44 years calls her "one of the most fearless individuals I have ever known. She will take on anyone, anything, if that is what she thinks is right.... I tell her there are times you have to compromise, but she is not one who will readily entertain the idea of compromise about anything."

* * *

Tucker herself has run for office three times—unsuccessfully—most recently for Congress in Philadelphia three years ago. She says she was urged to run by African American women who wanted representation, and she's not interested in doing it again. "Everything that's happened in my life," she says, "I never planned it. I never sought it."

Now she is focused on causes, like the Bethune–DuBois Fund, an organization she founded to provide educational and training programs for black youth, and a newly formed coalition of African American women intent on voter registration.

* * *

CLOUDY DAYS

The rap lawsuits are not the first time Tucker's activities have been questioned. She was fired as secretary of state of Pennsylvania in 1977 by Gov. Milton Shapp, who had hired her. She had been reprimanded two years earlier, after charges that she used state workers and resources to produce speeches for which she received $65,000 in 28 months.

She brushes aside questions about those problems, maintaining that they started when she refused to support Shapp's designated successor as governor. "That's when the henchmen moved in," she says.

In the battle over gangsta rap, opponents describe her as "robotic ... unable to discuss complicated issues." Industry executives say she has been promoting her own interests by singling out Time Warner for attention over other major rap distributors: Polygram, Sony and BMG. "She wasn't interested in a serious conversation about a complex issue," says one. "She was interested in going on 'Nightline.'"

* * *

"WE ... HAVE POWER"

Despite the lawsuits, Tucker claims victory in her gangsta rap campaign.

* * *

Tucker's masterstroke was to stand up at the Time Warner stockholder meeting in May and read Tupac Shakur and Snoop Doggy Dogg lyrics aloud. Through the summer and fall, she and Bennett—joined by Lieberman in the Senate—kept up a steady beat of news conferences, television appearances and radio ads. By September, the Warner Music Group had sold its $115 million interest in Interscope.

* * *

Nevertheless, the day after the Interscope sale, Tucker clenched her fist in triumph. "They said it couldn't be done," she crowed. "It shows that we the people have power."

———

Does a Song By Any Other Name Still Sound as Sweet? Digital Sampling and Its Copyright Implications

Comment, 43 AM. U. L.R. 231 (1993).

■ RANDY S. KRAVIS

INTRODUCTION

Much controversy has emerged over the new technology of digital sampling. Simply put, sampling is the process that recording artists use to include previously recorded portions of another artist's work in a new recording. While some people in the music industry believe that sampling without permission is tantamount to stealing, others view sampling as an art form no more plagiaristic than any other. The popularity of "rap" music, which relies heavily on the use of sampling, has pushed the technique into the spotlight of the music industry. As a result, a debate has arisen over the practice of sampling and its legal implications.

The primary area of debate focuses on the Copyright Act of 1976. The Act governs the making and the use of artistic creations such as books, works of art, and musical compositions. Although it requires artists to obtain permission before using another's sound recordings in certain instances, for the most part, the Act is ill equipped to deal effectively with digital sampling. Congress simply could not have foreseen the myriad of issues that the advanced technology of sampling would present.

* * *

Another test that the Copyright Act uses to determine whether a use is a fair use is the "effect on the market" test, which asks whether the imitation or re-creation of a copyrighted song adversely affects the market for the copyrighted song. Again, when it formulated the effect on the market test, Congress did not and could not have taken into account sampling, where actual sounds of a song are used. Some commentators have questioned whether Congress would have outlawed digital sampling under the Act if it could have foreseen the advent of such technologies. Nevertheless, because Congress could not have considered the unique nature of sampling when it created and last amended the Act, legal scholars must analyze digital sampling without direct congressional guidance.

Surprisingly, despite the confusion, debate, and controversy surrounding sampling and its widespread use, it was not until December 1991 in

Grand Upright Music Ltd. v. Warner Bros. Records, Inc. that a court handed down the first decision regarding the use of sampling. In that case, Judge Kevin Duffy for the U.S. District Court for the Southern District of New York enjoined the production and sale of rap artist Biz Markie's album "I Need a Haircut" because it contained sampled portions of Gilbert O'Sullivan's 1972 hit "Alone Again (Naturally)." In addition to issuing the injunction, Judge Duffy referred the case to the U.S. Attorney for consideration of possible criminal penalties.

The *Grand Upright Music* decision is significant for two reasons. First, the Southern District of New York, which issued the opinion, handles a large percentage of this country's copyright cases; thus the court has a substantial impact on copyright law. Second, the decision is the first and, so far, the only judicial attempt to provide guidance on applying current copyright law to digital sampling.

* * *

I. DIGITAL SAMPLING

* * *

While the use of the sampling process is a fairly recent phenomenon, digital sampling actually traces its roots back to the 1960s when disc jockeys (DJs) began experimenting with "dub," a form of art created when DJs mix different sounds together into a single musical work. Dub originated in Jamaica, where DJs mixed Jamaican and non-Jamaican records together. It continued to be solely a Jamaican practice until a Jamaican-born DJ named Kool DJ Herc, along with other early DJs, introduced dub in the United States by experimenting with early sound techniques that would become precursors to modern-day sampling.

II. COPYRIGHT LAW

The Copyright Act of 1976, which is the statutory body of law governing digital sampling, addresses four main issues: (1) What qualifies for copyright protection?; (2) If a work qualifies for protection, what rights does the owner of the copyright have with respect to the work?; (3) What constitutes infringement of that copyright?; and (4) If infringement is found, what remedies are available to the copyright owner? This Part addresses each question separately.

A. *What Qualifies for Copyright Protection?*

The 1976 Copyright Act protects only "original works of authorship fixed in any tangible medium of expression." Thus, for a work to qualify for copyright protection, it must satisfy certain criteria. First, a "work of authorship" must be at issue. The Act specifically lists seven categories that constitute works of authorship: literary works; dramatic works; pantomimes and choreographic works; pictorial, graphic, and sculptural works; motion pictures and audiovisual works; and sound recordings. Sampled songs are works of authorship because, as "musical ... works," they fall under the category of "sound recordings."

Second, only "original" works of authorship receive copyright protection under the Act. The Act itself does not define "original"; the courts, however, are in general agreement that the originality threshold is a very low one. In *L. Batlin & Son, Inc. v. Snyder*, for example, the U.S. Court of Appeals for the Second Circuit held that an author need only contribute something more than a "merely trivial" variation for the court to consider the work at issue to be original. The author's work simply has to be "recognizably his own." An original work must also possess "independent creation," but it need not be invention in the sense of striking uniqueness, ingeniousness, or novelty. Rather, an original work simply must be a distinguishable creation of the author.

Third, copyright law does not protect ideas, but expressions of those ideas in fixed forms. Thus, only ideas reduced to concrete form are copyrightable. For example, a copyright extends to the arrangement of words in a book, but not to the idea conveyed by the words. Similarly, a tune or melody that an individual hums is not protected. To gain protection, the melody must be recorded.

B.   Rights of the Copyright Owner

Once an author has met the criteria for establishing a valid copyright and has completed the proper copyright registration procedure, the author then has certain exclusive rights under § 106 of the Act with respect to the copyrighted work. These exclusive rights include the rights to reproduce the work, to prepare derivative works, and to sell copies of the work to the public. A copyright's term lasts for fifty years after the death of the sound recording artist.

C.   Infringement

Section 501(a) of the Copyright Act provides that "anyone who violates any of the exclusive rights of the copyright owner . . . is an infringer of the copyright." To show infringement of the copyright, a plaintiff must show proof of ownership of a valid copyright and demonstrate that the defendants copied the work. To prove actual copying, which is difficult to do, a plaintiff must establish the following two elements: "(1) defendant's access to the copyrighted work prior to creation of defendant's work, and (2) substantial similarity of both general ideas and expression between the copyrighted work and the defendant's work."

1.   Ownership

To prove copyright infringement, the owner of a sound recording must prove ownership. Under § 201 of the Act, the author of a particular work initially receives ownership of the copyright. In most cases, then, a copyright owner may prove ownership simply by showing authorship. Under certain exceptional circumstances, however, the author of a work is not the owner of the copyright. For example, if the author were hired to create the work, then the copyright would rest not in the author, but in the employer for whom the work was made. In this instance, the employer must demonstrate that the work was created for hire to establish rightful ownership. Similarly, if the author previously conveyed all or part of the copyright to someone else, then the new owner has the burden of proving proper receipt of copyright ownership.

2.   Copying

To prove infringement, the plaintiff in a copyright suit must prove that the defendant copied the sound recording by demonstrating that the defendant had "access" to the recording and that the two works are substantially similar.

a.   Access

Without proof of access, the similarity between two works may be purely coincidental. Courts generally agree that the test for access is whether the defendant had a reasonable opportunity to view the copyrighted work. In sampling cases, access is rarely an issue because, by definition, sampling involves the purposeful usurpation of, and thus access to, another's work.

b.   Substantial similarity

Unlike the access determination, the question of substantial similarity is an important issue in most sampling cases. The test for substantial similarity is whether a reasonable person would recognize that the defendant took the copyrighted work and incorporated it into a new work. A general impression of similarity is not sufficient to constitute "substantial" similarity. Rather, the "total concept" and "feel" of the two works must be similar. At the same time, however, a copyright owner does not have to show that every small detail of the protected work was duplicated. In fact, the duplication of only a small part of the work may be considered substantial if the part taken was an important and material part of the work.

3.   The defense of fair use

In determining whether an act constitutes infringement, courts recognize that certain acts, such as fair use, are defensible. Specifically, § 107 provides an affirmative defense to potential infringers of the fair use doctrine. Section 107 does not define "fair use," but merely lists four factors for courts to weigh in determining whether the use of a copyrighted work is fair. The Act is silent, however, as to how much weight courts should allocate to each factor. The Supreme Court has also provided little guidance, explaining only that "[s]ection 107 requires a case-by-case determination whether a particular use is fair."

The first factor listed in § 107 is the purpose and character of the use. If the work is used for nonprofit educational purposes, for example, fair use may be presumed. A work used for commercial purposes, however, would not constitute a fair use. The second consideration is the nature of the copyrighted work. Courts generally permit the use of a longer portion of a protected work if the work is an informational collection of facts as opposed to a creative piece. The third factor is the amount and substantiality of the portion used. When determining whether this element has been met, courts look to the same considerations set forth in the substantial similarity element of infringement; specifically, courts consider both quantitative and qualitative similarity. If a court finds substantial similarity, it generally will find that the use was not fair. The fourth and final factor is the effect of the use on the potential market for the copyrighted work. A use that produces a negative effect on the sales market for the original work will tend to deny a finding of fair use.

D. Remedies

Section 504 of the Copyright Act provides damage awards for the copyright owner once infringement has been proven. The Act states that the infringer is liable for either actual damages and profits or statutory damages. Actual damages generally are measured by the market value of profits lost by the copyright owner. Infringer's profits, which the owner is entitled to, are determined by deducting certain costs from the infringer's gross revenue. Statutory damages are available even without evidence that the plaintiff has suffered actual damages. The court has wide discretion in determining the amount of damages as long as it remains within the statutory limits.

* * *

Finally, if the court finds that the infringement is willful, the court can impose criminal sanctions. Courts are split, however, on the question of what level of intent constitutes willfulness. Some courts hold that only a general intent to act constitutes willfulness, even if the defendant did not realize that he or she was acting in an illegal manner; other courts require a specific intent to break the law.

III. THE CONTROVERSY SURROUNDING DIGITAL SAMPLING

A. The Debate Over Substantial Similarity

The legality of unauthorized digital sampling has divided the music industry. One issue that has caused much debate is the role of "substantial similarity" in a digital sampling suit. The controversy arises over the use of the word "actual" in § 114(b) of the Copyright Act. On one hand, this term can be viewed as prohibiting the usurpation of any exact sound from a song. But on the other hand, a plaintiff in a copyright suit must demonstrate substantial similarity between the two works in order to prove infringement. This substantial similarity requirement thus suggests that the Copyright Act might allow some actual use of a copyrighted song without that use rising to the level of infringement.

* * *

B. The Debate Over Originality

Proponents of sampling often argue that sampling is no different from other art forms that rely on older works, and should thus be accorded the favorable legal treatment that these other art forms presently receive. They do not understand why samplers are penalized when other artists also borrow from earlier works of art without criticism. They maintain that all artists borrow from past works and assert that even great composers such as Bach, Handel, and Vivaldi borrowed from preexisting works.

* * *

On the other hand, this argument based on artistic originality might be out of place in a legal context because it has been held that "artistic originality is not the same thing as the legal concept of originality in the Copyright Act." In *Gracen v. Bradford Exchange*, the Seventh Circuit held that although a slight change or diversion from the original work might constitute artistic originality, it does not necessarily constitute legal originality. Consequently, samplers' claims that their works are original and independent creations might be misplaced because they focus on artistic originality, not legal originality.

* * *

C. The Debate Over the Effect of Sampling on a Song's Market

The effect that sampling has on a song's potential market is one element courts use to decide whether the use of the song is a fair one. It is an affirmative defense for one accused of copyright infringement to argue that the infringement did not adversely affect the market for the copyrighted song. Given that digital samplers often borrow from older songs, samplers argue that use of these songs does not adversely affect their potential market because the people who would buy these older songs will not buy rap albums in their place. Therefore, even if it is conceded that sampling is a copyright infringement, it is still a fair use because it does not harm the market for the original song. In fact, some argue that sampling actually helps the potential market for older songs by reviving interest in relatively forgotten music.

Critics of sampling could suggest, however, that a market analysis that only examines the effect on the original song is incomplete because it fails to account for the effect on other potential or derivative uses of the song. For example, if the owner of an older song re-released the song as a rap version, any prior sampling would affect the market for that derivative work by potentially interfering with sales of the owner's new version. In this way, sampling may hurt the market for protected songs, thus proving to be an unfair use of the original songs.

* * *

Advocates of sampling could respond by asserting that § 107 does not mention the effect on the potential market for the musician. Rather, the Act only mentions the effect on the market for the actual work. Under this approach, while the effect on the common studio musician is unfortunate, it has no bearing on the question of fair use.

D. The Copyright Act's Ambiguous Legislative History

Both sides of the digital sampling debate have interpreted the language of the Copyright Act differently when arguing whether digital sampling constitutes copyright infringement. Attempting to find answers in the Act's legislative history, however, is difficult. When Congress last made major changes to the Act in 1976, digital sampling did not exist. Any analysis of legislative history thus can only speculate on what Congress would have done had it considered digital sampling. As a result, the Act's legislative history has spawned further debate over how Congress would have responded to digital sampling.

* * *

IV.   THE CASE: *GRAND UPRIGHT MUSIC LTD. v. WARNER BROS. RECORDS, INC.*

Before December 1991, the controversy surrounding the copyright implications of digital sampling could only take the form of a debate as to what the law should be with regards to sampling. With no judicial decisions addressing the issue and with a controlling statute that predated the development of sampling technology, the debate was necessarily and uncomfortably theoretical. On December 16, 1991, however, the Southern District of New York, "[a]fter many years of anticipation and speculation," announced the first judicial opinion to address the issues presented by digital sampling, *Grand Upright Music Ltd. v. Warner Bros. Records, Inc.*

A.   The Factual Background

Grand Upright Music Ltd., the alleged copyright owner of pop artist Gilbert O'Sullivan's 1972 hit "Alone Again (Naturally)," brought a copyright infringement action to enjoin all production and sales of rap artist Biz Markie's album "I Need a Haircut." Grand Upright Music based its claim on the fact that Biz Markie's album contained a song entitled "Alone Again" that used three words and a portion of the music from the master recording of the Gilbert O'Sullivan song. Before the infringement action arose, Biz Markie's attorney had tried to get permission to use the 1972 song from Terry O'Sullivan, the artist's brother and agent, by sending a letter requesting use of the song along with a cassette copy of Biz Markie's recording. Before the two reached an agreement, however, Biz Markie released the "I Need a Haircut" album. Mr. O'Sullivan subsequently refused to grant permission to use the song and, after repeated demands to remove the album from the market, he filed suit.

B.   The Opinion

The defendants in this case, Biz Markie and the record companies that produced "I Need a Haircut," conceded that the Biz Markie song used words and music from the Gilbert O'Sullivan song. On the basis of this admission, the district court concluded that Biz Markie's use constituted infringement of the original song's copyright and that the only remaining issue was whether Grand Upright Music was the true owner of the "Alone Again (Naturally)" copyright. The court ruled that Grand Upright Music was the owner of the copyright based on three categories of proof: (1) copies of the copyrights and deeds vesting title to the copyrights in Gilbert O'Sullivan and then from O'Sullivan to Grand Upright Music; (2) testimony of Gilbert O'Sullivan acknowledging Grand Upright Music as the copyright owner; and (3) the defendants' attempt to contact Gilbert and Terry O'Sullivan. With regard to the third element of proof of ownership, the court held that the defendants' attempt to discuss terms for use of the song with Terry and Gilbert O'Sullivan was evidence that the plaintiff owned a valid copyright. The court reasoned that the defendants would not have attempted to discuss terms with O'Sullivan if the latter were not the copyright owner.

The court further concluded that Biz Markie's use of the song violated Grand Upright Music's valid copyright to the song. As a result, the court enjoined the sale of Biz Markie's album. The court also found that the defendants intended "to sell thousands upon thousands of records" by knowingly violating the copyright. Consequently, the court referred the case to the U.S. Attorney for the Southern District of New York for possible criminal prosecution of the defendants for willful copyright infringement.

V. THE EFFECT OF *GRAND UPRIGHT MUSIC* ON THE LAW REGARDING DIGITAL SAMPLING

A. *The Decision's Effect on the Law Regarding Digital Sampling*

There are two reasons to believe that *Grand Upright Music* will have a strong impact on digital sampling law. First, the Southern District of New York, which decided *Grand Upright Music*, handles a substantial percentage of all the copyright and entertainment law cases in this country. The *Grand Upright Music* decision, which is binding authority on all cases that come out of the Southern District of New York, will thus serve as controlling authority on a large percentage of future digital sampling cases.

Second, because *Grand Upright Music* is the only judicial pronouncement on the issue of digital sampling, it is likely to be persuasive authority in other jurisdictions. Considering the vagueness of the outdated body of statutory law, and the lack of judicial assistance in applying the statutory law to digital sampling, future digital sampling cases from other jurisdictions will at least address the *Grand Upright Music* decision. Other jurisdictions, therefore, may use this case as a starting point from which to rule on digital sampling simply because it is the first and only court ruling on digital sampling. For purposes of a detailed legal review of this decision, then, this Note assumes that the *Grand Upright Music* decision will influence the law.

B. *How the Decision Will Influence the Law Regarding Digital Sampling*

Although long awaited as the first digital sampling decision, *Grand Upright Music* left many questions unanswered. One prominent entertainment lawyer said, " '[T]his isn't the seminal case everyone wanted.' " While the court ruled that Biz Markie's sampling violated the copyright law, the court failed to mention the elements necessary to prove copyright infringement, with the exception of the copyright ownership element. Although the decision failed to clear up many of the theoretical legal questions regarding digital sampling, it still will have a significant impact on the music and entertainment industry.

1. The impact on the questions of law presented by digital sampling

The *Grand Upright Music* decision explicitly focuses on ownership, one of the elements a plaintiff must demonstrate to prove infringement. This issue, however, is not the real problem that digital sampling brings to copyright law. Observers had hoped that this case would address some of the questions that the issue of fair use presents to digital sampling, such as sampling's effect on the market and the role of substantial similarity in a digital sampling suit. Yet, without addressing any defense of fair use issues, the court ruled that, once the plaintiff proved ownership, infringement had occurred by the simple fact that Biz Markie had sampled Gilbert O'Sullivan's song.

* * *

Grand Upright Music also fails to clarify the issue of willful infringement. In *Grand Upright Music*, the district court referred the case to the U.S. Attorney for possible criminal sanctions because it had found willful infringement. In particular, the defendants' actions and testimony indicated that they knew Mr. O'Sullivan owned a valid copyright. The court, however, omitted any discussion of whether willfulness requires a specific intent to break the law or only a broader intent to commit an act that is an infringement of a copyright. The fact that the defendants knew that they were sampling a copyrighted song without authorization was sufficient for the court to find the defendants guilty of copyright infringement. Nevertheless, the court's utter failure to explain what level of intent is needed for sampling to constitute infringement perpetuates the confusion surrounding willful infringement.

* * *

2. The impact on the music industry

Even though the court in *Grand Upright Music* did not expressly rule out the possibility that the limited use of a song may be legal, the court's strong condemnation of unauthorized sampling could be construed as a declaration that sampling constitutes infringement per se. Thus, while *Grand Upright Music* provides little guidance on the legal questions of digital sampling, it will still have a major impact on the music industry because it is a strong judicial denunciation of the practice of unauthorized sampling. For this reason, samplers will have to alter their behavior.

* * *

VI. SOLUTIONS

A. *Congress Should Amend the Copyright Act*

Grand Upright Music's shortcomings suggest that the Copyright Act is so outdated that it simply cannot provide answers to the digital sampling problem. A revision of the Act may thus be the only solution to the sampling dilemma.

* * *

A revision of the current copyright law to accommodate sampling would be consistent with both the Copyright Act's history of periodic adjustment due to technological advancements and the purposes of copyright law. The Copyright Act has two major objectives: securing an adequate return for the artist, and securing public access to artistic works through the prevention of monopolies. When copyright laws become outdated, new technologies escape regulation and the Act's policy goals are thwarted. * * *

B. Congress Should Institute a Compulsory Licensing Provision for Digital Sampling

Copyright law's two competing policy goals, public access to works of art and protection of copyright owners' rights to profit, are diametrically opposed objectives. For example, a prohibition on sampling would disregard the policy of access to others' works. At the same time, allowing unrestricted unauthorized sampling would compromise the copyright owners' interests in seeking an adequate return on their works. To achieve the optimal balance between these two goals, the law should take the middle ground.

* * *

CONCLUSION

In modern musical culture, digital sampling has emerged as a popular technique for exploring and reexamining older music. Because the sampling phenomenon is more far-reaching in its technological capabilities than any previous musical technology, sampling has transcended the scope of the existing law, forcing lawyers, musicians, and others in the music entertainment business to analyze this new musical technique in a legal vacuum, and leaving them only to speculate as to how the old law applies to sampling. As a result, much debate and controversy among those interested in the entertainment law field have produced a whole spectrum of opinions on digital sampling's place in the law. In fact, even the judiciary appears confused and undecided on how the law should treat sampling, as evidenced by the *Grand Upright Music* decision.

* * *

———

A NOTE ON ARTISTIC REPARATIONS

In the following excerpt, we catch a glimpse of black rock 'n' roll icon Little Richard's bitterness about the economic impact of racism that many black artists endured in the 1930s through 1970s. After he suffered bankruptcy, Little Richard describes his economic subordination in the industry as follows: "I was taken for everything except my toenails—and they would've got them as well, but they were too short to cut."

The exploitation of African American talent during this period is a double tragedy because many of the individual artists who are still alive today do not have a secure retirement, or the financial security of many of their less talented white contemporaries. The second misfortune is that the black music of this period is generally agreed around the world to be the most uniquely American contribution to music. It is a paradox that the cultural contributions of African American artists serve as the foundation of American cultural identity worldwide, while these contributions have not provided a foundation of stable wealth for the communities from which they emerged.

The difficulty in law is fashioning a legal theory that will permit the wealth of the music industry to be redirected to rectify past economic injustice. As we see in *Merchant v. Levy*, below, formal legal rules such as laches (delay in pursuing the claim), estoppel (preclusion to pursue the claim because of some earlier action by the claimant), or statutes of limitation (statutory time limitations imposed on the injured party's right to sue for redress) present formidable barriers to redress.

Can you think of other theories of compensation? What about reparations theory? Equitable restitution and constructive trusts? For a careful exploration of the moral and ethical premises of restitution, see Hanoch Dagan, *The Distributive Foundation of Corrective Justice*, 98 MICH. L. REV. 138 (1999) (exploring the corrective justice approach to the doctrine of restitution for wrongs and especially for appropriations); HANOCH DAGAN, THE FOURTH PILLAR: THE LAW AND ETHICS OF RESTITUTION (2004).

————

A Session With Little Richard

Jim Jerome, LIFE MAG., Dec. 1992, at p. 48.

With a crash of piano keys, a flash of mascaraed eyelashes and a dash of awop-bop-aloo-bop-awop-bam-boom, Little Richard baptized a new musical style.—born Richard Penniman in Macon, GA., and raised on gospel music, he ran away from home with Dr. Hudson's traveling medicine show.—he later toured small nightclubs in the south and cut records for RCA and the Peacock label in Houston.—commercial success eluded him—until September 14, 1955, when he entered J & M studios in New Orleans for Specialty Records. That recording session produced "Tutti Frutti," a hit in early 1956. More sessions quickly followed, and out of them came such rock standards as "Long Tall Sally," "Rip it Up," "Keep a Knockin" and "Good Golly, Miss Molly." Then, suddenly, during a tour of Australia in late 1957, Little Richard renounced rock and roll, saying he had dreamed of his own damnation. He went on to become a minister in the Seventh–Day

Adventist church, and over the years, while mounting several unsuccessful comebacks, he has preached against drugs and sex (particularly homosexuality), but it was his quavering falsetto shriek that gathered most converts. Jim Jerome talked with the 56–or 59–year-old musician (depending on whether you believe him or his mother) in a Hollywood hotel, his home away from his Riverside, Calif., home, as flamboyant and outrageous as ever. Little Richard didn't hesitate to claim his rightful place in the history of rock and roll.

"Tutti Frutti" was really an accident, wasn't it?

Yes. See, they wanted me to sing like Ray Charles and B.B. King. I did it just to record; it wasn't what I wanted. So after one session I got on the piano and did awop-bop-aloo-bop-awop-bam-boom. They said, "That's the hit. Ain't no one ever put out mess like that." I had to clean up the lyrics. I had "Tutti frutti, good booty" instead of "aw-rooty." And there was worse, believe me.

Does any one show stick in your mind?

I remember one of those early Madison Square Garden shows in New York—runnin' out there with my brothers and my entourage, the lights come up and those screams, and it just ran through my whole body like a shock. I stood there with my arms out, then I sat at the piano, screamin' to the top of my lungs and tears comin' out of my eyes. My orgasm was the stage, gettin' out there and touchin' the piano and goin' wild. You can't buy that feeling.

But money did buy you plenty.

I remember before one of his big New York shows Alan Freed walked up to me—it was my birthday or some celebration—and he handed me an envelope with $10,000 in it, all in hundred dollar bills. He kissed me on the jaw. I put it all in the trunk of my custom gold-and-white Cadillac with the leopard interior. I bought my mother a mansion in L.A., right behind Joe Louis, and my bed was packed with money. My sisters would just count it over and over.

What impact did racism have on your early career?

I was blocked from playing a lot of places. We'd have to drive all night in the car, 'cause there wasn't no blacks allowed in the hotel. If we wanted a sandwich, you had to go to the back door of a restaurant and ask the chef if he would fix you one. This is even after all of those big hits. And no hospitals for us if we got sick on the road down south.

Do you see any link between your music and rap?

Yes. When I see Hammer, I see me. Michael Jackson—I look at him, I see Little Richard. And he's the greatest entertainer ever lived. Little Richard suffered, he went through hell, he was denied, he was deprived. I helped build that bridge across despair. Now the road is paved. That's why Michael Jackson gets a billion-dollar guarantee.

So is Elvis the King of Rock and Roll?

I know they call him the King, but if he is, who crowned him? When was the ceremony—and why was I not invited? How can a white boy be King of Rock and Roll? I'm not downin' white singers. But I been imitated by more people. I, too, have been called the King of Rock and Roll. I been called the Queen. I earned the throne 'cause I am the Originator, the Architect, the Emancipator—The Founding Father of Rock and Roll.

The Fight Over The Golden Oldies

MACLEAN'S, March 2, 1987, at 36.

■ NICHOLAS JENNINGS

Even from an artist renowned for outrageous behavior, the action was a shocking sight. In August, 1984, Richard Penniman—better known as Little Richard, the flamboyant 1950s rocker—began picketing an office building in downtown Los Angeles. The rock star was not on strike; he was on a crusade. The offices belonged to ATV Music Corp., one of the world's largest song publishers. Little Richard's claim: that ATV, along with Specialty Records and Venice Music, owed him millions of dollars in royalties for *Tutti-Frutti, Good Golly Miss Molly* and other classic Little Richard hits. Four months later his $115–million lawsuit against those companies was thrown out of U.S. Federal Court.

Bankrupt: Now, Little Richard, 54, is pondering his next move. But in a recent *Maclean's* interview he said bitterly, "I was taken for everything except my toenails—and they would've got them as well, but they were too short to cut." Little Richard has a new recording contract with Warner Bros. and says that *Lifetime Friend,* his new album on that label, will be the first to earn him money in 30 years of recording.

* * *

Beatles: Even the biggest and presumably best-advised artists have made deals they now regret. Since 1969 Paul McCartney has tried unsuccessfully to recover ownership rights to the highly prized Beatles' songs he wrote with John Lennon, currently owned by ATV. The Beatles' songs are part of the corporation's catalogue, now valued at more than $65 million.

* * *

At last, however, artists have someone to champion their cause. He is Chuck Rubin, described by *The New York Times* as the "white knight of rock." Rubin, 48, runs the Artists Rights Enforcement Corp., a New York firm that seeks to regain royalties for performers. His list of about 200 clients reads like a *Who's Who* of early rock 'n' roll, with enough vintage pop songs to their credit to fill a rec room full of jukeboxes. Among them: The Shirelles (*I Met Him on a Sunday*); Huey (Piano) Smith (*Sea Cruise*); The Marvelettes (*Please Mr. Postman*); and the estate of Clyde McPhatter (*Money Honey*).

* * *

An even more bizarre case involves the estate of Frankie Lymon, the teenage singing sensation who died in 1968. Lymon and his group, the Teenagers, enjoyed a Top 10 hit in 1956 with *Why Do Fools Fall in Love,* which later was used on several TV shows. Rubin successfully won performance royalties for the artists, including Lymon's estate, in 1982. But it was not until a year later, while pursuing further royalties, that Rubin located Lymon's widow, Emira Lymon, a schoolteacher in Augusta, Ga. She was naturally delighted, but surprised that she was entitled to any royalties; she had been told by Lymon's attorney that she had no legal claim. When Rubin tried to help her renew the claim on her husband's composition, he discovered that Lymon's record company owner had come to court with two other women, each claiming to be the singer's widow and heir. The case is now pending in the New York courts. Rubin estimates that the royalties in question could be worth more than $1.4 million.

Payments: In some cases the loss of rights was clearly the artist's own fault. In 1957 Richard Berry sold copyrights to seven of his songs to his publisher for $750 because, he said later, he needed money to get married. One of those songs, a three-chord tune called *Louie Louie,* later became a rock classic, with more than 400 recorded versions. Had Berry retained ownership, industry experts say that he would have earned about $5 million from the song. But his story has a happy ending. Last year, after seven years of perseverance, Berry, 51, won his share of the copyright back and is now entitled to future payments.

* * *

Merchant v. Levy

92 F.3d 51 (2d Cir. 1996).

■ JON O. NEWMAN, CHIEF JUDGE.

BACKGROUND

Plaintiffs Merchant and Santiago are two of the original members of the singing group "The Teenagers," which was formed in 1955. Plaintiffs testified that in 1955 they jointly wrote the initial version of the song *Fools.* Frankie Lymon made a number of changes to the song when he subsequently joined the group, which then became known as "Frankie Lymon and The Teenagers." The jury found that Merchant, Santiago, and Lymon were co-authors of *Fools.* At the time Lymon was 12 years old and Plaintiffs were each 15.

In 1956 the Teenagers recorded *Fools* for Gee Records, then owned and operated by George Goldner, now deceased. Plaintiffs testified that they relied upon Goldner to handle the formalities of copyrighting the song, and that Goldner informed them that only two of the three authors could be listed on the copyright. Subsequently, Goldner filed the *Fools* copyright with the Copyright Office in 1956, listing himself and Lymon as sole co-authors. The Levy Defendants maintain that Goldner was properly listed as an author because he was personally involved in writing and arranging *Fools*. The Levy Defendants also contend that Goldner was a co-author of *Fools* under the "work for hire" doctrine because, during the Fools recording session, a saxophone solo composed by a studio musician was incorporated into the song. The jury, however, found that Goldner was not an author of *Fools*.

Sometime in the 1950s Lymon agreed to let Goldner exploit Lymon's interest in the song. In 1968 Lymon died, survived by his wife Emira Lymon.

In 1964, defendant Morris Levy purchased Goldner's interest in several music companies, including the music publishing company that held the copyright for *Fools*. In a letter to the Copyright Office dated June 24, 1965, Goldner stated that Levy, rather than Goldner, had co-authored *Fools* with Lymon. The copyright registration was amended to reflect this statement and, thereafter, the copyright was held by Levy's company, Big Seven Music.

Although *Fools* became a hit and continues to be popular today (Diana Ross has recorded a popular version), Plaintiffs have never received any royalties from their claimed co-authorship of *Fools*.

* * *

Beginning in the late 1970s, Plaintiffs took various steps in pursuit of their claim, including hiring an attorney and investigator to look into the status of the copyright. Plaintiffs did not take formal legal action, however, until 1987.

A.   Procedural History

Plaintiffs brought the instant Complaint against the Levy Defendants and Emira Lymon on October 7, 1987. Plaintiffs asked for a declaration that they were co-owners with Lymon of the copyright to *Fools* and for an accounting of royalties. Plaintiffs also alleged copyright infringement, Sherman Act and Lanham Act violations, unfair competition, fraud and misappropriation, and negligence and breach of fiduciary duty. Before trial the District Court (Vincent L. Broderick, Judge) dismissed all claims against Emira Lymon, but allowed the action to proceed against the Levy Defendants.

* * *

The Court granted Plaintiffs' basic request for a declaration of copyright co-ownership, rejecting the three defenses advanced by the Levy Defendants, all based on the long delay in Plaintiffs' assertion of their claim.

1. *Duress and Statute of Limitations*. The Court interpreted the three-year statute of limitations, applicable to civil copyright actions, 17 U.S.C. § 507(b), as limiting Plaintiffs' recovery to damages accruing within three years of the filing of the suit, rather than as an absolute bar to

Plaintiffs' cause of action. Merchant, 828 F. Supp. at 1056. The important question for the Court then became whether the statute of limitations had been tolled for any period before the filing of the suit, thereby allowing Plaintiffs to recover damages that accrued even prior to three years before the suit. *Id.*

 * * *

2. *Laches*. Responding to the Levy Defendants' laches defense, the Court, relying on equity's "clean hands" principle, refused to allow the Levy Defendants to profit from their "untoward actions" by asserting laches. *id.* at 1064.

3. *Equitable Estoppel*. As to equitable estoppel, which requires proof that a defendant was misled into justifiably believing that a plaintiff would not pursue its claims against the defendant, the Court determined that the Levy Defendants offered no evidence that Plaintiffs acted in a manner that justified a belief on the part of the Levy Defendants that their copyright was free from challenge. *id.*

B. Subsequent Proceedings

 * * *

In the final judgment entered on June 26, 1995, the Court awarded Plaintiffs an undivided one-half interest in the copyright to *Fools*. The Court also ordered the Levy Defendants and Windswept to pay money damages to Plaintiffs.

On this appeal Defendants challenge the District Court's subject matter jurisdiction, and also argue that the District Court erred in not dismissing the action for a declaration of copyright co-ownership as barred by the statute of limitations or laches. Defendants additionally contend that Plaintiffs failed to establish that they are joint authors of *Fools*. Plaintiffs cross-appeal, arguing that the Court should have applied the tolling doctrine of equitable estoppel to allow Plaintiffs to recover damages accruing from 1969 to 1984, the period during which the jury had found that Plaintiffs were subject to duress.

DISCUSSION

I. Subject Matter Jurisdiction

Federal courts have exclusive original jurisdiction over actions arising under the federal copyright laws. See 28 U.S.C. § 1338(a). As Judge Friendly has explained, an action "arises under" the copyright laws "if the complaint is for a remedy expressly granted by the [Copyright] Act, ... or asserts a claim requiring construction of the Act ... or, at the very least and perhaps more doubtfully, presents a case where a distinctive policy of the Act requires that federal principles control the disposition of the claim." *T.B. Harms Co. v. Eliscu*, 339 F.2d 823, 828 (2d Cir. 1964), *cert. denied*, 381 U.S. 915 (1965). Plaintiffs' action seeking to establish their rights to copyright co-ownership because of their status as co-authors of a joint work falls well within these jurisdictional boundaries.

* * *

II.   Statute of Limitations

We come finally to the dispositive issue. Plaintiffs filed the instant suit in 1987, primarily seeking a declaration of their copyright ownership rights and an accounting of profits. Civil actions under the Copyright Act are subject to a three-year statute of limitations. 17 U.S.C. § 507(b). Defendants argue that since Plaintiffs did not institute suit for a declaration of copyright co-ownership within three years of the accrual of their claim, they are now time-barred.

* * *

The District Court nevertheless awarded Plaintiffs a declaration of co-ownership rights and damages for a time period beginning three years before the commencement of their suit. The Court relied on our decision in *Stone, supra.* That decision, however, which was based on "highly idiosyncratic facts," 3 *Nimmer, supra*, § 12.05 at 12–108 n.2.2, does not insulate all civil actions under the copyright law from the general three-year statute of limitations. Rather, *Stone* stands for the narrow proposition that, in certain situations, the statute of limitations will not be applied to defeat the copyright co-ownership claim of an author's relative accruing more than three years before the lawsuit where uncertainty surrounded the relative's status as a member of the author's family. Instead, if the relative prevails on the merits and if the equities permit, the Court will grant the relative a declaration of copyright co-ownership, but permit damages only for the period starting three years prior to the suit. See *Stone*, 970 F.2d at 1051.

———

Three Wives & The Legacy of "Love"; A Courtroom Clash Over Frankie Lyman's '56 Song

WASH. POST, Mar. 30, 1988, at C1.

■ PAULA SPAN

It's been 32 years, but the song still shimmers and bops: first that calliope-like bass ("ehhh toom ah-ta toom ah-ta toom ah doe doe"), then a wash of "ooh-wahs," followed by the swooping soprano of 13–year-old Frankie Lymon, asking his immortal musical questions:

Why do birds sing so gay? Why does the rain fall from up above? And the true imponderable, "Why Do Fools Fall in Love?"

It is Frankie Lymon's only real legacy, that two minutes and 15 seconds of doo-wop. He recorded other songs, alone and with his group the Teenagers, but none has inspired the same affection. The only child he is known to have fathered died hours after her birth. He left no fortune; when he died of a heroin overdose 20 years ago, he was broke and troubled, trying again for a comeback he never achieved.

* * *

Depending on how the judge rules, the decision may reactivate a federal suit to wrest Lymon's royalties and publishing rights from the record industry executive who claims to own them. There may be further delays, though, while that executive faces federal extortion charges. Not to mention that two other members of the Teenagers have filed suit claiming they co-wrote "Why Do Fools Fall in Love."

* * *

ELIZABETH

They were there in Surrogate Court—the three would-be widows and their teams of lawyers and witnesses—for 10 days this past December and January, raking over the past.

Zola Taylor Lymon, now 50, one of the original Platters, had flown in from Los Angeles. Conscious of her stardom (Reporter: "Are you still performing in California?" Zola: "I perform all over the world"), she arrived at court daily in a limousine.

* * *

Neither Zola nor Elizabeth could quite figure Emira Eagle Lymon, the 48–year-old third wife from Augusta, Ga. Frankie marrying a schoolteacher? "She's a square," Zola decided, noticing that Emira was coming to court in sneakers. Zola and Elizabeth didn't get close to Emira; she didn't have anything much to say to them, either.

The essence of their dispute was which of the marriages was legally binding, given a certain laxity in some quarters about divorce. At the least, records and witnesses' recollections seem to indicate that Frankie Lymon did stand before a magistrate or minister on three occasions to promise himself to each of these women until death parted them, which turned out to be a fairly short time.

* * *

ZOLA

Zola Taylor had also been a teen-aged star. Her singing group, the Platters, was sometimes referred to as the Four Platters and a Dish; Zola, in her low-cut gowns, was the dish.

She and Frankie were riding a tour bus together in 1956, doing 81 one-nighters with a rock 'n' roll cavalcade that included Chuck Berry, the Coasters, the Penguins and Bo Diddley, as well as the Platters and the Teenagers. They became lovers, Zola testified, one night in Bangor, Maine, when Frankie had won $1,700 gambling with Clyde McPhatter and she had gotten "a little loaded drinking scotch and water." Zola, the older woman, was 17. Their affair continued off and on for several years.

* * *

The next month, according to Zola, she and Frankie drove to Tijuana and got married in a small chapel. The small wedding party celebrated by getting very drunk, not an uncommon state for Frankie at the time. Back in Los Angeles, the club where Zola was performing tossed a celebration, with a cake and champagne.

Zola has been unable to locate records documenting their Mexican wedding, or documenting her Mexican divorce from her previous marriage (her second). But her secretary and her booking agent both testified that they were witnesses to the wedding. Zola's attorneys argue that California law makes her a "putative spouse" entitled to share in Lymon's property.

* * *

EMIRA

By the time Pvt. Lymon was discharged a year later, he'd said "I do" once more. This time his bride was Emira Eagle, an educated, churchgoing elementary school teacher who lived with her family in nearby Augusta. Her sister's boyfriend introduced them; soon, Emira was cooking meals for Frankie and they were shopping for wedding rings. They were married in June 1967 at the Beulah Grove Baptist Church, with 50 members of Emira's family in attendance and a reception afterward at the Capri Lounge.

* * *

Key parts of this chronology are in dispute, of course. Emira's attorneys argue that Elizabeth and Frankie separated in mid–1965 and never lived together as man and wife thereafter, invalidating her claim to a common-law marriage. They point to the absence of documentation from Mexico as evidence that Zola and Frankie never married at all. Elizabeth's lawyers maintain her marriage is valid, which means that neither Zola's nor Emira's can be.

* * *

WHO WROTE THE BOOK OF "LOVE"?

* * *

Who wrote "Why Do Fools Fall in Love"? It is copyrighted in the names of Frankie Lymon and Morris Levy, head of Roulette Records, an independent label that bought out the Gee label, which originally released the record. Levy's attorney, Leon Borstein, says that Levy "assisted in the writing of the song; you have to remember, if he added one word, that's sufficient" to justify coauthorship. Borstein also says that Lymon, who was always pestering Levy for money, sold Levy the copyright to all his songs and that Levy has a signed document to that effect. "Remember, Frankie needed the money badly," Borstein says. "He had been busted in California again for drugs." The sum, he says, "might have been $1,500."

But in 1984 (as the original copyright term of the song was expiring) Emira Eagle Lymon brought suit in U.S. District Court in New York against Levy, his attorney, his record label and his publishing company.

Her complaint charges fraud, misappropriation and copyright infringement, among other offenses. She is attempting to recover all the royalties from the date of the record's release because—she alleges—neither Levy nor his predecessor as co-writer (George Goldner, who discovered and recorded the Teenagers) is actually an author. Borstein, Levy's attorney, says the charges are "complete speculation; there's absolutely no proof."

* * *

Jimmy Merchant and Herman Santiago, the two surviving members of the original Teenagers (Sherman Garnes, the inventive bass, and Joe Negroni were the others), say they wrote "Why Do Fools Fall in Love?" with Frankie Lymon, and they have filed their own federal suit against Levy et al., with Emira also named as a defendant.

* * *

Lymon's "Teenagers" Are No Fools; Win Rights to '50s Hit in Long Fight

Newsday, Nov. 19, 1992, at 45.

■ Pat Wechler

It took 36 years, but a federal jury in Manhattan Tuesday awarded the copyright to the 1956 hit song "Why Do Fools Fall in Love?" to Jimmy Merchant and Herman Santiago, members of the 1950s rock and roll group Frankie Lymon and the Teenagers, which first performed it.

The award of the copyright could mean millions of dollars in past and future royalties for Merchant and Santiago, who have been fighting since the late 1960s for a share in the song's success. An attorney for the performers said that at least 3 million records with the song—now an American classic—were sold over the years, including a 1981 album by Diana Ross that used the song as its title. All records and performances of the song since 1969, the date the jury chose to base past royalties on, will bring them additional royalties.

* * *

Juries decided the composers should be allowed to right old wrongs, despite statutes of limitations, because the composers of '50s and '60s hits—often underage and from poor and minority neighborhoods—were unaware that sizable royalties were being paid and that they should have been receiving a portion.

In both cases, attorneys for the record companies, which will owe the back royalties, are seeking to overturn the verdicts.

* * *

Attorneys for Merchant and Santiago argued in the successful suit that the two had been the composers of the song, along with Lymon, but that music mogul George Goldner filed in 1956 the song's copyright in Lymon's and his own name.

In the 1964, the copyright to "Fools" was transferred to another music entrepreneur, Morris Levy, who took over Goldner's operation and has been linked to organized crime in articles and books on the music industry. Both Levy and Goldner are dead.

Santiago testified that he and Merchant were threatened by Levy in 1969 not to try to get the copyright back or a portion of the royalties.

SWEET SOUND OF ROYALTIES

Songwriters earn two types of royalties—mechanical and performing. For classics such as "Why Do Fools Fall In Love?", the combined royalties can easily reach into the millions of dollars over time.

Mechanical royalties have to do with the actual recording of songs. The government has set a rate of 6.25 cents for each time the song is recorded, multiplied by the number of records cut that contain the song. That amount is paid to the music publishing company which then pays a portion to the composer, determined by agreements between the two.

Performing royalties relate to how many times the song is played on the radio or performed on television, in movies and in nightclubs. These royalties are collected by either of the nation's two performance rights societies—the American Society for Composers, Artists and Performers (ASCAP) or Broadcast Music Inc. (BMI).

BMI or ASCAP collect a set fee for use of a song licensed to them. After subtracting a fee for the collection service, a portion of the total collection for each three-month quarter is paid to the publishing company of the song, based on how popular the song has been in that quarter as determined by BMI and ASCAP, through random samplings of radio and other outlets. These royalties split equally between the company and the actual composer.

———

Malcolm X and the Hip Hop Culture

RECONSTRUCTION II, 100–03 (1993).

■ MARTHA BAYLES

The looming billboards, the full-page ads, the T-shirts, the baseball caps, the potato chips, the automobile air fresheners—they all say "X." To many admirers of Malcolm X, the hype surrounding Spike Lee's latest movie is an insult. How dare Lee reduce Malcolm X's extraordinary, ultimately tragic life to a logo, a trademark with no more depth than, say, the Batman symbol. As Jonathan Yardley wrote in the *Washington Post*: "This implacably serious man has become that most American of creatures, a brand-name superstar. It is impossible to imagine that anything more demeaning could be done, to his name and his memory." Even Malcolm's

widow, Betty Shabazz, expressed doubts, hiring a licensing firm to curb a
marketing juggernaut that, in her view, "had gotten out of hand."

* * *

This is not to say that there is nothing good about either hip-hop or
Lee's film making. On the contrary, that ubiquitous "X" looks a whole lot
better after seeing *Malcolm X*. My expectations for the film were modest,
because although Lee is gifted in many areas of filmmaking (such as
business, production design, hiring jazz composers and working with actors), he is deficient in the most important one, storytelling. To tell a good
story, you must be able to think straight, and Lee shows minimal interest
in that activity. Like so many other celebrities, black and white, who play
at politics from the vantage point of entertainment, Lee seems, (especially
in interviews) to have nothing invested in clarity, everything in obfusca-
tion—or, at best, in a clownish incoherence that would be funny if the
issues were not so grave.

* * *

Most people would agree that Malcolm X's legacy has something to do
with truth-seeking, and with being unafraid to change one's life, along with
one's mind, according to the truth one discovers. I hasten to add that by
"truth-seeking" I do not mean total historical accuracy. Was Malcolm X's
father a proud follower of Marcus Garvey, or did he beat his wife and
children? Probably both, but I don't care. Let the historians quibble about
whether Earl Little ever laid a hand on young Malcolm; God may be in the
details in health-care reform, but not in legend. What matters is that
Malcolm X's father was an upright, demanding, forceful man whose loss
destroyed the family and left his most brilliant son alone with the painfully
open question of what it means to be a black male in America. The film
gets that essential starting point right.

* * *

Malcolm X *was* Detroit Red, of course, and one of the most powerful
themes in his autobiography is his revulsion at the hypocrisy of whites,
including his girlfriend, Sophia, who secretly pursued sexual liaisons with
blacks. This theme is soft-pedaled in the film: there's a veil of contempt in
Denzel Washington's eyes when (as Malcolm) he orders Sophia to kiss his
foot and feed him like a baby. Later, there's more than a hint of revulsion
in the image of Sophia's white husband, a lumpish fellow sunk in an
armchair who doesn't even look up when she brings his TV dinner. And
finally, there's the judgment rendered through Laura, the black girl who
defies her strict upbringing to go with Malcolm, only to sink into drug
abuse and prostitution when be drops her for Sophia. Together, these
scenes evoke something of the indignation Malcolm X felt at the sick racist
stereotypes that reduce black men to the status of stud animals and expose
black women to every kind of exploitation.

* * *

Recall that Malcolm X, like so many of his followers, was a child of the
Great Migration. In addition to being a Garveyite, his father was also an

itinerant Baptist preacher, hailing from Georgia but preaching hellfire sermons among his fellow migrants in Philadelphia, Omaha, Milwaukee and East Lansing, Michigan. Malcolm's mother was a native of Grenada, also uprooted from the world of her black mother and the white man who had raped and impregnated her. Even before the Little family was torn apart, it must have experienced both the exhilaration and the terror of being set adrift in alien territory. It's no wonder that Malcolm and his siblings were drawn to the Nation of Islam; its peculiar ideology gave them, and millions like them, a way of coping with both the exhilaration and the terror.

* * *

The Nation of Islam appealed to this liberating impulse, but it was Malcolm X who expressed it most fully—because, although he was deeply serious, he was not, in Yardley's phrase, "implacably serious." The word "implacably" suggests a relentlessness, and especially a humorlessness, that were alien to the man. Hard as Washington works to imitate Malcolm X's oratorical style, his performance skimps on the quality that most intrigued listeners, both white and black. That quality, a function of Malcolm X's extraordinary courage and intelligence, was his comic sense. I don't mean this frivolously, that Malcolm X was a comedian. I mean comic in the classical sense of irony, detachment, distance on both one's circumstances and oneself. When Malcolm X laid down the rhetoric about the white man being a "pale thing" bred from dogs by the devil Yacub on the Isle of Patmos, the effect was, in the highest sense, satirical. The curl of his lip, the glint in his eye, seemed to say: "This is what you sound like, you dumb crackers. Try it on for size." More effective than the blind rage that followed his death, now sadly ritualized into the pumped-up woofing of young hip-hop poseurs, was this devastating mockery. Malcolm X didn't invent it; it has always been part of Afro–American culture. But he brought it out for the white folks to see.

Why was Malcolm X able to do this, when so many other angry people have not? Because he had also found a way to master the terror of his Great Migration upbringing—terror that came, as always, from uprootedness, from the loss of an accepted belief system by which human beings make sense of the cosmos and distinguish between right and wrong. On this level, the story of Malcolm X's youth is a descent into nihilism.

* * *

———

The Taming of Malcolm X

RECONSTRUCTION II, 93–99 (1993).

■ ALAN A. STONE

* * *

There are many conflicting opinions about Malcolm X, the man—what he came from, who he was, where he was going. But whether those opinions are derived from personal encounter, his autobiography, or other documentary sources, one thing seems clear: he was an intimidating human being—an electrifying presence, a burning firebrand, and a brilliant polemicist. Spike Lee, despite his obvious talents, seems to have been unwilling or unable to portray that intimidating presence. The movie lasts more than three hours and Denzel Washington is on the screen most of that time. But he never projects what Ossie Davis recognized as Malcolm's "style and hallmark, that shocking zing of fire and be damned to you." That real Malcolm X briefly appears at the end of the film to speak his famous phrase, "by any means necessary." You need only keep that jarring authentic moment in the center of your awareness as you reflect on the entire movie to get the measure of how much Lee fails to capture the real Malcolm.

* * *

Malcolm X has become increasingly important to African Americans since his death. Part of his importance is psychological. He is their hero, the oppressed Negro who transformed himself into a "Shining Black Prince," an archetype with whom proud young Black men and women, no matter how desperate their lives have become, can make a positive identification. Malcolm X's actual psychological identity as a young man is therefore of great importance. American history has made Washington (I can not tell a lie), Lincoln (Honest Abe who freed the slaves), J.F.K. (the president as martyred savior), into sanctified beings and by that hagiographic standard there is no basis for criticizing Lee's film. He has given African Americans their own saint. However, in the strange alchemy of history, Malcolm X is emerging as the most important African American of the twentieth century and to sanctify his memory is to mystify racism. The attempt here is therefore to analyze Lee's hagiographic version from a psychological perspective using the *Autobiography* and other sources as a standard for comparison to highlight the forces of racism in Malcolm's life which the hagiography suppresses.

* * *

Each of the big scenes during the first hour of the movie emphasize Malcolm, the child-rascal. Malcolm's first conk, sets the stage. As Shorty straightens Malcolm's hair, he quickly turns into a pain-stricken child as the lye reaches his scalp. That scene is reprised just before Malcolm goes to jail. Malcolm has to put his head in the toilet, when, at the crucial moment in his conking, he finds all the water in the apartment has been turned off. The two conk scenes are Lee's "comic" book ends for Malcolm's technicolor life of crime.

* * *

One of the reasons that *The Autobiography of Malcolm X* is a stunning book is because it is a psychologically coherent and believable indictment of life in a racist world whatever race the reader might be. Whether or not

Malcolm invented many of the facts he told Haley, Malcolm was telling his version of his own life and it is authentic in that sense. The *Autobiography* also had a sophisticated psychological agenda. This is how the *Autobiography* ends the section of Malcolm's life that Lee has made into a kind of glamorized musical comedy:

> I want to say before I go on that I have never previously told anyone my sordid past in detail. I haven't done it now to sound as though I might be proud of how bad, how evil, I was. But people are always speculating—why am I as I am? To understand that of any person, his whole life, from birth, must be reviewed. All of our experiences fuse into our personality. Everything that ever happened to us is an ingredient.

> Today, when everything that I do has an urgency, I would not spend one hour in the preparation of a book which had the ambition to perhaps titillate some readers. But I am spending many hours because the full story is the best way that I know to have it seen, and understood, that I had sunk to the very bottom of the American white man's society when—soon now, in prison—I found Allah and the religion of Islam and it completely transformed my life.

When Lee's Malcolm goes to jail he is still psychologically a child-man. Malcolm in contrast saw himself as an embittered hustler who had seen the most sordid side of life, and was appropriately nicknamed Satan by his fellow prisoners. Malcolm tells us how almost entirely by his own efforts he shaped that violent and ignorant man into something else in prison. In Lee's movie the child-man finds the good father in prison just as he found the good father in crime.

* * *

Malcolm believed that both of his parents had been destroyed by White racism; his father murdered by bigots and his mother driven mad by grief and a harassing White social worker. His extended family was all the more important to Malcolm and he kept up his ties with his brothers and sisters. His older step-sister, Ella, by the father's first marriage was a strong woman who took him in when he first came to Boston. It is to his older brother's Black Muslim home in Detroit that he goes when he is released from prison. Malcolm's brothers and sisters, however, are entirely absent from Lee's film. Lee's child-man is a virtual orphan and from prison he goes to the invented Baines' home. We are led to believe that the Black Muslim faith has become his family and Malcolm has found in Elijah the father he had lost in childhood.

Lee's Malcolm has a series of particularly touching scenes with the messenger, Elijah Muhammad who is uncannily portrayed by the actor Al Freeman, Jr. Elijah has a gentle exotic spirituality. He is the ultimate kind and wise father and Malcolm, according to Lee's stage direction, is "completely humble in his presence accepting his authority totally and without reservation." Lee's Malcolm has found the answer to his inner longing and his mission is to be the good son.

* * *

Malcolm made it clear in the *Autobiography* that he "adored" Elijah and Lee has found a way to make the scenes between the two men demonstrate that. Those scenes had stymied the previous screenwriters according to Lee. No doubt the earlier writers were unable to reconcile Malcolm's fiery independent personality with his subordination to Elijah. Lee's "tamed" Malcolm presents no such problem for him. He portrays a filial love affair made possible by Elijah's modesty and a Malcolm completely humble in the older man's presence. The scenes make for inspiring cinema, but as with Malcolm's relation to Baines, they also pose questions about his gullibility that are left unanswered when Malcolm leaves the Black Muslim faith. More importantly, just as Lee downplays the forces of White racism in Malcolm's early life, he downplays the Black racism that Malcolm espoused with his acceptance of Elijah Muhammad's religious beliefs.

* * *

The moments in the film which come closest to epic proportions are when Malcolm and his Black Muslim brothers confront police brutality. The mobilization of oppressed people transformed into a disciplined political force to be reckoned with by White America was Malcolm's dream and Lee captures it on film. Whatever criticism one has of the film's psychological veracity, this is surely a stirring moment of artistic and political achievement for Lee as an African American director.

* * *

Innocence and goodness are the constant elements of the Malcolm in Lee's film. That person is a denial not only of Malcolm's own righteous fury but of the contemporary Black rage that finds its sounding board in Malcolm's personality. Malcolm is the man who always knew the score. He was street-smart and self-educated. Malcolm never denied his rage, he used it. His conversion to the Black Muslim faith focused his grievances on the White man as the Blue-eyed devil. His rage was given an outlet in the focused hatred of Black racism which he embraced. His rage was turned from sordid self-destruction to constructive political and religious goals. From guns and hustling he came to polemics and sermons. He understood the traumas of his own family as part of the continuing degradation of slavery and White racism. Everything he said in his sermons and lectures had an impact because Malcolm X spoke as one who recognized the source of his pain. The people all know the awful truth when the angry prophet, the seer finally tells it. Malcolm, the angry prophet, who terrified his listeners with the truth, is what Lee has left out of his film.

* * *

Given the political pressures on Lee, the most difficult issue must have been the filmed account of the assassination. If Oliver Stone's film *J.F.K.* is the standard of comparison, then Lee deserves an Oscar for reasonableness.

Some Blacks believe that a White conspiracy involving the F.B.I. or the C.I.A. killed Malcolm. Minister Farrakhan apparently would have preferred the film to have featured that version of the assassination. His idea is that the growing hostility between Malcolm and the Nation of Islam gave the White power structure cover for their own ends. Others have alleged that Elijah Muhammad himself ordered members of "Temple no.25" in New Jersey to kill Malcolm. Of course, there are many conspiracy theories just as is the case with J.F.K., R.F.K., and Martin Luther King, Jr.

Lee's movie shows that White operatives of the F.B.I./C.I.A. had Malcolm under surveillance. But his screenplay leaves no doubt that the actual killers were Black Muslims. He writes: "Five Black men sit around a table. They do not speak. They are Thomas Haver, Ben Thomas, Lon Davis, William X and Wilbur Kinley. All are Muslims; all are the assassins."

* * *

Lee's depiction of the assassination is brilliant and conveys fanatic and desperate brutality. But then, in keeping with the tone he has established throughout his film, he takes us to South Africa where Black school children proudly announce their identification with Malcolm X who has been enshrined by Lee as the icon of Black pride and the catalyst of international Black unity. And finally there on the screen is the long suffering Nelson Mandela, who in his gentle demeanor is the antithesis of Malcolm X. In a voice, devoid of anger, he embraces Malcolm's credo. The prodigal son has found yet another godlike father.

* * *

The Marketing of Malcolm X; Is Spike Lee's Film Just Capitalizing on an Image?

WASH. POST, Nov. 4, 1996, at C1.

■ ELAINE RIVERA

Twenty-seven years after he was assassinated in an auditorium in upper Manhattan, and a few weeks before he is resurrected on the screen in Spike Lee's $34 million epic, Malcolm X is once again at the center of controversy.

* * *

The revolutionary black leader, who spent much of his life attacking white America, is suddenly big business.

* * *

Just what Malcolm's message is, and how he should be portrayed, remains a matter of some dispute. He began life in Omaha as Malcolm Little, transformed himself into a street hustler known as "Detroit Red," went to prison where he was introduced to the teachings of Elijah Muhammad, became a leader of Muhammad's Nation of Islam, which espoused a black separatist philosophy, then broke away to pursue a more international and interracial vision of human rights.

But the Nation of Islam, which Malcolm denounced in the last year of his life and which is now headed by Louis Farrakhan, is still selling Malcolm X tapes at its Harlem mosque. And some who condemned Malcolm for his militant views in the 1960s—or who have little idea of what he stood for—are now embracing him.

* * *

But Betty Shabazz, Malcolm X's widow and an administrator at Medgar Evers College in Brooklyn, says there is nothing wrong with marketing her husband's image.

"People want to be a part of Malcolm, and this is a way for them to do it," said Shabazz, who, as executor of her husband's estate, hired a management company earlier this year to license his name and likeness. "I think anyone who is wearing a hat or T-shirt has a basic understanding that Malcolm was for justice, equality and parity for all human beings."

Thulani Davis, who wrote the libretto for an opera about Malcolm's life, says it's all part of the process of transforming a man into a myth.

"Malcolm is a modern-day myth and a powerful one," said Davis, who has seen the movie and defends Lee's work. "If Spike is doing anything, he's making a movie about a hero."

* * *

The battle over Malcolm's legacy will likely heat up in coming weeks. Baraka says he plans to see the film, then make up his mind about Lee. But he says many people who rejected Malcolm when he was alive "are pimping off of him now."

* * *

————

NOTES AND QUESTIONS

1. What accounts for the alliance between black leaders and conservatives in the face of gangsta rap? Clarence Lusane argues that the alliance between C. Delores Tucker and William Bennett, a former Reagan official, against gangsta rap gives a false sense of cooperation between blacks and conservatives. *See* CLARENCE LUSANE, RACE IN THE GLOBAL ERA: AFRICAN AMERICANS AT THE MILLENNIUM 87 (1997). In particular, he argues that the seeming alliance between both groups ignores the social forces that have negatively impacted the black community.

Is this similar to the criticism that is being leveled at Bill Cosby for his harsh criticism of African Americans of "lower economic" status who have children who curse in public and commit acts of violence? Many blacks have complained that his comments only served to reinforce conservatives' negative stereotypes of blacks. Also, in what context should we assess the criticisms that Tucker and Cosby have leveled against rap music?

One writer likens the Cosby personal responsibility criticisms and counterreaction to them to the historic intellectual debates at the turn of the twentieth century between W.E.B. DuBois and Booker T. Washington. Kevin Merida, *Cos and Effect; Bill Cosby Sparked a Debate. Will His Own Troubles Snuff it Out?* WASH. POST, Feb. 20, 2005, at D01 (arguing that Cosby's "tough-love tour that had been sweeping the country . . . was the kind of thing that used to go on with a lot greater frequency, part of an honored tradition of unflinching dialogue that African Americans have practiced for generations").

2.   Role of race in gangsta rap. It has long been noted that the majority of gangsta rap fans are white and much has been made of that fact. It has given rise to questions over whether whites are only willing to accept certain images of blacks. In fact, if one looks at MTV and BET, there is a proliferation of rap videos that depict black rappers as pimps and gangsters with numerous scantily clad black women. Is the image prevalent because it is the one whites are most comfortable with? Would blacks still be on MTV and BET if the images were the exact opposite of those presently shown?

In *Pale Imitation of Gangsta Life Gives Everyone a Bad Rap*, Richard Roeper, a *Chicago Sun-Times* columnist, argues that the prevalence of negative black stereotypes in music and movies negatively impacts all blacks. Roeper, Apr. 24, 2003, *available at* www.freerepublic.com. According to Roeper, most of the stereotypes depict blacks as chicken-eating, 40-ounce drinking, dancing people. He finds these clichés embarrassing and troubling. Most recently, the movie *Soul Plane* debuted to heavy criticism. The film purports to be a black take on *Airplane* and is rife with black stereotypes: chicken, dancing, and 40 ounce bottles of malt liquor.

The black community has been divided over its perception of *Soul Plane*. Some like Anne-Marie Johnson, an actress in *Hollywood Shuffle,* assert that Hollywood depictions of blacks have not improved since *Shuffle*. Some contend that the images have grown worse. On the other hand, some like Walter Latham, creator of the successful *Original Kings of Comedy* tours, feel that blacks take the movies far too seriously. *See* Wiley A. Hall III, *Commentary: Movie Offers Nothing More than a Soul Pain*, BLACKAMERI-CAWEB.COM NEWS, June 04, 2004, http://blackamericaweb.com/site.aspx/baw-news/soulplane63.

3.   Gangsta rap and violence. In *Black Liberation in Conservative America*, Manning Marable suggests that violence rates have increased with the increasing popularity of gangsta rap. MANNING MARABLE, BLACK LIBERATION IN CONSERVATIVE AMERICA (1997). Marable cites the violent lyrics coming from his daughter's bedroom and suggests that the music and its message are inescapable.

How much of the blame placed on rap might be misplaced? Don't inner city problems run deeper than rap lyrics? Many commentators have criticized the glamorization of gangsta life by such rappers as Tupac, Notorious B.I.G., and Snoop Dogg. These critics believe that rap lyrics are responsible for the violence and strife in urban communities.

4. Malcolm X and black rage. Cornel West devotes much discussion to Malcolm X and the black rage he embodied. *See* Cornel West, Race Matters (1993). Malcolm X has long been associated with rage and fiery passion, but the articles suggest that Spike Lee drastically toned that part of his persona to make it more palatable to a mainstream audience. That argument can be made, but on the other hand, anytime a movie is made of one's life some parts are inevitably going to be left out. But, does concern over marketability or the movie's capacity account for Lee's decision to disregard some of the leader's more confrontational rhetoric?

5. Race and royalties. Black artists and musicians have long struggled to own their songs. Because of this, many have led impoverished lives and died broke. Nor is this a past phenomenon; one only has to look at the travails of modern artists such as TLC and Toni Braxton to see that unfair recording and publishing contracts are still prevalent. Even more telling is that both TLC and Braxton were top-selling artists who still could not fend off bankruptcy.

As the aforementioned articles about Little Richard and Frankie Lymon highlight, struggles with the recording industry are not new. The articles depict both artists as victims of record companies who did not possess the necessary business knowledge for the industry. However, ignorance of the business side of the recording industry does not completely account for the uneven playing field. In *Kraski, Clint Black Launch Equity*, Clint Black, a country artist, discusses how the recording business works: "The system pays artists advances against future royalties, meaning that the revenues from their album sales first must repay numerous recoupable items, including the cost of the record production and marketing." Chris Lewis, *Kraski, Clint Black Launch Equity*, Nashville City Paper, August 1, 2003. As Black's statement illustrates, artists face an uphill battle in securing fair contracts.

The following excerpt provides an inside look at the way independent recording studios and record labels exploited African American artists.

CHARLIE ROSE: Much has been said before in the world, and during these four decades, that a lot of these black artists didn't get what they earned.

AHMET ERTEGUN: Oh, that's true. * * * There were a lot of independent record companies in the '40s, that—it mushroomed because there was a shortage of shellac. * * * And a lot of small companies that found a way of getting shellac, a way of pressing records, started to press anything that they could do. So there are all these independent companies. Many of them made jazz records. Many of them made rhythm and blues records. Many of them made country records. They made the music that the majors didn't make because of the shortage. * * *

And as a result, these—a lot of these independent record companies were owned and run by people who were not really that interested in the music. All they cared about was making a fast buck. And they had no intention of paying anybody royalties. So many of these companies were owned by people who were ex-jukebox operators, or nightclub owners, or whatever. They made these records, and unfortunately many of them [ ] never paid any royalties. And they only paid the big artists something to keep them from leaving the label.

At the same time, the big artists . . . all made 5 percent. Records sold for 75 cents. And they made 5 percent of 75 cents. That was top, that was the top royalty. Beginning artists, like country artists were paid 1 percent or 2 percent. Race record artists were paid either nothing or 1 or 2 percent. * * * In those days, a big hit record sold 50,000 or 100,000 copies. And you know, 100,000 times a nickel is not a lot of money. You know, it's $5,000. * * * [M]y first employee at Atlantic Records was a bookkeeper, . . . because we in our naive way thought that we had to pay everybody their royalties, so we had to know how much was owed. So we had a bookkeeper to figure that out. And we paid our royalties, but many companies did not.

And so it's generally said that nobody got paid correctly, or got paid at all. [T]he people who made big hits in those days, compared to people who make big hits today, got very little.

A Conversation With Ahmet Ertegun, Music Producer, Founder of Atlantic Records, CHARLIE ROSE TRANSCRIPTS, Feb. 21, 2005. *See also* AHMET ERTEGUN, WHAT'D I SAY: THE ATLANTIC STORY (2001).

6. The Paradox of Hip-Hop Sampling. *The Washington Post* writer, John Balz, discusses the increasing number of lawsuits between rappers over the use of hooks and beats. Since rap is built on sampling and appropriating old sounds this is new and unexpected phenomenon. In the article Balz focuses on disputes between unknown artists and established rappers such as I.O.F. (It's Only Family) and Ludacris. Most of these disputes center on unknown artists' allegations that popular rappers steal their hooks and beats and turn them into popular songs.

As more rappers encounter appropriation disputes, one has to wonder whether the increasing number of lawsuits reflects the influence of corporate business on the nature of rap. When rap first began it was mainly a way to entertain at parties or in parks. However, in the thirty years since it was introduced, it is the most popular music in the United States and often the background for advertising in print and media. The introduction of corporate values into what started as a homegrown music enterprise makes it safe to assume that the financial gain of rap has made settling musical disputes through litigation an attractive option for rappers, who until recently, were happy to avoid judicial resolution of their conflicts over creative and intellectual property issues. John Balz, "Hip-Hopping Mad Over Beats and Hooks", *Washington Post*, May 8, 2005, at B01.

CHAPTER 6

CORRECTIVE STRUGGLES

"Let me give you a word of the philosophy of reform. The whole history of the progress of human liberty shows that all concessions yet made to her august claims, have been born of earnest struggle. . . . If there is no struggle there is no progress. Those who profess to favor freedom and yet depreciate agitation, are men who want crops without plowing up the ground, they want rain without thunder and lightening. They want the ocean without the awful roar of its many waters.

This struggle may be a moral one, or it may be a physical one, and it may be both moral and physical, but it must be a struggle. Power concedes nothing without a demand. It never did and it never will."[1]

Frederick Douglass, Canandaigua, New York, August 3, 1857.

Introduction

This final chapter presents, perhaps, the greatest challenge within our exploration of the meaning and dimensions of economic justice. We have framed this chapter with a set of premises that we now make explicit. First, this is not a chapter of "solutions." In order for there to be a solution, there must be a stable definition of the problem. Our experience is that race and identity subordination are dynamic, changing even as new efforts to redistribute power, realign economic resources, and eliminate inequality are proposed. In this chapter, we survey the landscape of corrective struggles in order to challenge identity-based economic inequality. We have undertaken this task, with modesty born of the recognition, that as Frederick Douglass said about the end of slavery, "power concedes nothing without a demand." We recognize that the ideas and legal remedies discussed here will be no more than hollow rhetoric without a strong connection to the lives of individual people who must resist the daily indignities of economic inequality and material deprivation. Second, as scholars, we are not committed to a fixed set of remedies. Our commitment is to the process of creative resistance to the economic inequalities that we have surveyed in elaborate detail in the preceding twelve chapters. Finally, we expect that, in keeping with our view of the dynamic nature of subordinating strategies, new theories will enter the debate about correc-

---

1. Frederick Douglass, The Significance of Emancipation in the West Indies, Address delivered in Canandaigua, New York (Aug. 3, 1857), *in* 3 THE FREDERICK DOUGLASS PAPERS 204 (John W. Blassingame ed., 1985).

tive justice, even as we go to press. We look forward to bringing the most promising ideas to future editions of this book.

We begin the chapter with two cases that represent significant milestones in the development of the Supreme Court jurisprudence on the constitutionality of minority set-asides in government contracting programs These programs represent explicit economic redistribution. *Croson*, the Richmond case, presents a fascinating opportunity to see the dynamic that ensues when a subordinated group captures a majority in a local legislature. *Metro Broadcasting* has been included, nothwithstanding the fact that it has been overruled by *Adarand Constructor v. Pena*, 515 U.S. 200 (1995). In *Metro Broadcasting*, the court adopted the distinction between benign racial classifications intended to assist members of subordinated groups and invidious discrimination that preserves age-old racial stigmas and subordination. Although this view was later repudiated, it is a valuable artifact of the evolution of Supreme Court jurisprudence addressing race-conscious remedies.

Educational opportunity, as we have seen from the beginning to the end of this book, is one of the most important access points to economic mobility. As we have discussed in earlier chapters, educational attainment is also the single biggest predictor of lifetime earnings. The Constitution, however, does not treat primary or secondary education as a fundamental interest, nor is wealth a suspect classification. These two holdings of the *Rodriguez* school financing case of the 1970s, have served to shatter the first rung on the ladder of equal educational access. The absence of well-financed, high quality public education at the primary and secondary level has meant that colleges and universities must select from a pool of applicants that bear all the marks of wealth- and race-based inequality. As Justices Ginsburg and Breyer observe in *Grutter v. Bollinger*, 539 U.S. 306 (2003) (Ginsberg, J. Concurring): "[a]s to public education, data for the years 2000–2001 show that 71.6% of African-American children and 76.3% of Hispanic children attended a school in which minorities made up a majority of the student body.... [I]t remains the current reality that many minority students encounter markedly inadequate and unequal educational opportunities." Grutter, 539 U.S. at 345–46. It is unsurprising, therefore, that we have the much-discussed test score and grade gap between applicants of color and poor white students on one hand, and the wealthy students who, on the other hand, are able to earn high test scores and strong grades through parental support and resources.

Decreasing economic mobility in recent years has meant that, as conservative editorial writer David Brooks notes, we have a "sticky ladder" in which parental wealth is the greatest predictor of future class status for any child born in America today. Brooks argues, with substantial research support, that we have an "inherited meritocracy." Poor whites and students from racially subordinated communities must overcome formidable financial and educational challenges to secure a college education. Thomas Shapiro documents the consequences of the wealth gap and the attitudes of meritocratic entitlement that underlie the structures of economic privilege for families at the top of the economic ladder.

The Supreme Court opinions in *Grutter* give us a fascinating view of all the major arguments that are made in the debate about race-conscious affirmative action admissions policies in higher education. Justice O'Connor's opinion in *Grutter* sets an ominous time limit of twenty-five years for constitutional approval of race-conscious admissions programs. Lani Guinier offers a deep analysis of the political dimensions of admissions policies and suggests a forward-looking alternative for making admissions decisions.

As we have seen in previous chapters, another important element of the American class system is marriage. In this country, we rely on heterosexual marriage to finance the bulk of family dependency needs, from child care to elder care to care of the sick and dying. As we have seen, the place of marriage in the economic order established in the 1950s asked wives to stay out of wage work in order to provide this dependent care, while husbands would receive a "family wage." Marriage also served as a legal access point for benefits such as private health insurance and social insurance. In recent decades, however, marriage as a system for providing dependent care has steadily broken down. As the industrial economy shifted to a service economy, the family wage disappeared, and the resulting economic pressures have forced more and more wives into wage work in order to keep families afloat. Meanwhile, social changes have led to higher divorce rates, a steadily rising age of first marriage, and increasing numbers of never-married people and single mothers. This chapter examines three groups of people caught in the crossfire of these changes: stay-at-home wives, working mothers, and same-sex couples. The human capital theory offers a useful conceptual intervention in the age-old story of individual ownership of degrees earned with spousal support during the term of a marriage. Treating discrimination against mothers as sex discrimination uses litigation as a tool for restructuring the workplace. Finally, we explore the question of same-sex marriage as an interplay of symbolic issues—religious values versus secular egalitarian values—with material issues, including the continuing viability of marriage as the major conduit for dependency care.

Finally, as we have in earlier chapters, we look at the international dimensions of economic inequality. We consider the role of cultural property, and the international development questions that arise from global poverty and economic inequality.

A.   Affirmative Action

City of Richmond v. J.A. Croson Co.

Supreme Court of the United States, 488 U.S. 469, 109 S.Ct. 706 (1989).

■ Justice O'Connor announced the judgment of the Court and delivered the opinion of the Court with respect to Parts I, III–B, and IV, and opinion with respect to Part II, in which the CHIEF JUSTICE and JUSTICE WHITE join, and an opinion with respect to Parts III–A and V, in which the CHIEF JUSTICE, JUSTICE WHITE, and JUSTICE KENNEDY join.

In this case, we confront once again the tension between the Fourteenth Amendment's guarantee of equal treatment to all citizens, and the use of race-based measures to ameliorate the effects of past discrimination on the opportunities enjoyed by members of minority groups in our society. In *Fullilove v. Klutznick, 448 U.S. 448 (1980),* we held that a congressional program requiring that 10% of certain federal construction grants be awarded to minority contractors did not violate the equal protection principles embodied in the Due Process Clause of the Fifth Amendment. Relying largely on our decision in *Fullilove,* some lower federal courts have applied a similar standard of review in assessing the constitutionality of state and local minority set-aside provisions under the Equal Protection Clause of the Fourteenth Amendment. * * *

I

On April 11, 1983, the Richmond City Council adopted the Minority Business Utilization Plan (the Plan). The Plan required prime contractors to whom the city awarded construction contracts to subcontract at least 30% of the dollar amount of the contract to one or more Minority Business Enterprises (MBE's). Ordinance No. 83–69–59, codified in Richmond, Va., City Code, § 12–156(a) (1985). The 30% set-aside did not apply to city contracts awarded to minority-owned prime contractors. * * *

The Plan defined an MBE as "[a] business at least fifty-one (51) percent of which is owned and controlled . . . by minority group members." * * * "Minority group members" were defined as "[c]itizens of the United States who are Blacks, Spanish-speaking, Orientals, Indians, Eskimos, or Aleuts." * * * There was no geographic limit to the Plan; an otherwise qualified MBE from anywhere in the United States could avail itself of the 30% set-aside. The Plan declared that it was "remedial" in nature, and enacted "for the purpose of promoting wider participation by minority business enterprises in the construction of public projects." * * * The Plan expired on June 30, 1988, and was in effect for approximately five years.

* * *

The Plan was adopted by the Richmond City Council after a public hearing. * * * Seven members of the public spoke to the merits of the ordinance: five were in opposition, two in favor. Proponents of the set-aside provision relied on a study which indicated that, while the general population of Richmond was 50% black, only 0.67% of the city's prime construction contracts had been awarded to minority businesses in the 5–year period from 1978 to 1983. It was also established that a variety of contractors' associations, whose representatives appeared in opposition to the ordinance, had virtually no minority businesses within their membership. * * *

There was no direct evidence of race discrimination on the part of the city in letting contracts or any evidence that the city's prime contractors had discriminated against minority-owned subcontractors. [Councilperson Kent said,] "[The public witnesses] indicated that the minority contractors were just not available. There wasn't a one that gave any indication that a minority contractor would not have an opportunity, if he were available."

* * *

[The district court upheld the plan. The court of appeals affirmed, applying the *Fullilove* standard and deferring to congressional findings of past discrimination. The Supreme Court vacated the decision for further consideration in light of its *Wygant* opinion.

The court of appeals struck down the plan on remand, holding that it violated the Equal Protection clause of the Fourteenth Amendment. Applying strict scrutiny according to its reading of *Wygant*, the court of appeals held that Richmond failed to show a compelling government interest for racial preferences because there was no findings of past discrimination by the local government in awarding contracts. Further, the 30% set aside figure was not narrowly tailored as the number was arbitrary. The Supreme Court affirms.]

II

The parties and their supporting *amici* fight an initial battle over the scope of the city's power to adopt legislation designed to address the effects of past discrimination. Relying on our decision in *Wygant*, appellee argues that the city must limit any race-based remedial efforts to eradicating the effects of its own prior discrimination. This is essentially the position taken by the Court of Appeals below. Appellant argues that our decision in *Fullilove* is controlling, and that as a result the city of Richmond enjoys sweeping legislative power to define and attack the effects of prior discrimination in its local construction industry. We find that neither of these two rather stark alternatives can withstand analysis.

* * *

[In *Fullilove v. Klutznick*, 448 U.S. 448 (1980), the Court upheld the Public Works Employment Act of 1977 set aside provision, which required grants to local and state governments to use 10% of the funds on minority business enterprises. MBE's were defined as businesses effectively controlled by "citizens of the United States who are Negroes, Spanish-speaking, Orientals, Indians, Eskimos, and Aleuts."

Chief Justice Burger announced the Court's judgment, which his opinion noted was not based on an traditional standard of scrutiny for equal protection claims. The inquiry instead asked whether congressional objectives were within the scope of Congress' power and whether it was permissible to carry out these objectives with racial and ethnic criteria under the equal protection of the Due Process clause. As Congress was given special remedial powers under § 5 of the Fourteenth Amendment and the legislative history evidenced past national discrimination against minority businesses in awarding federal construction grants, the objectives were permissible. The flexibility of the 10% set aside made the use of racial criteria permissible because waivers could be granted where there were too few MBEs or where an MBE price was unreasonable, even in light of past discrimination.

Justice Powell's concurring opinion noted that requirements for findings of past discrimination might vary based on the types of remedies and the authority of the government entity.]

Appellant and its supporting *amici* rely heavily on *Fullilove* for the proposition that a city council, like Congress, need not make specific findings of discrimination to engage in race-conscious relief. Thus, appellant argues "[i]t would be a perversion of federalism to hold that the federal government has a compelling interest in remedying the effects of racial discrimination in its own public works program, but a city government does not." * * *

What appellant ignores is that Congress, unlike any State or political subdivision, has a specific constitutional mandate to enforce the dictates of the Fourteenth Amendment. The power to "enforce" may at times also include the power to define situations which *Congress* determines threaten principles of equality and to adopt prophylactic rules to deal with those situations. * * *

That Congress may identify and redress the effects of society-wide discrimination does not mean that, *a fortiori*, the States and their political subdivisions are free to decide that such remedies are appropriate. Section 1 of the Fourteenth Amendment is an explicit *constraint* on state power, and the States must undertake any remedial efforts in accordance with that provision. To hold otherwise would be to cede control over the content of the Equal Protection Clause to the 50 state legislatures and their myriad political subdivisions * * *

> * * *

It would seem equally clear, however, that a state or local subdivision (if delegated the authority from the State) has the authority to eradicate the effects of private discrimination within its own legislative jurisdiction. This authority must, of course, be exercised within the constraints of § 1 of the Fourteenth Amendment. Our decision in *Wygant* is not to the contrary. *Wygant* addressed the constitutionality of the use of racial quotas by local school authorities pursuant to an agreement reached with the local teachers' union. It was in the context of addressing the school board's power to adopt a race-based layoff program affecting its own work force that the *Wygant* plurality indicated that the Equal Protection Clause required "some showing of prior discrimination by the governmental unit involved." * * *

Thus, if the city could show that it had essentially become a "passive participant" in a system of racial exclusion practiced by elements of the local construction industry, we think it clear that the city could take affirmative steps to dismantle such a system. It is beyond dispute that any public entity, state or federal, has a compelling interest in assuring that public dollars, drawn from the tax contributions of all citizens, do not serve to finance the evil of private prejudice. * * *

III

A

The Equal Protection Clause of the Fourteenth Amendment provides that "[n]o State shall ... deny to *any person* within its jurisdiction the equal protection of the laws." (Emphasis added.) As this Court has noted in the past, the "rights created by the first section of the Fourteenth Amendment are, by its terms, guaranteed to the individual. The rights established are personal rights." *Shelley v. Kraemer,* 334 U.S. 1, 22 (1948). The Richmond Plan denies certain citizens the opportunity to compete for a fixed percentage of public contracts based solely upon their race. To whatever racial group these citizens belong, their "personal rights" to be treated with equal dignity and respect are implicated by a rigid rule erecting race as the sole criterion in an aspect of public decision-making.

Absent searching judicial inquiry into the justification for such race-based measures, there is simply no way of determining what classifications are "benign" or "remedial" and what classifications are in fact motivated by illegitimate notions of racial inferiority or simple racial politics. Indeed, the purpose of strict scrutiny is to "smoke out" illegitimate uses of race by assuring that the legislative body is pursuing a goal important enough to warrant use of a highly suspect tool. The test also ensures that the means chosen "fit" this compelling goal so closely that there is little or no possibility that the motive for the classification was illegitimate racial prejudice or stereotype.

Classifications based on race carry a danger of stigmatic harm. Unless they are strictly reserved for remedial settings, they may in fact promote notions of racial inferiority and lead to a politics of racial hostility. * * * We thus reaffirm the view expressed by the plurality in *Wygant* that the standard of review under the Equal Protection Clause is not dependent on the race of those burdened or benefited by a particular classification. * * *

Our continued adherence to the standard of review employed in *Wygant* does not, as Justice Marshall's dissent suggests, * * * indicate that we view "racial discrimination as largely a phenomenon of the past" or that "government bodies need no longer preoccupy themselves with rectifying racial injustice." * * *

Under the standard proposed by Justice Marshall's dissent, "race-conscious classifications designed to further remedial goals," * * * are forthwith subject to a relaxed standard of review. * * *

Even were we to accept a reading of the guarantee of equal protection under which the level of scrutiny varies according to the ability of different groups to defend their interests in the representative process, heightened scrutiny would still be appropriate in the circumstances of this case. One of the central arguments for applying a less exacting standard to "benign" racial classifications is that such measures essentially involve a choice made by dominant racial groups to disadvantage themselves. If one aspect of the judiciary's role under the Equal Protection Clause is to protect "discrete and insular minorities" from majoritarian prejudice or indifference, * * * some maintain that these concerns are not implicated when the "white majority" places burdens upon itself. * * *

In this case, blacks constitute approximately 50% of the population of the city of Richmond. Five of the nine seats on the city council are held by blacks. The concern that a political majority will more easily act to the disadvantage of a minority based on unwarranted assumptions or incomplete facts would seem to militate for, not against, the application of heightened judicial scrutiny in this case. * * *

[In *University of California Regents v. Bakke*, 438 U.S. 265 (1978), the Court struck down a racial quotas in public university medical school admissions, which were intended to remedy past societal discrimination and minority under-representation in the medical profession. Four members of the Court found that excluding nonminority applicants from a fixed portion of seats violated Title VI of the Civil Rights Act of 1964. Justice Powell's concurrence found the quota system to be unconstitutional using heightened scrutiny under the Equal Protection clause of the Fourteenth Amendment. Under his analysis, racial preferences could only be justified based on findings of past discrimination in violation of statutes or the Constitution.]

In *Wygant*, * * * four Members of the Court applied heightened scrutiny to a race-based system of employee layoffs. Justice Powell, writing for the plurality, again drew the distinction between "societal discrimination" which is an inadequate basis for race-conscious classifications, and the type of identified discrimination that can support and define the scope of race-based relief. [A] plurality of four Justices reiterating the view expressed by Justice Powell in *Bakke* that "[s]ocietal discrimination, without more, is too amorphous a basis for imposing a racially classified remedy."

    * * *

B

We think it clear that the factual predicate offered in support of the Richmond Plan suffers from the same two defects identified as fatal in *Wygant*. The District Court found the city council's "findings sufficient to ensure that, in adopting the Plan, it was remedying the present effects of past discrimination in the *construction industry*." * * * Like the "role model" theory employed in *Wygant*, a generalized assertion that there has been past discrimination in an entire industry provides no guidance for a legislative body to determine the precise scope of the injury it seeks to remedy. It "has no logical stopping point." * * * "Relief" for such an ill-defined wrong could extend until the percentage of public contracts awarded to MBE's in Richmond mirrored the percentage of minorities in the population as a whole.

* * *

While there is no doubt that the sorry history of both private and public discrimination in this country has contributed to a lack of opportunities for black entrepreneurs, this observation, standing alone, cannot justify a rigid racial quota in the awarding of public contracts in Richmond, Virginia. Like the claim that discrimination in primary and secondary schooling justifies a rigid racial preference in medical school admissions, an amorphous claim that there has been past discrimination in a particular industry cannot justify the use of an unyielding racial quota.

It is sheer speculation how many minority firms there would be in Richmond absent past societal discrimination, just as it was sheer speculation how many minority medical students would have been admitted to the medical school at Davis absent past discrimination in educational opportunities. Defining these sorts of injuries as "identified discrimination" would give local governments license to create a patchwork of racial preferences based on statistical generalizations about any particular field of endeavor.

These defects are readily apparent in this case. The 30% quota cannot in any realistic sense be tied to any injury suffered by anyone. The District Court relied upon five predicate "facts" in reaching its conclusion that there was an adequate basis for the 30% quota: (1) the ordinance declares itself to be remedial; (2) several proponents of the measure stated their views that there had been past discrimination in the construction industry; (3) minority businesses received 0.67% of prime contracts from the city while minorities constituted 50% of the city's population; (4) there were very few minority contractors in local and state contractors' associations; and (5) in 1977, Congress made a determination that the effects of past discrimination had stifled minority participation in the construction industry nationally. * * *

None of these "findings," singly or together, provide the city of Richmond with a "strong basis in evidence for its conclusion that remedial action was necessary." * * * There is nothing approaching a prima facie case of a constitutional or statutory violation by *anyone* in the Richmond construction industry. * * *

The District Court accorded great weight to the fact that the city council designated the Plan as "remedial." But the mere recitation of a "benign" or legitimate purpose for a racial classification is entitled to little or no weight. * * * Racial classifications are suspect, and that means that simple legislative assurances of good intention cannot suffice.

The District Court also relied on the highly conclusionary statement of a proponent of the Plan that there was racial discrimination in the construction industry "in this area, and the State, and around the nation." * * *

Reliance on the disparity between the number of prime contracts awarded to minority firms and the minority population of the city of

Richmond is similarly misplaced. There is no doubt that "[w]here gross statistical disparities can be shown, they alone in a proper case may constitute prima facie proof of a pattern or practice of discrimination" under Title VII. *Hazelwood School Dist. v. United States.* * * * But it is equally clear that "[w]hen special qualifications are required to fill particular jobs, comparisons to the general population (rather than to the smaller group of individuals who possess the necessary qualifications) may have little probative value." * * *

In the employment context, we have recognized that for certain entry level positions or positions requiring minimal training, statistical comparisons of the racial composition of an employer's work force to the racial composition of the relevant population may be probative of a pattern of discrimination. * * * But where special qualifications are necessary, the relevant statistical pool for purposes of demonstrating discriminatory exclusion must be the number of minorities qualified to undertake the particular task. * * *

In this case, the city does not even know how many MBE's in the relevant market are qualified to undertake prime or subcontracting work in public construction projects. * * * Nor does the city know what percentage of total city construction dollars minority firms now receive as subcontractors on prime contracts let by the city.

To a large extent, the set-aside of subcontracting dollars seems to rest on the unsupported assumption that white prime contractors simply will not hire minority firms. * * * Indeed, there is evidence in this record that overall minority participation in city contracts in Richmond is 7 to 8%, and that minority contractor participation in Community Block Development Grant *construction* projects is 17 to 22%. * * * Without any information on minority participation in subcontracting, it is quite simply impossible to evaluate overall minority representation in the city's construction expenditures.

The city and the District Court also relied on evidence that MBE membership in local contractors' associations was extremely low. Again, standing alone this evidence is not probative of any discrimination in the local construction industry.

* * *

Finally, the city and the District Court relied on Congress' finding in connection with the set-aside approved in *Fullilove* that there had been nationwide discrimination in the construction industry. The probative value of these findings for demonstrating the existence of discrimination in Richmond is extremely limited. By its inclusion of a waiver procedure in the national program addressed in *Fullilove*, Congress explicitly recognized that the scope of the problem would vary from market area to market area. * * *

Moreover, as noted above, Congress was exercising its powers under § 5 of the Fourteenth Amendment in making a finding that past discrimination would cause federal funds to be distributed in a manner which reinforced prior patterns of discrimination. While the States and their subdivisions may take remedial action when they possess evidence that their own spending practices are exacerbating a pattern of prior discrimination, they must identify that discrimination, public or private, with some specificity before they may use race-conscious relief. Congress has made national findings that there has been societal discrimination in a host of fields. If all a state or local government need do is find a congressional report on the subject to enact a set-aside program, the constraints of the Equal Protection Clause will, in effect, have been rendered a nullity. * * *

* * *

In sum, none of the evidence presented by the city points to any identified discrimination in the Richmond construction industry. We, therefore, hold that the city has failed to demonstrate a compelling interest in apportioning public contracting opportunities on the basis of race. To accept Richmond's claim that past societal discrimination alone can serve as the basis for rigid racial preferences would be to open the door to competing claims for "remedial relief" for every disadvantaged group. The dream of a Nation of equal citizens in a society where race is irrelevant to personal opportunity and achievement would be lost in a mosaic of shifting preferences based on inherently unmeasurable claims of past wrongs. "Courts would be asked to evaluate the extent of the prejudice and consequent harm suffered by various minority groups. Those whose societal injury is thought to exceed some arbitrary level of tolerability then would be entitled to preferential classifications...." [*Bakke* (Powell, J.)] We think such a result would be contrary to both the letter and spirit of a constitutional provision whose central command is equality.

The foregoing analysis applies only to the inclusion of blacks within the Richmond set-aside program. There is *absolutely no evidence* of past discrimination against Spanish-speaking, Oriental, Indian, Eskimo, or Aleut persons in any aspect of the Richmond construction industry. The District Court took judicial notice of the fact that the vast majority of "minority" persons in Richmond were black. * * * It may well be that Richmond has never had an Aleut or Eskimo citizen. The random inclusion of racial groups that, as a practical matter, may never have suffered from discrimination in the construction industry in Richmond suggests that perhaps the city's purpose was not in fact to remedy past discrimination.

If a 30% set-aside was "narrowly tailored" to compensate black contractors for past discrimination, one may legitimately ask why they are forced to share this "remedial relief" with an Aleut citizen who moves to Richmond tomorrow? The gross overinclusiveness of Richmond's racial preference strongly impugns the city's claim of remedial motivation. * * *

IV

As noted by the court below, it is almost impossible to assess whether the Richmond Plan is narrowly tailored to remedy prior discrimination since it is not linked to identified discrimination in any way. We limit ourselves to two observations in this regard.

First, there does not appear to have been any consideration of the use of race-neutral means to increase minority business participation in city contracting. * * * Many of the barriers to minority participation in the construction industry relied upon by the city to justify a racial classification appear to be race neutral. * * *

Second, the 30% quota cannot be said to be narrowly tailored to any goal, except perhaps outright racial balancing. It rests upon the "completely unrealistic" assumption that minorities will choose a particular trade in lockstep proportion to their representation in the local population. * * *

Unlike the program upheld in *Fullilove*, the Richmond Plan's waiver system focuses solely on the availability of MBE's; there is no inquiry into whether or not the particular MBE seeking a racial preference has suffered from the effects of past discrimination by the city or prime contractors.

Given the existence of an individualized procedure, the city's only interest in maintaining a quota system rather than investigating the need for remedial action in particular cases would seem to be simple administrative convenience. But the interest in avoiding the bureaucratic effort necessary to tailor remedial relief to those who truly have suffered the effects of prior discrimination cannot justify a rigid line drawn on the basis of a suspect classification. * * * Under Richmond's scheme, a successful black, Hispanic, or Oriental entrepreneur from anywhere in the country enjoys an absolute preference over other citizens based solely on their race. We think it obvious that such a program is not narrowly tailored to remedy the effects of prior discrimination.

V

Nothing we say today precludes a state or local entity from taking action to rectify the effects of identified discrimination within its jurisdiction. If the city of Richmond had evidence before it that nonminority contractors were systematically excluding minority businesses from subcontracting opportunities, it could take action to end the discriminatory exclusion. Where there is a significant statistical disparity between the number of qualified minority contractors willing and able to perform a particular service and the number of such contractors actually engaged by the locality or the locality's prime contractors, an inference of discriminatory exclusion could arise. * * * Under such circumstances, the city could act to dismantle the closed business system by taking appropriate measures against those who discriminate on the basis of race or other illegitimate criteria. * * * In the extreme case, some form of narrowly tailored racial preference might be necessary to break down patterns of deliberate exclusion.

Nor is local government powerless to deal with individual instances of racially motivated refusals to employ minority contractors. Where such discrimination occurs, a city would be justified in penalizing the discriminator and providing appropriate relief to the victim of such discrimination. * * * Moreover, evidence of a pattern of individual discriminatory acts can, if supported by appropriate statistical proof, lend support to a local government's determination that broader remedial relief is justified. * * *

Even in the absence of evidence of discrimination, the city has at its disposal a whole array of race-neutral devices to increase the accessibility of city contracting opportunities to small entrepreneurs of all races. Simplification of bidding procedures, relaxation of bonding requirements, and training and financial aid for disadvantaged entrepreneurs of all races would open the public contracting market to all those who have suffered the effects of past societal discrimination or neglect. Many of the formal barriers to new entrants may be the product of bureaucratic inertia more than actual necessity, and may have a disproportionate effect on the opportunities open to new minority firms.

* * *

Proper findings in this regard are necessary to define both the scope of the injury and the extent of the remedy necessary to cure its effects. Such findings also serve to assure all citizens that the deviation from the norm of equal treatment of all racial and ethnic groups is a temporary matter, a measure taken in the service of the goal of equality itself. Absent such findings, there is a danger that a racial classification is merely the product of unthinking stereotypes or a form of racial politics. * * * Because the city of Richmond has failed to identify the need for remedial action in the awarding of its public construction contracts, its treatment of its citizens on a racial basis violates the dictates of the Equal Protection Clause. Accordingly, the judgment of the Court of Appeals for the Fourth Circuit is

  Affirmed.

■ JUSTICE STEVENS, concurring in part and concurring in the judgment.

A central purpose of the Fourteenth Amendment is to further the national goal of equal opportunity for all our citizens. In order to achieve that goal we must learn from our past mistakes, but I believe the Constitution requires us to evaluate our policy decisions—including those that govern the relationships among different racial and ethnic groups—primarily by studying their probable impact on the future. I therefore do not agree with the premise that seems to underlie today's decision, as well as the decision in *Wygant*, * * * that a governmental decision that rests on a racial classification is never permissible except as a remedy for a past wrong.[1] * * * I do, however, agree with the Court's explanation of why the

---

1. In my view the Court's approach to this case gives unwarranted deference to race-based legislative action that purports to serve a purely remedial goal, and overlooks the potential value of race-based determinations that may serve other valid purposes. With regard to the former point—as I explained at some length in *Fullilove* (dissenting opinion)—I am not prepared to assume that even a more narrowly tailored set-aside program supported by stronger findings would be constitutionally justified. Unless the legislature can identify both the particular victims and the particular perpetrators of past discrimination, which is precisely what a court does when it makes findings of fact and conclusions of law, a *remedial* justification for race-based legislation will almost certainly sweep too broadly. With regard to the latter point: I think it unfortunate that the Court in neither *Wygant* nor this case seems prepared to acknowledge that some race-

Richmond ordinance cannot be justified as a remedy for past discrimination, and therefore join Parts I, III–B, and IV of its opinion. I write separately to emphasize three aspects of the case that are of special importance to me.

First, the city makes no claim that the public interest in the efficient performance of its construction contracts will be served by granting a preference to minority-business enterprises. * * *

Second, this litigation involves an attempt by a legislative body, rather than a court, to fashion a remedy for a past wrong. Legislatures are primarily policymaking bodies that promulgate rules to govern future conduct. The constitutional prohibitions against the enactment of *ex post facto* laws and bills of attainder reflect a valid concern about the use of the political process to punish or characterize past conduct of private citizens. It is the judicial system, rather than the legislative process, that is best equipped to identify past wrongdoers and to fashion remedies that will create the conditions that presumably would have existed had no wrong been committed. * * *

Third, instead of engaging in a debate over the proper standard of review to apply in affirmative-action litigation, I believe it is more constructive to try to identify the characteristics of the advantaged and disadvantaged classes that may justify their disparate treatment. * * * In this case that approach convinces me that, instead of carefully identifying the characteristics of the two classes of contractors that are respectively favored and disfavored by its ordinance, the Richmond City Council has merely engaged in the type of stereotypical analysis that is a hallmark of violations of the Equal Protection Clause. Whether we look at the class of persons benefited by the ordinance or at the disadvantaged class, the same conclusion emerges.

[Justice Kennedy's opinion concurring in part and concurring in the judgment has been omitted].

■ JUSTICE SCALIA, concurring in the judgment.

I agree with much of the Court's opinion, and, in particular, with JUSTICE O'CONNOR's conclusion that strict scrutiny must be applied to all governmental classification by race, whether or not its asserted purpose is "remedial" or "benign." * * * I do not agree, however, with JUSTICE O'CONNOR's dictum suggesting that, despite the Fourteenth Amendment, state and local governments may in some circumstances discriminate on the basis of race in order (in a broad sense) "to ameliorate the effects of past discrimination." * * * The benign purpose of compensating for social disadvantages, whether they have been acquired by reason of prior discrimination or otherwise, can no more be pursued by the illegitimate means of

based policy decisions may serve a legitimate public purpose. I agree, of course, that race is so seldom relevant to legislative decisions on how best to foster the public good that legitimate justifications for race-based legislation will usually not be available. But unlike the Court, I would not totally discount the legitimacy of race-based decisions that may produce tangible and fully justified future benefits.

racial discrimination than can other assertedly benign purposes we have repeatedly rejected. * * * The difficulty of overcoming the effects of past discrimination is as nothing compared with the difficulty of eradicating from our society the source of those effects, which is the tendency—fatal to a Nation such as ours—to classify and judge men and women on the basis of their country of origin or the color of their skin. A solution to the first problem that aggravates the second is no solution at all.

* * *

A sound distinction between federal and state (or local) action based on race rests not only upon the substance of the Civil War Amendments, but upon social reality and governmental theory. * * * The struggle for racial justice has historically been a struggle by the national society against oppression in the individual States. * * * And the struggle retains that character in modern times. * * * An acute awareness of the heightened danger of oppression from political factions in small, rather than large, political units dates to the very beginning of our national history. * * *

In my view there is only one circumstance in which the States may act *by race* to "undo the effects of past discrimination": where that is necessary to eliminate their own maintenance of a system of unlawful racial classification. If, for example, a state agency has a discriminatory pay scale compensating black employees in all positions at 20% less than their nonblack counterparts, it may assuredly promulgate an order raising the salaries of "all black employees" to eliminate the differential. * * * This distinction explains our school desegregation cases, in which we have made plain that States and localities sometimes have an obligation to adopt race-conscious remedies. * * *

I agree with the Court's dictum that a fundamental distinction must be drawn between the effects of "societal" discrimination and the effects of "identified" discrimination, and that the situation would be different if Richmond's plan were "tailored" to identify those particular bidders who "suffered from the effects of past discrimination by the city or prime contractors." * * * In my view, however, the reason that would make a difference is not, as the Court states, that it would justify race-conscious action * * * but rather that it would enable race-neutral remediation. * * *

It is plainly true that in our society blacks have suffered discrimination immeasurably greater than any directed at other racial groups. But those who believe that racial preferences can help to "even the score" display, and reinforce, a manner of thinking by race that was the source of the injustice and that will, if it endures within our society, be the source of more injustice still. The relevant proposition is not that it was blacks, or Jews, or Irish who were discriminated against, but that it was individual men and women, "created equal," who were discriminated against. And the relevant resolve is that that should never happen again. Racial preferences appear to "even the score" (in some small degree) only if one embraces the proposition that our society is appropriately viewed as divided into races, making it right that an injustice rendered in the past to a black man should be compensated for by discriminating against a white. Nothing is worth that embrace. * * *

Since I believe that the appellee here had a constitutional right to have its bid succeed or fail under a decisionmaking process uninfected with racial bias, I concur in the judgment of the Court.

■ JUSTICE MARSHALL, with whom JUSTICE BRENNAN and JUSTICE BLACKMUN join, dissenting.

It is a welcome symbol of racial progress when the former capital of the Confederacy acts forthrightly to confront the effects of racial discrimination in its midst. In my view, nothing in the Constitution can be construed to prevent Richmond, Virginia, from allocating a portion of its contracting dollars for businesses owned or controlled by members of minority groups. * * *

A majority of this Court holds today, however, that the Equal Protection Clause of the Fourteenth Amendment blocks Richmond's initiative. The essence of the majority's position is that Richmond has failed to catalog adequate findings to prove that past discrimination has impeded minorities from joining or participating fully in Richmond's construction contracting industry. I find deep irony in second-guessing Richmond's judgment on this point. As much as any municipality in the United States, Richmond knows what racial discrimination is; a century of decisions by this and other federal courts has richly documented the city's disgraceful history of public and private racial discrimination. In any event, the Richmond City Council *has* supported its determination that minorities have been wrongly excluded from local construction contracting. Its proof includes statistics showing that minority-owned businesses have received virtually no city contracting dollars and rarely if ever belonged to area trade associations; testimony by municipal officials that discrimination has been widespread in the local construction industry; and the same exhaustive and widely publicized federal studies relied on in *Fullilove*, studies which showed that pervasive discrimination in the Nation's tight-knit construction industry had operated to exclude minorities from public contracting. These are precisely the types of statistical and testimonial evidence which, until today, this Court had credited in cases approving of race-conscious measures designed to remedy past discrimination.

More fundamentally, today's decision marks a deliberate and giant step backward in this Court's affirmative-action jurisprudence. Cynical of one municipality's attempt to redress the effects of past racial discrimination in a particular industry, the majority launches a grapeshot attack on race-conscious remedies in general. The majority's unnecessary pronouncements will inevitably discourage or prevent governmental entities, particularly States and localities, from acting to rectify the scourge of past discrimination. This is the harsh reality of the majority's decision, but it is not the Constitution's command.

I

As an initial matter, the majority takes an exceedingly myopic view of the factual predicate on which the Richmond City Council relied when it passed the Minority Business Utilization Plan. * * * The majority's refusal to recognize that Richmond has proved itself no exception to the dismaying pattern of national exclusion which Congress so painstakingly identified infects its entire analysis of this case.

* * *

The congressional program upheld in *Fullilove* was based upon an array of congressional and agency studies which documented the powerful influence of racially exclusionary practices in the business world. * * *

[T]here was "abundant evidence" in the public domain "that minority businesses ha[d] been denied effective participation in public contracting opportunities by procurement practices that perpetuated the effects of prior discrimination." [*Fullilove.*] Significantly, this evidence demonstrated that discrimination had prevented existing or nascent minority-owned businesses from obtaining not only federal contracting assignments, but state and local ones as well. * * *

The members of the Richmond City Council were well aware of these exhaustive congressional findings, a point the majority, tellingly, elides. * * *

So long as one views Richmond's local evidence of discrimination against the backdrop of systematic nationwide racial discrimination which Congress had so painstakingly identified in this very industry, this case is readily resolved.

II

* * * My view has long been that race conscious classifications designed to further remedial goals "must serve important governmental objectives and must be substantially related to achievement of those objectives" in order to withstand constitutional scrutiny. * * * Analyzed in terms of this two-pronged standard, Richmond's set-aside, like the federal program on which it was modeled, is "plainly constitutional." [*Fullilove* (MARSHALL, concurring in judgment).]

* * *

A

* * *

1

Turning first to the governmental interest inquiry, Richmond has two powerful interests in setting aside a portion of public contracting funds for minority-owned enterprises. The first is the city's interest in eradicating the effects of past racial discrimination. It is far too late in the day to doubt that remedying such discrimination is a compelling, let alone an important, interest. * * *

Richmond has a second compelling interest in setting aside, where possible, a portion of its contracting dollars. That interest is the prospective one of preventing the city's own spending decisions from reinforcing and perpetuating the exclusionary effects of past discrimination. * * *

The majority pays only lipservice to this additional governmental interest. * * * But our decisions have often emphasized the danger of the government tacitly adopting, encouraging, or furthering racial discrimination even by its own routine operations. * * *

The majority is wrong to trivialize the continuing impact of government acceptance or use of private institutions or structures once wrought by discrimination. When government channels all its contracting funds to a white-dominated community of established contractors whose racial homogeneity is the product of private discrimination, it does more than place its *imprimatur* on the practices which forged and which continue to define that community. It also provides a measurable boost to those economic entities that have thrived within it, while denying important economic benefits to those entities which, but for prior discrimination, might well be better qualified to receive valuable government contracts. In my view, the interest in ensuring that the government does not reflect and reinforce prior private discrimination in dispensing public contracts is every bit as strong as the interest in eliminating private discrimination—an interest which this Court has repeatedly deemed compelling. * * *

2

The remaining question with respect to the "governmental interest" prong of equal protection analysis is whether Richmond has proffered satisfactory proof of past racial discrimination to support its twin interests in remediation and in governmental nonperpetuation. Although the Members of this Court have differed on the appropriate standard of review for race-conscious remedial measures, * * * we have always regarded this factual inquiry as a practical one. Thus, the Court has eschewed rigid tests which require the provision of particular species of evidence, statistical or otherwise. At the same time we have required that government adduce evidence that, taken as a whole, is sufficient to support its claimed interest and to dispel the natural concern that it acted out of mere "paternalistic stereotyping, not on a careful consideration of modern social conditions." [*Fullilove* (MARSHALL, concurring in judgment).]

The varied body of evidence on which Richmond relied provides a "strong," "firm," and "unquestionably legitimate" basis upon which the city council could determine that the effects of past racial discrimination warranted a remedial and prophylactic governmental response. * * *

Richmond's reliance on localized, industry-specific findings is a far cry from the reliance on generalized "societal discrimination" which the majority decries as a basis for remedial action. * * * But characterizing the plight of Richmond's minority contractors as mere "societal discrimination" is not the only respect in which the majority's critique shows an unwillingness to come to grips with why construction-contracting in Richmond is essentially a whites-only enterprise. * * *

[M]ore fundamentally, where the issue is not present discrimination but rather whether *past* discrimination has resulted in the *continuing exclusion* of minorities from a historically tight-knit industry, a contrast between population and work force is entirely appropriate to help gauge the degree of the exclusion. * * * This contrast is especially illuminating in cases like this, where a main avenue of introduction into the work force—here, membership in the trade associations whose members presumably train apprentices and help them procure subcontracting assignments—is itself grossly dominated by nonminorities. * * *

When the legislatures and leaders of cities with histories of pervasive discrimination testify that past discrimination has infected one of their industries, armchair cynicism like that exercised by the majority has no place. * * * Disbelief is particularly inappropriate here in light of the fact that appellee Croson, which had the burden of proving unconstitutionality at trial, * * * has *at no point* come forward with *any* direct evidence that the city council's motives were anything other than sincere.

Finally, I vehemently disagree with the majority's dismissal of the congressional and Executive Branch findings noted in *Fullilove* as having "extremely limited" probative value in this case. * * * The majority concedes that Congress established nothing less than a "presumption" that minority contracting firms have been disadvantaged by prior discrimination. The majority, inexplicably, would forbid Richmond to "share" in this information, and permit only Congress to take note of these ample findings. * * * In thus requiring that Richmond's local evidence be severed from the context in which it was prepared, the majority would require cities seeking to eradicate the effects of past discrimination within their borders to reinvent the evidentiary wheel and engage in unnecessarily duplicative, costly, and time-consuming factfinding.

No principle of federalism or of federal power, however, forbids a state or local government to draw upon a nationally relevant historical record prepared by the Federal Government. * * * Of course, Richmond could have built an even more compendious record of past discrimination, one including additional stark statistics and additional individual accounts of past discrimination. But nothing in the Fourteenth Amendment imposes such onerous documentary obligations upon States and localities once the reality of past discrimination is apparent. * * *

B

In my judgment, Richmond's set-aside plan also comports with the second prong of the equal protection inquiry, for it is substantially related to the interests it seeks to serve in remedying past discrimination and in ensuring that municipal contract procurement does not perpetuate that discrimination. The most striking aspect of the city's ordinance is the similarity it bears to the "appropriately limited" federal set-aside provision upheld in *Fullilove*. * * *

The majority takes issue, however, with two aspects of Richmond's tailoring: the city's refusal to explore the use of race-neutral measures to increase minority business participation in contracting, and the selection of a 30% set-aside figure. The majority's first criticism is flawed in two respects. First, the majority overlooks the fact that since 1975, Richmond has barred both discrimination by the city in awarding public contracts and discrimination by public contractors. * * * The virtual absence of minority businesses from the city's contracting rolls, indicated by the fact that such businesses have received less than 1% of public contracting dollars, strongly suggests that this ban has not succeeded in redressing the impact of past discrimination or in preventing city contract procurement from reinforcing racial homogeneity. Second, the majority's suggestion that Richmond should have first undertaken such race-neutral measures as a program of city financing for small firms, * * * ignores the fact that such measures, while theoretically appealing, have been discredited by Congress as ineffectual in eradicating the effects of past discrimination in this very industry. * * *

As for Richmond's 30% target, the majority states that this figure "cannot be said to be narrowly tailored to any goal, except perhaps outright racial balancing." * * * The majority ignores two important facts. First, the set-aside measure affects only 3% of overall city contracting; thus, any imprecision in tailoring has far less impact than the majority suggests. But more important, the majority ignores the fact that Richmond's 30% figure was patterned directly on the *Fullilove* precedent. Congress' 10% figure fell "roughly halfway between the present percentage of minority contractors and the percentage of minority group members in the Nation." [*Fullilove* (Powell, concurring).] The Richmond City Council's 30% figure similarly falls roughly halfway between the present percentage of Richmond-based minority contractors (almost zero) and the percentage of minorities in Richmond (50%). In faulting Richmond for not presenting a different explanation for its choice of a set-aside figure, the majority honors *Fullilove* only in the breach.

III

* * *

Today, for the first time, a majority of this Court has adopted strict scrutiny as its standard of Equal Protection Clause review of race-conscious remedial measures. * * * This is an unwelcome development. A profound difference separates governmental actions that themselves are racist, and governmental actions that seek to remedy the effects of prior racism or to prevent neutral governmental activity from perpetuating the effects of such racism. * * *

Racial classifications "drawn on the presumption that one race is inferior to another or because they put the weight of government behind racial hatred and separatism" warrant the strictest judicial scrutiny because of the very irrelevance of these rationales. * * * By contrast, racial classifications drawn for the purpose of remedying the effects of discrimination that itself was race based have a highly pertinent basis: the tragic and indelible fact that discrimination against blacks and other racial minorities in this Nation has pervaded our Nation's history and continues to scar our society. * * *

In concluding that remedial classifications warrant no different standard of review under the Constitution than the most brutal and repugnant forms of state-sponsored racism, a majority of this Court signals that it regards racial discrimination as largely a phenomenon of the past, and that government bodies need no longer preoccupy themselves with rectifying racial injustice. I, however, do not believe this Nation is anywhere close to eradicating racial discrimination or its vestiges. In constitutionalizing its wishful thinking, the majority today does a grave disservice not only to those victims of past and present racial discrimination in this Nation whom government has sought to assist, but also to this Court's long tradition of approaching issues of race with the utmost sensitivity.

* * *

Today's decision, finally, is particularly noteworthy for the daunting standard it imposes upon States and localities contemplating the use of race-conscious measures to eradicate the present effects of prior discrimination and prevent its perpetuation. The majority restricts the use of such measures to situations in which a State or locality can put forth "a prima facie case of a constitutional or statutory violation." * * * In so doing, the majority calls into question the validity of the business set-asides which dozens of municipalities across this Nation have adopted on the authority of *Fullilove*.

* * *

To the degree that this parsimonious standard is grounded on a view that either § 1 or § 5 of the Fourteenth Amendment substantially disempowered States and localities from remedying past racial discrimination, * * * the majority is seriously mistaken. * * *

* * *

IV

The majority today sounds a full-scale retreat from the Court's long-standing solicitude to race-conscious remedial efforts "directed toward deliverance of the century-old promise of equality of economic opportunity." [*Fullilove*.] The new and restrictive tests it applies scuttle one city's effort to surmount its discriminatory past, and imperil those of dozens more localities. I, however, profoundly disagree with the cramped vision of the Equal Protection Clause which the majority offers today and with its application of that vision to Richmond, Virginia's, laudable set-aside plan. The battle against pernicious racial discrimination or its effects is nowhere near won. I must dissent.

■ JUSTICE BLACKMUN, with whom JUSTICE BRENNAN joins, dissenting.

* * *

Richmond, to its great credit, acted. Yet this Court, the supposed bastion of equality, strikes down Richmond's efforts as though discrimination had never existed or was not demonstrated in this particular litigation. * * *

So the Court today regresses. I am confident, however, that, given time, it one day again will do its best to fulfill the great promises of the Constitution's Preamble and of the guarantees embodied in the Bill of Rights—a fulfillment that would make this Nation very special.

Metro Broadcasting, Inc. v. F.C.C.

Supreme Court of the United States, 497 U.S. 547, 110 S.Ct. 2997 (1990).

■ JUSTICE BRENNAN delivered the opinion of the Court.

The issue in these cases, consolidated for decision today, is whether certain minority preference policies of the Federal Communications Commission violate the equal protection component of the Fifth Amendment. The policies in question are (1) a program awarding an enhancement for minority ownership in comparative proceedings for new licenses, and (2) the minority "distress sale" program, which permits a limited category of existing radio and television broadcast stations to be transferred only to minority-controlled firms. We hold that these policies do not violate equal protection principles.

I

A

The policies before us today can best be understood by reference to the history of federal efforts to promote minority participation in the broadcasting industry. * * *

Building on the results of the conference [on minority ownership policies], the recommendations of the task force [to encourage minority participation in broadcasting], the decision [in *TV 9, Inc. v. FCC*, 161 U.S. App. D.C. 349, 938 (1973) that a reasonable expectation of superior community service was sufficient to justify a preference for African American broadcasters], and a petition proposing several minority ownership policies, the FCC adopted in May 1978 its *Statement of Policy on Minority Ownership of Broadcasting Facilities*. After recounting its past efforts to expand broadcast diversity, the FCC concluded:

> [W]e are compelled to observe that the views of racial minorities continue to be inadequately represented in the broadcast media. This situation is detrimental not only to the minority audience but to all of the viewing and listening public. Adequate representation of minority viewpoints in programming serves not only the needs and interests of

the minority community but also enriches and educates the non-minority audience. It enhances the diversified programming which is a key objective not only of the Communications Act of 1934 but also of the First Amendment. * * *

Describing its actions as only "first steps," * * * the FCC outlined two elements of a minority ownership policy.

First, the Commission pledged to consider minority ownership as one factor in comparative proceedings for new licenses. * * *

Second, the FCC outlined a plan to increase minority opportunities to receive reassigned and transferred licenses through the so-called "distress sale" policy. * * * As a general rule, a licensee whose qualifications to hold a broadcast license come into question may not assign or transfer that license until the FCC has resolved its doubts in a noncomparative hearing. The distress sale policy is an exception to that practice, allowing a broadcaster whose license has been designated for a revocation hearing, or whose renewal application has been designated for hearing, to assign the license to an FCC-approved minority enterprise. * * *

II

It is of overriding significance in these cases that the FCC's minority ownership programs have been specifically approved—indeed, mandated—by Congress. In *Fullilove v. Klutznick*, 448 U.S. 448 (1980), Chief Justice Burger [gave deference to agency actions making racial preferences based on congressional instructions].

* * *

Our decision last Term in *Richmond v. J. A. Croson Co.*, 488 U.S. 469 (1989), concerning a minority set-aside program adopted by a municipality, does not prescribe the level of scrutiny to be applied to a benign racial classification employed by Congress. As JUSTICE KENNEDY noted, the question of congressional action was not before the Court, * * * and so *Croson* cannot be read to undermine our decision in *Fullilove*. In fact, much of the language and reasoning in *Croson* reaffirmed the lesson of *Fullilove* that race-conscious classifications adopted by Congress to address racial and ethnic discrimination are subject to a different standard than such classifications prescribed by state and local governments. * * *

We hold that the FCC minority ownership policies pass muster under the test we announce today. First, we find that they serve the important governmental objective of broadcast diversity. Second, we conclude that they are substantially related to the achievement of that objective.

A

Congress found that "the effects of past inequities stemming from racial and ethnic discrimination have resulted in a severe under-representation of minorities in the media of mass communications." [H. R. Conf. Rep. No. 97–765.] Congress and the Commission do not justify the minority ownership policies strictly as remedies for victims of this discrimination,

however. Rather, Congress and the FCC have selected the minority ownership policies primarily to promote programming diversity, and they urge
that such diversity is an important governmental objective that can serve
as a constitutional basis for the preference policies. We agree.

* * *

[T]he interest in enhancing broadcast diversity is, at the very least, an
important governmental objective and is therefore a sufficient basis for the
Commission's minority ownership policies. Just as a "diverse student
body" contributing to a "robust exchange of ideas" is a "constitutionally
permissible goal" on which a race-conscious university admissions program
may be predicated, [*Bakke* (opinion of Powell, J.),] the diversity of views
and information on the airwaves serves important First Amendment values. * * * The benefits of such diversity are not limited to the members of
minority groups who gain access to the broadcasting industry by virtue of
the ownership policies; rather, the benefits redound to all members of the
viewing and listening audience. As Congress found, "the American public
will benefit by having access to a wider diversity of information sources."
* * *

We also find that the minority ownership policies are substantially
related to the achievement of the Government's interest. One component of
this inquiry concerns the relationship between expanded minority ownership and greater broadcast diversity; both the FCC and Congress have
determined that such a relationship exists. Although we do not " 'defer' to
the judgment of the Congress and the Commission on a constitutional
question," and would not "hesitate to invoke the Constitution should we
determine that the Commission has not fulfilled its task with appropriate
sensitivity" to equal protection principles, *Columbia Broadcasting System,
Inc. v. Democratic National Committee*, [412 U.S. 94 (1973),] we must pay
close attention to the expertise of the Commission and the factfinding of
Congress when analyzing the nexus between minority ownership and
programming diversity. With respect to this "complex" empirical question,
we are required to give "great weight to the decisions of Congress and the
experience of the Commission." * * *

* * *

C

The judgment that there is a link between expanded minority ownership and broadcast diversity does not rest on impermissible stereotyping.
Congressional policy does not assume that in every case minority ownership and management will lead to more minority-oriented programming or
to the expression of a discrete "minority viewpoint" on the airwaves.
Neither does it pretend that all programming that appeals to minority
audiences can be labeled "minority programming" or that programming
that might be described as "minority" does not appeal to nonminorities.
Rather, both Congress and the FCC maintain simply that expanded minority ownership of broadcast outlets will, in the aggregate, result in greater
broadcast diversity. A broadcasting industry with representative minority

participation will produce more variation and diversity than will one whose ownership is drawn from a single racially and ethnically homogeneous group. The predictive judgment about the overall result of minority entry into broadcasting is not a rigid assumption about how minority owners will behave in every case but rather is akin to Justice Powell's conclusion in *Bakke* that greater admission of minorities would contribute, on average, "to the 'robust exchange of ideas.'"

* * *

D

We find that the minority ownership policies are in other relevant respects substantially related to the goal of promoting broadcast diversity. First, the Commission adopted and Congress endorsed minority ownership preferences only after long study and painstaking consideration of all available alternatives. * * * For many years, the FCC attempted to encourage diversity of programming content without consideration of the race of station owners.

* * *

Moreover, the considered nature of the Commission's judgment in selecting the particular minority ownership policies at issue today is illustrated by the fact that the Commission has rejected other types of minority preferences. For example, the Commission has studied but refused to implement the more expansive alternative of setting aside certain frequencies for minority broadcasters. * * * In addition, in a ruling released the day after it adopted the comparative hearing credit and the distress sale preference, the FCC declined to adopt a plan to require 45–day advance public notice before a station could be sold, which had been advocated on the ground that it would ensure minorities a chance to bid on stations that might otherwise be sold to industry insiders without ever coming on the market. * * * Soon afterward, the Commission rejected other minority ownership proposals advanced by the Office of Telecommunications Policy and the Department of Commerce that sought to revise the FCC's time brokerage, multiple ownership, and other policies.

* * *

The minority ownership policies are "appropriately limited in extent and duration, and subject to reassessment and reevaluation by the Congress prior to any extension or reenactment." [*Fullilove* (opinion of Burger, C. J.).] Although it has underscored emphatically its support for the minority ownership policies, Congress has manifested that support through a series of appropriations Acts of finite duration, thereby ensuring future reevaluations of the need for the minority ownership program as the number of minority broadcasters increases. In addition, Congress has continued to hold hearings on the subject of minority ownership. * * * Furthermore, there is provision for administrative and judicial review of all Commission decisions, which guarantees both that the minority ownership policies are applied correctly in individual cases, and that there will be frequent opportunities to revisit the merits of those policies. Congress and the Commission have adopted a policy of minority ownership not as an end in itself, but rather as a means of achieving greater programming diversity. Such a goal carries its own natural limit, for there will be no need for further minority preferences once sufficient diversity has been achieved. The FCC's plan, like the Harvard admissions program discussed in *Bakke*, contains the seed of its own termination. * * *

Finally, we do not believe that the minority ownership policies at issue impose impermissible burdens on nonminorities. * * *

In the context of broadcasting licenses, the burden on nonminorities is slight. The FCC's responsibility is to grant licenses in the "public interest, convenience, or necessity," * * * and the limited number of frequencies on the electromagnetic spectrum means that "[n]o one has a First Amendment right to a license." [*Red Lion*] Applicants have no settled expectation that their applications will be granted without consideration of public interest factors such as minority ownership. Award of a preference in a comparative hearing or transfer of a station in a distress sale thus contravenes "no legitimate firmly rooted expectation[s]" of competing applicants. [*Johnson.*]

Respondent Shurberg insists that because the minority distress sale policy operates to exclude nonminority firms completely from consideration in the transfer of certain stations, it is a greater burden than the comparative hearing preference for minorities, which is simply a "plus" factor considered together with other characteristics of the applicants. * * * The distress sale policy is not a quota or fixed quantity set-aside. Indeed, the nonminority firm exercises control over whether a distress sale will ever occur at all, because the policy operates only where the qualifications of an existing licensee to continue broadcasting have been designated for hearing and no other applications for the station in question have been filed with the Commission at the time of the designation. * * * Thus, a nonminority can prevent the distress sale procedures from ever being invoked by filing a competing application in a timely manner.

In practice, distress sales have represented a tiny fraction—less than 0.4 percent—of all broadcast sales since 1979. * * *

III

The Commission's minority ownership policies bear the *imprimatur* of longstanding congressional support and direction and are substantially related to the achievement of the important governmental objective of broadcast diversity. The judgment in No. 89–453 is affirmed, the judgment in No. 89–700 is reversed, and the cases are remanded for proceedings consistent with this opinion.

It is so ordered.

[Justice Stevens's concurring opinion has been omitted]

■ JUSTICE O'CONNOR, with whom the CHIEF JUSTICE, JUSTICE SCALIA, and JUSTICE KENNEDY join, dissenting.

At the heart of the Constitution's guarantee of equal protection lies the simple command that the Government must treat citizens "as *individuals*, not 'as simply components of a racial, religious, sexual or national class.' " *Arizona Governing Comm. for Tax Deferred Annuity and Deferred Compensation Plans v. Norris*, 463 U.S. 1073, 1083 (1983). Social scientists may debate how peoples' thoughts and behavior reflect their background, but the Constitution provides that the Government may not allocate benefits and burdens among individuals based on the assumption that race or ethnicity determines how they act or think. To uphold the challenged programs, the Court departs from these fundamental principles and from our traditional requirement that racial classifications are permissible only if necessary and narrowly tailored to achieve a compelling interest. This departure marks a renewed toleration of racial classifications and a repudiation of our recent affirmation that the Constitution's equal protection guarantees extend equally to all citizens. The Court's application of a lessened equal protection standard to congressional actions finds no support in our cases or in the Constitution. I respectfully dissent.

I

As we recognized [in *J. A. Croson*], the Constitution requires that the Court apply a strict standard of scrutiny to evaluate racial classifications such as those contained in the challenged FCC distress sale and comparative licensing policies. * * * The Court abandons this traditional safeguard against discrimination for a lower standard of review, and in practice applies a standard like that applicable to routine legislation. Yet the Government's different treatment of citizens according to race is no routine concern. This Court's precedents in no way justify the Court's marked departure from our traditional treatment of race classifications and its conclusion that different equal protection principles apply to these federal actions.

In both the challenged policies, the Federal Communications Commission (FCC) provides benefits to some members of our society and denies benefits to others based on race or ethnicity. Except in the narrowest of circumstances, the Constitution bars such racial classifications as a denial to particular individuals, of any race or ethnicity, of "the equal protection of the laws." U.S. Const., Amdt. 14, § 1. * * * The dangers of such classifications are clear. They endorse race-based reasoning and the conception of a Nation divided into racial blocs, thus contributing to an escalation of racial hostility and conflict. * * * Such policies may embody stereotypes that treat individuals as the product of their race, evaluating their thoughts and efforts—their very worth as citizens—according to a criterion barred to the Government by history and the Constitution. * * * Racial classifications, whether providing benefits to or burdening particular racial or ethnic groups, may stigmatize those groups singled out for different treatment and may create considerable tension with the Nation's widely shared commitment to evaluating individuals upon their individual merit. * * *

The Constitution's guarantee of equal protection binds the Federal Government as it does the States, and no lower level of scrutiny applies to the Federal Government's use of race classifications. * * * Consistent with this view, the Court has repeatedly indicated that "the reach of the equal protection guarantee of the Fifth Amendment is coextensive with that of the Fourteenth." [*United States v. Paradise*, 480 U.S. 149 (1987) (plurality opinion).]

Nor does the congressional role in prolonging the FCC's policies justify any lower level of scrutiny. As with all instances of judicial review of federal legislation, the Court does not lightly set aside the considered judgment of a coordinate branch. Nonetheless, the respect due a coordinate branch yields neither less vigilance in defense of equal protection principles nor any corresponding diminution of the standard of review.

* * *

The guarantee of equal protection extends to each citizen, regardless of race: The Federal Government, like the States, may not "deny to any person within its jurisdiction the equal protection of the laws." * * *

The Court's reliance on "benign racial classifications," * * * is particularly troubling. " 'Benign' racial classification" is a contradiction in terms. Governmental distinctions among citizens based on race or ethnicity, even in the rare circumstances permitted by our cases, exact costs and carry with them substantial dangers. To the person denied an opportunity or right based on race, the classification is hardly benign. * * * Untethered to narrowly confined remedial notions, "benign" carries with it no independent meaning, but reflects only acceptance of the current generation's conclusion that a politically acceptable burden, imposed on particular citizens on the basis of race, is reasonable. The Court provides no basis for determining when a racial classification fails to be "benevolent." By expressly distinguishing "benign" from remedial race-conscious measures, the Court leaves the distinct possibility that any racial measure found to be substantially related to an important governmental objective is also, by definition, "benign." * * *

This dispute regarding the appropriate standard of review may strike some as a lawyers' quibble over words, but it is not. The standard of review establishes whether and when the Court and Constitution allow the Government to employ racial classifications. A lower standard signals that the Government may resort to racial distinctions more readily. The Court's departure from our cases is disturbing enough, but more disturbing still is the renewed toleration of racial classifications that its new standard of review embodies.

II

Our history reveals that the most blatant forms of discrimination have been visited upon some members of the racial and ethnic groups identified in the challenged programs. Many have lacked the opportunity to share in the Nation's wealth and to participate in its commercial enterprises. It is undisputed that minority participation in the broadcasting industry falls markedly below the demographic representation of those groups, * * * and this shortfall may be traced in part to the discrimination and the patterns of exclusion that have widely affected our society. As a nation we aspire to create a society untouched by that history of exclusion, and to ensure that equality defines all citizens' daily experience and opportunities as well as the protection afforded to them under law.

   * * *

III

Under the appropriate standard, strict scrutiny, only a compelling interest may support the Government's use of racial classifications. Modern equal protection doctrine has recognized only one such interest: remedying the effects of racial discrimination. The interest in increasing the diversity of broadcast viewpoints is clearly not a compelling interest. It is simply too amorphous, too insubstantial, and too unrelated to any legitimate basis for employing racial classifications. The Court does not claim otherwise. Rather, it employs its novel standard and claims that this asserted interest need only be, and is, "important." This conclusion twice compounds the Court's initial error of reducing its level of scrutiny of a racial classification. First, it too casually extends the justifications that might support racial classifications, beyond that of remedying past discrimination. * * * Second, it has initiated this departure by endorsing an insubstantial interest, one that is certainly insufficiently weighty to justify tolerance of the Government's distinctions among citizens based on race and ethnicity. This endorsement trivializes the constitutional command to guard against such discrimination and has loosed a potentially far-reaching principle disturbingly at odds with our traditional equal protection doctrine.

An interest capable of justifying race-conscious measures must be sufficiently specific and verifiable, such that it supports only limited and carefully defined uses of racial classifications. In *Croson*, we held that an interest in remedying societal discrimination cannot be considered compelling. * * * We determined that a "generalized assertion" of past discrimination "has no logical stopping point" and would support unconstrained uses of race classifications. * * *

The asserted interest in these cases suffers from the same defects. * * * Like the vague assertion of societal discrimination, a claim of insufficiently diverse broadcasting viewpoints might be used to justify equally unconstrained racial preferences, linked to nothing other than proportional representation of various races. And the interest would support indefinite use of racial classifications, employed first to obtain the appropriate mixture of racial views and then to ensure that the broadcasting spectrum continues to reflect that mixture. We cannot deem to be constitutionally adequate an interest that would support measures that amount to the core constitutional violation of "outright racial balancing." [*Croson*.]

   * * *

IV

Our traditional equal protection doctrine requires, in addition to a compelling state interest, that the Government's chosen means be necessary to accomplish, and narrowly tailored to further, the asserted interest. * * * This element of strict scrutiny is designed to "ensur[e] that the means chosen 'fit' [the] compelling goal so closely that there is little or no possibility that the motive for the classification was illegitimate racial prejudice or stereotype." [*Croson* (opinion of O'CONNOR, J.).] The chosen means, resting as they do on stereotyping and so indirectly furthering the asserted end, could not plausibly be deemed narrowly tailored. The Court instead finds the racial classifications to be "substantially related" to achieving the Government's interest, * * * a far less rigorous fit requirement. The FCC's policies fail even this requirement.

A

The FCC claims to advance its asserted interest in diverse viewpoints by singling out race and ethnicity as peculiarly linked to distinct views that require enhancement. The FCC's choice to employ a racial criterion embodies the related notions that a particular and distinct viewpoint inheres in certain racial groups, and that a particular applicant, by virtue of race or ethnicity alone, is more valued than other applicants because he/she is "likely to provide [that] distinct perspective." [Brief for FCC.] The policies directly equate race with belief and behavior, for they establish race as a necessary and sufficient condition of securing the preference. The FCC's chosen means rest on the "premise that differences in race, or in the color of a person's skin, reflect real differences that are relevant to a person's right to share in the blessings of a free society. [T]hat premise is utterly irrational and repugnant to the principles of a free and democratic society." [*Wygant* (STEVENS, J., dissenting).] The policies impermissibly value individuals because they presume that persons think in a manner associated with their race. * * *

The majority addresses this point by arguing that the equation of race with distinct views and behavior is not "impermissible" in these particular cases. * * * Apart from placing undue faith in the Government and courts' ability to distinguish "good" from "bad" stereotypes, this reasoning repudiates essential equal protection principles that prohibit racial generalizations. * * *

B

Moreover, the FCC's selective focus on viewpoints associated with race illustrates a particular tailoring difficulty. * * *

Our equal protection doctrine governing intermediate review indicates that the Government may not use race and ethnicity as "a 'proxy for other, more germane bases of classification.'" [*Mississippi Univ. for Women v. Hogan*, 458 U.S. 718 (1982).] The FCC has used race as a proxy for whatever views it believes to be underrepresented in the broadcasting spectrum. This reflexive or unthinking use of a suspect classification is the hallmark of an unconstitutional policy. * * * The ill fit of means to ends is manifest. The policy is overinclusive: Many members of a particular racial or ethnic group will have no interest in advancing the views the FCC believes to be underrepresented, or will find them utterly foreign. The policy is underinclusive: It awards no preference to disfavored individuals who may be particularly well versed in and committed to presenting those views. The FCC has failed to implement a case-by-case determination, and that failure is particularly unjustified when individualized hearings already occur, as in the comparative licensing process. * * * Even in the remedial context, we have required that the Government adopt means to ensure that the award of a particular preference advances the asserted interest. * * *

　　* * *

The FCC seeks to avoid the tailoring difficulties by focusing on minority ownership rather than the asserted interest in diversity of broadcast viewpoints. The Constitution clearly prohibits allocating valuable goods such as broadcast licenses simply on the basis of race. * * * Yet the FCC refers to the lack of minority ownership of stations to support the existence of a lack of diversity of viewpoints, and has fitted its programs to increase ownership. * * * This repeated focus on ownership supports the inference that the FCC seeks to allocate licenses based on race, an impermissible end, rather than to increase diversity of viewpoints, the asserted interest. And this justification that links the use of race preferences to minority ownership rather than to diversity of viewpoints ensures that the FCC's programs, like that at issue in *Croson*, "cannot be said to be narrowly tailored to any goal, except perhaps outright racial balancing."
* * *

C

Even apart from these tailoring defects in the FCC's policies, one particular flaw underscores the Government's ill fit of means to ends. The FCC's policies assume, and rely upon, the existence of a tightly bound "nexus" between the owners' race and the resulting programming. * * *

Three difficulties suggest that the nexus between owners' race and programming is considerably less than substantial. First, the market shapes programming to a tremendous extent. Members of minority groups who own licenses might be thought, like other owners, to seek to broadcast programs that will attract and retain audiences, rather than programs that reflect the owner's tastes and preferences. * * * Second, station owners have only limited control over the content of programming. The distress sale presents a particularly acute difficulty of this sort. Unlike the comparative licensing program, the distress sale policy provides preferences to minority owners who neither intend nor desire to manage the station in any respect. * * * Whatever distinct programming may attend the race of an owner actively involved in managing the station, an absentee owner would have far less effect on programming.

Third, the FCC had absolutely no factual basis for the nexus when it adopted the policies and has since established none to support its existence. * * *

Even apart from the limited nature of the Court's claims, little can be discerned from the congressional action. First, the Court's survey does not purport to establish that the FCC or Congress has identified any particular deficiency in the viewpoints contained in the broadcast spectrum. Second, no degree of congressional endorsement may transform the equation of race with behavior and thoughts into a permissible basis of governmental action. Even the most express and lavishly documented congressional declaration that members of certain races will as owners produce distinct and superior programming would not allow the Government to employ such reasoning to allocate benefits and burdens among citizens on that basis. Third, we should hesitate before accepting as definitive any declaration regarding even the existence of a nexus. * * *

D

Finally, the Government cannot employ race classifications that unduly burden individuals who are not members of the favored racial and ethnic groups. * * * The challenged policies fail this independent requirement, as well as the other constitutional requirements. The comparative licensing and distress sale programs provide the eventual licensee with an exceptionally valuable property and with a rare and unique opportunity to serve the local community. The distress sale imposes a particularly significant burden. The FCC has at base created a specialized market reserved exclusively for minority controlled applicants. There is no more rigid quota than a 100% set-aside. * * * The Court's argument that the distress sale allocates only a small percentage of all license sales, * * * also misses the mark. This argument readily supports complete preferences and avoids scrutiny of particular programs: It is no response to a person denied admission at one school, or discharged from one job, solely on the basis of race, that other schools or employers do not discriminate.

* * *

■ JUSTICE KENNEDY, with whom JUSTICE SCALIA joins, dissenting.

Almost 100 years ago in *Plessy v. Ferguson, 163 U.S. 537 (1896),* this Court upheld a government-sponsored race-conscious measure, a Louisiana law that required "equal but separate accommodations" for "white" and "colored" railroad passengers. The Court asked whether the measures were "reasonable," and it stated that "[i]n determining the question of reasonableness, [the legislature] is at liberty to act with reference to the established usages, customs and traditions of the people, and with a view to the promotion of their comfort." * * * The *Plessy* Court concluded that the "race-conscious measures" it reviewed were reasonable because they served the governmental interest of increasing the riding pleasure of railroad passengers. The fundamental errors in *Plessy*, its standard of review and its validation of rank racial insult by the State, distorted the law for six decades before the Court announced its apparent demise in *Brown v. Board* *of Education.* * * * *Plessy*'s standard of review and its explication have disturbing parallels to today's majority opinion that should warn us something is amiss here.

* * * The interest the Court accepts to uphold the race-conscious measures of the Federal Communications Commission (Commission or FCC) is "broadcast diversity." Furthering that interest, we are told, is worth the cost of discriminating among citizens on the basis of race because it will increase the listening pleasure of media audiences. In upholding this preference, the majority exhumes *Plessy*'s deferential approach to racial classifications. The Court abandons even the broad societal remedial justification for racial preferences once advocated by JUSTICE MARSHALL, *e.g.,* [*Bakke* (separate opinion)] and now will allow the use of racial classifications by Congress untied to any goal of addressing the effects of past race discrimination. All that need be shown under the new approach, * * * is that the future effect of discriminating among citizens on the basis of race will advance some "important" governmental interest.

Once the Government takes the step, which itself should be forbidden, of enacting into law the stereotypical assumption that the race of owners is linked to broadcast content, it follows a path that becomes ever more tortuous. It must decide which races to favor. * * * The Court's reasoning provides little justification for welcoming the return of racial classifications to our Nation's laws.

I cannot agree with the Court that the Constitution permits the Government to discriminate among its citizens on the basis of race in order to serve interests so trivial as "broadcast diversity." In abandoning strict scrutiny to endorse this interest the Court turns back the clock on the level of scrutiny applicable to federal race-conscious measures. * * * Strict scrutiny is the surest test the Court has yet devised for holding true to the constitutional command of racial equality. * * *

The Court insists that the programs under review are "benign." JUSTICE STEVENS agrees. * * * A fundamental error of the *Plessy* Court was its similar confidence in its ability to identify "benign" discrimination: "We consider the underlying fallacy of the plaintiff's argument to consist in the assumption that the enforced separation of the two races stamps the colored race with a badge of inferiority. If this be so, it is not by reason of anything found in the act, but solely because the colored race chooses to put that construction upon it." * * * Although the majority is "confident" that it can determine when racial discrimination is benign, * * * it offers no explanation as to how it will do so.

    * * *

The history of governmental reliance on race demonstrates that racial policies defended as benign often are not seen that way by the individuals affected by them. * * * Although the majority disclaims it, the FCC policy seems based on the demeaning notion that members of the defined racial groups ascribe to certain "minority views" that must be different from those of other citizens. Special preferences also can foster the view that members of the favored groups are inherently less able to compete on their own. And, rightly or wrongly, special preference programs often are perceived as targets for exploitation by opportunists who seek to take advantage of monetary rewards without advancing the stated policy of minority inclusion.

* * *

Though the racial composition of this Nation is far more diverse than the first Justice Harlan foresaw, his warning in dissent is now all the more apposite: "The destinies of the two races, in this country, are indissolubly linked together, and the interests of both require that the common government of all shall not permit the seeds of race hate to be planted under the sanction of law." [*Plessy* (dissenting opinion).] Perhaps the Court can succeed in its assumed role of case-by-case arbiter of when it is desirable and benign for the Government to disfavor some citizens and favor others based on the color of their skin. Perhaps the tolerance and decency to which our people aspire will let the disfavored rise above hostility and the favored escape condescension. But history suggests much peril in this enterprise, and so the Constitution forbids us to undertake it. I regret that after a century of judicial opinions we interpret the Constitution to do no more than move us from "separate but equal" to "unequal but benign."

Note: The FCC affirmative action distress sale policy reviewed in *Metro Broadcasting* was justified, in part, based upon the agency's concern for increasing the public good of diverse viewpoints and images in the broadcast industry. In the article that follows, legal scholar Jerry Kang takes up directly the relationship of broadcast images to the reinforcement of racial bias. Kang, relying on the cognitive bias research that we considered in Chapter 1 at p. 54 above, offers a provocative "thought experiment" to redirect the broadcast media to the task of "disinfecting" racial bias from the national consciousness.

Trojan Horses of Race

118 HARV. L. REV. 1489 (2005).

■ JERRY KANG

* * *

Mugshot. Political scientists Frank Gilliam and Shanto Iyengar created variations of a local newscast: a control version with no crime story, a crime story with no mugshot, a crime story with a Black-suspect mugshot, and a crime story with a White-suspect mugshot. The Black and White suspects were represented by the same morphed photograph, with the only difference being skin hue—thus controlling for facial expression and features. The suspect appeared for only five seconds in a ten-minute newscast; nonetheless, the suspect's race produced statistically significant differences in a criminal law survey completed after the viewing. Having seen the Black suspect, White participants showed 6% more support for punitive remedies than did the control group, which saw no crime story. When participants were instead exposed to the White suspect, their support for punitive remedies increased by only 1%, which was not statistically significant.

* * *

Shooter Bias. Social cognitionist Joshua Correll created a video game that placed photographs of a White or Black individual holding either a gun or other object (wallet, soda can, or cell phone) into diverse photographic backgrounds. Participants were instructed to decide as quickly as possible whether to shoot the target. Severe time pressure designed into the game forced errors. Consistent with earlier findings, participants were more likely to mistake a Black target as armed when he in fact was unarmed (false alarms); conversely, they were more likely to mistake a White target as unarmed when he in fact was armed (misses). Even more striking is that Black participants showed similar amounts of "shooter bias" as Whites.

What is going on here? Quite simply, a revolution. These studies are the tip of the iceberg of recent social cognition research elaborating what I call "racial mechanics"—the ways in which race alters intrapersonal, interpersonal, and intergroup interactions. The results are stunning, reproducible, and valid by traditional scientific metrics. They seriously challenge current understandings of our "rational" selves and our interrelations.

* * *

I start by asking a fundamental question: "Where does bias come from?" One important source is vicarious experience with the racial other, transmitted through the media. If these experiences are somehow skewed, we should not be surprised by the presence of pervasive implicit bias. What, then, might we do about such media programming given the rigid constraints of the First Amendment? To be sure, private actors of good faith can voluntarily adopt best practices that decrease implicit bias and its manifestations. But can the state, through law, do anything?

If there is any room for intervention, it would be in the communications realm of broadcast, which enjoys doctrinal exceptionalism. In broadcast, notwithstanding the First Amendment, we tolerate the licensing of speakers. In broadcast, we tolerate suppression of speech we dislike, such as indecency and violence. In broadcast, we tolerate encouragement of speech we like, such as educational television and local-oriented programming. All this is in the name of the "public interest," the vague standard that Congress has charged the Federal Communications Commission with pursuing.

That "public interest" standard was recently reshaped in the controversial June 2003 Media Ownership Order. There, the FCC repeatedly justified relaxing ownership rules by explaining how such changes would increase, of all things, local news. Since local news was viewed as advancing "diversity" and "localism," two of the three core elements of the "public interest," any structural deregulation that would increase local news was lauded.

* * *

For a race paper, my using social cognition and applying it to communications law are unorthodox, but purposefully so. * * * One way to break current deadlocks is to turn to new bodies of knowledge uncovered by social science, specifically the remarkable findings of social cognition. Not only do they provide a more precise, particularized, and empirically grounded picture of how race functions in our minds, and thus in our societies, they also rattle us out of a complacency enjoyed after the demise of de jure discrimination. Further calls for equality are often derogated as whining by those who cannot compete in a modern meritocracy. Social cognition discoveries dispute that resentful characterization and make us reexamine our individual and collective responsibilities for persistent racial inequality. * * *

[I] am confident that the language, methodologies, and findings of social cognition provide trenchant additions to the philosophical, anthropological, sociological, literary, and political science modes of argument that have so far dominated critical race studies. For better and worse, law has turned sharply in favor of quantified and empirical analyses. Social cognition allows a phalanx of those who study race to take that same turn, instrumentally to fight fire with fire, and substantively to profit from a body of science that supports, particularizes, and checks what we intuit as the truth of our lived experiences. * * *

Another way to generate new insights is to view old topics through new lenses. That explains my invocation of the metaphor of "Trojan Horses," which is more familiar to cyberlaw than to critical race studies. This strategy further explains why I apply my social cognitive model of racial mechanics to FCC regulations. I start with the theory and evidence of racial mechanics.

* * *

II.   TROJAN HORSES

A.   *Tuning In to Broadcast*

* * *

To understand my choice of topic, we must start with a fundamental question: "Where do racial meanings come from?" Racial meanings that accrete in our schemas can, on the one hand, come from "direct experiences" with individuals mapped into those categories. On the other hand, the racial meanings can arise from what I call "vicarious experiences," which are stories of or simulated engagements with racial others provided through various forms of the media or narrated by parents and our peers. Given persistent racial segregation, we should not underestimate the significance of vicarious experiences. Even if direct experience with racial minorities more powerfully shapes our schemas, vicarious experiences may well dominate in terms of sheer quantity and frequency.

The next question becomes, "Why are racial meanings biased against racial minorities?" One hypothesis is that people encounter skewed data sets—or as the computer scientists say, "garbage in, garbage out." If these principally vicarious experiences, transmitted through electronic media, are somehow "skewed," then the racial meanings associated with certain racial categories should also be skewed. This analysis invites further study of culture and mass media policy, topics that social cognitionists have largely avoided.

Suppose that social cognitionists identify which types of vicarious experiences trigger and exacerbate bias and which ameliorate it. Private parties will obviously be free to act on the basis of such discoveries. Voluntary attempts to create a "diversity" of role models on television reflect some such impulse, in addition to financial self-interest since "diversity" is sometimes good for business. But what about collective action, mediated through the state and implemented through law?

* * *

In the 1934 Act, Congress created the FCC and charged it with managing the spectrum to further the "public convenience, interest, or necessity"—the public interest standard. In addition to regulating entry by assigning frequencies, the FCC has power to mold, at least softly, the content of broadcast. * * *

In its history, the FCC has promulgated (and the courts have enforced) regulations that restrict the broadcast of content deemed "bad," such as obscenity, indecency, and excessive commercialization. Specific to antiracism, the FCC, at the instruction of the courts, has revoked the broadcast licenses of stations that favored segregation and aired anti-Black racial epithets. Conversely, the FCC has also promulgated regulations that promote content deemed "good" through informational programming guidelines, community needs and interests ascertainment requirements, the fairness doctrine, and children's educational television guidelines. Specific to questions of race, the FCC has also tried to promote "good" and diverse content by increasing minority ownership of stations through affirmative action. Finally, the FCC has regulated market structure at each stage of production, distribution, and consumption. * * *

[G]iven constitutional law as we know it, if we are curious about what the state can do to combat implicit bias transmitted through vicarious experiences, broadcast is the prime site of inquiry.

B. *Redefining the Public Interest*

The touchstone for governmental management of broadcast is the "public interest" standard. That standard has recently been explicated in an unusual way. At least in the context of ownership policy, the public interest has been functionally equated with the local news.

In June 2003, a divided FCC lifted numerous media ownership restrictions in the name of the "public interest." Some of the changes permitted greater horizontal consolidation in local markets. Specifically, the FCC liberalized the local television multiple ownership rule and the local radio ownership rule. * * * I focus on how the FCC operationalized, and thus arguably redefined, the idea of the "public interest" by equating it with the production of local news.

* * *

Local news * * * played a starring role in one other component of the public interest: "localism." Localism has never been consistently defined in the Commission's analysis. * * * In its order, the FCC did not clarify the term, but it did establish a methodology for measuring localism. It focused again on "programming responsive to local needs and interests, and local news quantity and quality." For two out of the three fundamental components of the "public interest"—diversity and localism—the FCC highlighted the significance of local news production.

* * *

In sum, "local news" has become *the* critical component of the FCC's "public interest" analysis, at least in the media ownership context. Although local news has long played an important role in the idea of "public service," its predominance in the deregulation order is striking. The supervening norm that the FCC must pursue, the "public interest," has now become practically identical to the number of hours of local news a station broadcasts. But what in fact is on the local news?

C.   Local News

1.   Crime and Punishment.—Violent crime. Crime occupies a heavy share of broadcast news programming. This is true for national news. It is also true for local news, which is "the most widely used source of information about crime." The PEJ's annual study of local news programming consistently finds that local newscasts spend about a quarter of their time on crime stories.

* * *

Violent crime news stories frequently involve racial minorities, especially African Americans. One reason is that racial minorities are arrested for violent crimes more frequently on a per capita basis than Whites. Given our social cognition review, we can predict what watching local news might do to us. If subliminal flashes of Black male faces can raise our frustration, as shown by the Computer Crash study, would it be surprising that consciously received messages couched in violent visual context have impact, too? In fact, we have already seen in the Mugshot study, described in the Introduction, that even ephemeral exposure to race can alter our opinions about crime and punishment. That study, also conducted by Gilliam and Iyengar, is one of the more sophisticated studies in a line of newscast experiments finding similar results.

* * *

2.   Trojan Horse Viruses.—I now make explicit what I have so far left implicit: local news programs, dense with images of racial minorities committing violent crimes in one's own community, can be analogized to Trojan Horse viruses. A type of computer virus, a Trojan Horse installs itself on a user's computer without her awareness. That small program then runs in the background, without the user's knowledge, and silently waits to take action—whether by corrupting files, e-mailing pornographic spam, or launching a "denial of service" attack—which the user, if conscious of it, would disavow.

Typically, a Trojan Horse comes attached secretly to a program or information we actively seek. For instance, we might download a new program for a trial run, and embedded inside may be a Trojan Horse that installs itself without our knowledge. Or, we might browse some website in search of information, and a small javascript bug may be embedded in the page we view. Here is the translation to the news context: we turn on the television in search of local news, and with that information comes a Trojan Horse that alters our racial schemas. The images we see are more powerful than mere words. As local news, they speak of threats nearby, not in some abstract, distant land. The stories are not fiction but a brutal reality. They come from the most popular and trusted source.

* * *

How do we know violent crime stories can, like Trojan Horses, exacerbate implicit bias? The Mugshot study and other work by political scientists using the newscast paradigm are suggestive. Further evidence comes from studies that demonstrate media primings of racial schemas. For example, we now know that exposure to violent rap music can increase implicit bias against African Americans and that playing the video game Doom can increase one's implicit self-concept of aggressiveness—all the while having no statistically significant impact on one's explicit, self-reported views. Still further evidence comes indirectly from research Nilanjana Dasgupta calls the "third wave" of implicit bias research, which examines the malleability of implicit bias. This research demonstrates that implicit bias can be exacerbated or mitigated by the information environments we inhabit.

* * *

[C]onsuming positive images can decrease individuals' implicit bias, although they may register no difference on measures of explicit bias. Conversely, it seems reasonable to suppose that consuming negative images can exacerbate implicit bias. Recall the group in the Blair study instructed to imagine stereotypic women. And if mental imagery can produce such effects, watching direct portrayals in electronic media may well have an even stronger impact.

* * *

To summarize: Local news provides data that we use consciously in a rational analysis to produce informed opinions on, say, criminal punishment. But these newscasts also activate and strengthen linkages among certain racial categories, violent crime, and the fear and loathing such crime invokes. In this sense, the local news functions precisely like a Trojan Horse virus. We invite it into our homes, our dens, in through the gates of our minds, and accept it at face value, as an accurate representation of newsworthy events. But something lurks within those newscasts that programs our racial schemas in ways we cannot notice but can, through scientific measurements, detect. And the viruses they harbor deliver a payload with consequences, affecting how we vote for "three strikes and you're out" laws, how awkwardly we interact with folks, and even how quickly we pull the trigger.

3.   *The Accuracy Objection.*—A predictable objection is that the violent content, including crime committed by racial minorities, is a feature, not a bug. In other words, the data presented are not skewed and instead faithfully reflect a reality that the local news did not create. I have three responses to this "accuracy objection": the data are likely not fairly presented; our memories and abilities to see patterns are selective; and we interpret the data in self-serving ways.

First, the information broadcast is probably not fair and balanced. There is a prima facie case that the local media give disproportionate attention to violent crime, in which Black suspects feature prominently. Furthermore, ample evidence shows that the media treats Black-perpetrator stories differently, representing and portraying suspects in a more threatening manner than comparable White perpetrators. Specifically, Robert Entman explains that because of production biases in local newscasts, Black suspects are more likely to remain unnamed and in physical custody, and less likely to speak for themselves. As a result, while there is evidence that the statistical prominence of Blacks portrayed in crime news is "not that much out of line with the actual Black arrest rate," the emphasis on violent crime appears to skew public perceptions.

Second, even if local news accurately reflected reality, we see "illusory correlations." Whenever two salient events are noticed together, that combination leaves a deep impression in our memories and leads us to overestimate its frequency. Because racial minorities are numerical minorities (and therefore often salient) and because bad acts (for example, crimes) are also unusual and salient, when racial minorities commit bad acts, the information gets more deeply imprinted and weighted than is statistically warranted. * * *

Third, even if our recollections are accurate, our interpretations may be biased * * * even if the news conveys descriptively accurate information about the *mean* criminality of racial minority groups, the public still may seriously underestimate the *variance*. This would contribute to the fallacy of thinking that simply because 50% of crimes are committed by a group X, 50% of group X commit crimes. Consider how this tendency to view members of outgroups as monolithic could affect Arab Americans during our indefinite war on terror.

Another concern is the "fundamental attribution error" (FAE). The FAE is a general tendency to attribute the causes of behavior to dispositional, instead of situational, factors. In other words, we tend to underweight contingent, environmental factors that cause a particular action and

to highlight putatively stable factors such as personality traits instead.
* * *

* * *

[Kang considers the possibility of placing "caps" on local news stories concerning violent crimes.] After answering the empirical question, we must also make a final normative judgment. In other words, even if implicit bias does what I claim it does, is that important enough to count as "compelling"? First Amendment doctrine does not provide a clear test to answer such a question. So we reason through close analogy to other government interests that have been deemed "compelling." We know, for example, that "safeguarding the physical and psychological well-being" of children is a compelling interest. Drawing on equal protection case law, we know that remedying racial discrimination as well as pursuing educational diversity count as compelling interests. In the end, the government interest in decreasing implicit bias should be deemed "compelling" as well.

* * *

———

Grutter v. Bollinger

Supreme Court of the United States, 539 U.S. 306 (2003).

■ O'CONNOR, J., delivered the opinion of the Court, in which STEVENS, SOUTER, GINSBURG, and BREYER, JJ., joined, and in which SCALIA and THOMAS, JJ., joined in part insofar as it is consistent with the views expressed in Part VII of the opinion of THOMAS, J. GINSBURG, J., filed a concurring opinion, in which BREYER, J., joined. SCALIA, J., filed an opinion concurring in part and dissenting in part, in which THOMAS, J., joined. THOMAS, J., filed an opinion concurring in part and dissenting in part, in which SCALIA, J., joined as to Parts I–VII. REHNQUIST, C. J., filed a dissenting opinion, in which SCALIA, KENNEDY, and THOMAS, JJ., joined. KENNEDY, J., filed a dissenting opinion.

■ JUSTICE O'CONNOR delivered the opinion of the Court.

This case requires us to decide whether the use of race as a factor in student admissions by the University of Michigan Law School (Law School) is unlawful.

I

A

The Law School ranks among the Nation's top law schools. It receives more than 3,500 applications each year for a class of around 350 students. Seeking to "admit a group of students who individually and collectively are among the most capable," the Law School looks for individuals with "substantial promise for success in law school" and "a strong likelihood of succeeding in the practice of law and contributing in diverse ways to the well-being of others." * * * More broadly, the Law School seeks "a mix of students with varying backgrounds and experiences who will respect and learn from each other." * * *

The hallmark of [the law school's affirmative action] policy is its focus on academic ability coupled with a flexible assessment of applicants' talents, experiences, and potential "to contribute to the learning of those around them." * * * The policy requires admissions officials to evaluate each applicant based on all the information available in the file, including a personal statement, letters of recommendation, and an essay describing the ways in which the applicant will contribute to the life and diversity of the Law School. * * * In reviewing an applicant's file, admissions officials must consider the applicant's undergraduate grade point average (GPA) and Law School Admissions Test (LSAT) score because they are important (if imperfect) predictors of academic success in law school. * * * The policy stresses that "no applicant should be admitted unless we expect that applicant to do well enough to graduate with no serious academic problems."

      * * *

The policy aspires to "achieve that diversity which has the potential to enrich everyone's education and thus make a law school class stronger than the sum of its parts." * * * The policy does not restrict the types of diversity contributions eligible for "substantial weight" in the admissions process, but instead recognizes "many possible bases for diversity admissions." * * * The policy does, however, reaffirm the Law School's long-standing commitment to "one particular type of diversity," that is, "racial and ethnic diversity with special reference to the inclusion of students from groups which have been historically discriminated against, like African-Americans, Hispanics and Native Americans, who without this commitment might not be represented in our student body in meaningful numbers." * * * By enrolling a " 'critical mass' of [underrepresented] minority students," the Law School seeks to "ensure their ability to make unique contributions to the character of the Law School." * * *

The policy does not define diversity "solely in terms of racial and ethnic status." * * * Nor is the policy "insensitive to the competition among all students for admission to the Law School." * * * Rather, the policy seeks to guide admissions officers in "producing classes both diverse and academically outstanding, classes made up of students who promise to continue the tradition of outstanding contribution by Michigan Graduates to the legal profession." * * *

B

Petitioner Barbara Grutter is a white Michigan resident who applied to the Law School in 1996 with a 3.8 grade point average and 161 LSAT score. The Law School initially placed petitioner on a waiting list, but subsequently rejected her application. In December 1997, petitioner filed suit in the United States District Court for the Eastern District of Michigan against the Law School, the Regents of the University of Michigan, Lee Bollinger (Dean of the Law School from 1987 to 1994, and President of the University of Michigan from 1996 to 2002), Jeffrey Lehman (Dean of the Law School), and Dennis Shields (Director of Admissions at the Law School from 1991 until 1998). Petitioner alleged that respondents discriminated against her on the basis of race in violation of the Fourteenth Amendment, Title VI of the Civil Rights Act of 1964, and Rev Stat § 1977.

Petitioner further alleged that her application was rejected because the Law School uses race as a "predominant" factor, giving applicants who belong to certain minority groups "a significantly greater chance of admission than students with similar credentials from disfavored racial groups." Petitioner also alleged that respondents "had no compelling interest to justify their use of race in the admissions process." * * * Petitioner requested compensatory and punitive damages, an order requiring the Law School to offer her admission, and an injunction prohibiting the Law School from continuing to discriminate on the basis of race. * * * Petitioner clearly has standing to bring this lawsuit.

* * *

We granted certiorari * * * to resolve the disagreement among the Courts of Appeals on a question of national importance: Whether diversity is a compelling interest that can justify the narrowly tailored use of race in selecting applicants for admission to public universities. Compare *Hopwood v. Texas*, 78 F.3d 932 (5th Cir. 1996) (Hopwood I) (holding that diversity is not a compelling state interest), with *Smith v. University of Washington Law School*, 233 F.3d 1188 (9th Cir. 2000) (holding that it is).

II

A

We last addressed the use of race in public higher education over 25 years ago. In the landmark *Bakke* case, we reviewed a racial set-aside program that reserved 16 out of 100 seats in a medical school class for members of certain minority groups. * * * The decision produced six separate opinions, none of which commanded a majority of the Court. Four Justices would have upheld the program against all attack on the ground that the government can use race to "remedy disadvantages cast on minorities by past racial prejudice." [*Bakke*] (joint opinion of Brennan, White, Marshall, and Blackmun, JJ., concurring in judgment in part and dissenting in part). Four other Justices avoided the constitutional question altogether and struck down the program on statutory grounds. [*Id.*] (opinion of Stevens, J., joined by Burger, C. J., and Stewart and Rehnquist, JJ., concurring in judgment in part and dissenting in part). Justice Powell provided a fifth vote not only for invalidating the set-aside program, but also for reversing the state court's injunction against any use of race whatsoever. The only holding for the Court in *Bakke* was that a "State has a substantial interest that legitimately may be served by a properly devised admissions program involving the competitive consideration of race and ethnic origin." * * * Thus, we reversed that part of the lower court's judgment that enjoined the university "from any consideration of the race of any applicant." * * *

Since this Court's splintered decision in *Bakke*, Justice Powell's opinion announcing the judgment of the Court has served as the touchstone for constitutional analysis of race-conscious admissions policies. Public and private universities across the Nation have modeled their own admissions programs on Justice Powell's views on permissible race-conscious policies. * * * We therefore discuss Justice Powell's opinion in some detail.

Justice Powell began by stating that "the guarantee of equal protection cannot mean one thing when applied to one individual and something else when applied to a person of another color. If both are not accorded the same protection, then it is not equal." * * *

First, Justice Powell rejected an interest in "reducing the historic deficit of traditionally disfavored minorities in medical schools and in the medical profession" as an unlawful interest in racial balancing. * * * Second, Justice Powell rejected an interest in remedying societal discrimination because such measures would risk placing unnecessary burdens on innocent third parties "who bear no responsibility for whatever harm the beneficiaries of the special admissions program are thought to have suffered." * * * Third, Justice Powell rejected an interest in "increasing the number of physicians who will practice in communities currently underserved," concluding that even if such an interest could be compelling in some circumstances the program under review was not "geared to promote that goal." * * *

Justice Powell approved the university's use of race to further only one interest: "the attainment of a diverse student body." * * * In seeking the "right to select those students who will contribute the most to the 'robust exchange of ideas,' a university seeks to achieve a goal that is of paramount importance in the fulfillment of its mission." * * *

B

The Equal Protection Clause provides that no State shall "deny to any person within its jurisdiction the equal protection of the laws." U.S. Const., Amdt. 14, § 2. Because the Fourteenth Amendment "protects *persons*, not *groups*," all "governmental action based on race—a *group* classification long recognized as in most circumstances irrelevant and therefore prohibited—should be subjected to detailed judicial inquiry to ensure that the *personal* right to equal protection of the laws has not been infringed." *Adarand Constructors, Inc. v. Pena*, 515 U.S. 200, 227 (1995) (emphasis in original; internal quotation marks and citation omitted). We are a "free people whose institutions are founded upon the doctrine of equality." *Loving v. Virginia*, 388 U.S. 1, 11 (1967) (internal quotation marks and citation omitted). It follows from that principle that "government may treat people differently because of their race only for the most compelling reasons." [*Adarand*.]

We have held that all racial classifications imposed by government "must be analyzed by a reviewing court under strict scrutiny." *Ibid*. This means that such classifications are constitutional only if they are narrowly tailored to further compelling governmental interests. * * *

Strict scrutiny is not "strict in theory, but fatal in fact." [*Adarand*.] Although all governmental uses of race are subject to strict scrutiny, not all are invalidated by it. * * * When race-based action is necessary to further a compelling governmental interest, such action does not violate the constitutional guarantee of equal protection so long as the narrow-tailoring requirement is also satisfied.

* * *

III

A

* * *

We first wish to dispel the notion that the Law School's argument has been foreclosed, either expressly or implicitly, by our affirmative-action cases decided since *Bakke*. It is true that some language in those opinions might be read to suggest that remedying past discrimination is the only permissible justification for race-based governmental action. See, e.g., *Richmond v. J. A. Croson Co.*, [488 U.S. 469 (1989) (plurality opinion).] But we have never held that the only governmental use of race that can survive strict scrutiny is remedying past discrimination. Nor, since *Bakke*, have we directly addressed the use of race in the context of public higher education. Today, we hold that the Law School has a compelling interest in attaining a diverse student body.

The Law School's educational judgment that such diversity is essential to its educational mission is one to which we defer. The Law School's assessment that diversity will, in fact, yield educational benefits is substantiated by respondents and their *amici*. Our scrutiny of the interest asserted by the Law School is no less strict for taking into account complex educational judgments in an area that lies primarily within the expertise of the university. Our holding today is in keeping with our tradition of giving a degree of deference to a university's academic decisions, within constitutionally prescribed limits. * * *

We have long recognized that, given the important purpose of public education and the expansive freedoms of speech and thought associated with the university environment, universities occupy a special niche in our constitutional tradition. * * * In announcing the principle of student body diversity as a compelling state interest, Justice Powell invoked our cases recognizing a constitutional dimension, grounded in the First Amendment, of educational autonomy: "The freedom of a university to make its own judgments as to education includes the selection of its student body." [*Bakke*.] From this premise, Justice Powell reasoned that by claiming "the right to select those students who will contribute the most to the 'robust exchange of ideas,' " a university "seeks to achieve a goal that is of paramount importance in the fulfillment of its mission." * * * Our conclusion that the Law School has a compelling interest in a diverse student body is informed by our view that attaining a diverse student body is at the heart of the Law School's proper institutional mission, and that "good faith" on the part of a university is "presumed" absent "a showing to the contrary." * * *

As part of its goal of "assembling a class that is both exceptionally academically qualified and broadly diverse," the Law School seeks to "enroll a 'critical mass' of minority students." * * * The Law School's interest is not simply "to assure within its student body some specified percentage of a particular group merely because of its race or ethnic origin." [*Bakke.*] That would amount to outright racial balancing, which is patently unconstitutional. * * * Rather, the Law School's concept of critical mass is defined by reference to the educational benefits that diversity is designed to produce.

These benefits are substantial. As the District Court emphasized, the Law School's admissions policy promotes "cross-racial understanding," helps to break down racial stereotypes, and "enables [students] to better understand persons of different races." * * * These benefits are "important and laudable," because "classroom discussion is livelier, more spirited, and simply more enlightening and interesting" when the students have "the greatest possible variety of backgrounds." * * *

The Law School's claim of a compelling interest is further bolstered by its *amici*, who point to the educational benefits that flow from student body diversity. In addition to the expert studies and reports entered into evidence at trial, numerous studies show that student body diversity promotes learning outcomes, and "better prepares students for an increasingly diverse workforce and society, and better prepares them as professionals." [Brief for American Educational Research Association et al.]

These benefits are not theoretical but real, as major American businesses have made clear that the skills needed in today's increasingly global marketplace can only be developed through exposure to widely diverse people, cultures, ideas, and viewpoints. [Brief for 3M et al.; Brief for General Motors Corp.] What is more, high-ranking retired officers and civilian leaders of the United States military assert that, "based on [their] decades of experience," a "highly qualified, racially diverse officer corps . . . is essential to the military's ability to fulfill its principle mission to provide national security." [Brief for Julius W. Becton, Jr. et al.] The primary sources for the Nation's officer corps are the service academies and the Reserve Officers Training Corps (ROTC), the latter comprising students already admitted to participating colleges and universities. * * * At present, "the military cannot achieve an officer corps that is *both* highly qualified *and* racially diverse unless the service academies and the ROTC used limited race-conscious recruiting and admissions policies." [*Id.* (emphasis in original).] To fulfill its mission, the military "must be selective in admissions for training and education for the officer corps, *and* it must train and educate a highly qualified, racially diverse officer corps in a racially diverse setting." [*id.* (emphasis in original).] We agree that "it requires only a small step from this analysis to conclude that our country's

other most selective institutions must remain both diverse and selective."
* * *

* * *

Moreover, universities, and in particular, law schools, represent the training ground for a large number of our Nation's leaders. *Sweatt v. Painter*, 339 U.S. 629, 634 (1950) (describing law school as a "proving ground for legal learning and practice"). Individuals with law degrees occupy roughly half the state governorships, more than half the seats in the United States Senate, and more than a third of the seats in the United States House of Representatives. [See Brief for Association of American Law Schools.] The pattern is even more striking when it comes to highly selective law schools. A handful of these schools accounts for 25 of the 100 United States Senators, 74 United States Courts of Appeals judges, and nearly 200 of the more than 600 United States District Court judges. * * *

In order to cultivate a set of leaders with legitimacy in the eyes of the citizenry, it is necessary that the path to leadership be visibly open to talented and qualified individuals of every race and ethnicity. All members of our heterogeneous society must have confidence in the openness and integrity of the educational institutions that provide this training. As we have recognized, law schools "cannot be effective in isolation from the individuals and institutions with which the law interacts." [*Sweatt.*] Access to legal education (and thus the legal profession) must be inclusive of talented and qualified individuals of every race and ethnicity, so that all members of our heterogeneous society may participate in the educational institutions that provide the training and education necessary to succeed in America.

The Law School does not premise its need for critical mass on "any belief that minority students always (or even consistently) express some characteristic minority viewpoint on any issue." * * * To the contrary, diminishing the force of such stereotypes is both a crucial part of the Law School's mission, and one that it cannot accomplish with only token numbers of minority students. Just as growing up in a particular region or having particular professional experiences is likely to affect an individual's views, so too is one's own, unique experience of being a racial minority in a society, like our own, in which race unfortunately still matters. The Law School has determined, based on its experience and expertise, that a "critical mass" of underrepresented minorities is necessary to further its compelling interest in securing the educational benefits of a diverse student body.

B

Even in the limited circumstance when drawing racial distinctions is permissible to further a compelling state interest, government is still "constrained in how it may pursue that end: [T]he means chosen to accomplish the [government's] asserted purpose must be specifically and narrowly framed to accomplish that purpose." *Shaw v. Hunt*, 517 U.S. 899, 908 (1996). The purpose of the narrow tailoring requirement is to ensure that "the means chosen 'fit' th[e] compelling goal so closely that there is little or no possibility that the motive for the classification was illegitimate racial prejudice or stereotype." [*Croson* (plurality opinion).]

* * *

To be narrowly tailored, a race-conscious admissions program cannot use a quota system—it cannot "insulate each category of applicants with certain desired qualifications from competition with all other applicants." [*Bakke* (opinion of Powell, J.).] Instead, a university may consider race or ethnicity only as a " 'plus' in a particular applicant's file," without "insulating the individual from comparison with all other candidates for the available seats." [*id.*] * * *

We find that the Law School's admissions program bears the hallmarks of a narrowly tailored plan. As Justice Powell made clear in *Bakke*, truly individualized consideration demands that race be used in a flexible, nonmechanical way. * * *

We are satisfied that the Law School's admissions program, like the Harvard plan described by Justice Powell, does not operate as a quota. Properly understood, a "quota" is a program in which a certain fixed number or proportion of opportunities are "reserved exclusively for certain minority groups." [*Croson* (plurality opinion).] Quotas " 'impose a fixed number or percentage which must be attained, or which cannot be exceeded,' " *Sheet Metal Workers v. EEOC*, 478 U.S. 421, 445 (1986) (O'CONNOR, J., concurring in part and dissenting in part), and "insulate the individual from comparison with all other candidates for the available seats." [*Bakke* (opinion of Powell, J.).] In contrast, "a permissible goal . . . requires only a good-faith effort . . . to come within a range demarcated by the goal itself," [*Sheet Metal Workers*,] and permits consideration of race as a "plus" factor in any given case while still ensuring that each candidate "competes with all other qualified applicants," *Johnson v. Transportation Agency, Santa Clara Cty.*, 480 U.S. 616, 638 (1987).

* * *

The Law School's goal of attaining a critical mass of underrepresented minority students does not transform its program into a quota. As the Harvard plan described by Justice Powell recognized, there is of course "some relationship between numbers and achieving the benefits to be derived from a diverse student body, and between numbers and providing a reasonable environment for those students admitted." [*id.*] "Some attention to numbers," without more, does not transform a flexible admissions system into a rigid quota. [*Id.*] Nor, as Justice Kennedy posits, does the Law School's consultation of the "daily reports," which keep track of the racial and ethnic composition of the class (as well as of residency and gender), "suggest[ ] there was no further attempt at individual review save for race itself" during the final stages of the admissions process. * * * To the contrary, the Law School's admissions officers testified without contradiction that they never gave race any more or less weight based on the information contained in these reports. * * * Moreover, as Justice Kennedy concedes, * * * between 1993 and 2000, the number of African-American, Latino, and Native–American students in each class at the Law School varied from 13.5 to 20.1 percent, a range inconsistent with a quota.

The Chief Justice believes that the Law School's policy conceals an attempt to achieve racial balancing, and cites admissions data to contend that the Law School discriminates among different groups within the critical mass. * * * But, as the Chief Justice concedes, the number of underrepresented minority students who ultimately enroll in the Law School differs substantially from their representation in the applicant pool and varies considerably for each group from year to year. * * *

* * *

Here, the Law School engages in a highly individualized, holistic review of each applicant's file, giving serious consideration to all the ways an applicant might contribute to a diverse educational environment. The Law School affords this individualized consideration to applicants of all races. There is no policy, either *de jure* or *de facto*, of automatic acceptance or rejection based on any single "soft" variable. Unlike the program at issue in *Gratz v. Bollinger*, [123 S.Ct. 2411 (2003),] the Law School awards no mechanical, predetermined diversity "bonuses" based on race or ethnicity. * * * Like the Harvard plan, the Law School's admissions policy "is flexible enough to consider all pertinent elements of diversity in light of the particular qualifications of each applicant, and to place them on the same footing for consideration, although not necessarily according them the same weight." [*Bakke* (opinion of Powell, J.).]

We also find that, like the Harvard plan Justice Powell referenced in *Bakke*, the Law School's race-conscious admissions program adequately ensures that all factors that may contribute to student body diversity are meaningfully considered alongside race in admissions decisions. With respect to the use of race itself, all underrepresented minority students admitted by the Law School have been deemed qualified. By virtue of our Nation's struggle with racial inequality, such students are both likely to have experiences of particular importance to the Law School's mission, and less likely to be admitted in meaningful numbers on criteria that ignore those experiences. * * *

* * *

What is more, the Law School actually gives substantial weight to diversity factors besides race. The Law School frequently accepts nonminority applicants with grades and test scores lower than underrepresented minority applicants (and other nonminority applicants) who are rejected. * * * This shows that the Law School seriously weighs many other diversity factors besides race that can make a real and dispositive difference for nonminority applicants as well. By this flexible approach, the Law School sufficiently takes into account, in practice as well as in theory, a wide variety of characteristics besides race and ethnicity that contribute to a diverse student body. Justice Kennedy speculates that "race is likely outcome determinative for many members of minority groups" who do not fall within the upper range of LSAT scores and grades. * * * But the same could be said of the Harvard plan discussed approvingly by Justice Powell in *Bakke*, and indeed of any plan that uses race as one of many factors. * * *

Petitioner and the United States argue that the Law School's plan is not narrowly tailored because race-neutral means exist to obtain the educational benefits of student body diversity that the Law School seeks. We disagree. Narrow tailoring does not require exhaustion of every conceivable race-neutral alternative. * * *

We agree with the Court of Appeals that the Law School sufficiently considered workable race-neutral alternatives. The District Court took the Law School to task for failing to consider race-neutral alternatives such as "using a lottery system" or "decreasing the emphasis for all applicants on undergraduate GPA and LSAT scores." * * * But these alternatives would require a dramatic sacrifice of diversity, the academic quality of all admitted students, or both.

* * *

We acknowledge that "there are serious problems of justice connected with the idea of preference itself." [*Bakke* (opinion of Powell, J.).] Narrow tailoring, therefore, requires that a race-conscious admissions program not unduly harm members of any racial group. Even remedial race-based governmental action generally "remains subject to continuing oversight to assure that it will work the least harm possible to other innocent persons competing for the benefit." * * * To be narrowly tailored, a race-conscious admissions program must not "unduly burden individuals who are not members of the favored racial and ethnic groups." *Metro Broadcasting, Inc. v. FCC*, 497 U.S. 547, 630 (1990) (O'CONNOR, J., dissenting).

* * * We agree that, in the context of its individualized inquiry into the possible diversity contributions of all applicants, the Law School's race-conscious admissions program does not unduly harm nonminority applicants.

We are mindful, however, that "[a] core purpose of the Fourteenth Amendment was to do away with all governmentally imposed discrimination based on race." *Palmore v. Sidoti*, 466 U.S. 429, 432 (1984). Accordingly, race-conscious admissions policies must be limited in time. This requirement reflects that racial classifications, however compelling their goals, are potentially so dangerous that they may be employed no more broadly than the interest demands. Enshrining a permanent justification for racial preferences would offend this fundamental equal protection principle. We see no reason to exempt race-conscious admissions programs from the requirement that all governmental use of race must have a logical end point. The Law School, too, concedes that all "race-conscious programs must have reasonable durational limits." * * *

In the context of higher education, the durational requirement can be met by sunset provisions in race-conscious admissions policies and periodic reviews to determine whether racial preferences are still necessary to achieve student body diversity. Universities in California, Florida, and Washington State, where racial preferences in admissions are prohibited by state law, are currently engaged in experimenting with a wide variety of alternative approaches. Universities in other States can and should draw on the most promising aspects of these race-neutral alternatives as they develop. * * *

The requirement that all race-conscious admissions programs have a termination point "assure[s] all citizens that the deviation from the norm of equal treatment of all racial and ethnic groups is a temporary matter, a measure taken in the service of the goal of equality itself." [*Croson* (plurality opinion).]

We take the Law School at its word that it would "like nothing better than to find a race-neutral admissions formula" and will terminate its race-conscious admissions program as soon as practicable. * * * It has been 25 years since Justice Powell first approved the use of race to further an interest in student body diversity in the context of public higher education. Since that time, the number of minority applicants with high grades and test scores has indeed increased. * * * We expect that 25 years from now, the use of racial preferences will no longer be necessary to further the interest approved today.

   * * *

It is so ordered.

■ JUSTICE GINSBURG, with whom JUSTICE BREYER joins, concurring.

   * * *

It is well documented that conscious and unconscious race bias, even rank discrimination based on race, remain alive in our land, impeding realization of our highest values and ideals. * * * As to public education, data for the years 2000–2001 show that 71.6% of African-American children and 76.3% of Hispanic children attended a school in which minorities made up a majority of the student body. * * * And schools in predominantly minority communities lag far behind others measured by the educational resources available to them. [See Brief for National Urban League et al.]

However strong the public's desire for improved education systems may be, * * * it remains the current reality that many minority students encounter markedly inadequate and unequal educational opportunities. Despite these inequalities, some minority students are able to meet the high threshold requirements set for admission to the country's finest undergraduate and graduate educational institutions. As lower school education in minority communities improves, an increase in the number of such students may be anticipated. From today's vantage point, one may hope, but not firmly forecast, that over the next generation's span, progress toward nondiscrimination and genuinely equal opportunity will make it safe to sunset affirmative action.

■ CHIEF JUSTICE REHNQUIST, with whom JUSTICE SCALIA, JUSTICE KENNEDY, and JUSTICE THOMAS join, dissenting.

I agree with the Court that, "in the limited circumstance when drawing racial distinctions is permissible," the government must ensure that its means are narrowly tailored to achieve a compelling state interest. * * * I do not believe, however, that the University of Michigan Law School's (Law School) means are narrowly tailored to the interest it asserts. The Law School claims it must take the steps it does to achieve a " 'critical mass' " of underrepresented minority students. * * * But its actual program bears no relation to this asserted goal. Stripped of its "critical mass" veil, the Law School's program is revealed as a naked effort to achieve racial balancing.

As we have explained many times, "any preference based on racial or ethnic criteria must necessarily receive a most searching examination." [*Adarand* (quoting *Wygant*).] Our cases establish that, in order to withstand this demanding inquiry, respondents must demonstrate that their methods of using race "fit" a compelling state interest "with greater precision than any alternative means." [*Id.*]

Before the Court's decision today, we consistently applied the same strict scrutiny analysis regardless of the government's purported reason for using race and regardless of the setting in which race was being used. We rejected calls to use more lenient review in the face of claims that race was being used in "good faith" because "more than good motives should be required when government seeks to allocate its resources by way of an explicit racial classification system." [*Adarand*.] We likewise rejected calls to apply more lenient review based on the particular setting in which race is being used. Indeed, even in the specific context of higher education, we emphasized that "constitutional limitations protecting individual rights may not be disregarded." [*Bakke*.]

Although the Court recites the language of our strict scrutiny analysis, its application of that review is unprecedented in its deference.

Respondents' asserted justification for the Law School's use of race in the admissions process is "obtaining 'the educational benefits that flow from a diverse student body.' " * * *

In practice, the Law School's program bears little or no relation to its asserted goal of achieving "critical mass." Respondents explain that the Law School seeks to accumulate a "critical mass" of *each* underrepresented minority group. * * * But the record demonstrates that the Law School's admissions practices with respect to these groups differ dramatically and cannot be defended under any consistent use of the term "critical mass."

From 1995 through 2000, the Law School admitted between 1,130 and 1,310 students. Of those, between 13 and 19 were Native American, between 91 and 108 were African-Americans, and between 47 and 56 were Hispanic. If the Law School is admitting between 91 and 108 African-Americans in order to achieve "critical mass," thereby preventing African-American students from feeling "isolated or like spokespersons for their race," one would think that a number of the same order of magnitude would be necessary to accomplish the same purpose for Hispanics and

Native Americans. Similarly, even if all of the Native American applicants admitted in a given year matriculate, which the record demonstrates is not at all the case,* how can this possibly constitute a "critical mass" of Native Americans in a class of over 350 students? In order for this pattern of admission to be consistent with the Law School's explanation of "critical mass," one would have to believe that the objectives of "critical mass" offered by respondents are achieved with only half the number of Hispanics and one-sixth the number of Native Americans as compared to African-Americans. But respondents offer no race-specific reasons for such disparities. Instead, they simply emphasize the importance of achieving "critical mass," without any explanation of why that concept is applied differently among the three underrepresented minority groups.

These different numbers, moreover, come only as a result of substantially different treatment among the three underrepresented minority groups, as is apparent in an example offered by the Law School and highlighted by the Court: The school asserts that it "frequently accepts nonminority applicants with grades and test scores lower than underrepresented minority applicants (and other nonminority applicants) who are rejected." * * * Specifically, the Law School states that "sixty-nine minority applicants were rejected between 1995 and 2000 with at least a 3.5 [Grade Point Average (GPA)] and a [score of] 159 or higher on the [Law School Admissions Test (LSAT)]" while a number of Caucasian and Asian–American applicants with similar or lower scores were admitted. * * *

Review of the record reveals only 67 such individuals. Of these 67 individuals, 56 were Hispanic, while only 6 were African-American, and only 5 were Native American. This discrepancy reflects a consistent practice.

These statistics have a significant bearing on petitioner's case. Respondents have *never* offered any race-specific arguments explaining why significantly more individuals from one underrepresented minority group are needed in order to achieve "critical mass" or further student body diversity. They certainly have not explained why Hispanics, who they have said are among "the groups most isolated by racial barriers in our country," should have their admission capped out in this manner. * * * True, petitioner is neither Hispanic nor Native American. But the Law School's disparate admissions practices with respect to these minority groups demonstrate that its alleged goal of "critical mass" is simply a sham. Petitioner may use these statistics to expose this sham, which is the basis for the Law School's admission of less qualified underrepresented minorities in preference to her. Surely strict scrutiny cannot permit these sort of disparities without at least some explanation.

* * *

* Indeed, during this 5–year time period, enrollment of Native American students dropped to as low as *three* such students. Any assertion that such a small group constituted a "critical mass" of Native Americans is simply absurd.

The Court, in an unprecedented display of deference under our strict scrutiny analysis, upholds the Law School's program despite its obvious flaws. We have said that when it comes to the use of race, the connection between the ends and the means used to attain them must be precise. But here the flaw is deeper than that; it is not merely a question of "fit" between ends and means. Here the means actually used are forbidden by the Equal Protection Clause of the Constitution.

[Justice Kennedy's dissenting opinion has been omitted].

■ JUSTICE SCALIA, with whom JUSTICE THOMAS joins, concurring in part and dissenting in part.

* * *

[T]he "educational benefit" that the University of Michigan seeks to achieve by racial discrimination consists, according to the Court, of " 'cross-racial understanding,' " * * * and " 'better prepar[ation of] students for an increasingly diverse workforce and society,' " * * * all of which is necessary not only for work, but also for good "citizenship." * * * This is not, of course, an "educational benefit" on which students will be graded on their Law School transcript (Works and Plays Well with Others: B+) or tested by the bar examiners (Q: Describe in 500 words or less your cross-racial understanding). For it is a lesson of life rather than law—essentially the same lesson taught to (or rather learned by, for it cannot be "taught" in the usual sense) people three feet shorter and twenty years younger than the full-grown adults at the University of Michigan Law School, in institutions ranging from Boy Scout troops to public-school kindergartens. If properly considered an "educational benefit" at all, it is surely not one that is either uniquely relevant to law school or uniquely "teachable" in a formal educational setting. *And therefore:* If it is appropriate for the University of Michigan Law School to use racial discrimination for the purpose of putting together a "critical mass" that will convey generic lessons in socialization and good citizenship, surely it is no less appropriate—indeed, *particularly* appropriate—for the civil service system of the State of Michigan to do so. There, also, those exposed to "critical masses" of certain races will presumably become better Americans, better Michiganders, better civil servants. And surely private employers cannot be criticized—indeed, should be praised—if they also "teach" good citizenship to their adult employees through a patriotic, all-American system of racial discrimination in hiring. The nonminority individuals who are deprived of a legal education, a civil service job, or any job at all by reason of their skin color will surely understand.

Unlike a clear constitutional holding that racial preferences in state educational institutions are impermissible, or even a clear anticonstitutional holding that racial preferences in state educational institutions are OK, today's *Grutter-Gratz* split double header seems perversely designed to prolong the controversy and the litigation. * * *

■ JUSTICE THOMAS, with whom JUSTICE SCALIA joins as to Parts I–VII, concurring in part and dissenting in part.

Frederick Douglass, speaking to a group of abolitionists almost 140 years ago, delivered a message lost on today's majority:

"[I]n regard to the colored people, there is always more that is benevolent, I perceive, than just, manifested towards us. What I ask for the negro is not benevolence, not pity, not sympathy, but simply *justice*. The American people have always been anxious to know what they shall do with us.... I have had but one answer from the beginning. Do nothing with us! Your doing with us has already played the mischief with us. Do nothing with us! If the apples will not remain on the tree of their own strength, if they are worm-eaten at the core, if they are early ripe and disposed to fall, let them fall! ... And if the negro cannot stand on his own legs, let him fall also. All I ask is, give him a chance to stand on his own legs! Let him alone! ... [Y]our interference is doing him positive injury." What the Black Man Wants: An Address Delivered in Boston, Massachusetts, on 26 January 1865, reprinted in 4 The Frederick Douglass Papers 59, 68 (J. Blassingame & J. McKivigan eds. 1991) (emphasis in original).

Like Douglass, I believe blacks can achieve in every avenue of American life without the meddling of university administrators. Because I wish to see all students succeed whatever their color, I share, in some respect, the sympathies of those who sponsor the type of discrimination advanced by the University of Michigan Law School (Law School). The Constitution does not, however, tolerate institutional devotion to the status quo in admissions policies when such devotion ripens into racial discrimination. Nor does the Constitution countenance the unprecedented deference the Court gives to the Law School, an approach inconsistent with the very concept of "strict scrutiny."

No one would argue that a university could set up a lower general admission standard and then impose heightened requirements only on black applicants. Similarly, a university may not maintain a high admission standard and grant exemptions to favored races. The Law School, of its own choosing, and for its own purposes, maintains an exclusionary admissions system that it knows produces racially disproportionate results. Racial discrimination is not a permissible solution to the self-inflicted wounds of this elitist admissions policy.

The majority upholds the Law School's racial discrimination not by interpreting the people's Constitution, but by responding to a faddish slogan of the cognoscenti. Nevertheless, I concur in part in the Court's opinion. First, I agree with the Court insofar as its decision, which approves of only one racial classification, confirms that further use of race in admissions remains unlawful. Second, I agree with the Court's holding that racial discrimination in higher education admissions will be illegal in 25 years. * * * I respectfully dissent from the remainder of the Court's opinion and the judgment, however, because I believe that the Law School's current use of race violates the Equal Protection Clause and that the Constitution means the same thing today as it will in 300 months.

I

* * * The Constitution abhors classifications based on race, not only because those classifications can harm favored races or are based on illegitimate motives, but also because every time the government places citizens on racial registers and makes race relevant to the provision of burdens or benefits, it demeans us all. "Purchased at the price of immeasurable human suffering, the equal protection principle reflects our Nation's understanding that such classifications ultimately have a destructive impact on the individual and our society." [*Adarand* (Thomas, J., concurring in part and concurring in judgment).]

II

Unlike the majority, I seek to define with precision the interest being asserted by the Law School before determining whether that interest is so compelling as to justify racial discrimination. The Law School maintains that it wishes to obtain "educational benefits that flow from student body diversity." * * * This statement must be evaluated carefully, because it implies that both "diversity" and "educational benefits" are components of the Law School's compelling state interest. Additionally, the Law School's refusal to entertain certain changes in its admissions process and status indicates that the compelling state interest it seeks to validate is actually broader than might appear at first glance.

* * *

A distinction between these two ideas (unique educational benefits based on racial aesthetics and race for its own sake) is purely sophistic—so much so that the majority uses them interchangeably. * * * The Law School's argument, as facile as it is, can only be understood in one way: Classroom aesthetics yields educational benefits, racially discriminatory admissions policies are required to achieve the right racial mix, and therefore the policies are required to achieve the educational benefits. It is the *educational benefits* that are the end, or allegedly compelling state interest, not "diversity." * * *

One must also consider the Law School's refusal to entertain changes to its current admissions system that might produce the same educational benefits. The Law School adamantly disclaims any race-neutral alternative that would reduce "academic selectivity," which would in turn "require the Law School to become a very different institution, and to sacrifice a core part of its educational mission." * * * In other words, the Law School seeks to improve marginally the education it offers without sacrificing too much of its exclusivity and elite status.

The proffered interest that the majority vindicates today, then, is not simply "diversity." Instead the Court upholds the use of racial discrimination as a tool to advance the Law School's interest in offering a marginally superior education while maintaining an elite institution. Unless each constituent part of this state interest is of pressing public necessity, the

Law School's use of race is unconstitutional. I find each of them to fall far short of this standard.

III

A

A close reading of the Court's opinion reveals that all of its legal work is done through one conclusory statement: The Law School has a "compelling interest in securing the educational benefits of a diverse student body." * * * No serious effort is made to explain how these benefits fit with the state interests the Court has recognized (or rejected) as compelling * * * or to place any theoretical constraints on an enterprising court's desire to discover still more justifications for racial discrimination. In the absence of any explanation, one might expect the Court to fall back on the judicial policy of *stare decisis*. But the Court eschews even this weak defense of its holding, shunning an analysis of the extent to which Justice Powell's opinion in [*Bakke*] is binding, * * * in favor of an unfounded wholesale adoption of it.

　　* * *

B

Under the proper standard, there is no pressing public necessity in maintaining a public law school at all and, it follows, certainly not an elite law school. Likewise, marginal improvements in legal education do not qualify as a compelling state interest.

1

While legal education at a public university may be good policy or otherwise laudable, it is obviously not a pressing public necessity when the correct legal standard is applied. * * *

2

* * * Michigan has no compelling interest in having a law school at all, much less an *elite* one. Still, even assuming that a State may, under appropriate circumstances, demonstrate a cognizable interest in having an elite law school, Michigan has failed to do so here.

　　* * *

[T]he Law School trains few Michigan residents and overwhelmingly serves students, who, as lawyers, leave the State of Michigan. The Law School's decision to be an elite institution does little to advance the welfare of the people of Michigan or any cognizable interest of the State of Michigan. * * *

3

Finally, even if the Law School's racial tinkering produces tangible educational benefits, a marginal improvement in legal education cannot justify racial discrimination where the Law School has no compelling interest in either its existence or in its current educational and admissions policies.

IV

The interest in remaining elite and exclusive that the majority thinks so obviously critical requires the use of admissions "standards" that, in turn, create the Law School's "need" to discriminate on the basis of race. The Court validates these admissions standards by concluding that alternatives that would require "a dramatic sacrifice of . . . the academic quality of all admitted students," * * * need not be considered before racial discrimination can be employed. In the majority's view, such methods are not required by the "narrow tailoring" prong of strict scrutiny because that inquiry demands, in this context, that any race-neutral alternative work " 'about as well.' " * * * The majority errs, however, because race-neutral alternatives must only be "workable," * * * and do "about as well" *in vindicating the compelling state interest.* The Court never explicitly holds that the Law School's desire to retain the status quo in "academic selectivity" is itself a compelling state interest, and, as I have demonstrated, it is not. * * * Therefore, the Law School should be forced to choose between its classroom aesthetic and its exclusionary admissions system—it cannot have it both ways.

With the adoption of different admissions methods, such as accepting all students who meet minimum qualifications, * * * the Law School could achieve its vision of the racially aesthetic student body without the use of racial discrimination. The Law School concedes this, but the Court holds, implicitly and under the guise of narrow tailoring, that the Law School has a compelling state interest in doing what it wants to do. I cannot agree. * * *

A

The Court bases its unprecedented deference to the Law School—a deference antithetical to strict scrutiny—on an idea of "educational autonomy" grounded in the First Amendment. * * * In my view, there is no basis for a right of public universities to do what would otherwise violate the Equal Protection Clause.

* * *

B

1

The Court's deference to the Law School's conclusion that its racial experimentation leads to educational benefits will, if adhered to, have serious collateral consequences. The Court relies heavily on social science evidence to justify its deference. * * * The Court never acknowledges, however, the growing evidence that racial (and other sorts) of heterogeneity actually impairs learning among black students. * * *

* * *

The majority grants deference to the Law School's "assessment that diversity will, in fact, yield educational benefits." * * * It follows, therefore, that an HBC's [historically black college's] assessment that racial homogeneity will yield educational benefits would similarly be given deference. An HBC's rejection of white applicants in order to maintain racial homogeneity seems permissible, therefore, under the majority's view of the Equal Protection Clause. * * * Contained within today's majority opinion is the seed of a new constitutional justification for a concept I thought long and rightly rejected—racial segregation.

2

* * *

C

. . .

The sky has not fallen at Boalt Hall at the University of California, Berkeley, for example. Proposition 209's adopt[ion] of Cal. Const., Art. 1, § 31(a) [1996], bars the State from "granting preferential treatment . . . on the basis of race . . . in the operation of . . . public education." * * * [W]ithout deploying express racial discrimination in admissions * * * total underrepresented minority student enrollment at Boalt Hall now exceeds 1996 levels. Apparently the Law School cannot be counted on to be as resourceful. The Court is willfully blind to the very real experience in California and elsewhere, which raises the inference that institutions with "reputation[s] for excellence," * * * rivaling the Law School's have satisfied their sense of mission without resorting to prohibited racial discrimination.

V

Putting aside the absence of any legal support for the majority's reflexive deference, there is much to be said for the view that the use of tests and other measures to "predict" academic performance is a poor substitute for a system that gives every applicant a chance to prove he can succeed in the study of law. The rallying cry that in the absence of racial discrimination in admissions there would be a true meritocracy ignores the fact that the entire process is poisoned by numerous exceptions to "merit." For example, in the national debate on racial discrimination in higher education admissions, much has been made of the fact that elite institutions utilize a so-called "legacy" preference to give the children of alumni an advantage in admissions. This, and other, exceptions to a "true" meritocracy give the lie to protestations that merit admissions are in fact the order of the day at the Nation's universities. The Equal Protection Clause does not, however, prohibit the use of unseemly legacy preferences or many other kinds of arbitrary admissions procedures. What the Equal Protection Clause does prohibit are classifications made on the basis of race. So while legacy preferences can stand under the Constitution, racial discrimination cannot. I will not twist the Constitution to invalidate legacy preferences or otherwise impose my vision of higher education admissions on the Nation. The majority should similarly stay its impulse to validate faddish racial discrimination the Constitution clearly forbids.

* * *

[N]o modern law school can claim ignorance of the poor performance of blacks, relatively speaking, on the Law School Admissions Test (LSAT). Nevertheless, law schools continue to use the test and then attempt to "correct" for black underperformance by using racial discrimination in admissions so as to obtain their aesthetic student body. The Law School's continued adherence to measures it knows produce racially skewed results is not entitled to deference by this Court. * * *

Having decided to use the LSAT, the Law School must accept the constitutional burdens that come with this decision. The Law School may freely continue to employ the LSAT and other allegedly merit-based standards in whatever fashion it likes. What the Equal Protection Clause forbids, but the Court today allows, is the use of these standards hand-in-hand with racial discrimination. An infinite variety of admissions methods are available to the Law School. Considering all of the radical thinking that has historically occurred at this country's universities, the Law School's intractable approach toward admissions is striking.

* * *

VI

The absence of any articulated legal principle supporting the majority's principal holding suggests another rationale. I believe what lies beneath the Court's decision today are the benighted notions that one can tell when racial discrimination benefits (rather than hurts) minority groups, * * * and that racial discrimination is necessary to remedy general societal ills. This Court's precedents supposedly settled both issues, but clearly the majority still cannot commit to the principle that racial classifications are *per se* harmful and that almost no amount of benefit in the eye of the beholder can justify such classifications.

* * *

The Law School tantalizes unprepared students with the promise of a University of Michigan degree and all of the opportunities that it offers. These overmatched students take the bait, only to find that they cannot succeed in the cauldron of competition. And this mismatch crisis is not restricted to elite institutions. * * * Indeed, to cover the tracks of the aestheticists, this cruel farce of racial discrimination must continue—in selection for the Michigan Law Review * * * and in hiring at law firms and for judicial clerkships—until the "beneficiaries" are no longer tolerated. While these students may graduate with law degrees, there is no evidence that they have received a qualitatively better legal education (or become better lawyers) than if they had gone to a less "elite" law school for which they were better prepared. And the aestheticists will never address the real problems facing "underrepresented minorities," instead continuing their social experiments on other people's children.

Beyond the harm the Law School's racial discrimination visits upon its test subjects, no social science has disproved the notion that this discrimination "engenders attitudes of superiority or, alternatively, provoke[s] resentment among those who believe that they have been wronged by the government's use of race." [*Adarand* (Thomas, J., concurring in part and concurring in judgment).] "These programs stamp minorities with a badge of inferiority and may cause them to develop dependencies or to adopt an attitude that they are 'entitled' to preferences." [*Id.*]

It is uncontested that each year, the Law School admits a handful of blacks who would be admitted in the absence of racial discrimination. * * * Who can differentiate between those who belong and those who do not? The majority of blacks are admitted to the Law School because of discrimination, and because of this policy all are tarred as undeserving. This problem of stigma does not depend on determinacy as to whether those stigmatized are actually the "beneficiaries" of racial discrimination. When blacks take positions in the highest places of government, industry, or academia, it is an open question today whether their skin color played a part in their advancement. The question itself is the stigma—because either racial discrimination did play a role, in which case the person may be deemed "otherwise unqualified," or it did not, in which case asking the question itself unfairly marks those blacks who would succeed without discrimination. Is this what the Court means by "visibly open"? * * *

   * * *

VII

As the foregoing makes clear, I believe the Court's opinion to be, in most respects, erroneous. I do, however, find two points on which I agree.

   * * *

Under today's decision, it is still the case that racial discrimination that does not help a university to enroll an unspecified number, or "critical mass," of underrepresented minority students is unconstitutional.

   * * *

I * * * understand the imposition of a 25–year time limit only as a holding that the deference the Court pays to the Law School's educational judgments and refusal to change its admissions policies will itself expire. * * * With these observations, I join the last sentence of Part III of the opinion of the Court.

         * * *

For the immediate future, however, the majority has placed its *imprimatur* on a practice that can only weaken the principle of equality embodied in the Declaration of Independence and the Equal Protection Clause. "Our Constitution is color-blind, and neither knows nor tolerates classes among citizens." *Plessy v. Ferguson*, 163 U.S. 537, 559 (1896) (Harlan, J., dissenting). It has been nearly 140 years since Frederick Douglass asked the intellectual ancestors of the Law School to "[d]o nothing with us!" and the Nation adopted the Fourteenth Amendment. Now we must wait another 25 years to see this principle of equality vindicated. I therefore respectfully dissent from the remainder of the Court's opinion and the judgment.

* * *

———

Admissions Rituals as Political Acts: Guardians at the Gates of Our Democratic Ideals

117 HARV. L. REV. 113 (2003).

■ LANI GUINIER

* * *

Every year, selective colleges and universities engage in admissions rituals to reconstitute themselves. Institutions presumably align these high-stakes moments of civic pedagogy with their educational agenda: to produce knowledge, to promote learning, and to help individuals realize their intellectual, athletic, or artistic potential. The moment when admissions decisions are mailed is also fraught with political consequences that reach beyond the classroom to the boardroom, the legislature, and the kitchen table. At selective institutions of higher education, admissions decisions have a special political impact: rationing access to societal influence and power, and training leaders for public office and public life. Those admitted as students then graduate to become citizens who shape business, education, the arts, and the law for the next generation. Admissions decisions affect the individuals who apply, the institutional environments that greet those who enroll, and the stability and legitimacy of our democracy. They are political as well as educational acts.

* * *

Some have construed [the *Grutter* decision's focus on the role of higher education in democracy] as a warning, as Justice O'Connor's majority opinion in *Grutter* includes a puzzling clause stating that she expects the need for considerations of race in admissions decisions to expire after twenty-five years. According to former Harvard University President Derek Bok, for example, this twenty-five-year expectation is more than simply a reminder of the need to reevaluate race-consciousness in order to satisfy the narrow tailoring element of strict scrutiny: rather, it is a "warning to do something about the underlying problem." Universities, in other words, are not living up to their educational and democratic missions: they need to do more about the achievement gap that makes affirmative action necessary; the environmental gap that socially isolates white students who, unlike students of color, spend most of their time with same-race friends in college; and the teaching and learning gaps that disable professors from reaching out to mentor students of color.

At the same time, it is important to acknowledge that the appearance of sharp boundary lines in defining race is problematic for many members of the public and the Court. There is a pervasive reluctance to view race in categorical terms. This resistance to racial categorization affects members of the public, not just the crusaders against affirmative action who, despite their defeat at the Supreme Court, seem to have lost none of their zeal.

* * *

Properly deployed, racial literacy, or the ability to read race in conjunction with institutional and democratic structures, may enable the building of a coalition that starts a larger conversation at the point where educational selection and democratic values meet. Race, in other words, reveals rather than produces the stress on institutional resources that undermines the connection between education and democracy, a connection that the Court in *Grutter* and *Gratz* recognized as essential. Because race is inextricably intertwined with every period in American history, from our founding as a constitutional democracy to current patterns of private wealth formation, it is a formidable diagnostic and sociological tool. Used as a lens to peer beyond the pretense of the debate, race helps detect the deeper issues confronting public institutions of higher education.

* * *

I. The Democratic and Educational Missions of Higher Education: Admissions Judgments as Political Acts

* * *

Although education has been linked to opportunity since the early days of the republic, higher education was originally a province reserved for wealthy white men. During the first half of the twentieth century, women, Jews, and blacks were the victims of arbitrary quotas or formal exclusionary policies sanctioned by law. During the 1950s and 1960s, however, legal challenges, social movements, and a participatory conception of individual rights helped pressure these institutions of higher education to open their doors—albeit only a crack—to those who had been shut out. Institutions that had once been bastions of elite privilege began admitting women and people of color for the first time.

At the same time, American society increasingly highlighted the importance of higher education to democratic values by extending the opportunity to attend college to more people. The GI Bill, Pell Grants, the Cold War, and the move to a global and information economy made higher education instrumental to our society's understanding of the relationship between an educated populace, a representative group of leaders, a commitment to public service, and national security. These developments also turned college education into a primary engine for economic and social upward mobility in the last part of the century.

Meanwhile, as more people saw higher education as a necessity for societal as well as individual reasons, government funding for this essential public good shrunk: states shifted resources from education to the criminal justice system, the federal government cut Pell grants, and state revenues plummeted, leading to higher tuition and reduced financial aid. This shift in funding priorities was driven in part by an ideological shift during the Reagan era. Higher education was presented as a private benefit to be financed by the individual, instead of a public good to be funded by the government. As a result, higher education became a scarce, indispensable, and competitive individual resource.

As more people wanted in, colleges and universities became more selective. * * * Many of these institutions valued their "selectivity" as an element of their identity or chose for other reasons not to add sufficient resources to keep up with increased interest. * * *

[I]nstitutions began to seek a fair and efficient set of selection criteria that would preserve their elite status, which had been derived from association with bloodlines and reinforced by the appearance of unattainability. Institutions that once used evidence of "good character"—a proxy for privilege and wealth—switched to ostensibly more democratic indicia of merit. College admissions officers began to replace the pedigreed "natural" aristocracy of Edmund Burke's world that had dominated elite higher education through the middle of the twentieth century. In the 1950s a "meritocracy" began to substitute "aptitude" for "character" (or family) as the ticket into colleges and universities. Admissions would proceed from an open calculus rather than a set of private relationships. Excellence through brains, not blood, would become the basis for awarding scarce admission slots.

Excellence did not simply cloak elitism, however. It was also associated with a fairness principle, derived from scientifically designed, and thus presumably more objective, criteria. One of the primary vehicles for apportioning access to an increasingly popular yet scarce public resource was the introduction of standardized tests and other potentially objective measures of excellence; such tests enabled university administrators to compare individuals from different demographic, geographic, and social cohorts. This ability to compare had been previously either unnecessary for the public institutions that admitted almost every (white male) applicant, or reserved to headmasters at private prep schools.

Because of the perceived ability to manufacture objective evidence of desert, excellence became measurable. Applicants who outscored or outranked their peers on standardized aptitude tests were therefore presumed to be the most qualified, regardless of social class. The premium on allocating access to higher education more democratically and meritocratically led to the development of a testing industry that now functions as one of the primary gatekeepers to upward mobility.

Deciding who "deserves" to benefit from admission to selective colleges and universities now occurs within a "testocracy" that claims to sort, evaluate, and rank measurable mental aptitude. The resulting test scores, together with high school grades, purport to tell us in both real and relative terms about each applicant's potential capacity, which is then deemed the most important evidence of his or her "visible, rankable" merit.

To maintain their elite status in terms of democratic "merit" rather than inherited privilege, these institutions had to raise the stakes. Thus, applicants who receive the thick envelopes in April have higher SAT scores than their parents did a generation ago. Unfortunately, along with democratic "merit" came a sense of entitlement without the sense of obligation. Ambition replaced pedigree, but the public spiritedness * * * failed to materialize.

During the second half of the twentieth century, the pendulum swung dramatically from subjective measures of character to objective measures of excellence; for reasons I describe in the next Part, it soon swung back to more subjective evidence of character to supplement the quantifiable standards for measuring academic merit. But now character would mean motivation, work ethic, and the ability to overcome obstacles, rather than charisma, athletic skill, and the ability to fit in. Diversity rather than homogeneity became a value.

Moving back and forth from subjective to objective to subjective measures, the admissions pendulum never settled on a single, fixed view of merit. Without a stable template for admissions choices, shifts in the values and identities of those making the choices, as well as the process of selection itself, came to define qualification. Yet the choice of who attends institutions of higher education, both public and private, has personal, institutional, and societal implications. Thus, admissions decisions are both educational questions and political acts.

The task of constituting each class is a political act because it implicates the institution's sense of itself as a community, as well as the larger society's sense of itself as a democracy. Such acts allocate resources in a way that affects those who are admitted to the institution, those who are rejected, those who fail to apply, and those who simply use the institution's selection criteria as an interpretive guide. Thus, they affect all members of society, both directly, as described above, and indirectly, by helping determine future political, economic, and social leaders. Directly or indirectly, taxpayers support these institutions, which function as gateways to upward mobility and help legitimize democratic ideals of participation, fairness, and equal opportunity. At nonselective public colleges, the opportunity to attend is less a function of admissions criteria per se, and more a question of application fees and tuition costs, as well as historical patterns of recruitment, information networks, social capital, and location that determine the demographics of the student body and faculty.

* * *

The term "political act" also describes inputs that inflect the process of decisionmaking, not just the outputs that help define it. Beyond the democratic significance, the social consequences, and the individual benefits of gaining admission to these institutions, admissions choices have an internal political dynamic. They are located in the heads of the decisionmakers as well as in the world.

II: CONTEST, SPONSORED, AND STRUCTURAL MOBILITY:
ALTERNATIVE WAYS OF CONCEPTUALIZING THE
RELATIONSHIP BETWEEN EDUCATION
AND DEMOCRACY

In this Part, I explore two related aspects of admissions rituals: the process used to make admissions decisions, and the values or goals that seem to animate different views of the selection process. Starting with the goals that inform the process, I identify four important values associated with access to higher education: individualism, merit, democracy, and upward mobility. Of these four, the value that seems to integrate the other three with higher education is upward mobility. Yet although upward mobility is the value most closely associated with higher education in our collective imagination, all four values are closely intertwined.

Upward mobility and individualism are both core values of the American Dream; they legitimate our democratic ideal of equal opportunity for all. In his history of the French Enlightenment, Marshall Berman describes individualism in perhaps its most favorable light: the right to be yourself, particularly the right not to have your role or status ascribed to you, but to find it for yourself. Individualism was forged in a revolt against feudalism, a system based entirely on ascribed roles. Thus conceived, individualism is deeply connected to democratic ideals of opportunity and upward mobility.

Likewise, mobility in America means not just moving out, but also moving up; it refers to sociological as well as geographical relocation in order to take advantage of opportunity. Upward mobility also suggests that we live in a "classless" society—or at least a society in which class is floating, not fixed. At the same time, higher education has built into it the idea of nobility as well as mobility. After all, universities predate the modern state—they were historically limited to an elite. Higher education grants upward social mobility because it is a status marker, not merely a private contract that matches one's skills with an appropriate educational setting to enhance one's learning. In our society education means opportunity, higher education offers heightened opportunity, and elite higher education confers not just heightened opportunity, but also elevated status. Admissions officers may not view themselves as the "sorting hats" of our society, but many Americans construe the fat or thin envelopes mailed in April as serving just this purpose.

Like upward mobility and individualism, meritocracy formally rejects ascribed roles, awarding opportunity based on individual merit rather than inherited status. Those who succeed are presumed to be those who do their best because of effort, not birth. Meritocracy also associates selectivity with excellence. The opportunity to choose among many qualified applicants not only confers status; it automatically connotes merit. Indeed, merit has two ideas of mobility built into it. It suggests criteria for identifying individual capacity for upward mobility. It also suggests the potential to change individual capacity through educational opportunity—the opportunity to learn in an environment that values excellence, and the opportunity to learn after graduation as the educational credential opens economic and political doors.

* * *

The different processes that educational institutions employ to navigate these goals, however, reveal that the goals are often mutually inconsistent. Individualism, for example, is in tension with a democratic commitment to equal opportunity; not all who have been disadvantaged by reason of their group status benefit equally when some group members are treated as individuals. Moreover, when taken to extremes, individualism can be a divisive force, driving people to find comfort in racial stereotyping and animosity, which becomes the only respectable reason for their own failures. If "right living and hard work do lead to success," then those who fail have no one to blame but themselves—an uncomfortable conclusion. Stuck in dead-end jobs, denied access to selective institutions, or frustrated that they cannot pass on their own privileges to their children, poor and working-class whites sometimes find it easier to blame blacks, or some other scapegoat, for "stealing" the American Dream. Blacks become personally responsible for their own, as well as everyone else's, failures. This form of one-way individualism, which accepts responsibility for success but not failure, is not only dangerously polarizing; it also ignores the experience of racial disadvantage. Many Americans have been disadvantaged precisely because of their group identity; yet this reality does not recede by simple commitments to treat everyone as an individual. Because individualism values the individual over the group, and individual mobility over community stability, it can contribute to more general feelings of dislocation and disable groups of people from participating in public life.

Moreover, systems of selection often end up perpetuating inherited privilege, even as they disavow any connection to ascribed identity or natural aristocracies. A principled commitment to merit selection can perpetuate ascribed identities in covert ways that are often aligned with the identities and experiences of those in a position to define merit. Access to higher education can become a "world in which inequalities of power are natural, and individuals compete for well-being as individuals at the same time they occupy distinct social locations replete with social roles and expectations." Nor are commitments to democratic legitimacy or upward mobility necessarily satisfied by selecting just a few group members to succeed. Indeed, in many ways, the democratic role of higher education has atrophied; without significant infusions of public funds and other potential sources of accountability, it is in danger of becoming a rhetorical but unrealized ideal.

I borrow and adopt three sociological terms—contest, sponsored, and structural mobility—to help assess the often-confusing interaction among the values that underlie admissions decisions. These three concepts describe the means through which individual upward mobility can be achieved: pure competition, discretionary choice, or structural intervention.

A. Contest Mobility

The term "contest mobility" is a very rough proxy for upward mobility achieved through competitive success on standardized tests. Elite status is the goal and is achieved by the candidate's own efforts in an open contest. Numerical valuations of students provide a scoreboard for this contest, which is either won or lost, with no middle ground. Victors assume that their success, and their resulting elite status, is a justly won prize, not an opportunity for further growth. Since aptitude or ability is presumed to be fixed before the race, the best prepared, rather than the most diligent, win. The ultimate goal of contest mobility is the distribution of opportunity based on individual competition and quantifiable measures of merit.

* * *

Contest mobility reinforces the culture of meritocratic entitlement among its primary beneficiaries, upper-middle-class whites, who feel they have played by the rules and therefore deserve to win. [C]ommitment to the narrative of contest mobility has proved resistant to data refuting its validity and continues to remain extremely persuasive, particularly among affluent whites, whose children are the primary beneficiaries of the traditional admissions regime and its overreliance on narrow, "objective" indicia of success. Survey data suggest that well-educated, well-off whites are among the most antagonistic to affirmative action in higher education, even though they are more supportive of programs designed to increase the representation of people of color in legislatures, public sector jobs, and government contracting positions.

Explicit diversity criteria for admissions are controversial. They are seen as throwbacks to an earlier, now rebuked, age that relied on social criteria rather than mathematically derived ones. Critics argue that, because explicit diversity criteria categorize people rather than their output, they leave room for the subjective exercise of racial prejudice, thus subverting the fairness principle. These critics presume that, because scores are "earned," and diversity is not, diversity criteria allow less "deserving" students of color to gain admission over more "qualified" whites, even though the number of whites adversely affected by affirmative action is miniscule. For critics of affirmative action, diversity represents a dramatic departure from the background commitment to objective measures of merit. Diversity is therefore denigrated as both a process and a substantive goal. Diversity criteria bend the rules of contest mobility.

B. Sponsored Mobility

In order to admit more individuals from underrepresented demographic categories, colleges and universities have modified contest mobility by supplementing the contest with discretion. This hybrid alternative, which I call "sponsored mobility," refers to the contemporary version of the elitist system that was in place when James Conant was President of Harvard.*

---

* Following World War II . . . James Conant, then-President of Harvard University [proposed admissions reforms]. Conant wanted to see elite institutions shift from a WASP

In a system of sponsored mobility, modern elites—including admissions officers, alumni, and others who have already enjoyed the spoils of higher education—hand-pick a few candidates to ascend the ladder of higher education. Whereas contest mobility relies solely on a fixed set of "hard" numbers, sometimes called "skinny merit," sponsored mobility relies on an expandable set of "soft" criteria, which might be called "robust merit," to supplement the hard numbers.

Sponsored mobility is an intermediate position between pure contest mobility and structural mobility. This intermediate position allows decisionmakers some room to maneuver; it also acknowledges the limitations of the contest in determining the most "qualified" candidates. The use of soft variables is defended with hard data showing that a purely test-based system suffers from the fallacy of false precision.

Like the hereditary elite system it replaced, modern sponsored mobility retains a discretionary process. * * * This discretion is informed by interviews, letters of recommendation, extracurricular activities, and personal circumstances, including the applicant's race. Sponsored mobility is managed by professional admissions officers for the most part; however, alumni representatives and the headmasters of private secondary schools still play a role in "sponsoring" candidates to elite institutions. Students from elite private schools, for example, still enjoy disproportionate access to Harvard, Yale, and Princeton.

Sponsored mobility enables status elevation at the individual level, but when it comes to issues of diversity, institutions justify it in the name of the group. This justification may take several forms. An institution may believe that diversity in higher education is important because it allows students of all races to "see that people like themselves can succeed" and to "learn the value of interacting with people who are different." Or it may believe that diversity is essential to preserve a "stable polity." Or it may conclude that interracial interaction helps destabilize stereotypes and improve race relations more generally. Whatever the motivation, decisionmakers select a few deserving group members, whose presence then legitimates the institution's educational and democratic missions. The process values associated with sponsored mobility are elite selection and good-faith discretion.

* * *

Sponsored mobility suffers from four serious flaws: First, it enables the unconscious biases of a relatively homogeneous group to thrive by relying on the judgment of individuals who do not have to explain their choices to a third party. Admissions officers rarely enjoy longstanding relationships with the inner-city principals, high school guidance counselors, individual

establishment of hereditary privilege that emphasized entitlement and obligation, to a more democratic accounting that fostered an even greater sense of social responsibility and a less paternalistic view toward public service. In Conant's view, such educated talent would serve the nation in exchange for support from taxpayers. But while Conant wanted to disturb the view that college was a hereditary privilege, he also desired to maintain the elite and selective status of these institutions.

teachers, or community leaders who might know and recommend a student and who can offer information that may not be apparent from the student's file. Second, sponsored mobility does not adequately embrace the idea that individuals change in relation to their environments; thus, although it moderates notions of the intrinsic worth of individuals, sponsored mobility does not adjust sufficiently for the malleability of intelligence in response to effort or encouragement. Third, sponsored mobility perpetuates reliance on the same admissions processes that enabled the current decisionmakers to succeed. Not only do the decisionmakers sponsor students who look like or remind them of themselves, but they also sponsor students who succeeded under the same criteria they faced. This commitment to self-replication is backward-looking; it tends to encourage complacency rather than self-reflection and experimentation. Finally, because adherents of sponsored mobility do not publicly and continuously rethink the relationship between their selection criteria and their mission, their criteria tend to become ends in themselves.

* * *

In the end, sponsored mobility may be only marginally better than contest mobility at allocating access to higher education in a way that is consistent with democratic principles. Although sponsored mobility uses diversity to supplement the hard numbers, it still relies extensively on "the contest" to determine the winners; in this way, diversity becomes a stabilizing norm to legitimate the status quo. Contest mobility at least assumes that individual competition will create churn to upend a complacent view of the status quo. In addition, sponsored mobility gives power to a few decisionmakers to allocate opportunity to "deserving" individuals. Contest mobility gives that power to the institutions that manufacture or referee the rules of the contest, whether a testing bureaucracy or a news magazine; the contest then allocates opportunity to those who "earn" it on their own, with individual competition serving as a tool of accountability. Sponsored mobility, because of its tendency to operate behind closed doors and in isolation from the people who know the candidate best, often lacks such accountability. Because sponsored mobility is still beholden to the hard numbers, operates without much transparency, and tends to reward a limited range of individual attributes, it can also be perceived as a means to co-opt or pacify potential challengers to the governing regime. * * *

C.   Structural Mobility

In addition to contest mobility, which uses hard numbers to measure academic merit, and sponsored mobility, which employs expandable criteria to measure diversity, there is a third conception of the relationship between opportunity and admissions: "structural mobility." A system of structural mobility seeks to identify qualified students in relation to the greater role of higher education in the political, economic, and social structure of community. A commitment to structural mobility means that an institution's commitments to upward mobility, merit, democracy, and individualism are framed and tempered by an awareness of how structures, including the institution's own admissions criteria, tend to privilege some groups of people over others. Structural mobility would require universities to change those admissions policies to provide access to large numbers of people across class, race, and geographic lines, thereby changing the very structure of educational opportunity in this country. Advocates of structural mobility understand that opening access to higher education benefits the society as a whole, not just the individual admittees.

Structural mobility differs from both contest and sponsored mobility, which are dedicated to individual advancement through a market-oriented contest or a "vote of confidence." Structural mobility places the issue of merit firmly on the table and attempts to define it in the context of democratic values. It takes a future-oriented view of the role of higher education in a multiracial democracy by linking ideas about merit directly to ideas about public service and opportunity broadly construed.

Although structural mobility is committed to *community* advancement, it is not inconsistent with ideals of individualism. Rather, structural mobility values the individual in relation to the community. Because it privileges those who have already served, or those who want to serve, their communities, structural mobility focuses society's educational resources on those who are most likely to fulfill the aims of democracy.

For proponents of structural mobility, contest mobility's preoccupation with competitive individualism fails to fulfill Conant's dream of assembling a more publicly spirited elite; contest mobility promotes short-term winners of the wrong game. Sponsored mobility does a better job of elevating individuals who remain connected to their communities or to the taxpayers who helped subsidize their success, but only through a small segment of all admittees. Structural mobility extends the emphasis on community affiliation and linked fate to all admittees, not just those who bring racial diversity to college campuses. It links the institution and its students to their communities, thereby advancing the goals of public education at the local, state, and national levels. An institution committed to structural mobility might measure its success, for example, not only by the students it admits but also by the changes it precipitates in educational opportunity at the K–12 level. Finally, structural mobility is sustained by a broadly democratic and participatory process of self-reflective and racially literate experimentalism. In a world of structural mobility, individuals are given access to educational opportunities not because they win a "contest" or because they have been hand-picked by elites, but because the relevant stakeholders come together to make a set of public-minded choices.

* * *

All of the salient features of structural mobility—a commitment to public service, the participation of grassroots voluntary organizations or indigenous actors in the construction of the program, and the escalator effect that generates broad public support—connect to democratic values.

III: ENTER THE SUPREME COURT:
THE PROMISE AND THE CAUTION OF USING RACE
AS A LENS

Selective public institutions, such as the University of Michigan and the University of Michigan Law School, are in the position to choose among a number of qualified candidates who can do the work and be expected to graduate. Because their admissions decisions have broad social purposes and important individual consequences, these institutions must be able to articulate and defend their admissions criteria and processes to their respective constituencies. Four elements of the Supreme Court's decisions in *Grutter* and *Gratz* seem particularly relevant to the challenge facing institutions of higher education like the University of Michigan that are committed to maintaining their elite status while producing racially literate graduates who contribute to both the campus community and the larger society. These elements are: the value of race-conscious diversity as it is connected to the university's educational mission; a robust view of diversity that includes class and geography, not just race; the role of democratic values; and the relationship between data, demographics, and reflective practice to inform the way institutions operationalize the concepts of diversity and democracy.

* * *

Although *Gratz* identifies how numbers cannot capture an individual's worth (or at least are over- and underinclusive as used by the University of Michigan's undergraduate program), numbers can provide relevant information in the aggregate about relationships of groups of individuals to economic, social, and political power. And while numbers do not tell us all that we need to know about an individual (if we respect the notion that individuals are unique and cannot be compared along a single metric), numbers can provide context to help situate individuals within larger domains. Numbers are informative: they are tools for assisting in making judgments but should not be confused with proxies for those judgments. If numbers should not be outcome-determinative about race, then neither should they be outcome-determinative as proxies for individual "merit" generally.

There is a direct relationship between efforts to quantify race and efforts to quantify merit. Both are driven in part by efficiency concerns. In addition, the quantification of merit hides the discretion of those who develop the quantification tools—standardized tests—which are normed to reward upper-class and upper-middle-class whites. Thus, the decision by institutions like the University of Michigan's undergraduate program to use "hard edges" to capture race is a recognized compensatory response to the "hard edges" that define quantifiable notions of merit. Both are over- and underinclusive categories. But it is the underinclusiveness of the hard variables that contributes to the hyper-visibility of race.

To the extent "merit" is considered largely quantifiable—as opposed to a set of qualitative judgments that are essentially educated guesses about future potential made in the context of an institution's educational and

public missions—individualized assessments that include race as one variable are doomed to be somewhat mechanistic, albeit less transparently so, in
order to compensate for the preferences embedded in the hard variables.
This use of race is also vulnerable to continued attack by those who feel
excluded by the admissions choices being made (mostly working-class and
poor whites, but status-seeking upper-middle-class whites as well), unless
those choices reflect not only concerns about democratic legitimacy but also
a democratic process.

Yet the likely immediate consequence of *Grutter* is that trusted admissions officials are now freer to make their decisions without a great deal of
transparency. They need not give reasons for their choices, as long as they
avoid the mechanistic use of race. If, for example, the institution has a
backward-looking purpose, then it may rely on contest mobility and continue to use admission as a reward or prize. Many universities, however, do
not like to speak of their admissions slots as rewards; law schools in
particular have a mission to train public citizens who serve their clients
and society as a whole. Such institutions might therefore embrace sponsored mobility, since they may use subjective criteria to supplement the
hard variables in making predictions about who among their applicants are
likely to serve the public. * * *

There is a caution, in other words, voiced by the very different dissents
of Justices Ginsburg and Thomas. The caution is that elite self-replication
is the problem, not affirmative action. In this sense, sponsored mobility will
be co-opted by elites in the same way contest mobility was. Diversity will
not be an aesthetic fad; instead, it will become a fig leaf to hide a
commitment to the status quo. If admissions decisions are to be made in a
more democratic fashion—that is, with transparency and accountability to
the institution's public mission and to the taxpayers who subsidize it—then
much more than the physical aesthetics of these choices needs to be
obvious.

        * * *

Like Conant's version of contest mobility, which used "merit" to
replace "character" and ended up reproducing privilege, sponsored mobility
may also turn out to benefit only those who are already advantaged. It is
not the goal of diversity that is the problem. Nor does adverting to
democratic legitimacy justify that goal. The problem is the failure to adopt
safeguards that ensure that the goal remains connected to its justificatory
principle.

The *Grutter* opinion, in conjunction with Chief Justice Rehnquist's
opinion for the Court in *Gratz*, holds two other potential limitations as well
as a promise. Although the Court expects institutions to sponsor individuals of color rather than racially categorized groups, and to revisit their use
of race periodically in light of the availability of race-neutral alternatives,
the Court still, paradoxically, requires institutions to consider race differently from the way they consider merit. Simultaneously, the approval of
limited forms of race-consciousness may invite complacency rather than
vigilance. However, the Court's quixotic hope that consideration of race will

be unnecessary in twenty-five years may instead prompt universities to engage the public in a larger conversation about what type of society we want to live in and what higher education institutions must do to bring us closer to that goal. Ultimately, the promise is that the introduction of a soft deadline will trigger bold new experiments in which universities demonstrate renewed involvement in K–12 education, build relationships with local communities to garner more support, and consider multiple ways to realize their twin goals of educational excellence and democratic opportunity.

IV.   PURSUING THE PROMISE AND HEEDING THE WARNING:
RACIAL LITERACY AND THE ROLE OF HIGHER
EDUCATION IN OUR DEMOCRACY

Although the *Grutter* and *Gratz* decisions vindicate the principle of diversity, they do not explain how institutions of higher education should use that principle to help make admissions decisions. This lack of guidance appears to be intentional: as long as institutions do not weight race so heavily that it overdetermines admissions outcomes, their good faith is essentially presumed. It may be that Justice O'Connor and the *Grutter* majority presume good faith because they want the meaning of diversity to emerge from a process of experimentation, feedback, and reflection. It may be that the Court is not prepared to articulate a national definition of diversity and instead prefers for educational institutions to work out the meaning of diversity locally over time. This explanation is consistent with the way Justice O'Connor interpreted narrow tailoring in the context of sponsored mobility, as well as her preference for voluntary self-correction in other contexts.

To the extent that an institution is committed to diversifying its student body, the Court's lack of specificity gives the institution leeway to experiment with ways to link the broad concept of diversity to the specific educational mission of the institution and the public values it aims to serve. For institutions committed to racial diversity, the three forms of mobility are all presumably constitutional as long as they do not use race categorically, overtly, and decisively to fix outcomes. An institution may consider race implicitly in conjunction with class and geography, as is done in percentage plans; it may consider race explicitly as part of a holistic evaluation; and it may consider other indicia of merit that provide democratic legitimacy, such as evidence of an applicant's service commitments, pluck in the face of disadvantage, or residence in an underrepresented geographic area.

In the short term, individualized, holistic review of all candidates will bring colleges and law schools into compliance with *Grutter*. Individualized review will allow institutions to admit students of color "in meaningful numbers" to ensure that students from underrepresented communities contribute to the character of the school and, in the case of law schools, to the legal profession. But in the long run, using affirmative action simply to perpetuate the status quo will likely backfire for practical, financial, and political reasons. Universities may be dogged by complaints that they are not really following *Grutter*, that their methods are too subjective, that their procedures lack transparency, or that their policies leave the decision-making power firmly in the grasp of admissions bureaucrats. Moreover, institutions committed to affirmative action as an add-on will be hard-pressed to keep up with changing demographics: admissions practices that depend on the language of critical mass may unintentionally result in an upper-limit quota that artificially suppresses the number of black and Latino admittees, despite the burgeoning number of such students in the eighteen-to twenty-four-year-old age cohort.

   * * *

To gain a deeper understanding of the problem while garnering public confidence in their admissions practices, universities need to become racially literate. A racially literate institution uses race as a diagnostic device, an analytic tool, and an instrument of process.

As a diagnostic or evidentiary device, race helps identify the underlying problems affecting higher education. Racial literacy begins by redefining racism as a structural problem rather than a purely individual one. Race reveals the ways in which demography is often destiny—not just for people of color, but for working-class and poor whites as well. Race constantly influences access to public resources, while also revealing the influence of class and geographical variables. Racial literacy, therefore, continuously links the underrepresentation of blacks and Latinos to the underrepresentation of poor people generally. At a minimum, it reminds public institutions of higher learning that the "idea of access is deeply embedded in [their] genetic code" and thus, the underrepresentation of certain demographic groups illuminates their failure to fulfill their public responsibilities.

When race is engaged directly, as it was in Texas following *Hopwood*, [78 F.3d 932 (5th Cir. 1996),] it can shed light on the confluence of forces that are truly responsible for current public dissatisfaction and that adversely affect people of all colors. At one time, for example, it was commonly accepted that each generation should publicly subsidize educational opportunity for the next generation. Yet today, higher education is no longer the engine of upward mobility and democratic opportunity that it was once imagined to be. Nor has it remained focused on its original purpose: to train leaders who then go on to serve society. Instead, it has become "a national personnel department" that sorts and ranks people and grants "the high scorers a general, long-duration ticket to high status that can be cashed in anywhere." Selective universities, in particular, use their admissions practices to generate a permanent governing elite, in ways that are inconsistent with democratic values of equal opportunity, accountability, and service. * * *

Racial literacy sees the decline in government investment in higher education, along with the accompanying justificatory rhetoric of individual responsibility and individual "desert," as deeply problematic. Racial literacy suggests that admitting a more diverse class of students not only benefits individual students, but is also necessary to realize the social function and values of higher education, including democratic access, equal opportunity, and public service. The idea that each person is alone responsible for her fate and her tuition has allowed government support for higher education to plummet while costs skyrocket. Meanwhile, the goal of training future leaders—once the noble ambition of public institutions and their signature contribution to society—continues to atrophy.

* * *

Racial literacy helps institutions as they choose between contest, sponsored, and structural mobility. Using racially literate criteria to select among the three kinds of upward mobility is permissible under *Grutter*, is not jeopardized by *Gratz*, and is not only defensible, but may be politically necessary. Racial literacy discloses how all of these admissions processes use sociological proxies for assessing "merit" and future potential. Contest mobility purports to rank individuals, yet it relies on data that is closely aligned with group, not individual, attributes and assets, such as parents' education, grandparents' socioeconomic status, and other indicators of privilege. Sponsored mobility also purports to rank individuals, yet it fails to take account of group bias, which may depress individual performance, tilt the preferences of individual sponsors, and systematically distort the opportunity structure for talented individuals. Each type of mobility puts on the table a different understanding of whether merit is fixed or contextual, stable or responsive, real or imagined, performative or service-oriented. By situating merit within structures of opportunity, racial literacy encourages consideration of qualities that current admissions policies overlook. As a result, racially literate yet selective institutions may be able to relax their efforts to predict short-term outcomes and focus more on encouraging long-term commitments to service and community leadership.

* * *

Racial literacy also has a process dimension that uses race to guide participatory problem solving and accountability. In order to change the way race is understood, race has to be directly addressed rather than ignored. Race is often the subtext of public conversations about institutional goals. In fact, informed discussion about why education is now more desirable but less affordable or accessible often gets drowned out by inflammatory and polarizing rhetoric about race or by equally divisive rhetoric about individual responsibility and merit. By contrast, discussion among a diverse group of citizens about the ways race reveals rather than produces these social costs helps institutional policies become more transparent and thus more legitimate. * * *

Institutions could also make their processes more transparent by taking the views of various constituencies into account, even as they develop in the short term their new, holistic methods of reviewing candidate files. A broadly participatory process that includes the relevant stakeholders also helps satisfy the legitimacy concerns articulated by Justice O'Connor and modified by Justice Thomas's critique of elitism. Such a process would include professional educators and administrators, and would respect their expertise and specialized knowledge. But this process would also seek opportunities to communicate openly and engage with a group that is sufficiently diverse and informed to be critical, to mitigate the tendency of socially isolated decisionmakers to select those like themselves, to pay attention to issues of race and power, and to consider the connection between admissions and pedagogy.

* * *

It is out of a deliberative and interactive process that the institution should create its mission and explore the possibilities of reconstituting itself through admissions rituals. Such a process may generate a hybrid form of contest and sponsored mobility, similar to the choices made by the University of Michigan Law School and by the college post-*Gratz*. It is just as plausible, however, that a process that includes relevant stakeholders in a larger public conversation may prefer social engineering to yield structural mobility, similar to the GI Bill and current military programs, which provide educational opportunity in exchange for national or community service. Whatever the outcome, the process of choosing among contest, sponsored, and structural mobility must be understood as a political act with important societal, not just individual, consequences.

* * *

VI. CONCLUSION

* * * The *Grutter* and *Gratz* decisions may ultimately usher in a historical moment in which institutions of higher education explore issues of access to education and the scarcity of resources—issues that make limitations on that access deeply problematic in democratic terms. Universities need to explain themselves better to the broader public through a conversation rather than a declaration. It is not simply time for a public relations battle; rather, it is an occasion to align educational opportunity with its cousin, democratic participation. The question becomes who should get opportunity given the long-term goals of the institution or the needs of the larger society, rather than who "deserves" a prize because she won a race or because her presence will improve the institution's rankings in a news magazine. To find the answer, university leaders need to consider the long-term needs of the institution, the concerns of local, regional, and national constituencies, and the stability of the larger society, in a manner that is consistent with the expectation that the university will produce a new generation of citizens capable of assuming a broad range of leadership roles. The post-*Grutter* moment is an opportunity to talk more openly about, and investigate more thoroughly and in contemporary terms, the ways in which race helps reveal the relationship between education and democracy. It is a chance to make ourselves more racially literate and to understand the ways in which the choice among contest, sponsored, and structural mobility is a fundamentally political act.

By viewing their admissions decisions as political acts, in the virtuous sense of the phrase, universities can open the door to greater public support and confidence. Ultimately, this reevaluation of admissions choices may enable universities to join with others to create institutional structures that respond to the future while holding on to the best practices of the past. At the very least, it has the potential to transform the discussion from one fixated on ersatz preferences to one that actively confronts the reality of higher education's role in a multiracial democracy with the promise that education makes to us all.

NOTES AND QUESTIONS

1. **Origins of affirmative action.** In March 1961, President John F. Kennedy issued Executive Order 10925, in an effort to end employment discrimination among government contractors. It read in part, "The Contractor will take *affirmative action*, to insure that applicants are employed, and that employees are treated during employment, without regard to their race, creed, color, or national origin." Steven M. Cahn, *Introduction, in* THE AFFIRMATIVE ACTION DEBATE, xi (Steven M. Cahn ed., 2d ed. 2002) (emphasis added). Affirmative action emerged during the civil rights movement as a strategy for helping African Americans overcome the debilitating effects of racial oppression. It has since targeted other minority groups, notably Hispanics, Native Americans, and persons of Asian descent. Affirmative action refers to an array of programs that use race as a factor in the allotment of resources with the intent of benefiting racial minorities. It may take the form of generally increasing outreach to minorities, counting race as a "plus" factor in the allocation of resources, or directing a set amount of resources to minorities in specific "percentage plans." For an overview of federal affirmative action programs, see SAMUEL LEITER & WILLIAM M. LEITER, AFFIRMATIVE ACTION IN ANTIDISCRIMINATION LAW AND POLICY 7–22 (2002).

Affirmative action is among the most controversial issues in American law and politics, evoking strong feelings in both supporters and opponents. This controversy has been accompanied by uncertainty in the Supreme Court, which in thirty years of affirmative action jurisprudence has struggled to find a consistent legal framework with which to treat the issue. Political and public support for affirmative action has also been inconsistent. Democrats and the political left have historically supported affirmative action, while Republicans and conservatives have opposed it. In polls, the public generally expresses support for the goals of racial equality and diversity, but is less supportive of specific affirmative action measures. PETER H. SCHUCK, DIVERSITY IN AMERICA 170–72 (2003).

2. **The constitutionality of affirmative action.** Challenger to the constitutionality of affirmative action rest on the Equal Protection Clause of the Fourteenth Amendment. The Fourteenth Amendment reads, in part:

> *Section 1.* . . . No State shall make or enforce any law which shall abridge the privileges or immunities of citizens of the United States; nor shall any State deprive any person of life, liberty, or

property, without due process of law; nor deny any person within its jurisdiction the equal protection of the laws.

* * *

Section 5. The Congress shall have power to enforce, by appropriate legislation, the provisions of this article.

U.S. Const. amend. XIV, §§ 2, 5.

The Thirteenth, Fourteenth, and Fifteenth Amendments were passed in the wake of the Civil War to try and protect the rights of the South's newly-freed black population. These "Reconstruction Amendments" were deemed necessary because, after the Civil War, the Southern states quickly started passing so-called "Black Codes," which returned former slaves to a position of complete social and political subordination. Geoffrey Stone, et al., Constitutional Law 432–33 (4th ed. 2001). The language of the amendments appears to afford minorities strong protections against governmental discrimination. However, in the years during and after Reconstruction, the Supreme Court read the amendments narrowly, typified in the *Slaughter-House Cases*, 83 U.S. (16 Wall.) 36 (1873), and especially *Plessy v. Ferguson*, 163 U.S. 537 (1896), in which the court validated the Jim Crow system of "separate but equal." The Court interpreted the amendments as having one overriding purpose, the freeing of the slaves, and showed little inclination to interpret them more ambitiously. Bruce Ackerman, We the People: Foundations 81–105 (1991). As a result, governmentally sponsored racial discrimination persisted well into the twentieth century. The civil rights movement of the 1950s and 60s was in many ways an attempt to fulfill the initial promise of Reconstruction and its three constitutional amendments, and many consider affirmative action a valuable tool for the realization of this goal. *See* Eric Schnapper, *Affirmative Action and the Legislative History of the Fourteenth Amendment*, 71 Va. L. Rev. 753 (1985).

Affirmative action raises Fourteenth Amendment questions because by seeking to promote a remedy for racially subordinated groups, it does not adhere to the formalistic notions of equality. This is not to say it is unconstitutional. The term "equal protection" has bedeviled courts who have tried to elucidate its meaning and apply it to governmental classifications, but some principles have emerged. It does *not* mean that all laws must treat or effect all classes of persons identically. There are many federal, state, and local laws that single out certain groups for inclusion or exclusion in receiving a benefit or suffering a detriment. However, the guarantee of equal protection also means that there are classifications that the government *cannot* lawfully make. It has been the task of the Supreme Court to decide what these unlawful classifications are.

The modern Court's approach to this problem has been to create a system of levels of review when dealing with laws that treat a discreet group or groups differently from others. The two baseline levels of review are "rational basis" review and "strict scrutiny" review, though as *Metro Broadcasting* shows these are not exclusive. The majority of classifications made by the government are subject to low-level, "rational basis" review and are overwhelmingly, but not always, upheld. These are laws which the Court believes are a proper use of governmental power and are rationally related to a legitimate governmental interest. However, the Court has held that some classifications are, by their very nature, "suspect" and should be examined with heightened scrutiny. Race is the classic "suspect" classification, and classifications based on race are normally subject to "strict scrutiny," the most stringent form of judicial review.

Some examples may help to flesh out this discussion. In *New York City Transit Authority v. Beazer*, 440 U.S. 568 (1979), the Court asked whether it was constitutional for the Transit Authority to exclude from employment users of methadone, a drug used by heroin addicts as part of their rehabilitation treatment. The Court concluded that safety concerns provided a sufficient "rational basis" for this special classification, and that it was not constitutionally significant that some qualified potential employees would be injured by the plan. The Court said that because the law "does not circumscribe a class of persons characterized by some unpopular trait or affiliation, it does not create or reflect any likelihood of bias on the part of the ruling majority." *Id.* at 593. *Beazer* is an example of a governmental classification which does not affect people equally, but is nevertheless constitutional. Under rational basis review, the Court treats classifications with a great deal of deference, and explicitly does not examine the wisdom or effectiveness of the law.

On the other end of the spectrum are laws that explicitly disadvantage persons based on their race. In *Strauder v. West Virginia*, 100 U.S. (10 Otto) 303 (1880), a West Virginia law which said that blacks may not serve on juries was invalidated as blatant discrimination, which is constitutionally impermissible. *Strauder* is an older case, but today this kind of classification would be subjected to "strict scrutiny" and would obviously be invalidated.

Traditionally, rational basis review nearly always meant a law would be upheld, and strict scrutiny review almost guaranteed disallowance. There are, however, important exceptions. For an example of a law examined under rational basis but nevertheless invalidated, see *City of Cleburne v. Cleburne Living Center*, 473 U.S. 432 (1985) (holding unconstitutional a law which negatively affected the mentally retarded because it had no rational relation to a legitimate governmental interest, but was instead motivated by "negative attitudes, or fear"). For an example of racial classifications upheld under strict scrutiny, see *Korematsu v. United States*, 323 U.S. 214 (1944) (upholding the internment of Japanese–Americans during World War II because the action was motivated by "pressing public necessity" rather than "racial antagonism"). Note that *Korematsu* has been harshly criticized. *See, e.g.,* Eugene V. Rostow, *The Japanese–American Cases—A Disaster, in* THE MASS INTERNMENT OF JAPANESE AMERICANS AND THE QUEST FOR LEGAL REDRESS 189 (Charles McClain ed., 1994).

Between the extremes of *Beazer* and *Strauder*, there are many laws which do not clearly fit into a certain level of scrutiny. These include laws which do not explicitly make racial classifications but have disparate effects on minorities, or laws that make classifications that are less clearly "suspect," such as with women or homosexuals. See, generally, STONE ET AL., *supra* at 514–53. Affirmative action programs fall into this problematic category because of their unique position as laws which make racial classifications in the interest of *benefiting* racial minorities. This is using racial classification in quite a different way than the law in *Strauder*, and Courts have struggled to determine what level of scrutiny should apply to affirmative action programs.

3. The Bakke case. The Supreme Court first ruled on the substance of affirmative action in *Regents of University of California v. Bakke*, 438 U.S. 265 (1978). *Bakke* established the principle that voluntary use by government employers of race-conscious goals and timetables to remedy prior discrimination is not per se unconstitutional, but that explicit "quotas" are not allowable. The case involved an admissions plan at the University of California Davis Medical School, whereby sixteen seats out of a hundred were reserved for minority applicants. Four justices voted to uphold this aggressive affirmative action plan. Four justices voted to strike it down, but not on constitutional grounds. The deciding vote came from Justice Powell, who first articulated the view that affirmative action programs should be subjected to strict scrutiny. He wrote that all racial classifications, including those that are "benign," are suspect and should be treated under the strict scrutiny test. He did not believe that a general history of prior discrimination created a compelling governmental interest because in the *Bakke* case there were no judicial, administrative, or legislative findings of prior racial discrimination, and there were no findings that discrimination was a pervasive problem at the medical school. Justice Powell's other major contribution was his treatment of diversity as a rationale for affirmative action. He wrote that the interest in a diverse student body was reason enough to allow race to be used in admission decisions, but not a rigid system that isolated sixteen spots from competition with others. Justice Powell wrote only for himself, but his opinion has proven to be very influential in affirmative action decisions. Since *Bakke*, the thorny issues associated with affirmative action have led to an often sharply divided Court and few clear guidelines.

Justice Powell retired in 1987, and Justice Kennedy's appointment was seen as creating a strong conservative voting bloc on the Court. *Croson* was the first time that the Court issued a majority opinion in an affirmative action case. Many believed the case marked a shift away from a Supreme Court that had been relatively receptive to affirmative action programs. Taking a rather literalistic view of the Fourteenth Amendment, the Court found that the fact that "the Richmond Plan denies certain citizens the opportunity to compete for a fixed percentage of public contracts based solely upon their races" meant that the plan must be subjected to strict scrutiny, which it was found not to meet. The decision in *Metro Broadcasting* was therefore something of a surprise. It marked the first time a non-remedial rationale was used to validate an affirmative action plan. The other important deviation made in *Metro Broadcasting* was its use of an intermediate level of scrutiny in assessing the FCC plan.

The regime of intermediate scrutiny in affirmative action cases was short lived. In 1995, only 5 years after *Metro Broadcasting* was decided, the Court decided *Adarand Constructors v. Pena*, 515 U.S. 200 (1995), the last major case prior to *Grutter*. A majority of the Court overruled *Metro Broadcasting*'s intermediate scrutiny standard and held that strict scrutiny applies to *all* affirmative action programs. The attitude toward affirmative action among the members of the Court had shifted once again with the addition of Justice Thomas, and the decision evidences a loss of confidence in Congress's ability to deal with race. *See* Paul J. Mishkin, *Foreword: The Making of a Turning Point—*Metro *and* Adarand, 84 CAL. L. REV. 875 (1996). Justice Scalia wrote in concurrence that there should be *no* group-based remedies for discrimination, only for individual cases of active discrimination, but a majority of the court has never accepted this view. For a detailed review of the Supreme Court's affirmative action jurisprudence prior to *Grutter*, see GIRARDEAU A. SPANN, THE LAW OF AFFIRMATIVE ACTION (2000).

As these cases show, the Court has struggled to find a consistent view on affirmative action, disagreeing over what legal standard should apply and more generally about the value of affirmative action. In the public arena, affirmative action is perhaps best known for its contentiousness. Depending on how the issue is framed, the arguments on both sides are appealing. What makes affirmative action problematic is that it is not intended to compensate for specific acts of overt discrimination; rather, it works more broadly to attempt to correct the general discrimination that has led to the economic and political inequality that exists for minorities. In this way, it focuses on groups rather than individuals. Supporters of affirmative action believe that given this country's history of racial prejudice, race-conscious programs are necessary to compensate for the disadvantage that has been suffered by minorities. Discrimination is still a problem that cannot be overcome through colorblind policies, and active steps must be taken to eclipse racial injustice. In addition, diversity is a valuable goal in a society where racial misunderstanding has so often led to prejudice. Opponents argue that it is wrong to use race as a basis for the allocation of resources, no matter who the intended beneficiaries are. They believe it is unfair to reserve resources for minorities at the expense of whites who have not engaged in discriminatory conduct, and unjust to have "innocent whites" today pay for the sins of past generations. Many also argue that affirmative action has a stigmatizing effect on blacks, casting doubts on the legitimacy of their accomplishments as possibly the result of special treatment.

For more on the affirmative action debate, see generally Erwin Chemerinsky, *Making Sense of the Affirmative Action Debate*, *in* CIVIL RIGHTS AND SOCIAL WRONGS 86 (John Higham ed., 1997); BARBARA R. BERGMANN, IN DEFENSE OF AFFIRMATIVE ACTION (1996); Ronald Dworkin, *Affirming Affirmative Action*, N.Y. REV. OF BOOKS, Oct. 28, 1998, at 91; JOHN E. ROEMER, EQUALITY OF OPPORTUNITY (1998). On the possible stigmatization of the beneficiaries of affirmative action, see Linda Hamilton Krieger, *Civil Rights*

Perestroika: Intergroup Relations After Affirmative Action, 86 CAL. L. REV. 1251 (1998).

4.   Affirmative action and equal protection. The Fourteenth Amendment says nothing about heightened standards of scrutiny for racial classifications. What precisely is it that makes racial classifications so troubling and suited for heightened scrutiny? Are they illegitimate in themselves, or only in the context of this country's history of racism against blacks and other minorities? What is the difference between a class of shortmen and a class of racial minorities? In a famous footnote in *United States v. Carolene Products*, 304 U.S. 144 (1938), Justice Stone argued that "more searching judicial inquiry" for classifications involving race may be necessary because "prejudice against discrete and insular minorities may be a special condition, which tends seriously to curtail the operation of those political processes ordinarily to be relied upon to protect minorities." Consider Charles R. Lawrence, *The Id, the Ego, and Equal Protection: Reckoning with Unconscious Racism*, 39 STAN. L. REV. 317, 322 (1987):

> Traditional notions of intent do not reflect the fact that decisions about racial matters are influenced in large part by factors that can be characterized as neither intentional—in the sense that certain outcomes are self-consciously sought—nor unintentional— in the sense that the outcomes are random, fortuitous, and uninfluenced by the decisionmaker's beliefs, desires, and wishes.

> Americans share a common historical and cultural heritage in which racism has played and still plays a dominant role. Because of this shared experience, we also inevitably share many ideas, attitudes, and beliefs that attach significance to an individual's race and induce negative feelings and opinions about nonwhites. To the extent that this cultural belief system has influenced all of us, we are all racists. At the same time, most of us are unaware of our racism. We do not recognize the ways in which our cultural experience has influenced our beliefs about race or the occasions on which those beliefs affect our actions. In other words, a large part of the behavior that produces racial discrimination is influenced by unconscious racial motivation.

It is evident from this language that strict scrutiny was intended as a means of *protecting* minorities from the effects of discrimination, be it overt or unconscious. Ironically, the use of strict scrutiny in affirmative action cases has led to the defeat of laws intended to *benefit* racial minorities. Does this prove that strict scrutiny in affirmative action programs is inappropriate? What aspect of affirmative action should most inform the Court's decision about the proper level of scrutiny—its goals, its effects, or its actual operation?

In *Washington v. Davis*, 426 U.S. 229 (1976), the Court held that a law that only disproportionately impacts a minority group, but is not race-specific in its application, will be subject to rational basis review. Is there a meaningful difference between a law that explicitly disadvantages minorities and one that does so only in effect? How can the Court justify treating laws which empirically disadvantage minorities with rational basis review, while treating affirmative action laws with strict scrutiny review simply because they explicitly classify using race? For a discussion of the equal protection clause and affirmative action, see MICHEL ROSENFELD, AFFIRMATIVE ACTION AND JUSTICE (1991).

5.   Can racial classifications be benign? Affirmative action programs are considered "benign" forms of discrimination because they burden the majority, and are regarded as protecting rather than harming the political interests of minorities. Many opponents of affirmative action doubt the ability of the government to make benign racial classifications. Some believe that "benign racial classification" is a contradiction in terms, and that given the troubled history of racial classifications in this country the government should *never* allocate resources or give preference on the basis of race. This position is strongly articulated in Justice Kennedy's dissent in *Metro Broadcasting*, when he writes that the Court is not able to identify readily which racial classifications are benign, and equates the logic of affirmative action with the Supreme Court's infamous decision in *Plessy*. Is it true that racial classifications are so dangerous that they should never be used? Why should it be difficult to differentiate between laws that are designed to benefit a minority population and those that are designed to oppress minorities?

6.   Strict or intermediate scrutiny? Inside the courtroom, perhaps the most controversial issue regarding affirmative action has been what legal standard should apply. As Justice O'Connor wrote in *Croson*, this is not a mere quibble over lawyers' words. Strict scrutiny is a very difficult standard to meet, and prior to *Grutter* no affirmative action program had survived strict scrutiny. Many predicted that *Adarand* would mark the end of affirmative action programs, believing that strict scrutiny would be "strict in theory, fatal in fact." *Grutter* has proved these predictions wrong, at least in the context of higher education. Why was the intermediate scrutiny used in *Metro Broadcasting* abandoned so quickly?

Strict scrutiny dictates that "benign" racial classifications will only be upheld if they are narrowly tailored to achieve a compelling governmental interest. How does Justice O'Connor apply strict scrutiny in *Grutter*? Do you agree that diversity in a university is a compelling state interest? Is it likely that a set-aside program such as the one in *Croson* can meet the strict scrutiny standard? In limited circumstances, the Court has found the remedying of past discrimination to be compelling governmental interest, see *Shaw v. Hunt*, 517 U.S. 899 (1996), but has stipulated that the remedy must attack "identified discrimination" which must be identified with specificity. Why is the remedying of generalized, pervasive discrimination which certainly existed at one time in this country not a compelling interest? Note Justice Marshall's strong assertion in *Croson* that the "interest in ensuring that the government does not reflect and reinforce prior discrimination is every bit as strong as the interest in eliminating private discrimination...."

The Court in *Croson* believed that attempts to remedy generalized, societal discrimination "[have] no logical stopping point." Is the absence of a clear stopping point sufficient reason to invalidate a law? In *Croson*, why did the majority determine that strict scrutiny was necessary? What were the majority's specific objections to the affirmative action plan in question? Was it appropriate for the court to speculate that the real motivation for the law was not past discrimination but simply political favoritism among African-Americans, who held a majority of City Council seats? What is the relevancy of the dissent's mention of Richmond's history as the capital of the confederacy?

Metro Broadcasting represents a relatively brief period of time when the Supreme Court applied an intermediate level of scrutiny to affirmative action programs, holding that the governmental interest served by a given program need only be "important." How does the Court rationalize this lessened standard? How much was the Court's decision in *Metro Broadcasting* a result of deference to Congressional findings and the extensive review procedures of the FCC? Justice O'Connor contends in her *Metro Broadcasting* dissent that treating groups differently based on race "may stigmatize those groups singled out for different treatment and may create considerable tension with the Nation's widely shared commitment to evaluating individuals upon their individual merit." 497 U.S. at 604. What concern is it of the Court's if the beneficiaries of affirmative action are stigmatized in the eyes of some? Does such a commitment to individual merit exist in this country? What "merits" must one possess to secure a broadcasting license? Is it possible that some racial tension must be tolerated to correct the effects of America's history of racism?

7. Colorblindness versus race-consciousness. Justice Blackmun wrote in *Bakke* "In order to get beyond racism, we must first take account of race. There is no other way. And in order to treat some persons equally, we must treat them differently." 438 U.S. at 407. At the core of the debate over affirmative action is disagreement over whether it is possible to overcome the inequality caused by past racial discrimination without taking race into account in the remedy. Implicit in this debate is further disagreement over whether discrimination itself continues to be a problem. Some believe that while overt racism is seldom expressed in public, unconscious discrimination continues to be a very real problem, despite the improvements in race relations that have taken place over the last fifty years. Not only are colorblind solutions ineffective, they are actually detrimental because they mask the discrimination that still occurs and disengaging whites from the unique problems facing minorities. Consider:

> I believe that [whites] today, raised white in a racist society, are often ridden with white solipsism—not the consciously held belief that one race is inherently superior to all others, but a tunnel-vision which simply does not see nonwhite experience or existence as precious or significant, unless in spasmodic, impotent guilt-reflexes, which have little or no long-term, continuing momentum or political usefulness.... A remedial regime predicated on color-

blindness will have little influence at this deep level of social and legal consciousness because it cannot adequately challenge white attitudes or recognize a role for black self-definition.

T. Alexander Aleinikoff, *A Case for Race-consciousness*, 91 COLUM. L. REV. 1060, 1060 (1991). *See also* Williams, *supra* at 544; LANI GUINIER & GERALD TORRES, THE MINER'S CANARY: ENLISTING RACE, RESISTING POWER, TRANSFORMING DEMOCRACY 32–67 (2002).

Conservative opponents of affirmative action argue that discrimination based on race is largely a thing of the past, and that colorblind policies that simply treat everyone equally can be effective. To overcome racial prejudice and inequality we must move beyond race and treat people as individuals, because the race of a person tells us nothing about her abilities, beliefs, moral worthiness, etc. *See* STEPHAN THERNSTROM & ABIGAIL THERNSTROM, AMERICA IN BLACK AND WHITE, ONE NATION, INDIVISIBLE: RACE IN MODERN AMERICA (1997). Whether or not discrimination continues to be a problem, there is considerable evidence that whites and blacks continue to have strongly divergent opinions on issues of race. *See* DONALD R. KINDER & LYNN SANDERS, DIVIDED BY COLOR: RACIAL POLITICS AND DEMOCRATIC IDEALS (1996). For a rebuttal of the Thernstroms' position that examines a range of issues, including education, crime, poverty, and voting, see Michael K. Brown, Martin Carnoy et al., WHITEWASHING RACE: THE MYTH OF A COLOR-BLIND SOCIETY (2003).

8.   Purpose of affirmative action. As *Croson*, *Metro Broadcasting*, and *Grutter* show, affirmative action programs have been employed for a variety of purposes in a variety of contexts. The original rationale for affirmative action was to remedy inequality by directing the allocation of resources to those who have been historically disadvantaged by discrimination. The "set-aside" program in *Croson* was premised on the desire to counteract past discrimination and correct the disparities in access to wealth that exists between whites and minorities. The objection opponents make to set-aside programs is that it is unfair and counterproductive to disadvantage those who have not themselves engaged in the harmful, discriminatory conduct. In *Croson*, why was the large disparity between the percentage of blacks in the general population and their share of contracting dollars not proof enough that discrimination had put black businesses at a disadvantage? Does the Court offer any other explanation for this disparity?

Who was most likely to benefit from the plan in *Metro Broadcasting*? The broadcast licenses at issue in *Metro Broadcasting* are valuable commodities, yet the court uses a diversity rationale to uphold the plan. What are the economic implications of the decision? *Metro Broadcasting* has been harshly criticized as a thinly veiled attempt to further enrich a small amount of already wealthy blacks, and characterized as doing very little to help those who have actually been disadvantaged by discrimination. SCHUCK, *supra* at 142. Others have pointed out that once the remedial rationale is removed from affirmative action cases, it become very difficult to decide what groups should be receiving benefits. Paul J. Mishkin writes, "Once remedial justification is set aside, there appears to be no explanation why the goal of greater variety in broadcast content would not be equally (or better) served by including among the preferred groups others not defined by race—e.g., older people or Polish-Americans (who may be able to claim even less presence on the airwaves)." Mishkin, *supra* at 882. Even some supporters of the decision in *Metro Broadcasting* questioned the diversity rationale as being the exclusive inspiration for the court's decision:

> [A]lthough the majority described its measures as "not 'remedial' in the sense of being designed to compensate victims of past governmental or societal discrimination," its reasoning is clearly framed as a corrective for historical conditions that are hardly long buried in the shroud of some long-forgotten past, but whose effects are specifically identifiable and endlessly enumerable.

Patricia J. Williams, Metro Broadcasting, Inc. v. FCC: *Regrouping in Singular Times*, 104 HARV. L. REV. 525, 527 (1990).

The dissent in *Metro Broadcasting* strongly questions the correlation between a person's race and a specific set of views that have been underrepresented. In one sense this must be correct; it is impossible to predict someone's views based simply on the color of their skin. Nevertheless, there is a connection between culture and race, and perhaps while minority broadcasters will not bring any particular views that can immediately be identified as "diverse," increasing the minority broadcasting ownership will better represent "a shared heritage of language patterns, habits, history, and experience" that is "black culture." *See* Williams, *supra* at 529–30.

9. Controversy about affirmative action. Affirmative action, whatever its merits, is unquestionably a hot-button issue in American politics, and the divide has only deepened in the wake of *Grutter*. This may not be surprising given the strong feelings that issues of race inject into any issue. This is accompanied by the high stakes, such as seats in highly selective colleges, and the feeling by some whites that these seats are their societal entitlement. Some opponents of affirmative action have taken to inflammatory and silly methods to try and undermine its goals. At Roger Williams University in Rhode Island, members of the College Republicans who object to the university's use of race-based affirmative action, provoked controversy by awarding a whites-only scholarship, the "Students of Non-color Scholarship." Said the president of the group, "If you're going to have race-based scholarships on campus, you just cannot have it to one group of people and not the other. We say that's unequal treatment." The Republican National Committee denounced the award and severed all ties with the college group. *All Things Considered* (NPR radio broadcast Feb. 19, 2004). In another instance, the editor of the conservative magazine National Review has encouraged white college applicants to engage in "civil disobedience" by misrepresenting their race on college admissions forms. Mark Edmundson, *Civil Disobedience Against Affirmative Action*, N.Y. TIMES, Dec. 14, 2003, (Magazine) at 60.

Supporters of affirmative action have entered their fray as well. For example, some point out that white members of the elite have enjoyed the advantages of affirmative action by being the sons and daughters of alumni of elite institutions and being enrolled in prep schools that every year send many students to the nation's best universities. Supporters note the fact that George W. Bush's sub-par academic performance in high school and subsequent acceptance at Yale. "Bush clearly got [into Yale] because of affirmative action. Affirmative action for the son and grandson of alumni. Affirmative action for a member of a politically influential family. Affirmative action for a boy from a fancy prep school. These forms of affirmative action still go on." Michael Kinsley, *How Affirmative Action Helped George W.*, TIME, Jan. 27, 2003, at 70.

Despite the controversy that surrounds affirmative action, Neal Devins points out the overwhelming support that the *Grutter* decision received from universities, the business community, the military and politicians. Not a single university filed an amicus brief opposing affirmative action, the military submitted a very influential brief in support, and even the Bush administration, though supporting the plaintiff in the case, expressed support for racial diversity and did not suggest that all race-based preferences be done away with. Devins argues that as a political matter it would have been very difficult for the Supreme Court to have disallowed all considerations of race in college admissions, and that "affirmative action has become so entrenched that the costs of taking a stand against it are greater now than ever before." Neal Devins, *Explaining* Grutter v. Bollinger, 152 U. PA. L. REV. 347, 373 (2003). Should this support affect the Supreme Court's ruling? Is it proper for the Court to recognize when it is dealing with a socially and politically controversial issue and perhaps treat it differently than others?

10.   Value of diversity in higher education. There is broad disagreement as to whether diversity in the classroom is a worthwhile goal, and whether it should be achieved through affirmative action, as shown in the *Hopwood* decision. While *Grutter* has settled the legal question for now, the debate will continue. Supporters of affirmative action view diversity as promoting the inclusion of marginalized segments of the population, helping to abate the broader segregation that exists in society, breaking down stereotypes, and introducing different and previously underrepresented viewpoints into the classroom. Devon W. Carbado & Mitu Gulati, *What Exactly is Racial Diversity?*, 91 CAL. L. REV. 1149 (2003) (book review).

Conservative commentators are highly skeptical of the benefits of diversity, and agree with Justice Thomas's contention that the support for affirmative action shown by universities is merely evidence of elite institutions' desire to be "aesthetically" diverse. Who benefits from classroom diversity? Is it legitimate to expect members of a certain race to bring a set of views that will be different from the white majority? consider this attack from an opponent:

> Students of minority groups may be forceful and eloquent spokesmen for their own racial views. But so what? There are many

academic courses in which the questions of race and sex are marginal at best. In the arts and sciences, none of the math and science curriculum has a racial message; the same is true of large portions of social sciences and the humanities as well. Within the law school, tax, business, and procedural courses have little if any content related to race, and it would be odd to say that they could not be taught successfully without any reference to race, or indeed without any minority or female students. After all, many of the lawyers and professors who teach today received excellent education in these subjects before the advent of any affirmative action program.

Richard A. Epstein, *A Rational Basis for Affirmative Action: A Shaky but Classical Liberal Defense*, 100 MICH. L. REV. 2036, 2040–41 (2002).

Another critique of the diversity rationale is that it presumes that certain qualities "inhere in a racial group." SCHUCK, *supra* at 165. *See also* Charles R. Lawrence, *Two Views of the River: A Critique of the Liberal Defense of Affirmative Action*, 101 COLUM. L. REV. 928 (2001) (criticizing the diversity rationale while supporting affirmative action). Notice Justice Kennedy's claim in *Grutter* that diversity may be a convenient rationale that is not the true basis for support of affirmative action. If diversity does not benefit a university, why is affirmative action overwhelmingly supported by the country's most selective colleges and graduate schools? Admission to top universities increases one's access to elite professions and social circles. Is increasing diversity not only in the classroom but in the upper echelons of society a realistic goal for affirmative action?

Another facet of the debate over university admissions is the value of the traditional tools that universities use for admission decisions, namely grades and standardized tests. Opponents of affirmative action contend that college admission should be based solely on these and other merit-based standards. However, many believe that grades, and especially standardized tests such as the SAT and LSAT, are not predictive of success in college or law school, but do correlate quite closely to race and parental income. How would the elimination of standardized testing affect admissions to elite universities? GUINIER & TORRES, *supra* at 71. Lani Guinier proposes a "structural mobility" framework in which identification of qualified applicants would move beyond traditional indicators such as standardized tests. Take for example two applicants to an Ivy League school. One is a wealthy, white, "A" student from a top prep school who scores extremely well on standardized tests and has a full compliment of extracurricular activities. The other is a black, "B+" student, from a crumbling inner-city high school whose test scores and extracurriculars are good but less impressive. How should an admissions officer assess these two candidates? Is it possible to say who "deserves" admission? What is the goal of an admissions officer in making this decision? Is it who she thinks will better succeed in college? Succeed in life? Add more to the college's student body? Add more to society as a whole? Should the fact that the second student has very likely encountered many more obstacles in her achievements be relevant to an admissions decision?

11. *Gratz v. Bollinger.* *Gratz v. Bollinger*, 539 U.S. 244 (2003), decided on the same day as *Grutter*, dealt with the admissions policy at the undergraduate division of the University of Michigan. The University ranked applicants on a 150 point scale. Students were primarily awarded points for academic achievement, but up to 40 points were available based on qualifications unrelated to academics. An applicant received 20 points for membership in an underrepresented minority group, attendance at a predominately minority or disadvantaged high school, or recruitment for athletics. Other non-academic factors included 10 points for residence in Michigan, 4 points for children of alumni, and up to 3 points for an outstanding essay. This admissions policy was rejected by the Court, primarily because it did not include the individualized review present in *Grutter*, and therefore too closely resembled the kind of quota system disallowed in *Bakke*. Justice Powell wrote in *Bakke* that the fact of an applicant being a minority should be "considered without being decisive," but according to Justice Rehnquist's majority opinion, under Michigan's undergraduate plan "the factor of race [is] decisive for virtually every minimally qualified underrepresented minority applicant." Justice Souter's dissent saw a meaningful difference between the quota system in *Bakke* and the system at issue in *Gratz*, because the *Bakke* plan focused only on race, whereas this plan "lets all applicants compete for all places and values an applicant's offerings for any place not solely on the grounds of [race]." He contended that the "college simply does by a numbered scale what that law school accomplishes by 'holistic review'; the distinction does not imply that applicants to the undergraduate college are denied individualized consideration...."

12. Alternate approaches. Kevin Brown presents a bleak picture of the prospects for black enrollment in selective colleges and graduate schools if affirmative action were stopped. Kevin Brown, Hopwood: *Was This the African-American Nightmare or the African American Dream?* 2 Tex. F. on C.L. & C.R. 97 (1996):

> After the *Hopwood* decision, Texas instituted a plan in which the top 10 percent of students from every public school in the state are automatically accepted by state universities. Florida and California have adopted similar programs. The plan has been described as a compromise between race and merit-based solutions. An obvious goal of the plan is to have minority students from underperforming schools and bad neighborhoods be able to attend state universities, but by not explicitly involving race it ameliorates some of the supposed unfairness of affirmative action. The Texas plan also received support from poor, rural whites who have limited access to opportunities in higher education. Justice Souter criticized these plans in his *Gratz* dissent, writing that they suffer "the disadvantage of obfuscation ... the 'percentage plans' are just as race conscious as the point scheme (and fairly so), but they get their racially diverse results without saying directly what they are doing or why they are doing it." *Id.*

at 298. These plans may also have the effect of disadvantaging minority students who attend better schools and do well, but fall outside of the top 10 percent. Does the Texas plan strike you as an effective way to meet the goals of affirmative action without employing race-based preferences?

In California, Proposition 209 prohibited preferential treatment based on race in public education. Justice Thomas contends in *Grutter* that minority admissions at Boalt Hall, the elite law school at the University of California Berkeley, have not significantly suffered since Proposition 209's passage. For a contrary view, see ANDREA GUERRERO, SILENCE AT BOALT HALL: THE DISMANTLING OF AFFIRMATIVE ACTION (2002). One scholar at the University of California-Los Angeles has claimed, based on a statistical analysis of data collected at that university's law school, that eliminating race-conscious admissions programs in law schools would actually increase the number of minority lawyers, because African American law students who are presently unable to perform adequately at top-flight schools would go to lesser schools where they could succeed spectacularly and pass the bar in greater numbers. Richard H. Sander, *A Systematic Analysis of Affirmative Action in American Law Schools*, 57 STAN. L. REV. 367 (2004). Sander's analysis has been attacked by defenders of affirmative action. *See, e.g.,* David L. Chambers et al., *The Real Impact of Eliminating Affirmative Action in American Law Schools: An Empirical Critique of Richard Sander's Stanford Law Review Study*, 58 STAN. L. REV. (forthcoming May, 2005); Cheryl I. Harris & William C. Kidder, *The Black Student Mismatch Myth in Legal Education: The Systemic Flaws in Richard Sander's Affirmative Action Study*, J. BLACKS HIGHER EDUC. 102 (2005). How can we reconcile this controversy with Brown's article?

What kinds of measures might an elite university take to sustain minority enrollment without using explicit, race-based preferences? Is it possible that admissions officers may secretly or even subconsciously continue to give preferential treatment to minorities even after a formal affirmative action program is no longer in place? Justice Ginsburg predicts in her dissent in *Gratz* that this will take place. Is there a value to having race-based preferences out in the open?

Many have argued that affirmative action in college admissions should be based on class rather than race, pointing out that academic achievement is tied to economic status, and that the beneficiaries of race-based admissions preferences are mostly middle and upper-middle class blacks who are not as in need of assistance. *See* RICHARD D. KAHLENBERG, THE REMEDY: CLASS, RACE, AND AFFIRMATIVE ACTION (1996). Despite the victory of the University of Michigan's Law School in *Grutter*, the president of the university has expressed the desire "to create a more 'diverse diversity,' based on students from wider socioeconomic backgrounds ... not[ing] that poor kids are nearly as scarce on campus as minorities. Just one in five of Michigan's 25,000 undergrads comes from a family making less than $50,000 a year." Keith Naughton, *A New Campus Crusader*, NEWSWEEK, Dec. 29, 2003/Jan. 5, 2004, at 78. Who has the most to lose and the most to gain when affirmative action programs are in place? What should be made of poor white students who face great challenges in achieving high levels of educations—should they be the beneficiaries of affirmative action programs? Other proposals, such as those promoted by Shapiro, promote a focus on the root causes of why affirmative action is deemed necessary, namely the poor education available to minority students that renders them unable to compete on an equal footing. Is racial inequality too widespread and deeply-rooted a problem to be solved by affirmative action?

13.   Is affirmative action effective? Despite the inequality that still exists, minorities have enjoyed uneven, but noteworthy, improvement in economic and social status in the past fifty years. Some argue that affirmative action has been instrumental in this progress. William Bowen and Derek Bok contend that selective colleges have succeeded in educating "sizable numbers of minority students who have already achieved significant success and seem likely in time to occupy positions of leadership throughout society." WILLIAM BOWEN & DEREK BOK, THE SHAPE OF THE RIVER: LONG-TERM CONSEQUENCES OF CONSIDERING RACE IN COLLEGE AND UNIVERSITY ADMISSIONS (1998). Others attribute this progress to a variety of advances and changed circumstances for black Americans unrelated to affirmative action. SCHUCK, *supra* at 140. To what extent should effectiveness affect future decisions about affirmative action? Justice O'Connor's *Grutter* opinion contains the prediction that in twenty-five years affirmative action will no longer be necessary. Does this seem likely? Why would she feel compelled to include this speculation?

B.   THE WEALTH OF COMMUNITIES

The financial services infrastructure available to make loans and accept deposits is a critical component for creating and sustaining wealth. Two banking statutes, the Equal Credit Opportunity Act and the Community Reinvestment Act, were designed to correct the long-established patterns of discriminatory lending to women, and to poor and minority communities. In what follows, legal scholar Anthony Taibi questions whether either of these statutes contributes significantly to the reversal of financial subordination, and economic isolation that have been sustaining features of wealth and income inequality for Blacks, and other targets of racial discrimination. Taibi proposes, instead, a "community empowerment" paradigm in which local racial, cultural identities and civil institutions are accorded central importance beyond the formalistic model of markets and rational choice.

———

Banking, Finance, and Community Economic Empowerment: Structural Economic Theory, Procedural Civil Rights, and Substantive Racial Justice
107 HARV. L. REV. 1463 (1994).

■ ANTHONY D. TAIBI

> Practical men, who believe themselves to be quite exempt from any intellectual influences, are usually the slaves of some defunct economist.
>
> JOHN MAYNARD KEYNES

I. Introduction: Paradigms of the Relationship Between Civil Rights and Banking Regulation

The structure of America's financial system necessarily has a profound effect on the social and economic conditions of our neighborhoods and communities. The current small business credit crunch increasingly stifles those businesses that provide the bulk of new jobs and give regular people a chance for entrepreneurial independence. The continuing discrimination and redlining in both mortgage and consumer credit hinder the ability of Black people to buy and improve their homes and therefore block asset accumulation, stakeholding, and revitalization in Black communities. The ongoing consolidation of the banking industry has had and will continue to have a profound negative impact in low- and moderate-income communities and in non-White communities. Community investment is at the intersection of civil rights and economics, yet the prevailing civil rights paradigms fail to consider the structure of the banking system as a civil rights issue.

Two paradigms dominate civil rights discourse, neither of which aids in understanding how the structure of the financial system disempowers African-American and other non-elite communities. The equality paradigm, embodied in the Equal Credit Opportunity Act (ECOA), seeks to regulate financial institutions to ensure that banks treat like customers alike and make services available according to race neutral criteria. The affirmative action paradigm considers traditional equal treatment policy insufficient to erase the legacy of past discrimination. This latter model, embodied in the Community Reinvestment Act (CRA), seeks to ensure not only that banks apply race neutral criteria in evaluating individual loan applications, but also that banks actually lend in low- and moderate-income communities.

These two prevailing civil rights paradigms cannot address the structural nature of disinvestment, because they implicitly accept a neoclassical economic ideology that is incompatible with genuine reform. According to the neoclassical economic paradigm, every competitively profitable investment will find an investor; therefore, an unfunded investment could not possibly be competitively profitable. Although this postulate has a pleasingly simple logic, it simply is not true. All investments are made with at least some degree of uncertainty. Investment decisions are made before realization, and actual return at realization can be very different from initial assumptions: some investments do not live up to initial expectations and others outperform expectations. Neoclassical ideology refuses to acknowledge that cultural and psychological forces can be as powerful as market forces. To the extent that investors continue to undervalue community investments relative to other investments—due to racial, ethnic, or class biases, or because small investments for working people seem mundane—there is systematic market failure. Neoclassical thinkers would counter that, even if market failure does occur, in the long run, someone will discover the failure and enter the underserved market. Leaving aside for the moment the fact that disinvestment can sometimes become a self-fulfilling prophecy, that "long run" may last until long after our grandchildren are dead.

The equality paradigm implicitly embraces neoclassical assumptions in that it presupposes that the competition for funds in particular real-world marketplaces can operate as competition would in the neutral, rational, theoretically "perfect" market. Thus, the equality paradigm assumes that, to the extent that African-Americans and other people from disempowered communities have an "equal opportunity" to compete for a capital investment with other credit seekers, the outcome of that competition is fair or at least efficient.

The affirmative action paradigm reinforces neoclassical assumptions in more subtle ways. It too incorporates the neoclassical assumption that capital allocations determined in particular marketplaces are in fact "market efficient," but also posits equity as a distinct and competing value from procedural fairness and efficiency and seeks to subsidize favored groups to achieve a desired distributional outcome. It never questions the structure of marketplaces that routinely produce unacceptable results. To the extent that it accepts as given the institutional structures of American life (but for racial disparity), affirmative action reinforces the legitimacy of the very institutions that effectively disempower African-American and other non-elite communities. Thus, affirmative action turns the aspirations of disempowered groups into mere special interest pleadings, and demands for justice into supplications for charity. It divides the disempowered along the lines of who does and does not benefit from "special treatment" instead of uniting them in a common struggle.

Unwittingly accepting these neoclassical assumptions, progressive observers continue to describe community investment problems in terms of industry recalcitrance and insufficient political commitment toward reform. This is a tragic error. The disinvestment faced by lower-middle-class communities is structural—a product of the globalization of markets, capital, and production. Working-class, ethnic, and minority communities must control their own destinies by wresting control of local finance away from non-local institutions; they must not simply ask those institutions to invest a little more in local neighborhoods. The structural economic problems facing America's communities can be addressed in part by creating and reinforcing financial institutions that are community specific in their control, whether in the form of a broad-based community organization or simply a local business elite focused on profits but informed by a sense of its cultural roots.

Liberal perspectives do not treat building community institutions as an end in itself; their assumptions obscure how such institutions might be both fair and efficient given a different structural grounding. Of course, even in a reformed marketplace, not all socially desired investments will be competitive. Ensuring efficiency and structuring markets does not exhaust the role of politics. From health care to roads, from the environment to housing, American citizens must make decisions about whether and how to subsidize and to regulate. But as long as we are mired in the habits of mind engendered by liberal civil rights ideology and neoclassical economics, we will make these decisions myopically.

The creation of empowered communities requires more than new policies tied to community-based political organizations: it requires creating a new economic discourse. Although the "American Dream" of strong communities and financial independence remains an essential part of our culture and politics, the idea that the purpose of economic policy should be to promote this dream has not enjoyed intellectual respectability since the downfall of the Populist movement in the late nineteenth century. The assumptions of neoclassical economic ideology implicitly underlie and undermine the debate across the political spectrum. This Article represents merely a salvo in the battle of scholarly debates, op-ed pieces, think-tank projects, and efforts to shape our understanding of "common sense." Creating a discourse of populist community-empowerment economics and public policy is an ongoing project.

Although the racial dimension is among the most pressing and morally repugnant aspects of community disinvestment, the eroding job base, the small business credit crunch, and the globalization of capital are problems that affect all Americans. These issues are racial, but they require more than racial solutions. The small business credit crunch affects all communities, and U.S. home ownership rates have dropped precipitously in the last decade for all Americans. The "redundancy" of the American workforce to global corporations is now affecting white-collar professionals and middle managers, as well as Black and White working class people. If we are to create a new populist discourse about structural economic changes in our society, our movement must be transracial and have broad appeal across the economic spectrum. Opposing the economic and cultural colonization of our particular racial, ethnic, cultural, and religious communities requires a common struggle. Ironically, we can only promote our own group's interest if we work in concert with other groups.

The creation of a new civil rights consciousness requires that we examine the successes and the failures of existing policies that were informed by the two predominant civil rights paradigms. To that end, Part II examines the expression of the equality paradigm in the Equal Credit Opportunity Act (ECOA) and the effects and shortcomings of that Act. Part II then looks critically at liberal explanations of those shortcomings and offers an understanding of the ECOA's weaknesses from the perspective of community empowerment. Part III examines the manifestation of the affirmative action paradigm in the Community Reinvestment Act (CRA). A review and critique of the CRA's successes and failures demonstrate why a community-empowerment perspective can more effectively improve people's lives and create a multi-racial political consensus than can current paradigms. Part IV describes the emergence of the various types of institutions that comprise the community development financial institutions (CDFI) industry. A critique of the Clinton administration's proposed Community Development Banking and Financial Institutions Act of 1994, informed by a community-empowerment perspective, then reveals the failure of the bill to confront the imperatives of the already-established financial structure. The Article concludes by proposing a number of steps that the government should take if it truly wishes to embrace the community-empowerment paradigm as a model for its vision of the financial sector.

II. THE EQUAL CREDIT OPPORTUNITY ACT

A. Background and Aims

The Equal Credit Opportunity Act (ECOA) expresses traditional liberal civil rights policy in the credit arena. The ECOA serves two purposes. First, like other consumer credit legislation, such as the Truth in Lending Act and the Fair Credit Reporting Act, the ECOA is a consumer protection statute designed to provide accurate information to or about consumers involved in credit transactions. Second, the ECOA is an antidiscrimination statute, like the Equal Employment Opportunity Act (EEOA) and the Fair Housing Act (FHA), that seeks to promote wider credit availability by prohibiting the use of stereotypes in credit decisions. For example, the Act prohibits financial institutions from discriminating between otherwise credit-worthy customers on the basis of race, color, national origin, sex, marital status, age, receipt of public assistance income, or the exercise in good faith of the rights guaranteed under the Consumer Credit Protection Act.

ECOA compliance is enforced both by government agencies and through private litigation. The Act authorizes the Federal Reserve Board to prescribe regulations that clarify and amplify specific statutory provisions in light of the Act's legislative purpose. Overall administrative enforcement of the Act rests with the Federal Trade Commission, with limited authority delegated to several other federal agencies. The ECOA and its implementing Regulation B cover all phases of a credit transaction. Regulation B identifies and addresses in detail various phases of the credit-granting procedure, with particular focus on the application process, the evaluation process, and the reporting of reasons for adverse action.

* * *

As amended, the ECOA appeared to be an imposing piece of antidiscrimination legislation. Industry spokesmen feared a substantial increase in administrative activity and litigation, as toughened public and private enforcement mechanisms combined to promote compliance with the Act. As the next section demonstrates, however, the intervening years have produced few public enforcement actions and a only a trickle of private litigation.

B. The ECOA's Performance: Evidence of Inadequacy

Discrimination in lending decisions remains a serious problem. Both systematic study and anecdotal evidence demonstrate that widespread credit discrimination continues to block home ownership, as well as small business creation and expansion, and thereby community economic development in non-White communities. For example, a recent Federal Reserve Bank of Boston study concluded that, all other factors being equal, Black and Latino mortgage applicants are roughly sixty percent more likely to be denied a loan than White applicants. This study may even have underestimated the extent of mortgage loan discrimination by omitting those discouraged from applying for loans by pre-application screening processes, negative institutional reputation, or loan officers' attitudes. Indeed, another recent study revealed that the lack of applications from minority neighborhoods, rather than disproportionately low approval rates, is the principal reason that lenders fail to attain similar lending rates in minority neighborhoods and White neighborhoods in the lenders' service area. Home Mortgage Disclosure Act data from 1992 further revealed that the disparity between Blacks and Whites in gross denial rates for conventional home purchase loans has widened slightly: in 1992, Blacks were 2.26 times more likely to be denied loans than were Whites, compared with 2.16 times in 1991.

Business loans to Black-owned firms present an even more distressing picture. Available data are not as complete as the data on home mortgages because business lenders need not disclose the race of their borrowers, as mortgagees must under the Home Mortgage Disclosure Act; evaluation is also more difficult because business loans are less uniform than home mortgage loans. Nevertheless, the available evidence indicates that Black and White business owners with identical predictive traits—age, educational background, a close family member who is a business owner or self-employed professional, purchase of an ongoing concern, and possession of equity capital—do not receive equal treatment. Black-owned firms are denied loans more frequently than White-owned firms, and the business financing that is approved is usually for smaller amounts and on more onerous terms. Studies indicate that lender caution derived from inaccurate perceptions that similarly situated Black-owned firms are riskier than their White-owned counterparts undermines many otherwise viable Black businesses. It is thus unsurprising that, according to one 1993 study, eighty-three percent of Black entrepreneurs believe that lending bias is a very serious problem for Black-owned businesses, with another nine percent considering the issue a moderately serious problem.

C. Standard Liberal Proposals

The evidence of ongoing and pervasive lending discrimination is extremely persuasive, prompting both explanations and proposals for possible improvement. For example, the speculative nature of actual damages in discrimination cases makes statutory damages particularly important, causing some critics to propose amending the Act to include a minimum statutory recovery. Under such a scheme, even technical violations of the Act would carry a minimum $100 award, regardless of the actual damages. Although such an Amendment might have some marginal benefit for large consumer-credit class actions, as well as for suits in which many individuals claim mortgage discrimination, statutory damages would be of little help to individual small business claims, to which the technical aspects of the Act do not apply.

Other critics attribute the paucity of litigation under the ECOA to the fact that (1) although lenders must supply written notification of adverse action to individual consumers, the lenders need only provide a written statement of reasons if the consumer makes a written request; (2) business creditors need not be notified at all; and (3) a change in credit terms to which the applicant has agreed does not constitute an adverse action. * * *

Finally, some progressive critics target the historical lack of effort on the part of public enforcement bodies. The Justice Department did not file its first "pattern or practice" lawsuit until 1992; the amount of time that went by before the first suit was filed and the paucity of suits since then have left serious doubts about the government's commitment to reform. In creating the ECOA, however, Congress clearly envisioned that private litigation that alleged substantive discrimination crimination would be the main enforcement method. The Act uses the concept of the private attorney general to provide for generous class action recoveries and attorney's fee awards. Despite Congress's expectations, most of the few suits brought under the Act have been based on minor violations of the Act's technical and notification provisions. Only a tiny amount of private litigation has been reported since the enactment of the ECOA in 1974, and most of this litigation has focused on sex rather than on race. Indeed, only a handful of substantive discrimination claims, few of which rested on racial grounds, and only three class actions have been successfully prosecuted.

* * *

D. A Community–Empowerment Critique of the ECOA

This section presents a community-empowerment critique of the ECOA that attacks both the Act's unrealistic conceptual assumptions and its defective normative vision. This critique explains more compellingly than standard liberal analyses why the ECOA has met with such limited success in extending credit to Black people and shows why the Act's vision may ultimately be undesirable.

The equality paradigm embodied by the ECOA posits an acultural, meritocratic "thing" called "creditworthiness." The paradigm assumes that banks can measure "creditworthiness" objectively and neutrally, and that, having done so, banks have an equal incentive to lend equally to all similarly creditworthy customers. The notion of "equally qualified" borrowers, however, overlooks the cultural specificity of the proxies by which creditworthiness is judged. Rather than reflecting actual ability and willingness to repay debts, particular qualifications are in fact only indicia associated with, but not determinative of, what succeeded in a creditor's past—a past that was typically "White only." The available research suggests that certain credit-scoring-model criteria have different meanings for different populations. For example, credit-scoring systems have typically deemed frequent changes in residence a significant negative, indicative of instability. It may be, however, that for Black people facing housing discrimination and concomitant schooling problems for their children, frequent family moves indicate hard work and responsibility. Such frequent movers might in fact be excellent credit risks. Similarly, frequent job changes may have different meanings for different populations. Indeed, the Federal Financial Institutions Examination Council has concluded that traditional employment stability requirements are discriminatory.

* * *

In addition to the equality paradigm's unrealistic conceptual assumptions, its normative vision is inherently limited. Relatively little non-consumer credit is granted solely on the basis of objective information. For small business loans in general and start-up loans in particular, little lending can be done by the numbers alone. The decision to lend is ultimately based on an inherently subjective determination that the credit-seeker's project has merit and that the credit-seeker is of good character and will go the extra mile to repay debts. Lenders do look to objective criteria like collateral and credit history and may consider how similar projects have fared in the past, but a decision to lend is in the end a decision to trust the judgment of the debtor. Even in mortgage lending, the decision to grant credit often hinges on the lending officer's subjective sense of the applicant's creditworthiness and the officer's extra efforts to work with the borrower to make the numbers come out right. It is at these points that racism may enter the loan-granting process.

In conventional use, "racism" means allowing race, an irrelevant characteristic, to play a part in what ought to be a purely "rational" decision. Banker discretion thus creates an opportunity for conventionally understood racism (either intentional or unconscious) to enter the loan-granting process. However, although racism is conventionally understood to mean not just hate for the other, but affinity for one's own, such subjective moments are both utterly inevitable and potentially desirable. Furthermore, fully "rationalized" settings, with no discretion and thus no conventional racism, may permit worse forms of institutional racism.

* * *

A community-empowerment critique points out that subjective moments in the lending process are not always problematic. People are more comfortable with things that are familiar to them. As a matter of common sense, loan officers feel more comfortable lending money to people with whom they share a common rapport, who belong to institutions with which they are familiar, who have backgrounds similar to their own, who seek loans for homes or business projects in familiar neighborhoods, and whose business plans are for familiar projects. At worst, we can attribute this phenomenon to culturally embedded racist stereotypes that prevent loan officers from seeing good business opportunities. At best, we can see this as good business sense: it is prudent to invest only in neighborhoods that one knows, in projects that one understands, and with people whom one trusts. It not only appears unlikely that we can eliminate subjectivity—which is necessarily culturally bound—from the credit-granting process, but it also seems that we would not want to if we could; what separates good from bad investments in lower-middle-class neighborhoods and small businesses will often be unquantifiable, intangible qualities like the passion, character, and vision of the borrower, or the aesthetic quality of the houses on a particular block. We want lenders to take a chance, based on the intuition that a project will succeed, on projects whose numbers may be less than perfect. This point of subjectivity in the lending process is paradoxically the time when both the worst and the best lending practices might transpire.

* * *

[B]lacks and Whites of the same economic status typically attend different clubs and recreational facilities, send their children to different schools, and therefore serve on different PTA boards, attend different churches, and live in different neighborhoods. Without personal knowledge of a credit seeker's character and reputation in the community, a banker has no basis for a reputational judgment. Even the most well-meaning White loan officer will be unable to make character loans with an acceptable racial balance. To the extent that, in modern America, White people do not know Black people, reputational lending by White institutions cannot help being "discriminatory."

Hiring more employees from Black communities could never be more than a partial solution. To make a large, White-owned bank in a Black neighborhood more responsive to the needs of its customers by staffing that branch with African-Americans might well harm the careers of those African-American loan officers. The management fast track at most large corporations necessitates moving around from position to position rather than remaining in a single location. The best opportunities for career advancement and bonuses are unlikely to be found in lower-middle-class neighborhoods; requiring Black professionals to work in low-income areas might ghettoize these professionals and thereby run afoul of employment discrimination laws. In addition, such a solution would do nothing for the credit problems of lower-middle-class White people.

In summary, as long as the main business of the bank is outside of a particular local community, it is difficult to imagine how members of that community could be treated "equally" by the institution. Within the context of an economy and financial structure driven by highly mobile transnational capital and large corporate interests, community-based economic development will always be a charitable afterthought, not an economic imperative.

III.   The Community Reinvestment Act

Lending discrimination contributes to neighborhood disinvestment, but such discrimination is only a part of the story. Even if all lending discrimination were eliminated, it would have little impact on low-income neighborhoods. Many Americans cannot even conceive of having sufficient economic resources to own their own home; African-Americans are significantly overrepresented in this group. Because lending in lower-income and non-White communities cannot be improved within the framework of conventional business practices, stronger steps must be taken. Such a remedial purpose is envisioned by the Community Reinvestment Act.

The equality paradigm suggests that it is beyond the scope of public policy to remedy inequality that persists after fair and equal procedures have been established. Thus, procedural fairness has no necessary connection to fair outcomes: lending outcomes are considered beyond question as long as lending criteria are arguably rational and clearly non-racial. In contrast, the affirmative action model maintains that the lingering effects of past discrimination cannot be cured by equal treatment alone, but only by affirmative steps to make equal opportunity a reality. As President Johnson stated, "[y]ou do not take a person who, for years, has been hobbled by chains and liberate him, bring him to the starting line of a race and then say, 'you are free to compete with all the others,' and still justly believe that you have been completely fair." Under the more activist affirmative action paradigm, government policy at the intersection of civil rights and banking regulation must do more than simply demand procedural equality; regulations must ensure that an appropriate level of lending actually takes place in all communities.

In this spirit, in 1977, Congress passed the Community Reinvestment Act (CRA). The Act has recently attracted much attention. Unlike the Bush administration, whose attempts to disarm the CRA were thwarted by Congress, President Clinton made community reinvestment a centerpiece of his campaign's economic platform. Clinton promised to "[e]ase the credit crunch in our inner cities by passing a more progressive Community Reinvestment Act to prevent 'redlining'; and requiring financial institutions to invest in their communities." The battle over the CRA has been joined.

A. Background and Aims

The Community Reinvestment Act (CRA) places upon each insured depository institution a "continuing and affirmative obligation to help meet the credit needs of the local communities in which [it is] chartered" and requires that each such institution be assessed on its "record of meeting the credit needs of its entire community, including low-and moderate-income neighborhoods, consistent with the safe and sound operation of such institution." Congress determined that banks were redlining or neglecting important credit needs within their communities and that regulators' efforts to deter such behavior were inadequate.

Although redlining and discrimination are somewhat different, in the credit context, the two practices are clearly interrelated. Discrimination refers to the denial of credit to an individual applicant based on race. Redlining originally referred to the practice of literally drawing a red line around certain neighborhoods on a city map and refusing to make loans for property or businesses located within the demarcated zones. Today the term refers to any set of practices that "systematically den[ies] credit to applicants from low-and moderate-income, and minority neighborhoods." Redlining decisions are sometimes based on a perception that the housing stock in certain neighborhoods is in disrepair. The practice also derives from outright racial discrimination or from the related prejudice that property values in racially changing neighborhoods must decline. Furthermore, herd behavior may result if others follow one major lender's decision not to invest. Consequently, to the extent that Black people live in distinct communities, racially disparate rejection rates indicate that Black communities suffer from systematic under-investment—redlining.

* * *

Despite its weaknesses, the CRA did affect bank behavior by allowing community-based organizations and residents to intervene in expansion and merger application proceedings and to challenge the approval of expansion requests on the basis of alleged inadequacies in the CRA records of the applicants or institutions to be acquired. Public responses to bank expansion requests are authorized by statute or regulation. Regulators must review evidence presented through the public comment process. Community groups have thus brought an estimated three hundred challenges against expansion requests. Although only approximately fifteen applications have been denied outright on CRA grounds since the Act's inception, and although federal regulators have granted conditional approval imposing CRA requirements in only fifty to sixty cases, community groups have successfully used the CRA process to negotiate directly with the applicant institution. A majority of CRA challenges have been withdrawn after applicant institutions and local groups negotiated settlements. Such settlements often specify what measures the applicant institution must take to improve its record in low-and moderate-income and non-White communities. Although this informal dispute resolution mechanism is neither sanctioned nor enforced by regulators, it is preferred by many community groups. These agreements have generated between $7.5 and $20 billion in targeted loan commitments to low-and moderate-income areas, which far exceeds the conditions that would have been imposed by regulators. Thus, the success of the CRA-challenge process depends on how effectively community leaders can obtain specific commitments to community reinvestment from banks in independent negotiations. Furthermore, research suggests that CRA agreements have resulted in significant changes in the institutional behavior of lenders. In addition to the imposed and negotiated commitments, lenders have made additional unilateral commitments of some $23 billion to community-development lending while their expansion requests were pending. It is doubtful that these lenders would have made these commitments without the desire to head off CRA challenges. Further, in the current climate of accelerated merger activity in the banking industry, the primary CRA enforcement mechanism of denying permission for mergers may be increasingly powerful.

In addition, in 1989 Congress greatly enhanced the CRA's impact as part of the comprehensive Financial Institutions Reform, Recovery, and Enforcement Act (FIRREA). Among other changes, the 1989 Amendments mandated public disclosure of regulators' CRA evaluation results and greatly expanded the collection of Home Mortgage Disclosure Act data.

These Amendments sent a message to the regulatory agencies to strengthen their CRA enforcement, which has been amplified by the Clinton administration's proposed overhaul of the regulations under the CRA.

B.   The CRA's Performance: Evidence of Inadequacy

Although the CRA has fostered many negotiated partnerships for community lending, low- and moderate-income communities remain underserved by the banking industry. The extent to which these commitments have translated into actual changes in lending practices is unclear. Although eighty-nine percent of the nation's banks and thrifts received outstanding or satisfactory CRA grades from federal banking regulators, widespread evidence indicates that the industry continues to fall short of the law's mandates.

The inadequacy of the CRA is demonstrated both by continuing and pervasive lending discrimination and by evidence demonstrating that banks continue to neglect the credit needs of low-and moderate-income communities. Redlining of many kinds is pervasive and growing. Many of America's lower-and middle-class communities—whether White or Black, urban, rural, or small town—suffer from continuing disinvestment. Even if the CRA's goals were met, it is unclear that their fulfillment would reverse these long-term, structural declines.

C.   The CRA's Inherent Contradictions

The CRA has been sharply criticized from all sides. Liberals attack the Act's enforcement provisions as ineffective and argue that much of what passes for compliance is merely charitable donation instead of serious investment. Conservatives bemoan allegedly excessive compliance costs, anti-competitive effects, and inefficient impacts on market structure. To the extent that speakers on both sides of this debate are correct, these critiques highlight the limitations of the CRA strategy that creates the illusion of a fixed choice between healthy communities and profitable industry. This false dichotomy results from our intellectual and political failure to target directly the structure of the financial industry.

1.   Liberal Critiques of the CRA.—Liberal critics of the CRA see much of what passes for CRA compliance as mere public relations and charitable contribution to community-group causes. According to this view, CRA enforcement merely imposes the requirement of extensive paper trails for marginal activities that have little to do with substantive investment in low- and moderate-income communities. These critics argue that banks refuse to change the way they do business and look to please regulators rather than to comply with the spirit of the law.

Liberal critics argue persuasively that regulators must, among other things, be directed to see CRA evaluation as an integral part of a regulator's job rather than as an additional burden; that better guidelines should emphasize the CRA as an aspect of normal bank operations rather than as a charitable afterthought; that only substantive lending in low- and moderate-income communities rather than negotiated gifts to community groups or other causes should constitute compliance; and that regulators need help in forming substantive policies rather than formalistic rules and in reducing paperwork. Backed by substantial bipartisan political support, various liberal reform proposals have recently emerged on both the legislative and the new administration's regulatory agendas. * * *

The CRA Reform Act also imposes CRA-type duties on non-depository mortgage banks and mortgage insurance companies: "[e]ach mortgage bank shall have an ongoing responsibility to meet the credit needs of all the communities in which such bank makes a significant number of extensions of credit or extends a significant amount of credit, including extensions of credit in low- and moderate-income neighborhoods of such communities." This provision is significant because mortgage banks account for an large share of mortgage-origination activity. The Act would establish an Office of Mortgage Bank and Insurance Supervision within the Department of Housing and Urban Development and require mortgage banks and mortgage insurers to submit reports detailing their efforts at meeting community credit needs. If the Secretary of HUD found that a mortgage bank was maintaining an "inadequate level of community support," the Secretary could issue an order requiring the institution to file a plan within ninety days detailing "concrete goals and timetables for correcting identified deficiencies." The Secretary could further prohibit the bank from using any HUD-administered program or product until all identified deficiencies were met. Violations of such orders would be subject to administrative and judicial review, cease and desist orders, and civil monetary penalties. This portion of the Act could have a dramatic impact on the behavior of mortgage lenders.

The CRA Reform Act is a well-intentioned but inherently limited step in the right direction. Liberal critiques both accept the financial market as it is currently structured and generally fail to respond adequately to the very real difficulties that the CRA creates for financial institutions. Such difficulties are the domain of the conservative critiques to which we now turn.

2. Neoclassical and Conservative Critiques of the CRA.—Despite continuing disinvestment in lower-middle-class communities and clear lack of regulatory enforcement, industry spokespeople and conservative commentators argue that, at least in part as a consequence of the 1989 amendments:

> CRA-based challenges to bank mergers and other transactions subject to CRA scrutiny are now routine, even when the institution in question has received high marks for CRA compliance in recent examinations. Some deals are actually derailed by the statute, and the costs of consummating a transaction in the face of a CRA challenge can be substantial.

Conservative commentators and industry analysts level three main criticisms at the Act: (a) compliance costs are too high, (b) banks are put at a competitive disadvantage vis-a-vis their non-bank competitors, and (c) the Act impedes market trends toward consolidation.

(a) Compliance Costs.—There is considerable disagreement about the direct compliance costs of the CRA. The CRA has been targeted as the most costly banking regulation currently in force; more troubling still, some studies reveal that smaller banks face the highest relative compliance costs. Conservative critics also charge that CRA regulations are vague and standardless and that bankers thus have little guidance about compliance with the Act. The data are not conclusive, however. Charles A. Bowsher, the Comptroller General of the United States, argues that these industry studies of compliance costs suffer from "serious methodological problems"; the regulatory agencies concluded, based on data received from financial institutions, that the paperwork requirements of the CRA are less time-consuming than the paperwork requirements of other banking consumer regulations. Nevertheless, whatever the precise burden may be, and no matter how the proposed regulatory changes may alter that burden, the CRA does generate substantial paperwork and other bureaucratic compliance costs.

(b) Anti-competitive Effects.—It is also fairly clear that the CRA places depository institutions at a competitive disadvantage compared to their less regulated non-bank competitors. Depository institutions face competition in the lending market from a wide array of other institutions, including pension funds, life insurance companies, finance companies, mortgage banks, venture capital companies, mutual funds, and commercial paper markets. As Professors Macey and Miller argue, "[t]he CRA thus effectively imposes a special, discriminatory tax on banks and savings associations, which are thereby weakened relative to other financial institutions." Given the centrality of banks to a variety of community-development goals, banks' declining importance in the U.S. finance system is troubling. To the extent that the CRA contributes to this trend, such decline runs counter to the Act's own goals.

* * *

A second issue arises if we seek to cure the problem of differential impact by extending the CRA to cover other lenders. Although some non-bank intermediaries—mortgage banks and finance companies—often operate within a geographic community, others—mutual funds, investment banks, and pension funds—operate across extended geographic areas. To bring these lenders within the ambit of CRA regulation, the idea of meeting the credit needs of a lender's "entire community" would have to be reconsidered. Yet the inclusion of this latter group is feasible. If these institutions were given a "safe harbor" from regulatory oversight in return for investing a set percentage of their assets in certain approved investments, a highly sophisticated and liquid market for CRA-approved investments would develop rather quickly. As the last decade proved, Wall Street financiers can securitize almost any investment. In addition, there are several bills before Congress that would create secondary markets—government-sponsored enterprises (GSEs) or private market mechanisms—to facilitate the securitization of small business and community-development lending. The CRA, therefore, could conceivably be extended to more sophisticated lenders with minimal logistical barriers.

* * *

(c) Impact on Market Consolidation.—Professors Macey and Miller argue that the CRA impedes the "desirable process of bank mergers and acquisitions." They contend that the consolidation of the industry is inevitable, efficient, and by implication, socially unproblematic. Although bank merger activity continues to increase and CRA protests *can* delay, derail, or raise the costs of an attempted merger, determining the normative value of this effect is a difficult task that requires both consideration of the relevant economic evidence and sensitivity to the contested nature of the implicated political values.

* * *

However, even if we accept the deeply problematic assumption that banking industry mergers take place because they promote efficiency and economies of scale, we should not necessarily permit consolidation. Efficiency is only one of many social goals, and it is legitimate for society to consider other public policy goals and to accept some sacrifice of efficiency.

In a narrow society-as-aggregate-of-individuals welfare calculus, small businesses, community institutions, and traditional forms of authority have no independent significance. But the promotion of small businesses and community institutions may be a legitimate independent political end. Small businesses and family farmers are an important bulwark in the maintenance of community and not just another interest group. Small businesses have been the engine of economic innovation and the sector of much new job creation. Additionally, small Black-owned businesses provide the best employment opportunities for Black workers. Civil rights values will therefore be best served by a structure of finance that supports such businesses.

Greater banking consolidation is inimical to small business and community institutions. Many studies show that local independent banks give small businesses better credit terms and service than do larger, more distant lenders. Local banks can evaluate and monitor the creditworthiness of small local firms more easily than large banks, know more about their small businesses customers, provide more reliable sources of credit, keep loan personnel in place longer, provide better access to these personnel, and make lending decisions faster. Local independent banks tend, therefore, to depend more on the character of the borrower in granting credit than on requiring high collateral. Branches and subsidiaries of large banks, on the other hand, are more likely to rotate personnel and to maintain final approval authority in remote head offices. For this reason, the branches or subsidiaries of out-of-town banks tend to rely on higher collateral requirements and other standardized lending criteria and "to provide less than the amount of credit requested by small" businesses. Larger banks generally do not emphasize small business lending; they view such lending as less profitable than middle market and larger business loans. Larger banks that do compete for small business customers primarily focus on established small businesses.

* * *

3. Further Considerations for CRA Reformers.—Despite the limitations of the CRA as a tool of structural reform, the CRA framework will exist for some time. It is thus useful to consider how the Act could be made more effective. This section argues that, in addition to extending the CRA's reach to all financial intermediaries, the current open-ended examination of institutions' lending policies should be replaced with a determinate requirement that institutions invest a set portion of their funds in approved investments. Such an approach would both reduce the bureaucratic role in the lending process and ensure that financial institutions actually invest in community development. Although such reform stops well short of real structural change to the economic landscape, it offers the possibility that the CRA might more systematically improve the lives of low- and moderate-income Americans.

The simplest way to extend the CRA to all lenders would be to abandon the ideology of community reinvestment and replace it with a conventional affirmative action approach that requires lenders to meet lending volume goals for certain delineated minority groups. A reform of this type would be a terrible mistake. Although the racial dimension of community disinvestment is the most visible and morally repugnant aspect of this problem, the majority of the American people suffer from the effects of disinvestment. These issues are racial, but they are not only racial. If we are to create a new populist discourse about structural economic changes in our society, our movement must be transracial and have broad appeal across the economic spectrum. Communities can only promote their own interests if they work in concert with other communities.

I want to underscore the argument that the CRA's reach should be extended to all financial intermediaries. First, to the extent that there are costs associated with CRA compliance, the CRA puts banks at a competitive disadvantage to non-bank competitors. Given that banks are, for a variety of reasons, already in significant decline compared to their competitors, their use as a tool of reform is of declining importance to the financial structure. The victories won in the realm of banking will be increasingly irrelevant. Moreover, the increasing complexity of America's financial marketplace requires a more comprehensive and unified regulatory structure. More generally, over the past two decades, the United States financial system has been reshaped by the spread of multifunctional financial conglomerates and the emergence of an unregulated parallel banking system. Along with other powerful trends like securitization, these events have broken down the carefully compartmentalized credit and capital marketplace that was established by New Deal legislation sixty years ago. Check-cashing and pawn shops, along with home-repair second mortgage companies, offer expensive services to low-income people bypassed by mainstream financial firms. Mortgage banks constitute a less regulated parallel housing finance system and finance companies constitute a parallel business and consumer lending regime. The commercial paper market cuts banks out of the financing of corporate businesses. Mutual funds and similar services provide the public with depository-like services that banks once provided exclusively.

* * *

In poor neighborhoods, one can find many profitable but marginal, under-regulated, and exploitative institutions that fill this niche—check-cashing outlets, pawn shops, finance companies, rent-to-own stores, and home-repair second mortgage companies—but there are few conventional banks. The data indicate that community lending is no riskier than comparable lending at similar rates of return. The lack of interest that banks show toward these markets helps create the demand for fringe banking services; conventional financial institutions then cash in on the fringe banking boom by issuing lines of credit to finance companies, providing transactional services to check-cashing outlets, purchasing high-interest notes from second mortgage companies, and pursuing other such business services. Thus, conventional financial institutions do help service these markets—but in an indirect way that permits unscrupulous operators to extract a middleman's profit while the banks keep their hands clean. To the extent that these alternative financial service businesses' high prices reflect not the actual extra risks of such lending, but rather the transaction-cost effects of cultural biases, this trend represents a cultural tax on low-and moderate-income communities.

Given current political realities, the view of most CRA supporters that the existing regulatory structure should not be abolished may well be correct. Unless the investment requirements are set high enough, a safe harbor approach will not provide sufficient incentive even to institutions that could easily extend their efforts in low- and moderate-income communities. Nevertheless, if we are to create a politics that promotes market-based community empowerment, we must move beyond marginal improvement in the opportunities for home and small business ownership and ultimately seek to alter the economic power relationships that dominate life in America.

D. A Structural Critique of the CRA

* * *

The CRA is based on a very limited vision of the nature of the credit problems facing low-and moderate-income communities. Offering no plan for the structure of the financial industry, CRA-based reinvestment strategies assume that industry and firm structure are independent of the investment decisions that firms make. By raising the cost of mergers, the Act has arbitrary and uneven effects that depend upon the zeal of local community groups and the direction of the political winds. Moreover, the incentive structure of the CRA is perverse; in recognition for having engaged in a minimally acceptable level of community investment, a firm is rewarded by being allowed to contribute to undermining the long-term basis of community investment by further concentrating the market. The

CRA assumes that, with a little push, all financial institutions, regardless of size and structure, can be made to engage in significant community investment and that structural questions are separate issues. Lacking a vision of what the structure of the industry ought to be, the CRA cannot be a coherent tool of structural change.

For example, CRA ratings for banks are inexact and subjective. The Act's requirement that each depository institution "help meet the credit needs" "of its entire community, including low-and moderate-income neighborhoods, consistent with the safe and sound operation of such institution[s]" is simple and straightforward in the abstract but, as a practical matter, difficult to assess in a uniform, principled manner. The implementing regulations that are currently in place are very vague. Even under the Clinton administration's proposed new regulations, which are somewhat more determinate and emphasize performance over procedural requirements, the CRA will remain without an overall structural image for the banking industry. In an industry of banks of many types and sizes, without credit quotas and with institutional decisionmaking left to bank managers, the best the CRA can do is to prescribe inexact guidelines and then to ask that bureaucrats apply these guidelines to various real-world situations on a case-by-case basis. Unfortunately, as the literature on bureaucratic management suggests, in this sort of environment, more attention will be paid to the imperatives of the bureaucracy than to the underlying goal.

The structural inadequacy of the CRA is symptomatic of the affirmative action paradigm's insufficiency. Although the equality paradigm and the ECOA are inadequate, because they refuse to entertain the possibility that seemingly fair procedures often yield unfair outcomes, the affirmative action paradigm is inadequate because it refuses to inspect and reform the institutional structures that determine the unfair outcomes affirmative action seeks to redress. Like most affirmative action programs, the CRA does not address the way that the structural imperatives of the institutions it seeks to reform inevitably recreate the very difficulties that the Act attempts to eradicate. Unlike most affirmative action programs, the CRA does not take an individualistic and race-specific approach to regulation. The income and neighborhood-based approach mandated by the CRA is a strength of the Act, but the lack of a vision for the structure of the financial industry undermines the Act's ability to achieve its purpose; the CRA approach does not recognize the fundamental incompatibility of the regulatory requirements it seeks to impose with the system it leaves unquestioned. To borrow President Johnson's metaphor, affirmative action does not question the type of race being run or the awards that attend differences in performance.

IV. TOWARD A COMMUNITY-EMPOWERMENT PARADIGM

The above analysis implies that the existing paradigms of civil rights reform are deeply flawed and, in spite of some important gains won under them, hopelessly contradictory and unworkable. The equality paradigm begins with several flawed premises: that neutral standards of merit exist or could exist, that those standards can be measured objectively, and that assimilation to the culture of the standards is a positive social goal upon which we all ought to agree. The affirmative action paradigm, although more realistic than the equality paradigm, is even more problematic in its premises: it seeks to ameliorate directly inequalities produced through the usual course of business in institutional life, but never questions why such institutions continually produce unacceptable results. Racial inequality is not merely an aberration of institutions that are otherwise fair and neutral and that serve the needs of all Americans equally and unproblematically. Rather, racial inequality is simply the most visible manifestation of how institutions like banks, universities, and law firms fail to serve the lower-middle-class and non-elite cultural communities. To the extent that affirmative action accepts as a given the structure of American life (but for racial disparity), it reinforces the legitimacy of the very institutions that colonize and suppress the Black community and its culture, and other non-elite communities and their distinct cultures. The equality and affirmative action paradigms reflect the views of the big business and big government elites who promote them: that cultural identity and religious belief are pathologies that must be cured so that everyone can become national-market consumers and clients of state services.

A community-empowerment paradigm seeks to escape from our current racial impasse and to allow us both to keep our particular cultural and religious identities and to live in economically healthy communities. Traditional civil rights reformers, neoclassical conservatives, and most Marxists fail to see any positive role for racial, ethnic, and cultural identification beyond the shaping of subjective preferences for individual consumption items. Any greater cultural identification is seen as an atavistic impulse, exemplified by the Klan or the tragic situation in the former Yugoslavia, that should be replaced with universal standards that apply equally to everyone. Although few would contest that the concepts of market and jural equality have created much good for the human race, man does not live by bread and procedural rights alone. A realm of authority and meaning exists at a level between the individual and the state—a realm that cannot be comprehended by neoclassical commentators and traditional civil rights reformers. Non-rational processes and forms of authority pervade the institutions—family, church, friendship—that are most central to people's lives. The local institutions of civil society are not understandable in market or bureaucratic terms.

In advocating a move toward a community-empowerment paradigm, one need not be an extreme racial or cultural particularist. Rather, one need merely believe that there is nothing pathological or wicked about the desire most people have to bond with others with whom they feel a common link of family, language, history, religion, and tradition. The universalisms of the market and government bureaucracies weaken the bonds of community. It does not derogate the individual to realize that life is given meaning in the context of family, community, religion, and culture.

* * *

The current view—that procedural fairness and outcome fairness are necessarily in conflict—traps us between two undesirables: big business and big government. Community empowerment shows us that our real interests lie in establishing economic and political structures that strengthen community-based institutions and allow the issues that most directly touch people's lives to be decided at the local level. Community empowerment advances the interests of every non-elite American, regardless of race or ethnicity, and addresses problems of middle-class anomie as well as of lower-class hopelessness. Part of the struggle must be to create a financial structure that ensures that all Americans can buy and improve their own homes, start and maintain their own businesses, and serve their own people. A community-empowerment paradigm sees lower-and middle-class Blacks and Whites as united by their desires to resist the cultural and economic colonization of their respective communities and to engage in self-determination. Moreover, a community-empowerment approach may provide a more legitimate and enduring basis for transracial politics, because unlike existing civil rights paradigms, community empowerment is based on a genuine respect for our differences. Because the structural economic forces that are eroding our communities can only be understood in their larger context, the discussion of community-empowerment public policy begins with a sobering analysis of the local effects of globalization.

* * *

B. A Community–Empowerment Approach in Practice: Community Development Financial Institutions

Despite increasing globalization, some significant positive signs have appeared on the horizon. Quietly, over the past fifteen years, with little governmental support, a billion dollar community development financial institution (CDFI) industry has emerged. Development banks, credit unions, and loan funds have collectively extended more than $2 billion in loans and are currently capitalized with more than $700 million—much of it raised from within the communities served. Although assisted by banks receiving CRA credit for investing in CDFIs, the emergence of the CDFI industry is largely a testament to what can be achieved by committed and visionary grassroots activism coupled with the support of small business.

CDFIs exist in a variety of forms: some are bank holding companies or other insured depository institutions; others are unregulated non-profit corporations. All CDFIs are responsible financial intermediaries primarily devoted to developing the community in which they operate. They are structured so as to encourage community input in making policy. Thus, CDFIs express the community-empowerment mindset: they transcend the liberal-conservative dichotomy, they are not entirely market driven but are not charities, and they are not bureaucratic government programs. Rather, they are responsible local businesses dedicated to helping their local community, institutions, and people to help themselves.

* * *

There are a variety of traditional reasons to support the assistance of the CDFI industry. Developing credit in low-and moderate-income communities is vital to our nation's economic prospects. As corporate downsizing is expected to continue, small businesses will continue to provide the bulk of new job growth; as the conventional financial industry becomes more concentrated and increasingly neglects small business, and as the possibility of direct governmental aid becomes increasingly remote, the role of CDFIs becomes ever more crucial. In addition, CDFI lending programs encourage entrepreneurship, self-sufficiency, and creative problem solving—essential qualities for national and community economic prosperity, and for breaking the cycles of poverty and welfare dependency. Notably, CDFIs measure their success not only by institutional and client economic gains, but also by their contributions to building the civic infrastructure of businesses, professions, voluntary organizations, church groups, families, and other community institutions.

To serve our communities' growing need for locally controlled credit, a national commitment to CDFIs must be cultivated. Yet there is a notable tension between the need that community-empowerment institutions have for independence, local control, and freedom from bureaucratic red tape on the one hand, and their need for active restructuring of the financial marketplace by the federal government and more initial capital input on the other. Public policy aimed at fostering the CDFI movement must do the latter without treating CDFIs as charities. Existing public purpose lenders, particularly community-development banks, community-development credit unions, community-development loan funds, and microloan funds, constitute a solid basis for a national network of CDFIs and provide potential models for structuring new institutions. The discussion that follows offers a look at some of the major models for CDFIs and concludes with a consideration of the policies on the current legislative agenda aimed at fostering CDFIs.

1. Community–Development   Banks.—A   community-development bank—the most comprehensive of the CDFI models—provides for development credit for its community through the vehicle of a commercial bank, credit union, or savings and loan. It utilizes proactive subsidiaries or affiliates to carry out its mission to develop the community. A community-development bank incorporates a broad range of services rather than specializing in a product or credit service as do other CDFIs. The depository institution subsidiaries of community-development banks are, of course, legally identical to and bound by the same regulations as their conventional insured depository counterparts.

A community-development bank, like any financial institution, must be concerned with operating in a safe and sound manner. In addition, if the institution hopes to grow—both by building on its retained earnings and by attracting additional outside capital—then it must be reasonably profitable. Nevertheless, its primary goal is the impact that both its depository institution and other affiliates have on its community or target population. Thus, a development bank has a dual standard of performance; it must successfully operate a financial institution and support community empowerment and development. The successes of the industry to date demonstrate that these are not necessarily incompatible goals.

* * *

2. Community–Development   Credit   Unions.—Community-development credit unions (CDCUs) are regulated and federally insured depository institutions that are cooperatively owned and operated by their members on a one-person, one-vote system regardless of the amount on deposit. As non-profit cooperative institutions, credit unions are tax exempt. Although their services vary depending on the credit union's size, age, level of organization, and the desires of its members, most CDCUs offer only a basic set of retail banking services.

* * *

CDCUs serve as the only bank for many poor Americans. Members are provided with basic financial services—bank accounts; check cashing; financial planning; and personal, car, tuition, and home-repair loans. By bringing people into the financial mainstream, credit unions help members to develop mainstream creditworthiness. Membership in the credit union offers not only reduced costs for needed services like check cashing and bill paying, but also encouragement to save through regular deposits and payroll deductions. Most importantly, credit union membership encourages better attitudes toward sound personal financial management.

Lending is, of course, central to the mission of most CDCUs. All credit unions make loans to their members, but CDCUs strive to make loans that will contribute to community development as well as benefit individual members. CDCUs typically encourage loans that enable members to get and keep jobs, start and expand businesses, and improve members' property. Many CDCUs also work with other community-development organizations to make loans for such development projects as the rehabilitation of multi-family apartment buildings.

* * *

3. Community–Development Loan Funds.—Community-development loan funds (CDLFs) are unregulated and uninsured financial intermediaries that aggregate capital raised from individual and institutional social investors at below market interest rates. They lend this money primarily to non-profit and cooperative housing and business developers in low-income rural and inner-city communities. CDLFs emphasize financing projects that provide new economic opportunities and resources in their communities. By providing low-income people with an economic stake, CDLFs encourage participation in community-business, social, and political affairs. "CDLFs have been leaders in financing community land trusts, cooperative housing (including mobile home parks), and worker/community-owned businesses."

CDLFs provide credit that is neither affordable nor available from mainstream lenders. Frequently, CDLFs' borrowers cannot seek financing from mainstream institutions because they lack credit histories or require too much technical assistance. Because most community-development projects require multiple sources of funding, the loans necessary to make the projects work most often do not comport well with mainstream financial loan packages and must be individually tailored to the project. This lack of standardization means that few projects fit secondary market criteria; these projects are thus unattractive to conventional lenders. In other instances, the loans appear too risky to mainstream lenders, and sometimes the CDLFs engage in outright interest rate subsidy.

CDLFs also operate as a bridge to conventional permanent financing by providing a reliable, low-risk source of information and funding. Conventional lenders often commit to a project once a CDLF loan provides comfort about the adequacy of the project's collateral. CDLFs can provide such assurance because, by involving community members directly in loan fund decisionmaking, CDLFs are able to base lending decisions not only on by-the-numbers financial analysis, but also on direct knowledge of their borrowers, thereby reducing risk. In addition, CDLFs' small, cooperative structure allows low-cost provision of capital because of the superior access to information and a high degree of repayment loyalty. Despite the absence of traditional risk management policies, of the more than $100 million loaned by CDLFs, loan default losses have amounted to less than one percent of all loans made.

* * *

4. *Microloan Funds.*—Microloan fund programs "make very small, short term loans from a revolving loan fund to people who want to start up or expand very small ... businesses that are often part-time, home-based, and minority-owned." Microloan funds most often appear as one component among many in micro-enterprise development programs that promote and teach entrepreneurship by integrating both economic and human development among low-income people. These micro-enterprise ventures include such businesses as home day care, tailoring, catering and food service, hair and nail styling, engine repair, trucking, and retail sales. Pioneered in the developing world by Accion International and Bangladesh's Grameen Bank, microloan funds are relatively new to the United States; the first such fund was established here in 1983. Approximately 150 funds now exist in the United States, and their successes have engaged the interest of President Clinton and members of the Small Business Administration.

Many microloan programs rely on a peer-group lending model, in which a small group of would-be entrepreneurs come together for the purpose of obtaining credit; after training and analyzing each other's business plans, the group selects a plan to receive the first loan. If payments on the first loan remain current for a certain length of time, other members of the group are eligible to borrow. In most programs, if one member defaults, no one else is eligible to borrow. Members meet regularly to evaluate business plans, track repayments, exchange information, and lend mutual support. Group borrowing creates tremendous peer pressure to repay loans, and by assuming administrative tasks, participants lower operating costs.

                              * * *

E.   Toward Community Economic Empowerment

There are moments in history in which intense shifts in what constitutes common-sense occur. The Great Depression was such a time. In the wake of the Great Depression, the American people lost their faith in the financial system and the business leadership of the society. The persistence of the Depression and the revelation of scandals involving the most prominent financiers caused a massive shift—one that transcended class—in notions about the proper role of government and the appropriate structure of the financial economy. President Roosevelt's answer was the New Deal's restructuring of financial markets, which was part of the foundation for a generation of expanding economic opportunity. That system collapsed as a result of "deregulation and destabilizing macroeconomic policies." In a similar fashion, shortly after Richard Nixon announced, "I am now a Keynesian," the neoclassical ideal of laissez faire again became the dominant economic paradigm in the United States. We are once more about to undergo such a change in world view.

I have attempted to demonstrate how a community-empowerment paradigm highlights the inadequacy of dominant civil rights paradigms that are based on neoclassical economic thinking; far from solving the problems they address, civil rights paradigms have instead obscured how the structure of the financial system harms all non-rich Americans and their communities, with particularly deleterious effects on the communities of African-Americans. This Article attempts both to disrupt the dominant paradigms and to begin to replace them. The latter ambition requires ongoing commitment, debate, and discussion. The ideas that follow are thus presented as tenuous indicators of potentially fruitful avenues of exploration, designed as much to provoke discussion and suggest areas for further research as to advocate a particular political trajectory.

Changing the nature of financial policy requires a broad-based coalition. Financial debate in Washington currently expresses little more than the scramble for advantage of different segments of the financial industry: big banks versus small banks, securities firms versus banks, and insurance companies versus securities firms. Consumer groups and community activists typically engage in the politics of finance with little more than interest-group aspirations. To achieve far-reaching reform, these groups must go beyond thinking about a hot scandal or a few bits of legislation and integrate financial reform into a larger politics. The logical source of financial reform is all nonrich Americans, whose interests are not addressed by the current financial economy. The interests of those who seek community reinvestment and those who seek decent, union-wage work are linked with those whose savings are inadequate, unguaranteed, or poorly invested, or whose pensions are jeopardized by weak regulatory and guaranty mechanisms. "These seemingly irreconcilable positions can only dovetail to drive reform if both organizing tracks explicitly promote greater financial sector stability and more dynamism in the underlying economy." Savers and borrowers must work together to effect changes in regulatory policy and in the tax code to support a more long-term perspective for investors and managers and to strengthen the foundational assets of the paper economy. "No matter where they fall on the risk-reward spectrum, most non-rich capital suppliers and capital users win when their political demands define the public obligations of financial markets in terms of strengthening domestic employment and living standards."

* * *

V. CONCLUSION

According to the influential philosopher Thomas Kuhn, when old modes of thought no longer provide a satisfactory explanation of reality or a guide to future activity, a shift in paradigms takes place so that activity and analysis can progress. This Article argues that the old liberal and conservative paradigms have exhausted their power to explain, inspire, or guide public policy. A new community-empowerment paradigm, however, is emerging. I have avoided making any highly specific claims as to the content of this emerging paradigm because, like the modes of thought I believe it will supplant, it is more a sensibility and an approach than it is a body of doctrine.

* * *

As the major parties stumble in the old grooves and grope toward a new politics, a variety of thriving grassroots organizations are meeting in living rooms and union halls across America to organize working class communities around such issues as hazardous waste dumping, community investment, and affordable housing. Unlike those who lead major activist and lobbying groups, grassroots activists come not from the professional classes, but from among the more typically alienated lower middle classes. "For them, democracy means building their own political organizations, drawing people together in a relationship that leads to real political power. In a sense, they are reinventing democracy from the ground up, starting in their own neighborhoods."

Despite the many local successes that grassroots community groups have won, the community-organizing movement has developed neither a national political presence nor a coherent body of doctrine or theory. Liberals and conservatives, bereft of any workable plans to deal with the nation's ills, look increasingly to community-based organizations for ideas. Unfortunately, mainstream politicians too often attempt to use ideas from the community-organizing movement for their own purposes and develop government programs that adopt the form but reject the substance of community empowerment. Technocratic attempts to "empower" people without challenging the entrenched power of the dominant elite are hollow. This hollowness is evident in the administration's CDFI initiative; although President Clinton genuinely seeks to give low-income communities the tools with which they can help themselves, his plan refuses to confront how the financial industry's structure undermines the economic base of our communities. Politicians now quote the old saying "give a man a fish and you feed him for a day. Teach a man to fish and you feed him for life." A community-empowerment approach argues that what really matters is who owns the fish pond, because skills and tools are not enough to ensure long-term community prosperity, and because man does not live by bread alone.

* * *

Moral values and social policies must be understood in the material economic context out of which they emerge. Moral values in the abstract have little content, and social policies meant to effectuate these values will be of no avail without concrete structural analysis of the nature of the problems being addressed. Racial justice is a moral value, and although the problems caused by the absence of racial justice are manifest everywhere, our old paradigms and attendant mindset obscure the structure within which these problems exist. Manifestations of our absence of racial justice include disinvestment in African-American communities and the difficulties that African-American people face when seeking access to capital. Continuing to understand these social problems solely in terms of the old paradigms, however, will cause us to continue to make largely ineffective public policy. The Equal Credit Opportunity Act and the Community Reinvestment Act, for all their good intentions, have failed to stem the tide of structural economic forces that are disempowering African-American and other low- and moderate-income communities.

The lack of access to capital that disempowers Black people and their communities is only the most visible and extreme manifestation of how the economic structure disempowers all non-elite people and their communities. The old formulations of anti-discrimination, equal treatment, and affirmative action policies are not up to the task of challenging the structural imperatives of the emerging global financial system; indeed, these policies tend to legitimate the very structures that are doing the damage. Within a community-empowerment paradigm, the devastation of particular communities is understood within the structural economic context, and the intellectual, rhetorical, and cultural foundation is laid for the creation of a broad-based transracial politics that can challenge the power of the emerging global business and professional elite.

The Hidden Cost of Being African American

Oxford Univ. Press (2004) at 183–200 (2004).

■ Thomas Shapiro

CONCLUSION: ASSETS FOR EQUALITY

The enormous racial wealth gap perpetuates racial inequality in the United States. Racial inequality appears intransigent because the way families use wealth transmits advantages from generation to generation. Furthermore, the twenty-first century marks the beginning of a new racial dilemma for the United States: Family wealth and inheritances cancel gains in classrooms, workplaces, and paychecks, worsening racial inequality. I see no means of seriously moving toward racial equality without positive asset policies to address the racial wealth gap.

The racial wealth gap is more then obdurate historical legacy that lives in the present, because it also springs from contemporary public policy and institutional discrimination, not to mention individuals' behavior.

Children's Savings Accounts

Children growing up in families with assets go to school secure in the knowledge that their families will support their dreams and future wellbeing. However, many children in American grow up without such confidence. The majority of children come from families who cannot provide a positive asset legacy. About 4 in 10 of all children grow up in asset poor families. More distressing, over half of African American children grow up asset poor. What difference would it make if every child in America grew up knowing that (s)he had a net egg to use to go to college, buy a home, or start a business? As a result of acquiring start up money, they would be more confident and competent; they would feel more invested in themselves, their communities, and the future. They would have dreams and a way of making them come true. Benefits would accrue to individuals, families, and society as a whole.

There are many models for Children's Savings Accounts, such as initial government or private contributions at birth, matches of family contributions for low income families throughout the child's formative years, and limited use of account balances at age 18 and older. Imagine, for example, that every child born in the United States had an initial deposit of $1,000 in such an account. Additional yearly deposits would be encouraged and possibly tied to achievements such as school graduations, summer employment, and community service. Acquiring financial literacy throughout the school years would be a strong program component, providing a relevant and stimulating educational content. Government would match contributions from low income parents.

Individual Development Accounts

The vast majority of Americans have not accumulated many assets and are not about to inherit a large nest egg. This lack of assets impedes them from moving ahead, and they watch people jumping ahead who they know have not worked harder, have not tried harder, and do not deserve financial success any more than they do. Start up assets for opportunities like education, businesses and retirement could improve dramatically the lives of average Americans.

Latoya Miton, who would do anything for her daughter's education, dreams of moving to a community with better schools, even calculating sacrifices like going without telephone service and auto insurance. If Latoya's job of managing a dry-cleaning establishment paid a living wage and offered health and pension benefits, moving to Kirkwood, Missouri might not be just a dream. She is an ideal candidate for a program that motivates savings for future mobility. Smart and hardworking, she might use it for higher education or even start a dry-cleaning business of her own.

Individual Development Accounts (IDA) are the first and larges policy initiative in asset-development policy, spearheaded by Michael Sherraden's book *Assets and the Poor,* promoted by policy makers and advocacy groups, and backed by several national foundations. Individual Development Accounts reward savings by asset poor families who aim to buy their first home, acquire postsecondary education, or start a small business. For every dollar a family saves, matching funds that typically come from a variety of private and public sources provide strong incentive. The IDA Tax Credit would work by providing financial institutions with a dollar for dollar tax credit for every dollar they contribute as matching funds for IDAs, up to $500 per IDA per year.

Down Payment Accounts

Homeownership is a signature of the American Dream and, as I have emphasized throughout this book, frames class status, family identity, and schooling opportunities. We also know that homeownership provides the nexus for transformative assets of family wealth. For this reason, and others, I think a hallmark policy idea is Down Payment Accounts for first time homebuyers.

The chief purpose of Down Payment Accounts is to allow families to acquire assets for down payment and closing costs. How would these accounts work? Similar to the home mortgage interest deduction, renters could deduct a portion of their rent on their tax form and have it put aside in a dedicated account to match their own savings for homeownership on a one to one basis. This money would be used for first time homebuyers.

A revealing contrast is that in U.S. history government policies have been very effective in giving other kinds of families start ups to acquire property and assets. I am thinking specifically of the Homestead Act, begun in 1862, which provided up to 160 acres of land, self-reliance, and ultimately wealth to millions of American families. This remarkable government policy set in motion opportunities for upward mobility and a more secure future for oneself and one's children by giving nearly 1.5 million families title to 246 million acres of land, nearly the size of California and Texas combined. One study puts the number of homestead descendents living today at 46 million adults. This means that up to a quarter of the adult population potentially traces its legacy of property ownership, upward mobility, economic stability, class status, and wealth directly to one national policy—a policy that in practice essentially excluded African Americans.

Matching Social Assistance to Asset Policy

Traditional welfare policies have failed to launch families out of poverty, just as they have failed to promote independence and self reliance. Asset policies will not work by themselves, either. In tandem, asset and income policies promise supporting pillars for mobility. To make sure that asset building policies do not become a shell game simply transferring costs from federal to state or from public to private—or creaming monies from social assistance—policy need to be crafted so that asset and traditional social assistance policies synergize one another rather than cancel each other out. For example, Children's Savings Accounts should not replace a public commitment to higher education. Tuition at public institutions of higher education should not rise just because 18 year olds have accumulated a small net egg to make college affordable. A worst case scenario involves a family raiding their fledgling IDA account, losing matching payments in the process, to buy food at the end of the month because their food stamp allocation was too small. Families should not miss medical appointments, delay renewing prescriptions, stretch out the time between dental visits, or skip meals to scrape together money for monthly IDA contributions. These sacrifices to contribute to asset accounts are damaging bargains families should not be forced to consider because of public policy failures. One lesson from the national IDA demonstration project indicates that these temptations are real and should be avoided.

The single most important housing policy is the home mortgage interest deduction. Because it lowers taxes in proportion to a family's tax rate, the majority of this $55 billion subsidy goes to the highest income families; one third of it goes to families in the top 10 percent.

The nation's housing priorities must change. First, the dynamic housing markets—that is, laws of supply and demand incentives for new housing construction, and the location of new housing—must change. I like an idea that, instead of rewarding taxpayers who pay higher marginal tax rates, converts the interest one can deduct into a flat percentage rate. All families, say, could take 25% of home mortgage interest off their taxes, regardless of earnings or whether they choose the standard deduction or the itemized tax schedule.

Given the increasing prevalence of automated underwriting systems in scoring mortgage applications, fair lending enforcement agencies should develop tools to test for discrimination so that factors weighted against minorities do not become codified into uniform industry standards. Especially as loan pricing according to risk becomes common practice, lenders should be discouraged from generating greater profits by designing systems that make minorities appear to be riskier mortgages.

Mortgage lenders and insurance redliners should be held accountable for the racially specific damages they have imposed on communities of color. Why can't we sue predatory lenders and their suppliers of capital, mortgage and insurance redliners for what they have done to cities and communities?

Without these changes, the extra capital made available to families through various asset policies and other government policies would likely fail because the two tiered housing market would still generate more wealth for the affluent.

Where a family lives largely determines school quality and family wealth largely determines where people live. Local property taxes fund the leading portion of school finances, 45–50 percent; therefore, it is easy to understand how the wealth of a community, its resource base, governs educational resources and the opportunities that go with them. (The federal share is actually only about 5–10 percent, with the state contributing the remaining 45–50 percent.) The disadvantage of low resource communities and the advantage of higher resource communities can be addressed by shifting local school financing up to state and federal levels.

Part of the big picture I have been describing is how communities, families, and individuals try to trap resources and hoard them for their own benefit. Because individuals believe they can personally benefit from it, and because they do not trust government to act in the civic interest, they attempt to buy their way out of social problems on a one at a time basis. This encourages a privatized notion of citizenship at the expense of solutions that work for all.

We can no loner ignore tremendous wealth inequities as we struggle with the thorny issue of racial inequality. Without attending to how equal results—especially concerning wealth—we will continue to repeat the deep and disturbing patterns of racial inequality and conflict that plague our republic. A just society would not wish racial legacies and inheritance to block opportunities and make a mockery of merit, and just individual will rejoice to give merit and democracy a fairer chance to triumph.

NOTE: The following case represents an innovative use of the Uniform Commercial Code and common law doctrine of unconscioniability to challenge the propensity of banks to increase fee income by introducing new fees, for automatic teller transactions for example, or by raising existing fees, such as bounced check (NSF) fees. The trend to unlimited increases in bounced check fees became a point of consumer activism in the 1900's in the immediate aftermath of Federal rules ending the interest rate ceilings on deposit account. Banks lost the government protection from having to pay market rates of interest of deposit accounts, and were forced to compete for deposits by paying higher and higher interest rates. The deposit rate wars created pressures on the profitability of the once secure bank balance sheet. This pressure was relieved in the early 1980's by introducing fees that were unrelated to cost, and that were not disclosed to depositors when the initial deposit agreement was signed.

Although, the *Perdue* case represents a victory. It did not result in a permanent reconfiguration of the fee structure for bounced checks. It did, however, introduce the use of unconscionability doctrine in class actions by plaintiffs seeking to limit the fee structure imposed on retail deposit customers in the federally regulated banking industry. The unconscionability doctrine that you encountered in your contracts course served the more limited purpose of defending a single consumer against a default enforcement action by retail sellers who sought judicial enforcement of a variety of unfair terms contained in boilerplate agreements. When you finish reading

Perdue, can you think of any other retail price structures that might be suitable for unconscionability challenges?

Perdue v. Crocker National Bank

702 P.2d 503 (Cal. 1985).

■ Broussard, Justice

Plaintiff filed this class action to challenge the validity of charges imposed by defendant Crocker National Bank for the processing of checks drawn on accounts without sufficient funds. (The parties refer to such checks as NSF checks and to the handling charge as an NSF charge.) He appeals from a judgment of the trial court entered after that court sustained defendant's general demurrer without leave to amend.

On July 3, 1978, plaintiff filed suit on behalf of all persons with checking accounts at defendant bank and a subclass of customers who have paid NSF charges to the bank. The complaint first alleges a contract under which the bank furnishes checking service in return for a maintenance charge. It then asserts that "It is the practice of defendants to impose and collect a unilaterally set charge for processing checks presented against plaintiffs' accounts when such accounts do not contain sufficient funds to cover the amount of the check." "Defendants have at various times unilaterally increased the NSF charge to an amount the defendants deemed appropriate, without reference to any criteria, and defendants imposed and collected the said increased amount without any explanation or justification by defendants to plaintiffs." At the time of filing of the suit, the charge was $6 for each NSF check, whether the check was honored or returned unpaid, even though "the actual cost incurred by the defendants in processing an NSF check is approximately $0.30."

The bank requires each depositor to sign a signature card which it uses "to determine and verify the authenticity of endorsements on checks." In extremely small (6 point) type, the signature card states that the undersigned depositors "agree with Crocker National Bank and with each other that ... this account and all deposits therein shall be ... subject to all applicable laws, to the Bank's present and future rules, regulations, practices and charges, and to its right of setoff for the obligations of any of us." The card does not identify the amount of the charge for NSF checks, and the bank does not furnish the depositor with a copy of the applicable bank rules and regulations.

On the basis of these allegations, plaintiff asserts five causes of action: (1) for a judicial declaration that the bank's signature card is not a contract authorizing NSF charges; (2) for a judicial declaration that such charges are oppressive and unconscionable; (3) to recover damages for unjust enrichment derived from the bank's collection of illegal NSF charges; (4) to enjoin alleged unfair and deceptive practices—the bank's failure to inform customers of the contractual nature of the signature card, and its practice of waiving NSF charges as to certain preferred customers; and (5) to recover the difference between the NSF charges and defendant's actual expenses in processing NSF checks on the theory that the charges represent an unreasonable attempt to fix liquidated damages.

* * *

Plaintiff's third alleged cause of action is derivative; its charge of unjust enrichment depends upon a finding pursuant to some other cause of action that the NSF charges were invalid or excessive. This cause of action raises no issues for decision in the present appeal. The other four alleged causes of action, however, present independent and substantial issues. We review each in turn, applying the established principle that [factual allegations in the demurrer are assumed true upon review]. * * *

I. Plaintiff's First Cause of Action: Whether the Signature Card is a Contract Authorizing NSF Charges.

The complaint alleges that "The signature card prepared by the defendants does not identify the amount of any charge to be paid by the plaintiffs for processing NSF checks and is not an agreement for such payment. The card does not constitute mutual assent to NSF charges in any particular sum or at all and accordingly is not a contract conferring authority to do the acts complained of herein." "Based upon the language of the signature card, the plaintiffs believed and expected that the signature card was intended as a handwriting example for purposes of identification and verification only." Plaintiff therefore seeks a judicial declaration "as to whether the signature card is a valid or enforceable contract and . . . a lawful basis for the imposition of the NSF charge."

The cases unanimously agree that a signature card such as the Crocker Bank card at issue here is a contract.

* * *

Plaintiff argues, however, that even if a signature card is a contract to establish a checking account, it is not a contract authorizing NSF charges. He contends that the contract is illusory because it permits the bank to set and change the NSF charges at its discretion, and without assent from the customer except such as may be inferred from the fact that the customer does not cancel his account after the bank posts notice of its rates.[6]

Plaintiff relies on the rule that "[an] agreement that provides that the price to be paid, or other performance to be rendered, shall be left to the will and discretion of one of the parties is not enforceable." [*Automatic Vending Co. v. Wisdom*, 182 Cal. App. 2d 354 (1960).] That rule, however, applies only if the total discretion granted one party renders the contract lacking in consideration. * * * If there are reciprocal promises, as in the present case, the fact that the contract permits one party to set or change

---

6. Financial Code section 865.4, subdivision (b)(1) requires a bank to give customers 15 days' notice of any change in charges imposed on bank accounts.

the price charged for goods or services does not render the contract illusory. * * *

The recent decision in *Lazar v. Hertz Corp.*, [143 Cal. App. 3d 128 (1983)] offers an analogy to the present litigation. Hertz' car rental agreement permitted it to determine unilaterally the price charged for gas used to fill the tanks of returned rental cars. Plaintiff's suit alleged that Hertz fixed unreasonably high prices, in breach of its duty of good faith and fair dealing. Discussing this cause of action, the court said that "[the] essence of the good faith covenant is objectively reasonable conduct. Under California law, an open term in a contract must be filled in by the party having discretion within the standard of good faith and fair dealing." * * *

We conclude that plaintiff here is not entitled to a judicial declaration that the bank's signature card is not a contract authorizing NSF charges. To the contrary, we hold as a matter of law that the card is a contract authorizing the bank to impose such charges, subject to the bank's duty of good faith and fair dealing in setting or varying such charges. Plaintiff may, upon remand of this case, amend his complaint to seek a judicial declaration determining whether the charges actually set by the bank are consonant with that duty.

II.   Plaintiff's Second Cause of Action: Whether the Bank's NSF Charges are Oppressive, Unreasonable, or Unconscionable.

Plaintiff's second cause of action alleges that the signature card is drafted by defendant bank which enjoys a superior bargaining position by reason of its greater economic power, knowledge, experience and resources. Depositors have no alternative but to acquiesce in the relationship as offered by defendant or to accept a similar arrangement with another bank. The complaint alleges that the card is vague and uncertain, that it is unclear whether it is intended as an identification card or a contract, that it imposes no obligation upon the bank, and permits the bank to alter or terminate the relationship at any time. It then asserts that "The disparity between the actual cost to defendants and the amount charged by defendants for processing an NSF check unreasonably and oppressively imposes excessive and unfair liability upon plaintiffs." Plaintiff seeks a declaratory judgment to determine the rights and duties of the parties.

Plaintiff's allegations point to the conclusion that the signature card, if it is a contract, is one of adhesion. The term contract of adhesion "signifies a standardized contract, which, imposed and drafted by the party of superior bargaining strength, relegates to the subscribing party only the opportunity to adhere to the contract or reject it." [*Neal v. State Farm Ins. Co.*, 188 Cal. App. 2d 690 (1961).] The signature card, drafted by the bank and offered to the customer without negotiation, is a classic example of a contract of adhesion; the bank concedes as much.

In *Graham v. Scissor–Tail, Inc.*, [28 Cal. 3d 807 (1981),] we observed that

To describe a contract as adhesive in character is not to indicate its legal effect.... [A] contract of adhesion is fully enforceable according to its terms * * * unless certain other factors are present which, under established legal rules—legislative or judicial—operate to render it otherwise. * * * Generally speaking * * * there are two judicially imposed limitations on the enforcement of adhesion contracts or provisions thereof. The first is that such a contract or provision which does not fall within the reasonable expectations of the weaker or "adhering" party will not be enforced against him. * * * The second—a principle of equity applicable to all contracts generally—is that a contract or provision, even if consistent with the reasonable expectations of the parties, will be denied enforcement if, considered in its context, it is unduly oppressive or 'unconscionable.' * * *

In 1979, the Legislature enacted Civil Code section 1670.5, which codified the established doctrine that a court can refuse to enforce an unconscionable provision in a contract.[10] Section 1670.5 reads as follows:

(a) If the court as a matter of law finds the contract or any clause of the contract to have been unconscionable at the time it was made the court may refuse to enforce the contract, or it may enforce the remainder of the contract without the unconscionable clause, or it may so limit the application of any unconscionable clause as to avoid any unconscionable result.

(b) When it is claimed or appears to the court that the contract or any clause thereof may be unconscionable the parties shall be afforded a reasonable opportunity to present evidence as to its commercial setting, purpose, and effect to aid the court in making the determination.

* * *

Plaintiff bases his claim of unconscionability on the alleged 2,000 percent differential between the NSF charge of $6 and the alleged cost to the bank of $0.30. * * *

To begin with, it is clear that the price term, like any other term in a contract, may be unconscionable. * * * Allegations that the price exceeds cost or fair value, standing alone, do not state a cause of action. * * * Instead, plaintiff's case will turn upon further allegations and proof setting forth the circumstances of the transaction.

The courts look to the basis and justification for the price, * * * including "the price actually being paid by ... other similarly situated consumers in a similar transaction." [*Bennett v. Behring Corp.*, 466 F.Supp. 689 (S.D. Fla. 1979).] The cases, however, do not support defendant's contention that a price equal to the market price cannot be held unconscionable. * * * Thus courts consider not only the market price, but also

---

10. Section 1670.5 is based upon Uniform Commercial Code section 2–302, but expands coverage to include noncommercial contracts.

the cost of the goods or services to the seller, * * * the inconvenience imposed on the seller, * * * and the true value of the product or service. * * *

In addition to the price justification, decisions examine what Justice Weiner in *A & M Produce* called the "procedural aspects" of unconscionability. See *A & M Produce Co.*, [135 Cal. App. 3d 473 (1982).] Cases may turn on the absence of meaningful choice, * * * the lack of sophistication of the buyer, * * * and the presence of deceptive practices by the seller. * * *

Applying this analysis to our review of the complaint at hand, we cannot endorse defendant's argument that the $6 charge is so obviously reasonable that no inquiry into its basis or justification is necessary. In 1978 $6 for processing NSF checks may not seem exorbitant, but price alone is not a reliable guide. Small charges applied to a large volume of transactions may yield a sizable sum. The complaint asserts that the cost of processing NSF checks is only $0.30 per check, which means that a $6 charge would produce a 2,000 percent profit; even at the higher cost estimate of $1 a check mentioned in plaintiff's petition for hearing, the profit is 600 percent. Such profit percentages may not be automatically unconscionable, but they indicate the need for further inquiry.[15]

* * *

In short, the bank structured a totally one-sided transaction. The absence of equality of bargaining power, open negotiation, full disclosure, and a contract which fairly sets out the rights and duties of each party demonstrates that the transaction lacks those checks and balances which would inhibit the charging of unconscionable fees. In such a setting, plaintiff's charge that the bank's NSF fee is exorbitant, yielding a profit far in excess of cost, cannot be dismissed on demurrer. Under Civil Code section 1670.5, the parties should be afforded a reasonable opportunity to present evidence as to the commercial setting, purpose, and effect of the signature card and the NSF charge in order to determine whether that charge is unconscionable.

III.　Plaintiff's Fourth Cause of Action: Whether the Bank has Performed Acts of Unfair Competition.

Business and Professions Code section 17200 defines "unfair competition" to include any "unlawful, unfair, or fraudulent business practice." This language is intended to protect consumers as well as business competitors; its prohibitory reach is not limited to deceptive or fraudulent conduct but extends to any unlawful business conduct. * * *

The complaint charges two acts of unfair competition. First, it asserts that the "signature card is used in a manner which is unfair, deceptive and

---

15. We observe that the bank charges the same fee whether it honors or rejects an NSF check. The fee, consequently, cannot be intended as compensation for the credit risk arising from paying such a check, or for the interest on the amount loaned.

misleading, in that plaintiffs are led to believe that it is a signature card for identification purposes and the defendants treat the signature card, without disclosure of said fact, as the legal authority to impose the NSF charge on plaintiffs' checking accounts." Second, it asserts that "defendants arbitrarily and capriciously waive the NSF charge for preferred or commercial accounts," thus shifting the costs of processing NSF checks from those preferred customers to others whose accounts are charged.

Neither allegation is clear and precise. [W]e are uncertain whether plaintiff contends that the signature card itself is deceptive, or whether he contends that the bank employs misrepresentations or other deceptive practices in presenting the card to the depositor. If the latter is plaintiff's contention, the complaint should set out the challenged representations or practices.

It is, of course, clear that if plaintiff can show that the card or the manner in which it is presented to the customer is deceptive and misleading, he can prove a cause of action for unfair competition. Since he seeks only injunctive relief under this cause of action, he need not show that he himself was misled; he need only prove that "members of the public are likely to be deceived." * * * Thus the defect in plaintiff's allegation is not one of substance, but only of lack of certainty. Such a defect would not justify the sustaining of a demurrer without leave to amend. * * *

Plaintiff's assertion * * * that the bank arbitrarily waives NSF charges for some customers contains a more serious defect. Although price discrimination is often unlawful, depending upon the context of the act and the intent of the perpetrator, * * * "arbitrary" price discrimination in itself is not necessarily illegal. This defect is one of substance; while plaintiff's accusation * * * of deceptive and misleading practices describes acts of unfair competition, albeit in very general terms, his accusation of arbitrary waiver of NSF charges does not.

    * * *

IV. Plaintiff's Fifth Cause of Action:
Whether the Bank's Charge for NSF
Checks is an Unlawful Penalty.

[T]he complaint states that "[causing] NSF checks to be presented for payment is a breach by plaintiffs of their contractual obligations to defendant...." The NSF charge collected by defendants, however, "is a penalty and is not imposed to compensate defendants for damages incurred by plaintiffs' breach," and therefore violates Civil Code sections 1670 and 1671. The complaint concludes that "[plaintiffs] are entitled to recover the difference between the unlawful charges collected and defendants' actual damages...."

By these allegations, plaintiff seeks to invoke the rule that a contractual provision specifying damages for breach is valid only if it "[represents] the result of a reasonable endeavor by the parties to estimate a fair average compensation for any loss that may be sustained." [*Better Food Mkts. v. Amer. Dist. Teleg. Co.*, 40 Cal.2d 179 (1953).] An amount disproportionate to the anticipated damages is termed a "penalty." A contractual provision imposing a "penalty" is ineffective, and the wronged party can collect only the actual damages sustained.

Two Court of Appeal decisions have addressed plaintiff's contention and concluded that the writing of an NSF check is not a breach of contract, and thus the fee charged for processing the check is not a penalty. [See *Hoffman v. Security Pacific Nat. Bank*, 121 Cal. App. 3d 964 (1981) ("the depositor has no statutory or contractual obligation to refrain from drawing checks for amounts in excess of the balance in his account"); accord, *Shapiro v. United California Bank*, 133 Cal. App. 3d 256 (1982).]

We agree with those decisions * * * that because the depositor has never agreed to refrain from writing NSF checks, the writing of such a check is not a breach of contract. The fee that the bank may charge for processing such a check is limited by principles of good faith, reasonableness, unconscionability, and the like, but it is not limited to the amount which a bank could recover in a suit for breach of contract. We conclude that the court correctly sustained the demurrer to plaintiff's fifth cause of action without leave to amend.

* * *

―――――

NOTES AND QUESTIONS

1. Community economic development. The intransigence of urban poverty and discrimination against African Americans and other minorities has led politicians, legal scholars, and public policy advocates to look beyond affirmative action and to seek out different legal and economic strategies with which to attack inequality. Many of these proposals have been market-based, grounded in the theory that the most effective ways to alleviate the burden of discrimination and poverty are new approaches to economic development and investment in disadvantaged communities. During the economic boom of the 1990s "community economic development...emerged as the dominant approach to poverty alleviation, touted by politicians as a market-based alternative to outdated welfare policies and championed by civil rights leaders as a critical link to economic equality." Scott L. Cummings, *Community Economic Development as Progressive Politics: Towards a Grassroots Movement for Economic Justice*, 54 STAN L. REV. 399, 400 (2001). Similarly, some argue that the primary obstacle to minority advancement is the lack of assets such as inheritance and home-ownership. Asset-based policy, such as the measures Shapiro proposes in the second excerpted portion of his book, focuses on giving the poor monetary benefits they can use to lift themselves out of poverty. Financial assets are seen as providing the poor with the opportunity to attain the keys to success in American society, such homeownership, business ownership, and quality education. *See* MICHAEL SHERRADEN, ASSETS AND THE POOR: A NEW AMERICAN WELFARE POLICY (1991).

2. Economic versus social equality. The debate over whether blacks should focus on achieving economic or social equality goes back to the origins of the modern civil rights movement. Booker T. Washington emphasized economic self-sufficiency and downplayed the struggle for civil rights. W.E.B. DuBois rejected this "politically acquiescent strategy," and came to be identified with his concept of building a "Talented Tenth" of college-trained black leaders to direct the fight for racial equality. Cummings, *supra* at 410–11. Should the goals of economic and social equality be sought in the same manner? Does one naturally follow from the other?

3. Community Economic empowerment. The kind of community development encouraged by Anthony Taibi is a model of economic investment wherein the betterment of the individual and community reinforce each other. Taibi expresses skepticism about the value of affirmative action, writing "the affirmative action paradigm is inadequate because it refuses to inspect and reform the institutional structures that determine the unfair outcomes affirmative action seeks to redress." How might a proponent of affirmative action respond to this critique? His proposals are very consciously economic, and this approach has been criticized as ignoring the "political dimensions of poverty." The poor are not only economically disadvantaged. Their interests are also woefully underrepresented in mainstream political discourse, and some believe that it is only through political advocacy as well as sound economic policy that the problems of inequality can truly be eradicated. The localism emphasized by Taibi has also been criticized. Scott L. Cummings argues it inhibits multiracial solutions and "works within the existing spatial distribution of poverty and does not address the nexus between poverty concentration and residential segregation—leaving unchallenged the racial cleavages that dissect urban geographies." Cummings, *supra* at 457.

What is your assessment of Taibi's proposals? Is it true that by focusing so exclusively on economics and localism his proposals will fall short of the broad-based changes many deem necessary? Why does Taibi reject the "equality paradigm" and "affirmative action paradigm" as outmoded approaches to improving the lives of minorities and the poor?

4. Asset-based policy. Thomas Shapiro, in his book, *The Hidden Cost of Being African American: How Wealth Perpetuates Inequality* (2004), proposes several methods for providing actual monetary assets to those in need to try and foster "wealth" in disadvantaged communities. Affirmative action may also be seen as an attempt to put some minorities on the road to "wealth." What is the importance of "wealth"? Should the government take an active role in providing financial assets to those who lack them? If educational and employment opportunities are severely limited for many minorities, and the government does not take steps to improve the economic condition of minorities, what are the prospects for narrowing economic inequality?

5. Unconscionability doctrine. Judicially developed legal doctrine has also been used as a method for combating the problems of racial and social inequality. The doctrine of unconscionability represents an attempt to protect the interests of those who are disadvantaged in knowledge and/or resources in contractual dealings. The doctrine was introduced in the D.C. Circuit Court case *Williams v. Walker-Thomas Furniture Co.*, 350 F.2d 445 (D.C. Cir. 1965), in response to what the court regarded as oppressive and unfair credit arrangements in low-income communities. Judge Skelly-Wright wrote that in "many cases, the meaningfulness of choice is negated by gross inequality of bargaining power." *Id.,* at 450. Unconscionability can be seen as undermining the general legal principle of freedom of contract, an extension of market-based rational choice theory, in which individuals are viewed as autonomous actors with perfect information, who may enter into any contractual arrangement they choose, as long as it is not illegal. The argument that the unconscionability doctrine does not violate freedom of contract is that the target of the doctrine, contracts of adhesion, are *not* entered into freely and therefore do not enjoy the same deference as truly bargained-for transactions. Many perceive a fundamental unfairness in form contracts between one economically sophisticated corporation, which writes a lengthy contract in dense, legalistic language, and a party who has no knowledge of contract law and limited resources for finding a different contractual partner. Despite its good intentions, the usefulness of unconscionability has been widely questioned, and there is well-developed criticism of the paternalistic nature of the doctrine. Is it the individual consumer's responsibility to understand every contract he or she enters into?

6.   NSF fees and open price terms. One critic of the affirmative use of unconscionability doctrine to limit bank fees, argues that "[j]udicial attempts at limiting bank discretion in setting NSF and other fees have been wholly unsuccessful in compensating injured depositors. Rising prices and industry practices . . . are used to maximize the number of NSF checks and have created increasing consumer hostility." Stephanie J. Weber, Note, *Excessive Bank Fees: Theories of Liability and the Need for Legislative Action*, 25 U. MEM. L. REV. 1439, 1474 (1995). Is it inherently unfair for a contract to have an open price term which the seller may fill with little or no oversight, only a vague duty to engage in "good faith and fair dealing"? Are open price terms in contracts especially subject to abuse when sellers are dealing with individuals it knows have little business knowledge and will be less likely to mount a legal challenge? For an exhaustive discussion of unconscionability doctrine in California, see Harry G. Prince, *Unconscionability in California: A Need for Restraint and Consistency*, 46 HASTINGS L.J. 459 (1995).

7.   Economic effects of discrimination. Shapiro contends that "studies using matching white and black couples with identical job, income, and credit information consistently reveal discrimination by real estate agents and banks." He argues that despite the reduction in overt racism, blacks and other minorities continue to be the victims of unconscious discrimination and stereotyping in employment, housing, loan application, and any number of other areas. Many contend in even stronger terms that white subordination of minorities is alive and well. Eduardo Bonilla-Silva detects a "new racism," in which racial inequality is reproduced in subtler and less facially offensive ways. In the example of housing segregation, "covert behaviors and strategies have largely replaced Jim Crow practices and have maintained the same outcome." Eduardo Bonilla-Silva, *"New Racism,"* *Color–Blind Racism, and the Future of Whiteness in America, in* WHITE OUT: THE CONTINUING SIGNIFICANCE OF RACISM 271, 273 (Ashley "Woody" Doane & Eduardo Bonilla–Silva eds., 2003). *See also* GLENN C. LOURY, THE ANATOMY OF RACIAL INEQUALITY (2003).

The economic inequality that exists in the United States, and its relation to race, must have an explanation, and since very few people would contend that blacks are less intelligent or less naturally able to succeed, many draw the conclusion that the best possible explanation is the preservation of subtle forms of white prejudice. What is your experience with racial discrimination, either observing or experiencing it?

David Dante Troutt makes the argument that the promotion of the ideal white-American middle-class neighborhood, the "metamarket," has contributed to the development of ghettoes populated largely by minorities, the "antimarket":

> A metamarket * * * describes the dynamic interaction of wealth- and welfare-enhancing public and private forces that stabilize life in middle-income neighborhoods. Meta links not only economic and noneconomic factors, but also the cultural, political, public, and private forces. A metamarket's specific elements reflect degrees of realized psychic and cultural ideals regarding "the good life". * * *

> In contrast, the antimarket involves more than just ghetto. It is the antinorm of the metamarket, the urban place never designed to hold stability. The antimarket encompasses the economic, political, and psychic marginalization of inner-city consumers through the subversion of middle-class rules. Its elements typically include a low-credit, high-risk milieu of struggling stores, inadequate public and private services, a preponderance of undermaintained and disproportionately public rental housing, weak schools, unregulated and unlawful commerce, a lack of public safety, a dearth of political capital, and virtually no personal wealth. * * *

> African American ghetto poverty remains the quintessential form of inner-city or "underclass" poverty because exclusion of, and discrimination against, African Americans have been the most essential means to sustaining middle-class metamarkets. In many respects, such as the siting of undesirable land uses or the deprivation of basic public infrastructure and maintenance services, ghettoes have made middle-class residential markets possible.

David Dante Troutt, *Ghettoes Made Easy: The Metamarket/Antimarket Dichotomy and the Legal Challenges of Inner-City Economic Development,* 35 HARV. C.R.-C.L. L. REV. 427, 429–33 (2000); *see also* WILLIAM JULIUS WILSON, WHEN WORK DISAPPEARS: THE WORLD OF THE NEW URBAN POOR (1997).

Troutt also agues that the worst thing that can happen to a poor community is success, because of the inevitable gentrification and displacement of minorities that will follow. Troutt, *supra* at 502. Shapiro shows the importance that one's neighborhood can have for his or her economic prospects, especially with regards to property values and quality public education. There are some who argue that the increased economic viability of currently disadvantaged communities will benefit society. On the other hand, if society has limited resources, and whites are the overwhelming beneficiaries of them, is it likely they will support policies that transfer these resources to others? Is it possible for everyone to live in a good neighborhood and attend a good school? How do Shapiro's points about educational opportunity among African-Americans relate to the goals of affirmative action?

C.   RETHINKING THE FAMILY AS AN ECONOMIC INSTITUTION

In Re Marriage of Sullivan

691 P.2d 1020 (Cal. 1984).

■ BIRD, C. J.

Is a spouse, who has made economic sacrifices to enable the other spouse to obtain a professional education, entitled to any compensation for his or her contribution upon dissolution of the marriage?

I

Janet and Mark Sullivan were married in September of 1967. The following year, Mark (respondent) entered medical school at Irvine and Janet (appellant) began her final year of undergraduate college at UCLA.

Appellant gives the following abbreviated account of the ensuing years. From 1968 through 1971, respondent attended medical school. Until 1969, appellant worked part time while completing her undergraduate education. After graduation, she obtained a full-time position which she held through 1971.

In 1972, respondent began his internship at Portland, Oregon. Appellant gave up her full-time job to accompany him there. Shortly after the move, she obtained part-time employment.

The couple's daughter, Treisa, was born in May of 1974. Appellant ceased work until 1975 when she resumed part-time employment. From 1976 through 1977, she worked full-time. During this period, respondent completed his residency.

Both parties then moved back to California. Shortly afterward, they separated. In August 1978, respondent petitioned for dissolution of the marriage.

During the marriage, the couple had accumulated some used furniture and two automobiles, both with payments outstanding. This property was disposed of by agreement. Appellant received $500, some used furniture and her automobile, including the obligation to complete the payments.

At the dissolution proceeding, appellant sought to introduce evidence of the value of respondent's medical education. She argued that the education was obtained by the joint efforts and sacrifices of the couple, that it constituted the greatest asset of the marriage, and that—accordingly—both parties should share in its benefits.

The superior court rejected these arguments and granted respondent's motion *in limine* to exclude all evidence pertaining to the value of the education. At the same time, the court granted partial summary judgment to the effect that respondent's education did not constitute community property. The court indicated that it was barred from awarding appellant any compensation for her contribution to respondent's education by the rule of *In re Marriage of Aufmuth*, [89 Cal. App. 3d 446 (1979)] (professional education does not constitute community property).

In May of 1980, the court issued its interlocutory judgment of dissolution. Appellant was awarded no spousal support, but the court reserved jurisdiction for five years to modify that determination. The parties were awarded joint custody of their daughter. Respondent was ordered to pay appellant $250 per month for child support and to reimburse her for half the cost of the child's medical insurance. Finally, the court directed respondent to pay appellant $1,250 in attorney fees and $1,000 in costs.

Both parties appealed.

II

This court originally granted a hearing in this case primarily to determine whether a spouse, who has made economic sacrifices to enable the other spouse to obtain an education, is entitled to compensation upon dissolution of the marriage. While the case was pending before this court, the Legislature amended the Family Law Act to provide compensation in all cases not yet final on January 1, 1985. * * *

The Amendments provide for the community to be reimbursed, absent an express written agreement to the contrary, for "community contributions to education or training of a party that substantially enhances the earning capacity of the party." [Civ. Code, § 4800.3.] The compensable community contributions are defined as "payments made with community property for education or training or for the repayment of a loan incurred for education or training." * * * The reimbursement award may be reduced or modified where an injustice would otherwise result.[4] * * *

---

4. The reimbursement provision states in full: "Section 4800.3 is added to the Civil Code, to read:

4800.3. (a) As used in this section, 'community contributions to education or training' means payments made with community property for education or training or for the repayment of a loan incurred for education or training.

In addition to providing for reimbursement, the amendments require the court to consider, in awarding spousal support, "the extent to which the supported spouse contributed to the attainment of an education, training, or a license by the other spouse." Civ. Code, § 4801.

Since the property settlement in the present proceeding will not be final on January 1, 1985, appellant is entitled to the benefit of the new amendments. * * *

III

Respondent has cross-appealed from that portion of the trial court's judgment ordering him to pay $1,250 for appellant's attorney fees and $1,000 for her costs. He contends that the decision was an abuse of the trial court's discretion.

Civil Code section 4370 provides that "[in] respect to services rendered or costs incurred after the entry of judgment, the court may award such costs and attorneys' fees as may be reasonably necessary to maintain or defend any subsequent proceeding. . . ." The purpose of the award is to

(b) Subject to the limitations provided in this section, upon dissolution of marriage or legal separation:

(1) The community shall be reimbursed for community contributions to education or training of a party that substantially enhances the earning capacity of the party. The amount reimbursed shall be with interest at the legal rate, accruing from the end of the calendar year in which the contributions were made.

(2) A loan incurred during marriage for the education or training of a party shall not be included among the liabilities of the community for the purpose of division pursuant to Section 4800 but shall be assigned for payment by the party.

(c) The reimbursement and assignment required by this section shall be reduced or modified to the extent circumstances render such a disposition unjust, including but not limited to any of the following:

(1) The community has substantially benefited from the education, training, or loan incurred for the education or training of the party. There is a rebuttable presumption, affecting the burden of proof, that the community has not substantially benefited from community contributions to the education or training made less than 10 years before the com-

mencement of the proceeding, and that the community has substantially benefited from community contributions to the education or training made more than 10 years before the commencement of the proceeding.

(2) The education or training received by the party is offset by the education or training received by the other party for which community contributions have been made.

(3) The education or training enables the party receiving the education or training to engage in gainful employment that substantially reduces the need of the party for support that would otherwise be required.

(d) Reimbursement for community contributions and assignment of loans pursuant to this section is the exclusive remedy of the community or a party for the education or training and any resulting enhancement of the earning capacity of a party. However, nothing in this subdivision shall limit consideration of the effect of the education, training, or enhancement, or the amount reimbursed pursuant to this section, on the circumstances of the parties for the purpose of an order for support pursuant to Section 4801."

(e) This section is subject to an express written agreement of the parties to the contrary."

provide one of the parties, if necessary, with an amount adequate to properly litigate the controversy.

In making its determination as to whether or not attorney fees and costs should be awarded, the trial court considers the respective needs and incomes of the parties. * * * Further, the trial court is not restricted in its assessment of ability to pay to a consideration of salary alone, but may consider all the evidence concerning the parties' income, assets and abilities. * * *

Finally, a motion for attorney fees and costs in a dissolution proceeding is left to the sound discretion of the trial court. * * * In the absence of a clear showing of abuse, its determination will not be disturbed on appeal. * * *

Review of the total financial situation of each of the parties reveals that there is substantial evidence to support the trial court's order. The record reflects that the trial court considered the financial statements of both the appellant and respondent before making its award. Appellant's financial statement disclosed a net monthly income that was several hundred dollars less than her monthly expenses. Further, appellant's total separate property assets amounted to even less than her net monthly income. According to her statement, then, appellant's assets would have been depleted within a matter of months and her expenses would continue to exceed her net income.

Respondent's financial statement, prepared in the spring of 1980, also reflected monthly expenses which exceeded his net monthly income by over $800. Similarly, respondent's assets, although greater than appellant's, would also have been depleted within a few months if his income and expenses remained the same.

However, the court also had before it a comparative statement of respondent's business revenue and expenditures for the years 1978 and 1979, respondent's first two years of medical practice. Significantly, this comparative statement demonstrated that the fees which respondent collected during his second year of practice were more than double the fees he collected during the first. His annual net income increased by over $40,000 in one year. On the other hand, there was no corresponding statement or testimony to indicate any likelihood of an increase in appellant's income.

Given this evidence, this court can only conclude that the trial court made the reasonable inference that respondent's burgeoning medical practice would continue to flourish and that his income would increase dramatically. The facts of this case fall woefully short of establishing any abuse of discretion by the trial court. "[The] cases have frequently and uniformly held that the court may base its decision on the [paying spouse's] ability to earn, rather than his [or her] current earnings ..." for the simple reason that in cases such as this, current earnings give a grossly distorted view of the paying spouse's financial ability. [*Meagher v. Meagher*, 190 Cal. App. 2d 62 (1961).]

IV

That portion of the judgment ordering respondent to pay appellant's costs and attorney fees is affirmed. The judgment denying compensation for contributions to spousal education is reversed and the cause remanded for further proceedings consistent with the views expressed in this opinion. Appellant to recover costs on both appeals.

■ Mosk, J., dissenting in part.

While I agree this matter should be returned to the trial court for consideration in the light of recent legislation, I fear that inappropriate language in the majority opinion may mislead the bench and bar. Several times in the majority opinion—indeed, in framing a question at the outset—there is reference to "compensation" for contributions to education. I must assume the repetition of that term was calculated and not inadvertent.

At no place in the relevant legislation does the word "compensation" appear. With clarity and precision, the Legislature referred instead to "reimbursement." The terms are not synonymous; there is a significant distinction that extends beyond mere semantics. Reimbursement implies *re*-payment of a debt or obligation; that is what the Legislature obviously contemplated. Compensation, on the other hand, may be payment in any sum for any lawful purpose; the Legislature also obviously did not intend to give such a blank check to trial courts.

Furthermore, the majority, in their creative reference to "compensation," fail to emphasize to whom it is to be paid. It is not to an individual spouse, in response to the initial query of the majority. The Legislature was crystal clear: reimbursement is to be made to the *community*. The community consists of both the husband and the wife, not one or the other. Thus when reimbursement is made to the community, that reclaimed community asset should be divided between the husband and wife in the same manner as all other community property.

* * *

To review the legislation: Civil Code section 4800.3, subdivision (b)(1), provides "The *community* shall be *reimbursed* for community contributions to education or training of a party that substantially enhances the earning capacity of the party. The amount *reimbursed* shall be with interest. . . ." Subdivision (c) provides "The *reimbursement* and assignment required by this section shall be reduced or modified. . . ." Subdivision (d) is even more precise: "*Reimbursement for community contributions and assignment of loans pursuant to this section is the exclusive remedy of the community or a party* for the education or training and any resulting enhancement of the earning capacity of a party." (Italics added.)

One searches in vain in the statute for a single use of the word "compensation." Thus I find it curious that the majority choose to employ that term rather than to consistently adhere to "reimbursement," the only monetary claim authorized by the Legislature. I trust that trial courts will not be misled into making awards of any sums for any purpose other than that permitted in what the Legislature described with remarkable emphasis as "the exclusive remedy."

———

Beyond the Glass Ceiling: The Maternal Wall as a Barrier to Gender Equality

26 T. JEFFERSON L. REV. 1 (2003).

■ JOAN C. WILLIAMS

My subject is motherhood. More specifically, the intertwining of motherhood, economic vulnerability, and social stigma. We've all heard about the glass ceiling and I'm sad to say that the glass ceiling is alive and well in America. But most women never get near it because they are stopped long before by the maternal wall.

Over eighty percent of women become mothers. And although the wage gap between men and women is actually narrowing, the wage gap between mothers and other adults has actually risen in recent decades. Although young women now earn about ninety percent of the wages of men, mothers still earn only about sixty percent of the wages of fathers. This is what's called the family gap, as distinguished from the wage gap.

Much of this family gap stems from the ways we organize the relationship of market work to family work. We still define the ideal worker as someone who starts to work in early adulthood and works full-time, full force, for forty years straight, taking no time off for childbearing, childrearing, or really anything else. That's not an ungendered norm. Because, after all, who needs time off for childbirth? It's women. And who needs time off for childcare? American women still do seventy to eighty percent of it. In my book *Unbending Gender*, I argue that designing workplace ideals around this "ideal worker" means that they are designed around men's bodies and men's traditional life patterns in a way that discriminates against women.

For the past several years, with very generous support from the Alfred P. Sloan Foundation to the Program on Work/Life Law, I have followed up on this discrimination analysis through two interrelated efforts.

First, we did a comprehensive survey and looked at every state and federal case in the country that involved family caregivers suing when they felt that they had been unfairly treated. We looked at cases involving men as well as women; in fact, some of the most interesting cases involved men, although, of course, the overwhelming majority involved women. What we found was that family caregivers were beginning to sue, and were beginning to have some success when they sued on the basis of being unfairly disadvantaged due to caregiving responsibilities.

The second major effort, of which Professor William Bielby was a part, was to establish a Cognitive Bias Working Group, to bring together experienced litigators with law professors and social psychologists (both psychologists and sociologists). The Working Group reviewed the existing literature on stereotyping and cognitive bias and tried to shift the framework from thinking not only about *women as opposed to men*, but also about mothers—and fathers—on the front lines of family care. Today I will first discuss the case law. Then I'll discuss the patterns of stereotyping that affect family caregivers. I will end by situating my discussion within feminist theory.

First, the case law. As people know, there is no federal statute that forbids discrimination against adults with caregiving responsibilities. Some state statutes do this. The best ones that we found are in Alaska and D.C. D.C. really is the model here. It's a statute that forbids discrimination against people with family responsibilities. In the absence of that kind of statute, plaintiffs have used more than a dozen legal theories when they go into court to challenge what they see as bias, usually against mothers, sometimes against fathers.

For instance, there have been cases brought under the Equal Protection Act and the Equal Pay Act, as well as causes of action that have utilized state statutes such as D.C.'s. In addition, we found some causes of action brought under state common law theories, notably wrongful discharge. We found between twenty and thirty cases in which plaintiffs either won, settled successfully, or survived an employer's summary judgment motion—after which the parties often settle. The recoveries in some cases have been substantial. One reported tentative settlement was for $495,000; another settled for $625,000; and the settlement for another was $665,000. There have been jury verdicts in the millions. One jury verdict (later reversed) was for $3 million, and another in a Family Medical Leave Act case was for over $11 million. One company has actually now been sued three times by three different mothers.

These kinds of numbers can really make employers sit up and take notice. About three quarters of these successful cases were brought after 1990, with the majority brought in the past five years. Plaintiffs are winning in large part because of a very open pattern of stereotyping that occurs in these cases, what I call "loose lips." These are remarkably frank and open statements by employers reflecting the view that mothers don't belong in the workplace, and that fathers don't belong on the front lines of family care.

Here are some examples. In a Tenth Circuit case, *Moore v. Alabama*, a woman's supervisor looked at her walking across campus; she was eight months pregnant. He stared at her belly and said, "I was going to make you head of the office, but look at you now."

In a Virginia state wrongful discharge case, *Bailey v. Scott–Gallaher*, a mother called up her employer to find out when she was supposed to return from maternity leave. He told her that a mother's place was at home with her child, and that she was fired "because she was no longer dependable since she had delivered a child."

A third was the $3 million jury verdict, where the president of a woman's company said, "Look, you've got to decide, do you want a baby or do you want a career here?" All these cases involve what psychologists call hostile prescriptive stereotyping.

In fact, we find not only gender policing of women into caregiving roles, but also gender policing of men out of caregiving roles. Here the leading case is *Knussman v. Maryland*. In that case, Trooper Knussman wanted to take three months paid leave off under a Maryland state statute and the Family Medical Leave Act. Because his wife had been put on bed rest due to complications concerning the pregnancy, he wanted three months off after she delivered. His supervisor told him that in order for him to be eligible his wife would have to be "in a coma or dead."

These cases suggest that employers now know enough not to say, "we don't hire women here," but they don't get it when it comes to caregiving. The cases suggest that mothers encounter statements that track documented comments of gender stereotyping, which employers evidently consider no more than "hard truths" or "tough love" rather than gender bias. The result is hostile prescriptive stereotyping, in the forms of statements that prescribe traditionalist roles for both men and women. In addition to this pattern, we also see what's called benevolent stereotyping.

Here, the best story emerged from an interview on a project I co-direct with Cynthia Calvert, called the Project on Attorney Retention (PAR), which studies work/life issues in the legal profession. We heard of two lawyers, a husband and wife, who worked for the same firm. After they had a baby, the wife was sent home like clockwork at 5:30—after all, she had a baby to take care of. The husband was kept late almost every night—after all, he had a family to support. That's called benevolent stereotyping. It's stereotyping done in a very different tone of voice than hostile stereotyping, but the effect is much the same: the employer polices men and women into traditionalist bread-winner/housewife roles—clearly an inappropriate role for an employer to play.

Another example of benevolent stereotyping is in *Trezza v. The Hartford, Inc.* The Hartford is the company that's been sued three times by three different mothers. *Trezza* involved a woman who was going great guns until she had kids, and then, like many women, she began to experience problems. In one context she was not considered for a promotion; when she asked why, they told her that it was because the job required travel. That's benevolent stereotyping. The appropriate thing for the employer to do is to ask the woman what she wants to do; many mothers don't mind travel.

In the caregiver context, one key study by Susan Fiske and her colleagues, ranked stereotypes by perceived competence. Fiske and her colleagues found that businesswomen were rated as very high in competence, similar to businessmen and millionaires. Housewives, on the other hand, were rated as very low in competence—similar to—(here I quote the researchers) the elderly, blind, "retarded," and "disabled."

To see how the caregiver stereotype operates in practice, let's recall the famous story of the Boston attorney who returned from maternity leave and found she was given the work of a paralegal. She said, "I wanted to say, 'Look I had a baby, not a lobotomy.' " What happened? She was taken out of the high competence "business woman" category and put into the low competence caregiver category.

Understanding this process is very important for understanding the kinds of problems mothers often experience at one of three particular moments in time: when they get pregnant, return from maternity leave, or go on a flexible work arrangement.

In many workplaces, of course, mothers do not experience any problems. But, in some workplaces, stereotyping begins immediately when a woman gets pregnant. Thus, in one law firm case, a pregnant woman lawyer found that she was subject to rumors and isolated from participation in firm activities upon announcing her pregnancy. In other cases, as in the case of the Boston lawyer, the stereotyping occurs when a woman returns from maternity leave.

But, in many cases, women who have not had problems when they got pregnant or returned from maternity leave, find they do have problems if they go part-time or on a flexible work arrangement. For example, in work-family studies, there is a lot of talk now about the job detriments associated with the use of family friendly policies. Combining this finding with empirical social psychology suggests that the flexible work arrangements so often are viewed as career stoppers because they trigger the stereotype of the housewife or caregiver. This seems particularly true when the business-women-housewife studies are juxtaposed with another earlier study that shows that women who work part-time are viewed primarily as homemakers rather than as employees or workers and a more recent study that reports that working mothers are rated as more similar to housewives than to businesswomen.

The psychological literature that provides insights into what's going on with women also provides very important insight into what's going on with men. One significant study is by Monica Biernat and Diane Kobrynowicz. They compared the "good father" to the "good mother," and they found a lot of overlap. But they also found one key difference, in the time culture of parenthood. The "good mother" was viewed as someone who was always available to her children. Consequently, a man who rated himself as a very good father actually spent about the same amount of time away from his kids as a woman who rated herself as only an alright mother. When a woman cuts back her hours, she may trigger stigma of various sorts and cease to be considered an ideal worker, at least she'll often be considered an ideal mother. The same is not true of many fathers. Nick Townsend, in a wonderful recent book, *The Package Deal*, pointed out that our ideals of fatherhood retain a strong emphasis on fathers as the providers. And studies of masculinity by Scott Coltrane and others document how we still tie masculinity very tightly into the size of a paycheck. These studies help us understand why the chilly climate for mothers at work often becomes a frigid climate for fathers who take an active role in family care. This frigid climate can give rise to some troubling situations. For example, in another PAR interview, we heard of men who literally had been told different things about the availability of part-time work than the women in their law firms. This does not look good from a legal standpoint, for it involves disparate treatment of women and men.

The stigma that's associated with flexible work arrangements also reflects various patterns of unexamined bias. Here again, I will refer to an interview from PAR:

> Before I went part-time and people called and found that I wasn't at my desk, they assumed I was somewhere else at a business meeting. But after I went part-time, the tendency was to assume that I wasn't there because of my part-time schedule, even if I was out at a meeting. Also, before I went part-time, people sort of gave me the benefit of the doubt. They assumed that I was giving them as fast a turn-around as was humanly possible. This stopped after I went part-time. Then they assumed that I wasn't doing things fast enough because of my part-time schedule.

As a result, she said, she used to get top-of-the-scale performance reviews, but now she didn't, "even though, as far as I can tell, the quality of my work has not changed." Here we can identify three types of unexamined bias.

The first is attribution bias. When she was full-time and was not there, her co-workers attributed her absence to legitimate business reasons. But when she was part-time, and they found her not there, they attributed her absence to family reasons—even if she was at a business meeting.

The second kind of bias is called in-group favoritism. The in-group for this purpose is full-timers, and the out-group is part-timers, who are almost exclusively female. When the informant was in the in-group, she was given the benefit of the doubt. But after she went part-time, she was in the out-group and that stopped. The literature on in-group favoritism provides fascinating and important insights into objective rules, which have often been considered to be the key to eliminating bias. According to Marilyn Brewer, one of the leading scholars in this area, "Coldly objective judgment may be reserved for outsiders." Thus, when this attorney was in the in-group they gave her the benefit of the doubt, whereas when she went part-time they threw the book at her.

Finally, in this PAR interview, we recall the businesswoman housewife studies, and, in particular, the study that found that women employed part-time were viewed similar to "housewives." In other words, women who worked part-time were viewed more as housewives rather than as business-women.

The implication of all these studies is that the chilly climate for family caregivers at work, including the stigma that attaches to many part-time and other flexible work arrangements, stems in part from gender stereotyping. Gender stereotyping, in certain fact patterns, may be successfully challenged in court.

This is important for several reasons. It's important, first because this stereotyping could give rise to liability; that's an important message for employers. Yet, at this point, you need very particular sets of facts in order for liability to arise. But the case law suggests, even at this early point, that if an employer has a family-hostile workplace and an employee with "loose lips," family caregiving issues can take on a legal dimension. For an employer, that's a sobering message, because how many employers know what every single employee is doing? All an employer needs is a few employees with extremely traditional attitudes, and you are looking at a situation that could become very uncomfortable.

This is particularly true given that maternal wall cases can be litigated as "family values" cases. Consider the case of *Walsh v. National Computer Systems*. *Walsh* was the $625,000 case covered by CBS Nightly News when we issued our initial *New Glass Ceiling* report. The facts of this case are vivid: the plaintiff's supervisor is alleged to have thrown a phone book at her and told her to find a new pediatrician because her son got a series of ear infections. Jim Caster represented the mother. The story he told in court was that his client was being made to choose between being a good mother and being a good worker. "And you know," he said, "that made the jury really mad"—$625,000 mad.

These cases can, and should, be framed around family values. There is a very widespread and uncontroversial sense that children need and deserve time with their parents. That's one of the things that give these cases "legs."

Our case law survey not only shows that the threat of legal liability is real, it also has important implications outside the courtroom. The literature on the new institutionalism shows that once a social situation begins to be perceived through the lens of discrimination, employers often go far beyond what legal cases initially require. Take for example sexual harassment initiatives that end up with no dating policies.

Are no dating policies required by Title VII? Of course not. So why do they emerge? One reason is that, in the United States, anti-discrimination law operates as a language of social ethics. When people begin to see something as "discrimination" in the U.S., they begin to act quite differently, without tight reference to the specific contours of case law. This is a peculiarity of American legal culture.

The institutionalism reminds us that lawyers, as litigators, are not the key delivery system for law-fueled social change. What drives change on the ground is really the response of intermediaries to the threat of litigation. For example, in a recent speech to the Association of Work–Life Professionals, I said that for twenty years work/life professionals have tried to encourage employers to implement work-life policies with reference to the "business case"—the argument that family-friendly policies help employers' bottom line. Today, part of that business case is the potential for legal liability and work/life professionals stand to play a crucial role in shaping our sense of social entitlements in this arena.

At the Program on Work/Life Law, we work with employers, with employees, and with intermediaries such as work-life professionals and diversity experts. We're also working with attorneys on the management side as well as on the plaintiffs' side. Management side attorneys may ultimately play a more important role than plaintiffs' attorneys; if you're talking about fueling social change, the key role is not the lawyer as litigator, but lawyer as counselor. In response to the *New Glass Ceiling* report, one firm of management side employment lawyers advised their clients to review personnel policies to assess whether they adversely affect employees with family responsibilities; to "consider prorating at least some benefits for part-time employees"; to consider permitting flexible schedules and/or telecommuting unless this would impede productivity; to consider allowing employees to "borrow" sick leave from future years or other employees when they need it; and to avoid asking questions or making assumptions about employees' family situations, and "Instead, inquire about the ability to perform job functions and meet attendance and other job requirements."

* * *

Women don't need sameness if that means the ability to live up to the ideal worker norm without the flow of family work that supports men who are ideal workers. And they don't need difference if that means a marginalized mommy track. What they really need is simple equality. But what simple equality requires is deconstructing the ideal worker norm and replacing that with a norm of a balanced worker: a worker whose life requires him to balance work obligations and family obligations, because he is not relying on the erased labor of a stigmatized and economically vulnerable partner. We need to deconstruct gender, for men as well as for women—and to offer both men and women a re-imagined world where family work and market work mesh.

Seeking Normal? Considering Same–Sex Marriage

2 Sᴇᴀᴛᴛʟᴇ J. Soᴄ. Jᴜsᴛ. 459 (2004).

■ Joᴅɪ O'Bʀɪᴇɴ

Like many lesbians and gay men, until recently I'd given little personal thought to marriage. It was just another one of those cultural institutions that didn't apply to me. As a sociologist, I am well-versed in the discourses by which marriage is deconstructed in order to reveal its patriarchal (read inequitable and unjust) foundations. As a sexualities scholar, I am also well aware of the many economic and legal benefits that accompany state-sanctioned definitions of family. When discussions of marriage have come up in my own long-term relationships, the impetus has been consideration of these benefits. Like many same-sex couples, my partner and I have spent thousands of dollars to file legal papers that would enable us to act on one another's behalf, secure legal recognition of our joint property, and grant power of decision in matters such as a living will. Each of these considerations is focused around worst case, "what if" scenarios (what if one of us dies and the family tries to take away the house from the living partner? what if one of us is terminally ill and the other is not allowed to participate in medical decisions?).

The relevance of marriage ceremonies in my own life has involved the weddings of my six siblings. All lavish affairs, I have attended each in arm with my partner (and had her introduced as such to family friends and relatives). When I was contemplating a break-up, my Mormon mother (who opposed the break-up) reminded me sternly, "this is just like a divorce you know." My parents became much more open and accepting of my sexuality as soon as I found a nice girl with whom to take up housekeeping. Although it would never have occurred to any of my family that I should seek marriage, my partner and I at least felt some comfort in this family recognition. Although we were acknowledged, we were still separate— separate and but not equal in the eyes of the law, and separate as two lesbians in an extended family of prolific heterosexual Mormons. Separate and acknowledged is certainly not separate but equal.

The trouble with this equation, as many lesbian and gay families have discovered through difficult legal and social entanglements, is that when a situation of inequality exists, "acknowledgement" is at the whim of those who hold power. To borrow a phrase from the poet June Jordan, "there is difference and there is power; who has the power decides the meaning of difference." The current "marriage wars" can be viewed and analyzed as a battle for the power to define complete inclusion in U.S. culture. For many supporters of same-sex marriage, the battle is about the simple justice of being able to define one's own family and have this definition recognized and respected as a basic human right * * *. For others, the battle is about who holds the power to determine justice in any form—what some observers have referred to as the "just-us" justice defined by those who see themselves as the keepers of a pre-determined cultural truth.

RADICAL OR ASSIMILATIONIST?

The so-called struggle for gay marriage is additionally complicated by the fact that homosexuality is not a monolith. Lesbians and gay men represent a full spectrum of colors, creeds, political and religious affiliations and economic circumstances. There are lesbian and gay Republicans, lesbian and gay criminals, lesbian and gay ministers, lesbian and gay parents, and yes, some lesbians and gay men who would like to have their committed unions recognized by the state and possibly even blessed by their church. One of the long-standing debates in lesbian and gay studies and social movements centers on the question of "seeking the normal." There are two well-recognized discourses framing this debate. One is the argument that as marginal members of society, lesbians and gay men should push the boundaries of acceptance as far as we can by demanding recognition for even the queerest among us. The other is that assimilation is the best and most politically and socially rewarding route to general acceptance.

Both positions are strongly represented in lesbian and gay history. For instance, ACT–UP protests strove to focus public attention on the rights of HIV-positive gay men who were being discriminated against in health care on the basis of a distinctly non-normative sexuality. At the same time, Madison Avenue was actively courting lesbian and gay dollars by featuring same-sex relationships in mainstream advertising. This marketing era, now known as the "gay media marketing moment," is credited with providing an economic basis for mainstream awareness and increasing tolerance of homosexuality. In the United States, purchasing power is one route to increased political and public acceptance. As advertisers realized that gay dollars were just as green as straight ones and just as likely to increase sales, mainstream media became more bold in the portrayal of lesbians and gay men. We moved from being background characters usually intended to draw laughs or convey moral missives to front-and-center TV-land companions. The appearance of shows such as Ellen, Will and Grace, Queer as Folk, and Queer Eye for the Straight Guy brought lesbians and gays into the living rooms of middle America and paved the way for mildly edgy straight-based identities such as the "metrosexual" and "lesbian chic." Around this time, in the early 1990s, some queer studies scholars began to note that the original ACT–UP chant, "we're here, we're queer, get used to it," was beginning to look more and more like "we're here, we're queer, let's go to IKEA."

This assimilationist trend has had many critics. Some critiques focused on the raced (white), classed (upper-middle) and gendered (predominantly male) demographics of those featured in the positive media representations of lesbian and gay characters. Others noted the increasing polarization between legions of lesbians, gay men, and transgendered persons who don't fit the assimilation mold (i.e., young runaways, poor, "too butch" or "too feminine" or "too queer") and those who were buying homes, expensive vehicles and seeking to have children. Critics of various lesbian and gay task forces and rights groups advocates observed that these groups seemed increasingly concerned with winning "mainstream" assimilation battles (e.g., same-sex adoption rights, military service, and religious participation) than in fighting the longstanding battles against forms of brutal discrimination that mark the daily lives of many queer folk. The mainstreaming of some aspects of lesbian and gay life were accompanied by an increased distancing among self-described queers who either did not relate to these representations of "normalcy" or felt obligated to actively—resist the narrow definitions of acceptability they reinforced.

Mainstream inclusion as portrayed in media [and] popular culture has also not only drawn resistance from some queers, but has resulted in a growing tide of backlash rising among heteronormative groups, most notably evangelical Christians. These anti-gay groups perceive the arrival of lesbians and gay men in the media and the winning of some basic antidiscrimination legislation as signs of the proliferation of a radical "gay agenda." This backlash has escalated into a full-blown social movement organized around attempts to legislate political and cultural exclusion. Most recently, anti-gay groups, who perceive persistent gay advancement on the cultural terrain, have drawn the line of acceptance at marriage. Amidst this climate of overt hostility and attempts to create legal discrimination, many lesbians and gay men have felt compelled to redraw the battle lines and call for a unified fight in the struggle for matrimony. The battle for legal marriage, even more than the issue of gays in the military, has forced many uneasy alliances among otherwise widely diverse individuals who claim no other commonality than shared discrimination along the dimension of (non-normative) sexuality. Ironically, to the extent that a "gay agenda" does exist, it can be defined as the collective spirit of defense that has coalesced *in response* to an anti-gay political movement. Most individuals who share a marginalized social position (race, ethnicity, gender, religion, sexuality) understand the quandary presented by the call for solidarity that such "anti-movements" provoke.

THE TYRANNY OF SOLIDARITY AND RHETORICAL AMBIVALENCE

In the case, of same-sex marriage, the quandary of solidarity is manifest among lesbians and gay men who begin conversations by claiming, "I really don't believe in marriage, *but* ..." and then attempt to justify why all lesbians and gays must fight for the *right* to marry. The most common justification is framed in economic and legal terms. To date, there are 1,138 federal benefits automatically bestowed on legally married couples. Certainly this is a compelling instance of social (in)justice that should be addressed. But my own observations indicate that the rush for marriage is about much more than the economic and legal benefits the union provides. Long before questions about legalizing same-sex marriages appeared before the courts, lesbians and gay men were seeking the blessing of religious communities for committed unions.

In recent months much talk has been spun among proponents of same-sex marriage about the legal and economic benefits that accompany state-sanctioned definitions of the family. Intriguingly, less has been said about the seemingly more obvious and long-enduring symbolic aspects of marriage. Yet, it is the symbolic, or cultural, meaning of marriage that is the central point of struggle for those opposed to same-sex unions. Lesbian and gay rights activists are correct in their focus on the discrimination that is inherent in state-sanctioned benefits that accrue through adherence to one and only one culturally accepted definition of family. We miss the mark however when we assume that U.S. legal and economic policy is grounded solely in rational arguments based on the discourse of individual "rights." The mistake often made in such debates is a conflation of "is" and "ought"—according to advocates of same-sex marriage, the U.S. government "ought" to protect individual citizens from unequal treatment. In reality, however, U.S. economic and legal policy has always reflected (and often protected) cultural hierarchies of inclusion and belonging.

Thus, the two sides currently represented in the marriage debate are not arguing about the same thing. Anthropologically, marriage is one of the only uniformly recognized rites of passage and signs of cultural achievement and social inclusion in U.S. society. In its ideal form, the union is recognized by the state and blessed by a church, symbolizing its deeply rooted cultural significance and legitimacy. Opponents of same-sex marriage are scrambling to conserve/preserve this symbolic institution of inclusion and belonging precisely because there are so few symbolic achievements that cut across the many cultural divides the define the landscape of U.S. society. Proponents of same-sex marriage are arguing for governmentally recognized access to the economic and legal benefits that accompany marriage without (appearing to be) paying genuine homage to the cultural institution itself.

The preponderance of marriage = rights/benefits rhetoric can be interpreted as an expression of the lack of consensual solidarity among lesbians and gay men regarding cultural assimilation and normalcy. Queers who have never given much thought to the cultural institution of marriage, precisely because it doesn't seem to apply to us, now feel compelled to fight for the rights of same-sex couples to marry, but are only willing to do so within a framework of "equal access to benefits" logic. At the same time, many lesbian and gay couples are seeking not only the related economic benefits of marriage, but the full cultural package. And why wouldn't they? Culturally, we are saturated with notion that marriage is truly the pinnacle of inter-relational attainment (the "happiest moment of your life"). Given similar acculturation, it stands to reason that many lesbians and gay men would grow up desiring the same cultural rites of belonging. If for the sake of argument we assume that lesbians and gays want to win the battle for same-sex marriage, then the problem, from a political/rhetorical perspective, is not whether lesbians and gays should seek this form of cultural belonging, but the failure of same-sex marriage proponents to fully acknowledge the cultural significance of marriage and the desire of some queers to participate in it.

My interpretation is that lesbian and gay activists have been slow to engage in this line of defense ("we really do want to belong as fully as we possibly can") precisely because it requires articulating a desire for normalcy that many lesbians and gay men are loathe to acknowledge. Many of the activists at the front line of this debate are ambivalent about the level of cultural normalcy they want for themselves. Many are long-time critical feminists who have been key voices in deconstructing the normative family. At the same time, as cultural acceptance and belonging has increased for these individuals, largely oriented around economic, professional, and family achievements, they find themselves enjoying more and more of the cultural benefits of inclusion and belonging. It makes sense that they would want the full recognition (legal and even religious acknowledgement) that completes this cultural package. Is this radical? Will it revolutionize, or even reform, current cultural hierarchies of belonging? That's another question entirely.

* * *

CONSIDERATIONS AND COMPLICATIONS

Legal and political recognition of same-sex unions is probably inevitable in the near future. Whether it be in the form of civil unions or the full recognition of legal marriage as currently defined, this struggle will expand the repertoire for many lesbians and gay men regarding the freedom to choose "normalcy" if they so desire. At the same time, the institution itself, which stands as a citadel of normalcy, will have its walls of inclusion stretched while simultaneously strengthening and polishing its standing as the ultimate icon of cultural belonging. In this regard, the recognition of same-sex couples will be both radical and assimilationist.

At the same time, I don't expect that this expansion will change anything at all for single parents who are poor, or for extended families with dependent relatives who do not qualify for healthcare and related benefits under current guidelines for "dependency." Same-sex unions will not alter the current political/economic arrangement whereby an average individual has access to healthcare only through corporate employment or its equivalent for one or more family members recognized as such through the legal definition of marriage/family. Most middle-class and working poor citizens will still bear a disproportionate tax burden relative to benefits received. Should so many economic and legal benefits be connected, uncritically, to the cultural institution of marriage? Certainly not. As [Zac] Kramer argues * * * and as [Nancy] Polikoff and [Martha] Fineman have argued convincingly, welfare states (of which the United States is one) should define and convey benefits and assurances based on realistic estimations of dependency. To this end, Kramer, Polikoff and Fineman call for a complete redefinition of the family as a basis for assessing economic households.

I appreciate these more complicated analyses and add that the question of the same-sex marriage, particularly as it is sometimes framed in terms of the implications of "seeking normal" needs to be problematized more complexly still on at least two dimensions: we should seek more comprehensive/comprehending analyses of the *significance* of cultural institutions in shaping lives and in reinforcing cultural hierarchies that are a basis for resource allocation; and we should interrogate the methodological and rhetorical practices by which implications regarding "radical" and "assimilationist" are falsely dichotomized. I conclude with a brief discussion of each of these points.

1) We need to pay more attention to the meaning and significance inscribed in particular cultural institutions, in this case, the institution of marriage. Whether one agrees with this meaning, it is empirically unsound and politically foolish to ignore cultural significance. Feminists scholars, myself included, have been deconstructing the institution of marriage for decades; successfully demonstrating the tremendous social and economic burden this small unit (the "couple") carries in corporate capitalist economy as well as [its] tremendous "compulsory" grip on our sense of self and accomplishment. Despite these insights, we have not done the best job at achieving an additional feminist methodological creed, comprehending the

"field of relations" on its own terms. Clearly marriage stands for more than 1,138 federal benefits. We do ourselves and our work an injustice when we fail to explore the very complex, and often contradictory, reasons for the tenacity of marriage in its current cultural form.

Likewise, lesbians and gay men (and all heterosexuals for that matter) should reflect more critically on the reasons for wanting marriage. A desire for cultural acceptance and belonging is understandable, but we do ourselves an injustice when we fail to fully explore the meaning and implications of participation in any highly significant cultural institution. To the extent that marriage is seen as a pinnacle of cultural achievement and a marker of acceptance, same-sex marriages will do nothing to alter this equation except in allowing for the possibility that the two-person unit (who is now responsible for most social and economic welfare of the "family") can be a same-sex unit. Certainly, in a gender-role obsessed society such as this, same-sex marital units will be radical. But in terms of more general cultural equations connected to hierarchies of belonging and used to determine who gets what, we shouldn't fool ourselves into believing that same-sex unions will pose much of a challenge to the existing status quo.

2) We also need more complicated discourses about who seeks belonging and what that reflects and, in turn, what consequences it carries in terms of change to cultural institutions. We need classed/gendered/raced analyses of who is seeking belonging in so-called "normalizing" institutions. We need nuanced, complex studies of variations among these groups (e.g., gay Christians) before any conclusions can be drawn about what is and isn't radical. One noteworthy consequence of the debate over the *right* to marry for lesbians and gays is that it cuts across other cultural fault lines. The resulting shifts are causing some interesting shake-ups and creating some bridges across long entrenched fissures of difference. For instance, many traditionally conservative parents of lesbian and gay men find themselves speaking out in favor of same-sex marriage. They imagine the cultural acceptance it will convey on their otherwise ostracized child and end up breaking stride with long-established political, religious and cultural allies. Even the *Economist*, the top-buttoned British news weekly, covered the story complete with glossy front picture. [Its] stance? "What's all the fuss about?" From the libertarian perspective, which the magazine espouses, this position makes perfect sense. It doesn't sit so well, of course, with cultural conservatives who consider themselves economic libertarians. But is has been a reminder to many fence-sitting Republicans that it is possible for them to be more libertarian in their political views than they are conservative in their cultural commitments.

And my own stance? Some will find it contradictory, but that's often a consequence of the critical feminist inquiries I attempt to practice. Just as I understand why someone could find meaning and a sense of belonging as a queer practicing Christianity, I understand the considerable cultural draw of marriage. * * * I comprehend the significance of this cultural institution to spin a binding web of commitment to one another and to convey a deeper sense of belonging in society generally. However, this is not the form of inclusion I seek. While I understand the desire of many lesbians and gay men to have their unions recognized by state and religion, I prefer the recognition, acceptance, respect and love granted me by my (Mormon) family, my colleagues, students and friends. Personally, I have never been compelled by the marital bug. But I would be disappointed if my family did not understand the need to support same-sex marriage legislation as it has been currently framed—i.e., one is either pro or anti-gay human rights. * * * I support the fight for everyone to make choices regarding how they wish to author their own lives and the meaning they seek for themselves and those they wish to define as "family." Simultaneously, I work to educate others about the fundamental need to forge a strong disconnect between culturally accepted definitions of "family" and political economic assessments of the distribution of benefits and assurances for U.S. citizens. In contemporary U.S. society, the power to define difference and the power to define economic well-being rest too strongly in the same "family." The dismantling of this particular union is long overdue.

NOTES AND QUESTIONS

1.   Value of human capital. What is the relationship between *Sullivan* and the other materials in this chapter? States have taken different approaches to the issue of the educational contributions of the working spouse to the degree awarded upon divorce. California stands alone as the only community property jurisdiction that permits the community estate to be reimbursed for educational costs upon the dissolution of a marriage. New York courts have held that professional degrees, education leading to professional degrees, and professional licenses are marital property when earned during marriage. Raj Rajan, *Medical Degree in Divorce: New York Versus California*, 11 CONTEMP. LEGAL ISSUES 240 (1997). Texas courts have concluded that the costs of financial support incurred by the supporting spouse are not reimbursable even though made with community funds. Katherine M. Willis, *The True Value of an Education: The Texas Approach to Characterizing and Valuing a Professional Education Degree Upon Dissolution of Marriage*, 31 TEX. TECH L. REV. 1117 (2000).

Recall the discussion of non-marital contractual relationships in *Marvin* and *Whorton, supra* chapter 3. Consensual sexual relationships are by nature intimate and in many ways opaque to those outside them. Can courts do an adequate job of deciding what is "fair" when these relationships dissolve? Does the existence of separate family-law courts in many jurisdictions prove that normal courts do not have the necessary expertise in marital and sexual relationships to adjudicate regarding them?

The court in *Marvin* wrote:

The mores of the society have indeed changed so radically in regard to cohabitation that we cannot impose a standard based on alleged moral considerations that have apparently been so widely abandoned by so many. Lest we be misunderstood, however, we take this occasion to point out that the structure of society itself largely depends upon the institution of marriage, and nothing we have said in this opinion should be taken to derogate from that institution. The joining of the man and woman in marriage is at once the most socially productive and individually fulfilling relationship that one can enjoy in the course of a lifetime.

Marvin, 557 P.2d 684.

Is this stamp of approval for marriage appropriate for a court? Have societal attitudes towards marriage changed significantly since *Marvin* was decided in 1976?

2. Dependency, marriage, and the state. As the Williams excerpt points out, caretaking, which involves the dependency needs of both children and adults, has traditionally been considered a "private" matter and thus ceded to the heterosexual nuclear family, while at the same time supported by extensive state subsidies and extensive social privileges. This service to the larger society can be seen as a public good of economic and social value. In a time in which (1) divorce rates are very high; (2) women can no longer carry the entire burden of caretaking given the economic pressures forcing them into the workplace (not to mention many women's desire to work for wages); and (3) sexual minorities are both struggling for social recognition and denied access to marriage, what should state policy toward marriage and dependency look like? What are the "legitimate state interests" that the government should be able to directly support, or to indirectly incentivize? What should feminists and sexual minorities be fighting for?

3. Discrimination against homosexuals? Most agree that homosexuals have historically been a marginalized population, and that a moral and religious stigma attached to same-sex relationships has existed throughout this country's history. However, some do not believe that homosexuals deserve to be treated as a "minority" in the same sense that blacks and Hispanics are. This belief may stem from the view that gays are now generally accepted in society and have every opportunity to attain material success equivalent to straight people. Indeed, gays and lesbians are sometimes painted as an economically privileged group, on the theory that they are less likely to have children. Colorado for Family Values, the group supporting Colorado's Amendment 2, made the disputed claim that "gay and lesbian Americans enjoyed substantially better salaries and higher education levels, and that they tended to be managers and professionals who travel around the world on ample supplies of disposable income ... [thus] seeking to destroy the image of gays and lesbians as somehow disadvantaged before the law." Sharon E. Debbage Alexander, Romer v. Evans *and the Amendment 2 Controversy: The Rhetoric and Reality of Sexual Orientation Discrimination in America*, 6 TEX. F. ON C.R. & C.L. 261, 278 (2002). Others, especially those on the "Christian right" continue to believe that moral condemnation of homosexuality is acceptable.

Romer has been hailed by many as a landmark decision for the protection of the rights of homosexuals. In this view, Amendment 2 was struck down "for seeking to impose second-class status on gays and lesbians," and by striking down the law "the Supreme Court illuminated the core of equal protection: government must respect the principle that all persons have equal intrinsic worth." Supporters of the decision tend to have little doubt that Amendment 2 was inspired by hostility towards gays and lesbians, but even barring animosity they believe the law invalid because "the principle [of equal protection] bars laws that seek to entrench a social hierarchy—to keep a group 'in its place.' " Joseph S. Jackson, *Persons of Equal Worth:* Romer v. Evans *and the Politics of Equal Protection*, 45 UCLA L. REV. 453, 454 (1997). Why do you think Amendment 2 was passed? Should the legality of the Amendment be affected if it was principally inspired by hostility towards homosexuals? Scalia's dissent strongly criticizes the court's decision as having "no foundation in American constitutional law." If so, why did the court decide as it did? Was Amendment 2 the same as laws prohibiting polygamy, as Scalia suggests? Is the protection of "traditional sexual mores," endorsed by Scalia, an appropriate governmental goal?

The federal courts have not regarded homosexuals as a protected class. On the other hand, many states and municipalities have passed anti-discrimination laws that cover sexual orientation. For example, by 1999, eleven states and the District of Columbia had legislation prohibiting employment discrimination based on sexual orientation, and eighteen states and the District of Columbia prohibited discrimination based on sexual orientation in public employment specifically. By 1999, over half of the Fortune 500 companies included sexual orientation in their anti-discrimination policies, and anti-discrimination policies in universities had become commonplace. Alexander, *supra* at 271. Is the passage of anti-discrimination laws regarding homosexuals proof that they are discriminated against? If the claim made by CFV about homosexuals' material success is accurate, is that proof that they are not being discriminated against?

4. Homosexuality and the Supreme Court. The success of gays and lesbians before the Supreme Court has been mixed post-*Romer*. In *Lawrence v. Texas, supra* chapter 3, the court struck down laws which outlawed homosexual sex. But in *Boy Scouts of America v. Dale*, 530 U.S. 640 (2000), the Supreme Court allowed private discrimination against homosexuals by ruling that a New Jersey anti-discrimination law violated the Boy Scouts' First Amendment expressive association right to exclude homosexuals from membership.

Same-sex marriage abruptly moved to the foreground of gay and lesbian legal rights in 2003. As Phyllis Bossin recounts:

> The most dramatic legal development in the United States in 2003 was the Massachusetts Supreme Court's decision in *Goodridge v. Department of Public Health* [798 N.E.2d 941, *supra* at chapter 3.] It was without question the shot heard around the world, or at least around

the United States. The decision became a call to arms for conservatives to press for a federal constitutional amendment. Although the decision was based upon the Massachusetts, not the United States, Constitution, concern about the spread of legalized same-sex marriage was profound. Numerous amicus briefs were filed by groups presenting legal, religious, and mental health perspectives. The court had amassed before it a wealth of information related to all possible aspects of this highly controversial issue. It is clear from a reading of the opinion that the court weighed all of the information before it, and also considered much of the dicta of *Lawrence*, in rendering its opinion. The court distinguished the Massachusetts Constitution from the federal Constitution, noting that: "The Massachusetts Constitution is, if anything, more protective of individual liberty and equality than the Federal Constitution; it may demand broader protection for fundamental rights; and it is less tolerant of government intrusion into the protected sphere of private life."

The court divided the question before it—whether the marriage restriction violated the Massachusetts Constitution—into two queries: whether the restriction was a denial of equal protection and whether the restriction violated due process of law. It pointed out, however, that in matters of marriage and children, the two concepts overlap. The court recognized the substantial benefits enjoyed by those in marriages and pointed out that: "Because it fulfils yearnings for security, safe haven, and connection that express our common humanity, civil marriage is an esteemed institution, and the decision whether and whom to marry is among life's momentous acts of self-definition." The court then discussed some of the benefits attached to marriage that are not available to unmarried persons, concluding that: "It is undoubtedly for these concrete reasons, as well as for its intimately personal significance, that civil marriage has long been termed a 'civil right.'"

Significantly, the court analogized the prohibition on same-sex marriage to the earlier prohibition on interracial marriage, stating:

> As both *Perez* and *Loving* make clear, the right to marry means little if it does not include the right to marry the person of one's choice, subject to appropriate government restrictions in the interests of public health, safety and welfare. In this case, as in *Perez* and *Loving*, a statute deprives individuals of access to an institution of fundamental legal, personal, and social significance—the institution of marriage—because of a single trait: skin color in *Perez* and *Loving*, sexual orientation here. As it did in *Perez* and *Loving*, history must yield to a more fully developed understanding of the invidious quality of the discrimination.

After analyzing the safeguards of the Massachusetts Constitution to protect liberty and equality, the court found that: "The liberty interest in choosing whether and whom to marry would be hollow if the Commonwealth could, without sufficient justification, foreclose an individual from freely choosing the person with whom to share an exclusive commitment in the unique institution of civil marriage." The court went on to find that the marriage ban could not meet the rational basis test under either due process or equal protection analysis. * * *

The court stayed its order for 180 days to permit the legislature to enact legislation consistent with its decision. Subsequently, the legislature requested an advisory opinion from the court as to whether the enactment of a civil union law would comply with the court's order. The court unequivocally found that it would not. The court found that the proposed legislation suffered from an inherent defect, specifically, that it continued to define "marriage" as between one man and one woman and attempted to create an institution that is parallel but not the same as marriage. The court stated emphatically that "the history of our nation has demonstrated that separate is seldom, if ever, equal." Therefore, the court ordered that only full marriage rights for same-sex couples would pass constitutional muster.

Although the *Goodridge* decision made abundantly clear that the Massachusetts Constitution affords greater protections than does the United States Constitution and further acknowledged that its decision can and should go no further than the state's own borders, the national reaction to the decision was nothing short of mass hysteria. Afraid that homosexual marriage would be imposed throughout the land, Congress and many states urged the passage of constitutional amendments forever banning same-sex marriage.

Phyllis G. Bossin, *Same-Sex Unions: the New Civil Rights Struggle or an Assault on Traditional Marriage?*, 40 TUL. L. REV. 381 (2005).

5. Proposal to create Private Enforcement of Anti Discrimination Employment Policies Against Gays through Intellectual Property Law. Legal scholars Ian Ayres and Jennifer Gerarda Brown have proposed an interesting new corrective opinion to expand the range of possible remedies in the struggle against employment discrimination against homosexuals. Ayres and Brown have created a certification mark, a registered trademark. The trademark is **FE** in a circle. The symbol is called the "Fair Employment" mark. Registration with the Patent Office gives the trademark holder the right to enforce the terms of the mark. The non-discrimination policy is provided by Ayres and Brown on an online licensing site that states a detailed non-discrimination policy. Any employer, who adopts this mark, becomes liable to individual lawsuits from employees who believe they have suffered discrimination because of their sexual orientation. Although the conventional method for enforcing such licenses is for the holder of the intellectual property interest to police and initiate a lawsuit, this mark was created to extend "express third party beneficiary" status to any employee of a covered employer.

Why would any employer ever adopt this mark? If you were the lawyer for an employer with a good record of non-discrimination against homosexuals what advice would you give your client about whether or not to opt into the FE. What would be the relationship of this private remedy to any future federal employment discrimination law? What might the risk calculus for an employer look like? Are employers who are now free to discriminate, including, religious institutional employers, likely to adopt this mark? Would this work for race discrimination? As a matter of legal policy is privatizing antidiscrimination law a sound idea? Ian Ayres & Jennifer Gerarda Brown, "Privatizing Gay Rights with Nondiscrimination Promises Instead of Policies", *The Economists' Voice*: Vol. 2: No. 2, Article 11 (2002) *available at* http://www.bepress.com/ev/vol2/iss2/art11.

D.   REPARATIONS

The idea that the federal government owed former slaves material compensation for the economic, social, and psychological injuries of the "peculiar institution of slavery," gained currency with the end of the Civil War. On January 16, 1865, General Sherman's Special Field Order No. 15 granted to former slaves, who were the heads of households, 40 acres of land formerly belonging to land-owning whites in the low lands of South Carolina, and a mule to plow the land. ERIC FONER, RECONSTRUCTION: AMERICAN'S UNFINISHED REVOLUTIONS, 1863–1877 (1988). From this order, soon vetoed by President Johnson, grew the phrase, Forty Acres and a Mule, now emblematic of all forms of reparations for slavery. Through the years, virtually every black liberation movement, from Marcus Garvey to Martin Luther King, called upon the obligation of the federal government to provide redress to the descendents of former slaves.

The twenty-first century has witnessed a revival of earlier calls for reparations in the form of litigation seeking legal compensation for slavery. The defendants have ranged from insurance companies, to elite universities with proven ties to the profit from slavery. The contemporary reparations movement raises complex questions of legal standing, statutes of limitations, the problems of calculating damages, and identifying suitable plaintiffs.

Legal scholar, Roy Brooks takes up many of these questions in his book, *Atonement and Forgiveness: A New Model for Black Reparations*. In the passages that follow, Brooks advances his core conception of the atonement rationale for reparations.

Atonement and Forgiveness: A New Model for Black Reparations

UNIVERSITY OF CALIFORNIA PRESS, (2004) pages 155–63.

■ ROY L. BROOKS

THE ANATOMY OF REPARATIONS

Essence of Reparations

Once the perpetrator of an atrocity has apologized, it now has the burden of making its precious words believable. It must solidify its apology.

In other words, the perpetrator of an atrocity cannot expiate the sin it has committed against an innocent people until it has undertaken a great and heroic task of redemption. That task of redemption is a reparation. The second element of the atonement model, a reparation can thus be defined as *the revelation and realization of apology*. It is the act that transforms the rhetoric of apology into a meaningful, material reality. Simply saying "I'm sorry" is never enough when righting an atrocity.

A reparation is by nature asymmetrical. Only victims of the atrocity are eligible to receive a reparation. A scholarship program for African Americans as a form of redress for slavery is a reparation. But a scholarship program for "minority and women students" even when presented as a form of redress for slavery is no more a reparation than are Holocaust payments to American gentiles, including blacks. It is important to understand, however, that asymmetrical civil rights policies-reparations-are not intended to displace ongoing civil rights enforcement or other social reforms. On this point, I wholeheartedly agree with Elazar Barkan. I would add that symmetrical human rights measures, such as traditional U.S. civil rights legislation, are designed to be equally accessible to all victims of discrimination. Employment discrimination laws, for example, are open to blacks, other persons of color, women, and whites. Although there may be some duplication, symmetrical and asymmetrical human rights measures are not mutually exclusive. Japanese Americans who have received reparations from the federal government were not excluded from traditional civil rights laws or even precluded from participating in social welfare programs. That is how it should be. Symmetrical and asymmetrical human rights measures serve different purposes.

Forms of Reparations

Reparations can come in many forms. They need not be directed toward the victims personally nor involve cash payments. Indeed, when one looks

> at the ways in which governments have responded to atrocities committed under their authority, a pattern begins to emerge. A basic distinction is made between what can be called *compensatory* and *rehabilitative* reparations. Compensatory reparations are directed toward the individual victim or the victim's family. They are intended to be compensatory, but only in a symbolic sense; for nothing can undo the past or truly return the victim to the status quo ante. In contrast, rehabilitative reparations are directed toward the victim's group, or community. They are designed to benefit the victim's group, to nurture the group's self-empowerment and, thus, aid in the nation's social and cultural transformation.

Whether compensatory or rehabilitative, reparations can come in monetary or nonmonetary forms. Unrestricted cash payments or restricted cash payments (such as scholarship funds) given directly to the victims or their immediate families are monetary compensatory reparations. In contrast, unrestricted cash payments or restricted cash payments to the victim's group (such as, scholarship funds or an atonement trust fund that provides an estate for educational purposes or venture capital to eligible members of the victim's group) are examples of monetary rehabilitative reparation. Although nonmonetary reparations can be compensatory, such as a statute commemorating a family member, they are more likely to be rehabilitative. Affirmative action for the victim's group and a museum memorializing the slaves and educating the public about slavery's contribution to our nation are all examples of nonmonetary rehabilitative reparations.

The perpetrator of an atrocity ultimately has the responsibility of coming forward with an appropriate form of reparations. In so doing, the perpetrator must give due respect to the victims' needs or desires. This, of course, is a moral responsibility, part of the perpetrator's atonement. What follows are suggestions concerning the types of reparations that may be appropriate for slave redress. My intention is to be illustrative rather than comprehensive, yet to provide enough details so that we have a pretty good idea as to the direction in which the government ought to be moving.

Solidifying the Apology for Slavery and Jim Crow

There are no dearth of ways in which our government could make its apology for slavery and Jim Crow believable. Compensatory reparations in the form of government checks to slave descendants, usually broached in the context of the tort model, have received the most attention in the national debate. In my view, compensatory reparations are inappropriate for slave redress. Rehabilitative reparations are far more appropriate, for two reasons. First, they are structurally designed to reach a greater number of victims. As such, they are likely to be both more effective than compensatory reparations in solidifying the apology for slavery and Jim Crow and more helpful in fostering racial reconciliation. Second, rehabilitation reparations are narrowly tailored to the harms visited upon slaves and slave descendants. Slavery and Jim Crow operated at the group level-blacks were persecuted, not because of who they were individually, but because of who they were collectively. Rehabilitative reparations proceed at this level of generality; they speak more to the group than to the individual.

The two rehabilitative reparations I favor most are a museum of slavery and an atonement trust fund. The former would be a memorial to the slaves, and the latter would be a governmental response to some of the capital deficiencies today's blacks have inherited from their ancestors. As will become clear in a moment, the museum of slavery envisioned here is very different in structure and purpose from the "National Museum of African American History and Culture" President Bush signed into law in 2003. . . .

Slavery museums modeled on the Holocaust Museum in Washington, D.C., and the Simon Wiesenthal Center Museum of Tolerance in Los Angeles should be built in Washington, D.C.; and every state capital to commemorate the contributions slaves made to our country and educate Americans about them, as well as about the lingering effects slavery has on blacks today. These objectives can be realized through high-tech, interactive experiences. Visitors will be led back in time to witness the horrors of racial slavery, from capture in Africa, to the middle passage, and, finally, to the peculiar institution. Men, women, and children will be able to walk through a recreated slave ship in which hundreds of blacks were packed together for weeks like sardines in incredibly tight spaces as the ship made its way from West Africa to the American colonies (and later to the United States). Visitors will also be able to listen to recordings of slave narratives spoken by the slaves themselves. This experience should give the visitor a close-up view of life on the plantation, including the mind-numbing drudgery of working in the fields under the hot sun from sunup to sundown and the dehumanizing conditions of the slave quarters.

Reenactments of the debates on slavery at the Constitutional Convention in 1787 and in Congress on the eve of southern succession can be presented in a "Point of View Diner" that serves a menu of slave-related topics on video jukeboxes. Was the North's creation of a union with the South a necessary evil or merely a convenience? Was that union ultimately good for the slaves? Did Union soldiers fight to end slavery or to save the Union? Did Confederate soldiers fight to keep slavery or for states' rights? What contributions have slaves made to our nation? How are blacks disadvantaged by slavery? What is racism? Visitors will listen to the debates on these and similar topics, and then input their opinions as to which side of the debate won. After instant tabulation of the results, the visitors might be surprised to learn how little our opinions may have changed over time.

Some might argue that a museum of slavery would be a racially divisive reparation, because it would dwell on the darkest hour in our nation's past. But I believe it would have just the opposite effect. Like the fabulous 1970S TV series *Roots*—at the time, the most watched event in TV history—the museum of slavery will pull a racially divided nation together through a mixture of awareness, understanding, and, in some cases, empathy. The museum of slavery will, in fact, teach many valuable lessons. Among these are:

- Slavery was more than just another everyday tragedy. Millions of innocent lives were sacrificed and families were broken up for personal profit and the socioeconomic development of our country. Human beings were denied liberty at its worst so that other human beings could enjoy liberty at its fullest. We must take into our hearts and minds those who perished at the hands of our country. They were great Americans.

- We need to learn and remember, because none of us was there to see slavery, and because many Americans continue to suffer from the lingering effects of slavery-the psychology and socioeconomics of slavery.

- There is a line drawn in time between those who view human life, liberty, and well-being as expendable in pursuit of personal gain, and those who believe in the dignity of all human beings. We must always look down from time to time to see on which side of the line we stand.

- We must rededicate ourselves to the cause of freedom, tolerance, and human dignity, even when the tide of public opinion flows against us. These are the values that make our nation exceptional. These are the values worth fighting for.

- The emancipation of black slaves redefined our ideas of democracy and freedom. It made America a better nation, truer to her ideals. In this sense, emancipation and slavery transcended skin color.

- By remembering the nation's resolve to end slavery, we gain a positive racial perspective that enables us to move forward with probity and intelligence on racial matters. This racial outlook reminds us that we are on a mission of racial justice, that we must come together to complete this mission, that this is our history's call, which we must answer.

The museum of slavery, in short, will be a national symbol that gives voice to the millions of nameless slaves who made possible the aspirations of others. For the vast majority of Americans, the museum will challenge their thinking about slavery and, it may be hoped, transform them. Certainly, the construction of the museum will cost taxpayers money. But if it was worth constructing memorials to mourn the death of the some 3,000 innocent people who perished in the World Trade Center, the Pentagon, and on a field near Shanksville, Pennsylvania, at the hands of terrorists, then it is surely worth constructing a tribute to the millions of slaves who died in forced service to this country.

My second proposal is the atonement trust fund. As envisioned here, the federal government would finance, and reputable trust administrators selected by prominent black Americans would administer, a trust fund for every newborn black American child born within a certain period of time-five, ten, or more years. The Supreme Court seems to view racial progress in increments of twenty-five years, a generation, but the eligibility period can certainly be negotiated. The purpose of the trust fund is to provide a core group of blacks with one of the most important resources slavery and Jim Crow have denied them-financial capital, family resources, or an estate, handed down from generation to generation. Subject to the restrictions mentioned in a moment, each black child within this group would receive the proceeds from the trust fund annually or upon reaching a certain age. He or she would then have the financial wherewithal to take a meaningful step toward a successful future, including enrolling in and graduating from college. The atonement estate would also be ear-marked for elementary and secondary education, allowing parents to take their children out of inferior public schools.

Before sketching the contours of the atonement trust fund, I should like to take a moment to explain why this particular reparation applies only to slave descendants and not to other racial minorities, who, nonetheless, would continue to receive symmetrical social benefits. Slavery created and Jim Crow sustained a racial hierarchy based on color. Under this system of racial favoritism, presumptions of beauty and intelligence and other manifestations of group privilege are determined in large part by the group's proximity to the European (or white) phenotype. Asians, Latinos, or other racial groups whose phenotype is closer to the European model than that of blacks experience less disadvantage than blacks, although more than whites, *owing to slavery and Jim Crow.* This is true even among blacks. For example, in American society, black women who are admired for their beauty—such as Halle Berry, Tyra Banks, and Vanessa Williams—have predominantly European rather than Negroid features. One could argue, however, that because nonblack minorities experience at least some disadvantage from the lingering effects of slavery and Jim Crow-which is to say, the "black-white paradigm," or "black-white binary," which sees the color line only in black and white, is invalid-the atonement trust fund, which after all is designed to redress the lingering effects of slavery, should be made available to all racial minorities. But to do this, we would have to determine the relative degree of disadvantage each racial group actually sustains because of slavery and Jim Crow. We would have to determine, for example, what percentage of the social problems Latinos experience are fueled by the continuous flow of poor and unskilled immigrants into Latino communities, or how much harm slavery and Jim Crow visits on Asians who continue to experience housing discrimination yet have higher incomes and educational levels than even whites. This exercise would simply run the idea of reparations into the ground-it would make a mockery of an otherwise laudable principle. For that reason, a line has to be drawn somewhere.

I draw the line at blacks for several reasons. First, blacks were the *main target* of slavery and Jim Crow. No other American group inhabited the peculiar institution. No other American group sustained more casualties or lengthier suffering from slavery and Jim Crow. No other American group harbors as much ill will against the federal government for slavery and Jim Crow. Second, this gives blacks a connection to slavery and Jim Crow-both familial and psychological-that no other racial minority has. There is a collective memory here that only blacks have, and a collective emotional need that only the government can satisfy. Third, unlike Asians and Latinos, blacks did not volunteer for this tour of duty. Blacks were kidnapped from their homeland and brought to this country by brutal force, the likes of which we have not seen before or since in American history. In short, although blacks, Asians, Latinos, Native Americans, Indians, and other people of color are victims of what Joe Feagin calls "systemic racism" (or the "white-created" paradigm of racial subordination), they do not experience and hence do not react to racial subordination in exactly the same way. Each experiences a different pattern, or syndrome, of white oppression, which sometimes overlaps, and each reacts differently, from despair to disregard, from levels of resistance to total acceptance. White-on-black oppression is just different from other white-oppression syndromes, whether racial or gender. "As Patricia Rodriguez has observed, 'White means mostly privilege and black means overcoming obstacles, a history of civil rights. As a Latina, I can't try to claim one of these.'" Black Americans carry the weight of the atrocities-slavery and Jim Crow—for which atonement is being sought. But, again, all racial minorities, including blacks, should continue to receive the protection of symmetrical social measures, including the civil rights laws.

Although the atonement trust fund would apply primarily to blacks, several restrictions would be imposed on the management, transfer, and use of trust funds. Each trust fund would have a life of twenty-five years (the amount of time it would take each child to get through college or many graduate or professional schools) and be maintained by the federal government. A board of commissioners, consisting of reputable citizens selected by blacks, would oversee fund operations in their respective regions of the country. Commissioners and their staff would, for example, help fund recipients make the right choices in schools and business opportunities. All payments from the trust fund would be by electronic transfer. Recipients would never really see or handle the funds.

Money accumulated in the atonement trust fund would only be spent for education or to start or invest in a business. Good primary and secondary education, graduation from a prestigious college or university, and small businesses are important ingredients in building family resources and sustaining their accumulation from one generation to the next. The trust fund would provide resources to help black children escape poor-performing public schools, alleviate the financial burden that causes many black students to leave college before graduating, and finance business opportunities for blacks who do not go to college. Venture capital funds would not, however, be made available until the recipient's twenty-fifth birthday (or later). An eighteen-year-old simply lacks the maturity to know his or her aspirations or to make sound investment decisions. For that reason, vocational education and mandatory consultations with a managerial advisory board, consisting of retired business persons selected by the board of commissioners, would be additional requirements for the receipt of venture capital. Finally, wealthy black families would be excluded from the program. Because wealth is relative—$100,000 in Tupelo, Mississippi, is not the same as $100,000 in New York City—the income level would be set regionally by the board of commissioners.

The amount of money each black recipient should receive for education or business investment could be determined in numerous ways. One way is to base it on projected educational costs. A broader approach is offered by Boris I. Bittker, whose calculation operates upon the relevant assumption that the purpose of monetary relief is to close the considerable net family wealth gap between blacks and whites. Bittker takes the difference between the average earnings between whites and blacks (let us call this value EG, for earnings gap) and multiplies EG by the number of black Americans (BA) to arrive at the amount of money blacks as a group should receive. This sum (the reparations amount, or RA) is determined annually, and is the amount Congress funds each year until the net family wealth gap is closed. Bittker does not say how long it would take to close the net family wealth gap. I would suggest that the funding period be consistent with the life of the atonement trust fund-twenty-five years for each beneficiary. Bittker's formula, then, is roughly, EG × BA = RA.

Another approach, offered by a former student of mine, the attorney Darrell L. Pugh, takes the racial income gap figure (EG) and capitalizes it to determine the present value of the investment required to realize the income necessary to close the gap. "For example, assume an average income gap of $5,000 a year and an average market rate of return of zero per-cent. Under the capitalization approach, it would take $50,000 of investment capital per eligible worker to close the gap—5,000/.10 = $50,000. This figure could then be multiplied by the number of African Americans available in the adult workforce." Pugh's approach would permit funding to be phased in over time, "not only to encourage capacity building but to make the political feasibility of funding more likely."

Bittker and Pugh demonstrate that it is quite possible to calculate a monetary amount to be paid to slave descendants either per capita or through some program of eligibility like the atonement trust fund. Indeed, calculating the value of human life is rather routine in our society. Government agencies, juries, and insurance companies do it everyday. It is also important to note, as one thinks about the reparations calculations, that these calculations are always subject to second guessing. For example, when the Environmental Protection Agency did a cost-benefit analysis of a clean-air proposal that valued the life of a person over seventy years old at $1.4 million less than the life of a younger person-the so-called "senior death discount"—it was criticized by economists on several grounds, including that the calculation was faulty.

I offer the museum of slavery and atonement trust fund as forms of redress for slavery and Jim Crow, not as substitutes for ongoing civil rights reforms. The U.S. government still has an obligation to do what governments are supposed to do-protect its citizens from invidious discrimination. The museum of slavery and atonement trust fund should be viewed as special addenda to the struggle for racial justice in the United States. When viewed in juxtaposition to the milestones of this struggle—the abolition of slavery and Jim Crow—the museum of slavery and the atonement trust fund present easy burdens for our government. The hard question is whether white self-interest or perception of the public good will, once again, impede racial justice.

E.   REDRESS IN THE GLOBAL POLITICAL ECONOMY

What Role for Humanitarian Intellectual Property? The Globalization of Intellectual Property Rights

6 MINN. J.L. SCI. & TECH. 191 (2004).

■ SUSAN K. SELL

* * *

The 1995 Agreement on Trade–Related Aspects of Intellectual Property Rights (TRIPS), administered by the World Trade Organization (WTO), is the most important international law governing intellectual property rights. TRIPS extends patent rights to a wide variety of agricultural biotechnology innovations, including pharmaceutical products, pesticides, and plant varieties. It establishes a twenty-year patent term for these innovations. TRIPS requires states to provide adequate and effective enforcement mechanisms both internally and at their borders. The price of information and technology is increased under TRIPS because monopoly privileges are extended to patent-holders and TRIPS makes WTO dispute settlement procedures available to patent holders claiming violation of intellectually property rights. If a complaining government is successful in its claim, the WTO can authorize trade sanctions against the violating state. These settlement procedures and powers to punish make TRIPS a real force in the world.

Intellectual property rights reflect an inherent tension between the strong desire to promote and reward creative energy and the desire to make the fruits of that creativity available to the public. The granting of exclusive rights must be balanced against the economic effects of higher product and transaction costs and the potential "exclusion from the market of competitors who may be able to imitate or adapt the invention in such a way that social value is increased." Thus, the question is whether intellectual property rights should be treated as "a public goods problem for which the remedy is commodification, or a monopoly of information problem for which the remedy is unfettered competition[?]"

Strong intellectual property protection is justified by a market approach, because such protection provides incentives to "increase the number of commercially available products and thereby serve the public interest." However, it is important to question which public interests these rights serve. In the context of agricultural biotechnology, stakeholders include private sector seed companies, public corporations, research institutions, and resource-poor farmers. Intellectual property rights holders benefit from exclusive control of their innovations, as do those who have the resources to gain access to these innovations via the commercial market. Yet market-based solutions have failed to serve marginalized populations, such as the millions of people afflicted with HIV/AIDS and smallholder subsistence farmers in developing countries. The fact that smallholder farmers account for seventy-five percent of the world's undernourished population is evidence of this failure. In contemporary life science industries, market mechanisms fail to deliver innovation into the public domain. Indeed, "[i]nternational markets for technologies are inherently subject to failure due to distortions attributable to concerns about appropriability, problems of valuing information by buyers and sellers, and market power, all strong justifications for public intervention at both the domestic and global levels." There is a great need to strike a balance between a patent-holder's exclusive rights and the provision of agricultural technology to marginalized populations throughout the world. Solutions that will maximize the benefit of protecting innovation and yet minimize the risk of harm created by the potential overextension of this protection must be explored. It is therefore essential that policymakers consider "humanitarian" policies that promote social goals, such as protecting public health and alleviating malnutrition.

* * *

The contemporary global intellectual property regime is embedded in a broad structural context characterized by asymmetrical power relationships. Over the past thirty years, the globalization of financial markets and the shift towards an unfettered faith in laissez faire markets ideology pursued by the Reagan and Thatcher administrations has resulted in an increase in corporate transnational power vis-à-vis the state. States, seeking to be globally competitive, have liberalized markets, engaged in deregulation and privatization, and implemented new regulatory structures designed to promote efficiency and enforce market-friendly behavior. According to Philip Cerny, "[t]he institutions and practices of the state itself are increasingly marketized or 'commodified,' and the state becomes the spearhead of structural transformation to international market norms both at home and abroad." States have increasingly privatized once-public services, such as prisons, hospitals, military support services and even "mission-critical" functions, such as providing protection for the head of the 2003 Coalition Provisional Authority in Iraq, L. Paul Bremer III. The expansion of intellectual property rights and the privatization of federally funded research under the Bayh–Dole Act must be seen as an instance of this larger trend.

These broad economic changes have profoundly affected developing countries. Earlier models of economic development such as import-substituting industrialization, popular in Latin America and India, were discredited by economic stagnation and the debt crises of the 1970s–1980s. Meanwhile, the success of the East Asian "Tigers" vindicated export-led development and integration into global markets. Many developing countries subsequently reversed decades-old policies of economic nationalism in favor of market liberalization and privatization and consequently slashed public budgets. Governments in developing countries began to compete to attract foreign investment and eased former restrictions of foreign investors' activities. The new push toward export-led growth meant that developing countries needed access to industrialized country markets. The dependence of developing nations on trade gave the United States considerable economic leverage. Those developing countries sought access to the expansive United States market. Using the U.S. Trade Act of 1974, the Office of the United States Trade Representative, at the behest of high-technology firms, threatened trade sanctions against developing countries unless they adopted and enforced highly protective intellectual property policies. Such economic coercion was an important factor behind developing countries' ultimate acceptance of TRIPS.

This liberalizing agenda favors "finance capital and other mobile factors of production." Transnational firms in knowledge-intensive sectors such as pharmaceuticals, chemicals, software, and entertainment "have the resources, motivations and capabilities to roam the world searching for the kind of opportunities that promise lucrative rewards." These privileged sectors participate in "globalized" markets insofar as "there are a small number of participants who know one another and operate across countries with a common conception of control." TRIPS reflects the wishes of these privileged sectors and globalizes their preferred conception of control by establishing a high level of protection.

Beyond extending property rights, competitiveness concerns moved the United States to relax its antitrust policies. The Reagan administration codified this approach in the Antitrust Division's Merger Control Guidelines of 1982. Reflecting the influence of the Chicago School of Economics, the new guidelines abandoned the populist focus on market structure in favor of the Chicago school's focus on price theory. "In this view, only business practices that reduce output and increase prices are anti-competitive; business practices that expand output are pro-competitive." In contrast to earlier approaches, according to the Chicago school, "[h]igh levels of market concentration and the exercise of market power may be indicative of efficiencies." The 1982 guidelines presented an expanded definition of relevant markets. The guidelines allowed the introduction of non-structural factors, such as foreign competition or the possession of new technology that was important to long-term competitiveness. The Justice Department argued that "anti-trust laws should not be applied in a way that hinders the renewed emphasis on . . . competitiveness."

This new thinking removed most intellectual property licensing from antitrust scrutiny. As Thomas Hayslett points out, under Reagan's administration, "executive agencies viewed the economic incentives provided by intellectual property rights as legitimate means of extracting the full economic benefit from innovation." In effect then, "[i]ntellectual property rights acted as a 'magic trump card' allowing many previously suspect arrangements to proceed without challenge from the [Federal Trade Commission] or [Department of Justice]." Keith Maskus and Jerome Reichman suggest that today:

> There are virtually no products sold on the general products market that do not come freighted with a bewildering and overlapping array of exclusive property rights that discourage follow-on applications of

routine technical know-how. Weak enforcement of antitrust laws then further reinforces the barriers to entry erected upon this thicket of rights, while the need to stimulate and coordinate investment in complex innovation projects justifies patent pools, concentrations of research efforts, and predatory practices formerly thought to constitute misuses of the patent monopoly.

So-called patent "thickets" have proliferated, in which overlapping patent rights require those seeking to commercialize new technology to obtain licenses from multiple patent holders. "A growing thicket of rights surrounds gene fragments, research tools, and other upstream inputs of scientific research, and the resulting transaction costs impede and delay research and development undertaken in both the public and private sectors."

III.   ISSUES IN AGRICULTURE

What are the implications of the foregoing for agriculture? "Increasingly ... [intellectual property] rights have invaded the research commons itself and made it both costly and difficult to obtain cutting-edge technologies needed for public health, agricultural production, environmental protection, and the provision of other public goods." Critics of the increasing commodification of what was once treated as the public domain have raised at least six issues of concern: (1) threats to traditional agriculture and food security; (2) abuses of monopoly power; (3) increased dependence on costly commercial agriculture; (4) threats to biodiversity; (5) "biopiracy;" and (6) questions of benefit sharing. The discussion in this article focuses on the first three issues of concern.

Technological, judicial, and legislative changes together have produced a radical shift from public to private provision of seeds. As Professor Keith Aoki points out, "[t]he private seed market for grains was almost nonexistent at the beginning of the twentieth century, due to free government seed distribution and the widespread practice of farmer seed saving." According to Professor Aoki, "the intersection of biotechnical knowledge and methods and expanded legal protections for plant breeders transforms seed germplasm into a paradigm commodity." Legislative changes, including the United States Plant Variety Protection Act of 1970, "increased expectations of seed industry profits and thereby helped to stimulate an upsurge in mergers and acquisitions...." Life sciences corporations "emerged out of a wave of mergers, acquisitions, joint ventures and strategic partnerships involving companies in a wide range of fields such as chemicals, seeds, processed foods, dietary supplements and pharmaceuticals." Advances in biotechnology spurred the consolidation process throughout the 1970s and particularly in the 1980s. The 1973 development of the recombinant DNA technique, "which enabled foreign genes to be inserted into microorganisms," helped launch the era of commercial biotechnology. Notably, although "the Cohen–Boyer method for combining DNA from different organisms" was patented, "the patents were licensed nonexclusively and cheaply to encourage firms to take licenses rather than to challenge the patents." This technology had been federally funded, and "[m]any observers attribute the rapid progress of the biotechnology industry to the fact that this technology was made widely available rather than licensed exclusively to a single firm." In 1980, the U.S. Supreme Court ruled in Diamond v. Chakrabarty that a man-made, oil-eating bacterium could be patented. This case led to the expansion of rights to own living organisms and injected greater certainty into the development of commercial biotechnology. The ability to acquire patents on altered life forms helped biotechnology startup companies to raise venture capital.

The combination of expanded intellectual property rights and relaxed antitrust enforcement has led to marked economic concentration in the life sciences industries. The "vertical integration" of plant breeding, agrochemical, and food processing corporations has led to a situation in which the top ten seed companies control thirty percent of the world's $23 billion commercial seed market. Corporate plant breeders are obtaining broad patents that will have "far reaching" consequences. "Breeders are patenting entire species (cotton), economic characteristics (oil quality), plant reproductive behaviour (apomixes), and basic techniques in biotechnology (gene transfer tools)." Six major industrial groups now control most of the technology " 'which gives freedom to undertake commercial research and development in the area of [genetically modified] crops.' These are (i) Agrevo and Plant Genetic Systems (PGS); (ii) Du Pont and Pioneer; (iii) ELM, DNAP, Asgrow and Seminis; (iv) Monsanto, Calgene, DeKalb, Agracetus, PBI, Hybritech and Delta and Pine Land Co.; (v) Novartis; and (vi) Zeneca, Mogen and Avanta." Furthermore, six agricultural biotechnology companies alone hold seventy-five percent of all U.S. patents granted to the top thirty patent-holding firms: Monsanto, Du Pont, Syngenta, Dow, Aventis, and Grupo Pulsar. This combination of economic concentration with extensive and broad patenting means that a handful of global corporations are making huge inroads toward control of the world's food supply and are entangling farmers and indigenous peoples in an increasingly complex web of licensing and royalty obligations. As Keith Maskus and Jerome Reichman suggest:

> [T]he natural competitive disadvantages of follower countries may become reinforced by a proliferation of legal monopolies and related entry barriers that result from global minimum [intellectual property] standards. Such external restraints on competition could consign the poorest countries to a quasi-permanent status at the bottom of the technology and growth ladder.

The current system skews research towards rich and middle-income countries' markets and sectors. Most notably, there is a tendency in the public health sector to neglect tropical diseases in favor of focusing on cancer and so-called lifestyle afflictions, requiring drugs to combat obesity, balding, and erectile dysfunction. Consequently, only thirteen of 1,233 new drugs marketed between 1975 and 1997 were approved for tropical diseases in particular. As Professor Hammer suggests, "the rhetoric of strong intellectual property rights leading to innovation that meets social needs rings particularly hollow" for poorer countries most afflicted by tropical diseases. Similarly, there is a focus on the interests of higher-income markets in the agriculture sector, resulting in the development of crops unsuitable for subsistence and smallholder farming and a dearth of research beneficial for less lucrative micro-climates. The disproportionate emphasis on wealthier countries' market needs can be corrected through changes in private-public collaboration and through the allocation of more funding towards "the goal of helping subsistence farmers." Historically, seed companies preferred to develop hybrids because farmers must purchase new hybrid seed every planting season. Since the offspring of hybrid plants do not breed true-to-type, hybrid seeds offer a "form of biological protection." However, for plant varieties that lack this built-in biological protection, plant breeders can appeal to plant breeders' rights. Plant breeders' rights "generally do not encourage breeding related to minor crops with small markets." As a result, the private sector under invests in crops and technologies suitable for smallholder farmers, and these public goods are underprovided.

With the advent of genetic engineering, plant breeders sought to safeguard their investments through strong patent protections. Depending on national law, patents may be available for "the use of the new gene to transform a plant, on the transformation process, and most significantly on the transformed plant itself." The protection of transgenic plants enables genetic engineering firms to have "more confidence in their ability to reap the fruits of their research." That is because transfer or insertion of the patented gene into other plants constitutes patent infringement. Before the adoption of the 1991 Union for the Protection of New Varieties of Plants (UPOV91), plant breeders were forced to choose to protect their plant varieties with either a plant breeders' right or a patent. However, UPOV91 "removed the 1978 [UPOV's] ban on dual protection and now permits member states to protect the same plant variety with both a breeders' right and a patent." Professor Robert Lettington argues that this expansion of intellectual property rights into the agricultural sector has threatened the public sector's traditional focus on the needs of smallholder farmers. First of all, "private sector intellectual property rights may limit public sector access to innovations and germplasm that may be adaptable to smallholder needs and conditions while also limiting public sector research options due to concerns over the unhindered distribution of the products of its research." Second, the "failure of intellectual property systems to preserve the integrity of the public domain, and the consequent development of intellectual property rights strategies in public institutions, risks distorting research priorities to the detriment of smallholder farmers."

In developing countries, a large number of farmers are smallholders who do not participate in the transgenic seed market in any substantial way. Instead, these farmers engage in seed-saving, replanting, and "across-the-fence" exchange. This is particularly the case in many African countries where the public and private sectors play a minimal role in seed production and distribution. The smallholder farming sector plays an important role in contributing to national food needs. For example, such farmers produce "fifty-one percent of Latin America's maize, seventy-seven percent of its beans and sixty-one percent of its potatoes." In Africa, smallholder farmers produce the "majority of grains and legumes and almost all root, tuber and plantain crops." Furthermore, fifty to sixty percent of Peruvians and seventy to eighty percent of Kenyans depend on smallholder agriculture for their livelihood.

According to Professor Lettington, subsistence farmers traditionally save seeds for reuse, trade, and experimentation with new hybrids. Such experimentation contributes to the planet's biodiversity, as evidenced by the farmers in Professor Lettington's study who produced "as many as [thirty or forty] distinct varieties of potato, and [five or ten varieties] of maize, on farms of little more than a hectare." In the past, American laws covering plant varieties incorporated the notion of farmers' rights in which farmers retained their freedom to engage in these important and tradition-al activities. However, in August 1994 the U.S. Congress amended the Plant Variety Protection Act and removed the farmer's exemption. As a result, "it is now expressly illegal for farmers to sell or save seeds from proprietary crop varieties without receiving permission from breeders and paying royalties." Ironically, according to Professor Aoki, while the U.S. Patent Office in the "early 19th century began to collect and catalogue and make" seed freely available, by the early twenty-first century, the commo-dification of germplasm had transformed the U.S. patent office, into a "primary means" of attacking the longstanding "practice of farmer seed-saving." Grassroots activists are convinced that American industries are seeking these same results through TRIPS by pushing a particular inter-pretation of sui generis protection under Article 27.3(b).

Ultimately, TRIPS restricted the patenting of life forms, but Article 27.3(b) requires that members provide intellectual property protection for plant varieties or an "effective sui generis" system. However, there really is no consensus on what a sui generis system needs to include. Additionally, the negotiations leading to the adoption of Article 27 provide little guidance because they provide no record on the meaning of sui generis. American plant breeders have been pushing the UPOV as the model sui generis system. American support of UPOV may be due in part to how generous UPOV is to the corporate plant breeder. Fifty-one countries, many of which are industrialized, have joined the UPOV, which was last amended in 1991. The 1978 version of UPOV provided two limitations on the monopoly rights of plant breeders. First, other breeders could freely use UPOV-protected varieties for research purposes. Second, farmers could reuse the seed for the following year's harvest under certain conditions. The 1991 revision narrowed down the exemption for competing breeders, deleted the so-called farmers' privilege, and extended the breeders' monopoly right to the products of the farmer's harvest. "Although the UPOV system allows on-farm replanting, its rules restrict farmers' freedom to buy seed from sources other than the original breeders." UPOV91 "does not authorize farmers to sell or exchange seeds with other farmers for propagating purposes." To join UPOV today, nations must sign the 1991 treaty. Countries eschewing the UPOV system can adopt sui generis systems of protection that allow "farmers to acquire ... protected seed from any source and/or requiring protected varieties to display qualities that are genuinely superior to existing varieties."

In a comparative study of smallholder farming in Peru and Kenya, Robert J. L. Lettington did not find evidence that plant variety protection (PVP) legislation harmed smallholder agriculture. However, he argued that "the current system of PVP [legislation] is failing to create solutions to existing problems." In particular, PVP legislation has created incentives that direct resources away from subsistence farmers' needs in favor of those of large commercial agricultural enterprises. It also promotes the use of commercial seed as opposed to landraces or "wild" cultivars. "The end result has been a hastening of the deterioration of food security in these areas...." Professor Lettington suggests that governments that seek to limit the cost of seed in economically and climatically marginal areas may "need to place limits on the nature of intellectual property rights."

IV. THE REGULATORY ENVIRONMENT

In examining the regulatory environment in this context, the central question is what degree of discretion states have in limiting intellectual property rights to support smallholder agriculture. There are at least two dimensions to the answer: one addresses the letter of the law, the other addresses the broader context of asymmetrical power. Focusing on the formal features of intellectual property law, texts, and institutions, one sees plenty of room for state discretion and flexibility in adapting the global minimum standards to local concerns. However, this formal universe is embedded in a system of asymmetrical power relationships and global capitalism that constrain weaker states' abilities to exploit the flexibilities crafted into the law.

TRIPS provides substantial flexibility for developing countries. Article 27.3(b) specifies that countries may adopt an "effective sui generis system" to protect plant varieties. Under TRIPS, countries may adopt patent protection for plant varieties, UPOV91, an alternative sui generis system, or some combination of these forms of protection. While corporate plant breeders would prefer that developing countries adopt UPOV91 as their domestic legislative standard, these countries are by no means required to do so. The UPOV treaties are one type of sui generis protection designed to serve the interests of plant breeders. In a searching and thorough analysis of developing countries' options, Professor Laurence Helfer has arrayed the options on a spectrum ranging from maximum discretion to minimal discretion for developing countries to tailor their systems to meet their particular needs. States that adopt TRIPS and ratify or accede to UPOV91 have the least discretion. According to Professor Helfer, states wishing to retain maximum flexibility and discretion to serve the needs of smallholder agriculture would be well-advised to adopt TRIPS only.

The advantages of TRIPS are that its provisions on plant varieties "do not refer to or incorporate any preexisting intellectual property agreements, including the 1978 and 1991 UPOV Acts." TRIPS members are neither required "to become members of UPOV nor to enact national laws consistent with either UPOV Act in order to comply with their obligations under TRIP[S]." Article 27.3(b) preserves "significant leeway for national governments to work out the precise manner in which they will balance protection of IPRs against other international obligations and national objectives." "The chances are, that for a poor nation, neither a UPOV nor a regular patent approach will actually encourage private-sector research. Hence, such a nation is probably best-off adopting minimum compliance with TRIPS...." TRIPS, unlike UPOV91, preserves the right of subsistence farmers to exchange seed. For a nation in which the exchange is an issue, it would be wise to incorporate both subsistence farmer exemptions and research exemptions in national plant breeders' rights legislation. Countries wishing to adopt the stronger UPOV91 system should consider incorporating waivers or exemptions for subsistence and smallholder farmers. In countries lacking significant private sector competition, as is often the case in poor countries, public sector seed provision will be important to promote competition to stimulate both variety and lower prices.

Public-private partnerships in agriculture might stimulate the transfer of technology so that public sector seed providers could adapt technology to subsistence farmers' needs. In order for such arrangements to work, private firms would need to retain opportunities to capture economic benefits in the market sector, while keeping the technology affordable for the subsistence sector. This two-tiered arrangement has some parallels in the control of access to medicines and would require safeguards against diverting subsistence-priced technology into the market sector.

Focusing on TRIPS and the letter of the law, one can conclude, as does Professor Helfer, that:

> States that implement the four core TRIP[S] requirements in good faith—that is, states that grant breeders intellectual property rights and enforcement measures applicable to varieties in all species and botanical genera and that provide those same rights and measures to breeders from other TRIP[S] member states—are unlikely to have their laws challenged successfully.

However, public international law such as TRIPS is embedded in a broader context of asymmetrical power relationships between developed and developing countries, and between producers and consumers of the fruits of biotechnology. This context reduces the amount of leeway that poor states have in devising regulatory approaches most suitable for their individual needs and stages of development. In particular, developing countries increasingly have been subject to bilateral and regional pressure to surrender the flexibilities afforded by TRIPS. Bilateral investment treaties, bilateral intellectual property agreements, and regional free trade agreements concluded between the United States and developing countries and between the European Union and developing countries invariably have been considered to be "TRIPS–Plus."

For example, in the intellectual property provisions covering agriculture in the Central American Free Trade Agreement framework, developing countries are most often required to ratify or accede to UPOV91 as their sui generis system of protection and "to undertake 'all reasonable efforts' to make patent protection available for plants."

Furthermore, developing countries have failed to take full advantage of TRIPS flexibilities not only in the agricultural marketplace, but the pharmaceutical market as well. This is largely because such nations are eager to attract foreign investment and are concerned about alienating potential investors. They also are eager to have access to technologies that may aid in their development, provide reliable nutrition, and which have the potential to address a myriad of pressing social and economic problems. Most of these countries lack significant bargaining leverage and the capacity to resist the high-pressure tactics of the United States Trade Representative and the industries that it represents.

In these circumstances it is imperative that public institutions take the lead in assisting developing countries in the implementation of suitable legislation that conforms to their international legal obligations. Public institutions, such as land grant universities, must also continue to make the fruits of their research available to those who need it most on terms that the recipients accept. The 1980 Bayh–Dole Act allowed "grantees to seek patent rights in government-sponsored research results." The idea behind this was that many inventions with commercial potential lay fallow in university laboratories, and that patenting opportunities would give universities incentives to search research labs for significant and marketable inventions. The Bayh–Dole Act has resulted in at least a ten-fold increase of university patenting activity since 1979. This flurry of patenting activity has had the beneficial effect of generating revenue for cash-strapped public universities. For instance, the patent infringement award that the University of Minnesota won for the development of the drug Ziagen has provided much-needed funding for research and graduate student support. University patent portfolios also help to attract private sector funding, especially in biotechnology.

However, the Bayh–Dole Act also has created new divisions within universities. As Professors Arti Rai and Rebecca Eisenberg point out, the legislation makes no distinction between upstream and downstream research, and as a result, an increasing number of research tools have become patent-protected. An unintended consequence of the Bayh–Dole Act has been the dramatic reduction of open access to research tools. Technology transfer offices are charged with patenting and licensing technology to generate revenue for the institution. Research scientists are more interested in having access to "open science." The Bayh–Dole Act also has increased university collaboration with private sector biotechnology firms, raising many questions about academic freedom, research priorities, and incentives. Some critics have gone so far as to assert that universities have lost their sense of "public mission."

Yet the choices may not be so stark, and there may be ways to navigate the contours of the current system to better balance competing imperatives. For example, in the pharmaceutical sector, there could be clauses in agreements to allow a university to sublicense to generic manufacturers if its patent conflicts with efforts to distribute affordable drugs for HIV/AIDS victims in sub-Saharan Africa. Professors Rai and Eisenberg offer a similarly modest and sensible suggestion for publicly-funded research. They suggest that "decisions about the dividing line between the public domain and private property should be made by institutions that are in a position to appreciate the tensions between widespread access and preservation of commercial incentives without being unduly swayed by institutional interests that diverge from the overall public interest." In other words, they argue that public funding agencies should decide what fruits of their investments to patent. They also advocate addressing the upstream/downstream research tool issue by devising "a system that distinguishes cases in which proprietary claims make sense from cases in which they do not." Research tool exemptions would be useful to help to preserve the domain of "open science."

V. CONCLUSION

This brief overview of some major issues involved in intellectual property protection and agricultural biotechnology underscores the fact that "the institution of property is extremely complex, and more importantly, political." Yet we are no closer to resolving these controversies. "More often than not, rather than being an answer, the issue of property rights is only the beginning of a long series of vexing questions." Developing countries should do what they can to preserve their autonomy in adopting intellectual property policies that suit their levels of development. They should resist TRIPS-plus initiatives in bilateral and regional trade and investment agreements and insist upon TRIPS as their maximum standard. Developing nations should seek technical assistance that encourages them to use existing TRIPS flexibilities. They also need to participate in global standard-setting exercises concerning competition policy and address the ways in which they would prefer to regulate foreign firms' acquisition of local firms.

Promoting genuine competition is an important policy objective. "Nations in which there is limited private sector competition in the seed industry should ensure that public sector varieties are available in competition with private sector ones." Professor Lettington recommends:

> The activities of smallholder farmers, in particular the saving, use, exchange, and sale of farm-saved seed, should be explicitly stated as not subject to the rights of intellectual property rights holders. In accordance with the purposes and objectives of TRIPS, effort should be made to develop effective incentives for research targeted at smallholder farmers . . . . Limited exceptions to intellectual property rights should be permitted to promote the adaptation of protected products to the needs of smallholder farmers. These should apply to both research and development and to manufacturing and distribution.

Universities may feel caught between the conflicting imperatives of attracting private sector funding and generating revenue through patenting activity on the one hand, and promoting public goods through "humanitari-an intellectual property" policies on the other. It is clear that universities have an important role to play in preserving the balance between exclusion and access as well as paving the way to more informed, effective, and socially responsible agricultural intellectual property policies.

———

Civil Resistance and the "Diversity of Tactics" in the Anti–Globalization Movement: Problems of Violence, Silence, and Solidarity in Activist Politics

41 OSGOODE HALL L.J. 505 (2003).

■ JANET CONWAY

I. INTRODUCTION

With the November 1999 mobilization that shut down the World Trade Organization (WTO) meetings in Seattle, the "anti-globalization" move-ment erupted onto the world stage. Between the Seattle protest and the events of September 11, 2001 (9/11), massive and growing anti-globaliza-tion demonstrations confronted neo-liberal elites wherever they convened. These demonstrations, especially their North American and European variants, have been the forum for the emergence of a debate over "diversity of tactics." The debate has revolved around the acceptability of more disruptive or confrontational forms of direct action, the putative role of property damage, and the use of veiled threats of the escalation of violence in the struggle against neo-liberal globalization.

* * *

In the name of creativity, resistance, and democracy, many anti-globalization activists advocate "respect for diversity of tactics" as a non-negotiable basis of unity. Solidarity with the full range of resistance has meant that no tactics are ruled out in advance and that activists refrain from publicly criticizing tactics with which they disagree. However, embrac-ing diversity of tactics is not without ambiguity and risk: both strategically in terms of provoking repression and losing public support, but also in terms of democratic practice and culture within the movement itself where it may damage any prospect for broad coalition politics.

* * *

II. CIVIL DISOBEDIENCE AND DIRECT ACTION

The terms "civil disobedience" and "direct action" have been used interchangeably in both activist and academic circles; their meanings are often conflated. Further, the meaning of these terms often suffers as assumptions of illegality and violence are imported into their use.

Civil disobedience is a specific form of extra-parliamentary political action involving the deliberate, principled, and public breaking of a law that is perceived to be unjust. Acts of civil disobedience are premised on the existence of liberal democratic institutions and the rule of law. The public and principled breaking of a law by otherwise law-abiding persons is meant to call attention to the unjustness of that law, both through heroic witness (being willing to risk arrest or jail), and through using or gumming-up legal channels themselves (for example, through a trial). Classic examples of the use of civil disobedience from recent movement history include the lunch counter sit-ins of the civil-rights movement, the burning of draft cards in the anti-Vietnam War movement, and the blockades and occupations of the anti-nuclear movement.

Direct action is a larger and more generic category than is civil disobedience. The term refers to forms of political action that bypass parliamentary or bureaucratic channels to directly ameliorate or eliminate an injustice, or to slow down or obstruct regular operations of an unjust system or order. Strikes, street demonstrations, and occupations are classic forms of direct action.

Virtually all contemporary forms of direct action are in some sense symbolic as the action dramatizes conflict of system-wide problems. For example, the act of squatting (moving into and living in) in a vacant building may provide housing for a dozen homeless people thus directly ameliorating their situation. However, as forms of political action, most squats point to a much larger phenomenon of homelessness and create pressure for public agencies to act against the squat or to provide affordable housing. In this sense, a single squat constitutes direct action and is symbolic at the same time.

Direct action can be legal, illegal, or extra-legal (extra-legal is used here to refer to practices that are not currently contemplated by the law). It may or may not be an occasion of police action and arrests. While all civil disobedience is a form of direct action, not all direct action involves the intentional and principled breaking of an unjust law with the purpose of calling attention to it. Direct action can be situated anywhere on what young activists call "the violence/non-violence continuum." Likewise, direct action can be situated anywhere on the illegal/extra-legal/legal continuum. There is no necessary correlation between non-violence and legality or, as activist victims of police brutality are quick to point out, between violence and illegality.

Both civil disobedience and direct action can involve property destruction and can still be considered non-violent by many activists. Here, non-violence is generally understood to mean the eschewing of the use of physical force against another human being. Generally, the mass street actions of the anti-globalization movement have been forms of direct action, some of them legal but many of them not, and have been almost completely non-violent on the part of the protesters. Within the demonstrations, there have been numerous direct actions of a great variety of types. The intensifying debate over diversity of tactics in the movement must be understood within a context of expanding commitment to, and enactment of, a wide variety of expressions of direct action.

III. DIVERSITY OF TACTICS

The debate over diversity of tactics in the anti-globalization movement initially emerged in the context of the Seattle demonstrations in November 1999. By the April 2001 anti-Free Trade Area of the Americas (FTAA) demonstrations in Quebec City, there was a full and specific articulation of the meaning of the term. Respect for diversity of tactics implies support for a bundle of organizing approaches, attitudes, and tactics. Since the Seattle demonstrations, proponents of diversity of tactics in the Canadian anti-globalization movement have argued both for an escalation and for a diversification of tactics beyond the routines of lobbying and legal, stage-managed demonstrations. They have argued for the valuing of a wider range of political activity especially in the institutionalized power centres of the movement such as labour unions and non-governmental organizations (NGOs). Proponents of diversity of tactics have called for and have engaged in popular education, cultural work, and grassroots-community organizing. Driven by a sense of urgency resulting from mounting social and ecological crises, these activists have argued for a return to more militant and confrontational tactics, including direct action and civil disobedience. In the name of both escalation and diversity they have also called for and defended property destruction, from stickering, spray painting, and guerrilla murals, to window smashing and the defacing of signs.

Respect for diversity of tactics as an ethical framework presupposes the existence of "affinity groups" as the unit of organization and democratic decision making. Affinity group organizing has its roots in feminist, anarchist, and anti-nuclear movements in which small, autonomous groups decide on the nature of their participation in a direct action, organizing independently of any centralized movement authority. Commitment to affinity group organizing often implies a repudiation of representative forms of democracy, institutions of the liberal democratic state, as well as labour unions and more bureaucratized movement organizations. Respect for diversity of tactics is part of a commitment to and practice of direct and participatory democracy in which all practitioners participate directly in decision making about tactics within their affinity groups. Large-scale anti-globalization demonstrations have been organized in significant part by networks of affinity groups who gather in spokescouncils. Theoretically, these groups strive for consensus, but practically work towards coordination and mutual tolerance.

The decisive feature of respect for diversity of tactics is an ethic of respect for, and acceptance of, the tactical choices of other activists. This tolerance of pluralism involves an explicit agreement not to publicly denounce the tactics of other activists—most controversially, rock-throwing, window-breaking, garbage can burning, and vandalism. So respect for diversity of tactics precludes, for example, the kind of non-violence agreement proposed by the Direct Action Network (DAN) that undergirded the Seattle organizing. The debate about diversity of tactics first emerged under that name when DAN organizers and other key movement leaders condemned the people throwing rocks and breaking windows in Seattle.

By the time of the demonstrations in Quebec City, those who were advocating diversity of tactics were also repudiating the dogmatism of non-violence, which they understood to be an authoritarian move to render certain forms of political resistance illegitimate. They criticized the overly rigid violence/non-violence binary that characterizes much of the discourse around non-violence. They also critiqued the highly ritualized forms of civil disobedience that had evolved during the peace movement, where protesters passively handed themselves over to the police.

* * *

V.   PERSPECTIVES ON PROPERTY DESTRUCTION IN THE ANTI–GLOBALIZATION MOVEMENT

The most contentious debates about violence and non-violence in the North American anti-globalization movement revolve around the nature and status of property destruction as a tactic. Proponents of diversity of tactics specify that property damage includes such political staples as stickering, billboard "corrections," or graffiti. Few activists would dispute the value and creativity of these tactics, either within the context of large demonstrations and in their own right.

They rightly argue that the label violent is used somewhat indiscriminately, both within and beyond the movement, to refer to anyone acting outside the bounds of legitimate, that is routinized, legalized, and bureaucratized, forms of dissent. Those within the movement (including those engaged in non-violent direct action) tend to single out property damage, particularly window breaking, as violent. Notably, the debate here is not about physical violence against persons, but about whether destruction of property is encompassed within the meaning of violent.

The smashing of corporate windows, police cruisers, and media vehicles remain very controversial and have occasionally given rise to fisticuffs on the spot between activists who try to prevent those who attempt to pursue these tactics. Proponents of property destruction in Seattle pointed out the irony of self-proclaimed non-violent protesters physically tackling those targeting corporate property. They reject the notion that property destruction is violent unless it involves causing pain to, or death of, people. Rather than an expression of rage or reaction, proponents claim that property damage is "strategically and specifically targeted direct action against corporate interests." Proponents distinguish between private (capitalist) property and personal (use-value) property, targeting the former. They maintain that, as a tactic, property destruction unsettles middle-class culture and the reification of private property that is so entrenched in North America. "Property destruction allows for a change in landscape, a visual punctuation."

Therefore, proponents argue both ideologically and strategically for certain *kinds* of property destruction. But within the discourse of respect for diversity of tactics there seems to be little room for discussion between affinity groups of what kinds of property can be destroyed and what kinds of damage are appropriate. Further, there is little discussion between groups about the relation of these acts to the larger political context or to any broader movement strategy.

It is a fact that both the mainstream and alternative media are captivated by property destruction and the climate of uncertainty and disorder that it fosters through its threat of escalating conflict. Some forms of property destruction—notably window breaking—have trumped all other movement tactics in terms of the mass production of images. This fact is not recognized as problematic among the proponents of property destruction, despite their rhetoric of respect for (and presumably, a valuing of) diversity of tactics.

VI.   THE BLACK BLOC

Finally, while I support a clear distinction between the destruction of property and violence to people, discussions about property damage in the context of the anti-globalization movement are unavoidably haunted by the spectre of the Black Bloc and the host of political and strategic issues it raises. Because it is the most prominent apologist for, and practitioner of, property destruction, the Black Bloc's discourses and practices as a whole overdetermine the debate about property destruction in the context of the anti-globalization movement.

The Black Bloc originated in the European Autonomen movement in which masked and black-clad anarchists engaged in a range of militant and confrontational tactics and defend each other from the police. In Seattle, the Black Bloc concentrated their efforts on property damage and avoided engaging the police. In post-Seattle actions in Toronto, Ottawa, and Quebec City, the Black Bloc appeared to me to be a masked and costumed group of youths beating tattoos on poles and stop signs and marching in formation within large demonstrations. Yet in other situations, notably in Europe, all manners of mayhem have been attributed to the Black Bloc—hurling rocks, sticks, and Molotov cocktails at the police and looking for a fight. They played particularly explosive roles in Prague and Genoa.

* * *

Numerous activists do engage in various forms of property destruction without masks and without any identification with the Black Bloc. Moreover, many are explicitly non-violent in their interactions with police. There are also traditions of property destruction in the anti-nuclear movement that are part of traditions of non-violent civil disobedience. But in the current context of the anti-globalization movement, property destruction has also become a tactic favoured by the Black Bloc. And it is this relationship, created by the discourses and practices of the Black Bloc, between property destruction in the context of the large anti-globalization demonstrations and a readiness, even an eagerness, to confront the police physically, that has so problematized property destruction as an acceptable tactic in the current context. Furthermore, when property destruction is enacted by masked activists, it is also vulnerable to appropriation, manipulation, and escalation by masked others: the police or their paid agitators, fascists, or criminal elements, some of whom appear to have participated in Genoa.

According to George Lakey, at its best, non-violent protest is a form of prefiguration. Its power lies in its contrast to the violent power of the state in the theatre of protest—solidarity and pacifism in the face of naked aggression. However, these assumptions were challenged in Seattle, particularly by those who engaged in and defended property destruction, not as a form of violence, but as embodying a distinct (and more militant and therefore better) political and strategic logic. As such, property destruction continues to raise troubling and challenging questions for the movement. In the post-Seattle period, Barbara Ehrenreich states:

> Clearly the left, broadly speaking, has come to a creative impasse. We need to invent some new forms of demonstrating that minimize the danger while maximizing the possibilities for individual self-expression.... We need ways of protesting that are accessible to the uninitiated, untrained, nonvegan population as well as to the seasoned veteran. We need to figure out how to capture public attention while, as often as possible, directly accomplishing some not-entirely-symbolic purpose, such as gumming up a WTO meeting or, for that matter, slowing down latte sales at a Starbucks.

> Rock-throwing doesn't exactly fit these criteria, nor did the old come-as-you-are demos of the sixties. But neither do the elaborately choreographed rituals known as "nonviolent" civil disobedience.

* * *

IX. ELITE RETREAT TO KANANASKIS AND HARD LESSONS FOR THE MOVEMENT

In response to the events of Genoa, the June 2002 meeting of the G8 was set for the remote Rocky Mountain town of Kananaskis. With five thousand troops, fifteen hundred Royal Canadian Mounted Police (RCMP), and an enforced no-fly zone, it was the "largest security operation in Canadian history," with a price tag of three to 500,000,000 dollars. Activists spent months planning a week-long Solidarity Village only to be outspent and outmaneuvered by governments and security forces at every turn. Negotiations with the Stoney Point First Nation over use of land came to an abrupt halt amid accusations of federal interference. The City of Calgary refused permission to use parks. According to David Robbins, an organizer with the Council of Canadians, "there's a desire to disorganize and frustrate coherent organizing around this particular summit in order to create confrontation and discredit opposition to the G–8 and corporate globalization."

Nevertheless, several thousand people turned up to the summit, the snake march, and the picnic without a permit, to muddy corporate facades, and to demonstrate with and without their clothes on. Again, the actions were organized under the rubric of diversity of tactics. Significantly, unions, NGOs, and direct-action protesters in Canada were working together again after a post–9/11 hiatus. In Calgary, unionists were visible in all the activities, including the snake marches that disrupted traffic during Monday morning rush hour, and had participated in the convergence table leading up to and during the events. The demonstrations were completely non-violent, although not without some heated moments. Protesters actively intervened to defuse potentially explosive situations between police and the more confrontational activist factions. Police in Calgary were on bicycles and in soft hat rather than riot gear.

Several thousand people also turned up in Ottawa in response to a call to "take the capital." As in Calgary, the framework for organizing was respect for diversity of tactics. Coordinated separation of spaces allowed for different kinds of events, from an explicitly non-violent World March of Women-led "revolutionary knitting action" to a diversity of tactics, CLAC [La Convergence des Luttes Anti-Capitalistes]-led snake march. A large non-violent convergence march was organized on the second day around the theme that "no one is illegal" in response to repressive anti-terrorist laws.

In the lead-up to Calgary and Ottawa, new language had begun to appear among proponents of diversity of tactics advocating forms of resistance "that maximize respect for life." This did not mean that organizing, especially in Ottawa, was not extremely fractious. A refusal by CLAC, in the name of respect for diversity of tactics, to exclude violent tactics created a serious split in the Ottawa activist community. Most church-, labour-, and NGO-based activists (including Global Democracy Ottawa) simply stayed away from all Take the Capital activities. As a result, the CLAC-organized snake march in particular represented a much narrower cross-section of the movement; it was comprised almost exclusively of young people with a high proportion of self-identified anarchists, including a number who were masked and carrying batons. The batons were used to produce the trademark rhythmic drumming on any available metal surface—stop signs, guardrails, and street grates.

Throughout both the snake march and the "no one is illegal" march, CLAC organizer Jaggi Singh kept reiterating over the bullhorn that "anything could happen," and that people should and will directly confront actions they perceive to be unjust in ways that they deem legitimate. As a participant in both events, I experienced this rhetoric as inflammatory and manipulative. Singh was holding open the possibility of violence as an acceptable aspect of protest in general and in the context of the event in which we were participating. As someone willing to support a militant action organized under the rubric of diversity of tactics, I felt that my presence was being manipulated to support a threat of violent escalation over which I had no say.

On the other hand, the Raging Granny marching beside me had this to say: "Some of our members are uncomfortable taking part in these kinds of events because they're worried about what might happen. But, I think, when you consider the violence all around us, these (gesturing to the sea of young people) are just the lambs."

In Ottawa, there was some spray-painting and paint-bombing of banks. The windows of a police car were smashed during the snake march, but this action was immediately booed by protesters and did not escalate. Police were in regular uniform and kept their distance. Like the events in Calgary, Ottawa was acclaimed by police, press, and protesters alike as completely non-violent, despite the tensions created by those insisting on "solidarity with the full scope of resistance."

In the aftermath of these actions, Starhawk published what amounted to a thorough rethinking of diversity of tactics. Coming from an activist with demonstrated commitment to both non-violent direct action and respectful dialogue with the Black Bloc, her comments are especially persuasive. She argued that the time (post–9/11) and place (oil-rich and right-wing Calgary) demanded a powerful, militant, disruptive, and explicitly non-violent direct action. However, such action could not happen because diversity of tactics had become the movement's default mode.

Although offering a critique of the morality of much non-violence politics and the staleness of its tactics, Starhawk argues that a commitment to strategic non-violence opens up political space that diversity of tactics has, in effect, shut down:

> Strategic nonviolence lets us mobilize broadly around actions that are more than symbolic, that actually interfere with the operations of an institution of power. Unions and NGOs, and at-risk groups can support and participate in such actions, which contain many necessary roles at varied levels of risk.

> Committing to nonviolence as a strategic move for a particular action allows us to organize openly, without security culture and with broad participation in decision-making.... Transparency allows us to actually educate, mobilize, and inspire people to join us. While security culture may be necessary at times, it works against empowerment and direct democracy. People can only have a voice in the decisions that affect them if they know what is being decided....

> If we are to regain momentum in the post–9–11 climate for issues of global justice, we need actions that can mobilize large numbers of people to do more than simply march. We need to embrace discussion and debate, and trust that our movement is strong, resilient, and mature enough to tolerate our differences of opinion. We might agree that a diversity of tactics are [sic] needed in the long run to undermine global corporate capitalism, and still be willing to commit to strategic nonviolence for an action when it seems the strongest option. Otherwise, we end up without either diversity or tactics.

X. CONCLUSIONS

The first G8 summit in Europe since Genoa, 9/11, and the war in Iraq is currently taking place in Evian, France and with it has come the return of massive anti-globalization protests. Organizers claim that 120,000 people demonstrated in the mass march on Sunday, June 1, 2003. Through the winter of 2003, the anti-globalization movement was transformed by the explosion of a massive, global anti-war movement in opposition to an American-led attack on Iraq. On February 15, 2003, over four million people took to the streets in over six hundred towns and cities across the world in an extraordinary, globally-coordinated effort to prevent war. In January 2003, over 100,000 people gathered in Porto Alegre, Brazil for the third annual World Social Forum to march against the American Empire, to showcase the existence of political and economic alternatives to neo-liberalism, and to assert that another world is possible. Global opposition to neo-liberalism has been fueled by the war on Iraq. United States-led military aggression is increasingly recognized as an imperial civilizational project of global proportion.

In this new climate, the debate about diversity of tactics appeared increasingly marginalized. Organizers of mass anti-war demonstrations in Canada and elsewhere negotiated routes with police and marshaled the protests. Protesters carefully avoided property destruction or confrontation with police.

Anti-globalization activists were very prominent in the organizing and protesting against the war. But the movement against the war also broadened dramatically, incorporating many more people of color, notably from Muslim and Arab communities, and people who have never before protested anything. New movement coalitions included the more traditional peace groups with their strong traditions of pacifism and non-violent civil disobedience.

There will almost certainly be renewed debates within the movement about tactics. Property destruction has re-appeared in Lausanne, Switzerland, as part of the most recent round of anti-G8 protests. So have non-violent direct actions blockading roads and bridges. But these activities are in the wake of massive anti-war coalitions and demonstrations that may change the conditions for debate within the movement. Most powerfully, in the face of such naked use of deadly force by the United States, Starhawk's argument for strategic non-violence may have greater purchase in the movement.

In Canada, from the late 1990s into the early years of this century, the notion of "respect for diversity of tactics" held great appeal, especially among young activists. Against the historical backdrop of several decades of highly institutionalized forms of movement politics, it both named and validated important new activist practices in the face of growing global crises. More than ever, the movement and the world needs the creativity and courage of this new generation of activists in advancing non-violent strategies for social transformation. But in the face of unprecedented forces of power and domination, we also need to nurture the movement as a space of freedom and democracy, genuine diversity and pluralism, respect for life, and a love of peace in prefiguring the world we want.

NOTES AND QUESTIONS

1. Global security and poverty: In February of 2005, UN Secretary General Kofi Annan said "We will not defeat terrorism unless we also tackle the causes of conflict and misgovernment in developing countries. And we will not defeat poverty so long as trade and investment in any major part of the world are inhibited by fear of violence or instability."

In an extended interview with *Mother Jones* magazine, Jeffrey Sachs, an international development economist, author of *The End of Poverty*, laid out his own strategies for eradicating global poverty by 2025. Sachs headed a United Nations panel of development experts that were given the task of drafting global development goals to be met by the year 2015.

Why is it that decades of development economics haven't achieved the elimination of poverty? What makes Sachs' proposals so special? Is eradicating poverty a feasible goal to achieve in our lifetime? Sachs recently discussed his views with *Mother Jones Magazine*. Onnesha Roychoudhuri, *The End of Poverty: An Interview with Jeffrey Sachs*, MOTHER JONES MAG., May 6, 2005, *available at* http://www.motherjones.com/news/qa/2005/05/jeffrey_sachs.html.

2. Practical investment strategy. Sachs proposes that the "rich countries need to help poor countries make practical investments that are often really very basic.... For instance, one issue that has been tragically neglected ... is malaria. That's a disease that kills up to 3 million people every year." Sachs decries the failure to address this practical problem "that could be controlled quite dramatically and easily". Sachs argues that development issues got sidetracked during the post-911 crisis period. However, he notes that the tsunami in the Indian Ocean in which we could all see the scope of the devastation on our television screens, shifted discussion towards the plight of the world's poor.

3. The point seven percent solution. Sachs has proposed that the rich countries, such as the United States, devote 0.7 percent of our Gross National Product to development aid. This proposal has been criticized by former World Bank economist, William Easterly. Easterly calls instead for "piecemeal reform", in which more limited projects are tried, monitored and measured to see what really works before a major commitment is given. Sachs' reply to the piecemeal approach is that "I don't think that we should be choosing between whether a young girl has immunizations or water, or between whether her mother an father are alive, because they have access of treatment for AIDS, or whether she has a meal at school, or whether her father and mother, who are farmers are able to grow enough food to feed their family.... Those strike me as quite doable and practical things that can be done at once.... I am proposing that we help people help themselves."

4. Corruption. Rich countries frequently cite the problem of corruption as a reason to withhold significant contributions of foreign aid. Sachs says, "my experience is that there's corruption everywhere: in the U.S., in Europe, in Asia, and in Africa. It's a bit like infectious disease—you can control it, but it's very hard to eradicate it ... I don't have any magic solution for those situations....Nothing is done on trust. Everything should be done on a basis of measurement and monitoring.... Don't just send money: send bed nets, send in auditors, make targets quantitative."

5. Teaching development economics in the universities. Sachs proposes a major change in the way advanced students are taught development economics. "Students in economics write dissertations about countries that they never stepped foot in because their advisor gives them a database from Nigeria or Kenya or some place else, and they do their thesis that way. That is like becoming a doctor without ever seeing a patient. We don't do case studies" Sachs proposes that development economists be trained with "clinical economics." In this mode students would meet in the field of study, then conference with professors to analyze the results of their efforts. This would approximate the hospital "rounds" for residents in training.

6. Shocking disengagement of World Bank from the aids crisis. "I was absolutely shocked and aghast when I learned that in the late 1990s the World Bank and other donors weren't paying a penny to help treat people dying of AIDS.... Rarely do rich countries say, 'Look we're just not prepared to spend money to save poor people's lives'. Instead you get a lot of skepticism. 'You can't do this, this is impossible. We're doing everything we can after all. We've tried everything. Let's go slowly. Let's do one thing at a time' I don't buy those arguments."

7. Modern direct action. Attempts to affect social change through courts or legislatures can often be a cumbersome process, characterized by delays, compromises and setbacks. Social activists have often sought more immediate strategies, such as protests and boycotts. Socially and economically disruptive activity has the advantage of gaining immediate and widespread attention from the public, and they may be more forceful both in their methods and results. These tactics include risks as well. Their failure may also be more visible, and they may engender backlash from the public.

The most famous example of a boycott from the American civil rights movement is the Montgomery Bus Boycott. In 1955, Montgomery, Alabama had a municipal law which required black citizens to ride in the back of the city's buses. On December 1, Rosa Parks sparked the boycott when she was arrested for refusing to relinquish her seat at the front of the bus to white passengers. Over the weekend of December 3 and 4, the leaders of Montgomery's black community, including Dr. Martin Luther King, planned a large scale boycott of Montgomery's bus system, in protest of the South's segregation laws. Black ministers urged their congregations to join the boycott, and pamphlets were distributed throughout the city. The boycott was remarkably successful. According to the bus company receipts, about 90 percent of blacks who usually rode the buses joined the boycott and found other means of transportation. The boycott continued into 1956, during which time the leaders and participants of the boycott were subjected to harassment and violence. Bombs were set off at the houses of both

Dr. King and E. D. Nixon. In November of 1956, the Supreme Court declared that segregation on public buses was unconstitutional, and the boycott ended. *See* Thomas J. Gilliam, *The Montgomery Bus Boycott of 1955–56, in* THE WALKING CITY: THE MONTGOMERY BUS BOYCOTT (David J. Garrow ed., 1989).

The protest was an invaluable tool for the civil rights movement. Clayborne Carson describes the movement, or in his preferred term the "Black Freedom Struggle," as involving "local protest movements" engaged in by "thousands of protesters, including large numbers of working class blacks, and local organizers who were more concerned with local issues, including employment opportunities and political power, than with achieving national legislation." Clayborne Carson, *Civil Rights Reform and the Black Freedom Struggle, in* THE CIVIL RIGHTS MOVEMENT IN AMERICA 19, 23–4 (Charles W. Eagles ed., 1986). Martin Luther King highly valued the peaceful protest, and admired its participants. In his famous "Letter from a Birmingham Jail," Dr. King responded to criticism made by eight Alabama clergymen of the demonstrations going on in Birmingham in 1963. He wrote:

> I wish you had commended the Negro sit-inners and demonstrators of Birmingham for their sublime courage, their willingness to suffer and their amazing discipline in the midst of great provocation. One day the South will recognize its real heroes. They will be the James Merediths, with the noble sense of purpose that enables them to face jeering, and hostile mobs, and with the agonizing loneliness that characterizes the life of the pioneer. They will be old, oppressed, battered Negro women, symbolized in a seventy-two-year-old woman in Montgomery, Alabama, who rose up with a sense of dignity and with her people decided not to ride segregated buses, and who responded with ungrammatical profundity to one who inquired about her weariness: "My feets is tired, but my soul is at rest." They will be the young high school and college students, the young ministers of the gospel and a host of their elders, courageously and nonviolently sitting in at lunch counters and willingly going to jail for conscience' sake. One day the South will know that when these disinherited children of God sat down at lunch counters, they were in reality standing up for what is best in the American dream and for the most sacred values in our Judeo–Christian heritage, thereby bringing our nation back to those great wells of democracy which were dug deep by the founding fathers in their formulation of the Constitution and the Declaration of Independence.

8.   Protests and boycotts today. Today, protests and boycotts continue to be employed by social activists and others. The war in Iraq has led to worldwide demonstrations by those opposed to it. *See* Evelyn Nieves, *Worldwide Civil Disobedience; Protesters Speak and Act Out Against War,* WASH. POST, Mar. 21, 2003, at A28. On the other side, political pundit Bill O'Reilly has repeatedly called for a boycott of French goods for that country's refusal to support the United States' actions in Iraq. Bill O'Reilly, *No Brie for Me*, BillOReilly.com, Jul. 1, 2004, *available at* http://www.billo-reilly.com/site/product?pid=18712. The goals of protesting groups are not necessarily politically progressive causes, as evidenced by Baptists' boycott of Disney for its supposed friendliness to homosexuals. The goals of the civil rights movement are now nearly universally seen as laudable and worth the civil strife they caused, though of course they were not so understood at the time by everyone. How should society react to protesters and boycotters whose goals do not seem as worthwhile or important as those engaged in during the civil rights movement? Are protests valuable if they allow insular yet tenacious minorities to sway large majorities against their interests?

Does the boycott seem like an effective strategy for achieving long-term changes, or do they seem more appropriate for combating specific incidents of perceived injustice? The rationale behind the boycott is that by economically attacking one's opponent, boycotters will hurt the target of the boycott in tangible, undeniable ways. Is it possible that boycotts will harm those who are not responsible for the offending activity?

9. Boycotts in Colorado. Following the passage of Amendment 2, homosexual groups and others called for a boycott of the state of Colorado. The Conference of Mayors, the National Association of Hispanic Journalists, and the American Library Association were among dozens of groups which cancelled events they had planned in the state. The mayors of New York, Chicago and Los Angeles, among others, endorsed the boycott. The boycott gained nationwide attention, prompted by support from celebrities such as Barbara Streisand. Colorado's dependence on tourism caused special concern in the state's business community. The effects of the boycott appear to have been mixed. It attained some success in financial terms, and brought the Amendment 2 issue to national prominence. However, the boycott appears to have had limited effect on public opinion in Colorado. A *Denver Post* poll taken at the time reported that 94 percent of the 606 adults interviewed in mid-December said they had not changed their minds about Amendment Two in response to the boycott. There may even have been some backlash: 43 percent said the boycott had lessened their interest in repealing Amendment 2. *Homosexuals: Fuming on the Slopes*, THE ECONOMIST, Feb. 6, 1993, at 30. A similar boycott took place in Arizona as a result of the state's refusal to declare Martin Luther King Day a holiday. It involved more than 166 meeting cancellations, costing Arizona more than $190 million. In 1992, the holiday was declared in the state, and the boycott was given much of the credit. Shari Caudron, *The Colorado Boycott: A Wake-up Call to all Businesses?*, INDUSTRY WEEK, Mar. 1, 1993, at 48.

10. Anti-globalization struggles and guerrilla theater. In addition to the direct action tactics of violent and non-violent mass action described by Conway, activists in the anti-globalization movement have engaged in other kinds of tactics. In *No Logo: Taking Aim at the Brand Bullies* (1999), Naomi Klein describes "culture jamming," "the practice of parodying advertisements and hijacking billboards in order to drastically alter their messages." KLEIN, *supra* at 280. Klein explains:

> [J]ammers * * * insist that they aren't inverting ad messages but are rather improving, editing, augmenting or unmasking them. * * * A good jam, in other words, is an X-ray of the subconscious of a campaign, uncovering not an opposite meaning but the deeper truth hiding beneath the layers of advertising euphemisms. So, according to these principles, with a slight turn of the imagery knob, the now-retired Joe Camel turns into Joe Chemo, hooked up to an IV machine. That's what's in his future, isn't it? * * * Apple computers' "Think Different" campaign of famous figures both living and dead has been the subject of numerous simple hacks: a photograph of Stalin appears with the altered slogan "Think Really Different"; the caption for the ad featuring the Dalai Lama is changed to "Think Disillusioned" and the rainbow Apple logo is morphed into a skull * * *. My favorite truth-in-advertising campaign is a simple jam on Exxon that appeared just after the 1989 Valdez spill: "Shit Happens. New Exxon," two towering billboards announced to millions of San Francisco commuters.

KLEIN, *supra* at 281–82.

11. Grassroots global anti-poverty campaigns: The Jubilee movement. "Jubilee 2000" was an international grassroots campaign that mobilized twenty four million people over a five year period, beginning in 1996, to cancel the "unpayable debts of the poorest countries by the year 2000." The term comes from the Old Testament book of Leviticus, which describes a Year of Jubilee that comes once every fifty years, during

> which slaves are freed and debt is canceled. The Jubilee 2000 campaign—which launched the slogan "Drop the Debt"—was supported by celebrities, including musicians Bono of U2, Bob Geldof, Youssou Ndour, Thom Yorke and others, as well as by mainline Protestant and evangelical church organizations. In 1999, at the Cologne G8 Summit, world leaders agreed to $34 billion in debt relief for 22 countries, 18 of them in Africa.

> See *http://www.jubilee2000uk.org/* (visited June 9, 2005); Jeff M. Sellers, *How To Spell Debt Relief*, CHRISTIANITY TODAY, May 21, 2001, *available at* http://www.christianitytoday.com/ct/2001/007/6.64.html.

Grassroots organizing under the Jubilee name continues in various countries. According to the Jubilee USA Network website, the United States network began in 1997 "when a diverse gathering of people and organizations came together in response to the international call for Jubilee debt cancellation. Now over sixty organizations including labor, churches, religious communities and institutions, AIDS activists, trade campaigners and over 9,000 individuals are active members of the Jubilee USA Network. Together we are a strong, diverse and growing network dedicated to working for a world free of debt for billions of people." Jubilee USA

Network, *About the network*, *http://www.jubileeusa.org* (visited June 9, 2005).

12. Porto Allegre grassroots movement. In January 2001, as a counter to the World Economic Forum—an exclusive annual gathering of economic elites in Davos, Switzerland—a committee of Brazilian non-governmental organizations hosted the first "World Social Forum" in Porto Alegre, Brazil. The World Social Forum became an annual international grassroots event. According to its Charter of Principles, the World Social Forum:

> is an open meeting place for reflective thinking, democratic debate of ideas, formulation of proposals, free exchange of experiences and interlinking for effective action, by groups and movements of civil society that are opposed to neoliberalism and to domination of the world by capital and any form of imperialism, and are committed to building a planetary society directed towards fruitful relationships among Humankind and between it and the Earth.

World Social Forum Charter of Principles, available at http://www.forumsocialmundial.org.br/main.php?id_menu=4 & cd_language=2 (visited June 9, 2005).

Porto Alegre itself is a place open to alternatives to traditional economic practices. An article reports on "participatory budgeting" in the city:

> Porto Alegre is a regional capital of 1.3 million people which since 1989 has been governed by the Partido dos Trabalhadores (PT or Workers' Party), Brazil's largest Left-wing party. Its flagship policy—the Participatory Budget—involves thousands of city residents in decisions about municipal expenditures. In a country where public funds are typically spent through a mixture of corruption, patronage and obscure technocratism, this is a revolution in political practice.
>
> It sprang from a political party's desire to live up to its policy platform, an aim seldom achieved in the world of politics. Since it was formed in the 1980s, the Workers' Party proclaimed its commitment to both citizen participation and redirecting government priorities toward the poor. But when it was elected to municipal office in January 1989, the party found an administration deeply indebted, lacking basic supplies and with buildings and machinery in shambles. At the first neighbourhood assemblies to discuss the budget, community leaders called for hundreds of investments. Not a penny was available.
>
> The local government spent its first year controlling costs and passing tax increases in city council but opinion polls showed high levels of dissatisfaction. So a group within the administration proposed both participatory decision-making and that priority be given to basic infrastructure in the poorest neighbourhoods. This translated as a total commitment, backed by funds, to the decisions made by the neighbourhood budget assemblies.
>
> Since then, residents have met in their neighbourhoods annually to discuss needs for community infrastructure, electing delegates to

each of 16 'district budget forums'. Through intense and often conflictual negotiations among neighbourhood representatives, these delegates list priorities for each type of capital expenditure such as basic sanitation, street paving and parks. Every year, open assemblies in each district also elect two members to a city-wide Municipal Budget Council which devises criteria for distributing funds among districts and approves an investment plan that respects the priorities of each one.

This policy gained such popularity in its first years that the administration expanded the programme beyond neighbourhood issues when it was re-elected in 1992. A year later, a series of Thematic Forums were created to discuss city-wide expenditures in areas such as urban planning, transportation and economic development. These forums also elect members to the Municipal Budget Council.

As it has grown, the Council has gained force. Not only does it now approve the entire capital budget but it also deliberates on all city expenditures. Over time a series of other participatory councils have also been created to discuss more qualitative aspects of city programmes on issues such as housing, health, culture and the environment.

The timing was ideal for building support for the idea. The first half of the 1990s was a period of great popular outrage in Brazil against government corruption, leading to the impeachment of President Collor de Mello. By contrast, at a local level, the Participatory Budget demonstrated that the administration was committed to change by challenging 'back room decision-making', mobilizing large numbers of people and visibly improving the quality of life in the poorest neighbourhoods. While opposition politicians privately questioned participatory decision-making, which effectively eliminated them as patronage brokers, they were forced to approve the investment plans since their own supporters were increasingly participating. After just one electoral term, all candidates promised to maintain the Participatory Budget.

As the policy began to gain international recognition, the government also gained local popularity for being innovative and responsible. Those people participating in the Municipal Budget Council gained a certain 'moral authority'. This helped garner the support of groups that still questioned the policy, such as technical personnel within the bureaucracy who doubted the ability of ordinary people to make budget decisions. The result was a bureaucracy that worked better, responding with agility to the demands of budget participants.

One of the outstanding achievements of the Participatory Budget has been its effectiveness in bringing the poor into public decision-making. The poorest neighbourhoods participate in much greater numbers than middle-class ones where streets have already been paved, sewers built and children are sent to private schools. Surveys show assembly participants have lower incomes and education levels than averages for the city as a whole.

However, the most enduring value of the Participatory Budget is that citizen participation has now become a way of life, accepted by people as well as politicians as the modus operandi in all realms of public decision-making. What is more, citizen groups have grown and strengthened in response to increased opportunities for effectively influencing government actions. Contrary to the common assumption that civil society must strengthen before government will improve, in Porto Alegre a state-initiated policy that has encouraged civic organizing has helped consolidate the new practices at all levels.

While promoting citizen participation may often seem politically risky, in Porto Alegre it has helped build political success for the Workers' Party. Since 1989 the party has been re-elected three times and has gained a reputation for effective administration elsewhere. Today it governs five cities of more than a million people, including São Paulo, as well as three states. Its local successes have directly challenged the idea that the Workers' Party—a party once identified with radical social movements—does not know how to govern. These successes have served as credentials for the Workers' Party in this year's national election campaign, which delivered the presidency to the party's leader, 'Lula' da Silva.

By 2000, more than 100 Brazilian cities were implementing the policy (about half of which are not Workers' Party controlled). Not always have the results been so impressive as in Porto Alegre. In most cases participatory control has remained limited to a small portion of expenditures. Even so, it is clear that the policy has a tremendous potential to mobilize: in major Brazilian cities such as Belém, Brasília and Belo Horizonte, participatory budget programmes have involved hundreds of thousands of participants. In São Paulo alone, 55,000 people participated in budget forums this year.

Rebecca Abers, *Daring Democracy*, NEW INTERNATIONALIST 352 (December 2002), *available at http://www.newint.org/issue352/daring.htm*. In fall, 2004, however, the Workers' Party was voted out of office. The World Social Forum has now moved to a biannual schedule; the next meeting will be in 2007, in Africa.

COPYRIGHT PERMISSIONS

Professors Jordan and Harris, along with Foundation Press, would like to gratefully acknowledge the authors and copyright holders of the following works, who permitted their inclusion in this work:

Akerlof, George A. & Kranton, Rachel E., *Economics and Identity*, 115 Q.J. OF ECON. 715 (Aug. 2000). Copyright © 2000 by the Quarterly Journal of Economics. Reprinted by permission of The MIT Press.

Associated Press, *Uneasy Rider! Jury Finds Wynona Guilty in Shoplift Case*, N.Y. DAILY NEWS, Nov. 6, 2002. Copyright © 2002 by the Associated Press. Reprinted by permission.

Ayres, Ian, *Pervasive Prejudice? Unconventional Evidence of Race and Gender Discrimination* 3–7 (2001). Copyright © 2001 by Ian Ayres and the University of Chicago Press. Reprinted by permission.

Barnes, Anita C., *The Sexual Continuum: Transsexual Prisoners*, 24 NEW ENG. J. ON CRIM. & CIV. CONFINEMENT 599 (1998). Copyright © 1998 by Anita C. Barnes and the New England Journal on Criminal and Civil Confinement. Reprinted by permission.

Bayles, Martha, *Malcolm X and the Hip Hop Culture*, RECONSTRUCTION II 593–596 (1993). Copyright © 1993 by Randall Kennedy, Michael R. Klein Professor of Law, Harvard Law School. Reprinted by permission.

Becker, Gary S., *The Forces Determining Discrimination in the Market Place*, in *The Economics of Discrimination* 13–18 (2d. ed. 1971). Copyright © 1971 by The University of Chicago Press and Gary S. Becker. Reprinted by permission.

Brooks, Roy L., *Atonement and Forgiveness: A New Model for Black Reparations* 155–163 (2004). Copyright © 2004 by The University of California Press. Reprinted by permission.

Caldwell, Paulette M., *A Hair Piece: Perspective on the Intersection of Race and Gender*, 1991 DUKE L.J. 365 (1991). Copyright © 1991 by Paulette M. Caldwell. Reprinted by permission.

Carbado, Devon W. & Gulati, Mitu, *The Law and Economics of Critical Race Theory*, 112 YALE L.J. 1757, 1789–93, 1795–96, 1797–99, 1801–14 (2003) (book review). Reprinted by permission of The Yale Law Journal Company and William S. Hein from The Yale Law Journal, Vol. 112, pages 1757, 1789–93, 1795–96, 1797–99, 1801–14, in the format Textbook via the Copyright Clearance Center.

Chapkis, Wendy, *Dress as Success*, in *Beauty Secrets: Women and the Politics of Appearance* 79–80, 83–85, 88–93 (1986). Copyright © 1986 by Wendy Chapkis and South End Press. Reprinted by permission.

Clifford, James, *Identity in Mashpee*, in THE PREDICAMENT OF CULTURE: TWENTIETH-CENTURY ETHNOGRAPHY, LITERATURE, AND ART 277–346 (1988). "Identity in Mashpee" reprinted by permission of the publisher of THE PREDICAMENT OF CULTURE: TWENTIETH–CENTURY ETHNOGRA-

*

INDEX

†